REFRAMING

ORGANIZATIONS

Reframing Organizations, Sixth Edition is also available in **WileyPLUS Learning Space**—an interactive and collaborative learning environment that provides insight into learning strengths and weaknesses through a combination of dynamic and engaging course materials. With WileyPLUS Learning Space, students make deeper connections and get better grades by annotating course material and by collaborating with other students in the course.

With WileyPLUS Learning Space, you will find:

- A restructured digital text that features interactive content, videos, assignments, and social networking tools that enable interaction with instructors and encourage discussion between students

- Interactive features include a gradable test bank, videos to engage students with differing organizational scenarios, interactive graphics, practice questions to reinforce key concepts, exercise assignments, and a Leadership Orientations Self-Assessment to help students understand the way they instinctively think about and approach leadership

- The course also includes a full Instructor's Manual, including chapter-by-chapter teaching notes, lecture slides, sample syllabi, and other support materials

For more information and to request a free trial, visit http://www.wiley.com//college/sc/wpls/

An updated online Instructor's Guide with lecture slides and a Your Leadership Orientations Self-Assessment is also available at http://eu.wiley.com/WileyCDA/WileyTitle/productCd-1119281814.html

ARTISTRY, CHOICE, AND LEADERSHIP

6TH **EDITION**

REFRAMING ORGANIZATIONS

LEE G. BOLMAN
TERRENCE E. DEAL

JB JOSSEY-BASS™

A Wiley Brand

In Memory of Warren Bennis
Exemplar, Mentor, and Friend
With Appreciation for All He Gave Us

CONTENTS

PREFACE

This is the sixth release of a work that began in 1984 as *Modern Approaches to Understanding and Managing Organizations* and became *Reframing Organizations* in 1991. We're grateful to readers around the world who have told us that our books gave them ideas that make a difference—at work and elsewhere in their lives.

It is again time for an update, and we're gratified to be back by popular demand. Like everything else, organizations and their leadership challenges continue to evolve rapidly, and scholars are running hard to keep pace. This edition tries to capture the current frontiers of both knowledge and art.

The four-frame model, with its view of organizations as factories, families, jungles, and temples, remains the book's conceptual heart. But we have incorporated new research and revised our case examples extensively to keep up with the latest developments. We have updated a feature we inaugurated in the third edition: "Greatest Hits in Organization Studies." These features offer pithy summaries of key ideas from the some of the most influential works in the scholarly literature (as indicated by a citation analysis, described in the Appendix at the end of the book). As a counterpoint to the scholarly works, we have also added occasional summaries of management bestsellers. Scholarly and professional literature often run on separate tracks, but the two streams together provide a fuller picture than either alone, and we have tried to capture the best of both in our work.

Life in organizations has produced many stories and examples, and there is new material throughout the book. At the same time, we worked zealously to minimize bloat by tracking down and expunging every redundant sentence, marginal concept, or extraneous example. We've also tried to keep it fun. Collective life is an endless source of vivid examples as entertaining as they are instructive, and we've sprinkled them throughout the text.

We apologize to anyone who finds that an old favorite fell to the cutting-room floor, but we hope readers will find the book an even clearer and more efficient read.

As always, our primary audience is managers and leaders. We have tried to answer the question, what do we know about organizations and leadership that is genuinely relevant and useful to practitioners as well as scholars? We have worked to present a large, complex body of theory, research, and practice as clearly and simply as possible. We tried to avoid watering it down or presenting simplistic views of how to solve managerial problems. This is not a self-help book filled with ready-made answers. Our goal is to offer not solutions but powerful and provocative ways of thinking about opportunities and pitfalls.

We continue to focus on both management *and* leadership. Leading and managing are different, but they're equally important. The difference is nicely summarized in an aphorism from Bennis and Nanus: "Managers do things right. Leaders do the right thing." If an organization is overmanaged but underled, it eventually loses any sense of spirit or purpose. A poorly managed organization with a strong, charismatic leader may soar briefly—only to crash shortly thereafter. Malpractice can be as damaging and unethical for managers and leaders as for physicians.

Myopic managers or overzealous leaders usually harm more than just themselves. The challenges of today's organizations require the objective perspective of managers as well as the brilliant flashes of vision that wise leadership provides. We need more people in managerial roles who can find simplicity and order amid organizational confusion and chaos. We need versatile and flexible leaders who are artists as well as analysts, who can reframe experience to discover new issues and possibilities. We need managers who love their work, their organizations, and the people whose lives they affect. We need leaders who appreciate management as a moral and ethical undertaking, and who combine hardheaded realism with passionate commitment to larger values and purposes. We hope to encourage and nurture such qualities and possibilities.

As in the past, we have tried to produce a clear and readable synthesis and integration of the field's major theoretical traditions. We concentrate mainly on organization theory's implications for practice. We draw on examples from every sector and around the globe. Historically, organization studies has been divided into several intellectual camps, often isolated from one another. Works that seek to give a comprehensive overview of organization theory and research often drown in social science jargon and abstraction and have little to say to practitioners. Works that strive to provide specific answers and tactics often offer advice that applies only under certain conditions. We try to find a balance between misleading oversimplification and mind-boggling complexity.

The bulk of work in organization studies has focused on the private *or* public *or* nonprofit sector but not all three. We think this is a mistake. Managers need to understand similarities and differences among all types of organizations. All three sectors increasingly interpenetrate one another. Federal, state and local governments create policy that shapes or intends to influence organizations of all types. When bad things happen new laws are promulgated. Public administrators who regulate airlines, nuclear power plants, or pharmaceutical companies face the problem of "indirect management" every day. They struggle to influence the behavior of organizations over which they have very limited authority. Private firms need to manage relationships with multiple levels of government. The situation is even more complicated for managers in multinational companies coping with the subtleties of governments with very different systems and traditions. Around the world, voluntary and nongovernment organizations partner with business and government to address major social and economic challenges. Across sectors and cultures, managers often harbor narrow, stereotypic conceptions of one another that impede effectiveness on all sides. We need common ground and a shared understanding that can help strengthen organizations in every sector. The dialogue between public and private, domestic and multinational organizations has become increasingly important. Because of their generic application, the four frames offer an ecumenical language for the exchange. Our work with a variety of organizations around the world has continually reinforced our confidence that the frames are relevant everywhere. Translations of the book into many languages, including Chinese, Dutch, French, Korean, Norwegian, Russian, Spanish, Swedish, and Turkish, provide ample evidence that this is so. Political and symbolic issues, for example, are universally important, even though the specifics vary greatly from one country or culture to another.

The idea of *reframing* continues to be a central theme. Throughout the book, we show how the same situation can be viewed in at least four unique ways. In Part VI, we include a series of chapters on reframing critical organizational issues such as leadership, change, and ethics. Two chapters are specifically devoted to reframing real-life situations.

We also continue to emphasize artistry. Overemphasizing the rational and technical side of an organization often contributes to its decline or demise. Our counterbalance emphasizes the importance of art in both management and leadership. Artistry is neither exact nor precise; the artist interprets experience, expressing it in forms that can be felt, understood, and appreciated. Art fosters emotion, subtlety, and ambiguity. An artist represents the world to give us a deeper understanding of what is and what might be. In modern organizations, quality, commitment, and creativity are highly valued but often hard to find. They can be developed and encouraged by leaders or managers who embrace the expressive side of their work.

OUTLINE OF THE BOOK

As its title implies, the first part of the book, "Making Sense of Organizations," focuses on sense-making and tackles a perplexing question about management: Why is it that smart people so often do dumb things? Chapter 1, "The Power of Reframing," explains why: Managers often misread situations. They have not learned how to use multiple lenses to get a better sense of what they're up against and what they might do. Chapter 2, "Simple Ideas, Complex Organizations," uses well-known cases (such as 9/11) to show how managers' everyday thinking and theories can lead to catastrophe. We explain basic factors that make organizational life complicated, ambiguous, and unpredictable; discuss common fallacies in managerial thinking; and spell out criteria for more effective approaches to diagnosis and action.

Part II, "The Structural Frame," explores the key role that social architecture plays in the functioning of organizations. Chapter 3, "Getting Organized," describes basic issues that managers must consider in designing structure to fit an organization's strategies, tasks, and context. It demonstrates why organizations—from Amazon to McDonald's to Harvard University—need different structures in order to be effective in their unique environments. Chapter 4, "Structure and Restructuring," explains major structural pathologies and pitfalls. It presents guidelines for aligning structures to situations, along with cases illustrating successful structural change. Chapter 5, "Organizing Groups and Teams," shows that structure is a key to high-performing teams.

Part III, "The Human Resource Frame," explores the properties of both people and organizations, and what happens when the two intersect. Chapter 6, "People and Organizations," focuses on the relationship between organizations and human nature. It shows how managers' practices and assumptions about people can lead either to alienation and hostility or to commitment and high motivation. It contrasts two strategies for achieving effectiveness: "lean and mean," or investing in people. Chapter 7, "Improving Human Resource Management," is an overview of practices that build a more motivated and committed workforce—including participative management, job enrichment, self-managing workgroups, management of diversity, and organization development. Chapter 8, "Interpersonal and Group Dynamics," presents an example of interpersonal conflict to illustrate how managers can enhance or undermine relationships. It also discusses emotional intelligence and how group members can increase their effectiveness by attending to group process, including informal norms and roles, interpersonal conflict, leadership, and decision making.

Part IV, "The Political Frame," views organizations as arenas. Individuals and groups compete to achieve their parochial interests in a world of conflicting viewpoints, scarce resources, and struggles for power. Chapter 9, "Power, Conflict, and Coalition," analyzes the tragic loss of the space shuttles *Columbia* and *Challenger*, illustrating the influence of political dynamics in decision making. It shows how scarcity and diversity lead to conflict, bargaining, and games of power; the chapter also distinguishes constructive and destructive political dynamics. Chapter 10, "The Manager as Politician," uses leadership examples from a nonprofit organization in India and a software development effort at Microsoft to illustrate basic skills of the constructive politician: diagnosing political realities, setting agendas, building networks, negotiating, and making choices that are both effective and ethical. Chapter 11, "Organizations as Political Arenas and Political Agents," highlights organizations as both arenas for political contests and political actors influencing broader social, political, and economic trends. Case examples such as Walmart and Ross Johnson explore political dynamics both inside and outside organizations.

Part V explores the symbolic frame. Chapter 12, "Organizational Symbols and Culture," spells out basic symbolic elements in organizations: myths, heroes, metaphors, stories, humor, play, rituals, and ceremonies. It defines organizational culture and shows its central role in shaping performance. The power of symbol and culture is illustrated in cases as diverse as the U.S. Congress, Nordstrom department stores, the U.S. Air Force, Zappos, and a unique horse race in Italy. Chapter 13, "Culture in Action," uses the case of a computer development team to show what leaders and group members can do collectively to build a culture that bonds people in pursuit of a shared mission. Initiation rituals, specialized language, group stories, humor and play, and ceremonies all combine to transform diverse individuals into a cohesive team with purpose, spirit, and soul. Chapter 14, "Organization as Theater," draws on dramaturgical and institutional theory to reveal how organizational structures, activities, and events serve as secular dramas, expressing our fears and joys, arousing our emotions, and kindling our spirit. It also shows how organizational structures and processes—such as planning, evaluation, and decision making—are often more important for what they express than for what they accomplish.

Part VI, "Improving Leadership Practice," focuses on the implications of the frames for central issues in managerial practice, including leadership, change, and ethics. Chapter 15, "Integrating Frames for Effective Practice," shows how managers can blend the frames to improve their effectiveness. It looks at organizations as multiple realities and gives guidelines for aligning frames with situations. Chapter 16, "Reframing in Action," presents four scenarios, or scripts, derived from the frames. It applies the scenarios to the harrowing experience of a young manager whose first day in a new job turns out to be far more challenging than she expected. The discussion illustrates how leaders can expand their options and enhance their effectiveness by considering alternative approaches. Chapter 17, "Reframing Leadership," discusses limitations in traditional views of leadership and proposes a more comprehensive view of how leadership works in organizations. It summarizes and critiques current knowledge on the characteristics of leaders, including the relationship of leadership to culture and gender. It shows how frames generate distinctive images of effective leaders as architects, servants, advocates, and prophets.

Chapter 18, "Reframing Change in Organizations," describes four fundamental issues that arise in any change effort: individual needs, structural alignment, political conflict, and existential loss. It uses cases of successful and unsuccessful change to document key strategies, such as training, realigning, creating arenas, and using symbol and ceremony. Chapter 19, "Reframing Ethics and Spirit," discusses four ethical mandates that emerge from the frames: excellence, caring, justice, and faith. It argues that leaders can build more ethical organizations through gifts of authorship, love, power, and significance. Chapter 20, "Bringing It All Together," is an integrative treatment of the reframing process. It takes a troubled school administrator through a weekend of reflection on critical difficulties he faces. The chapter shows how reframing can help managers move from feeling confused and stuck to discovering a renewed sense of clarity and confidence. The Epilogue describes strategies and characteristics needed in future leaders. It explains why they will need an artistic combination of conceptual flexibility and commitment to core values. Efforts to prepare future leaders have to focus as much on spiritual as on intellectual development.

Lee G. Bolman
Brookline, Massachusetts

Terrence E. Deal
San Luis Obispo, California

July 2017

ACKNOWLEDGMENTS

We noted in our first edition, "Book writing often feels like a lonely process, even when an odd couple is doing the writing." This odd couple keeps getting older (ancient, to be more precise) and—some would say—even odder and grumpier. It seems like only yesterday we were young, vibrant new authors, but that was 40 years ago. To our amazement, we're still at it and have remained close friends. The best thing about teaching and book writing is that you learn so much from your readers and students, and we have been blessed to have so many of both.

Students at Stanford, Harvard, Vanderbilt, the University of Missouri–Kansas City, the University of La Verne, and the University of Southern California have given us invaluable criticism, challenge, and support over the years. We're grateful to the many readers who have responded to our open invitation to write and ask questions or share comments. They have helped us write a better book. (The invitation is still open—our contact information is in "The Authors.") We wish we could personally thank all of the leaders and managers who helped us learn in seminars, workshops, and consultations. Their knowledge and wisdom are the foundation and touchstone for our work.

We want to thank all the colleagues and readers in the United States and around the world who have offered valuable comments and suggestions, but the list is very long and our memories keep getting shorter. Bob Marx, of the University of Massachusetts, deserves special mention as a charter member of the frames family. Bob's interest in the frames, creativity in developing teaching designs, and eye for video material have aided our thinking and teaching immensely. Conversations with Dick Scott and John Meyer of Stanford University have helped us explore the nuances of institutional theory. Ellen Harris, of

Harvard and Outward Bound, provided many thoughtful comments on the manuscript. Susan Griggs, of the University of Denver, offered a provocative critique of our handling of issues related to gender and leadership. Elena Granell de Aldaz, of the Institute for Advanced Study of Management in Caracas, collaborated with us on developing a Spanish-language adaptation of *Reframing Organizations* as well as on a more recent project that studied frame orientations among managers in Venezuela. We are proud to consider her a valued colleague and wonderful friend. Azarm Ghareman, a clinical psychologist, deepened our understanding of Carl Jung's view of the important role symbols play in human experience. Captain Gary Deal, USN, at the Eisenhower School, National Defense Institute, teaches leadership and the frames to high-ranking officers from all branches of the military and government services. Dr. Peter Minich, a transplant surgeon, now brings the world of leadership to physicians. Major Kevin Reed, of the United States Air Force, and Jan and Ron Haynes, of FzioMed, all provided valuable case material. Richard and Sharon Pescatore have been a valuable source for insights into Hewlett-Packard. The irrepressible Charlie Alfano and co-owner Audrey of Alfano Motorcars (San Luis Obispo) have provided us a glimpse of key ingredients for success in a sales organization (the Alfanos also own a dealership in Phoenix). Angela Schmiede of Menlo College has broadened our views of the ways the frames can contribute to undergraduate education.

A number of friends and colleagues at the Organizational Behavior Teaching Conference have given us many helpful ideas and suggestions. We apologize for any omissions, but we want to thank Anke Arnaud, Carole K. Barnett, Max Elden, Kent Fairfield, Cindi Fukami, Olivier Hermanus, Jim Hodge, Earlene Holland, Scott Johnson, Mark Kriger, Hyoungbae Lee, Larry Levine, Mark Maier, Magid Mazen, Thomas P. Nydegger, Dave O'Connell, Lynda St. Clair, Mabel Tinjacá, Susan Twombly, and Pat Villeneuve. We can only wish to have succeeded in implementing all the wonderful ideas we received from these and other colleagues.

Lee is grateful to all his Bloch School colleagues and particularly to Nancy Day, Pam Dobies, Dave Donnelly, Doranne Hudson, Jae Jung, Tusha Kimber, Sandra Kruse-Smith, Rong Ma, Brent Never, Roger Pick, Stephen Pruitt, Laura Rees, David Renz, Marilyn Taylor, and Bob Waris. Terry's colleagues Carl Cohn, Stu Gothald, and Gib Hentschke, of the University of Southern California, have offered both intellectual stimulation and moral support. Sharon Conley, Professor at the University of Santa Barbara, is a constant source of ideas and feedback. Her work keeps us attuned closely to the world of education. Terry's recent (2013) team-teaching venture with President Devorah Lieberman and Professor Jack Meek of the University of La Verne showed what's possible when conventional boundaries are trespassed in a class of aspiring undergraduate leaders. This experience led to the founding of the Terrence E. Deal Leadership Institute.

Others to whom our debt is particularly clear are the late Chris Argyris, Sam Bacharach, Cliff Baden, Margaret Benefiel, Estella Bensimon, Bud Bilanich, Bob Birnbaum, Barbara Bunker, Tom Burks, Ellen Castro, Carlos Cortés, Linton Deck, Patrick Faverty, Dave Fuller, Jim Honan, Tom Johnson, Bob Kegan, James March, Grady McGonagill, Judy McLaughlin, John Meyer, Kevin Nichols, Harrison Owen, Regina Pacheco, Donna Redman, Peggy Redman, Michael Sales, Joan Vydra, Karl Weick, Jilie Wheeler, Roy Williams, and Joe Zolner. Thanks again to Dave Brown, Phil Mirvis, Barry Oshry, Tim Hall, Bill Kahn, and Todd Jick of the Brookline Circle, now in its fourth decade of searching for joy and meaning in those lives devoted to the study of organizations.

Outside the United States, we are grateful to Poul Erik Mouritzen in Denmark; Rolf Kaelin, Cüno Pumpin, and Peter Weisman in Switzerland; Ilpo Linko in Finland; Tom Case in Brazil; Einar Plyhn and Haakon Gran in Norway; Peter Normark and Dag Bjorkegren in Sweden; Ching-Shiun Chung in Taiwan; Helen Gluzdakova and Anastasia Vitkovskaya in Russia; and H.R.H. Prince Philipp von und zu Lichtenstein.

Closer to home, Lee also owes more than he can say to the recently retired Bruce Kay, whose genial and unflappable approach to work, coupled with high levels of organization and follow-through, had a wonderfully positive impact while he took on the challenge of bringing a modicum of order and sanity to Lee's professional functioning. We also continue to be grateful for the enduring support and friendship of Linda Corey, our long-time resident representative at Harvard, and Homa Aminmadani, a delightful character and irreplaceable assistant, who now splits her time between Nashville and Teheran.

The couples of the Edna Ranch Vintners Guild—the Pecatores, Donners, Hayneses, Alfanos, and Andersons—link efforts with Terry in exploring the ups, downs, and mysteries of the art and science of wine making. Three professional winemakers, Romeo "Meo" Zuech of Piedra Creek Winery, Brett Escalera of Consilience and TresAnelli, and Bob Shiebelhut of Tolosa offer advice that applies to leadership as well as winemaking. Meo reminds us, "Never overmanage your grapes," and Brett prefaces answers to all questions with "It all depends."

We're delighted to be well into the fourth decade of our partnership with Jossey-Bass and Wiley. We're grateful to the many friends who have helped us over the years, including Bill Henry, Steve Piersanti, Lynn Luckow, Bill Hicks, Debra Hunter, Cedric Crocker, Byron Schneider, Kathe Sweeney, and many others. In recent years, Jeanenne Ray has been a wonderful editor and friend. Jenny Ng and Lauren Freestone of Wiley have done vital and much-appreciated work backstage in helping to get all the pieces of this edition together and keep the process moving forward.

Lee's six children—Edward, Shelley, Lori, Scott, Christopher, and Bradley—and three grandchildren—James, Jazmyne, and Foster—all continue to enrich his life and contribute to his growth. Terry's daughter Janie, a chef, has a rare talent of almost magically transforming simple ingredients into fine cuisine. Special mention also goes to Terry's deceased parents, Bob and Dorothy Deal. Both lived long enough to be pleasantly surprised that their oft-wayward son could write a book. Equal mention is due to Lee's parents, Eldred and Florence Bolman.

We again dedicate this book to our wives, who have more than earned all the credit and appreciation that we can give them. Joan Gallos, Lee's spouse and closest colleague, combines intellectual challenge and critique with support and love. She has been an active collaborator in developing our ideas, and her teaching manual for previous editions has been a frame-breaking model for the genre. Her contributions have become so integrated into our own thinking that we are no longer able to thank her for all the ways that the book has gained from her wisdom and insights.

Sandy Deal's psychological training enables her to approach the field of organizations with a distinctive and illuminating slant. Her successful practice produces examples that have helped us make some even stronger connections to the concepts of clinical psychology. She is one of the most gifted diagnosticians in the field, as well as a delightful partner whose love and support over the long run have made all the difference. She is a rare combination of courage and caring, intimacy and independence, responsibility and playfulness.

To Joan and Sandy, thanks again. As the years accumulate (rapidly), we love you even more.

Lee G. Bolman
Brookline, Massachusetts

Terrence E. Deal
San Luis Obispo, California

July 2017

PART ONE

Making Sense of Organizations

Sit no longer at your dusty window
I urge you to break the gaze
from your oh so cherished glass

—Gian Torrano Jacobs
Journeys through the Windows of Perception
Reprinted by permission of the poet, Gian Torrano Jacobs.

Introduction
The Power of Reframing

By the second decade of the twenty-first century, the German carmaker Volkswagen and the U.S. bank Wells Fargo were among the world's largest, most successful, and most admired firms. Then both trashed their own brand by following the same script. It's a drama in three acts:

Act I: Set daunting standards for employees to improve performance.

Act II: Look the other way when employees cheat because they think it's the only way to meet the targets.

Act III: When the cheating leads to a media firestorm and public outrage, blame the workers and paint top managers as blameless.

In Wells Fargo's case, the bank fired more than 5,000 lower-level employees but offered an exit bonus of $125 million to the executive who oversaw them (Sorkin, 2016).

Volkswagen CEO Martin Winterkorn was known as an eagle-eyed micromanager but pleaded ignorance when his company admitted in 2015 that it had been cheating for years on emissions tests of its "clean" diesels. He was quickly replaced by Matthias Müller, who claimed that he didn't know anything about VW's cheating either. Müller also explained why VW wasn't exactly guilty: "It was a technical problem. We had not the interpretation of the American law . . . We didn't lie. We didn't understand the question first" (Smith and Parloff, 2016). Apparently VW was smart enough to design clever software to fudge emissions tests but not smart enough to know that cheating might be illegal.

The smokescreen worked for years—VW sold a lot of diesels to consumers who wanted just what Volkswagen claimed to offer, a car at the sweet spot of low emissions, high performance, and great fuel economy. The cheating apparently began around 2008, seven years before it became public, when Volkswagen engineers realized they could not make good on the company's public, clean-diesel promises (Ewing, 2015). Bob Lutz, an industry insider, described VW's management system as "a reign of terror and a culture where performance was driven by fear and intimidation" (Lutz, 2015). VW engineers faced a tough choice. Should they tell the truth and lose their jobs now or cheat and *maybe* lose their jobs later? The engineers chose option B. The story did not end happily. In January, 2017, VW pleaded guilty to cheating on emissions tests and agreed to pay a fine of $4.3 billion. In the same week, six VW executives were indicted for conspiring to defraud the United States.[1] In Spring of 2017, VW's legal troubles appeared to be winding down in the United States, at a total cost of more than $20 billion, but were still ramping up in Germany, where authorities had launched criminal investigations (Ewing, 2017).

The story at Wells Fargo was similar. For years, it had successfully billed itself as the friendly, community bank. It ran warm and fuzzy ads around themes of working together and caring about people. The ads did not mention that in 2010 a federal judge ruled that the bank had cheated customers by deliberately manipulating customer transactions to increase overdraft fees (Randall, 2010), nor that in August, 2016, the bank agreed to pay a $4.1 million penalty for cheating student borrowers. But no amount of advertising would have helped in September, 2016, when the news broke that employees in Wells Fargo branches, under pressure from their bosses to sell more "solutions," had opened some two million accounts that customers didn't want and usually didn't know about, at least not until they received an unexpected credit card in the mail or got hit with fees on an account they didn't know they had.

None of it should have been news to Wells Fargo's leadership. Back in 2005, employees began to call the firm's human resources department and ethics hotline to report that some of their coworkers were cheating (Cowley, 2016). The bank sometimes solved that problem by firing the whistleblowers. Take the case of a branch manager in Arizona. While covering for a colleague at another branch, he found that employees were opening accounts for fake businesses. He called HR, which told him to call the ethics hotline. Ethics asked him for specific data to support the allegations. He pulled data from the system and reported it. A month later, he was fired for improperly looking up account information.

In 2013, the *Los Angeles Times* ran a story about phony accounts in some local branches. Wells Fargo's solution was not to lower the flame under the pot but to try and screw down the lid even tighter. They kept up the intense push for cross-selling but sent employees to ethics seminars where they were instructed not to open accounts customers didn't want. CEO John Stumpf achieved plausible deniability by proclaiming that he didn't want "want anyone ever offering a product to someone when they don't know what the benefit is, or the customer doesn't understand it, or doesn't want it, or doesn't need it" (Sorkin, 2016, p. B1). But despite his public assurances, the incentives up and down the line still rewarded sales rather than ethical squeamishness. Many employees felt they were in a bind: they'd been told not to cheat, but that was the best way to keep their jobs (Corkery and Cowley, 2016). Like the VW engineers, many decided to cheat now and hope that later never came.

Maybe leaders at Volkswagen and Wells Fargo knew about the cheating and hoped it would never come to light. Maybe they were just out of touch. Either way, they were clueless—failing to see that their companies were headed for costly public-relations nightmares. But they are far from alone. Cluelessness is a pervasive affliction for leaders, even the best and brightest. Often it leads to personal and institutional disaster. But, sometimes there are second chances.

Consider Steve Jobs. He had to fail before he could succeed. Fail he did. He was fired from Apple Computer, the company he founded, and then spent 11 years "in the wilderness" (Schlender, 2004). During this time of reflection he discovered capacities as a leader—and human being—that set the stage for his triumphant second act at Apple.

He failed initially for the same reason that countless managers stumble: like the executives at VW and Wells Fargo, Jobs was operating on a limited understanding of leadership and organizations. He was always a brilliant and charismatic product visionary. That enabled him to take Apple from startup to major computer vendor, but didn't equip him to lead Apple to its next phase. Being fired was painful, but Jobs later concluded that it was the best thing that ever happened to him. "It freed me to enter one of the most creative periods of my life. I'm pretty sure none of this would have happened if I hadn't been fired from Apple. It was awful-tasting medicine, but I guess the patient needed it."

During his period of self-reflection, Jobs kept busy. He focused on Pixar, a computer graphics company he bought for $10 million, and on NeXT, a new computer company that he founded. One succeeded and the other didn't, but he learned from both. Pixar became so successful it made Jobs a billionaire. NeXT never made money, but it developed technology that proved vital when Jobs was recalled from the wilderness to save Apple from a death spiral.

His experiences at NeXT and Pixar provided two vital lessons. One was the importance of aligning an organization with its strategy and mission. He understood more clearly that he needed a great company to build great products. Lesson two was about people. Jobs had always understood the importance of talent, but now he had a better appreciation for the importance of relationships and teamwork.

Jobs's basic character did not change during his wilderness years. The Steve Jobs who returned to Apple in 1997 was much like the human paradox fired 12 years earlier—demanding and charismatic, charming and infuriating, erratic and focused, opinionated and curious. The difference was in how he interpreted what was going on around him and how he led. To his long-time gifts as a magician and warrior, he had added newfound capacities as an organizational architect and team builder.

Shortly after his return, he radically simplified Apple's product line, built a loyal and talented leadership team, and turned his old company into a hit-making machine as reliable as Pixar. The iMac, iPod, iPhone, and iPad made Jobs the world's most admired chief executive, and Apple passed ExxonMobil to become the world's most valuable company. His success in building an organization and a leadership team was validated as Apple's business results continued to impress after his death in October 2011. Like many other executives, Steve Jobs seemed to have it all until he lost it—but most never get it back.

Martin Winterkorn had seemed to be on track to make Volkswagen the world's biggest car company, and Wells Fargo CEO John Stumpf was one of America's most admired bankers. But both became so cocooned in imperfect worldviews that they misread their circumstances and couldn't see other options. That's what it means to be clueless. You don't know what's going on, but you think you do, and you don't see better choices. So you do more of what you know, even though it's not working. You hope in vain that steady on course will get you where you want to go.

How do leaders become clueless? That is what we explore next. Then we introduce *reframing*—the conceptual core of the book and our basic prescription for sizing things up. Reframing requires an ability to think about situations from more than one angle, which lets you develop alternative diagnoses and strategies. We introduce four distinct frames—

structural, human resource, political, and symbolic—each logical and powerful in capturing a detailed snapshot. Together, they help to paint a more comprehensive picture of what's going on and what to do.

VIRTUES AND DRAWBACKS OF ORGANIZED ACTIVITY

There was little need for professional managers when individuals mostly managed their own affairs, drawing goods and services from family farms and small local businesses. Since the dawn of the industrial revolution some 200 years ago, explosive technological and social changes have produced a world that is far more interconnected, frantic, and complicated. Humans struggle to avoid drowning in complexity that continually threatens to pull them in over their heads (Kegan, 1998). Forms of management and organization effective a few years ago are now obsolete. Sérieyx (1993) calls it the organizational big bang: "The information revolution, the globalization of economies, the proliferation of events that undermine all our certainties, the collapse of the grand ideologies, the arrival of the CNN society which transforms us into an immense, planetary village—all these shocks have overturned the rules of the game and suddenly turned yesterday's organizations into antiques" (pp. 14–15).

Benner and Tushman (2015) argue that the twenty-first century is making managers' challenges ever more vexing:

> The paradoxical challenges facing organizations have become more numerous and strategic (Besharov & Smith, 2014; Smith & Lewis, 2011). Beyond the innovation challenges of exploration and exploitation, organizations are now challenged to be local and global (e.g., Marquis & Battilana, 2009), doing well and doing good (e.g., Battilana & Lee, 2014; Margolis & Walsh, 2003), social and commercial (e.g., Battilana & Dorado, 2010), artistic or scientific and profitable (e.g., Glynn, 2000), high commitment and high performance (e.g., Beer & Eisenstadt, 2009), and profitable and sustainable (e.g., Eccles, Ioannou, & Serafeim, 2014; Henderson, Gulati, & Tushman, 2015; Jay, 2013). These contradictions are more prevalent, persistent, and consequential. Further, these contradictions can be sustained and managed, but not resolved (Smith, 2014).

The demands on managers' wisdom, imagination and agility have never been greater, and the impact of organizations on people's well-being and happiness has never been more consequential. The proliferation of complex organizations has made most human activities more formalized than they once were. We grow up in families and then start our own. We work for business, government, or nonprofits. We learn in schools and universities. We worship in churches, mosques, and synagogues. We play sports in teams, franchises, and leagues. We join clubs and associations. Many of us will grow old and die in hospitals or nursing homes. We build these enterprises because of what they can do for us. They offer goods, entertainment, social services, health care, and almost everything else that we use or consume.

All too often, however, we experience a darker side of these enterprises. Organizations can frustrate and exploit people. Too often, products are flawed, families are dysfunctional, students fail to learn, patients get worse, and policies backfire. Work often has so little meaning that jobs offer nothing beyond a paycheck. If we believe mission statements and public pronouncements, almost every organization these days aims to nurture its employees and delight its customers. But many miss the mark. Schools are blamed for "mis-educating," universities are said to close more minds than they open, and government is criticized for corruption, red tape, and rigidity.

The private sector has its own problems. Manufacturers recall faulty cars or inflammable cellphones. Producers of food and pharmaceuticals make people sick with tainted products. Software companies deliver bugs and "vaporware." Industrial accidents dump chemicals, oil, toxic gas, and radioactive materials into the air and water. Too often, corporate greed, incompetence, and insensitivity create havoc for communities and individuals. The bottom line: We seem hard-pressed to manage organizations so that their virtues exceed their vices. The big question: Why?

Management's Track Record

Year after year, the best and brightest managers maneuver or meander their way to the apex of enterprises great and small. Then they do really dumb things. How do bright people turn out so dim? One theory is that they're too smart for their own good. Feinberg and Tarrant (1995) label it the "self-destructive intelligence syndrome." They argue that smart people act stupid because of personality flaws—things like pride, arrogance, and an unconscious desire to fail. It's true that psychological flaws have been apparent in brilliant, self-destructive individuals such as Adolf Hitler, Richard Nixon, and Bill Clinton. But on the whole, the best and brightest have no more psychological problems than everyone else. The primary source of cluelessness is not personality or IQ but a failure to make sense of complex situations. If we misread a situation, we'll do the wrong thing. But if we don't know we're seeing things inaccurately, we won't understand why we're not getting the results we want. So we insist we're right even when we're off track.

Vaughan (1995), in trying to unravel the causes of the 1986 disaster that destroyed the *Challenger* space shuttle and its crew, underscored how hard it is for people to surrender their entrenched conceptions of reality:

> They puzzle over contradictory evidence, but usually succeed in pushing it aside—until they come across a piece of evidence too fascinating to ignore, too clear to misperceive, too painful to deny, which makes vivid still other signals they do not want to see, forcing them to alter and surrender the world-view they have so meticulously constructed (p. 235).

So when we don't know what to do, we do more of what we know. We construct our own psychic prisons and then lock ourselves in and throw away the key. This helps explain a number of unsettling reports from the managerial front lines:

- Hogan, Curphy, and Hogan (1994) estimate that the skills of one half to three quarters of American managers are inadequate for the demands of their jobs. Gallup (2015) puts the number even higher, estimating that more than 80 percent of American managers lack the talent they need. But most probably don't realize it: Kruger and Dunning (1999) found that the less competent people are, the more they overestimate their performance, partly because they don't know good performance when they see it.

- About half of the high-profile senior executives that companies hire fail within two years, according to a 2006 study (Burns and Kiley, 2007).

- The annual value of corporate mergers has grown more than a hundredfold since 1980, yet evidence suggests that 70 to 90 percent "are unsuccessful in producing any business benefit as regards shareholder value" (KPMG, 2000; Christensen, Alton, Rising, and Waldeck, 2011). Mergers typically benefit shareholders of the acquired firm but hurt almost everyone else—customers, employees, and, ironically, the buyers who initiated the deal (King et al., 2004). Stockholders in the acquiring firm typically suffer a 10 percent loss on their investment (Agrawal, Jaffe, and Mandelker, 1992), while consumers feel that they're paying more and getting less. Despite this dismal record, the vast majority of the managers who engineered mergers insisted they were successful (KPMG, 2000; Graffin, Haleblian, and Kiley, 2016).

- Year after year, management miscues cause once highly successful companies to skid into bankruptcy. In just the first quarter of 2015, for example, 26 companies went under, including six with claimed assets of more than $1 billion. (Among the biggest were the casino giant, Caesars Entertainment, and the venerable electronics retailer, RadioShack.)

Small wonder that so many organizational veterans nod in assent to Scott Adams's admittedly unscientific "Dilbert principle": "the most ineffective workers are systematically moved to the place where they can do the least damage—management" (1996, p. 14).

Strategies for Improving Organizations

We have certainly made a noble effort to improve organizations despite our limited ability to understand them. Legions of managers report to work each day with hope for a better future in mind. Authors and consultants spin out a torrent of new answers and promising solutions. Policymakers develop laws and regulations to guide or shove organizations on the right path.

The most universal improvement strategy is upgrading management talent. Modern mythology promises that organizations will work splendidly if well managed. Managers are supposed to see the big picture and look out for their organization's overall well-being. They have not always been equal to the task, even when armed with the full array of modern tools and techniques. They go forth with this rational arsenal to try to tame our wild and primitive workplaces. Yet in the end, irrational forces too often prevail.

When managers find problems too hard to solve, they hire consultants. The number and variety of advice givers keeps growing. Most have a specialty: strategy, technology, quality, finance, marketing, mergers, human resource management, executive search, outplacement, coaching, organization development, and many more. For every managerial challenge, there is a consultant willing to offer assistance—at a price.

For all their sage advice and remarkable fees, consultants often make little dent in persistent problems plaguing organizations, though they may blame the clients for failing to implement their profound insights. McKinsey & Co., "the high priest of high-level consulting" (Byrne, 2002a, p. 66), worked so closely with Enron that its managing partner (Rajat Gupta, who eventually went to jail for insider trading) sent his chief lawyer to Houston after Enron's collapse to see if his firm might be in legal trouble.[2] The lawyer reported that McKinsey was safe, and a relieved Gupta insisted bravely, "We stand by all the work we did. Beyond that, we can only empathize with the trouble they are going through. It's a sad thing to see" (p. 68).

When managers and consultants fail, government recurrently responds with legislation, policies, and regulations. Constituents badger elected officials to "do something" about a variety of ills: pollution, dangerous products, hazardous working conditions, discrimination, and low performing schools, to name a few. Governing bodies respond by making "policy." But policymakers don't always understand the problem well enough to get the solution right, and a sizable body of research records a continuing saga of perverse ways in which the implementation process undermines even good solutions (Bardach, 1977; Elmore, 1978; Freudenberg and Gramling, 1994; Gottfried and Conchas, 2016; Peters, 1999; Pressman and Wildavsky, 1973). Policymakers, for example, have been trying for decades to reform U.S. public schools. Billions of taxpayer dollars have been spent. The result? About as successful as America's switch to the metric system. In the 1950s Congress passed legislation mandating adoption of metric standards and measures. More than six decades later, if you know what a hectare is or can visualize the size of a 300-gram package of crackers, you're ahead of most Americans. Legislators did not factor into their solution what it would take to get their decision implemented against longstanding custom and tradition.

In short, the difficulties surrounding improvement strategies are well documented. Exemplary intentions produce more costs than benefits. Problems outlast solutions. Still, there are reasons for optimism. Organizations have changed about as much in recent decades as in the preceding century. To survive, they had to. Revolutionary changes in technology, the rise of the global economy, and shortened product life cycles have spawned a flurry of efforts to design faster, more flexible organizational forms. New organizational models flourish in companies such as Pret à Manger (the socially conscious U.K. sandwich shops), Google (the global search giant), Airbnb (a new concept of lodging) and Novo-Nordisk (a Danish pharmaceutical company that includes environmental and social metrics in its bottom line). The dispersed collection of enthusiasts and volunteers who provide content for Wikipedia and the far-flung network of software engineers who have developed the Linux operating system provide dramatic examples of possibilities in the digital world. But despite such successes, failures are still too common. The nagging question: How can leaders and managers improve the odds for themselves as well for their organizations?

FRAMING

Goran Carstedt, the talented executive who led the turnaround of Volvo's French division in the 1980s, got to the heart of a challenge managers face every day: "The world simply can't be made sense of, facts can't be organized, unless you have a mental model to begin with. That theory does not have to be the right one, because you can alter it along the way as information comes in. But you can't begin to learn without some concept that gives you expectations or hypotheses" (Hampden-Turner, 1992, p. 167). Such mental models have many labels—maps, mind-sets, schema, paradigms, heuristics, and cognitive lenses, to name a few.[3] Following the work of Goffman, Dewey, and others, we have chosen the label *frames,* a term that has received increasing attention in organizational research as scholars give greater attention to how managers make sense of a complicated and turbulent world (see, e.g., Foss and Webber, 2016; Gray, Purdy, and Ansari, 2015; Cornelissen and Werner, 2014; Hahn et al., 2014; Maitlis and Christianson, 2014). In describing frames, we deliberately mix metaphors, referring to them as windows, maps, tools, lenses, orientations, prisms, and perspectives, because all these images capture part of the idea we want to convey.

A frame is a mental model—a set of ideas and assumptions—that you carry in your head to help you understand and negotiate a particular "territory." A good frame makes it easier to know what you are up against and, ultimately, what you can do about it. Frames are vital because organizations don't come with computerized navigation systems to guide you turn-by-turn to your destination. Instead, managers need to develop and carry accurate maps in their heads.

Such maps make it possible to register and assemble key bits of perceptual data into a coherent pattern—an image of what's happening. When it works fluidly, the process takes the form of "rapid cognition," the process that Gladwell (2005) examines in his best seller *Blink*. He describes it as a gift that makes it possible to read "deeply into the narrowest slivers of experience. In basketball, the player who can take in and comprehend all that is happening in the moment is said to have 'court sense'" (p. 44). The military stresses situational awareness to describe the same capacity.

Dane and Pratt (2007) describe four key characteristics of this intuitive "blink" process:

- It is nonconscious—you can do it without thinking about it and without knowing how you did it.
- It is very fast—the process often occurs almost instantly.
- It is holistic—you see a coherent, meaningful pattern.
- It results in "affective judgments"—thought and feeling work together so you feel confident that you know what is going on and what needs to be done.

The essence of this process is matching situational cues with a well-learned mental framework—a "deeply held, nonconscious category or pattern" (Dane and Pratt, 2007, p. 37). This is the key skill that Simon and Chase (1973) found in chess masters—they could instantly recognize more than 50,000 configurations of a chessboard. This ability enables grand masters to play 25 lesser opponents simultaneously, beating all of them while spending only seconds on each move.

The same process of rapid cognition is at work in the diagnostic categories physicians rely on to evaluate patients' symptoms. The Hippocratic Oath to "do no harm" requires physicians to be confident that they know what they're up against before prescribing a remedy. Their skilled judgment draws on a repertoire of categories and clues, honed by training and experience. But sometimes they get it wrong. One source of error is anchoring: doctors, like leaders, sometimes lock on to the first answer that seems right, even if a few messy facts don't quite fit. "Your mind plays tricks on you because you see only the landmarks you expect to see and neglect those that should tell you that in fact you're still at sea" (Groopman, 2007, p. 65).

That problem tripped up leaders at Volkswagen, Wells Fargo, and countless other organizations. Organizations are at least as complex as the human body, and the diagnostic categories less well defined. That means that the quality of your judgments depends on the information you have at hand, your mental maps, and how well you have learned to use them. Good maps align with the terrain and provide enough detail to keep you on course. If you're trying to find your way around Beijing, a map of Chicago won't help. In the same way, different circumstances require different approaches.

Even with the right map, getting around will be slow and awkward if you have to stop and study at every intersection. The ultimate goal is fluid expertise, the sort of know-how that lets you think on the fly and navigate organizations as easily as you drive home on a familiar route. You can make decisions quickly and automatically because you know at a glance where you are and what you need to do next.

There is no shortcut to developing this kind of expertise. It takes effort, time, practice, and feedback. Some of the effort has to go into learning frames and the ideas behind them. Equally important is putting the ideas to use. Experience, one often hears, is the best teacher, but that is true only if one learns from it. McCall, Lombardo, and Morrison (1988, p. 122) found that a key quality among successful executives was they were great learners, displaying an "extraordinary tenacity in extracting something worthwhile from their experience and in seeking experiences rich in opportunities for growth."

Reframing

Frames define the questions we ask and solutions we consider (Berger 2014). John Dewey defined freedom as the power to choose among known alternatives. When managers' options are limited they make mistakes but too often fail to understand the source. Take a simple example: "What is the sum of 5 plus 5?" The only right answer is "10." Ask a different way, "What two numbers add up to ten? Now the number of solutions is infinite (once you include fractions and negative numbers). The two questions differ in how they are framed. Albert Einstein once observed: "If I had a problem to solve and my whole life depended on the solution, I would spend the first fifty-five minutes determining the question to ask, for once I know the proper question, I could solve the problem in five minutes" (Seelig, 2015, p. 19). Asking the right question enhances the ability to break frames. Why do that? A news story from the summer of 2007 illustrates. Imagine yourself among a group of friends enjoying dinner on the patio of a Washington, DC, home. An armed, hooded intruder suddenly appears and points a gun at the head of a 14-year-old guest. "Give me your money," he says, "or I'll start shooting." If you're at that table, what do you do? You could faint. Or freeze. You could try a heroic frontal attack. You might try to run. Or you could try to break frame by asking an unexpected question. That's exactly what Cristina "Cha Cha" Rowan did.

> "We were just finishing dinner," [she] told the man. "Why don't you have a glass of wine with us?"
>
> The intruder had a sip of their Chateau Malescot St-Exupéry and said, "Damn, that's good wine."
>
> The girl's father . . . told the intruder to take the whole glass, and Rowan offered him the bottle.
>
> The robber, with his hood down, took another sip and a bite of Camembert cheese. He put the gun in his sweatpants . . .
>
> "I think I may have come to the wrong house," the intruder said before apologizing. "Can I get a hug?"
>
> Rowan . . . stood up and wrapped her arms around the would-be robber. The other guests followed.
>
> "Can we have a group hug?" the man asked. The five adults complied.
>
> The man walked away a few moments later with a filled crystal wine glass, but nothing was stolen, and no one was hurt. Police were called to the scene and found the empty wine glass unbroken on the ground in an alley behind the house (Hagey, 2007).

In one stroke, Cha Cha Rowan redefined the situation from a robbery— "we might all be killed"—to a social occasion—"let's offer our guest some wine and include him in our party." Like her, artistic managers frame and reframe experience fluidly, sometimes with extraordinary results. A critic once commented to Cézanne, "That doesn't look anything like a sunset." Pondering his painting, Cézanne responded, "Then you don't see sunsets the way I do." Like Cézanne and Rowan, leaders have to find ways of asking the right question to shift points of view when needed. This is not easy, which is why "most of us passively accept decision problems as they are framed, and therefore rarely have an opportunity to discover the extent to which our preferences are *frame-bound* rather than *reality-bound*" (Kahneman, 2011, p. 367).

Caldicott (2014) sees reframing as vital for leadership: "One distinguishing difference between leaders that succeed at driving collaboration and innovation versus those that fail is their ability to grasp Complexity. This skill set involves framing difficult concepts quickly, synthesizing data in a way that drives new insight, and building teams that can generate future scenarios different from the world they see today." A growing body of psychological research shows that reframing can improve performance across a range of tasks. Autin and Croizet (2012) gave students a difficult task on which they all struggled. Some students were taught to reframe the struggle as a normal sign of learning. That intervention increased confidence, working memory, and reading comprehension on subsequent tasks. Jamieson et al. (2010) found that they could improve scores on the Graduate Record Exam by reframing anxiety as an aid to performance. The old song lyric, "accentuate the positive and eliminate the negative," is powerful advice.

Like maps, frames are both windows on a terrain and tools for navigating its contours. Every tool has distinctive strengths and limitations. The right tool makes a job easier; the wrong one gets in the way. Tools thus become useful only when a situation is sized up accurately. Furthermore, one or two tools may suffice for simple jobs but not for more complex undertakings. Managers who master the hammer and expect all problems to behave like nails find life at work confusing and frustrating. The wise manager, like a skilled carpenter, wants at hand a diverse collection of high-quality implements. Experienced managers also understand the difference between possessing a tool and knowing when and how to use it. Only experience and practice foster the skill and wisdom to take stock of a situation and use suitable tools with confidence and skill.

The Four Frames

Only in the past 100 years or so have social scientists devoted much time or attention to developing ideas about how organizations work, how they should work, or why they often fail. In the social sciences, several major schools of thought have evolved. Each has its own concepts, assumptions, and evidence, espousing a particular view of how to bring social collectives under control. Each tradition claims a scientific foundation. But a theory can easily become a theology that preaches a single, parochial scripture. Modern managers must sort through a cacophony of voices and visions for help.

Sifting through competing voices is one of our goals in writing this book. We are not searching for or advocating the one best way. Rather, we consolidate major schools of organizational thought and research into a comprehensive framework encompassing four perspectives. Our goal is usable knowledge. We have sought ideas powerful enough to capture the subtlety and complexity of life in organizations yet simple enough to be useful. Our distillation has drawn much from the social sciences—particularly sociology, psychology, political science, and anthropology. Thousands of managers and scores of organizations have helped us sift through social science research to identify ideas that work in practice. We have sorted insights from both research and practice into four major frames—structural, human resource, political, and symbolic (Bolman and Deal, 1984). Each is used by academics and practitioners alike and can be found, usually independently, on the shelves of libraries and bookstores.

Four Frames: As Near as Your Local Bookstore

Imagine a harried executive browsing online or at her local bookseller on a brisk winter day in 2017. She worries about her company's flagging performance and wonders if her own job might soon disappear. She spots the black cover of *How to Measure Anything: Finding the Value of "Intangibles" in Business*. Flipping through the pages, she notes topics like measuring the value of information and the need for better risk analysis. She is drawn to phrases such as "A key step in the process is the calculation of the economic value of information . . . [A] proven formula from the field of decision theory allows us to compute a monetary value for a given amount of uncertainty reduction"[4] (p. 35). "This stuff may be good," the executive tells herself, "but it seems a little too stiff and numbers-driven."

Next, she finds *Lead with LUV: A Different Way to Create Real Success*. Glancing inside, she reads, "Many of our officers handwrite several thousand notes each year. Besides being loving, we know this is meaningful to our People because we hear from them if we miss something significant in their lives like the high school graduation of one of their kids. We just believe in accentuating the positive and celebrating People's successes"[5] (p. 7). "Sounds nice," she mumbles, "but a little too touchy-feely. Let's look for something more down to earth."

Continuing her search, she looks at *Power: Why Some People Have It and Others Don't*. She reads, "You can compete and triumph in organizations of all types . . . if you understand the principles of power and are willing to use them. Your task is to know how to prevail in the political battles you will face"[6] (p. 5). She wonders, "Does it really all come down to politics? It seems so cynical and scheming. How about something more uplifting?"

She spots *Tribal Leadership: Leveraging Natural Groups to Build a Thriving Organization*. She ponders its message: "Tribal leaders focus their efforts on building the tribe, or, more precisely, upgrading the tribal culture. If they are successful, the tribe recognizes them as leaders, giving them top effort, cult-like loyalty, and a track record of success"[7] (p. 4). "Fascinating," she concludes, "but seems a little too primitive for modern organizations."

In her book excursion, our worried executive has rediscovered the four perspectives at the heart of this book. Four distinct metaphors capture the essence of each of the books she examined: organizations as factories, families, jungles, and temples or carnivals. But she leaves more confused than ever. Some titles seemed to register with her way of thinking. Others fell outside her zone of comfort. Where should she go next? How can she put it all together?

Factories

The first book she stumbled across, *How to Measure Anything,* provides counsel on how to think clearly and make rational decisions, extending a long tradition that treats an organization as a factory. Drawing from sociology, economics, and management science, the structural frame depicts a rational world and emphasizes organizational architecture, including planning, strategy, goals, structure, technology, specialized roles, coordination, formal relationships, metrics, and rubrics. Structures—commonly depicted by organization charts—are designed to fit an organization's environment and technology. Organizations allocate responsibilities ("division of labor"). They then create rules, policies, procedures, systems, and hierarchies to coordinate diverse activities into a unified effort. Objective indicators measure progress. Problems arise when structure doesn't line up well with current circumstances or when performance sags. At that point, some form of reorganization or redesign is needed to remedy the mismatch.

Families

Our executive next encountered *Lead with LUV: A Different Way to Create Real Success,* with its focus on people and relationships. The human resource perspective, rooted in psychology, sees an organization as an extended family, made up of individuals with needs, feelings, prejudices, skills, and limitations. From a human resource view, the key challenge is to tailor organizations to individuals—finding ways for people to get the job done while feeling good about themselves and their work. When basic needs for security and trust are unfulfilled, people withdraw from an organization, join unions, go on strike, sabotage, or quit. Psychologically healthy organizations provide adequate wages and benefits and make sure employees have the skills, support, and resources to do their jobs.

Jungles

Power: Why Some People Have It and Others Don't is a contemporary application of the political frame, rooted in the work of political scientists. This view sees organizations as arenas, contests, or jungles. Parochial interests compete for power and scarce resources. Conflict is rampant because of enduring differences in needs, perspectives, and lifestyles among contending individuals and groups. Bargaining, negotiation, coercion, and compromise are a normal part of everyday life. Coalitions form around specific interests and change as issues come and go. Problems arise when power is concentrated in the wrong places or is so widely dispersed that nothing gets done. Solutions arise from political skill and acumen—as Machiavelli suggested 500 years ago in *The Prince* (1961).

Temples and Carnivals

Finally, our executive encountered *Tribal Leadership: Leveraging Natural Groups to Build a Thriving Organization,* with its emphasis on culture, symbols, and spirit as keys to organizational success. The symbolic lens, drawing on social and cultural anthropology, treats organizations as temples, tribes, theaters, or carnivals. It tempers the assumptions of rationality prominent in other frames and depicts organizations as cultures, propelled by rituals, ceremonies, stories, heroes, history, and myths rather than by rules, policies, and managerial authority. Organization is also theater: actors play their roles in an ongoing drama while audiences form impressions from what they see on stage. Problems arise when actors blow their parts, symbols lose their meaning, or ceremonies and rituals lose their potency. We rekindle the expressive or spiritual side of organizations through the use of symbol, myth, and magic.

The FBI and the CIA: A Four-Frame Story

A saga of two squabbling agencies illustrates how the four frames provide different views of the same situation. Riebling (2002) documents the long history of head-butting between America's two major intelligence agencies, the Federal Bureau of Investigation and the Central Intelligence Agency. Both are charged with combating espionage and terrorism, but the FBI's authority is valid primarily within the United States, while the CIA's mandate covers everywhere else. Structurally, the two agencies have always been disconnected. The FBI is housed in the Department of Justice and reports to the attorney general. The CIA reported through the director of central intelligence to the president until 2004, when reorganization put it under a new director of national intelligence.

At a number of major junctures in American history (including the assassination of President John F. Kennedy, the Iran-Contra scandal, and the 9/11 terrorist attacks), each agency held pieces of a larger puzzle, but coordination snafus made it hard for anyone to see all the pieces, much less put them together. After 9/11, both agencies came under heavy criticism, and each blamed the other for lapses. The FBI complained that the CIA had failed to tell them that two of the terrorists had entered the United States and had been living in California since 2000 (Seper, 2005). But an internal Justice Department investigation also concluded that the FBI didn't do very well with the information it did have. Key signals were never "documented by the bureau or placed in any system from which they could be retrieved by agents investigating terrorist threats" (Seper, 2005, p. 1).

Structural barriers between the FBI and the CIA were exacerbated by the enmity between the two agencies' patron saints, J. Edgar Hoover and "Wild Bill" Donovan. When Hoover first became FBI director in the 1920s, he reported to Donovan, who didn't trust him and tried unsuccessfully to get him fired. When World War II broke out, Hoover lobbied to get the FBI identified as the nation's worldwide intelligence agency. He fumed when President Franklin D. Roosevelt instead created a new agency and made Donovan its director. As often happens, cooperation between two units was chronically hampered by a rocky personal relationship between two top dogs who never liked one another.

Politically, the relationship between the FBI and CIA was born in turf conflict because of Roosevelt's decision to give responsibility for foreign intelligence to Donovan instead of to Hoover. The friction persisted over the decades as both agencies vied for turf and funding from Congress and the White House.

Symbolically, different histories and missions led to very distinct cultures. The FBI, which built its image with the dramatic capture or killing of notorious gang leaders, bank robbers, and foreign agents, liked to generate headlines by pouncing on suspects quickly and publicly. The CIA preferred to work in the shadows, believing that patience and secrecy were vital to its task of collecting intelligence and rooting out foreign spies.

Senior U.S. officials have known for years that tension between the FBI and CIA damages U.S. security. But most initiatives to improve the relationship have been partial and ephemeral, falling well short of addressing the full range of issues.

Multiframe Thinking

The overview of the four-frame model in Exhibit 1.1 shows that each of the frames has its own image of reality. You may be drawn to some and put off by others. Some perspectives may seem clear and straightforward, while others seem puzzling. But learning to apply all four deepens your appreciation and understanding of organizations. Galileo discovered this when he devised the first telescope. Each lens he added contributed to a more accurate image of the heavens. Successful managers take advantage of the same truth. Like physicians, they reframe, consciously or intuitively, until they understand the situation at hand. They use more than one lens to develop a diagnosis of what they are up against and how to move forward.

Exhibit 1.1.
Overview of the Four-Frame Model.

	Frame			
	Structural	**Human Resource**	**Political**	**Symbolic**
Metaphor for organization	Factory or machine	Family	Jungle	Carnival, temple, theater
Supporting disciplines	Sociology, management science	Psychology	Political science	Anthropology, dramaturgy, institutional theory
Central concepts	Roles, goals, strategies, policies, technology, environment	Needs, skills, relationships	Power, conflict, competition, politics	Culture, myth, meaning, metaphor, ritual, ceremony, stories, heroes
Image of leadership	Social architecture	Empowerment	Advocacy and political savvy	Inspiration
Basic leadership challenge	Attune structure to task, technology, environment	Align organizational and human needs	Develop agenda and power base	Create faith, belief, beauty, meaning

This claim about the advantages of multiple perspectives has stimulated a growing body of research. Dunford and Palmer (1995) discovered that management courses teaching multiple frames had significant positive effects over both the short and long term—in fact, 98 percent of their respondents rated reframing as helpful or very helpful, and about 90 percent felt it gave them a competitive advantage. Other studies have shown that the ability to use multiple frames is associated with greater effectiveness for managers and leaders (Bensimon, 1989, 1990; Birnbaum, 1992; Bolman and Deal, 1991, 1992a, 1992b; Heimovics, Herman, and Jurkiewicz Coughlin, 1993, 1995; Wimpelberg, 1987). Similarly, Pitt and Tepper (2012) found that double-majoring helped college students develop both creative and integrative thinking. As one student put it, "I'm never stuck in one frame of mind because I'm always switching back and forth between the two" (p. 40). Multiframe thinking requires moving beyond narrow, mechanical approaches for understanding organizations. We cannot count the number of times managers have told us that they handled some problem the "only way" it could be done. That was United Airline's initial defense in April 2017, when video of a bloodied doctor being dragged off a plane went viral. United's CEO wrote that "our agents were left with no choice" because the 69-year-old physician had refused to give up his seat. After a few days in public-relations hell, United announced that the only choice was a bad one, and they would never do it again. It may be comforting to think that failure was unavoidable and we did all we could. But it can be liberating to realize there is always more than one way to respond to any problem or dilemma. Those who master reframing report a liberating sense of choice and power. Managers are imprisoned only to the extent that their palette of ideas is impoverished.

Akira Kurosawa's classic film *Rashomon* recounts the same event through the eyes of several witnesses. Each tells a different story. Similarly, organizations are filled with people who have divergent interpretations of what is and should be happening. Each version contains a glimmer of truth, but each is a product of the prejudices and blind spots of its maker. Each frame tells a different story (Gottschall, 2012), but no single story is comprehensive enough to make an organization fully understandable or manageable. Effective managers need frames to generate multiple stories, the skill to sort through the alternatives, and the wisdom to match the right story to the situation.[8]

Lack of imagination—Langer (1989) calls it "mindlessness"—is a major cause of the shortfall between the reach and the grasp of so many organizations—the empty chasm between noble aspirations and disappointing results. The gap is painfully acute in a world where organizations dominate so much of our lives. Taleb (2007) depicts events like the 9/11 attacks as "black swans"—novel events that are unexpected because we have never seen them before. If every swan we've observed is white, we expect the same in the future. But fateful, make-or-break events are more likely to be situations we've never experienced before. Imagination or mindfulness is our best chance for being ready when a black swan sails into view, and multiframe thinking is a powerful stimulus to the broad, creative mind-set imagination requires.

Engineering and Art

Exhibit 1.2 presents two contrasting approaches to management and leadership. One is a rational-technical mind-set emphasizing certainty and control. The other is an expressive, artistic conception encouraging flexibility, creativity, and interpretation. The first portrays managers as technicians; the second sees them as artists.

Exhibit 1.2.
Expanding Managerial Thinking.

How Managers Often Think	How Managers Might Think
Oversimplify reality (for example, blame problems on individuals' flaws and errors).	Think holistically about a full range of significant issues: people, power, structure, and symbols.
Regardless of the problems at hand, rely on facts, logic, restructuring.	Use feeling and intuition as well as logic, bargaining as well as training, celebration as well as reorganization.
Cling to certainty, rationality, and control while fearing ambiguity, paradox, and "going with the flow."	Develop creativity, risk-taking, and playfulness in response to life's dilemmas and paradoxes, and focus as much on finding the right question as the right answer, on finding meaning and faith amid clutter and confusion.
Rely on the "one right answer" and the "one best way."	Show passionate, unwavering commitment to principle, combined with flexibility in understanding and responding to events.

Artists interpret experience and express it in forms that can be felt, understood, and appreciated by others. Art embraces emotion, subtlety, ambiguity. An artist reframes the world so others can see new possibilities. Modern organizations often rely too much on engineering and too little on art in searching for quality, commitment, and creativity. Art is not a replacement for engineering but an enhancement. Many engineering schools are currently developing design programs to stimulate creative thinking. Artistic leaders and managers help us look and probe beyond today's reality to new forms that release untapped individual energies and improve collective performance. The leader as artist relies on images as well as memos, poetry as well as policy, reflection as well as command, and reframing as well as refitting.

CONCLUSION

As organizations have become pervasive and dominant, they have also become harder to understand and manage. The result is that managers are often nearly as clueless as their subordinates (the Dilberts of the world) think they are. The consequences of myopic management and leadership show up every day, sometimes in small and subtle ways, sometimes in catastrophes. Our basic premise is that a primary cause of managerial failure is faulty thinking rooted in inadequate ideas. Managers and those who try to help them too often rely on narrow models that capture only part of organizational life.

Learning multiple perspectives, or frames, is a defense against thrashing around without a clue about what you are doing or why. Frames serve multiple functions. They are sources of new question, filters for sorting essence from trivia, maps that aid navigation, and tools for solving problems and getting things done. This book is organized around four frames rooted in both managerial wisdom and social science knowledge. The structural approach focuses on the architecture of organization—the design of units and subunits, rules and roles, goals and policies. The human resource lens emphasizes understanding people—their strengths and foibles, reason and emotion, desires and fears. The political view sees organizations as competitive arenas of scarce resources, competing interests, and struggles for power and advantage. Finally, the symbolic frame focuses on issues of meaning and faith. It puts ritual, ceremony, story, play, and culture at the heart of organizational life.

Each of the frames is powerful and coherent. Collectively, they make it possible to reframe, looking at the same thing from multiple lenses or points of view. When the world seems hopelessly confusing and nothing is working, reframing is a powerful tool for gaining clarity, regaining balance, generating new questions, and finding options that make a difference.

Notes

1. Tabuchi, H., Ewing, J., and Apuzzo, M. 2017. "6 Volkswagen Executives Charged as Company Pleads Guilty in Emissions Case." *New York Times*, January 12. https://www.nytimes.com/2017/01/11/business/volkswagen-diesel-vw-settlement-charges-criminal.html?_r=0
2. Enron's reign as history's greatest corporate catastrophe was brief. An even bigger behemoth, WorldCom, with assets of more than $100 billion, thundered into Chapter 11 seven months later, in July 2002. Stock worth more than $45 a share two years earlier fell to nine cents.
3. Among the possible ways of talking about frames are schemata or schema theory (Fiedler, 1982; Fiske and Dyer, 1985; Lord and Foti, 1986), representations (Frensch and Sternberg, 1991; Lesgold and Lajoie, 1991; Voss, Wolfe, Lawrence, and Engle, 1991), cognitive maps (Weick and Bougon, 1986), paradigms (Gregory, 1983; Kuhn, 1970), social categorizations (Cronshaw, 1987), implicit theories (Brief and Downey, 1983), mental models (Senge, 1990), definitions of the situation, and root metaphors.
4. Douglas W. Hubbard, *How to Measure Anything: Finding the Value of Intangibles in Business* (New York: Wiley, 2010), p. 35.

5. Ken Blanchard and Colleen Barrett, *Lead with LUV: A Different Way to Create Real Success* (Upper Saddle River, NJ: FT Press, 2010), p. 7.

6. Jeffrey Pfeffer, *Power: Why Some People Have It and Others Don't* (New York: Harper Business, 2010), p. 5.

7. Dave Logan, John King, and Halee Fischer-Wright, *Tribal Leadership: Leveraging Natural Groups to Build a Thriving Organization* (New York: Harper Business, 2011), p. 4.

8. A number of scholars (including Allison, 1971; Bergquist, 1992; Birnbaum, 1988; Elmore, 1978; Morgan, 1986; Perrow, 1986; Quinn, 1988; Quinn, Faerman, Thompson, and McGrath, 1996; and Scott, 1981) have made similar arguments for multiframe approaches to groups and social collectives.

Simple Ideas, Complex Organizations

Precisely one of the most gratifying results of intellectual evolution is the continuous opening up of new and greater prospects.

—Nikola Tesla[1]

September 11, 2001 brought a crisp and sunny late-summer morning to America's east coast. Perfect weather offered prospects of on-time departures and smooth flights for airline passengers in the Boston-Washington corridor. That promise was shattered for four flights bound for California when terrorists commandeered the aircraft. Two of the hijacked aircraft attacked and destroyed the Twin Towers of New York's World Trade Center. Another slammed into the Pentagon. The fourth was deterred from its mission by the heroic efforts of passengers. It crashed in a vacant field, killing all aboard. Like Pearl Harbor in December 1941, 9/11 was a day that will live in infamy, a tragedy that changed forever America's sense of itself and the world.

Why did no one foresee such a catastrophe? In fact, some had. As far back as 1993, security experts had envisioned an attempt to destroy the World Trade Center using airplanes as weapons. Such fears were reinforced when a suicidal pilot crashed a small private plane onto the White House lawn in 1994. But the mind-set of principals in the national security network was riveted on prior hijackings, which had almost always ended in negotiations. The idea of a suicide mission, using commercial aircraft as missiles, was never incorporated into homeland defense procedures.

In the end, 19 highly motivated young men armed only with box cutters were able to outwit thousands of America's best minds and dozens of organizations that make up the country's homeland defense system. Part of their success came from fanatical determination, meticulous planning, and painstaking preparation. We also find a dramatic version of an old story: human error leading to tragedy. But even the human-error explanation is too simple. In organizational life, there are almost always systemic causes upstream of human failures, and the events of 9/11 are no exception.

The United States had a web of procedures and agencies aimed at detecting and monitoring potential terrorists. Had those systems worked flawlessly, the terrorists would not have made it onto commercial flights. But the procedures failed, as did those designed to respond to aviation crises. Similar failures have marked many other well-publicized disasters: nuclear accidents at Chernobyl and Three Mile Island, the botched response to Hurricane Katrina on the Gulf Coast in 2005, and the deliberate downing of a German jet in 2015 by a pilot who was known to suffer from severe depression. In business, the fall of giants like Enron and WorldCom, the collapse of the global financial system, the Great Recession of 2008–2009, and Volkswagen's emissions cheating scandal of 2015 are among many examples of the same pattern. Each illustrates a chain of misjudgment, error, miscommunication, and misguided action that our best efforts fail to avert.

Events like 9/11 and Katrina make headlines, but similar errors and failures happen every day. They rarely make front-page news, but they are familiar to most people who work in organizations. In the remainder of this chapter, we discuss how organizational complexity intersects with fallacies of human thinking to obscure what's really going on and lead us astray. We describe some of the peculiarities of organizations that make them so difficult to figure out and manage. Finally, we explore how our deeply held and well-guarded mental models cause us to fail—and how to avoid that trap.

COMMON FALLACIES IN EXPLAINING ORGANIZATIONAL PROBLEMS

Albert Einstein once said that a thing should be made as simple as possible, but no simpler. When we ask students and managers to analyze cases like 9/11, they often make things simpler than they really are. They do this by relying on one of three misleading and oversimplified explanations.

The first and most common is *blaming people.* This approach casts every failure as a product of individual blunders. Problems result from egotism, bad attitudes, abrasive personalities, neurotic tendencies, stupidity, or incompetence. It's an easy way to explain anything that goes wrong. After scandals like the ones that hit Volkswagen and Wells Fargo Bank in 2016, the hunt is on for someone to blame, and top executives became the prime target of reporters, investigators, and talk-show comedians.

As children, we learned it was important to assign blame for every broken toy, stained carpet, or wounded sibling. Pinpointing the culprit is comforting. Assigning blame resolves ambiguity, explains mystery, and makes clear what to do next: punish the guilty. Corporate scandals often have their share of culpable individuals, who may lose their jobs or even go to jail. But there is usually a larger story about the organizational and social context that sets the stage for individual malfeasance. Targeting individuals while ignoring larger system failures oversimplifies the problem and does little to prevent its recurrence.

Greatest Hits from Organization Studies

Hit Number 8: James G. March and Herbert A. Simon, *Organizations* (New York: Wiley, 1958)

March and Simon's pioneering 1958 book *Organizations* sought to define an emerging field by offering a structure and language for studying organizations. It was part of the body of work that helped Simon earn the 1978 Nobel Prize for economics.

March and Simon offered a cognitive, social-psychological view of organizational behavior, with an emphasis on thinking, information processing, and decision making. The book begins with a model of behavior that presents humans as continually seeking to satisfy motives based on their aspirations. Aspirations at any given time are a function of both individuals' history and their environment. When aspirations are unsatisfied, people search until they find better, more satisfying options. Organizations influence individuals primarily by managing the information and options, or "decision premises," that they consider.

March and Simon followed Simon's earlier work (1947) in critiquing the economic view of "rational man," who maximizes utility by considering all available options and choosing the best. Instead, they argue that both individuals and organizations have limited information and limited capacity to process what they have. They never know all the options. Instead, they gradually alter their aspirations as they search for alternatives. Home buyers often start with a dream house in mind, but gradually adapt to the realities of what's available and what they can afford. Instead of looking for the best option—"maximizing"—individuals and organizations instead "satisfice," choosing the first option that seems good enough.

Organizational decision making is additionally complicated because the environment is complex. Resources (time, attention, money, and so on) are scarce, and conflict among individuals and groups is constant. Organizational design happens through piecemeal bargaining

(continued)

(continued)

that holds no guarantee of optimal rationality. Organizations simplify the environment to reduce the demands on limited information-processing and decision-making capacities. They simplify by developing "programs"—standardized routines for performing repetitive tasks. Once a program is in place, the incentive is to stay with it as long as the results are marginally satisfactory. Otherwise, the organization is forced to expend time and energy to innovate. Routine tends to drive out innovation because individuals find it easier and less taxing to stick to programmed tasks (which are automatic, well-practiced, and more certain of success). Thus, a student facing a term-paper deadline may find it easier to "fritter"—make tea, straighten the desk, text friends, and browse the Web—than to struggle to write a good opening paragraph. Managers may sacrifice quality to avoid changing a familiar routine.

March and Simon's book falls primarily within the structural and human resource views. But their discussions of scarce resources, power, conflict, and bargaining recognize the reality of organizational politics. Although they do not use the term *framing*, March and Simon affirm its logic as an essential component of choice. Decision making, they argue, is always based on a simplified model of the world. Organizations develop unique vocabulary and classification schemes, which determine what people are likely to see and respond to. Things that don't fit an organization's mind-set are likely to be ignored or reframed into terms the organization can understand.

When it is hard to identify a guilty individual, a second popular option is *blaming the bureaucracy*. Things go haywire because organizations are stifled by rules and red tape or by the opposite, chaos resulting from a lack of clear goals, roles, and rules. One explanation or the other usually applies. When things aren't working, then the system needs either more or fewer rules and procedures, and tighter or looser job descriptions.

By this reasoning, tighter financial controls could have prevented the subprime mortgage meltdown of 2008. The tragedy of 9/11 could have been thwarted if agencies had had better protocols for such a terrorist attack. But piling on rules and regulations is a direct route to bureaucratic rigidity. Rules can inhibit freedom and flexibility, stifle initiative, and generate reams of red tape. The Commission probing the causes of 9/11 concluded: "Imagination is not a gift associated with bureaucracy." When things become too tight, the solution is to "free up" the system so red tape and rigid rules don't stifle creativity and bog things down. An enduring storyline in popular films is the free spirit who triumphs in the end over silly rules and mindless bureaucrats (examples include the cult classics *Office Space* and *The Big Lebowski*). But many organizations vacillate endlessly between being too loose and too tight.

A third fallacy attributes problems to *thirsting for power*. Enron collapsed, you can say, because key executives were more interested in getting rich and expanding their turf than in advancing the company's best interests. This view sees organizations as jungles teeming with predators and prey. Victory goes to the more adroit, or the more treacherous. You need to play the game better than your opponents—and watch your back.

Each of these three perspectives contains a kernel of truth but oversimplifies a knottier reality. Blaming people points to the perennial importance of individual responsibility. People who are rigid, lazy, bumbling, or greedy do contribute to some of the problems we see in organizations. But condemning individuals often distracts us from seeing system weaknesses and offers few workable options. If, for example, the problem is someone's abrasive or pathological personality, what do we do? Even psychiatrists find it hard to alter character disorders, and firing everyone with a less-than-ideal personality is rarely a viable option. Training can go only so far in ensuring semi-flawless individual performance.

The blame-the-bureaucracy perspective starts from a reasonable premise: Organizations exist to achieve specific goals. They usually work better when strategies, goals, and policies are clear (but not excessive), jobs are well defined (but not constricting), control systems are in place (but not oppressive), and employees behave prudently (but not callously). If organizations always operated that way, they would presumably work a lot better than most do. In practice, this perspective is better at explaining how organizations should work than why they often don't. Managers who cling to logic and procedures become discouraged and frustrated when confronted by intractable irrational forces. Year after year, we witness the introduction of new control systems, hear of new ways to reorganize, and are dazzled by emerging management strategies, methods, and gurus. Yet old problems persist, seemingly immune to every rational cure we devise. As March and Simon point out, rationality has limits.

The thirst-for-power view highlights enduring, below-the-surface features of organizations. Dog-eat-dog logic offers a plausible analysis of almost anything that goes wrong. People both seek and despise power but find it a convenient way to explain problems and get their way. Within hours of the 9/11 terror attacks, a senior FBI official called Richard Clarke, America's counterterrorism czar, to tell him that many of the terrorists were known members of Al Qaeda.

"How the fuck did they get on board then?" Clarke exploded.

"Hey, don't shoot the messenger. CIA forgot to tell us about them."

In the context of its chronic battles with the CIA, the FBI was happy to throw the CIA under the bus: "We could have stopped the terrorists if CIA had done their job."

The tendency to blame what goes wrong on people, the bureaucracy, or the thirst for power is part of our mental wiring. But there's much more to understanding a complex situation than assigning blame. Certain universal peculiarities of organizations make them especially difficult to understand or decipher.

PECULIARITIES OF ORGANIZATIONS

Human organizations can be exciting and challenging places. That's how they are often depicted in management texts, corporate annual reports, and fanciful managerial thinking. But they can also be deceptive, confusing, and demoralizing. It is a big mistake to assume that organizations are either snake pits or rose gardens (Schwartz, 1986). Managers need to recognize characteristics of life at work that create opportunities for the wise as well as hidden traps for the unwary. A case from the public sector provides a typical example:

When Bosses Rush In

Helen Demarco arrived in her office to discover a clipping from the local paper. The headline read, "Osborne Announces Plan." Paul Osborne had arrived two months earlier as Amtran's new chief executive. His mandate was to "revitalize, cut costs, and improve efficiency."

After 20 years, Demarco had achieved a senior management position at the agency. She had little contact with Osborne, but her boss reported to him. Demarco and her colleagues had been waiting to learn what the new chief had in mind. She was startled as she read the newspaper account. Osborne's plan made technical assumptions directly related to her area of expertise. "He might be a change agent," she thought, "but he doesn't know much about our technology." She immediately saw the new plan's fatal flaws. "If he tries to implement this, it'll be the worst management mistake since the Edsel."

Two days later, Demarco and her colleagues received a memo instructing them to form a committee to work on the revitalization plan. When the group convened, everyone agreed it was crazy.

"What do we do?" someone asked.

"Why don't we just tell him it won't work?" said one hopeful soul.

"He's already gone public! You want to tell him his baby is ugly?"

"Not me. Besides, he already thinks a lot of us are deadwood. If we tell him it's no good, he'll just think we're defensive."

"Well, we can't go ahead with it. It'll never work and we'd be throwing away money."

"That's true," said Demarco thoughtfully. "But what if we tell him we're conducting a study of how to implement the plan?"

Her suggestion was approved overwhelmingly. The group informed Osborne that they were moving ahead on the "implementation study" and expected excellent results. They got a substantial budget to support their "research." They did not say that the real purpose was to buy time and find a way to minimize the damage without alienating the boss.

Over time, the group assembled a lengthy technical report, filled with graphs, tables, and impenetrable jargon. The report offered two options. Option A, Osborne's original plan, was presented as technically feasible but well beyond anything Amtran could afford. Option B, billed as a "modest downscaling" of the original plan, was projected as a more cost-effective alternative.

When Osborne pressed the group on the huge cost disparity between the two proposals, he received a barrage of complicated cost-benefit projections and inscrutable technical terms. Hidden in a fog was the reality that even Option B offered few benefits at a very high cost. Osborne argued and pressed for more information. But given the apparent facts, he agreed to proceed with Option B. The "Osborne plan" was announced with fanfare and widely heralded as another instance of Paul Osborne's talent for revitalizing ailing organizations. Osborne had moved on to work his management magic on another organization by the time the plan came online, and his successor had to defend the underwhelming results.

Helen Demarco came away with deep feelings of frustration and failure. The Osborne plan, in her view, was a wasteful mistake, and she had knowingly participated in a charade. But, she rationalized to herself, she had no other choice. Osborne was adamant. It would have been career suicide to try to stop him.

You might have noticed that Helen Demarco's case is more than a little similar to the scandals at Volkswagen in 2015 and Wells Fargo in 2016. At the Geneva International Motor Show in 2012, VW CEO Martin Winterkorn proclaimed that by 2015 the company would cut its vehicles' carbon dioxide emissions by 30 percent from 2006 levels. It was an ambitious goal that would have beat the targets set by European regulators to combat global warming.

But just like Paul Osborne, Winterkorn had set the bar too high. The engineers saw no way to meet the boss's goals, but no one wanted to tell him it couldn't be done. So, they cheated instead. There was a precedent because VW's cheating on diesel emissions had started back in 2008, and observers reported that "an ingrained fear of delivering bad news to superiors" (Ewing, 2015, p. B3) was a feature of VW's culture.

Like Helen Demarco and her colleagues, the VW engineers had other options but couldn't see them. Paul Osborne and Martin Winterkorn both thought they were providing bold leadership to vault their organizations forward. They were tripped up in part by human fallibility but also by how hard it can be to know what's really going on in any organization. Managerial wisdom and artistry require a well-honed understanding of four key characteristics of organizations.

First, *organizations are complex*. The behavior of the people who populate them is notoriously hard to predict. Large organizations in particular include a bewildering array of people, departments, technologies, strategies. and goals. Moreover, organizations are open systems dealing with a changing, challenging, and erratic environment. Things can get even messier across multiple organizations. The 9/11 disaster resulted from a chain of events that involved several separate systems. Almost anything can affect everything else in collective activity, generating causal knots that are hard to untangle. After an exhaustive investigation, our picture of 9/11 is woven from sundry evidence, conflicting testimony, and conjecture.

Second, *organizations are surprising.* What you expect is often not what you get. Paul Osborne saw his plan as a bold leap forward; Helen and her group considered it an expensive albatross. In their view, Osborne was going to make matters *worse* by trying to improve them. He might have achieved better results by spending more time with his family and letting his organization take care of itself. Martin Winterkorn was stunned when the hidden cheating blew up in his face, costing him his job and hitting VW with devastating financial and reputational damage.

The solution to yesterday's problems often creates tomorrow's obstacles. A friend of ours headed a retail chain. In the firm's early years, he had a problem with two sisters who worked in the same store. To prevent this from recurring, he established a nepotism policy prohibiting members of the same family from working for the company. Years later, two key employees met at work, fell in love, and began to live together. The president was startled when they asked if they could get married without being fired. Taking action in a cooperative venture is like shooting a wobbly cue ball into a scattered array of self-directed billiard balls. Balls bounce in so many directions that it is impossible to know how things will eventually sort out.

Third, *organizations are deceptive.* They camouflage mistakes and surprises. After 9/11, America's homeland defense organizations tried to conceal their confusion and lack of preparedness for fear of revealing strategic weaknesses. Volkswagen engineers developed software whose only purpose was to cheat on emissions tests, hoping that no one would ever see through their deception. Helen Demarco and her colleagues disguised obfuscation as technical analysis.

It is tempting to blame deceit on individual weakness. Yet Helen Demarco disliked fraud and regretted cheating—she simply believed it was her best option. Sophisticated managers know that what happened to Paul Osborne happens all the time. When a quality initiative fails or a promising product tanks, subordinates often clam up or cover up. They fear that the boss will not listen or will kill the messenger. Internal naysayers at Volkswagen and Wells Fargo Bank were silenced until outsiders "blew the whistle." A friend in a senior position in a large government agency put it simply: "Communications in organizations are rarely candid, open, or timely."

Fourth, *organizations are ambiguous.* Complexity, unpredictability, and deception generate rampant ambiguity, a dense fog that shrouds what happens from day to day. It is hard to get the facts and even harder to know what they mean or what to do about them. Helen Demarco never knew how Paul Osborne really felt, how receptive he was to other points of view, or how open he was to compromise. She and her peers piled on more mystery by conspiring to keep him in the dark.

Exhibit 2.1.
Sources of Ambiguity.

- We are not sure what the problem is.

- We are not sure what is really happening.

- We are not sure what we want.

- We do not have the resources we need.

- We are not sure who is supposed to do what.

- We are not sure how to get what we want.

- We are not sure how to determine if we have succeeded.

Source: Adapted from McCaskey (1982).

Ambiguity has many sources. Sometimes available information is incomplete or vague. Different people may interpret the same information in a variety of ways, depending on mind-sets and organizational doctrines. At other times, ambiguity is intentionally manufactured as a smoke screen to conceal problems or avoid conflict. Much of the time, events and processes are so intricate, scattered, and uncoordinated that no one can fully understand—let alone control—the reality. Exhibit 2.1 lists some of the most important sources of organizational uncertainty.

ORGANIZATIONAL LEARNING

How can lessons be extracted from surroundings that are complex, surprising, deceptive, and ambiguous? It isn't easy. Decades ago, scholars debated whether the idea of organizational learning made sense: Could organizations actually learn, or was learning inherently individual? That debate lapsed as experience verified instances in which individuals learned and organizations didn't, or vice versa. Complex firms such as Apple, Zappos, and Southwest Airlines have "learned" capabilities far beyond individual knowledge. Lessons are enshrined in acknowledged protocols and shared cultural codes and traditions. At the same time, individuals often learn even when systems cannot.

Several perspectives on organizational learning are exemplified in the work of Peter Senge (1990), Barry Oshry (1995), and Chris Argyris and Donald Schön (1978, 1996). Senge sees a core-learning dilemma: "We learn best from our experience, but we never directly experience the consequences of many of our decisions" (p. 23). Learning is relatively easy when the link between cause and effect is clear. But complex systems often sever that connection: causes remote from effects, solutions detached from problems, and feedback absent, delayed, or misleading (Cyert and March, 1963; Senge, 1990). Wells Fargo's aggressive push for cross-selling led to cheating from coast to coast, but that was mostly invisible at headquarters, which kept its eyes on the financial results—until the scandal blew up.

Senge emphasizes the value of "system maps" that clarify how a system works. Consider the system created by Robert Nardelli at Home Depot. Nardelli had expected to win the three-way competition to succeed management legend Jack Welch as CEO of General Electric. He was stunned when he learned he didn't get the job. But within a week, he was hired as Home Depot's new CEO. He was a big change from the company's free-spirited founders, who had built the wildly successful retailer on the foundation of an uninhibited, entrepreneurial "orange" culture. Managers ran their stores using "tribal knowledge," and customers counted on friendly, knowledgeable staff for helpful advice.

Nardelli revamped Home Depot with a heavy dose of command-and-control, discipline, and metrics. Almost all the top executives and many of the frontline managers were replaced, often by ex-military hires. At first, it seemed to work—profits improved, and management experts hailed Nardelli's success. He was even designated Best Manager of 2004 on the cover of *Business Week* (Business Week, 2005). But employee morale and customer service went steadily downhill. The founders had successfully promoted a "make love to the customers" ethic, but Nardelli's toe-the-line stance pummeled Home Depot to last place in its industry for consumer satisfaction. A website, Home Depot Sucks.com, gave customers a place to vent their rage. As criticism grew, Nardelli tried to keep naysayers at bay, but his efforts failed to placate customers, shareholders, or his board. Nardelli abruptly left Home Depot at the beginning of 2007.

The story is one of many examples of tactics that look good until long-term costs become apparent. A corresponding systems model might look like Exhibit 2.2. The strategy might be cutting training to improve short-term profitability, drinking martinis to relieve stress, offering rebates to entice customers, or borrowing from a loan shark to cover gambling debts. In each case, the results look good at first, and the costs only emerge much later.

Oshry (1995) agrees that system blindness is widespread but highlights causes rooted in troubled relationships between groups that have little grasp of what's going on outside their own neighborhood. Top managers feel overwhelmed by complexity, responsibility, and overwork. They are chronically dissatisfied with subordinates' lack of initiative and

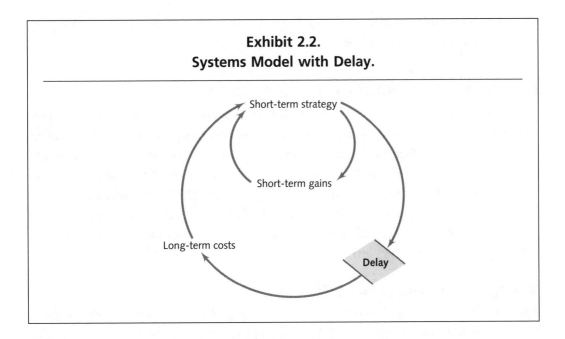

**Exhibit 2.2.
Systems Model with Delay.**

Short-term strategy

Short-term gains

Long-term costs

Delay

creativity. Middle managers, meanwhile, feel trapped between contradictory signals and pressures. The top tells them to take risks but then punishes mistakes. Their subordinates expect them to intervene with the boss and improve working conditions. Top and bottom tug in opposite directions, causing those in the middle to feel pulled apart, confused, and weak. At the bottom, workers feel helpless, unacknowledged, and demoralized. "They give us bad jobs, lousy pay, and lots of orders but never tell us what's really going on. Then they wonder why we don't love our work." Unless you can step back and see how system dynamics create these patterns, you muddle along blindly, unaware of better options.

Both Oshry and Senge argue that our failure to read system dynamics traps us in cycles of blaming and self-defense. Problems are always someone else's fault. Unlike Senge, who sees gaps between cause and effect as primary barriers to learning, Argyris and Schön emphasize managers' fears and defenses. As a result, "the actions we take to promote productive organizational learning actually inhibit deeper learning" (1996, p. 281).

According to Argyris and Schön, our behavior obstructs learning because we avoid undiscussable issues and tiptoe around organizational taboos. That often seems to work because we avoid conflict and discomfort in the moment, but we create a double bind. We can't solve problems without dealing with issues we have tried to hide but discussing them would expose our cover up. Facing that double bind, Volkswagen engineers hid their cheating until outsiders finally caught on. Desperate maneuvers to hide the truth and delay the inevitable made the day of reckoning more catastrophic.

COPING WITH AMBIGUITY AND COMPLEXITY

Organizations try to cope with a complicated and uncertain world by making it more simple. One approach to simplification is to develop better systems and technology to collect and process data. Another is to break complex issues into smaller chunks and assign slices to specialized individuals or units. Still another approach is to hire or develop professionals with sophisticated expertise in handling thorny problems. These and other methods are helpful but not always sufficient. Despite the best efforts, as we have seen, surprising—and sometimes appalling—events still happen. We need better ways to anticipate problems and wrestle with them once they arrive.

Making Sense of What's Going On

Some events are so clear and unambiguous that it is easy for people to agree on what is going on. Determining whether a train is on schedule, a plane landed safely, or a clock is keeping accurate time is fairly straightforward. But most of the important issues confronting leaders are not so clear cut. Will a reorganization work? Was a meeting successful? Why did a consensual decision backfire? In trying to make sense of complicated and ambiguous situations, humans are often in over their heads, their brains too taxed to decode all the complexity around them. At best managers can hope to achieve "bounded rationality," which Foss and Webber (2016) describe in terms of three dimensions:

1. *Processing capacity:* Limits of time, memory, attention, and computing speed mean that the brain can only process a fraction of the information that might be relevant in a given situation.

2. *Cognitive economizing:* Cognitive limits force human decision makers to use cognitive short-cuts—rules of thumb, mental models, or frames—in order to cut complexity and messiness down to manageable size.

3. *Cognitive biases:* Humans tend to interpret incoming information to confirm their existing beliefs, expectations, and values. They often welcome confirming information while ignoring or rejecting disconfirming signals (Foss and Webber, 2016).

Benson (2016) frames cognitive biases in terms of four broad tendencies that create a self-reinforcing cycle (see Exhibit 2.3). To cope with information overload, we filter out

Exhibit 2.3.
Cognitive Biases.

Cognitive Challenge	Solution	Risk
Too much data to process	Filter out everything except what we see as important and consistent with our current beliefs	Miss things that are important or could help us learn
Tough to make sense of a confusing, ambiguous world	Fill in gaps, make things fit with our existing stories and mental models	Create and perpetuate false beliefs and narratives
Need to act quickly	Jump to conclusions—favor the simple and obvious over the messy and complex	Quick decisions and actions lead to mistakes and get us in trouble
Memory overload	Discard specifics to form generalities or use a few specifics to represent the whole	Error and bias in memory reinforce current mind-sets and biases in information-processing

Source: Adapted from Benson, 2016.

most data and see only what seems important and consistent with our current mind-set. That gives us an incomplete picture, but we fill in the gaps and make everything fit with our current beliefs. Then, in order to act quickly instead of getting lost in thought, we favor the easy and obvious over the complex or difficult. We then code our experience into memory by discarding specifics and retaining generalities or by using a few specifics to represent a larger whole. This reinforces our current mental models, which then shape how we process experience in the future.

To a greater or lesser degree, we all use these cognitive short-cuts. In the early days of his presidency, Donald Trump's tweet storms and off-the-cuff communications provided prominent examples. In March, 2017, he tweeted that his predecessor, Barack Obama, was a "bad (or sick) guy" for tapping Trump's phones prior to the election. Trump apparently based this claim on an article from the right-wing website Breitbart. Since the charge aligned with Trump's world view, he figured it must be true and continued to insist he was right even after investigators concluded it never happened.

Decisions, whether snap judgments or careful calculations, work only if we have adequately sized up the situation. As one highly placed female executive reported to us, "I thought I'd covered all the bases, but then I suddenly realized that the rest of my team were playing football."

Managers regularly face an unending barrage of puzzles or "messes." To act without creating more trouble, they must first grasp an accurate picture of what is happening. Then they must move to a deeper level, asking, "What is *really* going on here?" When this step is omitted, managers too often form superficial analyses and pounce on the solutions nearest at hand or most in vogue. Market share declining? Try strategic planning. Customer complaints? Put in a quality program. Profits down? Time to reengineer or downsize.

A better alternative is to think, to probe more deeply into what is really going on, and to develop an accurate diagnosis. The process is more intuitive than analytic: "[It] is in fact a cognitive process, faster than we recognize and far different from the step-by-step thinking we rely on so willingly. We think conscious thought is somehow better, when in fact, intuition is soaring flight compared to the plodding of logic" (DeBecker, 1997, p. 28).

The ability to size up a situation quickly is at the heart of leadership. Admiral Carlisle Trost, former Chief of Naval Operations, once remarked, "The first responsibility of a leader is to figure out what is going on . . . That is never easy to do because situations are rarely black or white, they are a pale shade of gray . . . they are seldom neatly packaged."

It all adds up to a simple truth that is easy to overlook. The world we perceive is, for the most part, the image we construct in our minds. Ellen Langer, the author of *Mindfulness* (1989), captures this viewpoint succinctly: "What we have learned to look for in situations determines mostly what we see" (Langer, 2009, p. 33). The ideas or theories we hold determine whether a given situation is foggy or clear, mildly interesting or momentous, a paralyzing disaster, or a genuine learning experience. Personal theories are essential because of a basic fact about human perception: in any situation, there is simply too much happening for us to attend to everything. To help us understand what is going on and what to do next, well-grounded, deeply ingrained personal theories offer two advantages: they tell us what is important and what is safe to ignore, and they group scattered bits of information into manageable patterns. Mental models shape reality.

Research in neuroscience has called into question the old adage, "Seeing is believing." It has been challenged by its converse: "Believing is seeing." The brain constructs its own images of reality and then projects them onto the external world (Eagleman, 2011). "Mental models are deeply held internal images of how the world works, images that limit us to familiar ways of thinking and acting. Very often, we are not consciously aware of our mental models or the effects they have on our behavior" (Senge, 1990, p. 8). Reality is therefore what each of us believes it to be. Shermer (2012) tells us that "beliefs come first, explanations for beliefs follow." Once we form beliefs, we search for ways to explain and defend them. Today's experience becomes tomorrow's fortified theology.

In November, 2014, two police officers in Cleveland received a radio report of a "black male sitting on a swing pulling a gun out of his pants and pointing it at people" in a city park (Holloway, 2015). Arriving at the site, one officer spotted the suspect and saw him reach for his gun. The officer immediately shot and killed the suspect. The officer might have responded differently if the radio report had included two additional details. The caller who made the initial report had said that the suspect might be a juvenile, and the gun was probably fake. The gun was a toy replica of a Colt semiautomatic pistol. The victim, Tamir Rice, was 12 years old, but, at 195 pounds, might have looked like an adult on a quick glance.

Perception and judgment involve matching situational cues with previously learned mental models. In this case, the perceptual data were hard to read, and expectations were prejudiced by a key missing clue—the radio operator had never mentioned the possibility of a child with a toy. The officer was expecting a dangerous gunman, and that is what he saw.

Impact of Mental Models

Changing old patterns and mind-sets is difficult. It is also risky; it can lead to analysis paralysis, confusion, and erosion of confidence. This dilemma exists even if we see no flaws in our current thinking because our theories are often self-sealing. They block us from recognizing our errors. Extensive research documents the many ways in which individuals spin reality to protect existing beliefs (see, for example, Garland, 1990; Kühberger, 1995; Staw and Hoang, 1995). In one corporate disaster after another, executives insist that they were not responsible but were the unfortunate victim of circumstances.

Extensive research on the "framing effect" (Kahneman and Tversky, 1979) shows how powerful subtle cues can be. Relatively modest changes in how a problem or decision is framed can have a dramatic impact on how people respond (Shu and Adams, 1995; Gegerenzer, Hoffrage, and Kleinbölting, 1991). One study found that doctors responded more favorably to a treatment with "a one-month survival rate of 90 percent" than one with "a 10 percent mortality rate in the first month," even though the two are statistically identical (Kahneman, 2011).

Many of us sometimes recognize that our mental models or maps influence how we interpret the world. It is less widely understood that what we expect often determines what we get. Rosenthal and Jacobson (1968) studied schoolteachers who were told that certain students in their classes were "spurters"—students who were "about to bloom." The so-called spurters, who had been randomly selected, achieved above-average gains on achievement tests. They really *did* spurt. Somehow, the teachers' expectations were communicated to and assimilated by the students. Medical science is still probing the placebo effect—the power of sugar pills to make people better (Hróbjartsson and Gøtzsche, 2010). Results are attributed to an unexplained change in the patient's belief system. When patients believe they will get better, they do. Similar effects have been replicated in countless reorganizations, new product launches, and new approaches to performance appraisal. All these examples show how hard it is to disentangle reality from the models in our minds.[2]

Japan has four major spiritual traditions, each with unique beliefs and assumptions: Buddhism, Confucianism, Shintoism, and Taoism. Though they differ greatly in history, traditions, and basic tenets, many Japanese feel no need to choose only one. They use all four, taking advantage of the strengths of each for suitable purposes or occasions.[3] The four frames can play a similar role for managers in modern organizations. Rather than portraying the field of organizational theory as fragmented, we present it as pluralistic. Seen this way, the field offers a rich spectrum of mental models or lenses for viewing organizations. Each theoretical tradition is helpful. Each has blind spots. Each tells its own story about organizations. The ability to shift nimbly from one to another helps redefine situations so they become understandable and manageable. The ability to reframe is one of the most powerful capacities of great artists. It can be equally powerful for managers and leaders.

CONCLUSION

Because organizations are complex, surprising, deceptive, and ambiguous, they are formidably difficult to comprehend and manage. Our preconceived theories, models, and images determine what we see, what we do, and how we judge what we accomplish. Narrow, oversimplified mental models become fallacies that cloud rather than illuminate managerial action. The world of most managers and administrators is a world of messes: complexity, ambiguity, value dilemmas, political pressures, and multiple constituencies. For managers whose images blind them to important parts of this messy reality, it is a world of frustration and failure. For those with better theories and the intuitive capacity to use them with skill and grace, it is a world of excitement and possibility. A mess can be defined as both a troublesome situation and a group of people who eat together. The core challenge of leadership is to move an organization from the former to something more like the latter.

In succeeding chapters, we look at four perspectives, or frames, that have helped managers and leaders find clarity and meaning amid the confusion of organizational life. The frames are grounded in both the cool rationality of management science and the hot fire of actual practice. You can enhance your chances of success with an artful appreciation of how to use the four lenses to understand and influence what's really going on.

Notes

1. The Wonder World to Be Created by Electricity, *Manufacturer's Record*, September 9, 1915.
2. These examples all show thinking influencing reality. A social constructivist perspective goes a step further to say that our thinking *constructs* social reality. In this view, an organization exists not "out there" but in the minds and actions of its constituents. This idea is illustrated in an old story about a dispute among three baseball umpires. The first says, "Some's balls, and some's strikes, and I calls 'em like they are." The second counters, "No, you got it wrong. Some's balls, and some's strikes, and I calls 'em the way I sees them." The third says, "You guys don't really get it. Some's balls, and some's strikes, but they ain't nothin' until I call 'em." The first umpire is a realist who believes that what he sees is exactly what is. The second recognizes that reality is influenced by his own perception. The third is the social constructivist—his call makes them what they are. This distinction is particularly important in the symbolic frame, which we return to in Chapter 12.
3. A similar phenomenon occurs in other East Asian cultures. In both China and Vietnam, for example, Buddhism, Confucianism, Taoism and native folk religions (including ancestor worship) live comfortably alongside of one another.

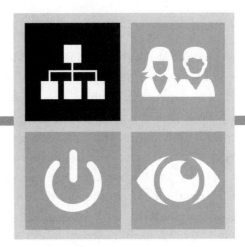

PART TWO

The Structural Frame

A frame is a coherent set of ideas or beliefs forming a prism or lens that enables you to see and understand more clearly what's going on in the world around you. In Part II, we embark on the first stage of a tour that will take us to four very different ways of making sense of life at work or elsewhere. Each frame will be presented in three chapters: one that introduces the basic concepts and two that focus on key applications and extensions. We begin with one of the oldest and most popular ways of thinking about organizations: the structural frame.

If someone asked you to describe your organization—your workplace, your school, or even your family—what image would come to mind? A likely possibility is a traditional organization chart: a series of boxes and lines depicting job responsibilities and levels. The chart might be shaped roughly like a pyramid, with a small number of bosses at the top and a much larger number of employees at the bottom. Such a chart is only one of many images that reflect the structural view. The frame is rooted in traditional rational images but goes much deeper to develop versatile and powerful ways to understand social architecture and its consequences.

We begin Chapter 3 with cases contrasting the structural features of racing crews, Amazon, and rescue efforts in New York City's 9/11 terrorist attacks. We then highlight the basic assumptions of the structural view, with emphasis on two key dimensions: dividing work and coordinating it thereafter. We emphasize how structural design depends on an organization's circumstances, including its goals, strategy, technology, and environment. In addition, we show why tightly controlled, top-down forms may work in simple, stable situations but fall short in more fluid and ambiguous ones.

In Chapter 4, we turn to issues of structural change and redesign. We describe basic structural tensions, explore alternatives to consider when new circumstances require revisions, and discuss challenges of the restructuring process. We compare traditional organization charts with "Mintzberg's Fives," a more abstract rendering of structural alternatives. We close the chapter with examples of successful structural change.

Finally, in Chapter 5, we apply structural concepts to groups and teams. When teams work poorly, members often blame one another for problems that reflect design flaws rather than individual failings. We begin with the SEAL Team Six operation to track down Osama bin Laden. We examine structural options in five-person teams and then contrast the games of baseball, American football, and basketball to show how optimal structure depends on what a team is trying to do and under what conditions. We close by examining the architectural design of high-performance teams.

Getting Organized

Organizing is what you do before you do something, so that when you do it, it is not all mixed up.

—A. A. Milne

Watching an eight-oar racing crew skim along the Charles River is like watching a highly choreographed ballet group perform *Swan Lake.* To a coxswain's cadence, eight oars at exactly 90 degrees enter the water in unison. A collective pull "in swing" propels the shell smoothly forward as eight oars leave the water at a precise perpendicular angle. If any oarsman muffs just one of these strokes or "catches a crab," the shell is thrown off kilter. Close coordination welds eight rowers into a harmonious crew.

It looks straightforward to an outside observer, an effortless ballet in motion. But structurally it is more complicated. All members of a crew are expected to row smoothly and quickly. But expectations for individuals vary depending on the seat they occupy. Bow seats one, two, and three have the greatest potential to disrupt the boat's direction, so they must be able to pull a perfect oar one stroke after another. Rowers in seats four, five, and six are the boat's biggest and strongest. They are often referred to as the "engine," providing the boat's raw power. Seat seven's rower provides a conduit between the engine room and the "stroke oar" in seat eight. The "stroke oar" sits directly facing the coxswain and rows at the requested rate of speed and power, setting the pace and intensity for the other rowers.

The coxswain is responsible for steering the shell, but also serves as captain. Coxswains vocally determine both the rate and degree of power of the oar strokes. They know their rowers physically and psychologically and how to inspire their best efforts. They also know opponents' strengths and weaknesses. Before a race, the coxswain develops a strategy but must be ready to alter it as a situation demands. A good coxswain is "a quarterback, a cheerleader, and a coach all in one. He or she is a deep thinker, canny like a fox, inspirational, and in many cases the toughest person in the boat" (Brown, 2014, p. 232).

The individual efforts are also integrated by shared agreement that the team effort transcends the individual. All rowers have to optimize their strokes for the benefit of the boat. Coordination and cooperation among individuals of different statures and strengths assures the unified and beautiful symphony that a crew in motion becomes. In crew racing competition, structure is vital to top performance.

Structure is equally critical in larger organizations. Jeff Bezos, one of the world's most admired CEOs, is passionate about structure and process at the company he founded, Internet giant Amazon. He makes the company's strategy crystal clear. Embracing the familiar credo that the "customer is always right," Bezos is riveted on figuring out what the customer wants and delivering it with speed and precision. His "culture of metrics" coddles Amazon's 250 million shoppers, not its quarter million employees.

Amazon tracks its performance against some 500 measurable goals; almost 80 percent relate directly to customer service. Even the smallest delay in loading a Web page is carefully scrutinized, because Amazon has found that ". . . a .01 second delay in page rendering can translate into a 1 percent drop in customer activity" (Anders, 2012). Supervisors measure and monitor employees' performance, observing behavior closely to see where steps or movements can be streamlined to improve efficiency.

Amazon is a classic example of a highly developed organizational structure—clear strategy, focus on the mission, well-defined roles, and top-down coordination. Some employees grumble about the working conditions and the fast pace, but many others find the tempo exhilarating. Bezos makes it clear: The customer is number one. Period. Amazon began as an online bookstore, but now it sells almost anything that can be shipped or downloaded. The company lost money for many years after its founding in 1995. But in recent years, it has been consistently profitable, and its 2015 annual report noted that it had achieved $100 billion in sales faster than any company in history (Amazon, 2015).

The benefits of getting structure right are obvious under normal conditions and even more so when organizational architecture meets unexpected crises. Recall the horror of 9/11 and the breakdown in coordination between New York City's fire and police departments as they confronted the aftermath of terrorist strikes on the World Trade Center. That day saw countless inspiring examples of individual heroism and personal sacrifice. At the risk of their own lives, emergency personnel rescued thousands of people. Many died in the effort. But extraordinary individual efforts were hindered or thwarted by breakdowns in communication, command, and control. Police helicopters near the north tower radioed that it was near collapse more than twenty minutes before it fell. Police officers got the warning, and most escaped. But there was no link between fire and police radios, and the commanders in the two departments could not communicate because their command posts were three blocks apart. It might not have helped even if they had talked, because the fire department's radios were notoriously unreliable in high-rise buildings.

The breakdown of communication and coordination magnified the death toll—including 121 firefighters who died when the north tower collapsed. The absence of a workable structure undermined the heroic efforts of highly dedicated, skilled professionals who gave their all in an unprecedented catastrophe (Dwyer, Flynn, and Fessenden, 2002).

The contrast between Amazon's operations and the rescue efforts at the World Trade Center highlights a core premise of the structural lens. The right combination of goals, roles, relationships, and coordination is essential to organizational performance. This is true of all organizations: families, clubs, hospitals, military units, businesses, schools, churches, and public agencies. The right structure combats the risk that individuals, however talented, will become confused, ineffective, apathetic, or hostile. The purpose of this chapter and the next two is to identify the basic ideas and inner workings of a perspective that is fundamental to collective human endeavors.

We begin our examination of the structural frame by highlighting its core assumptions, origins, and basic forms. The possibilities for designing an organization's social architecture are almost limitless, but any option must address two key questions: How do we allocate responsibilities across different units and roles? And, once we've done that, how do we integrate diverse efforts in pursuit of common goals? In this chapter, we explain these basic issues, describe the major options, and discuss imperatives to consider when designing a structure to fit the challenges of a unique situation.

STRUCTURAL ASSUMPTIONS

The central beliefs of the structural frame reflect confidence in rationality and faith that a suitable array of roles and responsibilities will minimize distracting personal static and maximize people's performance on the job. Where the human resource approach (to be discussed in Chapters 6 through 8) emphasizes dealing with issues by changing people (through coaching, training, rotation, promotion, or dismissal), the structural perspective argues for putting people in the right roles and relationships. Properly designed, these formal arrangements support and accommodate both collective goals and individual differences.

Six assumptions undergird the structural frame:

1. Organizations exist to achieve established goals and objectives and devise strategies to reach those goals.

2. Organizations increase efficiency and enhance performance through specialization and appropriate division of labor.

3. Suitable forms of coordination and control ensure that diverse efforts of individuals and units mesh.

4. Organizations work best when rationality prevails over personal agendas and extraneous pressures.

5. Effective structure fits an organization's current circumstances (including its strategy, technology, workforce, and environment).

6. When performance suffers from structural flaws, the remedy is problem solving and restructuring.

ORIGINS OF THE STRUCTURAL PERSPECTIVE

The structural view has two principal intellectual roots. The first is the work of industrial analysts bent on designing organizations for maximum efficiency. The most prominent of these, Frederick W. Taylor (1911), was the father of time-and-motion studies; he founded an approach that he labeled "scientific management." Taylor broke tasks into minute parts and retrained workers to get the most from each motion and moment spent at work. Other theorists who contributed to the scientific management approach (Fayol, [1919] 1949; Urwick, 1937; Gulick and Urwick, 1937) developed principles focused on specialization, span of control, authority, and delegation of responsibility.

A second pioneer of structural ideas was the German economist and sociologist Max Weber, who wrote around the beginning of the twentieth century. At the time, formal organization was a relatively new phenomenon. Patriarchy rather than rationality was still the primary organizing principle. A father figure—who ruled with almost unlimited authority and power—dominated patriarchal organizations. He could reward, punish, promote, or fire on personal whim. Seeing an evolution of new structural models in late-nineteenth-century Europe, Weber described "monocratic bureaucracy" as an ideal form that maximized efficiency and norms of rationality. His model outlined several major features that were relatively novel at the time, although they are commonplace now:

- A fixed division of labor
- A hierarchy of offices
- A set of rules governing performance
- A separation of personal from official property and rights
- The use of technical qualifications (not family ties or friendship) for selecting personnel
- Employment as primary occupation and long-term career (Weber, 1947)

After World War II, Blau and Scott (1962), Perrow (1986), Thompson (1967), Lawrence and Lorsch (1967), Hall (1963), and others rediscovered Weber's ideas. Their work inspired a substantial body of theory and research amplifying the bureaucratic model. They examined relationships among the elements of structure, looked closely at why organizations develop one structure over another, and analyzed the effects of structure on morale, productivity, and effectiveness.

Greatest Hits from Organization Studies

Hit Number 5: James D. Thompson, *Organizations in Action: Social Science Bases of Administrative Theory* (New York: McGraw-Hill, 1967)

"Organizations act, but what determines how and when they will act?" (p. 1). That guiding question opens Thompson's compact, tightly reasoned book. He answers that "organizations do some of the basic things they do because they must—or else! Because they are expected to produce results, their actions are expected to be reasonable, or rational" (p. 1). As Thompson sees them, organizations operate under "norms of rationality," but uncertainty makes rationality hard to achieve. "Uncertainties pose major challenges to rationality, and we will argue that technologies and environments are basic sources of uncertainty for organizations. How these facts of organizational life lead organizations to design and structure themselves needs to be explored" (p. 1).

Thompson looked for a way to meld two distinct ways of thinking about organizations. One was to see them as closed, rational systems (as in Taylor's scientific management and Weber's theory of bureaucracy). The second viewed them as open, natural systems in which "survival of the system is taken to be the goal, and the parts and their relationships are presumably determined through evolutionary processes" (p. 6). Thompson tried to build on a "newer tradition" emerging from the work of March and Simon (1958, number 8 of our greatest hits in organization studies) and Cyert and March (1963, number 3). This tradition viewed organizations as "problem facing and problem solving" in a context of limited information and capacities.

(continued)

With these premises, Thompson developed a series of propositions about how organizations design and manage themselves as they seek rationality in an uncertain world. The two primary sources of uncertainty, in his view, are technology and the environment. He distinguished three kinds of technology—pooled, sequential, and reciprocal—each making different demands on communication and coordination. Because demands and intrusions from the environment threaten efficiency, organizations try to increase their ability to anticipate and control the environment and attempt to insulate their technical core from environmental fluctuations. Still another source of uncertainty is the "variable human." The more uncertainty an organization faces, the more discretion individuals need to cope with it, but there is the risk that discretion will run amok. "Paradoxically, the administrative process must reduce uncertainty but at the same time search for flexibility" (Thompson, pp. 157–158).

STRATEGY

Strategy comes from a Greek word that originally referred to the art of military leaders. It was imported into the business context in the twentieth century as a way to talk about an organization's overall approach to goals and methods. Strategy has been defined in many ways. Mintzberg (1987), for example, offers five of them, all beginning with the letter P:

1. Plan: a conscious and intentional course of action.
2. Perspective: an organization's way of framing where it wants to go and how it intends to get there.
3. Pattern: a consistent pattern of decisions.
4. Position: the way an organization positions itself in relationship to its environment.
5. Ploy: a plan or decision whose purpose is to provoke a reaction from competitors.

Some of Mintzberg's Ps focus on thinking while others are more about action. All are elements of a coherent strategy. Roberts (2004) argues that the job of the general manager is to define a strategy that includes objectives, a statement of scope, a specification of the organization's competitive advantage, and the logic for how the organization will succeed. Structural logic dictates that an organization's success requires alignment of strategy, structure, and environment. But, as Chandler noted in 1962, "structure follows strategy." A good strategy needs to be specific enough to provide direction but elastic enough to adapt to changing circumstances.

Eastman Kodak provides a classic case in point. Kodak developed a strategy that made it a dominant player in the film industry for many decades, but stayed with its approach too long and finally ended in bankruptcy. In 1880, George Eastman developed a formula for gelatin-based dry plates, the basis for the then nascent field of photography. For the next 125 years the company's strategy sought to capitalize on this technology by introducing products such as the Kodak Brownie camera, Kodachrome, the Kodak Instamatic camera, and gold standard motion picture film—as well as producing thousands of patents in related fields. Pursuing this strategy the company's performance soared. At its zenith, Kodak employed over 145,000 people and earned billions of dollars in sales (Brachmann, 2014). It was one of America's best-known and most-admired companies.

Threats to Kodak's film-based strategy surfaced as early as 1950 with the introduction of instant photography and the Polaroid camera. In the 1980s, Fujifilm, an upstart Japanese competitor, was able to mass produce film and sell it at a cheaper price to discount retailers like Walmart. Kodak couldn't compete and lost a large share of the film market (Brachmann, 2014).

The death knell for Kodak came in the midseventies with the invention of the digital camera. Ironically, it was invented in one of the company's labs by one of its own engineers. Upper management's reaction: "It's cute but don't tell anyone about it" (Chunka, 2012). Kodak's protection of its film-based strategy and inability to see that digital would capture the market led to its decline and eventual bankruptcy filing in January, 2012.

What kept Kodak from adapting to a changing world? The strategy led to an organizational structure that channeled the activities and thinking of top management in one primary direction: film! In that context, any effort to promote digital cameras required swimming upstream against a strong current.

A similar thing happened at Xerox. Xerox researchers had developed the concepts for the graphical user interface and mouse, but the company's structure and business model were built around photocopying, not computers. Steve Jobs at Apple and Bill Gates at Microsoft immediately saw the market potential that Xerox executives missed. Kodak and Xerox, like many other companies, were never able to capitalize on their own inventions because they fell outside the corporate strategy. Christensen (1997) calls it "the innovator's dilemma," and notes that one reason firms get stuck in the past is that standard cost-benefit analysis usually tells them that they will get a better return by investing in the tried and true instead of something new and unproven. As at Kodak and Xerox, the game is usually lost before the numbers tell a different story.

STRUCTURAL FORMS AND FUNCTIONS

Structure provides the architecture for pursuing an organization's strategic goals. It is a blueprint for expectations and exchanges among internal players (executives, managers, employees) and external constituencies (such as customers, competitors, regulators, and clients). Like an animal's skeleton or a building's framework, structure both enhances and constrains what an organization can do. The alternative design possibilities are virtually infinite, limited only by human preferences and capacities, technological limits, and constraints in the surroundings.

We often assume that people prefer structures with more choices and latitude (Leavitt, 1978), but this is not always the case. A study by Moeller (1968), for example, explored the effects of structure on teacher morale in two school systems. One was loosely structured and encouraged wide participation in decision making. Centralized authority and a clear chain of command characterized the other. Moeller was surprised to find the opposite of what he expected: Faculty morale was higher in the district with a tighter structure. Teachers seemed to prefer clarity of expectations, roles, and lines of authority.

United Parcel Service, "Big Brown," provides a contemporary example of the benefits of structural certainty and clarity. In the company's early days, UPS delivery employees were "scampering messenger boys" (Niemann, 2007). Since then, computer technology has curtailed employee discretion, and every step from pickup to delivery is highly programmed. Detailed instructions specify placement of packages on delivery trucks. Drivers follow computer-generated routes (which minimize mileage and left turns to save time and gas). Newly scheduled pickups automatically download into the nearest driver's route plan.

UPS calculates in advance the numbers of steps to your door. If a driver sees you while walking briskly to your door, you'll receive a friendly greeting. Look carefully and you'll probably notice the automated van lock the driver carries. Given such a tight leash, you might expect demoralized employees. But, the technology makes the job easier and enables drivers to be more productive. As one driver remarked to us with a smile, "We're happy robots."

Do these examples prove that a tighter structure is better? Sometimes the opposite is true. Adler and Borys (1996) argue that the type of structure is as important as the amount or rigidity. There are good rules and bad ones. Formal structure enhances morale if it helps us get our work done. It has a negative impact if it gets in our way, buries us in red tape, or makes it too easy for management to control us. Equating structure to rigid bureaucracy confuses "two very different kinds of machines, those designed to de-skill work and those designed to leverage users' skills" (p. 69).

Structure, then, need not be machinelike or inflexible. Structures in stable environments are often hierarchical and rules oriented. But recent years have witnessed remarkable inventiveness in designing structures emphasizing flexibility, participation, and quality. A prime example is BMW, the luxury automaker whose success formula relies on a combination of stellar quality and rapid innovation. "Just about everyone working for the Bavarian automaker—from the factory floor to the design studios to the marketing department—is encouraged to speak out. Ideas bubble up freely and there is never a penalty for proposing a new way of doing things, no matter how outlandish. The company has become an industry benchmark for high-performance premium cars, customized production, and savvy brand management" (Edmondson, 2006, p. 72. Copyright © 2006 McGraw-Hill Companies, Inc.).

Dramatic changes in technology and the business environment have rendered old structures obsolete at an unprecedented rate, spawning a new interest in organizational design (Nadler, Gerstein, and Shaw, 1992; Bryan and Joyce, 2007; Roberts, 2004). Pressures of globalization, competition, technology, customer expectations, and workforce dynamics have prompted organizations worldwide to rethink and redesign structural prototypes. A swarm of items compete for managers' attention—money, markets, people, and technological competencies, to name a few. But a significant amount of time and attention must be devoted to social architecture—designing structures that allow people to do their best:

> CEOs often opt for the ad hoc structural change, the big acquisition, or a focus on where and how to compete. They would be better off focusing on organizational design. Our research convinces us that in the digital age, there is no better use of a CEO's time and energy than making organizations work better. Most companies were designed for the industrial age of the past century, when capital was the scarce resource, interaction costs were high and hierarchical authority and vertically integrated structures were the keys to efficient operation. Today superior performance flows from the ability to fit these structures into the present century's very different sources of wealth creation (Bryan and Joyce, 2007, p. 1).

BASIC STRUCTURAL TENSIONS

Two issues are central to structural design: how to allocate work (differentiation) and how to coordinate diverse efforts after parceling out responsibilities (integration). Even in a group as small and intimate as a family, it is important to settle issues concerning who does what, when the "what" gets done, and how individual efforts mesh to ensure harmony. Every family will find an arrangement of roles and synchronization that works—or suffer the fallout.

Division of labor—or allocating tasks—is the keystone of structure. Every living system creates specialized roles to get important work done. Consider an ant colony: "Small workers . . . spend most of their time in the nest feeding the larval broods; intermediate-sized workers constitute most of the population, going out on raids as well as doing other jobs. The largest workers . . . have a huge head and large powerful jaws. These individuals are . . . soldiers; they carry no food but constantly run along the flanks of the raiding and emigration columns" (Topoff, 1972, p. 72).

Like ants, humans long ago discovered the virtues of specialization. A job (or position) channels behavior by prescribing what someone is to do—or not do—to accomplish a task. Prescriptions take the form of job descriptions, procedures, routines, protocols, or rules (Mintzberg, 1979). On one hand, these formal constraints can be burdensome, leading to apathy, absenteeism, and resistance (Argyris, 1957, 1964). On the other, they help to ensure predictability, uniformity, and reliability. If manufacturing standards, aircraft maintenance, hotel housekeeping, or prison sentences were left solely to individual discretion, problems of quality and equity would abound.

Once an organization spells out positions or roles, managers face a second set of key decisions: how to group people into working units. They have several basic options (Mintzberg, 1979):

- Function: Groups based on knowledge or skill, as in the case of a university's academic departments or the classic industrial units of research, engineering, manufacturing, marketing, and finance.
- Time: Units defined by when they do their work, as by shift (day, swing, or graveyard shift).
- Product: Groups organized by what they produce, such as detergent versus bar soap, wide-body versus narrow-body aircraft.
- Customer: Groups established around customers or clients, as in hospital wards created around patient type (pediatrics, intensive care, or maternity), computer sales departments organized by customer (corporate, government, education, individual), or schools targeting students in particular age groups.
- Place: Groupings around geography, such as regional or international offices in corporations and government agencies or neighborhood schools in different parts of a city.
- Process: Grouping by a complete flow of work, as with "the order fulfillment process. This process flows from initiation by a customer order, through the functions, to delivery to the customer" (Galbraith, 2001, p. 34).

Creating roles and units yields the benefits of specialization but creates challenges of coordination and control—how to ensure that diverse efforts mesh. Units tend to focus on their separate priorities and strike out on their own, as New York's police and fire departments did on 9/11. The result is *suboptimization*—individual units may perform splendidly in terms of their own goals, but the whole may add up to much less than the sum of the parts. This problem plagued Tom Ridge, who was named by President George W. Bush as the director of homeland security in the aftermath of the 9/11 terrorist attacks. His job was to resolve coordination failures among the government's many different units that dealt with security. But he was more salesman and preacher than boss, and he lacked the authority to compel compliance. Ridge's slow progress led President Bush to create a cabinet-level Department of Homeland Security. The goal was to cluster independent security agencies under one central authority.

As often happens, the new structure created its own problems. Folding the Federal Emergency Management Agency into the mix reduced FEMA's autonomy and shifted its priorities toward security and away from its core mission of disaster relief. The same agency that had responded nimbly to hurricanes and earthquakes in the 1990s was slow and ponderous in the aftermath of Hurricane Katrina and lacked authority and budget to move without a formal okay from the new Secretary of Homeland Security (Cooper and Block, 2006).

Successful organizations employ a variety of methods to coordinate individual and group efforts and to link local initiatives with system-wide goals. They do this in two primary ways: vertically, through the formal chain of command, and laterally, through meetings, committees, coordinating roles, or network structures. We next look at each of these strategies in detail.

VERTICAL COORDINATION

With vertical coordination, higher levels coordinate and control the work of subordinates through authority, rules and policies, and planning and control systems.

Authority

The most basic and ubiquitous way to harmonize the efforts of individuals, units, or divisions is to designate a boss with formal authority. Authorities—executives, managers, and supervisors—are charged with keeping action aligned with strategy and objectives. They do this by making decisions, resolving conflicts, solving problems, evaluating performance and output, and distributing rewards and sanctions. A chain of command is a hierarchy of managerial and supervisory strata, each with legitimate power to shape and direct the behavior of those at lower levels. It works best when authority is both endorsed by subordinates and authorized by superiors (Dornbusch and Scott, 1975). In military organizations such as an aircraft carrier or a commando team, for example, the chain of command is usually clear and universally accepted. In schools and human service organizations authority relations are often fuzzier or more contested.

Rules and Policies

Rules, policies, standards, and standard operating procedures are developed to ensure that individual behavior is predictable and consistent. Rules and policies govern conditions of work and specify standard ways of completing tasks, handling personnel issues, and relating to customers and others. The goal is to ensure the handling of similar situations in comparable ways and to avoid "particularism" (Perrow, 1986)—responding to specific issues based on personal whims or political pressures. Two citizens' complaints about a tax bill are supposed to be treated similarly, even if one citizen is a prominent politician and the other a shoe clerk. Once a situation is defined as fitting a particular rule, the course of action is clear, straightforward and, in an ideal world, almost automatic.

A standard is a benchmark to ensure that goods and services maintain a specified level of quality. Measurement against the standard makes it possible to identify and fix problems. During the 1970s and 1980s, American manufacturing standards lagged, while Japanese manufacturers were scrupulous in ensuring that high standards were widely known and universally accepted. In one case, an American company ordered ball bearings from a Japanese plant. The Americans insisted on what they saw as a daunting standard—no more than 20 defective parts per thousand. The order arrived with a separate bag of 20 defective bearings and a note: "We were not sure why you wanted these, but here they are." More recently, pressure for world-class quality has spawned growing interest in "Six Sigma," a statistical standard of near perfection (Pyzdek, 2003). Although Six Sigma has raised quality standards in many companies around the world, its laser focus on measurable aspects of work processes and outcomes has sometimes hampered creativity in innovative companies such as 3M (Hindo, 2007, pp. 8–12). Safe and measurable may crowd out the elusive breakthroughs a firm needs.

Standard operating procedures (SOPs) reduce variance in routine tasks that have little margin for error. Commercial airline pilots typically fly with a different crew every month. Cockpit actions are tightly intertwined, the need for coordination is high, and mistakes can kill. SOPs consequently govern much of the work of flying a plane. Pilots are trained extensively in the procedures and seldom violate them. But a significant percentage of aviation accidents occur in the rare case in which someone does. More than one airplane has crashed on takeoff after the crew missed a required checklist item.

SOPs can fall short, however, in the face of "black swans" (Taleb, 2007)—freak surprises that the SOPs were never designed to handle. In the 9/11 terrorist attacks, pilots followed standard procedures for dealing with hijackers: cooperate with their demands and try to get the plane on the ground quickly. These SOPs were based on a long history of hijackers who wanted to make a statement, not wreak destruction on a suicide mission. Passengers on United Airlines flight 93, who had learned via cell phones that hijackers were using aircraft as bombs rather than bully pulpits, abandoned this approach. They lost their lives fighting to regain control of the plane, but theirs was the only one of four hijacked jets that failed to devastate a high-profile building.

Planning and Control Systems

Reliance on planning and control systems—forecasting and measuring—has mushroomed since the dawn of the computer era. Retailers, for example, need to know what's selling and what isn't. Point-of-sale terminals now yield that information instantly. Data flow freely up and down the hierarchy, greatly enhancing management's ability to oversee performance and respond in real time.

Mintzberg (1979) distinguishes two major approaches to control and planning: performance control and action planning. Performance control specifies results (for example, "increase sales by 10 percent this year") without specifying how to achieve them. Performance control measures and motivates individual efforts, particularly when targets are reasonably clear and calculable. Locke and Latham (2002) make the case that clear and challenging goals are a powerful incentive to high performance. Performance control is less successful when goals are ambiguous, hard to measure, or of dubious relevance. A notorious example was the use of enemy body counts by the U.S. military to measure combat effectiveness in Vietnam. Field commanders became obsessed with "getting the numbers up," and were often successful. The numbers painted a picture of progress, even as the war was being lost. Meanwhile, as an unintended consequence, American troops had an incentive to kill unarmed civilians in order to raise the count (Turse, 2013).

Action planning specifies how to do something—methods and time frames as in "increase this month's sales by using a companywide sales pitch" (Mintzberg, 1979, pp. 153–154). Action planning works best when it is easier to assess how a job is done than to measure its outcome. This is often true of service jobs. McDonald's has clear specifications for how counter employees are to greet customers (for example, with a smile and a cheerful welcome). United Parcel Service has a detailed policy manual that specifies how a package should be delivered. The objective is customer satisfaction, but it is easier to monitor employees' behavior than customers' reactions. An inevitable risk in action planning is that the link between action and outcome may fail. When that happens, employees may get bad results by doing just what they're supposed to do. Unions sometimes use this as a bargaining chip by telling employees to "work to rule"—scrupulously observing every detail in every procedure—because it is often an effective way to slow work to a crawl.

LATERAL COORDINATION

Behavior in organizations is often remarkably untouched by commands, rules, and systems. Lateral techniques—formal and informal meetings, task forces, coordinating roles, matrix structures, and networks—pop up to fill the gaps. Lateral forms are typically less formal and more flexible than authority-based systems and rules. They are often simpler and quicker as well.

Meetings

Formal gatherings and informal exchanges are the cornerstone of lateral coordination. All organizations have regular meetings. Boards confer to make policy. Executive committees gather to make strategic decisions. In some government agencies, review committees (sometimes known as "murder boards") convene to examine proposals from lower levels. Formal meetings provide the lion's share of lateral harmonization in relatively simple, stable organizations—for example, a railroad with a predictable market, a manufacturer with a stable product, or a life insurance company selling standard policies.

But in fast-paced, turbulent environments, more spontaneous and informal contacts and exchanges are vital to take up slack and help glue things together. Pixar, the animation studio whose series of hits includes *Toy Story* (*1*, *2*, and *3*); *Finding Nemo* (and *Dory*); *Monsters, Inc.*; *WALL-E*; and *Up*, relies on a constant stream of informal connections among managers, artists, and engineers in its three major groups. Technologists develop graphics tools, artists create stories and pictures, and production experts knit the pieces together in the final film. "What makes it all work is [Pixar's] insistence that these groups constantly talk to each other. So a producer of a scene can deal with the animator without having to navigate through higher-ups" (Schlender, 2004, p. 212).

Task Forces

When organizations face complex and fast-changing environments, demand for lateral communication mushrooms. Additional face-to-face coordination devices are needed. Task forces assemble when new problems or opportunities require collaboration of diverse specialties or functions. High-technology firms and consulting firms rely heavily on project teams or task forces to synchronize the development of new products or services.

Coordinating Roles

Coordinating roles or groups use persuasion and negotiation to help dovetail the efforts of different units. They are boundary-spanners with diplomatic status who are artful in dealing across specialized turfs. For example, a product manager in a consumer goods company, responsible for the performance of a laundry detergent or low-fat snack, spends much of the day pulling together functions essential to the product's success such as R&D, manufacturing, marketing, and sales.

Matrix Structures

Until the mid-twentieth century, most companies were functionally organized. Responding to strategic complexity during the late 1950s and early 1960s, many companies shed their functional structures in favor of divisional forms pioneered by DuPont and General Motors in the 1920s. Beginning in the mid-1960s, many organizations in unwieldy environments began to develop matrix structures, even though they are often cumbersome (Peters, 1979; Davis and Lawrence, 1978.) When organizations figure out how to make matrix structures work, they solve many problems (Vantrappen and Wirtz, 2016). By the mid-1990s, Asea Brown Boveri (ABB), the Swiss-based electrical engineering giant, had grown to encompass some 1,300 separate companies and more than 200,000 employees worldwide. To hold this complex collection together, ABB developed a matrix structure crisscrossing approximately 100 countries with about 65 business sectors (Rappaport, 1992). Each subsidiary reported to both a country manager (Sweden, Germany, and so on) and a sector manager (power transformers, transportation, and the like).

The design carried the inevitable risk of confusion, tension, and conflict between sector and country managers. ABB aimed for structural cohesion at the top with a small executive coordinating committee (11 individuals from seven countries in 2016), an elite cadre of some 500 global managers, and a policy of communicating in English, even though it was a second language for most employees. Variations on ABB's structure—a matrix with business or product lines on one axis and countries or regions on another—are common in global corporations. Familiar brands like Starbucks and Whole Foods rely on matrix structures to support their successful international operations (Business Management, 2015).

Networks

Networks have always been around, more so in some places than others. Cochran (2000) describes how both Western and Japanese firms doing business in China in the nineteenth and twentieth centuries had to adapt their hierarchical structures to accommodate powerful social networks deeply embedded in Chinese culture. One British firm tried for years, with little success, to limit the control of "Number Ones" (powerful informal leaders who headed local networks based on kinship and village) over the hiring and wages of its workforce. The proliferation of information technology beginning in the 1980s led to an explosive growth of digital networks—everything from small local grids to the global Internet. These powerful new lateral communication devices often supplanted vertical strategies and spurred the development of network structures within and between organizations (Steward, 1994). Powell, Koput, and Smith-Doerr (1996) describe the mushrooming of "interorganizational networks" in fast-moving fields like biotechnology, where knowledge is so complex and widely dispersed that no organization can go it alone. They give an example of research on Alzheimer's disease that was carried out by thirty-four scientists from three corporations, a university, a government laboratory, and a private research institute.

Many large global corporations have evolved into interorganizational networks (Ghoshal and Bartlett, 1990; Gulati and Gargiulo, 1999). Horizontal linkages supplement and some-times supplant vertical coordination. Such a firm is multicentric: initiatives and strategy emerge from many places, taking shape through a variety of partnerships and joint ventures.

Designing a Structure That Works

In designing a structure that works, managers have a set of options for dividing the work and coordinating multiple efforts. Structure needs to be designed with an eye toward strategy, the nature of the environment, the talents of the workforce, and the available resources (such as time, budget, and other contingencies). The options are summarized in Exhibit 3.1.

Vertical or Lateral?

Vertical coordination is often efficient but not always effective and depends on employees' willingness to follow directives from above. More decentralized and interactive lateral forms of coordination are often needed to keep top-down control from stifling initiative and creativity. Lateral coordination is often more effective but costlier than its vertical counter-parts. A meeting, for example, provides an opportunity for face-to-face dialogue and decision making but may squander time and energy. Personal and political agendas may undermine the meeting's purpose.

Ad hoc groups such as task forces can foster creativity and integration around pressing problems but may divert attention from ongoing operating issues. The effectiveness of coordinators who span boundaries depends on their credibility and skills in handling others.

Exhibit 3.1.

Basic Structural Options.

Division of labor: Options for differentiation

	Function
	Time
	Product
	Customers or clients
	Place (geography)
	Process

Coordination: Options for integration

Vertical	Authority
	Rules and policies
	Planning and control systems
Lateral	Meetings
	Task forces
	Coordinating roles
	Matrix structures
	Networks

Coordinators are also likely to schedule meetings that take still more time from actual work (Hannaway and Sproull, 1979). Matrix structures provide lateral linkage and integration but are notorious for creating conflict and confusion. Multiple players and decision nodes make networks inherently difficult to manage. Organizations have to use both vertical and horizontal procedures for coordination. The optimal blend of the two depends on the unique challenges in a given situation. Vertical coordination is generally superior if an environment is stable, tasks are well understood and predictable, and uniformity is essential. Lateral communications work best for complex tasks performed in a turbulent environment. Every organization must find a design that works for its circumstances, and inherent structural tradeoffs rarely yield easy answers or perfect solutions.

Consider the contrasting structures of McDonald's and Harvard University (highly regarded organizations in two very different industries), and Amazon and Zappos (two successful Internet retailers with very different structures).

McDonald's and Harvard: A Structural Odd Couple

McDonald's, the company that made the Big Mac a household word, has been enormously successful. For 40 years after its founding in the 1950s, the company was an unstoppable growth engine that came to dominate the worldwide fast-food business. McDonald's has a relatively small staff at its world headquarters near Chicago; the vast majority of its employees are salted across the world in more than 36,000 local outlets. But despite its size and geographic reach, McDonald's is a highly centralized, tightly controlled organization. Most big decisions are made at headquarters.

Managers and employees of McDonald's restaurants have limited discretion about how to do their jobs. Their work is controlled by technology; machines time the preparation of French fries and measure soft drinks. The parent company uses powerful systems to ensure that customers get what they expect and a Big Mac tastes about the same whether purchased in New York, Beijing, or Moscow. Cooks are not expected to develop creative new versions of the Big Mac or Quarter Pounder. Creative departures from standard product lines are neither encouraged nor tolerated on a day-to-day basis, though the company has adapted to growth and globalization with a mantra of "freedom within a framework," increasing its receptivity to new ideas from the field. The Big Mac and Egg McMuffin were both created by local franchisees, and burgers-on-wheels home delivery was pioneered in traffic-choked cities like Cairo and Taipei (Arndt, 2007b).

All that structure might sound oppressive, but a major McDonald's miscue in the 1990s resulted from trying to loosen up. Responding to pressure from some frustrated franchisees, McDonald's in 1993 stopped sending out inspectors to grade restaurants on service, food, and ambience. When left to police themselves, some restaurants slipped badly. Customers noticed, and the company's image sagged. Ten years later, a new CEO brought the inspectors back to correct lagging standards (David, 2003).

Year after year, Harvard University appears at or near the top of lists of the world's best universities. Like McDonald's, it has a small administrative group at the top, but in most other respects the two organizations diverge. Even though Harvard is more geographically concentrated than McDonald's, it is significantly more decentralized. Nearly all of Harvard's activities occur within a few square miles of Boston and Cambridge, Massachusetts. Most employees are housed in the university's several schools: Harvard College (the undergraduate school), the graduate faculty of arts and sciences, and various professional schools. Each school has its own dean and its own endowment and, in accordance with Harvard's philosophy of "every tub on its own bottom," largely controls its own destiny. Schools have fiscal autonomy, and individual professors have enormous discretion. They have substantial control over what courses they teach, what research they do, and which university activities they pursue, if any. Faculty meetings are typically sparsely attended. If a dean or a department head wants a faculty member to chair a committee or offer a new course, the request is more often a humble entreaty than an authoritative command.

The contrast between McDonald's and Harvard is particularly strong at the level of service delivery. Individual personality is not supposed to influence the quality of McDonald's hamburgers, but Harvard courses are the unique creations of individual professors. Two schools might offer courses with the same title but different content and widely divergent teaching styles. Efforts to develop standardized core curricula founder on the autonomy of individual professors.

Structural Differences in the Same Industry

Harvard and McDonald's operate in very different industries, but you will sometimes find very different structures among enterprises operating in a similar business environment. Take Amazon and Zappos.

Both companies are online retailers who ship a variety of goods to customers across America. Both are successful and known for their customer service. We have noted that Amazon gets it done with a tight structure that relies on sophisticated technology, precise measurement, close supervision, and zealous focus on customers, often to the exclusion of employees' satisfaction and welfare.

Contrast this with the Zappos structure, erected on a "culture of happiness" rather than a "culture of metrics." Tony Hsieh, Zappos CEO, is just as focused on the customer as Amazon CEO Jeff Bezos, but he has chosen a very different structure to get there. Structurally, Amazon and Zappos are mirror images of one another. Amazon steers customers toward interaction with its website rather than its employees. Zappos wants highly motivated, happy employees, immersed in an environment of "weirdness and fun," who will create a personal, emotional contact with customers.

Zappos fulfillment operations take place in two large warehouses in Kentucky where goods are received and merchandise is shelved, picked, packed, and shipped. Work is fast paced, intense, and often strenuous. Amazon workers have been known to say they are "treated like a piece of crap" (Soper, 2011, p. 1), but Zappos makes working conditions a primary concern. The warehouses are air-conditioned, and lunch breaks are embellished with free food, video games, and karaoke—the equivalent of adding several dollars to the hourly rate. One employee summed it up: "It's a hot boring job, and we may not get paid top dollar, but with our benefits and free food, it really makes a difference."

In 2013, Hsieh concluded that Zappos was developing too much bureaucracy and proposed a "holocratic" form that eliminated jobs and the organization chart. Managers were replaced by "lead links" of self-managing teams, and individuals were charged to use the "Role Marketplace" (Bernstein et al., 2016, p. 10) to look for work that interested them and needed to be done. The new system turned off some employees, and Zappos lost almost a fifth of its workforce. The transition to holocracy required major investments of time and energy as everyone struggled to figure out how the new system was supposed to work. Things got worse before they got better, as is typical of structural change. But, working

(continued)

(continued)

within the holocracy framework in 2015, Zappos achieved a 75 percent year-over-year increase in profits (Bernstein et al., 2016). The long-term impact on Zappos' free-wheeling culture remains to be seen, but, despite a rocky start, there are signs that this experiment may not be as crazy as it seems.

Zappos and Amazon achieve customer satisfaction through entirely different structural arrangements. What makes the story even more interesting is that Amazon paid over $1 billion to buy Zappos in November 2009. More than a year later, Zappos CEO Tony Hsieh sent a memo to employees saying the culture was still intact, Zappos was still in charge of its own destiny, and business was better than ever (Zappos Blogs, 2011). That was still true five years later in 2016.

Structural Imperatives

Why do McDonald's and Harvard or Zappos and Amazon have such different structures? Is one more effective than the other? Or has each evolved to fit its unique circumstances? In fact, there is no such thing as an ideal structure. Every organization needs to respond to a universal set of internal and external parameters (outlined in Exhibit 3.2). These parameters, or contingencies, include the organization's size, age, core process, environment, strategy and goals, information technology, and workforce characteristics. All these combine to point toward an optimal social architecture.

Exhibit 3.2.
Structural Imperatives.

Dimension	Structural Implications
Size and age	Complexity and formality typically increase with size and age.
Core process	Structure must align with core processes or technologies.
Environment	Stable environment rewards simpler structure; uncertain, turbulent environment requires a more complex, flexible structure.
Strategy and goals	Variation in clarity, suitability, and consistency of strategy requires appropriate structural adaptations.
Information technology	Information technology permits flatter, more flexible, and more decentralized structures.
Nature of the workforce	More educated and professional workers need and want greater autonomy and discretion.

Size and Age

Size and age affect structural shape and character. Problems crop up if growth (or downsizing) occurs without fine-tuning roles and relationships. A small, entrepreneurial organization typically has simple, informal architecture. Growth spawns formality and complexity (Greiner, 1972; Quinn and Cameron, 1983). If carried too far, this leads to the suffocating bureaucratic rigidity often seen in large, mature enterprises.

In the beginning, McDonald's was not the tightly controlled company it is today. It began as a single hamburger stand in San Bernardino, California, owned and managed by the McDonald brothers. They virtually invented the concept of fast food, and their stand was phenomenally successful. The two tried to expand by selling franchise rights, with little success. They were making more than enough money, disliked travel, and had no heirs. If they were richer, said one brother, "we'd be leaving it to a church or something, and we didn't go to church" (Love, 1986, p. 23).

The concept took off when Ray Kroc arrived on the scene. He had achieved modest success selling milk shake machines to restaurants. When many of his customers began to ask for the McDonald's milk shake mixer, he decided to visit the brothers. Seeing the original stand, Kroc realized the potential: "Unlike the homebound McDonalds, Kroc had traveled extensively, and he could envision hundreds of large and small markets where a McDonald's could be located. He understood the existing food services businesses, and understood how a McDonald's unit could be a formidable competitor" (Love, 1986, pp. 39–40). Kroc persuaded the McDonald brothers to let him take over the franchising effort. The rest is history (or Hollywood, which tells its version of this story in the 2016 film, *The Founder*).

Core Process

Structure forms around an organization's basic method of transforming raw materials into finished products. Every organization has at least one core technology that includes raw materials, activities that turn inputs into outputs, and underlying beliefs about the links among inputs, activities, and outcomes (Dornbusch and Scott, 1975).

Core technologies vary in clarity, predictability, and effectiveness. Assembling a Big Mac is relatively routine and programmable. The task is clear, most potential problems are known in advance, and the probability of success is high. Its relatively simple core technology allows McDonald's to rely mostly on vertical coordination.

In contrast, Harvard's two core processes—research and teaching—are far more complex and less predictable. Teaching objectives are knotty and amorphous. Unlike hamburger buns, students are active agents. Which teaching strategies best yield desired results is more a matter of faith than of fact. Even if students could be molded predictably, mystery surrounds the knowledge and skills they will need to succeed in life. This uncertain technology, greatly dependent on the skills and knowledge of highly educated professionals, is a key source of Harvard's loosely coordinated structure.

Core technologies often evolve, and significant technical innovation calls for corresponding structural alterations (Barley, 1990). In recent decades, struggles to integrate new technologies have become a fateful reality for many firms (Henderson and Clark, 1990; Christensen, 1997). Existing arrangements often get in the way. Companies are tempted to shoehorn innovative technologies into a box that fits their existing operations. As we saw with the decline and fall of Kodak, a change from film to digital photography, slide rules to calculators, or "snail mail" to e-mail gives an advantage to new players less committed to the old ways. In his study of the disk drive industry from 1975 to 1994, Christensen (1997) found that innovation in established firms was often blocked less by technical challenges than by marketers who argued, "Our customers don't want it." By the time the customers did want it, someone else had grabbed the market.

Some organizations are more susceptible than others to outside influences. Public schools, for example, are highly vulnerable to external pressures because they have limited capacity to claim the resources they need or to shape the results they are supposed to produce. In contrast, an institution like Harvard is insulated from such intrusions by its size, elite status, and large endowment. It can afford to offer low teaching loads, generous salaries, and substantial autonomy to its faculty. A Harvard diploma is taken as sufficient evidence that instruction is having its desired effect.

Strategy and Goals

Strategic decisions are future oriented, concerned with long-term direction (Chandler, 1962; Mintzberg, 1994; Roberts, 2004). Across sectors, a major task of organizational leadership is "the determination of long-range goals and objectives of an enterprise, and the adoption of courses of action and allocation of resources necessary for carrying out these goals" (Chandler, p. 13).

A variety of goals are embedded in strategy. In business firms, goals such as profitability, growth, and market share are relatively specific and easy to measure. Goals of educational or human services organizations are typically more diffuse: "producing educated men and women" or "improving individual well-being." This is another reason Harvard adopts a more decentralized, loosely integrated system of roles and relationships.

Historically, McDonald's had fewer, more quantifiable, and less controversial goals than those of Harvard. This aligned well with the centralized, top-down McDonald's structure.

But that structure has become more complex as the company's size and global reach have fostered levels of decentralization that allowed outlets in India to offer vegetarian cuisine and those in France to run ads attacking Americans and American beef (Tagliabue, 1999; Stires, 2002; Arndt, 2007).

Understanding linkages among goals, structure, and strategy requires a look beyond formal statements of purpose. Schools, for example, are often criticized if structure does not coincide with the official goal of scholastic achievement. But schools have other, less visible goals. One is character development, often espoused with little follow-through. Another is the taboo goal of certification and selection, as schools channel students into tracks and sort them into careers. Still a third goal is custody and control—keeping kids off the streets, out from underfoot and temporarily away from the job market. Finally, schools often herald honorific goals such as excellence. Strategy and goals shape structure, but the process is often complex and subtle (Dornbusch and Scott, 1975).

Information Technology

New technologies continue to revolutionize the amount of information available and the speed at which it travels. Once accessible exclusively to top-level or middle managers, information is now easy to get and widely shared. New media have made communication immediate and far reaching. With the press of a key, anyone can reach another person—or an entire network. All this makes it easier to move decisions closer to the action.

In the 2003 invasion of Iraq, for example, U.S. and British forces had an obvious advantage in military hardware. They also had a powerful structural advantage because their superior information technology let them deploy a much more flexible and decentralized command structure. Commanders in the field could change their plans immediately in response to new developments. Iraqi forces, meanwhile, had a much slower, more vertical structure that relied on decisions from the top. A major reason that Iraqi resistance was lighter than expected in the early weeks was that commanders had no idea what to do when they were cut off from their chain of command (Broder and Schmitt, 2003).

Later, however, the structure and technology so effective against Iraq's military had more difficulty with an emerging resistance movement that evolved into a loosely connected structure of entrepreneurial local units that could adapt quickly to U.S. tactics. New technologies like the Internet and cell phones enabled the resistance to structure itself as a network of loosely connected units, each pursuing its own agenda in response to local conditions. The absence of strong central control in such networks can be a virtue because local units can adapt quickly to new developments and the loss of any one outpost does little damage to the whole.

Nature of the Workforce

Human resource requirements have also changed dramatically in recent decades. Many lower-level jobs now require higher levels of skill. A better-educated workforce expects and often demands more discretion in daily work routines. "Millennials" typically ask for higher salaries and more favorable working conditions than their predecessors. Increasing specialization has professionalized many functions. Professionals typically know more than their supervisors about technical aspects of their work. They expect autonomy and prefer reporting to professional colleagues. Trying to tell a Harvard professor what to teach is an exercise in futility. In contrast, giving too much discretion to a low-skilled McDonald's worker could become a disaster for both employee and customers.

Dramatically different structural forms are emerging as a result of changes in workforce demographics. Deal and Kennedy (1982) predicted early on the emergence of the atomized or network organization, made up of small, autonomous, often geographically dispersed work groups tied together by information systems and organizational symbols. Drucker makes a similar observation in noting that businesses increasingly "move work to where the people are, rather than people to where the work is" (1989, p. 20).

Challenges of Global Organization

In sum, numerous forces affecting structural design create a knotty mix of challenges and tensions. It is not simply a matter of deciding whether we should be centralized like McDonald's or Amazon or decentralized like Harvard or Zappos. Many organizations find that they have to do both and somehow accommodate the competing structural tensions.

Two electronics giants, Panasonic (formerly Matsushita) in Japan and Philips in the Netherlands, have competed with one another around the globe for more than half a century. Historically, Panasonic developed a strong headquarters, while Philips was more decentralized, with strong units in different countries. The pressures of global competition pushed both to become more alike. Philips struggled to gain the efficiencies that come from selling the same products around the world. Meanwhile, as Panasonic gradually discovered, "No company can operate effectively on a global scale by centralizing all key decisions and then farming them out for implementation. It doesn't work . . . No matter how good they are, no matter how well supported analytically, the decision-makers at the center are too far removed from individual markets and the needs of local customers" (Ohmae, 1990, p. 87).

CONCLUSION

The structural frame looks beyond individuals to examine the social architecture of work. Though sometimes equated with red tape, mindless memos, and rigid bureaucrats, the approach is much broader and more subtle. It encompasses the freewheeling, loosely structured entrepreneurial task force as well as the more tightly controlled railway company or postal department. If structure is overlooked, an organization often misdirects energy and resources. It may, for example, waste time and money on massive training programs in a vain effort to solve problems that have much more to do with social architecture than with people's skills or attitudes. It may fire managers and bring in new ones, who then fall victim to the same structural flaws that doomed their predecessors.

At the heart of organizational design are the twin issues of differentiation and integration. Organizations divide work by creating a variety of specialized roles, functions, and units. They must then use both vertical and horizontal procedures to mesh the many elements together. There is no one best way to organize. The right structure depends on prevailing circumstances and considers an organization's goals, strategies, technology, people, and environment. Understanding the complexity and variety of design possibilities can help create formal prototypes that work for, rather than against, both people and collective purposes.

Structure and Restructuring

When society requires to be rebuilt, there is no use in attempting to rebuild it on the old plan.

—John Stuart Mill

In 2004, a crisis over journalistic standards ensnared the British Broadcasting Corporation (BBC) in a flurry of parliamentary hearings, resignations, and public recrimination. The controversy so tarnished the respected institution's reputation that top officials took steps to ensure that it would never happen again.

They initiated a number of structural changes: a journalism board to monitor editorial policy, guidelines on journalistic procedures, forms to flag trouble spots that managers were required to complete, and a 300-page volume of editorial guidelines. The cumulative effect of the changes was a multilayered bureaucracy that limited managerial discretion and fostered a hierarchy of approve-disapprove boxes. These were to be passed up the chain of command as an alternative to probing questions at lower levels in the organization.

Some cures make the patient worse, and this newly restructured system resulted in two crises more damaging than the one in 2004. In October 2012, the BBC came under heavy fire when it became known that it had broadcast a glowing tribute to a well-known former BBC TV host, Jimmy Savile, but killed an investigative report detailing evidence that Savile had been a serial child molester. The following month, the BBC aired a report wrongly accusing a member of Margaret Thatcher's government of being a pedophile.

Postmortem investigations attributed both errors directly to BBC's restructured, highly bureaucratized system.

In another case, when Larry Summers, an economist and former treasury secretary, became president of Harvard University in 2001, he soon concluded that the venerable university needed a structural overhaul, and he subsequently issued a series of presidential directives. He attacked the undergraduate grading system, in which half of the students received As and 90 percent graduated with honors. He stiffened standards for awarding tenure, encouraged more foreign study, and directed faculty (especially senior professors) to spend more time with students. He stepped across curricular boundaries to call for an emphasis on educational reform and more interdisciplinary courses. He proposed a center for medicine and science to encourage more applied research. Finally, he announced a bold move to build an additional campus across the Charles River to house new growth and development. Summers's initiatives aimed to tighten Harvard's famously decentralized structure and to imbue the president's office with more clout.

Restructuring worked about as well for Summers as it had for the BBC—he was forced out after serving the shortest term for a Harvard president in more than a century. Reorganizing or restructuring is a powerful but high-risk approach to improvement. Major initiatives to redesign structure and processes often prove neither durable nor beneficial. Designing a structure, putting all the parts in place, and satisfying every interested party is difficult and hazardous. Although restructuring is a manager's strategy of choice to improve performance, a Boston Group Study estimates 50 percent of the efforts fail (BSG, 2012). Other estimates put the misfire rate even higher (HBR, 2000).

But it is also true that, over the past 100 years, management innovations such as decentralization, capital budgeting techniques, and self-governing teams have done more than any other kind of innovation to allow companies to cross new performance thresholds (Hamel, 2006). American automakers scratched their heads for 20 years trying to figure out what made Toyota so successful. They tried all kinds of process innovations but finally reached the conclusion that Toyota had simply given their employees more authority to make decisions and solve problems (Hamel, 2006).

An organization's structure at any moment represents its resolution of an enduring set of basic tensions or dilemmas, which we discuss in opening this chapter. Then, drawing on the work of Henry Mintzberg and Sally Helgesen, we describe two views of the alternatives organizations may consider in aligning structure with mission and environment. We conclude with case examples illustrating both opportunities and challenges that managers encounter when attempting to create more workable and successful structural designs.

STRUCTURAL DILEMMAS

Finding an apt system of authority, roles, and relationships is an ongoing, universal struggle. Managers rarely face well-defined problems with clear-cut solutions. Instead, they confront enduring structural dilemmas, tough trade-offs without easy answers.

Differentiation versus Integration

The tension between assigning work and synchronizing sundry efforts creates a classic dilemma, as seen in Chapter 3. The more complex a role structure (lots of people doing many different things), the harder it is to sustain a focused, tightly coupled enterprise. Recall the challenge facing Larry Summers as he tried to bring a higher level of coordination to a highly decentralized university. As complexity grows, organizations need more sophisticated—and more costly—coordination strategies. Lateral strategies need to supplement top-down rules, policies, and commands.

Gap versus Overlap

If key responsibilities are not clearly assigned, important tasks fall through the cracks. Conversely, roles and activities can overlap, creating conflict, wasted effort, and unintended redundancy. A patient in a prestigious teaching hospital, for example, called her husband and pleaded with him to rescue her. She couldn't sleep at night because hospital staff, especially nurses' aides and interns, kept waking her, often to repeat a procedure or administer a medication that someone else had done a short time before. Conversely, when she wanted something, pressing her nurses' call button rarely produced any response.

The new cabinet-level Department of Homeland Security, created in the wake of the 9/11 terrorist attacks, was intended to reduce gaps and overlaps among the many agencies responsible for responding to domestic threats. Activities incorporated into the new department included immigration, border protection, emergency management, and intelligence analysis. Yet the two most prominent antiterrorism agencies, the FBI and the CIA—with their long history of mutual gaps, overlaps, and bureaucratic squabbling—remained separate and outside the new agency (Firestone, 2002).

Underuse versus Overload

If employees have too little work, they become bored and get in other people's way. Members of the clerical staff in a physician's office were able to complete most of their tasks during the morning. After lunch, they filled their time talking to family and friends. As a result, the office's telephone lines were constantly busy, making it difficult for patients to ask questions and schedule appointments. Meanwhile, clients and routine paperwork swamped the nurses, who were often brusque and curt because they were so busy. Patients complained about impersonal care. Reassigning many of the nurses' clerical duties to office staff created a better structural balance.

Lack of Clarity versus Lack of Creativity

If employees are unclear about what they are supposed to do, they often tailor their roles to fit personal preferences instead of shaping them to meet system-wide goals. This frequently leads to trouble. Most McDonald's customers are not seeking novelty and surprise in their burgers and fries. But when responsibilities are over-defined, people conform to prescribed roles and protocols in "bureaupathic" ways. They rigidly follow job descriptions, regardless of how much the service or product suffers.

"You lost my bag!" an angry passenger shouted, confronting an airline manager.

The manager responded, "How was the flight?"

"I asked about my bag," said the passenger.

"That's not my job," the manager replied. "Check with baggage claim."

The passenger did not leave as a satisfied customer.

Excessive Autonomy versus Excessive Interdependence

If the efforts of individuals or groups are too autonomous, people often feel isolated. School-teachers may feel lonely and unsupported because they work in self-contained classrooms and rarely see other adults. Yet efforts to create closer teamwork have repeatedly run aground because of teachers' difficulties in working together. In contrast, if too tightly connected, people in roles and units are distracted and spend too much time on unnecessary coordination. IBM lost an early lead in the personal computer business in part because new initiatives required so many approvals—from levels and divisions alike—that new products were overdesigned and late to market. The same problem hindered Hewlett-Packard's ability to innovate in the late 1990s.

Too Loose versus Too Tight

One critical structural challenge is how to hold an organization together without holding it back. If structure is too loose, people go astray, with little sense of what others are doing. But rigid structures stifle flexibility and encourage people to waste time trying to beat the system.

We can see some of the perils of a loose structure in the former accounting firm Andersen Worldwide, indicted in 2002 for its role in the Enron scandal. Efforts to shred documents and alter memos at Andersen's Houston office went well beyond questionable accounting procedures. At its Chicago headquarters, Andersen had an internal audit team, the Professional Standards Group, charged with reviewing the work of regional offices.

Unlike other large accounting firms, Andersen let frontline partners closest to the clients overrule the internal audit team. This fostered local discretion that was a selling point to customers but came back to haunt the firm. As a result of the lax controls, "the rainmakers were given the power to overrule the accounting nerds" (McNamee and Borrus, 2002, p. 33).

The opposite problem is common in managed health care. Insurance companies give clerks far from the patient's bedside the authority to approve or deny treatment or to review medical decisions, often frustrating physicians and patients. Doctors lament spending time talking to insurance representatives that would be better spent seeing patients. Insurance providers sometimes deny treatments that physicians see as urgent. In one case, a hospital-based psychologist diagnosed an adolescent as likely to commit sexual assault. The insurer questioned the diagnosis and denied hospitalization. The next day, the teenager raped a five-year-old girl.

Goal-less versus Goal-bound

In some situations, few people know what the goals are; in others, people cling closely to goals long after they have become irrelevant or outmoded. In the 1960s, for example, the Salk vaccine virtually eradicated polio. This medical breakthrough also brought to an end the existing goal of the March of Dimes organization, which for years had championed finding a cure for the crippling disease. The organization rebounded by shifting its strategy to focus on preventing birth defects.

Irresponsible versus Unresponsive

If people abdicate their responsibilities, performance suffers. However, adhering too rigidly to policies or procedures can be equally harmful. In public agencies, "street-level bureaucrats" (Lipsky, 1980) who deal with the public are often asked, "Could you do me this favor?" or "Couldn't you bend the rules a little bit in this case?" Turning down every request, no matter how reasonable, alienates the public and perpetuates images of bureaucratic rigidity and red tape. But agency workers who are too accommodating create problems of inconsistency and favoritism.

STRUCTURAL CONFIGURATIONS

Structural design rarely starts from scratch. Managers search for options among the array of possibilities drawn from their accumulated wisdom and the experiences of others. Templates and frameworks can offer options to stimulate thinking. Henry Mintzberg and Sally Helgesen offer two abstract conceptions of structural possibilities.

Mintzberg's Fives

As the two-dimensional lines and boxes of a traditional organization chart have become increasingly archaic, students of organizational design have developed a variety of new structural images. One influential example is Mintzberg's five-sector "logo," depicted in

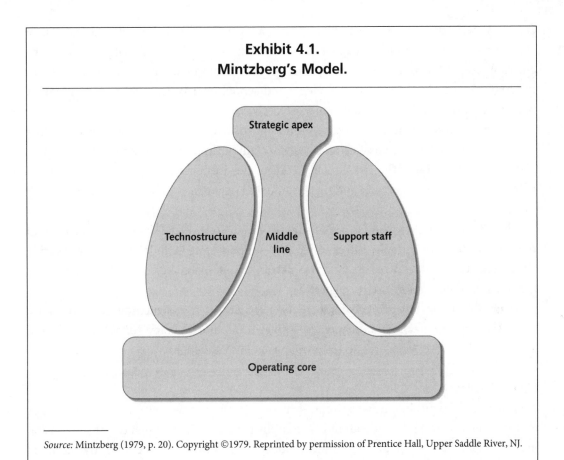

Exhibit 4.1.
Mintzberg's Model.

Strategic apex

Technostructure

Middle
line

Support staff

Operating core

Source: Mintzberg (1979, p. 20). Copyright ©1979. Reprinted by permission of Prentice Hall, Upper Saddle River, NJ.

Exhibit 4.1. Mintzberg's model clusters various functions into groupings and shows their relative size and influence in response to different strategies and external challenges. His schema provides a rough atlas of the structural terrain that can help managers get their bearings. It assists in sizing up the lay of the land before assembling a structure that conforms to the prevailing circumstances. One of the distinctive features of Mintzberg's image is expanding the typical two-dimensional view of structure into a more comprehensive portrayal. In doing this, he is able to capture more of the complexity and issues in formal dealings.

At the base of Mintzberg's image is the *operating core,* consisting of workers who produce or provide products or services to customers or clients: teachers in schools, assembly-line workers in factories, physicians and nurses in hospitals, and flight crews in airlines.

Directly above the operating core is the *administrative component:* managers who supervise, coordinate, control, and provide resources for the operators. School principals, factory supervisors, and echelons of middle management fulfill this role. At the top of Mintzberg's figure, senior managers in the strategic apex track developments in the environment, determine the strategy, and shape the grand design. In school systems, the strategic apex includes superintendents and school boards. In corporations, the apex houses the board of directors and senior executives.

Two more components sit alongside the administrative component. The *technostructure* houses specialists, technicians, and analysts who standardize, measure, and inspect outputs and procedures. Accounting and quality control departments in industry, audit departments in government agencies, and flight standards departments in airlines perform such functions.

The *support staff* performs tasks that support or facilitate the work of others throughout the organization. In schools, for example, the support staff includes nurses, secretaries, custodians, food service workers, and bus drivers. These people often wield influence far greater than their station might suggest.

From this basic blueprint, Mintzberg (1979) derived five structural configurations: simple structure, machine bureaucracy, professional bureaucracy, divisionalized, and adhocracy. Each creates a unique set of management challenges.

Simple Structure

New businesses typically begin as simple structures with only two levels: the strategic apex and an operating level. Coordination is accomplished primarily through direct supervision and oversight, as in a small mom-and-pop operation. Mom or pop constantly monitors what is going on and exercises complete authority over daily operations. William Hewlett and David Packard began their business in a garage, as did Apple Computer's Steve Jobs and Steve Wozniak. Simple structure has the virtues of flexibility and adaptability. One or two people control the operation and can turn on a dime when needed. But virtues can become vices. Authorities can block as well as initiate change, and they can punish capriciously as well as reward handsomely. A boss too close to day-to-day operations is easily distracted by immediate problems, neglecting long-range strategic issues. A notable exception was Panasonic founder Konosuke Matsushita, who promulgated his 250-year plan for the future of the business when his young company still had less than 200 employees.

Machine Bureaucracy

McDonald's is a classic machine bureaucracy. Members of the strategic apex make the big decisions. Managers and standardized procedures govern day-to-day operations. Like other machine bureaucracies, McDonald's has large support staffs and a sizable techno-structure that sets standards for the cooking time of French fries or the assembly of a Big Mac or Quarter Pounder.

For routine tasks, such as making hamburgers and manufacturing automotive parts, a machine-like operation is both efficient and effective. A key challenge is how to motivate and satisfy workers in the operating core. People quickly tire of repetitive work and standardized procedures. Yet offering too much creativity and personal challenge in, say, a McDonald's outlet could undermine consistency and uniformity—two keys to the company's success.

Like other machine bureaucracies, McDonald's deals constantly with tension between local managers and headquarters. Local concerns and tastes weigh heavily on decisions of middle managers. Top executives, aided by analysts armed with reams of data, rely more on generic and abstract information. Their decisions are influenced by corporation-wide concerns. As a result, a solution from the top may not always match the needs of individual units. Faced with declining sales and market share, McDonald's introduced a new food preparation system in 1998 under the marketing banner "Made for you." CEO Jack Greenberg was convinced the new cook-to-order system would produce the fresher, tastier burgers needed to get the company back on the fast track. However, franchisees soon complained that the new system led to long lines and frustrated customers. Unfazed by the criticism, Greenberg invited a couple of skeptical financial analysts to flip burgers at a McDonald's outlet in New Jersey so they could see firsthand that the concerns were unfounded. The experiment backfired. The analysts agreed with local managers that the system was too slow and decided to pass on the stock (Stires, 2002). The board replaced Greenberg at the end of 2002.

Professional Bureaucracy

Harvard University affords a glimpse into the inner workings of a professional bureaucracy. As in other organizations that employ large numbers of highly educated professionals to perform core activities, Harvard's operating core is large relative to other structural parts, although the technostructure has grown in recent years to accommodate mandated programs such as racial equity or gender sensitivity. At the operating sphere, each individual school, for example, has its own local approach to teaching evaluations; there is no university-wide profile developed by analysts. Few managerial levels exist between the strategic apex and the professors, creating a flat and decentralized profile.

Control relies heavily on professional training and indoctrination. Insulated from formal interference, professors have almost unlimited academic freedom to apply their expertise as they choose. Freeing highly trained experts to do what they do best produces many benefits but leads to challenges of coordination and quality control. Tenured professors, for example, are largely immune from formal sanctions. As a result, universities have to find other ways to deal with incompetence and irresponsibility. Faced with a professor whose teaching performance was moving from erratic to bizarre, a Harvard dean did the one thing he felt he could do—he relieved the professor of teaching responsibilities while continuing to pay his full salary. The dean was not very disappointed when the professor quit in anger (Rosovsky, 1990).

A professional bureaucracy responds slowly to external change. Waves of reform typically produce little impact because professionals often view any change in their surroundings as an annoying distraction. The result is a paradox: Individual professionals may strive to be at the forefront of their specialty, whereas the institution as a whole changes at a glacial pace. Professional bureaucracies regularly stumble when they try to exercise greater control over the operating core; requiring Harvard professors to follow standard teaching methods might do more harm than good.

Harvard president Larry Summers tripped over this challenge in a famous case when he suggested that superstar African American studies professor Cornel West redirect his scholarly efforts. Summers gave his advice to West in private, but West's pique made the front page of the *New York Times* (Belluck and Steinberg, 2002). Summers's profuse public apologies failed to deter the offended professor from decamping to Princeton, where he stayed for 14 years before returning to Harvard in 2016. In professional bureaucracies, professionals often win struggles between the strategic apex and the operating core. Hospital administrators learn this lesson quickly, and often painfully, in their dealings with physicians.

Divisionalized Form

In a divisionalized organization (see Exhibit 4.2), the bulk of the work is done in quasiautonomous units, such as freestanding campuses in a multi-campus university, areas of expertise in a large multispecialty hospital, or independent business units in a Fortune 500 firm (Mintzberg, 1979). Johnson and Johnson, for example, is among the largest companies in the world (#39 on the Fortune 500 in 2016). It has 250 operating companies lodged in virtually every country. Its medical device division is the world's largest. Its pharmaceutical division is even bigger. Its consumer products division produces a wide assortment of well-known brands, such as Neutrogena, Tylenol, Band-Aids, and Rogaine. It also makes contact lenses and tuberculosis medicines.

Although J&J's divisions often have little in common, the company's executives argue that there is a level of shared synergy and stability that have paid off over time. Despite

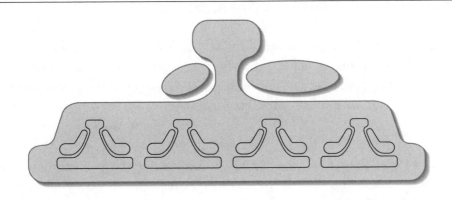

Exhibit 4.2.
Divisionalized Form.

Source: Mintzberg (1979, p. 393). Copyright © 1979. Reprinted by permission of Pearson Education, Inc., New York, New York.

setbacks in the Tylenol crisis of 1982 and a series of product recalls in 2010 and 2012, J&J had raised its dividend for 53 consecutive years and was one of only two U.S. companies with an AAA credit rating.

One of the oldest businesses in the United States, Berwind Corporation began in coal-mining in 1886. It now houses divisions in business sectors as diverse as manufacturing, financial services, real estate, and land management. Each division serves a distinct market and supports its own functional units. Division presidents are accountable to the corporate office in Philadelphia for specific results: profits, sales growth, and return on investment. As long as they deliver, divisions have relatively free rein. Philadelphia manages the strategic portfolio and allocates resources based on its assessment of market opportunities.

Divisionalized structure offers economies of scale, resources, and responsiveness while controlling economic risks, but it creates other tensions. One is a cat-and-mouse game between headquarters and divisions. Headquarters wants oversight, while divisional managers try to evade corporate control:

> Our top management likes to make all the major decisions. They think they do, but I've seen one case where a division beat them. I received . . . a request from the division for a chimney. I couldn't see what anyone would do with a chimney . . .

[But] they've built and equipped a whole plant on plant expense orders. The chimney is the only indivisible item that exceeded the $50,000 limit we put on plant expense orders. Apparently they learned that a new plant wouldn't be formally received, so they built the damn thing (Bower, 1970, p. 189).

Another risk in the divisionalized form is that headquarters may lose touch with operations. As one manager put it, "Headquarters is where the rubber meets the air." Divisionalized enterprises become unwieldy unless goals are measurable and reliable information systems are in place (Mintzberg, 1979).

Adhocracy

Adhocracy is a loose, flexible, self-renewing organic form tied together primarily through lateral means. Usually found in a diverse, freewheeling environment, adhocracy functions as an "organizational tent," exploiting benefits that structural designers traditionally regarded as liabilities: "Ambiguous authority structures, unclear objectives, and contradictory assignments of responsibility can legitimize controversies and challenge traditions. Incoherence and indecision can foster exploration, self-evaluation, and learning" (Hedberg, Nystrom, and Starbuck, 1976, p. 45). Inconsistencies and contradictions in an adhocracy become paradoxes whereby a balance between opposites protects an organization from falling into an either-or trap.

Ad hoc structures thrive in conditions of turbulence and rapid change. Examples are advertising agencies, think-tank consulting firms, and the recording industry. A successful and durable example of an adhocracy is W. L. Gore, producer of Gore-Tex, vascular stents, dental floss, and many other products based on its pioneering development of advanced polymer materials. When he founded the company in 1958, Bill Gore conceived it as an organization where "there would be no layers of management, information would flow freely in all directions, and personal communications would be the norm. And individuals and self-managed teams would go directly to anyone in the organization to get what they needed to be successful" (Hamel, 2010).

Half a century later, Gore has more than 10,000 employees (Gore calls them "associates") and some $3 billion in annual sales but still adheres to Bill Gore's principles. In Gore's "lattice" structure, people don't have bosses. Instead, the company relies on "natural leaders"—individuals who can attract talent, build teams, and get things done. One test: If you call a meeting and no one comes, you're probably not a leader. When Gore's CEO retired in 2005, the board polled associates to find out whom they would be willing to follow. They weren't given a slate—they could nominate anyone. No one was more surprised than Terri Kelly when she became the people's choice. She acknowledges that Gore's approach carries a continuing risk of chaos. It helps, she says, that the culture has clear norms and values, but "Our leaders have to do an incredible job of internal selling to get the organization to move. The process is sometimes frustrating, but we believe that if you spend more time up front, you'll have associates who are not only fully bought-in, but committed to achieving the outcome. Along the way, they'll also help to refine the idea and make the decision better" (Hamel, 2010).

Helgesen's Web of Inclusion

Mintzberg's five-sector imagery adds a new dimension to the conventional line-staff organization chart but retains some of the traditional image of structure as a top-down pyramid. Helgesen argues that the idea of hierarchy is primarily a male-driven depiction, quite different from structures created by female executives:

> The women I studied had built profoundly integrated and organic organizations in which the focus was on nurturing good relationships; in which the niceties of hierarchical rank and distinction played little part; and in which lines of communication were multiplicitous, open, and diffuse. I noted that women tended to put themselves at the center of their organizations rather than at the top, thus emphasizing both accessibility and equality, and that they labored constantly to include people in their decision making (Helgesen, 1995, p. 10).

Helgesen coined the expression "web of inclusion" to depict an organic social architectural form more circular than hierarchical. The web builds from the center out. Its architect works much like a spider, spinning new threads of connection and reinforcing existing strands. The web's center and periphery are interconnected; action in one place ripples across the entire configuration, forming "an interconnected cosmic web in which the threads of all forces and events form an inseparable net of endlessly, mutually conditioned relations" (Fritjof Capra, quoted in Helgesen, 1995, p. 16). Consequently, weaknesses in either the center or the periphery of the web undermine the strength of the natural network.

A famous example of web organization is "Linux, Inc.," the loose organization of individuals and organizations that has formed around Linus Torvalds, the creator of the open-source operating system Linux, whose many variants power most of the world's supercomputers, cell phones, stock markets, and Web domains. "Linux, Inc." is anything but a traditional company: "There's no headquarters, no CEO, and no annual report. It's not a single company, but a cooperative venture. More than 13,000 developers from more than 1,300 companies along with thousands of individual volunteers have contributed to the

Linux code. The Linux community, Torvalds says, is like a huge spider web, or better yet, multiple spider webs representing dozens of related open-source projects. His office is 'near where those webs intersect'" (Hamm, 2005).

Freewheeling web or lattice structures may encounter increasing challenges as an organization gets bigger. When Meg Whitman became CEO of Internet phenomenon eBay in 1998, she joined an organization of fewer than 50 employees configured in an informal web around founder Pierre Omidyar. When she tried to set up appointments with her new staff, she was surprised to learn that scheduled meetings were a foreign concept in a company where no one kept a calendar. Omidyar had built a company with a strong culture and powerful sense of community but no explicit strategy, no regular meetings, no marketing department, and almost no other identifiable structural elements. Despite the company's phenomenal growth and profitability, Whitman concluded that it was in danger of imploding without more structure and discipline. Omidyar agreed. He had worked hard to recruit Whitman because he believed she brought the big-company management experience that eBay needed to keep growing (Hill and Farkas, 2000).

GENERIC ISSUES IN RESTRUCTURING

Eventually, internal or external changes force every structure to adjust, but structural change is rarely easy, When the Roman Catholic Church elevated a new pope, Francis, in March, 2013, many hoped that he would represent a breath of fresh air after the troubled reign of his predecessor. But a well-placed insider noted how difficult this would be, even for a supposedly absolute ruler: "There have been a number of Popes in succession with different personalities, but the structure remains the same. Whoever is appointed, they get absorbed by the structure. Instead of you transforming the structure, the structure transforms you" (Donadio and Yardley, 2013).

When the time for restructuring comes, managers need to take account of tensions specific to each structural configuration. Consultants and managers often apply general principles and specific answers without recognizing key differences across architectural forms. Reshaping an adhocracy, for example, is different from restructuring a machine bureaucracy, and reweaving a web is very different from nudging a professional bureaucracy. Falling victim to the one-best-system or one-size-fits-all mentality is a route to disaster. But the comfort of a well-defined prescription lulls too many managers into a temporary comfort zone. They don't see the iceberg looming ahead until they crash into it.

Mintzberg's depiction suggests general principles to guide restructuring across a range of circumstances. Each major component of his model exerts its own pressures. Restructuring triggers a multidirectional tug-of-war that eventually determines the shape of the emerging configuration. The result may be a catastrophe unless leaders acknowledge and manage various pushes and pulls.

The strategic apex—top management—tends to exert centralizing pressures. Through commands, rules, or less obtrusive means, top managers continually try to develop a unified mission or strategy. Deep down, they long for a simple structure they can control. By contrast, middle managers resist control from the top and tend to pull the organization toward balkanization. Navy captains, school principals, plant managers, department heads, and bureau chiefs become committed to their own domain and seek to protect and enhance their unit's parochial interests. Tensions between centripetal forces from the top and centrifugal forces from middle management are especially prominent in divisional structures but are critical issues in any restructuring effort.

The technostructure exerts pressures to standardize; analysts want to measure and monitor the organization's progress against well-defined criteria. Depending on the circumstances, they counterbalance (or complement) top administrators, who want to centralize, and middle managers, who seek greater autonomy. A college professor who wants to use a Web-based simulation game, for example, may find that it takes weeks or months to negotiate the rules and procedures that the university's information technology units have put in place. Issues that seem critical to IT may seem like trivial annoyances to the professor and vice-versa. Technocrats feel most at home in a machine bureaucracy.

The support staff pulls in the direction of greater collaboration. Its members usually feel happiest when authority is dispersed to small work units. There they can influence, directly and personally, the shape and flow of everyday work and decisions. In one university, a new president created a new governance structure that, for the first time, included support staff along with faculty and administrators. The staff loved it, but when they came up with a proposal for improvements to the promotion and tenure process, the faculty was not amused. Meanwhile, the operating core seeks to control its own destiny and minimize influence from the other components. Its members often look outside—to a union or to their professional colleagues—for support.

Attempts to restructure must acknowledge the natural tensions among these competing interests. Depending on the configuration, any component may have more or less influence on the final outcome. In a simple structure, the boss has the edge. In machine bureaucracies, the techno structure and strategic apex possess the most clout. In professional bureaucracies, chronic conflict between administrators and professionals is the dominant tension, while members of the techno structure play an important role in the wings. In the adhocracy, a variety of actors can play a pivotal role in shaping the emerging structural patterns.

Beyond internal negotiations a more crucial issue lurks. A structure's effectiveness ultimately depends on its fit with the organization's strategy, environment, and technology. Natural selection weeds out the field, determining survivors and victims. The major players must negotiate a structure that meets the needs of each component and still enables the organization to survive, if not thrive.

Why Restructure?

Restructuring is a challenging process that consumes time and resources with no guarantee of success, as the BBC and Harvard cases at the beginning of the chapter illustrate. Organizations typically embark on that path when they feel compelled to respond to major problems or opportunities. Various pressures can lead to that conclusion:

- *The environment shifts.* At American Telephone & Telegraph, once the telephone company for most of the United States, a mandated shift from regulated monopoly to a market with multiple competitors required a massive reorganization of the Bell System that played out over decades. When AT&T split off its local telephone companies into regional "Baby Bells," few anticipated that eventually one of the children (Southwest Bell) would swallow up the parent and appropriate its identity.

- *Technology changes.* The aircraft industry's shift from piston to jet engines profoundly affected the relationship between engine and airframe. Some established firms faltered because they underestimated the complexities; Boeing rose to lead the industry because it understood the issues (Henderson and Clark, 1990).

- *Organizations grow.* Digital Equipment thrived with a very informal and flexible structure during the company's early years, but the same structure produced major problems when it grew into a multibillion-dollar corporation.

- *Leadership changes.* Reorganization is often the first initiative of new leaders. It is a way for them to try to put their stamp on the organization, even if no one else sees a need to restructure.

Miller and Friesen (1984) studied a sample of successful as well as troubled firms undergoing structural change and found that those in trouble typically fell into one of three configurations:

- *The impulsive firm:* A fast-growing organization, controlled by one individual or a few top people, in which structure and controls have become too primitive and the firm is increasingly out of control. Profits may fall precipitously, and survival may be at stake.

Many once-successful entrepreneurial organizations stumble at this stage because they have failed to evolve beyond their simple structure.

- *The stagnant bureaucracy:* An older, tradition-dominated organization with an obsolete product line. A predictable and placid environment has lulled everyone to sleep, and top management is slavishly committed to old ways. Management thinking is too rigid or information systems are too primitive to detect the need for change, and lower-level managers feel ignored and alienated. Many old-line corporations and public agencies fit into this group of faltering machine bureaucracies.

- *The headless giant:* A loosely coupled, divisional organization that has turned into a collection of feudal baronies. The strategic apex is weak, and most of the initiative and power resides in autonomous divisions. With little strategy or leadership at the top, the firm is adrift. Collaboration is minimal because departments compete for resources. Decision making is reactive and crisis-oriented. WorldCom is an example of how bad things can get in this situation. CEO Bernie Ebbers built the company rapidly from a tiny start-up in Mississippi to a global telecommunications giant through some 65 acquisitions. But "for all its talent in buying competitors, the company was not up to the task of merging them. Dozens of conflicting computer systems remained, local network systems were repetitive and failed to work together properly, and billing systems were not coordinated. 'Don't think of WorldCom the way you would of other corporations,' said one person who has worked with the company at a high level for many years. 'It's not a company, it's just a bunch of disparate pieces. It's simply dysfunctional'" (Eichenwald, 2002, p. C-6).

Miller and Friesen (1984) found that even in troubled organizations, structural change is episodic: Long periods of little change are followed by brief episodes of major restructuring. Organizations are reluctant to make major changes because a stable structure reduces confusion and uncertainty, maintains internal consistency, and protects the existing equilibrium. The price of stability is a structure that grows increasingly misaligned with the environment. Eventually, the gap gets so big that a major overhaul is inevitable. Restructuring, in this view, is like spring cleaning: We accumulate debris over months or years until we are finally forced to face up to the mess.

Making Restructuring Work: Three Case Examples

In this section, we look at three case examples of restructuring. Some represent examples of reengineering, which rose to prominence in the 1990s as an umbrella concept for emerging trends in structural thinking. Hammer and Champy promised a revolution in how organizations were structured: "When a process is reengineered, jobs evolve from narrow and task oriented to multidimensional. People who once did as they were instructed now make choices and decisions on their own instead. Assembly-line work disappears. Functional departments lose their reason for being. Managers stop acting like supervisors and behave more like coaches. Workers focus more on customers' needs and less on their bosses' whims. Attitudes and values change in response to new incentives. Practically every aspect of the organization is transformed, often beyond recognition" (1993, p. 65).

More than half of all Fortune 500 companies jumped on the reengineering bandwagon in the mid-1990s, but only about a third of those efforts were successful. Champy admitted in a follow-up book, *Reengineering Management* (1995), that reengineering was in trouble, and attributed the shortfall to flaws in senior management thinking.

Some reengineering initiatives have indeed been catastrophic, a notorious example being the long-haul bus company Greyhound Lines. As the company came out of bankruptcy in the early 1990s, a new management team announced a major reorganization, with sizable cuts in staffing and routes and development of a new, computerized reservation system. The initiative played well on Wall Street, where the company's stock soared, but poorly on Main Street as customer service and the new reservations system collapsed. Rushed, underfunded, and insensitive to both employees and customers, it was a textbook example of how not to restructure. Eventually, Greyhound's stock crashed, and management was forced out. One observer noted wryly, "They reengineered that business to hell" (Tomsho, 1994, p. A1). Across many organizations, reengineering was a cover for downsizing the workforce, often with disappointing results.

Nevertheless, despite the many disasters, there have also been examples of notable restructuring success. Here we discuss three of them, drawn from different eras and industries.

Citibank's Back Room

The "back room" at Citibank—charged with processing checks and other financial instruments—was in trouble when John Reed took charge in 1970 (Seeger, Lorsch, and Gibson, 1975). Productivity was down, errors were frequent, and expenses were rising almost 20 percent every year. Reed soon determined that the area needed dramatic structural change. Traditionally, the department was a service for the bank's customer-contact offices, structured as a machine bureaucracy. Reed decided to think of it as an independent factory—a free-standing, high-volume production facility. He imported high-level executives from the automobile industry. One was Robert White, who came from Ford to become the primary architect of the new structure for the back room.

White began by cutting costs, putting in new computer systems, and developing a financial control system to forecast and measure performance. In effect, the strategy tightened the machine bureaucracy. Later on, White concluded that "we hadn't gone back to the basics enough. We found that we did not really understand the present processes completely" (Seeger, Lorsch, and Gibson, 1975, p. 8).

They embarked on a detailed study of how the back room's processes worked and developed a detailed flowchart. This helped them realize that the current structure was, in effect, one very large functional pipeline. Everything flowed into "preprocessing" at the front end of the pipe, then to "encoding," and on through a series of functional areas until it eventually came out at the other end. Reed and White decided to break the pipe into several smaller lines, each carrying a different "product" and supervised by a single manager with responsibility for an end-to-end process. The key insight was to change the structure from machine bureaucracy to a divisionalized form. Along with the change, White instituted extensive performance measures and tight accountability procedures—69 quality indicators and 129 different standards for time lines.

As Mintzberg's model predicts, the operating core strongly resisted this intrusion. Reed and White implemented the new structure virtually overnight, and the short-term result was chaos and a major breakdown in the system. It took two weeks to get things working again, and five months to recover from the problems generated by the transition. Once past that crisis, the new system dramatically improved operating results: Production was up; costs and errors were down. The back room became a major source of competitive advantage.

The Citibank restructuring was strongly driven from the top down and focused primarily on internal efficiencies. This has been true of many, but by no means all, restructuring efforts.

Beth Israel Hospital

Boston's Beth Israel Hospital illustrates a health care restructuring effort that sought to move toward greater autonomy and teamwork. When Joyce Clifford became Beth Israel's director of nursing, she found a top-down pyramid common in many hospitals:

> The nursing aides, who had the least preparation, had the most contact with the patients. But they had no authority of any kind. They had to go to their supervisor to ask if a patient could have an aspirin. The supervisor would then ask the head nurse, who would then ask a doctor. The doctor would ask how long the patient had been in pain. Of course, the head nurse had absolutely no idea, so she'd have to track down the aide to ask her, and then relay that information back to the doctor. It was ridiculous, a ludicrous and dissatisfying situation, and one in which it was impossible for the nurse to feel any satisfaction at all. The system was hierarchical, fragmented, impersonal, and [overmanaged] (Helgesen, 1995, p. 134).

(continued)

(*continued*)

Within units, responsibilities of nurses were highly specialized: some were assigned to handling medications, others to monitoring vital signs, still others to taking blood pressure readings. Add to the list specialized housekeeping roles—bedpan, bed making, and food services. A patient received repeated interruptions from virtual strangers. No one really knew what was going on with any individual patient.

Clifford instituted a major structural revamp, changing a pyramid with nurses at the bottom to an inclusive web with nurses at the center. The concept, called primary nursing, places each patient in the charge of a primary nurse. The nurse takes information upon admission, develops a comprehensive care plan, assembles a team to provide round-the-clock care, and lets the family know what to expect. A nurse manager sets goals for the unit, deals with budget and administrative matters, and makes sure that primary nurses have ample resources to provide quality care.

As the primary nurses assumed more responsibility, connections with physicians and other hospital workers needed reworking. Instead of simply carrying out physicians' orders, primary nurses became professional partners, attending rounds and participating as equals in treatment decisions. Housekeepers reported to primary nurses rather than to housekeeping supervisors. Housekeepers assigned to specific patients made the patient's bed, attended to the patient's hygiene, and delivered food trays. Laundry workers brought in clean items on demand rather than making a once-a-day delivery. Sophisticated technology gave all personnel easy access to patient information and administrative data.

Primary nurses learned from performing a variety of heretofore menial tasks. Bed making, for example, became an opportunity to evaluate a patient's condition and assess how well a treatment plan was working. Joyce Clifford's role also transformed, from top-down supervisor to web-centered coordinator:

> A big part of my job is to keep nurses informed on a regular basis of what's going on out there—what the board is doing, what decisions are confronting the hospital as a whole, what the issues are in health care in this country. I also let them know that I'm trying to represent what the nurses here are doing—to our vice-presidents, to our board, and people in the outside world . . . to the nursing profession and the health care field as a whole (Helgesen, 1995, p. 158).

Beth Israel's primary nursing concept, initiated in the mid-1970s, produced significant improvement in both patient care and nursing morale. Nursing turnover declined dramatically (Springarn, 1982), and the model's success made it highly influential and widely copied both in the United States and abroad. But even successful change won't work forever. Over the years, changes in the health care system put Beth Israel's model under increasing pressure. More patients with more problems but shorter hospital stays made nurses' jobs much harder at the same time that cost pressures forced reductions in nursing staff. Beth Israel chose to update its approach by creating interdisciplinary "care teams." Instead of assembling an ad hoc collection of care providers for each new patient, ongoing teams of nurses, physicians, and support staff provided interdisciplinary support to primary nurses (Rundall, Starkweather, and Norrish, 1998).

Ford Motor Company

In 2006, after Ford Motor Company chalked up a $13 billion loss, Chairman William Ford III concluded that the way to save the company his great-grandfather had founded was to hire a strong and experienced outsider who could take on the entrenched mind-sets and infighting among executives and divisions at Ford. He took a gamble on a noncar guy, Alan Mulally, an engineer with a long career at Boeing and a reputation for turning around struggling businesses.

Arriving at Ford, Mulally encountered many surprises. Bureaucracy was so entrenched and top-down that it was considered bad form for a subordinate to invite a superior to lunch. Ford was struggling, but no one wanted to admit it, so executives brought thick books of minutiae to meetings, using a flurry of details to obfuscate problems or shift blame to someone else. They resorted to doublespeak to avoid admitting that they didn't know the answers to questions.

Mulally soon concluded that Ford needed a major overhaul of a "convoluted management structure riddled with overlapping responsibilities and tangled chains of command" (Hoffman, 2012, p. 142). He flattened the hierarchy, cut out two layers of senior management, and increased his number of direct reports. He sold off secondary brands like Volvo and Land Rover and streamlined Ford's product line to aim for fewer models with higher quality. He implemented what had worked at Boeing: a matrix structure that crisscrossed the already-strong regional organizations with upgraded global functional units. So, for example, the head of communications or purchasing in Ford Europe would report to both the regional president in Europe and to a corporate vice-president back at headquarters in the United States.

Mulally believed this structure would bring the balance Ford needed: "It made each business unit fully accountable, but also made sure that each key function, from purchasing to product development, was managed globally in order to maximize efficiencies and economies of scale" (Hoffman, 2012, p. 143). He emphasized teamwork, collaboration across divisions, and an end to blaming, hiding mistakes, and hoarding cost figures. Division presidents were instructed to act as one company, not as airtight silos.

It worked. After losing market share for 13 straight years, Ford gained share in 2009, turned a profit in 2010, and achieved its highest profits in more than a decade in 2011. Mulally turned 65 in 2011 amid speculation about when he would retire. Board chair William Ford III expressed the hope that he would stay forever, but Mulally chose to retire two years later in 2014.

Principles of Successful Structural Change

Too many efforts to change structure fail. The Citibank, Beth Israel, and Ford Motor Company initiatives succeeded by following several basic principles of successful structural change:

- They did the hard work of carefully studying the existing structure and process so that they fully understood how things worked—and what wasn't working. (Many efforts at structural change fail because they start from an inadequate picture of current roles, relationships, and processes.)

- The change architects developed a new conception of the organization's goals and strategies attuned to the challenges and circumstances of the time.

- They designed the new structure in response to changes in strategy, technology, and environment.

- Finally, they experimented as they moved along, retaining things that worked and discarding those that did not.

CONCLUSION

At any given moment, an organization's structure represents its best effort to align internal activities with outside pressures and opportunities. Managers work to juggle and resolve enduring organizational dilemmas: Are we too loose or too tight? Are employees under-worked or overwhelmed? Are we too rigid, or do we lack standards? Do people spend too much or too little time harmonizing with one another? Structure represents a resolution of contending claims from various groups.

Mintzberg differentiates five major components in organizational structure: strategic apex, middle management, operating core, techno structure, and support staff. These components configure in unique designs: machine bureaucracy, professional bureaucracy, simple structure, divisionalized form, and adhocracy. Helgesen adds a less hierarchical model, the web of inclusion.

Changes, whether driven from inside or outside, eventually require some form of structural adaptation. Restructuring is a sensible but high-risk move. In the short term, structural change invariably produces confusion and resistance; things get worse before they get better. In the end, success depends on how well the new model aligns with environment, task, and technology. It also hinges on the route taken in putting the new structure in place. Effective restructuring requires both a fine-grained, microscopic assessment of typical problems and an overall, topographical sense of structural options.

Organizing Groups and Teams

Alone we can do so little; together we can do so much.

—Helen Keller

On May 2, 2011, Stealth Hawk helicopters carried two units of SEAL Team Six Red Squadron for Operation Neptune Spear—the assault on Osama bin Laden's lair in Abbottabad, Pakistan. The outcome of their mission "to interdict a high value target in a nonpermissive environment" has taken its place in history, though there are conflicting accounts of the actual combat. The fog of war invites many interpretations.

Red Squadron's success owed much to awesome weaponry and the unsurpassed courage and pluck of its highly trained operators. But many after-the-fact commentators agree that the real secret of its success is the astonishing teamwork built into a SEAL's experience from the beginning.

Teamwork is an integral part of Basic Underwater Demolition (BUD/S) training, the toughest school in the military. Classes begin with 200 recruits, but few make it to the end of the program. Sometimes no one from a class graduates. Applicants endure extreme, if not inhuman, physical and mental challenges. Teams of eight are assigned 200-pound inflatable rubber boats that they must carry with them at all times. During chow time or bathroom breaks, a team member must guard the boat. The team gets punished for any individual infractions. When anyone drops out, other members of the team have to fill in. Sometimes a crew of two or three is responsible for the heavy vessel.

Survivors of the initial BUD/S ordeal move on to SEAL Teams. Those who seek a place on legendary Team Six apply for the Green Team. Past training intensifies during the year of Green Team rigor. In addition to tougher physical challenges, candidates for SEAL Team Six train in intense, close-quarters combat in a simulated terrorist "kill house," using live ammunition. An inch or two between men under combat conditions may mean the difference between life and death. Candidates sometimes wound or kill teammates during this phase of training. During Green Team exercises, members of the three Team Six squadrons—Gold, Blue, and Red—choose new men for their units.

The squadrons exist in a relatively simple structure. The Admiral who heads Joint Secret Operations Command (JSOC) reports directly to the Secretary of Defense, who in turn answers to the President. Those relations follow strict protocol. The Team Six commander reports to the head of JSOC and has authority over the leaders who command the three squadrons; "The heart of each Squadron are the teams, each led by a senior enlisted SEAL and made up of half a dozen operators apiece . . . Assault squadrons are accompanied by intelligence analysts and support personnel" (Owen and Maurer, 2012, p. 37). Teams consist of snipers, shooters, explosive experts, and other operators required for a specific mission.

In the case of Operation Neptune Spear these included a translator, a CIA agent, and a dog named Cairo. The chain of command from the JSOC Admiral to the operators is clear but very informal: casual civilian dress, first names, very little protocol. But in battle, Team Six operational units are highly regimented: "Every assaulter knew both his place in the chain of command and what to do if communications were lost to operations center" (Pfarrer, 2011, p. 181). The mission's detailed plan relied on highly sophisticated intelligence. When the two helicopters landed in bin Laden's compound, every operator knew his role and relation to others. Lateral coordination was precise, achieved mainly through terse "SEAL Talk" and nonverbal hand signals. When one helicopter crashed, the teams quickly modified their plans and team structure. From BUD/S training on, a focus on teamwork returned a huge dividend for the operatives of Red Squadron, Team Six, and the nation. When the team assembled for recognition at the White House, President Barack Obama asked, "Which of you fired the final round?" In unison, the members of Red Squadron responded, "We all did!"

Teams that work well regularly make an enormous difference in the business world as well. Consider "six teams that changed the world" (*Fortune*, 2006). There was the remarkable group that Thomas Edison pulled together, including an English machinist, a Swiss clockmaker, a German glass blower, and a Princeton-trained mathematician. They worked in concert with Edison's inventive genius to produce an astonishing array of novel products, including the phonograph and the lightbulb.

Or how about Lockheed's legendary Skunk Works, a team that built a series of breakthrough aircraft: the F-104 Starfighter, the U-2, and SR-71 spy planes? The name came from the team's initial quarters—a circus tent with bad odors. It was World War II, and space was tight. Designers were quartered away from the main offices and worked side by side with metal workers to help assure that breakthrough designs were practical. Cumbersome bureaucratic procedures were streamlined by team leader Kelly Johnson's "14 rules and practices." In addition to Skunk Works' own innovations, the concept of its team structure has spawned thousands of corporate imitators.

Then, of course, there's the well-known team of four driven malcontents, later expanded to dozens, who believed you could build a personal computer easy enough to use and inexpensive enough to be affordable. Their ultimate goal was to unleash personal creativity. Steve Jobs of Apple headed up the super-stealth project, housed in a two-story building near a gas station. Competition with other projects and with Apple's leadership was fierce, but, despite the quarreling, the Macintosh was born in 1983, marking a turning point in the history of personal computing.

MasterCard was struggling in 1997. Six major advertising campaigns had failed to close the gap with Visa. In desperation the company hired McCann Erickson, who assigned a creative team of three to the case. The trio's breakthrough came with the tagline "some things money can't buy." The first ad was set at a baseball game featuring everyday transactions with the setup, "priceless." The ad and its successors helped MasterCard turn the tables on Visa.

Ford faced a difficult challenge in the 1980s. The Japanese were making serious inroads in the American automobile market. Taurus, Ford's best-selling car, needed a major redesign, but executives knew too well of past problems with the design process. Every function had a different view. Designers initially presented a new concept. Engineering very often maintained the design was not feasible, finance typically argued it was too costly, and manufacturing was sure to argue that it couldn't be built. Competing voices typically slowed down or shut down the smooth transition from concept to finished product.

This time, Ford decided too much was at stake and put 700 people, representatives from each group, in the same place, under a tough manager, to work it out. The concept was Team Taurus. The result was Motor Trend's Car of the Year in 1986.

In all these cases, teams of diverse individuals, typically working at a distance from the existing hierarchy, sparked major breakthroughs. Well-organized small teams have the ability to produce results that often elude the grasp of large organizations.

Around the globe, much of the work in organizations gets done in groups or teams. When these units work well, they elevate the performance of ordinary individuals to extraordinary heights. When teams malfunction, as too often happens, they erode the potential contributions of even the most talented members. What determines how well groups perform? As the examples illustrate, the performance of a small group depends heavily on structural design and clarity. A key ingredient of a top-notch team is an appropriate blueprint of roles and relationships aligned with common goals or missions.

In this chapter, we explore the structural features of small groups and teams to show how restructuring can improve group performance. We begin by describing various design options for teams, accenting the relationship between design and task. Next, using sports as an analogy, we discuss patterns of team configuration, coordination, and interdependence suited to different situations. Then we describe the characteristics of high-performing teams. Finally, we discuss the pros and cons of self-managing teams—a hot topic in recent years.

TASKS AND LINKAGES IN SMALL GROUPS

Groups choose among a range of options to develop a structure that maximizes individuals' contributions while minimizing the chronic problems that plague small groups. The nature of the work or task provides a key to shaping group structure. Tasks vary in complexity, clarity, predictability, and volatility (Hærem, Pentland, and Miller, 2015). The task-structure relationship in small groups is parallel to that in larger organizations.

Contextual Variables

As we saw in Chapter 4, simple tasks align with basic structures—clearly defined roles, elementary forms of interdependence, and coordination by plan or command. Projects that are more complex or volatile generally require more complicated structural forms: flexible roles, reciprocal give-and-take, and synchronization through lateral dealings and communal feedback. If a situation becomes exceptionally ambiguous and fast paced, particularly when time is a factor, groups may be unable to make decisions quickly enough without centralized authority and tight scripts. Planning a SEAL Team Six mission or transplanting a kidney is not the same as painting a house or setting up a family outing. Performance and morale suffer, and troubles multiply when groups lack an appropriate structure.

Getting structure right requires careful consideration of pertinent contextual variables, some of which are vague or tough to assess:

- What is our mission?
- What actions are required?

- Who should do what?
- Who is in charge?
- How should we make decisions?
- How do we coordinate efforts?
- What do individual members care about most: time, quality, participation?
- What are the special skills and talents of each group member?
- How does this group relate to others?
- How will we determine success?

Some Fundamental Team Configurations

A high percentage of employees' and managers' time is spent in meetings and working groups of three to twelve people. To illustrate design options, we examine several fundamental structural configurations from studies of five-member teams. These basic patterns are too simple to apply to larger, more complex systems, but they help to illustrate how different structural forms respond to a variety of challenges.

The first is a one-boss arrangement; one person has authority over others (see Exhibit 5.1). Information and decisions flow from the top. Group members offer

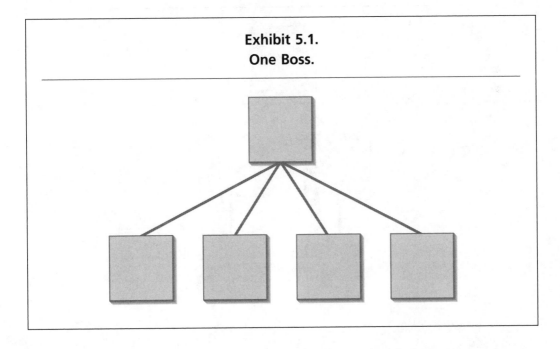

**Exhibit 5.1.
One Boss.**

information to and communicate primarily with the official leader rather than with one another. This array is efficient and fast and works best in relatively simple and straightforward situations when it is easy for the boss to stay on top of things. Circumstances that are more complicated or volatile can overload the boss, producing delays or bad decisions, unless the person in charge has an unusual level of skill, expertise, and energy. Subordinates quickly become frustrated with directives that are late or out of touch.

A second alternative creates a management level below the boss (see Exhibit 5.2). Two individuals have authority over specific areas of the group's work. Information and decisions flow through them. This arrangement works when a task is divisible; it reduces the boss's span of control, freeing up time to concentrate on mission, strategy, or relationships with higher-ups. But adding a new layer limits access from the lower levels to the boss. Communication becomes slower and more cumbersome, and may eventually erode morale and performance.

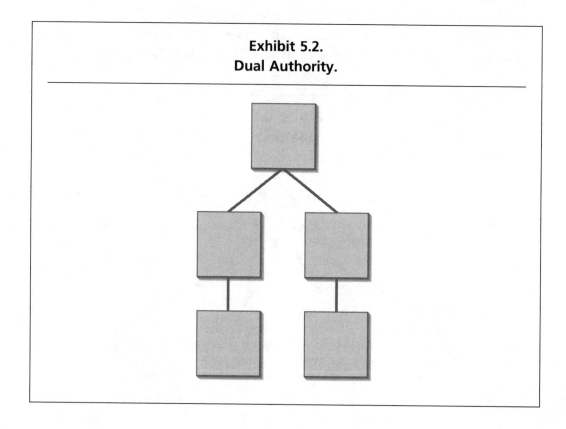

Exhibit 5.2.
Dual Authority.

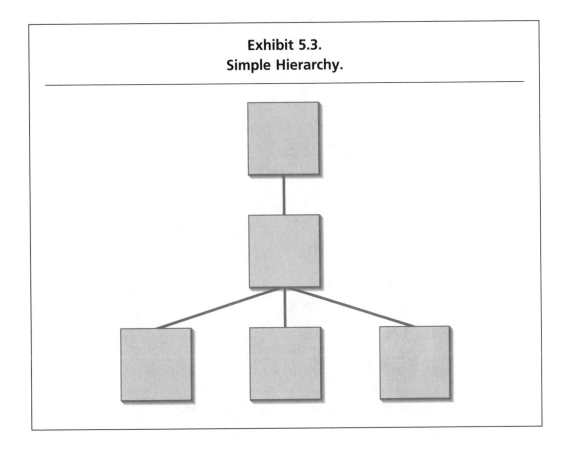

**Exhibit 5.3.
Simple Hierarchy.**

Another option is a simple hierarchy with a middle manager who reports to the boss and, in turn, supervises and communicates with others (see Exhibit 5.3). A similar arrangement at the White House frees the President to focus on mission and external relations while leaving operational details to the chief of staff. Although this type of hierarchy further limits access to the top, it can be more efficient than a dual-manager arrangement. At the same time, friction between operational and top-level managers is commonplace, and number two may be tempted to usurp number one's position.

A fourth option is a circle network, where information and decisions flow sequentially from one group member to another (see Exhibit 5.4). Each can add to or modify whatever comes around. This design relies solely on lateral coordination and simplifies communication. Each person has to deal directly with only two others; transactions are therefore easier to manage. However, one weak link in the chain can undermine the entire enterprise. The circle can bog down with complex tasks that require more reciprocity.

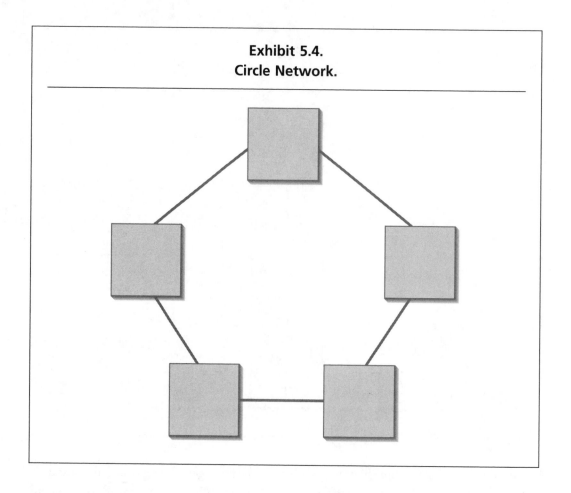

Exhibit 5.4.
Circle Network.

A final possibility sets up what small group researchers call the all-channel, or star, network (see Exhibit 5.5). This design, familiar to Team Six operators, is similar to Helgesen's web of inclusion. It creates multiple connections so that everyone can talk to anyone else. Information flows freely; decisions sometimes require touching multiple bases. Morale in an all-channel network is usually high. The arrangement works well if a task is amorphous or complicated, requiring substantial mutual adjustment, particularly if each member brings distinct knowledge or skill. But this structure can be time consuming, and decision making may slow to a crawl, making it cumbersome and inefficient for simpler undertakings or for groups that have difficulty coming to agreement. It works best when team members bring well-developed communication skills, enjoy participation, tolerate ambiguity, embrace diversity, are able to manage conflict, and agree on how the team will make decisions.

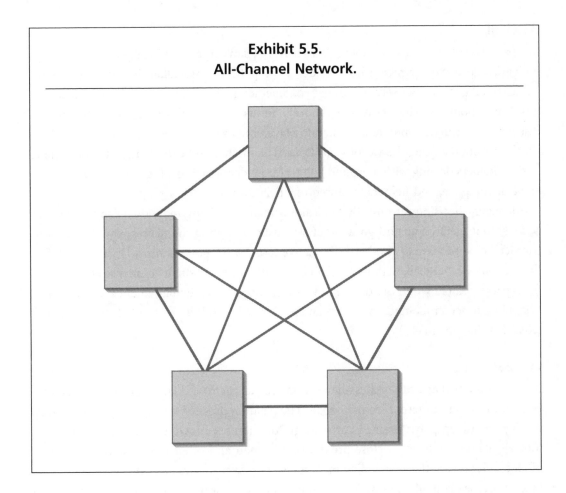

Exhibit 5.5.
All-Channel Network.

TEAMWORK AND INTERDEPENDENCE

Even in the relatively simple case of five-person groups, the formal network is critical to team functioning. In the give-and-take of larger organizations, things get more complicated. We can get a fresh perspective and sharpen our thinking about structure in groups by looking beyond typical work organizations. Making the familiar strange often helps the strange become familiar.

Team sports, among the world's most popular pastimes, offer a helpful analog to clarify how teamwork varies depending on the nature of the game. Every competition calls for its own unique patterns of interaction. Because of this, distinctive structures are required for different sports. Social architecture is thus remarkably different for baseball, football, and basketball.

Baseball

Baseball player Pete Rose once noted, "Baseball is a team game, but nine men who meet their individual goals make a nice team" (Keidel, 1984, p. 8). In baseball, as in cricket and other bat-and-ball games, a loosely integrated confederacy makes a team. Individual efforts are mostly autonomous, seldom involving more than two or three players at a time. Significant distances, particularly on defense, separate players. Loose connections reduce the need for synchronization among the various positions. The pitcher and catcher need to coordinate, as do infielders dealing with a ground ball or outfielders playing a high fly. But batters are alone at the plate, and fielders are often on their own to make a play.

Managers' decisions are mostly tactical, normally involving individual substitutions or actions. Managers come and go without seriously disrupting the team's play. Players can transfer from one team to another with relative ease. John Updike summed it up well: "Of all the team sports, baseball, with its graceful intermittence of action, its immense and tranquil field sparsely salted with poised men in white, its dispassionate mathematics, seemed to be best suited to accommodate, and be ornamented by, a loner. It is an essentially lonely game" (Keidel, 1984, pp. 14–15).

Football

American football and other chess-like sports such as rugby and curling create a structural configuration very different from baseball. These games proceed through a series of moves, or plays. Between plays, teams plan strategy for the next move. Unlike baseball players, football players perform in close proximity. Linemen and offensive backs hear, see, and often touch one another. Each play involves every player on the field. A prearranged plan links efforts sequentially. The actions of linemen pave the way for the movement of backs; a defensive team's field position becomes the starting point for the offense, and vice versa. In the transition from offense to defense, specialty platoons play a pivotal role.

Efforts of individual players are tightly synchronized. George Allen, former coach of the Washington Redskins, put it this way: "A football team is a lot like a machine. It's made up of parts. If one part doesn't work, one player pulling against you and not doing his job, the whole machine fails" (Keidel, 1984, p. 9).

Tight connections among parts require a football team to be well integrated, mainly through planning and top-down control. The primary units are the offensive, defensive, and specialty platoons, each with its own coordinator. Under the direction of the head coach, the team uses scouting reports and other surveillance to develop a strategy or game plan in advance. During the game, the head coach typically makes strategic decisions. Assistants or designated players on either offense or defense make tactical decisions (Keidel, 1984).

A football team's tight-knit character makes it tougher to swap players from one team to another. Irv Cross, of the Philadelphia Eagles, once remarked, "An Eagles player could never make an easy transition to the Dallas Cowboys; the system and philosophies are just too different" (Keidel, 1984, p. 15). Unlike baseball, football requires intricate strategy and tightly meshed execution.

Basketball

In basketball and similar games, like soccer (football everywhere but North America), hockey, and lacrosse, players perform in even closer proximity to one another than football players do. In quick, rapidly moving transitions, offense becomes defense—with the same players. Efforts of individuals are reciprocal; each player depends on the performance of others. Each may be involved with any of the others. Anyone can handle the ball or attempt to score.

Basketball is much like improvisational jazz. Teams require a high level of spontaneous, mutual adjustment. Everyone is on the move, often in an emerging pattern rather than a predetermined course. A successful basketball season depends heavily on a flowing relationship among team members who read and anticipate one another's moves. Players who play together a long time develop a sense of what their teammates will do. A team of newcomers has trouble adjusting to individual predispositions or quirks. Unlike football, basketball has no platoons. It is wholly a harmonized group effort.

Coaches, who sit or roam the sidelines, serve as integrators. Their periodic interventions reinforce team cohesion, helping players coordinate laterally on the move. Unlike baseball teams, basketball teams cannot function as a collection of individual stars. During the 2016 basketball season, the rather dismal performance of the Los Angeles Lakers was attributed to it being a loose array of individual stars rather than a well-knit unified team. Conversely, the San Antonio Spurs became one of the most consistently successful teams in professional basketball by emphasizing teamwork. According to LeBron James, that's how the Spurs beat his team in the 2014 NBA championships: "It's all for the team and it's never about the individual. That's the brand of basketball, and that's how team basketball should be played" (Ginsburg, 2014).

Duke University's women's basketball success in 2000 documented the importance of group interdependence and cohesion. The team won because players could anticipate the actions of others. The individual "I" deferred to the collective "we." Passing to a teammate was valued as highly as making the shot. Basketball is "fast, physically close, and crowded, 20 arms and legs in motion, up, down, across, in the air. The better the team, the more precise the passing into lanes that appear blocked with bodies" (Lubans, 2001, p. 1).

DETERMINANTS OF SUCCESSFUL TEAMWORK

In sports and elsewhere, structural profiles of successful teams depend on the game—what a team is trying to do. Keidel (1984) suggests several important questions in designing an appropriate structure:

- What is the nature and degree of dealings among individuals?
- What is the spatial distribution of unit members?
- Where does authority reside?
- How are efforts integrated?
- Which word best describes the required structure: conglomerate, mechanistic, or organic?
- What sports metaphor captures the task of management: filling out the line-up card, preparing the game plan, or influencing the game's flow?

Appropriate team structures can vary, even within the same organization. For example, a senior research manager in a pharmaceutical firm observed a structural progression in discovering and developing a new drug: "The process moves through three distinct stages. It's like going from baseball to football to basketball" (Keidel, 1984, p. 11).

In basic research, individual scientists work independently to develop a body of knowledge. As in baseball, individual labors are the norm. Once a promising drug is identified, it passes from developmental chemists to pharmacy researchers to toxicologists. If the drug receives preliminary federal approval, it moves to clinical researchers for experimental tests. These sequential relationships are reminiscent of play sequences in football. In the final stage ("new drug application"), physicians, statisticians, pharmacists, pharmacologists, toxicologists, and chemists work closely and reciprocally to win final approval from the Food and Drug Administration. Their efforts resemble the closely linked and flowing patterns of a basketball team (Keidel, 1984).

Jan Haynes, former executive vice president of FzioMed, a California developer of new biomedical approaches to preventing scar tissue following surgical procedures, echoes the pharmaceutical executive's observations. She adds, "In sports a game lasts only a short period of time. In our business, each game goes on for months, even years. It more closely resembles cricket. A single game can go on for days and still end in a draw. Our product has been in the trial stage for several years and we still don't have final approval."

Ron Haynes, the firm's chairman, points out the challenge of adapting his leadership style as the rules of the game change: "I moved from manager to owner of an expansion team where we have several games being played simultaneously in the same stadium. If our leadership can't shift quickly from one to another, our operation won't get the job done right." Doing the right job requires a structure that evolves to fit what FzioMed is trying to accomplish.

TEAM STRUCTURE AND TOP PERFORMANCE

In developing their book *The Wisdom of Teams*, Katzenbach and Smith (1993) interviewed hundreds of participants on more than fifty teams. Their sample encompassed thirty enterprises in settings as diverse as Motorola, Hewlett-Packard, Operation Desert Storm, and the Girl Scouts. They drew a clear distinction between undifferentiated "groups" and sharply focused teams: "A team is a small number of people with complementary skills, who are committed to a common purpose, set of performance goals and approach for which they hold themselves mutually accountable" (p. 112).

Katzenbach and Smith's research highlights six distinguishing characteristics of high-quality teams:

- *High-performing teams shape purpose in response to a demand or an opportunity placed in their path, usually by higher management.* Top managers clarify the team's charter, rationale, and challenge while giving the team flexibility to work out goals and plans of operation. By giving a team clear authority and then staying out of the way, management releases collective energy and creativity.

- *High-performing teams translate common purpose into specific, measurable performance goals.* "If a team fails to establish specific performance goals or if those goals do not relate directly to the team's overall purpose, team members become confused, pull apart, and revert to mediocre performance. By contrast, when purpose and goals are built on one another and are combined with team commitment, they become a powerful engine of performance" (p. 113).

- *High-performing teams are of manageable size.* Katzenbach and Smith fix the optimal size for an effective team somewhere between two and twenty-five people: "Ten people are far more likely than fifty to work through their individual, functional, and hierarchical differences toward a common plan and to hold themselves jointly accountable for the results" (p. 114). More members mean more structural complexity, so teams should aim for the smallest size that can get the job done.

- *High-performing teams develop the right mix of expertise.* The structural frame stresses the critical link between specialization and expertise. Effective teams seek out the full range of necessary technical fluency; "product development teams that include only marketers or engineers are less likely to succeed than those with the complementary skills of both" (p. 115). In addition, exemplary teams find and reward expertise in problem solving, decision making, and interpersonal skills to keep the group focused, on task, and free of debilitating personal squabbles.

- *High-performing teams develop a common commitment to working relationships.* "Team members must agree on who will do particular jobs, how schedules will be set and adhered to, what skills need to be developed, how continuing membership in the team is to be earned, and how the group will make and modify decisions" (p. 115). Effective teams take time to explore who is best suited for a particular task as well as how individual roles come together. Achieving structural clarity varies from team to team, but it takes more than an organization chart to identify roles and pinpoint one's place in the official pecking order and layout of responsibilities. Most teams require a clear understanding of who is going to do what and how people relate to each other in carrying out diverse tasks. An effective team "establishes a social contract among members that relates to their purpose and guides and obligates how they will work together" (Katzenbach and Smith, 1993, p. 116).

- *Members of high-performing teams hold themselves collectively accountable.* Pinpointing individual responsibility is crucial to a well-coordinated effort, but effective teams find ways to hold the collective accountable: "Teams enjoying a common purpose and approach inevitably hold themselves responsible, both as individuals and as a team, for the team's performance" (p. 116). Recall the members of SEAL Team Six Red Squadron when President Obama asked who fired the shot that killed bin Laden: "We all did!"

In an influential article, Brian Dumaine (1994) highlights a common error in creating teams: "Teams often get launched in a vacuum, with little or no training or support, no changes in the design of their work, and no new systems like e-mail to help communication between teams. Frustrations mount, and people wind up in endless meetings trying to figure out why they are a team and what they are expected to do." A focused, cohesive structure is a fundamental underpinning for high-performing teams. Even highly skilled people zealously pursuing a shared mission will falter and fail if group structure constantly generates inequity, confusion, and frustration.

SELF-MANAGING TEAMS: STRUCTURE OF THE FUTURE?

The sports team analogy discussed earlier assumed some role for a manager or coach. But what about teams that manage themselves organically from the bottom up? Self-managing work teams are groups of employees with the following characteristics (Wellins et al., 1990, cited in Kirkman and Shapiro, 1997):

- They manage themselves (plan, organize, control, staff, and monitor).
- They assign jobs to members (decide who works on what, where, and when).
- They plan and schedule work (control start-up and ending times, the pace of work, and goal setting).
- They make production- or service-related decisions (take responsibility for inventory, quality control decisions, and work stoppage).
- They take action to remedy problems (address quality issues, customer service needs, and member discipline and rewards).

Self-directed teams typically produce better results and higher morale than groups operating under more traditional top-down control (Cohen and Ledford, 1994; Emery and Fredendall, 2002). However, getting such teams started and giving them the resources they need to be effective is a complex undertaking. Many well-known firms—such as Microsoft, Boeing, Google, W. L. Gore, Southwest Airlines, Harley-Davidson, and Goldman Sachs—have found ways to reap the benefits of self-directed teams without being overwhelmed by logistical snafus or reverting to the traditional command-and-control structure.

Saturn

General Motors's launch of Saturn in 1983 was one of the most ambitious experiments ever in the creation of self-managed teams. The goal was to create a different kind of company to build a different kind of car. Companywide, Saturn employees had authority to make team decisions within a few flexible guidelines. Restrictive rules and ironclad top-down work procedures were left behind as the company moved away from what employees called the "old world" of General Motors.

Saturn teams designated their own working relationships. Prior to a shift, team members conferred in a team center for 5 to 10 minutes. They determined the day's rotations. A team of ten would have ten jobs to do and typically rotated through them, except rotation was more frequent for jobs involving heavy lifting or stress. Every week the plant shut down to let teams review quality standards, budget, safety and the ergonomics of assembly. Not only did the team have dominion over its own operation, any member had the authority to stop the entire assembly line if some irregularity was spotted.

The team concept was a major factor in what made Saturn tick and a widely publicized feature of its initial success. The hoopla overlooked the fact that self-managing teams were not invented by Saturn. Other companies, such as Whole Foods, had been perfecting the idea for a long time.

Whole Foods

Whole Foods Markets offer more than a typical shopping trip. They are also a culinary and gourmet experience. Fruit and vegetables are artistically displayed with neatly arranged stems and leaves pointing in the same direction. Fresh meat and seafood are attractively arrayed. Table-ready prepared items look homemade and hard to resist. Health-conscious customers know that, as much as possible, the produce is organic, the meat is free of hormones and chemicals, and the seafood is from sustainable sources. Whole Foods's focus on a mission of helping people eat well and improving the quality of their lives has made it the largest natural and organic food company in the United States—and still growing.

Whole Foods began in 1980 with a merger between two small natural foods stores in Austin, Texas. By 2016, the company had grown to more than 450 stores in the United States, Canada, and the United Kingdom, producing $15 billion in sales.

Whole Foods's team structure plays an essential role in the company's success. From top to bottom, everyone at Whole Foods is a team member.

> Teams and team members—not positions, stores or regions—are central to the operational core of Whole Foods and the building blocks of the organization. Each Whole Foods location is built around eight to 10 teams, grouped from departments like produce, meat, prepared foods and checkout. The teams have a remarkable degree of autonomy, helping to decide what to order, how to price items and how to run promotions. Even outside the store, a team focus continues up the chain of command all the way to the top. Store leaders in the region are considered a team. Even the regional presidents form a team (Burkus, 2016).

At the top, Whole Foods's founder, John Mackey, and his co-CEO are part of the five-person "E Team" which has been together for years and makes decisions by consensus (Gaar, 2010).

Teams at the operating level have significant decision making authority. They control what is stocked, how merchandise is displayed, pricing, and labor expenditures. The attention to detail, customer service, and candor in team meetings is noteworthy, as an example from a store in Massachusetts illustrates (Fishman, 1996a):

The meeting of the bakery team is convened at 9:15 PM after the store closed. Aimee Morgida, the store manager, chairs the meeting because the first item on the agenda is the introduction of Debbie Singer, the new team leader. She's the fourth new leader in four years. Morgida admits the team has been through a lot, but adds that she's convinced that the right person is now in place. Singer says that she loves bakery, merchandising, and fast-pace retail but "this is your meeting, I want to hear from you. The ensuing conversation suggests that team members are concerned more about service issues than the new leader:

> Louise speaks first. "A lot of customers want a breakdown on the calories in the muffins and the scones"—something the bakery has been promising for a while. "A lot of people have voiced concern that everything has sugar. A few more nonfat items would definitely be welcomed."
>
> Carmen speaks next. She worries that the bakery's ordering has become sloppy, that the team is requesting too much product, paying full price for perishables that it marks down at the end of night or donates to charity. "Are we losing too much merchandise?" she asks. "Just putting it at 'a dollar off' and bagging it?" There is general agreement (Fishman, 1996a).

Morgida, the store manager, used the second half of the meeting to emphasize customer service and boost team spirits. Usually at Whole Foods a team deals with such issues on its own, but Morgida knows that the leadership changes may have taken a toll and she wants to give Singer a running start. She also knows that the holidays are approaching, a time when everyone in the retail business needs a boost:

> "Has everybody tried the pastries? You need to try them because people will ask, what do you recommend? What do you think? If you don't like something, you can tell them, but you need to tell them why. Try everything.
>
> "Around most holidays, customers are really tense. Just let it roll off; do whatever it takes to make people happy. If something's wrong, the question to ask is, 'What can I do to make it right?' Because customers always have something in their minds that would make it right" (Fishman, 1996a).

She told the story of a misplaced birthday-cake order—a scramble for another cake, her own decorating job, and the final personal touch: the face-to-face delivery to the customer's home.

"I don't care if we're giving things away," she stresses. "Because God forbid we screw up someone's holiday. If we screw it up, they'll tell all their friends at dinner. If we screw it up and fix it, they'll tell their friends that, too." (Fishman, 1996a).

Shortly before the meeting adjourned, team members brought up holiday staffing. Several wanted to give more hours to Hadja, a part-timer from India with spotty English. Morgida is initially skeptical but she listens.

"I know her English is not very good," says Sylvia, "but she's great to have around."

"She knows how to take care of customers," adds Patty. "I'm not sure how she does it, but she really communicates with them."

Morgida shrugs. "Okay, go ahead and put her on" (Fishman, 1996a).

A new hire needs a two-thirds vote from the team to stay on. Team members are tough on new hires because bonuses are tied to team performance. Teams are measured against sales, growth, and productivity against other teams in their store and against similar teams in other stores and regions (Quenllas, 2013). Bonuses are awarded to teams, not individuals.

Team decisions benefit from an information-rich, unusually transparent environment. In most stores, daily sales figures are posted by team, including figures for the previous year. Once a month stores get detailed financial numbers including sales, product costs, wages, and salaries for all stores. A yearly morale survey assesses employee confidence in team, store, and regional leaders as well as their fears and frustrations (Fishman, 1996a).

Any team member has access to sensitive data such as store sales, team sales, profit margins, and salaries, including fellow team members, individuals in other stores, and even the CEO. Such access to information is so unusual that the SEC has designated all Whole Foods employees as insiders in terms of stock trading (Fishman, 1996a). All that information spurs competition. Teams, stores, and regions compete intensely to outdo each other in quality, service, and profitability (Fishman, 1996b).

Stores also benchmark themselves against two peer review systems. The most intense is the periodic Store Tour. During this choreographed assessment, a group of as many as forty visitors from another region spends two days scrutinizing every aspect of a local Whole Foods operation. The group includes leaders from the region, store teams, and operation teams. Reviews and performance audits become a matter of record (Fishman, 1996b).

The Customer Snapshot (TCS) review is a surprise inspection every Whole Foods experiences ten times a year. A representative from headquarters or a region spends a day rating a store on 300 measures. TCS results from each store are shared with every other store once a month. Both the Store Tour and TCS review results are keen points of competition (Fishman, 1996b).

Whole Foods's team approach is remarkably consistent with ideas advanced by Rensis Likert in 1961: that every member of an organization should be part of an effective work group characterized by commitment to the team, interaction skills, and high performance goals, and that the leader of each group should be a "linking pin" who is also a member of a group at the next higher level (Likert, 1961). That's how it works at Whole Foods. Autonomous, self-managing teams have both the knowledge and the motivation to solve problems and find opportunities. Information transparency and periodic reviews ensure that teams have benchmarks to assess how well they're doing and where they could or should be able to improve. Contrast that with typical top-down approaches that train employees to hide problems and wait for orders from above, and it's easy to see how strong, self-managing teams can produce many benefits for customer service and business success.

CONCLUSION

Every group evolves a structure that may help or hinder effectiveness. Conscious attention to lines of authority, communication, responsibilities, and relationships can make a huge difference in group performance. A team structure emphasizing hierarchy and top-down control tends to work well for simple, stable tasks. As work becomes more complex or the environment gets more turbulent, structure must also develop more multifaceted and lateral forms of communication and coordination.

Sports analogies can help clarify teamwork options. It helps to understand whether the game you are playing is more like baseball, football, basketball, or some other game. Many teams never learn a key to getting structure right: Vary the structure in response to changes in task and circumstance. Make sure you know the game you're in and the field you're playing on. Organization and team structures can be complex but can be understood and adjusted. Leaders must recognize when the rules of the game change and redesign the structure accordingly.

Effective teams typically have a clear purpose, measurable goals, the right mix of expertise, a common commitment to working relationships, collective accountability, and manageable size.

An increasing number of progressive organizations are emphasizing self-managing teams that run themselves, assign jobs to members, plan and schedule work, and solve problems. With the right structure and the necessary information and autonomy, such teams can develop levels of collaboration and motivation that lead to high performance.

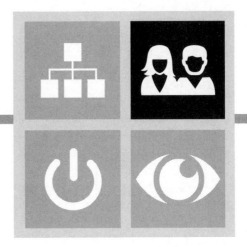

PART THREE

The Human Resource Frame

"Our most important asset is our people."

"Organizations exploit people—chew them up and spit them out."

Which of these two views of the relationship between people and organizations seems more accurate? How you answer affects everything you do at work.

The human resource frame centers on what organizations and people do to and for one another. We begin in Chapter 6 by laying out basic assumptions, focusing on the fit between human needs and organizational requirements. Organizations generally hope for a cadre of talented, highly motivated employees who give their best. Often though, these same organizations rely on outdated assumptions and counterproductive practices that cause workers to give less and demand more.

After examining how organizations err in Chapter 6, we turn in Chapter 7 to a discussion of how smart managers and progressive organizations find better ways to manage people. We describe "high-involvement" or "high-commitment" practices that build and retain a talented and motivated workforce.

In Chapter 8, we examine issues in interpersonal relations and small groups. We describe competing strategies for managing relationships and look at how personal and interpersonal dynamics can make or break a group or team.

People and Organizations

Who first invented work and tied the free and holy-day
rejoicing spirit down to the ever-haunting importunity of
business and, oh, most sad, to this dry drudgery of the desk's
dead wood?

—Charles Lamb

I s it all dry drugery? Schwartz and Porath (2014) say that's the reality for white collar workers, who aren't eager to go to work, don't feel they get much appreciation while they're there, have trouble getting everything done, and doubt that their work makes much of a contribution. They arrive home deflated and haunted by round-the-clock demands.

Schwartz and Porath could have been writing about Amazon where "workers are encouraged to tear apart one another's ideas in meetings, toil long and late (emails arrive past midnight, followed by text messages asking why they were not answered), and held to standards that the company boasts are 'unreasonably high' . . . [Amazon] is conducting a little-known experiment in how far it can push white-collar workers, redrawing the boundaries of what is acceptable" (Kantor and Streitfeld, 2015).

Amazon is tough on the white-collar employees at its Seattle headquarters, and even tougher on the blue-collar workers who move its goods.

Amazon came under fire in 2011 when workers in an eastern Pennsylvania warehouse toiled in more than 100-degree heat with ambulances waiting outside, taking away laborers as they fell. After an investigation by the local newspaper, the company installed air-conditioning (Kantor and Streitfeld, 2015).

Amazon is not alone. Apple's design and technological savvy have captured the affection and loyalty of consumers around the globe, but the company has earned lower marks for treatment of the offshore workers who make its products. In 2012, the huge success of products like the iPad and iPhone was great news for Apple but not so good for the Chinese employees who made them. Long hours, low pay, and intense pressure to ramp up production triggered strikes and a worker riot that shut one plant down for a day. Apple's products were cutting edge, but its people management evoked centuries-old images of sacrificing people for profits and reinforced popular stereotypes of bosses as heartless and insensitive (Amar, 2004; Duhigg and Barboza, 2012).

But not all companies view employees as merely a means to the greater end of profits, as a contrasting case illustrates:

Early one March afternoon, three electricians who worked for Nucor Corporation got bad news. In Hickman, Arkansas, the company's steel mill was dead in the water because its electric grid had failed. All three employees dropped what they were doing to head for Arkansas. One drove from Indiana, arriving at 9 PM that night. The other two flew from North Carolina to Memphis, then drove 2 more hours, arriving after midnight. All three camped out at the plant and worked 20-hour shifts with local staff to get the grid back up.

The electricians volunteered—they didn't need a boss to tell them that Nucor had to get the mill back on line. Their herculean effort was a big help to the company but brought them no immediate financial reward, even though their initiative helped Hickman post a quarterly record for tons of steel shipped (Byrnes and Arndt, 2006).

At Nucor, this story is not particularly unusual:

In an industry as Rust Belt as they come, Nucor has nurtured one of the most dynamic and engaged workforces around. Its nonunion employees don't see themselves as worker bees waiting for instructions from above. Nucor's flattened hierarchy and emphasis on pushing power to the front line have given its employees the mindset of owner-operators. It's a profitable formula: Nucor's 387% return to shareholders over the past five years soundly bests almost all other companies in the Standard & Poor's 500-stock index (Byrnes and Arndt, 2006, p. 58).

What's in it for the workers? Their base pay is nothing special—it's below the industry average. But when Nucor has a good year, as it often does, they get big bonuses, based on their own output and the company's success. That's one reason electricians would grab a plane to help jump-start a plant in Arkansas. It's also why a new plant manager at Nucor can expect supportive calls from experienced colleagues who want to help out. At Nucor, work is more than a job. It's about pride. Employees enjoy seeing their names listed on the covers of corporate publications, including the annual report. They're proud that their company, which turns scrap metal into steel, is the world's largest recycler. And they're exhilarated when they can draw on their intelligence and creativity to demonstrate that American workers can still compete.

Companies like Nucor are too rare. In the context of strikes and boycotts across China protesting "inhumane" management practices at Walmart in late 2016, a company spokesperson offered the usual boilerplate, "Our employees are our most valuable asset" (Hernández, 2016). Most companies claim to value their people, but fewer live up to those words. In practice, employees are often treated as pawns to be moved where needed and sacrificed when necessary.

In this chapter, we focus on the human side of organizations. We start by summarizing the assumptions underlying the human resource view. Next, we examine how people's needs are either satisfied or frustrated at work. Then we look at today's changing employment contract and its impact on both people and organizations.

HUMAN RESOURCE ASSUMPTIONS

Amazon and Nucor represent different stances in a perennial debate about the relationship between people and organizations. One side sees individuals as objects or tools, important not so much in themselves as in what they can do for the organization. The opposing camp holds that the needs of individuals and organizations can be aligned, engaging people's talent and energy while profiting the enterprise. This debate has intensified with globalization and the growth in size and power of modern institutions. Can people find freedom and dignity in a world dominated by economic fluctuations and a push for cost reduction and short-term results? Answers are not easy. They require a sensitive understanding of people and their symbiotic relationship with organizations.

The human resource frame evolved from early work of pioneers like Mary Parker Follett (1918) and Elton Mayo (1933, 1945), who questioned a deeply held managerial assumption that employees had no right beyond a paycheck, and their duty was to work hard and follow orders. Pioneers of the human resource frame criticized this view on two grounds: It was unjust, and it was bad psychology. They argued that people's skills, attitudes, energy, and commitment are vital resources that can make or break an enterprise. The human resource frame is built on core assumptions that highlight this linkage:

- Organizations exist to serve human needs rather than the converse.
- People and organizations need each other. Organizations need ideas, energy, and talent; people need careers, salaries, and opportunities.
- When the fit between individual and system is poor, one or both suffer. Individuals are exploited or exploit the organization—or both become victims.
- A good fit benefits both. Individuals find meaningful and satisfying work, and organizations get the talent and energy they need to succeed.

Organizations ask, "How do we find and retain people with the skills and attitudes to do the work?" Workers want to know, "How well will this place work for me?" These two questions are closely related, because "fit" is a function of at least three things: how well an organization responds to individual desires for useful work; how well jobs let employees express their skills and sense of self; and how well work fulfills individual financial and lifestyle needs (Cable and DeRue, 2002).

Human Needs

The concept of need is controversial—at least in some academic circles. Some theorists argue that the idea is too vague and ethereal. Others say that people's needs are so variable and influenced by their surroundings that the concept offers little help in explaining behavior (Salancik and Pfeffer, 1977). Goal-setting theory (Locke and Latham, 2002, 2004) suggests that managers do better to emphasize specific performance goals than to worry about employees' psychic needs. Economists like Jensen and Meckling (1994) argue that people's willingness to trade off one thing for another (time for money or sleep for entertainment) disproves the idea of need.

Despite this academic skepticism, needs are a central element in everyday psychology. Parents worry about the needs of their children, politicians promise to meet the needs of constituents, and managers make an effort to understand the needs of workers. That's how Wegmans, a grocery chain that perennially ranks high on *Fortune* magazine's list of best places to work (number two in 2017), states its philosophy: "We set our goal to be the very best at serving the needs of our customers. Every action we take should be made with this in mind. We also believe that we can achieve our goal only if we fulfill the needs of our own people" (Wegmans, 2016).

Common sense tells us that needs are important because we all have them. But identifying what needs we have—long term or at any given time—is more elusive. A horticultural analogy may help clarify. A gardener knows that every plant has specific requirements. The right combination of temperature, moisture, soil, and sunlight allows a plant to grow and flourish. Plants do their best to get what they need. They orient leaves sunward to get more light and sink roots deeper in search of water. A plant's capabilities generally increase with maturity. Highly vulnerable seedlings become more self-sufficient as they grow (better able to fend off insects and competition from other plants). These capabilities decline as a plant nears the end of its life cycle.

Human needs are similar. Conditions or elements in the environment allow people to survive and grow. Basic needs for oxygen, water, and food are clear; the idea of universal psychic needs is more controversial. A genetic, or "nature," perspective posits that certain psychological needs are essential to being human (Lawrence and Nohria, 2001; Maslow, 1954; McClelland, 1985; Pink, 2009; White, 1960). A "nurture" view, in contrast, suggests that people are so shaped by environment, socialization, and culture that it is fruitless to talk about common psychic needs.

In extreme forms, both nature and nurture arguments are misleading. You don't need an advanced degree in psychology to recognize that people are capable of enormous amounts of learning and adaptation. Just about any parent with more than one child knows that many psychological characteristics, such as temperament, are present at birth.

Most scholars see human behavior as resulting from the interplay between heredity and environment. Genes initially determine potential and predispositions. Research has identified connections between genetic patterns and behavioral tendencies such as antisocial behavior. But learning profoundly modifies innate directives, and research in behavioral genetics regularly concludes that genes and environment interact in complex ways to determine how people act (Baker, 2004).

The nature-nurture seesaw suggests a more useful way to think about human needs. A need can be defined as a genetic predisposition to prefer some experiences over others. Needs energize and guide behavior and vary in potency at different times. We enjoy the company of others, for example, yet we sometimes want to be alone. Because genetic instructions cannot anticipate all situations, both the form and the expression of each person's inborn needs are significantly tailored by experiences after birth.

WORK AND MOTIVATION: A BRIEF TOUR

Why do people do one thing rather than another? Why, for example, do they work hard, or not hard, or not at all? Despite decades of research, answers remain contested and elusive, but we can briefly summarize some of the major ideas in an ongoing dialogue.

An old formula (Maier, 1967) tells us that Performance = Ability × Motivation. If you have both talent and desire, you'll do well. Theories of motivation seek to explain the desire part of that formula. One of the oldest views, still popular among many managers and economists, is that the primary thing people care about is money: they do what they believe will get them more of it. Playing a hit man in the 2012 film *Killing Them Softly*, Brad Pitt summarizes this view with the observation, "America isn't a country. It's a business. Now give me my money." Money is a powerful incentive, and focusing on financial rewards simplifies the motivation problem—just offer people money for doing what you want. But the classic highwayman's demand—"Your money or your life!"—reminds us that money isn't the only thing people care about and is not always the most important thing. Managers and organizations that focus only on money will miss other opportunities to motivate. But what else is important beyond money?

A number of theorists have developed models of workplace motivation, and some of the better-known examples are summarized in Exhibit 6.1. Each model develops its own list of the things that people want, and no item appears on every list. But there is broad agreement that people want things that go beyond money, such as doing good work, getting better at what they do, bonding with other people, and finding meaning and purpose. There is also alignment with a distinction that was central to Herzberg's (1966) "two-factor" theory. Herzberg argued that extrinsic factors, like working conditions and company policies, can make people unhappy but don't really motivate them to be more productive. He insisted that the things that motivate are intrinsic to the work itself—things like achievement, responsibility, and recognition for work well done. All these theories converge on the view that motivating people requires understanding and responding to the range of needs they bring to the workplace.

Maslow's Hierarchy of Needs

One of the oldest and most influential of the models in Exhibit 6.1 was developed by the existential psychologist Abraham Maslow (1954). He started with the notion that people are motivated by a variety of wants, some more fundamental than others. The desire for food dominates the lives of the chronically hungry, but people move on to other things when they have enough to eat. Maslow grouped human needs into five basic categories, arrayed in a hierarchy from lowest to highest (Exhibit 6.2).

In Maslow's view, basic needs for physical well-being and safety are "prepotent"; they have to be satisfied first. Once lower needs are fulfilled, individuals move up to social needs (for belongingness, love, and inclusion) and ego needs (for esteem, respect, and recognition). At the top of the hierarchy is self-actualization—developing to one's fullest

Exhibit 6.1.
Models of Motivation at Work.

Author(s)	Needs/Motives at Work
Maslow (1943, 1954)	Hierarchy of needs (physiological, safety, love/belonging, esteem, self-actualization)
Herzberg, Mausner, and Snyderman (1959); Herzberg (1966)	Two-factor theory: Motivators/satisfiers: achievement, recognition, work itself, responsibility, advancement, pay Hygiene factors/dissatisfiers: company policies, supervision, interpersonal relationships, working conditions, pay
McClelland (1961)	Three needs: achievement, power, affiliation
Hackman and Oldham (1980)	Three critical psychological states: meaningfulness of work, responsibility for outcomes, knowledge of results
Lawrence and Nohria (2002)	Four drives: D1 (acquire objects and experiences that improve our status relative to others); D2 (bond with others in mutually beneficial, long-term relationships); D3 (learn about and make sense of ourselves and the world around us); D4 (defend ourselves, our loved ones, our beliefs, and our resources)
Pink (2009)	Three drives: autonomy (people want to have control over their work); mastery (people want to get better at what they do); purpose (people want to be part of something bigger than themselves)

and actualizing one's ultimate potential. The order is not ironclad. Parents may sacrifice themselves for their children, and martyrs sometimes give their lives for a cause. Maslow believed that such reversals occur when lower needs are so well satisfied early in life that they recede into the background later on.

Attempts to validate Maslow's theory have produced mixed results, partly because the theory is hard to test (Alderfer, 1972; Latham and Pinder, 2005; Lawler and Shuttle, 1973; Schneider and Alderfer, 1973; Wahba and Bridwell, 1976). Some research suggests that the theory is valid across cultures (Ajila, 1997; Rao and Kulkarni, 1998), but the many

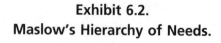

Exhibit 6.2.
Maslow's Hierarchy of Needs.

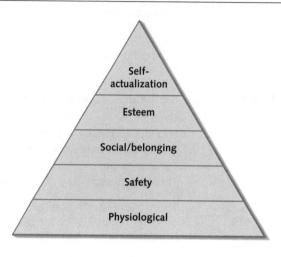

Source: Conley, 2007. Copyright © 1979. Reprinted by permission of Pearson Education, Inc., New York, New York.

theories of motivation developed since Maslow attest that the jury is still out on whether people have the needs Maslow posited or that the satisfaction of one need leads to activation of another.

Despite the modest evidence, Maslow's view has been widely accepted and enormously influential in managerial practice. Take, for example, the advice that the *Manager's Guide* at Federal Express offers employees: "Modern behavioral scientists such as Abraham Maslow . . . have shown that virtually every person has a hierarchy of emotional needs, from basic safety, shelter, and sustenance to the desire for respect, satisfaction, and a sense of accomplishment. Slowly these values have appeared as the centerpiece of progressive company policies, always with remarkable results" (Waterman, 1994, p. 92). Chip Conley, founder of a California hotel chain, put it simply: "I came to realize my climb to the top wasn't going to be on a traditional corporate ladder; instead it was going to be on Maslow's Hierarchy of Needs pyramid" (Conley, 2007). Academic skepticism didn't prevent him, FedEx, Joie de Vivre hotels, or Airbnb from building a highly successful management philosophy based on Maslow's theory, because the ideas carry a powerful message. If you manage solely by carrot and stick, you'll get only a part of the energy and talent that people have to offer.

Theory X and Theory Y

Douglas McGregor (1960) built on Maslow's theory by adding another important idea: that managers' assumptions about people tend to become self-fulfilling prophecies. McGregor argued that most managers harbor "Theory X" assumptions that subordinates are passive and lazy, have little ambition, prefer to be led, and resist change. Most conventional management practices, in his view, had been built on either "hard" or "soft" versions of Theory X. The hard version emphasizes coercion, tight controls, threats, and punishments. Over time, it generates low productivity, antagonism, militant unions, and subtle sabotage—conditions that were turning up in workplaces across the United States at the time. Soft versions of Theory X try to avoid conflict and keep everyone happy. The usual result is superficial harmony with undercurrents of apathy, indifference, and smoldering resentment.

McGregor's key point was that a hard or soft Theory X approach is self-fulfilling: If you treat people as if they're lazy and need to be directed, they live down to your expectations. Managers who say they know from experience that Theory X is the only way to get anything done are missing a key insight: The fact that people respond to you in a certain way may say more about you than about them. McGregor advocated a different way to think about people that he called Theory Y. Maslow's hierarchy of needs was the foundation:

> The man whose needs for safety, association, independence, or status are thwarted is sick as surely as the man who has rickets. And his sickness will have behavioral consequences. We will be mistaken if we attribute his resultant passivity, hostility, and refusal to accept responsibility to his inherent human nature. These forms of behavior are symptoms of illness—of deprivation of his social and egoistic needs (McGregor, 1960, pp. 35–36).

Theory Y's key proposition is that "the essential task of management is to arrange conditions so that people can achieve their own goals best by directing efforts toward organizational rewards" (McGregor, 1960, p. 61). If individuals find no satisfaction in their work, management has little choice but to rely on Theory X and external control. Conversely, the more managers align organizational requirements with employee self-interest, the more they can rely on Theory Y's principle of self-direction.

Personality and Organization

Like his contemporary McGregor, Chris Argyris (1957, 1964) saw a basic conflict between human personality and prevailing management practice. Argyris argued that people have basic "self-actualization trends"—akin to the efforts of a plant to reach its biological potential. From infancy into adulthood, people advance from dependence to independence, from a narrow to a broader range of skills and interests. They move from a short time perspective (interests quickly developed and forgotten, with little ability to anticipate the future) to a much longer-term horizon. The child's impulsivity and limited self-knowledge are replaced by a more mature level of self-awareness and self-control.

Like McGregor, Argyris believed that organizations often treated workers like children rather than adults—a view eloquently expressed in Charlie Chaplin's 1936 film *Modern Times*. In a classic scene, Chaplin's character works furiously on an assembly line, trying to tighten bolts on every piece that slides past. Skill requirements are minimal, and he has no control over the pace of his work. An efficiency expert uses Chaplin as the guinea pig for a new machine designed to feed him lunch while he continues to tighten bolts. It goes haywire and begins to assault Chaplin with food—pouring soup on his lap and shoving bolts into his mouth. The film's message is clear: Industrial organizations abuse workers and treat them like infants.

Argyris and McGregor saw person-structure conflict built into traditional principles of organizational design and management. The structural concept of task specialization defines jobs as narrowly as possible to improve efficiency. But the rational logic often backfires. Consider the experience of autoworker Ben Hamper. His observations mirror a story many other U.S. workers could tell:

> I was seven years old the first time I ever set foot inside an automobile factory. The occasion was Family Night at the old Fisher Body plant in Flint where my father worked the second shift. If nothing else, this annual peepshow lent a whole world of credence to our father's daily grumble. The assembly line did indeed stink. The noise was very close to intolerable. The heat was one complete bastard.
>
> After a hundred wrong turns and dead ends, we found my old man down on the trim line. His job was to install windshields using this goofy apparatus with large suction cups that resembled an octopus being crucified. A car would nuzzle up to the old man's work area and he would be waiting for it, a cigarette dangling from his lip, his arms wrapped around the windshield contraption as if it might suddenly rebel and bolt off for the ocean. Car, windshield. Car, windshield. Car,

windshield. No wonder my father preferred playin' hopscotch with barmaids (Hamper, 1992, pp. 1–2).

Following in his father's and grandfather's footsteps, Ben Hamper became an auto-worker—the pay was good, and he didn't know anything else. He soon discovered a familiar pattern. His career began decades after Argyris and McGregor questioned the fallacies of traditional management, but little had changed. Hamper held down a variety of jobs, each as mindless as the next: "The one thing that was impossible to escape was the monotony. Every minute, every hour, every truck, and every movement was a plodding replica of the one that had gone before" (1992, p. 41).

The specialization Ben Hamper experienced in the auto plant calls for a clear chain of command to coordinate discrete jobs. Bosses direct and control subordinates, thus encouraging passivity and dependence. The conflict worsens at lower levels of the hierarchy—narrower, more mechanized jobs, more directives, and tighter controls. As people mature, conflict intensifies. Leann Bies was 44 with a bachelor's degree in business when she started work as a licensed electrician at a Ford truck plant in 2003, and "for two years they treated me as if I were dumber than a box of rocks. You get an attitude if you are treated that way" (Uchitelle, 2007, p. 10).

Argyris argued that employees try to stay sane by looking for ways to escape these frustrations. He identified six options:

1. *They withdraw—through chronic absenteeism or simply by quitting.* Ben Hamper chronicled many examples of absenteeism and quitting, including a friend who lasted only a couple of months:

   My pal Roy was beginning to unravel in a real rush. His enthusiasm about all the money we were makin' had dissipated and he was having major difficulty coping with the drudgery of factory labor. His job, like mine, wasn't difficult. It was just plain monotonous . . .

   The day before he quit, he approached me with a box-cutter knife sticking out of his glove and requested that I give him a slice across the back of the hand. He felt sure this ploy would land him a few days off. Since slicing Roy didn't seem like a solid career move, I refused. Roy went down the line to the other workers where he received a couple of charitable offers to cut his throat, but no dice on the hand. He wound up sulking back to his job. After that night, I never saw Roy again (1992, pp. 40, 43).

2. *They stay on the job but withdraw psychologically, becoming indifferent, passive, and apathetic.* Like many other workers, Ben Hamper didn't want to quit, so he looked for ways to cope with the tedium. His favorite was to "double up" by making a deal with another worker to take turns covering each other's job. This made it possible to get full pay for half a day's work:

What a setup. Dale and I would both report to work before the 4:30 horn. We'd spend a half hour preparing all the stock we'd need for the evening. At 5:00, I would take over the two jobs while Dale went to sleep in a makeshift cardboard bed behind our bench . . . I'd work the jobs from 5:00 until 9:24, the official lunch period. When the line stopped, I'd give Dale's cardboard coffin a good kick. It was time for the handoff. I would give my ID badge to Dale so that he could punch me out at quitting time, (1992, p. 61).

If doubling up didn't work, workers invented other diversions, like Rivet Hockey (sailing rivets into a coworker's foot or leg) and Dumpster Ball (kicking cardboard boxes high enough to clear a dumpster).

3. *They resist by restricting output, deception, featherbedding, or sabotage.*[1] Hamper reports what happened when the company removed a popular foreman because he was "too close to his work force" (1992, p. 205):

With a tight grip on the whip, the new bossman started riding the crew. No music. No Rivet Hockey. No horseplay. No drinking. No card playing. No working up the line. No leaving the department. No doubling-up. No this, no that. No questions asked.

No way. After three nights of this imported bullyism, the boys had had their fill. Frames began sliding down the line minus parts. Rivets became cross-eyed. Guns mysteriously broke down. The repairmen began shipping the majority of the defects, unable to keep up with the repair load.

Sabotage was drastic, but it got the point across and brought the new foreman into line. To survive, the foreman had to fall into step. Otherwise, he would be replaced, and the cycle would start anew.

4. *They try to climb the hierarchy to better jobs.* Moving up works for some, but there are rarely enough "better" jobs to go around, and many workers are reluctant to take

promotions. Hamper reports what happened to a coworker who tried to crack down after he was promoted to foreman:

For the next eight days, we made Calvin Moza's short-lived career switch sheer hell. Every time he'd walk the aisle, someone would pepper his steps with raining rivets. He couldn't make a move without the hammers banging and loud chants of "suckass" and "brown snout" ringin' in his ears. He got everything he deserved (1992, p. 208).

Hamper found his own escape: he started to moonlight as a writer during one of automaking's periodic layoffs. Styling himself "The Rivethead," he wrote a column about factory life from the inside. His writing eventually led to a best-selling book, as well as film and radio gigs. Most of his buddies weren't as fortunate.

5. *They form alliances (such as labor unions) to redress the power imbalance.* Union movements grow out of workers' desire for a more equal footing with management. Argyris cautioned, however, that union "bosses" might run their operations much like factories, because they knew no other way to manage. In the long run, employees' sense of powerlessness would change little. Ben Hamper, like most autoworkers, was a union member, yet the union is largely invisible in his accounts of life on the assembly line. He rarely sought union help and even less often got any. He appreciated wages and benefits earned at the bargaining table, but nothing in the labor agreement protected workers from boredom, frustration, or the feeling of powerlessness.

6. *They teach their children to believe that work is unrewarding and hopes for advancement are slim.* Researchers in the 1960s began to note that children of farmers grew up believing hard work paid off, while the offspring of urban blue-collar workers did not. As a result, many U.S. companies began to move facilities away from old industrial states like Michigan (where Ben Hamper worked) to more rural states like North Carolina and Tennessee, in search of employees who still embodied the work ethic. Argyris predicted, however, that industry would eventually demotivate even the most committed workforce unless management practices changed. In recent decades, manufacturing and service jobs have been moving offshore to low-wage enclaves around the world, continuing the search for employees who will work hard without asking for too much in return.

Hamper's account of life on the line is a vivid illustration of Argyris's contention that organizations treat adults like children. The company assigned an employee to wander through the plant dressed in costume as "Howie Makem, the Quality Cat." (Howie was mostly greeted with groans, insults, and an occasional flying rivet.) Message boards were plastered with inspirational phrases like "Riveting is fun." A plant manager would emerge from his usual invisibility to give an annual speech promising to talk more with workers. All this hypocrisy took its toll: "Working the Rivet Line was like being paid to flunk high school the rest of your life. An adolescent time warp in which the duties of the day were just an underlying annoyance" (Hamper, 1992, p. 185).

The powerlessness and frustration that Hamper experienced are by no means unique to factory work. Bosses who treat office workers like children are a pop culture staple—including the pointy-haired martinet in *Dilbert* and the pathetically clueless boss in the television series *The Office.* In public education, many teachers and parents lament that increasing emphasis on high-stakes standardized tests alienates teachers and turns them into "deskilled clerks" (Giroux, 1998). Batstone sees frustration as pervasive among workers at every level: "Corporate workers from the mailroom to the highest executive office express dissatisfaction with their work. They feel crushed by widespread greed, selfishness, and quest for profit at any cost. Apart from their homes, people spend more time on the job than anywhere else. With that kind of personal stake, they want to be part of something that matters and contribute to a greater good. Sadly, those aspirations often go unmet" (2003, p. 1).

Argyris and McGregor formed their views on the basis of observations of U.S. organizations in the 1950s and 1960s. Since then, investigators have documented similar conflicts between people and organizations around the world. Orgogozo (1991), for example, contended that typical French management practices caused workers to feel humiliation, boredom, anger, and exhaustion "because they have no hope of being recognized and valued for what they do" (p. 101). She depicted relations between superiors and subordinates in France as tense and distant because "bosses do everything possible to protect themselves from the resentment that they generate" (p. 73).

Early on, human-resource ideas were often ignored by scholars and managers. The dominant "assembly-line" mentality enjoyed enough economic success to persist. The frame's influence has grown with the realization that misuse of human resources depresses profits as well as people. Legions of consultants, managers, and researchers now pursue answers to the vexing human problems of organizations.

HUMAN CAPACITY AND THE CHANGING EMPLOYMENT CONTRACT

In recent years, global trends have pushed organizations in two conflicting directions. On one hand, global competition, rapid change, shorter product life cycles and the rise of mobile apps have produced a turbulent, intensely competitive world, placing an enormous premium on the ability to adapt quickly to shifts in the environment. One way to adapt is to minimize fixed human assets. Beginning in the late twentieth century, more and more organizations turned to downsizing, outsourcing, and using part-time and temporary employees to cope with business fluctuations. In the United States, public universities have coped with a decline in state funding by shifting to more part-time adjunct instructors and fewer full-time faculty. Uber, emblematic of the "gig economy," has fought doggedly to keep its drivers classified as "independent contractors" rather than employees. Volkswagen opened a manufacturing plant in Brazil in which subcontractors employed 80 percent of the workforce. Even in Japan, traditional notions of lifetime careers have eroded in the face of "a bloated work force, particularly in the white collar sector, which proved to be an economic drag" (WuDunn, 1996, p. 8). Around the world, employees looking for career advice have been told to count on themselves rather than employers. Give up on job security, the advice often goes, and focus instead on developing skills and flexibility that will make you marketable.

On the other hand, some of the same global forces push in another direction—toward growing dependence on well-trained, loyal human capital. That was why the online real estate firm Redfin chose to run counter to the usual pattern for both tech start-ups and the real estate business. Employing more than 1,000 agents in 2016, Redfin "gives its agents salaries, health benefits, 401(k) contributions and, for the most productive ones, Redfin stock, none of which is standard for contractors" (Wingfield, 2016), because CEO Glenn Kelman believes that full-time employees provide better customer service.

Organizations have become more complex as a consequence of globalization and a more information-intensive economy. More decentralized structures, like the networks discussed in Chapter 3, have proliferated in response to greater complexity and turbulence. These new configurations depend on a higher level of skill, intelligence, and commitment across a broader spectrum of employees. A network of decentralized decision nodes is a blueprint for disaster if the dispersed decision makers lack the capacity or desire to make sensible choices. Skill requirements have been changing so fast that individuals are hard pressed to keep up. The result is a troubling gap: organizations struggle to find people who bring the skills and qualities needed, while individuals with yesterday's skills face dismal job prospects.

The shift from a production-intensive to an information-intensive economy is not helping to close the gap. There used to be more jobs that involved *making things*. In the first three decades after World War II, high-paying jobs in developed nations were heavily concentrated in blue-collar work (Drucker, 1993). These jobs generally required little formal training and few specialized skills, but they afforded pay and benefits to sustain a comfortable and stable lifestyle. No more. Whereas workers in manufacturing jobs accounted for more than a third of U.S. workers in the 1950s, by 2010 they were less than a tenth of the workforce (Matthews, 2012), dropping to a low of around 11.5 million jobs in early 2010. During the next five years, there were signs of a rebound (U. S. Bureau of Labor Statistics, 2016), and manufacturing jobs began to come back to traditional factory states like Indiana, Michigan, and Ohio (Baily and Katz, 2012). But the growth was concentrated in high-skill jobs in industries like aerospace, medical equipment, and automobiles. When U.S. automobile manufacturers began to replace retiring workers in the mid-1990s, they emphasized quick minds more than strong bodies and put applicants "through a grueling selection process that emphasized mental acuity and communication skills" (Meredith, 1996, p. 1).

This skill gap is even greater in many developing nations. Until late in the twentieth century, China's population of 1.3 billion people consisted largely of farmers and workers with old-economy skills. Beginning in the 1980s, China began a gradual shift to a market economy, reducing regulations, encouraging foreign investment, and selling off fading state-owned enterprises. Results were dramatic: China's economy shifted from almost entirely state-owned in 1980 to 70 percent private by 2005. China became one of the world's fastest-growing economies, with compound growth at 7 to 8 percent a year in the early twenty-first century, but unemployment mushroomed as state-owned enterprises succumbed to nimbler—and leaner—domestic and foreign competitors. China's reported unemployment rate was low by comparison to many western nations, but it still meant millions of Chinese were looking for work, and many observers suspected that the official numbers understated the problem.

Simultaneous pressures to increase flexibility and employee skills create a vexing human resource dilemma. Should an organization seek adaptability (through a downsized, outsourced, part-time workforce) or loyalty (through a long-term commitment to people)? Should it seek high skills (by hiring the best and training them well) or low costs (by hiring the cheapest and investing no more than necessary)?

Lean and Mean: More Benefits Than Costs?

The advantages of a smaller, more flexible workforce seem compelling: lower costs, higher efficiency, and greater ability to respond to business fluctuations. After the recession in 2008, the U.S. economy shed roughly 5 million jobs (Coy, Conlin, and Herbst, 2010), albeit just a fraction of the some 50 million lost worldwide (Schwartz, 2009).

Downsizing works best when new technology and smart management combine to enable fewer people to do more. In recent decades, manufacturing jobs have been shrinking around the globe because of changes in technology (Kenny, 2014). Yet even when it works, shedding staff risks trading short-term gains for long-term decay. "Chainsaw Al" Dunlap became a hero of the downsizing movement as chief executive of Scott Paper, where he more than doubled profits and market value. His strategy? Cut people—half of management, half of research and development, and a fifth of blue-collar workers. Financial outcomes were impressive at first, but employee morale sank, and Scott lost market share in every major product line. Dunlap did not stay around long enough to find out if he had sacrificed Scott's future for short-term gains. After less than two years on the job, he sold the company to its biggest competitor and walked away with almost $100 million for his efforts (Byrne, 1996).

Despite eliminating millions of jobs, many firms have found benefits elusive. Markels and Murray (1996) reported that downsizing often turned into "dumbsizing": "Many firms continue to make flawed decisions—hasty, across-the-board cuts—that come back to haunt, on the bottom line, in public relationships, in strained relationships with customers and suppliers, and in demoralized employees." In shedding staff, firms often found that they also sacrificed knowledge, skill, innovation, and loyalty (Reichheld, 1993, 1996). Multiple studies have found that cutting people hurts more often than it helps performance (Cascio, Young, and Morris, 1997; Gertz and Baptista, 1995; Love and Kraatz, 2005; Mellahi and Wilkinson, 2006). Nevertheless, more than half of the companies in a 2003 survey admitted that they would make cuts that hurt in the long term if that's what it took to meet short-term earnings targets (Berenson, 2004).

Downsizing and outsourcing often have a corrosive effect on employee motivation and commitment. A 2009 Conference Board survey found that "only 45% of workers surveyed were satisfied with their jobs, the lowest in 22 years of polling" (Coy, Conlin, and Herbst, 2010, p. 1). Workers reported that the mood in the workplace was angrier and colleagues were more competitive, and a 2012 survey found employee loyalty at a seven-year low.

Investing in People

Employers often fail to invest the time and resources necessary to develop a cadre of committed, talented employees. Precisely for that reason, a number of authors (including Cascio and Boudreau, 2008; Lawler, 1996; Lawler and Worley, 2006; Pfeffer, 1994, 1998, 2007; and Waterman, 1994) have made the case that a skilled and motivated workforce is a powerful source of competitive advantage. Consistent with core human resource assumptions, high-performing companies do a better job of understanding and responding to the needs of both employees and customers. As a result, they attract better people who are motivated to do a superior job.

The most successful company in the U.S. airline industry for many decades, Southwest Airlines, paid employees a competitive wage but had an enormous cost advantage because its highly committed workforce was so productive. Competitors tried to imitate Southwest's approach but rarely succeeded because "the real difference is in the effort Southwest gets out of its people. That is very, very hard to duplicate" (Labich, 1994, p. 52).

Ewing Kauffman started a pharmaceutical business in a Kansas City basement that he grew into a multibillion-dollar company (Morgan, 1995). His approach was heavily influenced by his personal experiences as a young pharmaceutical salesman:

> I worked on straight commission, receiving no salary, no expenses, no car, and no benefits in any way, shape, or form—just straight commission. By the end of the second year, my commission amounted to more than the president's salary. He didn't think that was right, so he cut my commission. By then I was Midwest sales manager and had other salesmen working for me under an arrangement whereby my commission was 3 percent of everything they sold. In spite of the cut in my commission, that year I still managed to make more than the president thought a sales manager should make. So this time he cut the territory, which was the same as taking away some of my income. I quit and started Marion Laboratories.
>
> I based the company on a vision of what it would be. When we hired employees, they were referred to as "associates," and they shared in the success of the company. Once again, the two principles that have guided my entire career, which were based on my experience working for that very first pharmaceutical company, are these: "Those who produce should share in the profits," and "Treat others as you would be treated" (Kauffman, 1996, p. 40).

Few managers in the 1950s shared Kauffman's faith, and many are still skeptics. An urgent debate is under way about the future of the relationship between people and organizations. The battle of lean-and-mean versus invest-in-people continues. In pipe manufacturing, two of the dominant players are crosstown rivals in Birmingham, Alabama. One is McWane, which compiled an abysmal record on safety and environmental protection—9 deaths, 400 safety violations, and 450 environmental violations between 1995 and 2002 (Barstow and Bergman, 2003b) that "culminated in an $8 million fine imposed in April 2009. Four former plant managers were sentenced to federal prison for what authorities said was wrongdoing at the plant, including the cover-up of evidence in the 2000 death of Alfred 'Alfie' Coxe in a forklift accident" (Salamone, 2016).

The other is American Cast Iron Pipe (Acipco), which was the first firm in its industry to appear on *Fortune*'s list of the best places to work in America and was named one of Birmingham's most admired companies in 2012. Barstow and Bergman write that "several statistical measures show how different Acipco is from McWane. At some McWane plants, turnover rates approach 100 percent a year. Acipco—with a work force of about 3,000, three-fifths the size of McWane—has annual turnover of less than half a percent; 10,000 people recently applied for 100 openings" (2003c, p. A15).

Which of these two competing visions works better? Financially, it is difficult to judge, because both companies are privately held. Both have achieved business success for roughly a century. But in January 2003, at the same time that *Fortune* was lauding Acipco for its progressive human resource practices, the *New York Times* and a television documentary pilloried McWane for its callous disregard of both people and the law. By 2012, a chastened McWane was describing itself as an industry leader in employee safety and offered data suggesting that safety problems in its plants had declined steadily.

CONCLUSION

The human resource frame highlights the relationship between people and organizations. Organizations need people (for their energy, effort, and talent), and people need organizations (for the many intrinsic and extrinsic rewards they offer), but their respective needs are not always well aligned. When the fit between people and organizations is poor, one or both suffer: individuals may feel neglected or oppressed, and organizations sputter because individuals withdraw their efforts or even work against organizational purposes. Conversely, a good fit benefits both: individuals find meaningful and satisfying work, and organizations get the talent and energy they need to succeed.

Global competition, turbulence, and rapid change have heightened an enduring organizational dilemma: Is it better to be lean and mean or to invest in people? A variety of strategies to reduce the workforce—downsizing, outsourcing, use of temporary, part-time, or contract workers—have been widely applied to reduce costs and increase flexibility. But they risk a loss of talent and loyalty that leads to organizations that are mediocre, even if flexible. Emerging evidence suggests that downsizing has often produced disappointing results. Many highly successful organizations have gone in another direction: investing in people on the premise that a highly motivated and skilled workforce is a powerful competitive advantage.

NOTES

1. Featherbedding is a colloquial term for giving people jobs that involve little or no work. This can occur for a variety of reasons: union pressures, nepotism (employing family members), or "kicking someone upstairs" (moving an underperformer into a job with no significant responsibilities).

Improving Human Resource Management

*Far and away the best prize that life offers is
the chance to work hard at work worth doing.*

—Theodore Roosevelt

Google, with more than 500 applicants for every job opening in recent years, is harder to get into than Harvard. In 2017 it was once again number one on *Fortune's* list of the best places to work (*Fortune*, 2017). Its king-of-the-Internet image helps, but the search giant knows it takes more to hire and retain the brainy, high-energy geeks who keep the place going and growing. As one Googler put it, "The company culture truly makes workers feel they're valued and respected as a human being, not as a cog in a machine. The perks are phenomenal. From three prepared organic meals a day to unlimited snacks, artisan coffee and tea to free personal-fitness classes, health clinics, on-site oil changes, haircuts, spa truck, bike-repair truck, nap pods, free on-site laundry rooms, and subsidized wash and fold. The list is endless" (*Fortune*, 2016).

Few go as far as Google, but a growing number of enlightened companies are finding their own ways to attract and develop human capital. They see talent and motivation as business essentials. That idea has taken a couple of centuries to gain traction, and many companies still don't get it. They adhere to the old view that anything you give to employees siphons money from the bottom line—like having your pocket picked or your bank account drained.

A pioneer of a more progressive approach was a Welshman, Robert Owen, who ran into fierce opposition. Born in 1771, Owen became a wildly successful entrepreneur before the age of 30 by exploiting the day's hot technology—textile mills. Owen was heavily attacked because he was the only capitalist of his time who believed it was bad for business to work eight-year-olds in 13-hour factory shifts. At his New Lanark (Scotland) knitting mill, bought in 1799, Owen took a new approach:

> Owen provided clean, decent housing for his workers and their families in a community free of contagious disease, crime, and gin shops. He took young children out of the factory and enrolled them in a school he founded. There he provided preschool, day care, and a brand of progressive education that stresses learning as a pleasurable experience (along with the first adult night school). The entire business world was shocked when he prohibited corporal punishment in his factory and dumbfounded when he retrained his supervisors in humane disciplinary practices. While offering his workers an extremely high standard of living compared to other workers of the era, Owen was making a fortune at New Lanark. This conundrum drew twenty thousand visitors between 1815 and 1820 (O'Toole, 1995, pp. 201, 206).

Owen tried to convince fellow capitalists that investing in people could produce a greater return than investments in machinery. But the business world dismissed him as a wild radical whose ideas would harm the people he wanted to help (O'Toole, 1995).

Owen was at least 100 years ahead of his time. A century later, when Henry Ford announced in 1914 that he was going to shorten the workday to 8 hours and double the wages of his blue-collar workers from $2.50 to $5.00 per day, he also came under heavy fire from the business community. The *Wall Street Journal* opined that he was "committing economic blunders, if not crimes" (Harnish et al., 2012). The *Journal* got it wrong. Ford's profits doubled over the next two years as productivity soared and employee turnover plunged. Ford later said the five dollars per day was the best cost-cutting move he ever made.

Only in the late twentieth century did more business leaders begin to believe that investing in people is a way to make money. In recent years, periodic waves of restructuring and downsizing have raised age-old questions about the relationship between the individual and the organization. A number of persuasive reports suggest Owen was right: An excellent route to long-term success is investing in employees and responding to their needs (Applebaum et al., 2000; Barrick et al., 2015; Collins and Porras, 1994; Deal and Jenkins, 1994; Farkas and De Backer, 1996; Becker and Huselid, 1998; Lawler, 1996; Levering and Moskowitz, 1993; Pfeffer, 1994, 1998, 2007; Schwartz and Porath, 2014; Waterman, 1994).

Changes in the business environment have made human resource management more critical than ever. "A skilled and motivated work force providing the speed and flexibility required by new market imperatives has increased the importance of human resource management issues at a time when traditional sources of competitive advantage (quality, technology, economies of scale, etc.) have become easier to imitate" (Becker and Huselid, 1998, p. 54). Yet many organizations still don't believe it, and others only flirt with the idea:

> Something very strange is occurring in organizational management. Over the past decade or so, numerous rigorous studies conducted both within specific industries and in samples across industries have demonstrated the enormous economic returns obtained through the execution of what are variously labeled as high involvement, high performance, or high commitment management practices . . . But even as positive results pile up, trends in actual management practice are often moving exactly opposite to what the evidence advocates (Pfeffer, 1998, p. xv).

Why would managers resist better ways of managing people? One reason is that Theory X managers fear losing control or indulging workers. A second is that investing in people requires time and persistence to yield a payoff. Faced with relentless pressure for immediate results, executives often conclude that slashing costs, changing strategy, or reorganizing is more likely to produce a quick hit. A third factor is the dominance of a "financial" perspective that sees the organization as simply a portfolio of financial assets (Pfeffer, 1998). In this view, human resources are subjective, soft, and suspect in comparison to hard financial numbers.

GETTING IT RIGHT

Despite such barriers, many organizations get it right. They understand the need to develop an approach to people that flows from the organization's strategy and human capital needs (Barrick et al., 2015; Becker and Huselid, 1998). Their practices are not perfect but good

Exhibit 7.1.
Basic Human Resource Strategies.

Human Resource Principle	Specific Practices
Build and implement an HR strategy.	Develop and share a clear philosophy for managing people. Build systems and practices to implement the philosophy.
Hire the right people.	Know what you want. Be selective.
Keep them.	Reward well. Protect jobs. Promote from within. Share the wealth.
Invest in them.	Invest in learning. Create development opportunities.
Empower them.	Provide information and support. Encourage autonomy and participation. Redesign work. Foster self-managing teams. Promote egalitarianism.
Promote diversity.	Be explicit and consistent about the organization's diversity philosophy. Hold managers accountable.

enough. The organization benefits from a talented, motivated, loyal, and free-spirited workforce. Employees in turn are more productive, innovative, and willing to go out of their way to get the job done. They are less likely to make costly blunders or to jump ship when someone offers them a better deal. That's a potent edge—in sports, business, or elsewhere. Every organization with productive people management has its own distinct approach, but most include variations on strategies summarized in Exhibit 7.1 and examined in depth in the remainder of the chapter.

Develop and Implement an HR Philosophy

"Systematic and interrelated human resource management practices" provide a sustainable competitive advantage. The key is a philosophy or credo that makes explicit an organization's core beliefs about managing people (Becker and Huselid, 1998, p. 55). The credo then has to be translated into specific management practices. Most organizations lack a philosophy, or they ignore the one they claim to have. A philosophy provides direction; practices make it real.

Wegmans, a supermarket chain in the northeastern United States that consistently gets top marks for both customer satisfaction and employee well-being, has been on Fortune's list of the 100 Best Companies to Work every year since 1998. It offers a succinct statement of "What We Believe:"

> At Wegmans, we believe that good people, working toward a common goal, can accomplish anything they set out to do.
>
> In this spirit, we set our goal to be the very best at serving the needs of our customers. Every action we take should be made with this in mind.
>
> We also believe that we can achieve our goal only if we fulfill the needs of our own people (Wegmans, 2016).

Hire the Right People

Strong companies know the kinds of people they want and hire those who fit the mold. Southwest Airlines became the most successful carrier in the U.S. airline industry by hiring people with positive attitudes and well-honed interpersonal skills, including a sense of humor (Farkas and De Backer, 1996; Labich, 1994; Levering and Moskowitz, 1993). In one case, interviewers asked a group of pilots applying for jobs at Southwest to change into Bermuda shorts for the interviews. Two declined. They weren't hired (Freiberg and Freiberg, 1998).

Even though Hertz had a 40-year head start, Enterprise overtook them in the 1990s to become the biggest firm in the car rental business. Enterprise wooed its midmarket clientele by deliberately hiring "from the half of the class that makes the top half possible"—college graduates more successful in sports and socializing than the classroom. Recruiting for people skills more than "book smarts" helped Enterprise build exceptional levels of customer service (Pfeffer, 1998, p. 71). In contrast, Microsoft's formidably bright CEO, Bill Gates, insisted on "intelligence or smartness over anything else, even, in many cases, experience" (Stross, 1996, p. 162). Google wants smarts, too, but believes teamwork is equally important—one reason that its hiring is team-based (Schmidt and Varian, 2005).

The principle seems to apply globally, as illustrated by a study of successful midsized companies in Germany (Simon, 1996). Turnover was rare in these firms except among new hires: "Many new employees leave, or are terminated, shortly after joining the work force, both sides having learned that a worker does not fit into the firm's culture and cannot stand its pace" (p. 199). Zappos tries to accelerate the process by offering new hires a cash bonus to quit after they complete the company's orientation program. Few take the money and run, but Zappos wants to keep only people who love the company's idiosyncratic culture.

Keep Employees

To get people they want, companies like Google, Southwest Airlines, and Wegmans offer attractive pay and benefits. To keep them, they protect jobs, promote from within, and give people a piece of the action. They recognize the high cost of turnover—which for some jobs and industries can run well over 100 percent a year. Beyond the cost of hiring and training replacements, turnover hurts performance because newcomers' lack of experience, skills, and local knowledge increases errors and reduces efficiency (Kacmar et al., 2006). This is true even at the CEO level. CEOs who move from one organization to another perform less well on average than those who are hired from inside (Elson and Ferrere, 2012).

Reward Well

In a cavernous, no-frills retail warehouse setting, where bulk sales determine stockholder profits, knowledgeable, dependable service usually isn't part of the low-cost package. Don't try to tell that to Costco Wholesale Corp., where employee longevity and high morale are as commonplace as overloaded shopping carts. "We like to turn over our inventory faster than our people," says Jim Sinegal, Costco founder and CEO until he retired in 2012. Costco, a membership warehouse store headquartered in Washington State, by 2016 had become the world's second largest retailer (after Walmart) with more than 700 stores across the United States and beyond.

Costco has a counterintuitive success formula: Pay employees more and charge customers less than its biggest competitor, Sam's Club (a Walmart subsidiary). A great way to lose money? Costco has been the industry's most profitable firm in recent years. How? In Sinegal's view, the answer is easy: "If you pay the best wages, you get the highest productivity. By our industry standards, we think we've got the best people and the best productivity when we do that." Costco paid its employees about 70 percent more than Sam's Club but generated twice as much profit per worker (Cascio, 2006). Compared with competitors, Costco achieved higher sales volumes, faster inventory turnover, lower shrinkage, and higher customer satisfaction (RetailSails 2012; American Customer Satisfaction Index, 2016). Costco illustrates a general principle: Pay should reflect value added. Paying people more than they contribute is a losing proposition. But the reverse is also true: It makes sense to pay top dollar for exemplary contributions of skilled, motivated, and involved employees (Lawler, 1996).

"This is the lesson Costco teaches," says retailing guru Doug Stephens. "You don't have to be Nordstrom selling $1,200 suits in order to pay people a living wage. That is what Walmart has lost sight of. A lot of people working at Walmart go home and live below the poverty line. You expect that person to come in and develop a rapport with customers who may be spending more than that person is making in a week? You expect them to be civil and happy about that?" (Stone, 2013).

To get and keep good people, selective organizations also offer attractive benefits. Firms with "high-commitment" human resource practices are more likely to offer work and family benefits, such as daycare and flexible hours (Osterman, 1995). Take software powerhouse SAS:

> Just about every benefit known to corporate America—on-site child care, swimming pools, medical clinics, fitness centers, car detailings, nail salons, shoe repairs—are on offer at this software company based in Research Triangle Park, North Carolina. Said one employee: "I get massages, pick up prescriptions, get my hair done, take photography classes, get physical therapy. The list is endless." But the employee quickly added: "It's not just about the 'what.' It's about the place itself. The campus is beautiful and quite tranquil. I can take a walk during lunch and find myself far away. I know it sounds corny, but I enjoy just driving into campus in the morning" (*Fortune*: SAS Institute, 2016).

Why spend that much? In an industry where turnover rates hover around 20 percent, SAS maintains a level below 4 percent, which results in about $50 million a year in HR-related savings, according to a Harvard Business School study. "The well-being of our company is linked to the well-being of our employees," says SAS CEO Jim Goodnight (Stein, 2000, p. 133).

Protect Jobs

Job security might seem anachronistic today, a relic of more leisurely, paternalistic times. In a turbulent, highly competitive world, is long-term commitment to employees possible? Yes, but it's not easy. Companies (and even countries) historically offering long-term security have abandoned their commitment in the face of severe economic pressures. During the first year of the recession of 2008–2009, American businesses laid off close to 2.5 million workers (Bureau of Labor Statistics, 2012). In China, a government report counted more than 25 million layoffs from 1998 to 2001, many of them unskilled older workers ("China Says 'No' . . . ," 2002; Lingle, 2002; Smith, 2002). Many state-owned enterprises foundered when economic reforms forced them to sink or swim in a competitive market.

Yet many firms continue to honor job security as a cornerstone of their human resource philosophy. Publix, an employee-owned, Fortune 500 supermarket chain in the southeastern United States, has never had a layoff since its founding in 1930. Similarly, Lincoln Electric, the world's largest manufacturer of arc welding equipment, has honored since 1914 a policy that no employee with more than three years of service will be laid off. This commitment was tested when the company experienced a 40-percent year-to-year drop in demand for its products. To avoid layoffs, production workers became salespeople. They canvassed businesses rarely reached by the company's regular distribution channels. "Not only did these people sell arc welding equipment in new places to new users, but since much of the profit of this equipment comes from the sale of replacement parts, Lincoln subsequently enjoyed greater market penetration and greater sales as a consequence" (Pfeffer, 1994, p. 47).

Japan's Mazda, facing similar circumstances, had a parallel experience: "At the end of the year, when awards were presented to the best salespeople, the company discovered that the top 10 were all former factory workers. They could explain the product effectively, and when business picked up, the fact that factory workers had experience talking to customers yielded useful ideas about product characteristics" (Pfeffer, 1994, p. 47).

Promote from Within

Costco promotes more than 80 percent of its managers from inside the company, and 90 percent of managers at FedEx started in a nonmanagerial job. Promoting from within offers several advantages (Pfeffer, 1998):

- It encourages both management and employees to invest time and resources in upgrading skills.
- It is a powerful performance incentive.
- It fosters trust and loyalty.
- It capitalizes on knowledge and skills of veteran employees.
- It avoids errors by newcomers unfamiliar with the company's history and proven ways.
- It increases the likelihood that employees will think for the longer term and avoid impetuous, shortsighted decisions. Highly successful corporations rarely hire a chief executive from the outside; less effective companies do so regularly (Collins and Porras, 1994).

Share the Wealth

Employees often feel little responsibility for an organization's performance because they expect gains in efficiency and profitability to benefit only executives and shareholders. People-oriented organizations have devised a variety of ways to align employee rewards more directly with business success. These include gain-sharing, profit-sharing, and employee stock ownership plans (ESOPs). Scanlon plans, first introduced in the 1930s, give workers an incentive to reduce costs and improve efficiency by offering them a share of gains. Profit-sharing plans at companies like Nucor give employees a bonus tied to overall profitability or to the performance of their local unit.

Both gain-sharing and profit-sharing plans usually have a positive impact on performance and profitability, although some have worked better than others. Success depends on how well these plans are integrated into a coherent human resource philosophy. Kanter (1989a) suggests that gain-sharing plans have spread slowly because they require broader changes in managing people: cross-unit teams, suggestion systems, and more open communication of financial information (Kanter, 1989a). Similar barriers have slowed the progress of ESOPs:

> To be effective, ownership has to be combined with ground-floor efforts to involve employees in decisions through schemes such as work teams and quality-improvement groups. Many companies have been doing this, of course, including plenty without ESOPs. But employee-owners often begin to expect rights that other groups of shareholders have: a voice in broad corporate decisions, board seats, and voting rights. And that's where the trouble can start, since few executives are comfortable with this level of power-sharing (Bernstein, 1996, p. 101).

Nevertheless, there have been many successful ESOPs. Thousands of firms participate (Rosen, Case, and Staubus, 2005), and most of the plans have been successful (Blasi, Kruse, and Bernstein, 2003; Blair, Kruse, and Blasi, 2000; Kruse, Blasi, and Park, 2010). Employee ownership tends to be a durable arrangement and to make the company more stable—less likely to fail, be sold, or to lay off employees (Blair, Kruse, and Blasi, 2000). When first introduced, employee ownership tends to produce productivity gains that persist over time (Kruse, 1993). A plan's success depends on effective implementation of three elements of the "equity model" (Rosen et al., 2005, p. 19):

- Employees must have a significant ownership share in the company.
- The organization needs to build an "ownership culture" (p. 34).
- It is important that "employees both learn and drive the business disciplines that help their company do well" (p. 38).

All those characteristics can be found at Publix, America's largest employee-owned business. Publix has become a fixture on *Fortune's* list of most admired companies and its list of best places to work, while achieving the highest customer satisfaction ratings in its industry (American Customer Satisfaction Index, 2016).

Bonus and profit-sharing plans spread rapidly in the boom years of the 1990s. The benefits often went mostly to top managers, but many successful firms shared benefits more widely. Skeptics noted a significant downside risk to profit-sharing plans: They work when there are rewards but breed disappointment and anger if the company experiences a financial downturn. A famous example is United Airlines, whose employees took a 15-percent pay cut in return for 55-percent ownership of the company in 1994. Initially, it was a huge success. Employees were enthusiastic when the stock soared to almost $100 a share. But, like most airlines, United experienced a financial crunch after 9/11. Employees were crushed when bankruptcy left their shares worthless and their pensions underfunded.

Invest in Employees

Undertrained workers harm organizations in many ways: shoddy quality, poor service, higher costs, and costly mistakes. A high proportion of petrochemical industry accidents involve contract employees (Pfeffer, 1994), and in postinvasion Iraq some of America's more damaging mistakes were the work of private security contractors, who often had less training and discipline than their military counterparts.

Many organizations are reluctant to invest in developing human capital. The costs of training are immediate and easy to measure; the benefits are long term and less certain. Training temporary or contract workers carries added disincentives. Yet many companies report a sizable return on their training investment. An internal study at Motorola, for instance, found a gain of $29 for every dollar invested in sales training (Waterman, 1994), and an analysis of the effects of training programs over the period 1960 to 2000 found consistently positive effects, "comparable to or larger than other organizational interventions designed to improve performance" (Pfeffer, 2007, p. 30).

Empower Employees

Progressive organizations give power to employees as well as invest in their development. Empowerment includes keeping employees informed, but it doesn't stop there. It also involves encouraging autonomy and participation, redesigning work, fostering teams, promoting egalitarianism, and infusing work with meaning.

Provide Information and Support

A key factor in Enron's dizzying collapse was that few people fully understood its financial picture. Eight months before the crash, *Fortune* reporter Bethany McLean asked CEO Jeffrey Skilling, "How, exactly, does Enron make money?" Her March 2001 article in *Fortune* pointed out that the company's financial reports were almost impenetrable and the stock price could implode if the company missed its earnings forecasts.

Over the last few decades, a philosophy sometimes called "open-book management" has begun to take root in progressive companies. The movement was inspired by the near-death experience of an obscure plant in Missouri, Springfield Remanufacturing (now SRC Holdings). SRC was created in 1983 when a group of managers and employees purchased it from International Harvester for about $100,000 in cash and $9 million in debt. It was one of history's most highly leveraged buyouts (Pfeffer, 1998; Stack and Burlingham, 1994). Less debt had strangled many companies, and CEO Jack Stack figured the business could make it only with everyone's best efforts. He developed the open-book philosophy as a way to survive. The system was built around three basic principles (Case, 1995):

- All employees at every level should see and learn to understand financial and performance measures.

- Employees are encouraged to think like owners, doing whatever they can to improve the numbers.

- Everyone gets a piece of the action—a stake in the company's financial success.

Open-book management works for several reasons. First, it sends a clear signal that management trusts people. Second, it creates a powerful incentive for employees to contribute. They can see the big picture—how their work affects the bottom line and how the bottom line affects them. Finally, it furnishes information they need to do a better job. If efficiency is dropping, scrap is increasing, or a certain product has stopped selling, employees can pinpoint the problem and correct it.

Open-book strategies have been applied mostly in relatively small companies, but they've also worked for Whole Foods, the natural foods supermarket chain, and Hilcorp, the largest privately owned U.S. business in the oil and gas industry. Whole Foods "collects and distributes information to an extent that would be unimaginable almost anywhere else. Sensitive figures on store sales, team sales, profit margins, even salaries, are available to every person in every location" (Fishman, 1996a). Hilcorp attained notoriety in December, 2015, when CEO Jeffrey Hildebrand came through on his promise to give every employee

$100,000 if the company met its five-year goals to "to double Hilcorp's oilfield production rate, net oil and gas reserves, and equity value." The bonuses cost Hildebrand more than $100 million, but he could afford it—the company's success had made him a very wealthy man. The checks went out in time for Christmas.

Encourage Autonomy and Participation

Information is necessary but not sufficient to fully engage employees. The work itself needs to offer opportunities for autonomy, influence, and intrinsic rewards. The Theory X approach assumes that managers make decisions and employees follow orders. Treated like children, employees behave accordingly. As companies have faced up to the costs of this downward spiral in motivation and productivity, they have developed programs under the generic label of participation to give workers more opportunity to influence decisions about work and working conditions. The results have often been remarkable.

A classic illustration comes from a group of women who painted dolls in a toy factory (Whyte, 1955). In a newly reengineered process, each woman took a toy from a tray, painted it, and put it on a passing hook. The women received an hourly rate, a group bonus, and a learning bonus. Although management expected little difficulty, production was disappointing and morale took a dive. Workers complained that the room was too hot and the hooks moved too fast.

Reluctantly, the foreman followed a consultant's advice and met face to face with the employees. After hearing the women's complaints, he agreed to bring in fans. Though he and the engineer who designed the manufacturing process expected no benefit, morale improved. Discussions continued, and the employees came up with a radical suggestion: let them control the belt's speed. The engineer was vehemently opposed; he had carefully calculated the optimal speed. The foreman was skeptical but agreed to give the suggestion a try. The employees developed a complicated production schedule: start slow at the beginning of the day, increase the speed once they had warmed up, slow it down before lunch, and so on.

Results were stunning. Morale skyrocketed. Production increased far beyond the most optimistic calculations. That became a problem when the women's bonuses escalated to the point that they were earning more than workers with more skill and experience. The experiment ended unhappily. The women's high pay created dissension in the ranks. Instead of trying to expand a concept that had worked so well, management chose to restore harmony by reverting to a fixed speed for the belt. Production plunged, morale plummeted, and most of the women quit.

Successful examples of participative experiments have multiplied across sectors and around the globe. A Venezuelan example is illustrative. Historically, the nation's health care was provided by a two-tier system: small-scale, high-quality private care for the affluent and a large public health care system for others. The public system, operated by the ministry of health, was in a state of perpetual crisis. It suffered from overcentralization, chronic deficits, poor hygiene, decaying facilities, and constant theft of everything from cotton balls to X-ray machines (Palumbo, 1991). A small group of health care providers founded Ascardio to provide cardiac care in a rural area (Palumbo, 1991; Malavé, 1995). Participation was a key to remarkably high standards of patient care. A key innovation was the General Assembly, which brought together doctors, technical staff, workers, board members, and community representatives where they discussed everything from individual performance issues to the system-wide implications of salary increases ordered by the President of Venezuela (Malavé, 1995, p. 16). Arteta (2006) argued that Ascardio's skill at learning has helped it to survive and grow in a very turbulent environment as Venezuela lurched from one economic and political crisis to another.

Studies of participation show it to be a powerful tool to increase both morale and productivity (Appelbaum et al., 2000; Blumberg, 1968; Katzell and Yankelovich, 1975; Levine and Tyson, 1990). A study of three industries—steel, apparel, and medical instruments—found participation consistently associated with higher performance (Appelbaum et al., 2000). Workers in high-performance plants had more confidence in management, liked their jobs better, and received higher pay. The authors suggested that participation improves productivity through two mechanisms: increasing effectiveness of individual workers and enhancing organizational learning (Appelbaum et al., 2000).

Lam, Huang, and Chan (2015) found that participation only works when it rises above a threshold level—managers need to be fully committed, and to include information sharing and effective leadership in the package. Efforts at fostering participation have sometimes failed because of managers' ambivalence—even if they like the idea, they often fear subordinates will abuse it. When managers are conflicted, participation is often more rhetoric than reality (Argyris, 1998; Argyris and Schön, 1996) and turns into "bogus empowerment" (Ciulla, 1998, p. 63; Heller, 2003). Without realizing it, managers often mandate participation in a controlling, top-down fashion, sending mixed messages—"It's your decision, but do what I want." Such contradictions virtually guarantee failure. Fast, Burris, and Bartel (2014) report that the less confidence managers had in their own effectiveness, the less likely they were to welcome employee input. That suggests that insecure, defensive managers set up a self-destructive spiral: They need help but avoid getting it.

Redesign Work

In the name of efficiency, many organizations spent much of the twentieth century trying to oust the human element by designing jobs to be simple, repetitive, and low skill. The analogue in education is "teacher-proof" curricula and prescribed teaching techniques. When such approaches dampen motivation and enthusiasm, managers and reformers habitually blame workers or teachers for being uncooperative and resistant to change. Only in the late twentieth century did opinion shift toward the view that problems might have more to do with jobs than with workers. A key moment occurred when a young English social scientist took a trip to a coal mine:

> In 1949 trade unionist and former coal miner Ken Bamforth, a postgraduate fellow training for industrial fieldwork in London, was encouraged to return to his former industry to report on work organization. At a newly opened coal seam, Bamforth noticed an interesting development. Technical improvements in roof control had made it possible to mine "shortwall," and the men in the pits, with the support of their union, proposed to reorganize the work process. Instead of each miner being responsible for a separate task, as was the custom, workers organized relatively autonomous groups. Small groups rotated tasks and shifts among themselves with a minimum of supervision. To take advantage of new technical opportunities, they revived a tradition of small group autonomy and responsibility dominant in the days before mechanization (Sirianni, 1995, p. 1).

Bamforth's observations helped to spur the "sociotechnical systems" movement (Rice, 1953; Trist and Bamforth, 1951), which sought to integrate structural and human resource considerations. Trist and Bamforth noted that the old method isolated individual workers and disrupted informal groupings that offered potent social support in a difficult and dangerous environment. They argued for the creation of "composite" work groups, in which individuals would be cross-trained in multiple jobs so each group could work relatively autonomously. Their approach made only modest headway in England in the 1950s but got a boost when two Tavistock researchers, Eric Trist and Fred Emery, were invited to Norway. Their ideas were welcomed, and Norway became a pioneer in work redesign.

At about the same time, in a pioneering American study, Frederick Herzberg (1966) asked employees about their best and worst work experiences. "Good feelings" stories featured achievement, recognition, responsibility, advancement, and learning; Herzberg called these motivators. "Bad feelings" stories clustered around company policy and administration, supervision, and working conditions; Herzberg labeled these hygiene factors. Motivators dealt mostly with work itself; hygiene factors bunched up around the work context. Herzberg concluded that attempts to motivate workers with better pay and fringe benefits, communications programs, or human relations training missed the point. Instead, he saw "job enrichment" as central to motivation. Enrichment meant giving workers more freedom and authority, more feedback, and greater challenges.

Hackman and his colleagues extended Herzberg's ideas by identifying three critical factors in job redesign: "Individuals need (1) to see their work as meaningful and worthwhile, more likely when jobs produce a visible and useful 'whole,' (2) to use discretion and judgment so they can feel personally accountable for results, and (3) to receive feedback about their efforts so they can improve" (Hackman et al., 1987, p. 320).

Experiments with job redesign have grown significantly in recent decades. Many efforts have been successful, some resoundingly so (Kopelman, 1985; Lawler, 1986; Yorks and Whitsett, 1989; Pfeffer, 1994; Parker and Wall, 1998; Mohr and Zoghi, 2006). Typically, job enrichment has a stronger impact on quality than on productivity. Workers find more satisfaction in doing good work than in simply working harder (Lawler, 1986). Most workers prefer redesigned jobs, although some still favor old ways. Hackman emphasized that employees with "high growth needs" would welcome job enrichment, while others with "low growth needs" would not. Organizational context also makes a difference. Job redesign produced greater benefit in situations where working conditions were poor to begin with (Morgeson et al., 2006).

Recent decades have witnessed a gradual reduction in dreary, unchallenging jobs. Routine work has been increasingly redesigned or turned over to machines, robots, and computers. But significant obstacles block the progress of job enrichment, and monotonous jobs will not soon disappear. One barrier is the lingering belief that technical imperatives make simple, repetitive work efficient and cheap. Another is the belief that workers produce more in a Theory X environment. A third barrier is economic; many jobs cannot be altered without major investments in redesigning physical plant and machinery. A fourth barrier is illustrated in the doll-manufacturing experiment: When it works, job enrichment leads to pressures for system-wide change. Workers with enriched jobs often develop higher opinions of themselves. They may demand more—sometimes increased benefits, other times career opportunities or training for new tasks (Lawler, 1986).

Foster Self-Managing Teams

From the beginning, the sociotechnical systems perspective emphasized a close connection between work design and teamwork. Another influential early advocate of teaming was

Rensis Likert, who argued in 1961 that an organization chart should depict not a hierarchy of individual jobs but a set of interconnected teams.[1] Each team would be highly effective in its own right and linked to other teams via individuals who served as "linking pins." It took decades for such ideas to take hold, but an increasing number of firms now embrace the idea. One is Whole Foods Market, the grocery chain discussed in Chapter 5. The firm cites "featured team members" on its website, and its "Declaration of Interdependence" pledges, "We Support Team Member Excellence and Happiness."

The central idea in the autonomous team approach is giving groups responsibility for a meaningful whole—a product, subassembly, or complete service—with ample autonomy and resources and with collective accountability for results. Teams meet regularly to determine work assignments, scheduling, and current production. Supervision typically rests with a team leader, who may be appointed or may emerge from the group. Levels of authority and discretion vary across situations. Some teams have authority to hire, fire, determine pay rates, specify work methods, and manage inventory. In other cases, the team's scope of decision making is narrower, focusing on issues of production, quality, and work methods.

The human resource concept of teams overlaps with the structural approach to teams (Chapter 5) but emphasizes that teams rarely work without ample training. Workers need group skills and a broader range of technical skills so that each member understands and can perform someone else's job. "Pay for skills" gives team members an incentive to keep expanding their range of competencies (Manz and Sims, 1995).

Promote Egalitarianism

Egalitarianism implies a democratic workplace where employees are an integral part of the decision-making process. This idea goes beyond participation, often viewed as a matter of style and climate rather than shared authority. Even in participative systems, managers still make key decisions. Broader, more egalitarian sharing of power is resisted worldwide (Heller, 2003). Managers have often resisted organizational democracy—the idea of building worker participation into the formal structure to protect it from management interference. Most U.S. firms report some form of employee involvement, but the approaches (such as a suggestion box or quality circle) "do not fundamentally change the level of decision-making authority extended to the lowest levels of the organization" (Ledford, 1993, p. 148). American organizations make less use of workforce involvement than evidence of effectiveness warrants (Pfeffer, 1998; Ledford, 1993).

Formal efforts to democratize the workplace are more common in some parts of Europe. Norway, for example, legally mandated worker participation in decision making in 1977 (Elden, 1983, 1986). Major corporations pioneered efforts to democratize and improve the quality of work life. Three decades later, the results of the "Norwegian model" look impressive—Norway came in at number one on the 2017 World Happiness Report (Worldhappiness.report, 2017) and is regularly at or near the top of rankings for "best country to live in," with a strong economy, broad prosperity, low unemployment, and excellent health care (Barstad, Ellingsen, and Hellevik, 2005; Garfield, 2015).

The Brazilian manufacturer Semco offers another dramatic illustration of organizational democracy in action (Killian, Perez, and Siehl, 1998; Semler, 1993). Ricardo Semler took over the company from his father in the 1980s and gradually evolved an unorthodox philosophy of management. At Semco, workers hire new employees, evaluate bosses, and vote on major decisions. In one instance, employees voted to purchase an abandoned factory that Semler didn't want and then proceeded to turn it into a big success. "In a 10-year recessionary period in Brazil, Semco's revenues still grew 600 percent, profits were up 500 percent, productivity was up 700 percent, and for the last 20+ years, employee turnover remains at an incredibly low 1–2 percent per year. They have no managers, no HR department, no written policies (just a few written beliefs) and no office hours. Everyone works in small, self-motivated, self-managed work teams who make their own decisions regarding salary, hiring, firing, and who leads the team for the next six months" (Blakeman, 2014).

Is organizational democracy worth the effort? Harrison and Freeman (2004) conclude that the answer is yes. Even if it does not produce economic gains, it produces other benefits such as reduced stress (Kalleberg, Nesheim, and Olsen, 2009). Still, many managers and union leaders oppose the idea because they fear losing prerogatives they see as essential to success. Union leaders and critical management theorists sometimes argue that democracy is a management ploy to get workers to accept gimmicks in place of gains in wages and benefits or as a wedge that might come between workers and their union.

Organizations that stop short of formal democracy can still become more egalitarian by reducing both real and symbolic status differences (Pfeffer, 1994, 1998). In most organizations, it is easy to discern an individual's place in the pecking order from such cues as office size and access to perks like limousines and corporate jets. Organizations that invest in people, by contrast, often reinforce participation and job redesign by replacing symbols of hierarchy with symbols of cooperation and equality. Semco, for example, has no organization chart, secretaries, or personal assistants. Top executives type letters and make their own photocopies. Nucor has no executive dining rooms, and the chief executive "flies commercial, manages without an executive parking space, and really does make the coffee in the office when he takes the last cup" (Byrnes and Arndt, 2006, p. 60).

Reducing symbolic differences is helpful, but reducing material disparities is important as well. A controversial issue is the pay differential between workers and management. In the 1980s, Peter Drucker suggested that no leader should earn more than 20 times the pay of the lowest-paid worker. He reasoned that outsized gaps undermine trust and devalue workers. Corporate America paid little heed. In 1980, big-company CEOs earned about 40 times as much as the average worker. By 2015, with an average annual compensation of $13.8 million, they were earning more than 200 times as much (Chamberlain, 2015). In the year it went bankrupt, Enron was a pioneer in the golden paycheck movement, handing out a total of $283 million to its five top executives (Ackman, 2002). The controversial drug company, Mylan, which came under fire in 2016 for stunning price increases on its most profitable product, the EpiPen, paid its top five managers a total of $300 million over five-year period—significantly more generous than much bigger and more profitable competitors like Johnson & Johnson and Pfizer (Maremont, 2016).

In contrast, a number of progressive companies, such as Costco, Whole Foods, and Southwest Airlines, have traditionally underpaid their CEOs by comparison with their competitors. Whole Foods Markets limits executives' pay to 19 times the average employee salary, and CEO John Mackey asked the board in 2007 to set his salary at $1/year (Gaar, 2010). It was newsworthy that Southwest's CEO received "less than $1 million in 2006 even as the carrier posted its 34th straight year of profits" (Roberts, 2007). In the same year, United Airlines, fresh out of bankruptcy, unintentionally united all five of its unions in protest against the estimated take-home pay of $39 million for its CEO (Moyers, 2007).

Promote Diversity

A good workplace is serious about treating everyone well—workers as well as executives; women as well as men; Asians, African Americans, and Hispanics as well as whites; gay as well as straight employees. Sometimes companies support diversity because they think it's the right thing to do. Others do it more grudgingly because of bad publicity, a lawsuit, or government pressure.

In 1994, Denny's Restaurants suffered a public relations disaster and paid $54 million to settle discrimination lawsuits. The bill was even higher for Shoney's, at $134 million. Both restaurant chains got religion as a result (Colvin, 1999). So did Coca-Cola, which settled a class action suit by African American employees for $192 million in November 2000 (Kahn, 2001), and Texaco, after the company's stock value dropped by half a billion dollars in the wake of a controversy over racism (Colvin, 1999).

Denny's transformation was so thorough that the company has frequently appeared on lists of best companies for minorities (Esposito et al., 2002; Daniels et al., 2004).

In the end, it makes good business sense for companies to promote diversity. If a company devalues certain groups, word tends to get out and customers become alienated. In the United States, more than half of consumers and workers are female, and about one fourth are Asian, African American, or Latino. California, New Mexico, and Texas are the first states in which non-Hispanic whites are no longer a majority—except for multiethnic Hawaii, in which whites have never been a majority. The same will eventually be true of the United States as a whole. When talent matters, it is tough to build a workforce if your business practices write off a sizable portion of potential employees. That's one reason so many public agencies in the United States have long-standing commitments to diversity. One of the most successful is the U.S. Army, as exemplified in Colin Powell's ability to rise through the ranks to head the Joint Chiefs of Staff and subsequently to become the nation's secretary of state.

In industries where talent is a vital competitive edge, private employers have moved aggressively to accommodate gay employees:

> As a high-profile supporter of gay rights, Raytheon of course provides health-care benefits to the domestic partners of its gay employees. It does a lot more, too. The company supports a wide array of gay-rights groups, including the Human Rights Campaign, the nation's largest gay-advocacy group. Its employees march under the Raytheon banner at gay-pride celebrations and AIDS walks. And it belongs to gay chambers of commerce in communities where it has big plants. Why? Because the competition to hire and retain engineers and other skilled workers is so brutal that Raytheon doesn't want to overlook anyone. To attract openly gay workers, who worry about discrimination, a company like Raytheon needs to hang out a big welcome sign. "Over the next ten years we're going to need anywhere from 30,000 to 40,000 new employees," explains Heyward Bell, Raytheon's chief diversity officer. "We can't afford to turn our back on anyone in the talent pool" (Gunther, 2006, p. 94).

Promoting diversity comes down to focus and persistence. Forward-looking organizations take it seriously and build it into day-to-day management. They tailor recruiting practices to diversify the candidate pool. They develop a variety of internal diversity initiatives, such as mentoring programs to help people learn the ropes and get ahead. They tie executive bonuses to success in diversifying the workforce. They work hard at eliminating the glass ceiling. They diversify their board of directors. They buy from minority vendors. It takes more than lip service, and it doesn't happen overnight. Many organizations still don't get the picture, but others have made impressive strides.

GETTING THERE: TRAINING AND ORGANIZATION DEVELOPMENT

Noble human resource practices are more often espoused than implemented. Why? One problem is managerial ambivalence. Progressive practices cost money and alter the relationship between superiors and subordinates. Managers are skeptical about a getting a positive return on the investment and fearful of losing control. Moreover, execution requires levels of skill and understanding that are often in short supply. Beginning as far back as the 1950s, chronic difficulties in improving life at work spurred the rise of the field of organization development (OD), an array of ideas and techniques designed to help managers convert intention to reality.

Group Interventions

Working in the 1930s and 1940s, social psychologist Kurt Lewin pioneered the idea that change efforts should emphasize the group rather than the individual (Burnes, 2006). His work was instrumental in the development of a provocative and historically influential group intervention: sensitivity training in "T-groups." The T-group (T for training) was a serendipitous discovery. At a conference on race relations in the late 1940s, participants met in groups, and researchers in each group observed and took notes. In the evening, researchers reported their observations to program staff. Participants got wind of it, and asked to be included in these evening sessions. They were fascinated to hear new and surprising things about themselves and their behavior. Researchers recognized that they had discovered something important and developed a program of "human relations laboratories." Trainers and participants joined in small groups, working together and learning from their work at the same time.

As word spread, T-groups began to supplant lectures as a way to develop human relations skills. But research indicated that T-groups were better at changing individuals than organizations (Gibb, 1975; Campbell and Dunnette, 1968), and practitioners experimented with a variety of new methods, including "conflict laboratories" for situations involving friction among organizational units and "team-building" programs to help groups work more effectively. "Future search" (Weisbord and Janoff, 1995), "open space" (Owen, 1993, 1995), and other large-group designs (Bunker and Alban, 1996, 2006) brought sizable numbers of people to work on key challenges together. Mirvis (2006, 2014) observes that even though the T-group itself may have become passé, it gave birth to an enormous range of workshops and training activities that are now a standard part of organizational life.

One famous example of a large-group intervention is the "Work-Out" conferences initiated by Jack Welch when he was CEO of General Electric. Frustrated by the slow pace of change in his organization, Welch convened a series of town hall meetings, typically with 100 to 200 employees, to identify and resolve issues "that participants thought were dumb, a waste of time, or needed to be changed" (Bunker and Alban, 1996, p. 170). Decisions had to be reached on the spot. The conferences were generally viewed as highly successful and spread throughout the company.

Survey Feedback

In the late 1940s, researchers at the University of Michigan began to develop surveys to measure patterns in organizational behavior. They focused on motivation, communication, leadership, and organizational climate (Burke, 2006). Rensis Likert helped found the Survey Research Center at the University of Michigan and produced a 1961 book, *New Patterns of Management*, that became a classic in the human resource tradition. Likert's survey data confirmed earlier research showing that "employee-centered" supervisors, who focused more on people and relationships, typically managed higher-producing units than "job-centered" supervisors, who ignored human issues, made decisions themselves, and dictated to subordinates.

The research paved the way for survey feedback as an approach to organizational improvement. The process begins with questionnaires aimed at people issues. The results are tabulated, then shared with managers. The data might show, for example, that information within a unit flows well but that decisions are made in the wrong place and employees don't feel that management listens. Members of the work unit, perhaps with the help of a consultant, discuss the results and explore how to improve effectiveness. A variant on the survey feedback model, increasingly standard in organizations, is 360-degree feedback, in which managers get survey feedback about how they are seen by subordinates, peers, and superiors.

Evolution of OD

T-groups and survey research spawned the field of organizational development (OD) in the 1950s and 1960s. Since then, OD has continued to evolve as a discipline (Burke, 2006;

Gallos, 2006; Mirvis, 1988, 2006). In 1965, few managers had heard of OD; 30 years later, few had not. Most major organizations (particularly in the United States) have experimented with OD: General Motors, the U.S. Postal Service, IBM, the Internal Revenue Service, Texas Instruments, Exxon, and the U.S. Navy have all developed their own versions.

Surveying the field in 2006, Mirvis saw significant innovation and ferment emanating from both academic visionaries and passionate "disciples" (Mirvis, 2006, p. 87). He also saw "exciting possibilities in the spread of OD to emerging markets and countries; its broader applications to peace making, social justice, and community building, and its deeper penetration into the mission of organizations" (p. 88). Returning to the same question in 2014, Mirvis found a similar answer: "[S]omething more—concepts extending beyond conventional behavioral science—has led to revolutionary advances in the practice of change in the past two decades" (Mirvis, 2014, p. 371). Among those advances, he mentions appreciative inquiry and ideas from the arts, spirituality, and chaos-and-complexity science.

CONCLUSION

When individuals find satisfaction and meaning in work, organizations profit from the effective use of their talent and energy. But when satisfaction and meaning are lacking, individuals withdraw, resist, or rebel. In the end, everyone loses. Progressive organizations implement a variety of "high-involvement" strategies for improving human resource management. Some approaches strengthen the bond between individual and organization by paying well, offering job security, promoting from within, training the workforce, and sharing the fruits of organizational success. Others empower workers and give work more significance through participation, job enrichment, teaming, egalitarianism, and diversity. No single method is likely to be effective by itself. Success typically requires a comprehensive strategy undergirded by a long-term human resource management philosophy. Ideas and practices from organization development often play a significant role in supporting the evolution of more comprehensive and effective human resource practices.

NOTE

1. Likert pronounced his last name Lick-ert.

Interpersonal and Group Dynamics

Coming together is a beginning. Keeping together is progress. Working together is success.

—Henry Ford

Anne Barreta

Anne Barreta was excited but scared when she became the first woman and the first Hispanic American ever promoted to district marketing manager at the Hillcrest Corporation. She knew she could do the job, but she expected to be under a microscope. Her boss, Steve Carter, was very supportive. Others were less enthusiastic—like the coworker who smiled as he patted her on the shoulder and said, "Congratulations! I just wish I was an affirmative action candidate."

Anne was responsible for one of two districts in the same city. Her counterpart in the other district, Harry Reynolds, was 25 years older and had been with Hillcrest 20 years longer. Some said that the term "good old boy" could have been invented to describe Harry. Usually genial, he had a temper that flared quickly when someone got in his way. Anne tried to maintain a positive and professional relationship but often found Harry to be condescending and arrogant.

Things came to a head one afternoon as Anne, Harry, and their immediate subordinates were discussing marketing plans. Anne and Harry were disagreeing politely. Mark, one of Anne's subordinates, tried to support her views, but Harry kept cutting him off. Anne saw Mark's frustration building, but she was still surprised when he angrily told Harry, "If you'd listen to anyone besides yourself and think a little before you open your mouth, we'd make a lot more progress." With barely controlled fury, Harry declared that "this meeting is adjourned" and stormed out.

(continued)

A day later, Harry phoned to demand that Anne fire Mark. Anne tried to reason with him, but Harry was adamant. Worried about the fallout, Anne talked to Steve, their mutual boss. He agreed that firing Mark was too drastic but suggested a reprimand. Anne agreed and informed Harry. He again became angry and shouted, "If you want to get along in this company, you'd better fire that guy!" Anne calmly replied that Mark reported to her. Harry's final words were, "You'll regret this!"

Three months later, Steve called Anne to a private meeting. "I just learned," he said, "that someone's been spreading a rumor that I promoted you because you and I are having an affair." Anne was stunned by a jumble of feelings—confusion, rage, surprise, shame. She groped for words, but none came.

"It's crazy, I know," Steve continued. "But the company hired a private detective to check it out. Of course, they didn't find anything. So they're dropping it. But some of the damage is already done. I can't prove it, but I'm pretty sure who's behind it."

"Harry?" Anne asked.

"Who else?"

Managers spend most of their time relating to other people—in conversations and meetings, in groups and committees, over coffee or lunch, on the phone, or on the net (Kanter, 1989b; Kotter, 1982; Mintzberg, 1973; Watson, 2000). The quality of their relationships figures prominently in how satisfied and how effective they are at work. But people bring patterns of behavior to the workplace that have roots in early life. These patterns do not change quickly or easily on the job. Thompson (1967) and others have argued that the socializing effects of family and society shape people to mesh with the workplace. Schools, for example, teach students to be punctual, complete assignments on time, and follow rules. But schools are not always fully successful, and future employees are shaped initially by family—a decentralized cottage industry that seldom produces raw materials exactly to corporate specifications.

People can become imperfect cogs in the bureaucratic machinery. They form relationships to fit individual styles and preferences, often ignoring what the organization requires. They may work but never *only* on their official assignments. They also express personal and social needs that often diverge from formal rules and requirements. A project falters, for example, because no one likes the manager's style. A committee bogs down because of interpersonal tensions that everyone notices but no one mentions. A school principal spends most days dealing with a handful of abrasive and vocal teachers who generate far more than their share of discipline problems and parent complaints. Protracted warfare arises because of personal friction between two department heads.

This chapter begins by looking at basic sources of effective (or ineffective) interpersonal relations at work. We examine why individuals are often blind to self-defeating personal actions. We describe theories of interpersonal competence and emotional intelligence, explaining how they influence office relationships. We explore different ways of understanding individual style preferences. Finally, we discuss key human-resource issues in the functioning of groups and teams: informal roles, norms, conflict, and leadership.

Greatest Hits from Organization Studies

Hit Number 6: M. S. Granovetter, "Economic Action and Social Structure: The Problem of Social Embeddedness." *American Journal of Sociology*, 1985, 91(3), 481–510

The central question in Granovetter's influential article is a very broad one: "How behavior and institutions are affected by social relations." Much of his approach is captured in a quip from James Duesenberry that "economics is all about how people make choices; sociology is all about how they don't have any choices to make" (1960, p. 233). Classical economic perspectives, Granovetter argues, assume that economic actors are atomized individuals whose decisions are little affected by their relationships with others. "In classical and neoclassical economics, therefore, the fact that actors may have social relations with one another has been treated, if at all, as a frictional drag that impedes competitive markets" (Granovetter, 1985, p. 484). Conversely, Granovetter maintains that sociological models are often "oversocialized" because they depict "processes in which actors acquire customs, habits, or norms that are followed mechanically and automatically, irrespective of their bearing on rational choice" (p. 485). The truth, in Granovetter's view, lies between these two extremes: "Actors do not behave or decide as atoms outside a social context, nor do they adhere slavishly to a script written for them by the particular intersection of social categories that they happen to occupy. Their attempts at purposive action are instead embedded in concrete, ongoing systems of social relations" (p. 487). Granovetter's argument may sound familiar, since it aligns with a central theme in our book: Actors make choices, but their choices are inevitably shaped by social context.

To illustrate his argument, Granovetter critiques another influential perspective: Oliver Williamson's analysis of why some decisions get made in organizational hierarchies and others are made in markets (Williamson, 1975, number 12 on our list of scholars' hits). Williamson proposed that repetitive decisions involving high uncertainty were more likely to be made in hierarchies because organizations had advantages of information and control—people knew and had leverage over one another. Granovetter counters that Williamson underestimates the power of relationships in cross-firm transaction and overemphasizes the advantages of hierarchy. A central

(continued)

(continued)

point in Granovetter's argument is that relationships often trump structure: "The empirical evidence that I cite shows . . . that even with complex transactions, a high level of order can often be found in the market—that is, across firm boundaries—and a correspondingly high level of disorder within the firm. Whether these occur, instead of what Williamson expects, depends on the nature of personal relations and networks of relations between and within firms" (p. 502).

INTERPERSONAL DYNAMICS

In organizations, as elsewhere in life, many of the greatest highs and lows stem from relations with other people. Three recurrent questions about relationships regularly haunt managers:

- What is really happening in this relationship?
- What motives are behind other peoples' behavior?
- What can I do about it?

All were key questions for Anne Barreta. What was happening between her and Harry Reynolds? Did he really start the rumor? If so, why? How should she deal with someone who seemed so difficult and devious? Should she talk to him? What options did she have?

To some observers, what's happening might seem obvious: Harry resents a young minority woman who has become his peer. He becomes even more bitter when she rejects his demand to fire Mark and then seeks revenge through a sneak attack. The case resembles many others in which men dominate or victimize women. What should Anne, or any woman in similar circumstances, do? Confront the larger issues? That might help in the long run, but a woman who initiates confrontation risks being branded a troublemaker (Collinson and Collinson, 1989). Should Anne try to sabotage Harry before he gets her? If she does, will she kindle a mêlée in which everyone loses?

Human resource theorists maintain that constructive personal responses are possible even in highly politicized situations. Argyris (1962), for example, emphasizes the importance of "interpersonal competence" as a basic managerial skill. He shows that managers' effectiveness is often impaired because they overcontrol, ignore feelings, and are blind to their impact on others.

Argyris and Schön's Theories for Action

Argyris and Schön (1974, 1996) carry the issue of interpersonal effectiveness a step further. They argue that individual behavior is controlled by personal theories for action—

assumptions that inform and guide behavior. Argyris and Schön distinguish two kinds of theory. *Espoused theories* are accounts individuals provide whenever they try to describe, explain, or predict their behavior. *Theories-in-use* guide what people actually do. A theory-in-use is an implicit program or set of rules that specifies how to behave.

Argyris and Schön discovered significant discrepancies between espoused theories and theories-in-use, which means that people aren't doing what they think they are. Managers typically see themselves as more rational, open, concerned for others, and democratic than others see them. Such blindness is persistent because people learn little from their experience. A major block to learning is a self-protective model of interpersonal behavior that Argyris and Schön refer to as Model I (see Exhibit 8.1).

Exhibit 8.1.
Model I Theory-in-Use.

Core Values (Governing Variables)	Action Strategies	Consequences for Behavioral World	Consequences for Learning
Define and achieve your goals.	Design and manage the environment unilaterally.	You will be seen as defensive, inconsistent, fearful, selfish.	Self-sealing (so you won't know about negative consequences of your actions).
Maximize winning, minimize losing.	Own and control whatever is relevant to your interests.	You create defensiveness in interpersonal relationships.	Single-loop learning (you don't question your core values and assumptions).
Minimize generating or expressing negative feelings.	Unilaterally protect yourself (from criticism, discomfort, vulnerability, and so on).	You reinforce defensive norms (mistrust, risk avoidance, conformity, rivalry, and so on).	You test your assumptions and beliefs privately, not publicly.
Be rational.	Unilaterally protect others from being upset or hurt (censor bad news, hold private meetings, and so on).	Key issues become undiscussable.	Unconscious collusion to protect yourself and others from learning.

Source: Adapted from Argyris and Schön (1996), p. 93.

Model I

Lurking in Model I is the core assumption that an organization is a dangerous place where you have to look out for yourself or someone else may do you in. This assumption leads individuals to follow a predictable set of steps in their attempts to influence others. We can see the progression in the exchanges between Harry and Anne:

1. *Assume that the problem is caused by the other side.* Harry seems to think that Mark and Anne cause his problems; Mark is insulting, and Anne protects him. Anne, for her part, blames Harry for being biased, unreasonable, and devious. Both are employing a basic assumption at the core of Model I: "I'm okay, you're not." So long as problems are someone else's fault, the other, not you, needs to change.

2. *Develop a private, unilateral diagnosis and solution.* Harry defines the problem and tells Anne how to solve it: fire Mark. When she declines, he apparently develops another, sneakier strategy: covertly undermine Anne.

3. *Since the other person is the cause of the problem, get that person to change.* Use one or more of three basic strategies: (1) facts, logic, and rational persuasion (tell others why you're right); (2) indirect influence (ease in, ask leading questions, manipulate the other person); or (3) direct critique (tell the other person directly what they are doing wrong and how they should change). Harry starts out logically, moves quickly to direct critique, and, if Steve's diagnosis is correct, finally resorts to subterfuge and sabotage.

4. *If the other person resists or becomes defensive, that confirms that the other person is at fault.* Anne's refusal to fire Mark presumably verifies Harry's perception of her as an ineffective troublemaker. Harry confirms Anne's perception that he's unreasonable by stubbornly insisting that firing is the only sufficient punishment for Mark.

5. *Respond to resistance through some combination of intensifying pressure and protecting or rejecting the other person.* When Anne resists, Harry intensifies the pressure. Anne tries to soothe him without firing Mark. Harry apparently concludes that Anne is impossible to deal with and that the best tactic is sabotage. He may even believe his rumor is true because, in his mind, it's the best explanation of why Anne got promoted.

6. *If your efforts are less successful than hoped, it is the other person's fault.* You need feel no personal responsibility. Harry does not succeed in getting rid of Mark or Anne. He stains Anne's reputation but damages his own in the process. Everyone is hurt. But Harry is unlikely to see the error of his ways. The incident may confirm to Harry's colleagues that he is temperamental and devious. Such perceptions will probably block Harry's promotion to a more senior position. But Harry may persist in believing that

he is right and Anne is wrong, because no one wants to confront someone as defensive and cranky as Harry.

The result of Model I assumptions is minimal learning, strained relationships, and deterioration in decision making. Organizations that rely too much on this model are rarely happy places to work.

Model II

How else can a situation like Anne's be handled? Argyris and Schön's Model II offers basic guidelines:

1. *Emphasize common goals and mutual influence.* Even in a situation as difficult as Anne's, developing shared goals is possible. Deep down, Anne and Harry both want to be successful. Neither benefits from mutual destruction. At times, each needs help and might learn and profit from the other. To emphasize common goals, Anne might ask Harry, "Do we really want an ongoing no-win battle? Wouldn't we both be better off if we worked together to develop a better outcome?"

2. *Communicate openly; publicly test assumptions and beliefs.* Model II suggests that Anne talk directly to Harry and test her assumptions. She *believes* Harry deliberately started the rumor, but she is not *certain*. She suspects Harry will lie if she confronts him, another untested assumption. Anne might say, for example, "Harry, someone started a rumor about me and Steve. Do you know anything about how that story might have been started?" The question might seem dangerous or naive, but Model II suggests that Anne has little to lose and much to gain. Even if she does not get the truth, she lets Harry know she is aware of his game and is not afraid to call him on it.

3. *Combine advocacy with inquiry.* Advocacy includes statements that communicate what an individual actually thinks, knows, wants, or feels. Inquiry seeks to learn what others think, know, want, or feel. Exhibit 8.2 presents a simple model of the relationship between advocacy and inquiry.

Model II emphasizes integration of advocacy and inquiry. It asks managers to express openly what they think and feel and to actively seek understanding of others' thoughts and feelings. Harry's demand that Anne fire Mark combines *high* advocacy with *low* inquiry. He tells her what he wants while showing no interest in her point of view. Such behavior tends to be seen as assertive at best, dominating or arrogant at worst. Anne's response is low in

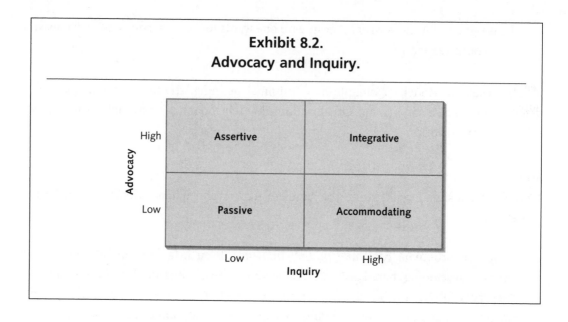

Exhibit 8.2.
Advocacy and Inquiry.

	Inquiry Low	**Inquiry High**
Advocacy High	Assertive	Integrative
Advocacy Low	Passive	Accommodating

both advocacy and inquiry. In her discomfort, she tries to get out of the meeting without making concessions. Harry might see her as unresponsive, apathetic, or weak.

Model II counsels Anne to combine advocacy and inquiry in an open dialogue. She can tell Harry what she thinks and feels while testing her assumptions and trying to learn from him. This is difficult to learn and practice. Openness carries risks, and it is hard to be effective when you are ambivalent, uncomfortable, or frightened. It gets easier as you become more confident that you can handle others' honest responses. Anne's ability to confront Harry depends a lot on her self-confidence and interpersonal skills. Beliefs can be self-fulfilling. If you tell yourself that it's too dangerous to be open and that you do not know how to deal with difficult people, you will probably be right. But tell yourself the opposite, and you may also be right.

The Perils of Self-Protection

When managers feel vulnerable, they revert to self-defense. They skirt issues or attack others and escalate games of camouflage and deception (Argyris and Schön, 1978). Feeling inadequate, they try to hide their inadequacy. To avoid detection, they pile subterfuge on top of camouflage. This generates even more uncertainty and ambiguity and makes it difficult or impossible to detect errors. As a result, an organization often persists in following a course everyone privately thinks is a path to disaster. No one wants to be the one to speak the truth. Who wants to be the messenger bearing bad news?

The result is often catastrophe, because critical information never reaches decision makers. You might think it difficult to ignore a major gap between what we're doing and what we think we're doing, but it's not, because we get so much help from others. You can see this happening in the following conversation between Susan, a cubicle-dwelling supervisor in an insurance company, and one of her subordinates, Dale. Dale has been complaining that he's underpaid and overqualified for his mail clerk job. As he regularly reminds everyone, he is a *college graduate*. Susan has summoned Dale to offer him a new position as an underwriting trainee.

What Susan is thinking:	What Susan and Dale say:
	Susan: We're creating a new trainee position and want to offer it to you. The job will carry a salary increase, but let me tell you something about the job first.
I wonder if his education makes him feel that society owes him a living without any relationship to his abilities or productivity.	*Dale:* Okay. But the salary increase has to be substantial so I can improve my standard of living. I can't afford a car. I can't even afford to go out on a date.
	Susan: You'll start as a trainee working with an experienced underwriter. It's important work, because selecting the right risks is critical to our results. You'll deal directly with our agents. How you handle them affects their willingness to place their business with us.
How can he be so opinionated when he doesn't know anything about underwriting? How's he going to come across to the people he'll have to work with? The job requires judgment and willingness to listen.	*Dale:* I'm highly educated. I can do anything I set my mind to. I could do the job of a supervisor right now. I don't see how risk selection is that difficult.
	Susan: Dale, we believe you're highly intelligent. You'll find you can learn many new skills working with an experienced underwriter. I'm sure many of the things you know today came from talented professors and teachers. Remember, one of the key elements in this job is your willingness to work closely with other people and to listen to their opinions.
That's the first positive response I've heard.	*Dale:* I'm looking for something that will move me ahead. I'd like to move into the new job as soon as possible.
	Susan: Our thought is to move you into this position immediately. We'll outline a training schedule for you. On-the-job and classroom, with testing at the end of each week.
We owe him a chance, but I doubt he'll succeed. He's got some basic problems.	*Dale:* Testing is no problem. I think you'll find I score extremely high in anything I do.

Dale is puzzled that no one seems to appreciate his talents. He has no clue that his actions continually backfire. He tries to impress Susan, but almost everything he says confirms his shortcomings and makes things worse. His constant self-promotion reinforces his public persona: opinionated, defensive, and a candidate for failure. But Dale doesn't know this because Susan doesn't tell him. At the moment that Susan is worrying that Dale will offend colleagues by not listening to them, she tells him, "We think you're intelligent." Susan has good reason to doubt Dale's ability to listen: He doesn't seem to hear her very well. If he can't listen to his boss, what's the chance he'll hear anyone else? But Susan ends the meeting still planning to move Dale into a new position in which she expects that he'll fail. She colludes in the likely disaster by skirting the topic of Dale's self-defeating behavior. In protecting herself and Dale from a potentially uncomfortable encounter, Susan helps to ensure that no one learns anything.

There's nothing unusual about the encounter between Susan and Dale—similar things happen every day in workplaces around the world. The Dales of the world dig themselves into deep holes. The Susans help them to remain oblivious as they dig. Argyris calls it "skilled incompetence"—using well-practiced skills to produce the opposite of what you intend. Dale wants Susan to recognize his talents. Instead, he strengthens her belief that he's arrogant and naive. Susan would like Dale to recognize his limitations but unintentionally reassures him that he's fine as he is.

Salovey and Mayer's Emotional Intelligence

The capacity that Argyris (1962) labeled *interpersonal competence* harked back to Thorndike's definition of *social intelligence* as "the ability to understand and manage men and women, boys and girls—to act wisely in human relations" (1920, p. 228). Salovey and Mayer (1990) updated Thorndike by coining the term *emotional intelligence* as a label for skills that include awareness of self and others and the ability to handle emotions and relationships. Salovey and Mayer discovered that individuals who scored relatively high in the ability to perceive accurately, understand, and appraise others' emotions could respond more flexibly to changes in their social environments and were better able to build supportive social networks (Cherniss, 2000; Salovey et al., 1999). In the early 1990s, Daniel Goleman popularized Salovey and Mayer's work in his best-selling book *Emotional Intelligence*.

Interpersonal skills and emotional intelligence are vital, because personal relationships are a central element of daily life. Many improvement efforts fail not because managers' intentions are incorrect or insincere but because they are unable to handle the social challenges of change. Take the case of a manufacturing organization that proudly announced its "Put Quality First" program. A young manager was assigned to chair a quality team where she worked. Excited about an opportunity to demonstrate leadership, she and her team began eagerly. But her plant manager dropped in and out of team meetings, staying long enough to dismiss any new ideas as impractical or unworkable. The team's enthusiasm quickly faded. The plant manager hoped to demonstrate accessibility and "management by walking around." No one had the courage to tell him he was killing the initiative.

Management Best Sellers

Daniel Goleman, *Emotional Intelligence* (New York: Bantam, 1995)

Daniel Goleman didn't invent the idea of emotional intelligence but he made it famous. His bestselling *Emotional Intelligence* focused more on children and education than on work, but it was still a hit with the business community. It was followed by articles in the *Harvard Business Review* and a small industry producing books, exercises, and training programs aimed at helping people improve their emotional intelligence (EI). Goleman's basic argument is that EI, rather than intellectual abilities (or intelligence quotient, IQ), accounts for most of the variance in effectiveness among managers, particularly at the senior level.

In a sequel, *Primal Leadership*, Goleman, Boyatzis, and McKee (2002) define four dimensions of emotional intelligence. Two are internal (self-awareness and self-management), and two are external (social awareness and relationship management). Self-awareness includes awareness of one's feelings and one's impact on others. Self-management includes a number of positive psychological characteristics, among them emotional self-control, authenticity, adaptability, drive for achievement, initiative, and optimism. Social awareness includes empathy (attunement to the thoughts and feelings of others), organizational awareness (sensitivity to the importance of relationships and networks), and commitment to service. The fourth characteristic, relationship management, includes inspiration, influence, developing others, catalyzing change, managing conflict, and teamwork.

Critics have two main complaints about Goleman's work: They say there's nothing new, just an updating of old ideas and common sense, and they maintain that Goleman is better at explaining why EI is important than at suggesting practical ideas for enhancing it. It is true that Goleman borrowed the EI label from Salovey and Mayer, and the idea of multiple forms of intelligence was developed earlier by Howard Gardner (1993) at Harvard and Robert J. Sternberg (1985) at Yale. The dimensions of EI in *Primal Leadership* (inspiration, teamwork, and so forth) could have been culled from the leadership literature of recent decades. But even if Goleman is offering old wine in new bottles, his work has found a large and receptive audience because of the way he has packaged and framed the issue. He has offered a way to think about the relative importance of intellectual and social skills, arguing that managers with high IQ but low EI are a danger to themselves and others. A growing body of research supports this proposition (Druskat, Sala and Mount, 2005).

MANAGEMENT STYLES

Argyris and Schön's work on theories for action and Salovey and Mayer's work on emotional intelligence emphasizes universal competencies—qualities useful to anyone. A contrasting research stream focuses on how individuals diverge in personality and behavior. A classic experiment (Lewin, Lippitt, and White, 1939) compared autocratic, democratic, and laissez-faire leadership in a study of boys' clubs. Leadership style had a powerful impact on both productivity and morale. Under autocratic leadership, the boys were productive but joyless. Laissez-faire leadership led to aimlessness and confusion. The boys strongly preferred democratic leadership, which produced a more productive and positive group climate.

Countless theories, books, workshops, and tests have been devoted to helping managers identify their own and others' personal or interpersonal styles. Are leaders introverts or extroverts? Are they friendly helpers, tough battlers, or objective thinkers? Are they higher in dominance, influence, stability, or conscientiousness? Do they behave more like parents or like children? Are they superstars concerned for both people and production, "country club" managers who indulge employees, or hard-driving taskmasters who ignore human needs and feelings (Blake and Mouton, 1969)?

In the 1980s, the Myers-Briggs Type Indicator (Myers, 1980) became (and has remained) a popular tool for examining management styles. Built on principles from Jungian psychology, the inventory assesses four dimensions: introversion versus extroversion, sensing versus intuition, thinking versus feeling, and perceiving versus judging. Based on scores on those dimensions, it categorizes an individual into one of sixteen types. The Myers-Briggs approach suggests that each style has its strengths and weaknesses and none is universally better than the rest. It also makes the case that interpersonal relationships are less confusing and frustrating if individuals understand and appreciate both their own style and those of coworkers.

One or both of the authors of this book, for example, are ENFPs (extroverted, intuitive, feeling, perceiving). ENFPs tend to be warmly enthusiastic, high-spirited, ingenious, and imaginative. But they dislike rules and bureaucracy, their desks are usually messy, and they tend to be disorganized, impatient with details, and uninterested in planning. One of us was once paired with an ISTJ (introverted, sensing, thinking, judging), who was true to her type—serious, quiet, thorough, practical, and dependable. The task was managing an educational program, but the relationship got off to a rocky start. The ISTJ arrived at meetings with a detailed agenda and a trusty notepad. Her ENFP counterpart arrived with enthusiasm and a few vague ideas. As decisions were reached, the ISTJ carefully wrote down both her assignments and his on a to-do list. Her counterpart made brief, semilegible notes on random scraps of paper. She followed through on all her tasks in a timely manner. He often lost the notes and did only the assignments that he remembered. She became distraught at his lack of organization. He got annoyed at her bureaucratic rigidity. The relationship might have collapsed had not the two discussed their respective Myers-Briggs styles and recognized that they needed one other; each brought something different but essential to the relationship and the undertaking.

A number of other measures of personality or style, in addition to the Myers-Briggs, are widely used in management development, but none is popular with academic psychologists. They prefer the "Big 5" model of personality, on the ground that it has stronger research support (Goldberg, 1992; John, 1990; Judge et al., 2002; Organ and Ryan, 1995). As its name implies, the model interprets personality in terms of five major dimensions. The labels for these dimensions vary from one author to another, but a typical list includes extroversion (displaying energy, sociability, and assertiveness), agreeableness (getting along with others), conscientiousness (a tendency to be orderly, planning oriented, and hard-working), neuroticism (difficulty in controlling negative feelings), and openness to experience (preference for creativity and new experience). For popular use, though, the Big 5 has its disadvantages. Compared with the Myers-Briggs, it conveys stronger value judgments. It is hard to argue, for example, that being disagreeable and neurotic are desirable leadership qualities. Moreover, some of the labels (such as neuroticism) make more sense to psychologists than to laypeople.

Despite the risk of turning managers into amateur psychologists, it helps to have shared language and concepts to make sense of the elusive, complex world of individual differences. When managers are blind to their own preferences and personal style, they usually need help from others to learn about it. Their friends and colleagues may be more ready to lend a hand if they have some way to talk about the issues. Tests like the Myers-Briggs provide a shared framework and language.

GROUPS AND TEAMS IN ORGANIZATIONS

Groups can be wonderful or terrible, conformist or creative, productive or stagnant. Whether paradise or wasteland, groups are indispensable in the workplace. They solve problems, make decisions, coordinate work, promote information sharing, build commitment, and negotiate disputes (Handy, 1993). As modern organizations rely less on hierarchical coordination, groups have become even more important in forms such as self-managing teams, quality circles, and virtual groups whose members are linked by technology. In Chapter 5, we discussed the structural issues that are vital to group functioning. Here we turn our attention to equally important human issues.

Groups have both assets and liabilities (Collins and Guetzkow, 1964; Hackman, 1989; McGrath, 1984; Cohen and Bailey, 1997). They have more knowledge, diversity of perspective, time, and energy than individuals working alone. Groups often improve communication and increase acceptance of decisions. On the downside, groups may overrespond to social pressure or individual domination, bog down in inefficiency, waste time, or let personal agendas smother collective purposes (Maier, 1967).

Groups operate on two levels: an overt, conscious level focused on *task* and a more implicit level of *process*, involving group maintenance and interpersonal dynamics (Bales, 1970; Bion, 1961; Leavitt, 1978; Maier, 1967; Schein, 1969). Many people see only confusion in groups. The practiced eye sees much more. Groups, like modern art, are complex and subtle. A few basic dimensions offer a map for bringing clarity and order out of apparent chaos and confusion. Our map emphasizes four human elements in group process: informal roles, informal norms, interpersonal conflict, and leadership in decision making.

Informal Roles

In groups, as in organizations, the fit between the individual and the larger system is a central human resource concern. The structural frame emphasizes the importance of formal roles, traditionally defined by a title (one's position in the hierarchy) or a formal job description. In groups and teams, individual roles are often much more informal and implicit on both task and personal dimensions. The right set of *task roles* helps get work done and makes optimal use of each member's resources. But without a corresponding set of informal roles, individuals feel frustrated and dissatisfied, which may foster unproductive or disruptive behaviors.

Parker (2008) conceptualizes four different informal roles that group members can take in order to contribute to group success. His roles align loosely with our four-frame model:

1. Contributors: task-oriented, structural-frame individuals who help a group develop plans and tactics for moving ahead on the task at hand.

2. Collaborators: big picture, more symbolic types who help a group clarify long-term directions.

3. Communicators: process-oriented, human resource–frame individuals who serve as facilitators and consensus builders.

4. Challengers: political-frame individuals who ask tough questions and push the group to take risks and achieve higher standards.

As Parker's model suggests, every work group has a range of roles that need to be filled. The roles are often fluid, evolving over time as the group moves through phases of its work. Groups do better when task roles align with characteristics of individuals, who bring different interests (some love research but hate writing), skills (some are better at writing, others are better presenters), and varying degrees of enthusiasm (some may be highly committed to the project, while others drag their feet). It is risky, for example, to assign the writing of a final report to a poor writer or to put the most nervous member on stage in front of a demanding audience.

Anyone who joins a group hopes to find a comfortable and satisfying personal role. Imagine a three-person task force. One member, Karen, is happiest when she feels influential and visible. Bob prefers to be quiet and inconspicuous. Teresa finds it hard to participate unless she feels liked and valued. In the early going in any new group, members send implicit signals about roles they prefer, usually without realizing they are doing it. In their first group meeting, Karen jumps in, takes the initiative, and pushes for her ideas. Teresa smiles, compliments other people, asks questions, and says she hopes everyone will get along. Bob mostly just watches.

If the three individuals' preferred roles dovetail, things may go well. Karen is happy to have Bob as a listener, and Bob is pleased that Karen lets him be inconspicuous. Teresa is content if she feels that Karen and Bob like her. Now suppose that Tony, who likes to be in charge, joins the group. Karen and Tony may collide—two alphas who want the same role. The prognosis looks bleaker. But suppose that another member, Susan, signs on. Susan's mission in life is to help other people get along. If Susan can help Karen feel visible, Teresa feel loved, and Tony feel powerful while Bob is left alone, everyone will be happy—and the group should be productive.

Some groups are blessed with a rich set of resources and highly compatible individuals, but many are less fortunate. They have a limited supply of talent, skill, and motivation. They have areas of both compatibility and potential conflict. The challenge is to capitalize on their assets while minimizing liabilities. Unfortunately, many groups fail to identify or discuss the hurdles they face. Avoidance often backfires. Neglected challenges come back to haunt team performance, often at the worst possible moment, when a deadline looms and everyone feels the heat.

It usually works better to deal with issues early on. A major consulting firm produced a dramatic improvement in effectiveness and morale by conducting a team-building process when new "engagement teams" formed to work on client projects. Members discussed the roles they preferred, the resources each individual brought and thoughts about how the group might operate. Initially, many skeptics viewed the team building as a waste of time with doubtful benefits. But the investment in group process at the front end more than paid for itself in effectiveness down the road.

Informal Group Norms

Every group develops informal rules to live by—norms that govern how the group functions and how members conduct themselves. We once observed two families in adjacent sites in the same campground. At first glance, both were alike: two adults, two small children, California license plates. Further observation made it clear that the families had very different unwritten rules.

Family A practiced a strong form of "do your own thing." Everyone did what he or she wanted, and no one paid much attention to anyone else. Their two-year-old wandered around the campground until he fell down a 15-foot embankment. He lay there wailing while a professor of leadership pondered the risks and rewards of intervening in someone else's family. Finally, he rescued the child and returned him to his parents, who seemed oblivious and indifferent to their son's mishap.

Family B, in contrast, was a model of interdependence and efficiency, operating like a well-oiled machine. Everything was done collectively; each member had a role. A drill sergeant would have admired the speed and precision with which they packed for departure. Even their three-year-old approached her assigned tasks with purpose and enthusiasm.

Like these two families, groups evolve informal norms for "how we operate" (The cultural implications of this idea will be elaborated in Part Five, The Symbolic Frame.) Eventually, such rules are taken for granted as a fixed social reality. The parents in Family A envied Family B. They were plainly puzzled as they asked, "How did they ever get those kids to help out like that? *Our* kids would never do that!"

Google, like most contemporary organizations, depends a lot on teams, so much so that they started a research project to try to find the secret sauce that made some teams work better than others (Duhigg, 2016). Google studied research by Wooley et al. (2010), which found that teams have a kind of collective IQ—some teams do better than others across a range of different tasks. Team IQ was not related to the intelligence of individual members nor to intuitively plausible factors like cohesion or satisfaction. But more effective groups had higher sensitivity—members were better at reading one another's feelings. They were also more egalitarian—no one dominated, and everyone got a turn. The study also found that the more women on a team the better, maybe because women tend to have higher social sensitivity.

The Google team connected this work to Edmondson's (1999) study of psychological safety: "a shared belief held by members of a team that the team is safe for interpersonal risk-taking." Teams with more psychological safety learned better, and teams that learned better performed better. The Google researchers concluded that teams would perform better if they developed norms of shared participation, emotional attunement, and psychological safety (Duhigg, 2016).

With norms, as with roles, early intervention helps. Do we want to be task oriented, no nonsense, and get on with the job? Or would we prefer to be more relaxed and playful? Do we insist on full attendance at every meeting, or should we be more flexible? Must people be unerringly punctual, or would that cramp our style? If individuals miss a deadline, do we stone them or gently encourage them to do better? Do we prize boisterous debate or courtesy and restraint? Groups develop norms to answer such questions.

Informal Networks in Groups

Like informal norms, informal networks—patterns of who relates to whom—help to shape groups. *Remember the Titans*, a feel-good Hollywood film, tells a story of two football teams whose black and white players were suddenly thrust together as a result of school desegregation. Their coach took them off-site for a week of team building where black and white players roomed together and soon developed bonds. Those relationships became a critical feature of the team's ability to win a state championship.

The Titans, like any team, can be viewed as an informal social network—a series of connections that link members to one another. When the team was first formed, it consisted of two different networks separated by suspicion and antagonism across racial boundaries. The coach intuitively understood something that research has confirmed—informal bonds among members make a big difference. Teams with more informal ties are more effective and more likely to stay together than teams in which members have fewer connections (Balkundi and Harrison, 2006).

Interpersonal Conflict in Groups

Many of the worst horror stories about group life center on personal conflict. Interpersonal strife can block progress and waste time. It can make things unpleasant at best, painful at worst. Some groups experience little conflict, but most encounter predictable differences in goals, perceptions, preferences, and beliefs. The larger and more diverse the group, the greater the likelihood of conflict.

A subtle but powerful source of conflict in groups is two distinct levels of cognition (Healey, Vuori, and Hodgkinson, 2015). One level is conscious and verbal and is reflected in the conversations that members have about what the group is here to do and how it should go about doing it. Another is an unconscious level of "hot" cognition—emotionally charged attitudes, goals, and stereotypes that operate outside of awareness. Conflict between those two levels of cognition can occur both within and between individuals but is hard to recognize and decode because unconscious processes are at work. A team might agree, for example, that "we'll share leadership and work collaboratively." But suppose that one member has an unconscious goal of being in charge, and another member holds unconscious stereotypes that lead him or her to doubt the capabilities of certain teammates. Both might do things that seem to violate the group's verbal contract while believing that they are just trying to help move things along. They may be puzzled and feel misunderstood if anyone questions their actions.

How can a group cope with interpersonal conflict? The Model I manager typically relies on two strategies: "pour oil on troubled waters" and "might makes right." As a result, things usually get worse instead of better. The oil-on-troubled-waters strategy views conflict as something to avoid: minimize it, deny it exists, smooth it over, bury it, or circumvent it. Suppose, for example, that Tony in our hypothetical group says that the group needs a leader, and Karen counters that a leader would selfishly dominate the group. Teresa, dreading conflict, might try to bypass it by saying, "I think we're all basically saying the same thing" or "We can talk about leadership later; right now, why don't we find out a little more about each other?"

Smoothing tactics may work if the issue is temporary or peripheral. In such cases, conflict may disappear on its own, much to everyone's relief. But conflict suppressed early in a group's life tends to resurface later—again and again. If smoothing tactics fail and conflict persists, another option is might-makes-right. If Tony senses conflict between Karen and himself, he may employ Model I thinking: Because we disagree, and I am right, she is the problem; I need to get her to shape up. Tony may try any of several strategies to change Karen. He may try to convince her he's right. He may push others in the group to side with him and put pressure on Karen. He may subtly, or not so subtly, criticize or attack her. If Karen thinks she is right and Tony is the problem, the two are headed for a collision that may be painful for everyone.

If Model I is a costly approach to conflict, what else might a group do? Here are some guidelines that often prove helpful.

Develop skills. More organizations are recognizing that group effectiveness depends on members' ability to understand what is happening and contribute effectively. Skills like listening, communicating, managing conflict, and building consensus are critical building blocks in a high-performing group.

Agree on the basics. Groups too often plunge ahead without taking the time to agree on goals and procedures. Down the road, people continue to stumble over unresolved issues.

Shared understanding and commitment around the basics are a powerful glue to hold things together in the face of the inevitable stress of group life.

Express conflict productively. Weingart et al. (2015) argue that how conflict is expressed makes a big difference in whether it turns productive or destructive. They focus on two dimensions of conflict expression. One is directness. "I think your statement is wrong" is direct. "Maybe," is indirect. The other dimension is "intensity of opposition" (Weingart et al., 2015, p. 235). Intensity is high when people become entrenched and start attacking each other. An example: "No way you can change my mind, because your idea is stupid." Low intensity of opposition is expressed through indications of interest in dialogue and willingness to be influenced. For example: "We disagree, but I'd like to understand your thinking better." Weingart et al. suggest that groups handle conflict best when they express it directly but minimize oppositional intensity. In other words, they are tough and direct on substance but gentle on one another.

Search for common interests. How does a group reach agreement if it starts out divided? It helps to keep asking, "What do we have in common? If we disagree on the issue at hand, how can we put it in a more inclusive framework where we can all agree?" If Tony and Karen clash on the need for a leader, where do they agree? Perhaps both want to do the task well. Recognizing commonalities makes it easier to confront differences. It also helps to remember that common ground is often rooted in complementary differences (Lax and Sebenius, 1986). Karen's desire to be visible is compatible with Bob's preference to be in the background. Conversely, similarity (as when Karen and Tony both want to lead) is often a source of conflict.

Experiment. If Tony is sure the group needs a leader (namely, him) and Karen is equally convinced it does not, the group could bog down in endless debate. Susan, the group's social specialist, might propose an experiment: Because Karen sees it one way and Tony sees it another, could we try one meeting with a leader and one without to see what happens? Experiments can be a powerful response to conflict. They offer a way to move beyond stalemate without forcing either party to lose face or admit defeat. Parties may agree on a test even if they can't agree on anything else. Equally important, they may learn something that moves the conversation to a more productive plane.

Doubt your infallibility. This was the advice that Benjamin Franklin offered his fellow delegates to the U.S. constitutional convention in 1787: "Having lived long, I have experienced many instances of being obliged by better information, or fuller consideration, to change opinions even on important subjects, which I once thought right, but found to be otherwise. It is therefore that the older I grow, the more apt I am to doubt my own judgment, and to pay more respect to the judgment of others" (Rossiter, 1966).

Groups typically possess diverse resources, ideas, and outlooks. A group that sees diversity as an asset and a source of learning has a good chance for a productive discussion and resolution of differences. Conflict can be a good thing—conflict about ideas promotes effectiveness, even though personal conflict gets in the way (Cohen and Bailey, 1997). In the heat of the moment, though, a five-person group can easily turn into five teachers in search of a learner or a lynch mob in search of a victim. At such times, it helps if at least one person asks, "Are we all sure we're infallible? Are we really hearing one another?"

Treat differences as a group responsibility. If Tony and Karen are on a collision course, it is tempting for others to stand aside. But all will suffer if the team fails. The debate between Karen and Tony reflects personal feelings and preferences but also addresses leadership as an issue of shared importance.

Leadership and Decision Making in Groups

A final problem that every group must resolve is the question of navigation: "How will we set a course and steer the ship, particularly in stormy weather?" Groups often get lost. Meetings are punctuated with statements like "I'm not sure where we're going" or "Does anyone know what we're talking about?"

Leadership helps groups develop a shared sense of direction and commitment. Otherwise, a group becomes rudderless or moves in directions that no one supports. Noting that teams are capable of very good and very bad performance, Hackman emphasizes that a key function of leadership is setting a compelling direction for the team's work that "is challenging, energizes team members and generates strong collective motivation to perform well" (2002, p. 72). Another key function of leadership in groups, as in organizations, is managing relationships with external constituents. Druskat and Wheeler found that effective leaders of self-managing teams "move back and forth across boundaries to build relationships, scout necessary information, persuade their teams and outside constituents to support one another, and empower their teams to achieve success" (2003, p. 435).

Still a third key leadership function is helping the group manage time. Maruping et al. (2015) found that time pressure hurts team performance when it is badly managed and leads to last-minute chaos and panic. But time pressure improves performance when leadership helps the group organize to deal with it through "scheduling of interim milestones, synchronization of tasks, and restructuring of priorities. These efforts result in higher team performance" (Maruping et al., 2015, p. 2014).

Though leadership is essential, it need not come from only one person. A single leader focuses responsibility and clarifies accountability. But the same individual may not be equally effective for all tasks and circumstances. Groups sometimes do better with a shared and fluid approach, regularly asking, "Who can best take charge in *this* situation?" Katzenbach and Smith (1993) discovered that a key characteristic of high-performance teams was mutual accountability, fostered when leaders were willing to step back and team members were prepared to share the leadership.

Leadership, whether shared or individual, plays a critical role in group effectiveness and individual satisfaction. Leaders who overcontrol or understructure tend to produce frustration and ineffectiveness (Maier, 1967). Good leaders are sensitive to both task and process. They enlist others actively in managing both. Effective leaders help group members communicate, work together, and do what they are there to do. Less-effective leaders try to dominate and get their own ideas accepted.

CONCLUSION

Employees hire on to do a job but always bring social and personal baggage with them. At work, they spend much of their time interacting with others, one to one and in groups. Both individual satisfaction and organizational effectiveness depend heavily on the quality of interpersonal relationships and team dynamics.

Individuals' social skills are a critical element in the effectiveness of relationships at work. Interpersonal dynamics are counterproductive as often as not. People frequently employ theories-in-use (behavioral programs) that emphasize self-protection and the control of others. Argyris and Schön developed an alternative model built on values of mutuality and learning. Salovey and Mayer, as well as Goleman, underscore the importance of emotional intelligence—social skills that include awareness of self and others and the ability to handle emotions and relationships.

Small groups are often condemned for wasting time while producing little, but groups *can* be both satisfying and efficient. In any event, organizations cannot function without them. Managers need to understand that groups always operate at two levels: task and process. Both levels need to be considered if groups are to be effective. Among the significant process issues that groups have to manage are informal roles, group norms, interpersonal conflict, and leadership.

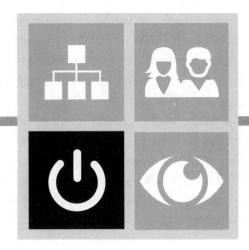

PART FOUR

The Political Frame

When you ponder the word *politics*, what images come to mind? Are any of them positive or helpful? For many people, the answer is no. Around the globe, politics and politicians are widely despised and viewed as an unavoidable evil. In organizations, phrases like "they're playing politics" or "it was all political" are invariably terms of disapproval.

Similar attitudes surround the idea of *power*, a concept that is central in political thinking. In her last interview, only days before she was assassinated in December 2007, Benazir Bhutto was asked whether she liked power. Her response captured the mixed feelings many of us harbor: "Power has made me suffer too much. In reality I'm ambivalent about it. It interests me because it makes it possible to change things. But it's left me with a bitter taste" (Lagarde, 2008, p. 13).

A jaundiced view of politics constitutes a serious threat to individual and organizational effectiveness. Viewed from the political frame, politics is the realistic process of making decisions and allocating resources in a context of scarcity and divergent interests. This view puts politics at the heart of decision making.

We introduce the elements of the political frame in Chapter 9. We begin by examining the dynamics lurking behind the tragic losses of the space shuttles *Columbia* and *Challenger*. We also lay out the perspective's key assumptions and discuss basic issues of power, conflict, and ethics.

In Chapter 10, we look at the constructive side of politics. The chapter is organized around basic skills of the effective organizational politician: setting agendas, mapping the political terrain, networking, building coalitions, and negotiating. We also offer four principles of moral judgment to guide in dealing with ethically slippery political issues.

Chapter 11 moves from the individual to the organization. We look at organizations as both arenas for political contests and active political players or actors. As arenas, organizations play an important role in shaping the rules of the game. As players or actors, organizations are powerful tools for achieving the agenda of whoever controls them. We close with a discussion of the relative power of organizations and society. Will giant corporations take over the world? Or will other institutions channel and constrain their actions?

Power, Conflict, and Coalition

*Politics [is] a strife of interests masquerading
as a contest of principles.*

—Ambrose Bierce

Early in the morning of February 1, 2003, the U.S. space shuttle *Columbia* was returning to earth from a smooth and successful mission. Suddenly something went terribly wrong. The crew was flooded with emergency signals—the noise of alarms and the glare of indicator lights signaling massive system failure. The craft tumbled out of control and was finally blown apart. Cabin and crew were destroyed (Wald and Schwartz, 2003a, 2003b).

After months of investigation, a blue-ribbon commission concluded that *Columbia*'s loss resulted as much from organizational as technical failures. Breakdowns included: "the original compromises that were required to gain approval for the shuttle, subsequent years of resource-constraints, fluctuating priorities, schedule pressures, mischaracterization of the shuttle as operational rather than developmental, and lack of an agreed national vision for human space flight" (*Columbia* Accident Investigation Board, 2003, p. 9).

In short, politics brought down the shuttle. It all sounded sadly familiar, and the investigation board emphasized that there were many "echoes" of the loss of the space shuttle *Challenger* 17 years earlier. Then, too, Congressional committees and a distinguished panel had spent months studying what happened and developing recommendations to keep it from happening again. But as the *Columbia* board said bluntly: "The causes of the institutional failure responsible for *Challenger* have not been fixed" (*Columbia* Accident Investigation Board, 2003, p. 195).

Flash back to 1986. After a series of delays, *Challenger* was set to launch on January 28. At sunrise, it was clear but very cold at Cape Canaveral, Florida. The weather was more like New Hampshire, where Christa McAuliffe was a high school teacher. Curtains of ice greeted ground crews as they inspected the shuttle. The temperature had plunged overnight to a record low of 24 degrees Fahrenheit (–4 degrees Celsius). Temperatures gradually warmed, but it was still brisk at 8:30 AM. *Challenger's* crew of seven astronauts noted the ice as they climbed into the capsule. As McAuliffe, the first teacher to venture into space, entered the ship, a technician offered her an apple. She beamed and asked him to save it until she returned. At 11:38 AM, *Challenger* lifted off. A minute later, there was a massive explosion in the booster rockets. Millions watched their television screens in horror as the shuttle and its crew were destroyed.

On the eve of the launch, an emergency teleconference had been called between NASA and the Morton Thiokol Corporation, the contractor for the shuttle's solid-fuel rocket motor. During the teleconference, Thiokol engineers pleaded with superiors and NASA to delay the launch. They feared cold temperatures would cause a failure in synthetic rubber O-rings sealing the rocket motor's joints. If the rings failed, the motor could blow up. The problem was simple and familiar: Rubber loses elasticity at cold temperatures. Freeze a rubber ball and it won't bounce; freeze an O-ring and it might not seal. Engineers recommended strongly that NASA wait for warmer weather. They tried to produce a persuasive engineering rationale, but their report was hastily thrown together, and the data seemed equivocal (Vaughan, 1995). Meanwhile, Thiokol and NASA both faced strong pressure to get the shuttle in the air:

> Thiokol had gained the lucrative sole source contract for the solid rocket boosters thirteen years earlier, during a bitterly disputed award process. Some veteran observers called it a low point in squalid political intrigue. At the time of the award, a relatively small Thiokol Chemical Company in Brigham City, Utah, had considerable political clout. Both the newly appointed chairman of the Senate Aeronautics and Space Science Committee, Democratic Senator Frank Moss, and the new NASA administrator, Dr. James Fletcher, were insiders in the tightly knit Utah political hierarchy. By summer 1985, however, Thiokol's monopoly was under attack, and the corporation's executives were reluctant to risk their billion-dollar contract by halting shuttle flight operations long enough to correct flaws in the booster joint design (McConnell, 1987, p. 7).

Meanwhile, NASA managers were experiencing their own political pressures. As part of the effort to build congressional support for the space program, NASA had promised that the shuttle would eventually pay for itself in cargo fees, like a boxcar in space. Projections of profitability were based on an ambitious plan: 12 flights in 1984, 14 in 1985, and 17 in 1986. NASA had fallen well behind schedule—only five launches in 1984 and eight in 1985. The promise of "routine access to space" and self-supporting flights looked more and more dubious. With every flight costing taxpayers about $100 million, NASA needed a lot of cash from Congress, but prospects were not bright. NASA's credibility was eroding as the U.S. budget deficit soared.

Such was the highly charged context in which Thiokol's engineers recommended canceling the next morning's launch. The response from NASA officials was swift and pointed. One NASA manager said he was "appalled" at the proposal, and another said, "My God, Thiokol, when do you want me to launch? Next April?" (McConnell, 1987, p. 196). Senior managers at Thiokol huddled and decided, against the advice of engineers, to recommend the launch. NASA accepted the recommendation and launched Flight 51-L the next morning. The O-rings failed almost immediately, and the flight was destroyed (Bell and Esch, 1987; Jensen, 1995; McConnell, 1987; Marx et al., 1987; Vaughan, 1990, 1995).

It is deeply disturbing to see political agendas corrupting technical decisions, particularly when lives are at stake. We might be tempted to explain *Challenger* by blaming individual selfishness and questionable motives. But such explanations are little help in understanding what really happened or in avoiding a future catastrophe. Individual errors typically occur downstream from powerful forces channeling decision makers over a precipice no one sees until too late. With *Columbia* and *Challenger*, key decision makers were experienced, highly trained, and intelligent. If we tried to get better people, where would we find them? Even if we could, how could we ensure that parochial interests and political gaming would not ensnare them? The *Columbia* investigating board recognized this reality, concluding, "NASA's problems cannot be solved simply by retirements, resignations, or transferring personnel" (*Columbia* Accident Investigation Board, 2003, p. 195).

Both *Columbia* and *Challenger* were extraordinary tragedies, but they illustrate political dynamics that are everyday features of organizational life. The political frame does not blame politics on individual foibles such as selfishness, myopia, or incompetence. Instead, it proposes that interdependence, divergent interests, scarcity, and power relations inevitably spawn political activity. It is naive and romantic to hope organizational politics can be eliminated, regardless of individual players. Managers can, however, learn to acknowledge, understand, and manage political dynamics, rather than shy away from them. In government, politics is a way of life rather than dirty pool. Chris Matthews calls it hardball: "Hardball is clean, aggressive Machiavellian politics. It is the discipline of gaining and holding power, useful to any profession or undertaking, but practiced most openly and unashamedly in the world of public affairs" (1999, p. 13).

This chapter seeks to explain why political processes are universal, why they won't go away, and how they can be handled adroitly. We first describe the political frame's basic assumptions and explain how they work. Next, we depict organizations as freewheeling coalitions rather than as formal hierarchies. Coalitions are tools for exercising power, and we contrast power with authority and highlight tensions between authorities (who try to keep things under control) and partisans (who try to influence a system to get what they want). We also delineate multiple sources of power. Because conflict is normal among members of a coalition, we underscore the role it plays across organizations. Finally, we discuss an issue at the heart of organizational politics: Do political dynamics inevitably undermine moral principles and ethics?

POLITICAL ASSUMPTIONS

The political frame views organizations as roiling arenas, hosting ongoing contests arising from individual and group interests. Five propositions summarize the perspective:

- Organizations are coalitions of different individuals and interest groups.
- Coalition members have enduring differences in values, beliefs, information, interests, and perceptions of reality.
- Most important decisions involve allocating scarce resources—deciding who gets what.
- Scarce resources and enduring differences put conflict at the center of day-to-day dynamics and make power the most important asset.
- Goals and decisions emerge from bargaining and negotiation among competing stakeholders jockeying for their own interests.

Political Propositions and the *Challenger*

All five propositions of the political frame came into play in the *Challenger* incident:

Organizations are coalitions. NASA did not run the space shuttle program in isolation. The agency was part of a complex coalition of contractors, Congress, the White House, the military, the media—even the American public. Consider, for example, why Christa

McAuliffe was aboard. Her expertise as a teacher was not critical to the mission. But the American public was getting bored with white male pilots in space. Moreover, as a teacher, McAuliffe represented a national commitment to universal education. Human interest was good for NASA and Congress; it built public support for the space program. McAuliffe's participation was a media magnet because it was a great human-interest story. Symbolically, Christa McAuliffe represented all Americans; everyone flew with her.

Coalition members have enduring differences. NASA's hunger for funding competed with the public's interest in lower taxes. Astronauts' concerns about safety were at odds with pressures on NASA and its contractors to maintain an ambitious flight schedule.

Important decisions involve allocating scarce resources. Time and money were both in short supply. Delay carried a high price—not just in dollars but also in further erosion of support from key constituents. On the eve of the *Challenger* launch, key officials at NASA and Morton Thiokol struggled to balance these conflicting pressures. Everyone from President Ronald Reagan to the average citizen was clamoring for the first teacher to fly in space. No one wanted to tell the audience the show was off.

Scarce resources and enduring differences make conflict central and power the most important asset. The teleconference on the eve of the launch began as a debate between the contractor and NASA. As sole customer, NASA was in the driver's seat. When managers at Morton Thiokol sensed NASA's level of disappointment and frustration, the scene shifted to a tense standoff between engineers and managers. Managers relied on their authority to override the engineers' technical expertise and recommended the launch.

Goals and decisions emerge from bargaining, negotiation, and jockeying for position among competing stakeholders. Political bargaining and powerful allies had propelled Morton Thiokol into the rocket motor business. Thiokol's engineers had been attempting to focus management's attention on the booster joint problem for many months. But management feared that acknowledging a problem, in addition to costing time and money, would erode the company's credibility. A large and profitable contract was at stake.

Implications of the Political Propositions

The assumptions of the political frame explain that organizations are inevitably political. A coalition forms because its members need each other, even though their interests may only partly overlap. The assumption of enduring differences implies that political activity is more visible and dominant under conditions of diversity than of homogeneity. Agreement and harmony are easier to achieve when everyone shares similar values, beliefs, and cultural ways.

The concept of scarce resources suggests that politics will be more salient and intense in difficult times. Schools and colleges, for example, have lived through alternating eras of feast and famine related to peaks and valleys in economic and demographic trends. When money and students are plentiful (as they were in the 1960s and again in the 1990s), administrators spend time designing new buildings and initiating innovative programs. Work is fun when you're delivering good news and constituents applaud. Conversely, when resources dry up, you may have to shutter buildings, close programs, and lay off staff. Conflict mushrooms, and administrators often succumb to political forces they struggle to understand and control.

Differences and scarce resources make power a key resource. Power in organizations is basically the capacity to make things happen. Pfeffer defines power as "the potential ability to influence behavior, to change the course of events, to overcome resistance, and to get people to do things they would not otherwise do" (1992, p. 30). Social scientists often emphasize a tight linkage between power and dependency: If A has something B wants, A has leverage. In much of organizational life, individuals and groups are interdependent; they need things from one another, and power relationships are multidirectional. From the view of the political frame, power is a "daily mechanism of our social existence" (Crozier and Friedberg, 1977, p. 32).

The final proposition of the political frame emphasizes that goals are not set by edict at the top but evolve through an ongoing process of negotiation and bargaining. Few organizations have a unitary apex. Who, for example, is at the head of a public company? The CEO? This is the structural view, but the CEO reports to the board. The board, in turn, is elected by and accountable to shareholders. And the shareholders are typically a large and scattered group of absentee owners. They have little time, interest, or capacity to influence the organization in which each has a sliver of ownership. But if a corporate raider or a hedge fund acquires a major ownership stake, the stage is set for a contest for control of the company.

This political view of organization might seem strange in light of traditional assumptions of control from the top. Yet the same dynamics of conflict, coalitions, and power are found at every level of human affairs. Mann (1986, 2013) tells us that's how society works. Society is not a cohesive unit but is "constituted of multiple, overlapping and intersecting networks of power" (1986, p. 1). David Eagleman says that the same is true of the human brain. He presents data from psychology and neuroscience to show that almost all of our mental activity takes place outside awareness. Here's what he says is going on politically inside your brain: "Small groups are constantly making decisions and sending out messages to other groups. Out of these local interactions, emerge larger coalitions. By the time you read a mental headline, the important action has already transpired, the deals are done. You have surprisingly little access to what happened behind the scenes. Entire political movements gain ground-up support and become unstoppable movements before you ever catch wind of them as a feeling or intuition or thought that strikes you. You're the last one on the chain of command to hear the information" (Eagleman, 2011, p. 6).

Multiple constituents jockey for influence at every level, from the individual brain to global society. This is especially apparent in the public sector. When Xi Jinping came to power as head of China's Communist Party in November 2012, his first public speech made no mention of Marx or Mao but emphasized the need to solve the problem of "corruption [and] being out of touch with the people" (Demick, 2012). Xi understood that corruption represented a potentially fatal threat to the party's continued dominance. But the party elite he hoped to influence included more than 80 billionaires (Anderlini, 2013; van Kerckhove, 2013), perhaps the largest concentration of wealth the world has ever seen.

Those superrich included both successful entrepreneurs and members of the so-called black collar class, Communist officials whose sway over business created opportunities to trade power for cash. Xi knew that something had to be done about rampant corruption, but he was up against formidable opposition from party and government officials who were in no hurry to change a system that was making them and their families rich. When Xi launched a new austerity campaign in 2013, ordering the elite to cut back on lavish banquets and similar luxuries, a new catchphrase became popular in Chinese officialdom, "Eat quietly, take gently and play secretly" (Jacobs, 2013).

The challenges Xi faced in fighting corruption mirrored those that had hindered China's efforts for more than a decade to protect intellectual property. When it joined the World Trade Organization in 2001, the Chinese government promised to get serious about protecting intellectual property, ensuring that products carrying brands such as Coca-Cola, Microsoft, Sony, and Rolex were authentic. The central government passed laws, threw the book at the occasional unlucky offender, blustered in the media, and put pressure on local governments. Yet 15 years later, name-brand knockoffs and pirated music continued to be sold all over China and Western tourists in Beijing still encountered a steady stream of vendors offering "Rolex" watches at amazing prices (Powell, 2007).

Why have the antipiracy efforts had limited impact? The Chinese government is far from monolithic and is only one of many players in a complex power game. Newly affluent Chinese consumers want foreign brands. Businesses understand that a homemade carbonated fluid can fetch a better price if it carries an American brand name. The problem has been so widespread that Coca-Cola's Chinese affiliate found itself not only raiding factories but also chasing pirates who slapped Coke labels on bottles in delivery trucks while on route to retail outlets.

Pirates are often local businesses with plenty of *guanxi* (connections) who share the loot with local government and police officials. As one *New York Times* reporter discovered when he was imprisoned for several hours in a toy factory, "Factory bosses can overrule the police, and Chinese government officials are not as powerful as you might suspect" (Barboza, 2007, p. 4–3). Moreover, the concept of intellectual property rights is new to many Chinese. They find it hard to see the merit of punishing a hard-working Chinese entrepreneur in order to protect a foreign corporation. In short, multiple power centers and continuing divisions have limited officials' ability to translate intention into action.

ORGANIZATIONS AS COALITIONS

Academics and managers alike have usually assumed that organizations have, or ought to have, clear and consistent goals set at the top. In a business, the owners or top managers set goals such as growth and profitability. Goals in a government agency are presumably set by the legislature and elected executives. The political frame challenges such views. Cyert and March articulate the difference between structural and political views of goals:

> To what extent is it arbitrary, in conventional accounting, that we call wage payments "costs" and dividend payments "profit" rather than the other way around? Why is it that in our quasigenetic moments we are inclined to say that in the beginning there was a manager, and he recruited workers and capital? . . . The emphasis on the asymmetry has seriously confused the understanding of organizational goals. The confusion arises because ultimately it makes only slightly more sense to say that the goal of a business enterprise is to maximize profit than to say that its goal is to maximize the salary of Sam Smith, assistant to the janitor (1963, p. 30).

Cyert and March are saying something like this: Sam Smith, the assistant janitor; Jim Ford, the foreman; and Celestine Cohen-Peters, the company president are all members of a grand coalition, Cohen-Peters Enterprises. All make demands on resources and bargain to get what they care about. Cohen-Peters has more authority than Jones or Ford and, in case of disagreement, she will often win—but not always. Her influence depends on how much power she mobilizes in comparison with that of Smith, Ford, and other members of the coalition. Xerox had a close brush with bankruptcy in 2001 under a CEO who had come from the outside and never mastered the politics at the top of the organization. The firm was adrift, and the captain lost control of his ship. His successor, Anne Mulcahy, was a canny insider who built the relationships and alliances she needed to get Xerox back on course.

If political pressures on goals are visible in the private sector, they are blatant in the public arena. As in the *Challenger* incident, public agencies operate amid a welter of constituencies, each making demands and trying to get its way. The result is a confusing multiplicity of goals, many in conflict. Consider Gazprom, Russia's biggest company and the world's largest producer of natural gas. Gazprom supplies most of the natural gas in Eastern Europe and 25 percent or more in France, Germany, and Italy. It began as a state ministry under Mikhail Gorbachev, became a public stock company under Boris Yeltsin, and then turned semipublic under Vladimir Putin, with the Russian government the majority stockholder.

Many observers felt that Gazprom functioned as an extension of government policy. Prices for gas exports seemed to correlate with how friendly a government was to Moscow. "If people take us for the state, that doesn't make us unhappy," said Sergey Kouprianov, a company spokesman. "We identify with the state" (Pasquier and Chevelkina, 2007, p. 43). Russian President Vladimir Putin returned the sentiment. Gazprom produced a quarter of Russia's government revenues, and Putin saw hydrocarbons substituting for the Red Army as a lever to project Russian power. At the same time, Russian consumers got their gas at about 20 percent of market price. When the company tried for a domestic price increase in 2006, it was blocked by a government that was thinking ahead to the next presidential election. Was this giant in business to benefit customers, management, stockholders, the Kremlin, or Russian citizens? All of the above and more, because all were participants in the grand and messy Gazprom coalition.

Greatest Hits from Organization Studies

Hit Number 3: Richard M. Cyert and James G. March, *A Behavioral Theory of the Firm* (Upper Saddle River, NJ: Prentice Hall, 1963)

Coming in at number three on the scholars' lists of greatest hits is a 40-year-old book by an economist, Richard Cyert, and a political scientist, James G. March. Cyert and March defined their basic purpose as developing a predictive theory of organizational decision making rooted in a realistic understanding of how decisions actually get made. They rejected as unrealistic the traditional economic view of a firm as a unitary entity (a corporate "person") with a singular goal of maximizing profits. Cyert and March chose instead to view organizations as coalitions made up of individuals and subcoalitions. This view implied a central idea of the political frame: goals

(continued)

(continued)

emerge out of a bargaining process among coalition members. Cyert and March also insisted that "side payments" are critical, because preferences are only partly compatible and decisions rarely satisfy everyone. A coalition can survive only if it offers sufficient inducements to keep essential members on board. This is not easy, because resources—money, time, information, and decision-making capacity—are limited.

In analyzing decision making, Cyert and March developed four "relational concepts," implicit rules that firms use to make decisions more manageable:

1. *Quasiresolution of conflict.* Instead of resolving conflict, organizations break problems into pieces and farm pieces out to different units. Units make locally rational decisions (for example, marketers do what they think is best for marketing). Decisions are never fully consistent but need only be aligned well enough to keep the coalition functioning.
2. *Uncertainty avoidance.* Organizations employ a range of simplifying mechanisms—such as standard operating procedures, traditions, and contracts—that enable them to act as if the environment is more predictable than it is.
3. *Problemistic search.* Organizations look for solutions in the neighborhood of the presenting problem and grab the first acceptable solution.
4. *Organizational learning.* Over time, organizations evolve their goals and aspiration levels, altering what they attend to and what they ignore, and changing search rules.

POWER AND DECISION MAKING

At every level in organizations, alliances form because members have interests in common and believe they can do more together than apart. To accomplish their aims, they need power. Power can be viewed from multiple perspectives. Structural theorists typically emphasize authority, the legitimate prerogative to make binding decisions. In this view, managers make rational decisions (optimal and consistent with purpose), monitor to ensure that decisions are implemented, and assess how well subordinates carry out directives. In contrast, human resource theorists place less emphasis on power and more on empowerment (Bennis and Nanus, 1985; Block, 1987). More than structuralists, they emphasize limits of authority and tend to focus on influence that enhances mutuality and collaboration. The implicit hope is that participation, openness, and collaboration substitute for sheer power.

The political frame views authority as only one among many forms of power. It recognizes the importance of individual (and group) needs but emphasizes that scarce resources and incompatible preferences cause needs to collide. Politically, the issue is how competing groups articulate preferences and mobilize power to get what they want. Power, in this view, is not evil: "We have to stop describing power always in negative terms: [as in] it excludes, it represses. In fact, power produces; it produces reality" (Foucault, 1975, p. 12).

Authorities and Partisans

Gamson (1968) describes the relationship between two antagonists—partisans and authorities—that are often central to the politics of both organizations and society. By virtue of the office they hold, authorities are entitled to make decisions binding on their subordinates. Any member of the coalition who wants to exert bottom-up pressure is a potential partisan. Gamson describes the relationship in this way: "Authorities are the recipients or targets of influence, and the agents or initiators of social control. Potential partisans have the opposite roles—as agents or initiators of influence, and targets or recipients of social control" (p. 76).

In a family, parents function as authorities and children as partisans. Parents make binding decisions about bedtime, television viewing, or which child uses a particular toy. Parents initiate social control, and children are the recipients of parental decisions. Children in turn try to influence the decision makers. They argue for a later bedtime or point out the injustice of giving one child something another wants. They try to split authorities by lobbying one parent after the other has refused. They may form a coalition (with siblings, grandparents, and so on) in an attempt to strengthen their bargaining position.

Authority is essential to anyone in a formal position because social control depends on it. Officeholders can exert control only so long as partisans respect or fear them enough that their authority or power remains intact. If partisans are convinced that existing authorities are too evil or incompetent to continue, they will risk trying to wrest control—unless they regard the authorities as too formidable. Conversely, if partisans trust authority and see it as legitimate, they will accept and support it in the event of an attack (Gamson, 1968; Baldridge, 1971). In almost any instance of unrest or revolution, there is a sharp cleavage between rebels and loyalists.

If partisan opposition becomes too powerful, authority systems may collapse. The process can be very swift, as illustrated by events in Eastern Europe in 1989 and the Arab Spring of 2011–2013. In both cases, established regimes had lost legitimacy years earlier but held on through coercion and control of access to decision making. When massive demonstrations erupted, authorities faced an unnerving choice: activate the police and army in the hope of preserving power or watch their authority fade away. Authorities in China and Romania in 1989, Libya in 2011, and Egypt and Syria in 2012, chose the first course. It led to bloodshed in every case, but only the Chinese were able to quash their opposition quickly. Elsewhere, authorities' attempts to quell dissent with force were futile, and their legitimacy evaporated.

The period of evaporation is typically heady but always hazardous. When the old regime collapses, the question is whether new authority can reconstitute itself quickly enough to avoid chaos. Authorities and partisans both have reason to fear a specter such as Bosnia and Liberia in the 1990s, Somalia for the last 25 years, Iraq in the aftermath of U.S. intervention or Syria since the Arab Spring of 2011. All are tragic examples of chronic turmoil and misery, with no authority strong enough to bring partisan strife under control.

Sources of Power

Authorities and partisans both have many potential sources of power. A number of social scientists (Baldridge, 1971; French and Raven, 1959; Kanter, 1977; Mann, 1986; Pfeffer, 1981, 1992; Russ, 1994) have tried to identify the various wellsprings of power. The list includes:

- *Position power (authority).* Positions confer certain levels of legitimate authority. Professors assign grades; judges settle disputes. Positions also place incumbents in more or less powerful locations in communications and power networks. It is as helpful to be in the right unit as it is to hold the right job. A lofty title in a backwater department may not carry much weight, but junior members of a powerful unit may have substantial clout (Pfeffer, 1992).

- *Control of rewards.* The ability to deliver jobs, money, political support, or other rewards brings power. Political bosses and tribal chiefs, among others, cement their power base by delivering services and jobs to loyal supporters (Mihalopoulos and Kimberly, 2006).

- *Coercive power.* Coercive power rests on the ability to constrain, block, interfere, or punish. A union's ability to walk out, students' capacity to sit in, and an army's ability to clamp down exemplify coercive power. A chilling example is the rise of suicide attacks in recent decades from about three a year worldwide in the 1980s to about one a day in 2016 (Chicago Project on Security and Terrorism, 2016). They were only about 3 percent of terror incidents but accounted for almost half the fatalities (Pape, 2006, p. 4).

- *Information and expertise.* Power flows to those with the information and know-how to solve important problems. It flows to marketing experts in consumer products industries, to the faculty in elite universities, and to political consultants who help politicians get elected.

- *Reputation.* Reputation builds on expertise. In almost any field, people develop records of accomplishment based on their prior performance. Opportunities and influence flow to people with strong reputations, like the Hollywood superstars whose presence in a film sells tickets. Boivie, Graffin, and Gentry (2016) found that the reputation of the analyst, the CEO, and the firm all influenced how a firm's stock price changed in response to a buy or sell recommendation from a Wall Street analyst.

- *Alliances and networks.* Getting things done in an organization involves working through a complex network of individuals and groups. Friends and allies make things a lot easier. Kotter (1982) found that a key difference between more and less successful senior managers was attentiveness to building and cultivating ties with friends and allies. Managers who spent too little time building networks had much more difficulty getting things done.

- *Access and control of agendas.* Organizations and political systems typically give some individuals and groups more access than others to decision arenas. When decisions are made, the interests of those with "a seat at the table" are well represented, while the concerns of absentees are often distorted or ignored (Lukes, 1974; Brown, 1986). Access often comes at a price. Shani and Westphal (2016) found that journalists who wrote negative stories about a firm's leadership soon found that CEOs from other firms stopped taking their calls. Because the journalists needed access to do their jobs, they tilted toward more flattering articles about corporate leaders.

- *Framing.* Control of meaning and symbols is what Mann (1986, 2013) refers to as ideological power. "Establishing the framework within which issues will be viewed and decided is often tantamount to determining the result" (Pfeffer, 1992, p. 203). Elites and opinion leaders often have substantial ability to shape meaning and articulate myths that express identity, beliefs, and values. Viewed positively, this fosters meaning and hope. Viewed cynically, elites can convince others to accept and support things not in their best interests (Brown, 1986; Lakoff, 2004). Lakoff argued that Republican electoral success in 2000 and 2004 owed much to skill in framing issues—recasting, for example, the "estate tax" (which sounds like a tax on the rich) into the "death tax" (which sounds like adding insult to injury).

- *Personal power.* Individuals who are attractive and socially adept—because of charisma, energy, stamina, political smarts, gift of gab, vision, or other characteristics—are imbued with power independent of other sources. French and Raven (1959) used the term *referent power* to describe influence that comes when people like you or want to be like you. John Kennedy and Ronald Reagan expanded their influence because they brought levels of charm, humor, and ease that Jimmy Carter and George W. Bush lacked.

A significant form of personal power is skill in the application of influence tactics. After reviewing research on persuasion, Cialdini (2008, 2016) developed a list of six techniques that skilled practitioners use to influence others, often without the targets realizing how they have been hooked:

1. *Reciprocation:* If I do something for you (send you a card, give you a small gift, or make some effort on your behalf), you're likely to feel you should do something for me as well.

2. *Commitment and consistency:* If I can get you to take a small step in my direction (maybe getting you to agree that you see at least some positive features in the product or idea I'm selling), I can leverage your desire to be consistent and to live up to your commitments.

3. *Social proof:* If I offer evidence that everyone (at least everyone you like) is doing it, you're more likely to do it as well. (Bars and cafes often salt the tip jar with cash to cue you that tipping is what people do. Sport and film stars might have no more product knowledge than you do, but you may still want the shoes they wear or the cosmetic they use.)

4. *Liking:* The more you like me (perhaps because I tell you how much I like you, or how well you'll do on this task, or how much we have in common), the better the chance you'll do what I ask.

5. *Authority:* If the boss, or someone with a badge or a fancy title, asks you to do it, you probably will.

6. *Scarcity:* We put a higher value on something that is scarce or about to become unavailable. (If I can convince you that the price is going up, there are only a few items left, what you want is very rare, or this is your last chance, you're more likely to buy.)

Partisans' multiple sources of power are always a constraint on authorities' capacity to make binding decisions. Officeholders who rely solely on position power generate resistance and get outflanked, outmaneuvered, or overrun by others more versatile in exercising multiple forms of power. Kotter (1985) argues that managerial jobs come with a built-in "power gap" because position power is rarely enough to get the job done. Expertise, rewards, coercion, allies, access, reputation, framing, and personal power help close the gap.

Power can be volatile, rising and falling with changes in circumstances. An organization that sets new profit records each year is rarely besieged by complaints and demands for change. As many corporate leaders have learned, however, the first bad quarter triggers a stream of calls and letters from board members, stockholders, and financial analysts. In the boom of the late 1990s, "everyone" was getting rich in the stock market, and charismatic CEOs such as Jack Welch of General Electric and Jean-Marie Messier of France's Vivendi became popular heroes. But when the economy, the market, and the image of business crashed in the first years of the new century, so did these heroic images. In 2002, Welch found himself deeply embarrassed by public revelation of the generous postretirement payouts his old company was bestowing on him. In the same year, Messier was booted out by board members dissatisfied with the company's stock price and his arrogant "American" leadership style.

Clark Kerr once remarked ruefully that his primary tasks as chancellor of the University of California at Berkeley seemed to be providing "sex for the students, parking for the faculty, and football for the alumni." The remark was half-facetious, but it reflects an important grain of truth: A president's power lies particularly in *zones of indifference*—areas only a few people care much about. The zone of indifference can expand or contract markedly, depending on how an organization is performing in the eyes of its major constituents. In the late 1960s, many college presidents lost their jobs because they were blamed for student unrest. Among them was Kerr, who remarked that he left the job just as he entered it, "fired with enthusiasm." Managers need to track shifting boundaries of zones of indifference so as not to blunder into decisions that stir up unanticipated firestorms of criticism and resistance.

Distribution of Power: Overbounded and Underbounded Systems

Organizations and societies differ markedly in how power is distributed. Alderfer (1979) and Brown (1983) distinguish between overbounded and underbounded systems. In an *overbounded system*, power is highly concentrated and everything is tightly regulated. In an *underbounded system*, power is diffuse and the system is very loosely controlled. An overbounded system regulates politics with a firm hand; an underbounded system encourages conflict and power games.

If power is highly regulated, political activity is often forced under wraps. Before the emergence of Mikhail Gorbachev and glasnost ("openness") in the 1980s, it was common for Westerners to view the Soviets as a vast, amorphous mass of like-minded people, brainwashed by decades of government propaganda. It was not true, but even so-called experts on Soviet affairs misread the underlying reality (Alterman, 1989). Ethnic, political, philosophical, and religious differences simmered quietly underground so long as the Kremlin maintained a tightly regulated society. Glasnost took the lid off, leading to an outpouring of debate and dissent that rapidly caused the collapse of the old order in the Soviet Union and throughout Eastern Europe. Almost overnight, much of Eastern Europe went from overbounded to underbounded. Most nations in Eastern Europe have since evolved into stable democracies, but many other countries have been less fortunate.

The war in Iraq, beginning in 2003, brought down the overbounded Saddam Hussein regime and created a power vacuum that attracted a host of contenders vying for supremacy. By 2006, Iraq had the formal elements of a new government, including a constitution and an elected parliament, but Iraq has struggled ever since to bring conflict and chaos under control. The Arab Spring, which began with unrest in Tunisia in 2010, brought unrest and revolt to many countries in the Middle East and North Africa, including Libya, Egypt, Syria, Bahrain, and Yemen. Fear of a similar fate drives the leaders of China's ruling Communist party to mount an ongoing, massive effort to stem the tides of criticism and dissent welling up from China's more than 700 million Internet users.

CONFLICT IN ORGANIZATIONS

The political frame stresses that the combination of scarce resources and divergent interests produces conflict as surely as night follows day. Conflict is not something that can or should be stamped out. Other frames view conflict differently. The structural frame, in particular, views conflict as an impediment to effectiveness. Hierarchical conflict raises the possibility that lower levels will ignore or subvert management directives. Conflict among major partisan groups can undermine leadership's ability to function. Such dangers are precisely why the structural perspective finds virtue in a well-defined, authoritative chain of command, and why those in authority so often work to keep conflict under control.

From a political perspective, conflict is not necessarily a problem or a sign that something is amiss. Organizational resources are in short supply; there is rarely enough to give everyone everything they want. Individuals compete for jobs, titles, and prestige. Departments compete for resources and power. Interest groups vie for policy concessions. If one group controls the policy process, others may be frozen out. Conflict is normal and inevitable. It's a natural byproduct of collective life.

The political prism puts more emphasis on strategy and tactics than on resolution of conflict. Conflict has benefits as well as costs: "a tranquil, harmonious organization may very well be an apathetic, uncreative, stagnant, inflexible, and unresponsive organization. Conflict challenges the status quo [and] stimulates interest and curiosity. It is the root of personal and social change, creativity, and innovation. Conflict encourages new ideas and approaches to problems, stimulating innovation" (Heffron, 1989, p. 185).

An organization can experience too much or too little conflict (Brown, 1983; Heffron, 1989; Jehn, 1995). Leaders may need to tamp down or stoke up the intensity, depending on the situation (Heifetz and Linsky, 2002). More important than the amount of conflict is how it is managed. Poorly managed conflict leads to infighting and destructive power struggles like those in the *Challenger* and *Columbia* cases. Well-handled conflict, on the other hand, can stimulate creativity and innovation that make an organization a livelier, more adaptive, and more effective place (Kotter, 1985).

Conflict is particularly likely to occur at boundaries, or interfaces, between groups and units. Horizontal conflict occurs in the boundary between departments or divisions; vertical conflict occurs at the border between levels. Cultural conflict crops up between groups with differing values, traditions, beliefs, and lifestyles. Cultural quarrels in the larger society often seep into the workplace, generating tension around gender, ethnic, racial, and other differences.

But organizations also house their own value disputes. The world of management is different from that of frontline employees. Workers who move up the ladder sometimes struggle with elusive adjustments required by their new role. A classic article described foremen as both "master and victim of doubletalk" (Roethlisberger, 1945) because of the pressures they felt from above to side with management, and from below to think and talk like a worker.

The management challenge is to recognize and manage interface conflict. Like other forms, it can be productive or debilitating. One of the most important tasks of unit managers or union representatives is to be a persuasive advocate for their group on a political field with many players representing competing interests. They need negotiation skills to develop alliances and cement deals that enable their group to move forward "without physical or psychological bloodshed and with wisdom as well as grace" (Peck, 1998, p. 71).

MORAL MAZES: THE POLITICS OF GETTING AHEAD

Does a world of power, self-interest, conflict, and political games inevitably develop into a dog-eat-dog jungle in which the strong devour the weak and selfishness trumps everything else? Is an unregulated organization invariably a nasty, brutish place where values and ethics are irrelevant? The corporate ethics scandals of recent years reinforced a recurrent suspicion that the morals of the marketplace amount to no morals at all.

Jackall (1988) views the corporation as a world of cabals and alliances, dominance and submission, conflict and self-interest, and "moral mazes." He suggests that "wise and ambitious managers resist the lulling platitudes of unity, though they invoke them with fervor, and look for the inevitable clash of interests beneath the bouncy, cheerful surface of corporate life" (p. 37). Moving up the ladder inevitably involves competition for the scarce resource of status. The favored myth is that free and fair competition ensures that, at least in the long run, better performers win.

But assessing performance in managerial work is fraught with ambiguity. There are multiple criteria, some of which can be assessed only through subjective judgment by the boss and others. It is often hard to separate individual performance from group performance or a host of other factors, including good or bad luck. It may make a difference who is judging. Did Thiokol engineers who fought to stop the launch of *Challenger* deserve high grades for their persistence and integrity or low grades because they did not do a better job of persuading their bosses? When some of those same engineers went public with their criticism, were they demonstrating courage or disloyalty? Whistleblowers are regularly lauded by the press yet pilloried or banished by employers. This is exemplified by *Time* magazine's 2002 Person of the Year award, given to three women who blew the whistle on their employers: Enron, WorldCom, and the FBI. By the time they received the award, all had moved on from workplaces that viewed them more as traitors than as exemplars of courage and integrity.

Managers frequently learn that getting ahead is a matter of personal "credibility," which comes from doing what is socially and politically correct. Definitions of political correctness reflect tacit forms of power deeply embedded in organizational patterns and structure (Frost, 1986). Because getting ahead and making it to the top dominate the attention of many managers (Dalton, 1959; Jackall, 1988; Ritti and Funkhouser, 1982), both organizations and individuals need to develop constructive and positive ways to engage in the political game. The question is not whether organizations will have politics but rather what kind of politics they will have.

Jackall's view is bleak:

> Bureaucracy breaks apart the ownership of property from its control, social independence from occupation, substance from appearances, action from responsibility, obligation from guilt, language from meaning, and notions of truth from reality. Most important, and at the bottom of all these fractures, it breaks apart the traditional connection between the meaning of work and salvation. In the bureaucratic world, one's success, one's sign of election, no longer depends on an inscrutable God, but on the capriciousness of one's superiors and the market; and one achieves economic salvation to the extent that one pleases and submits to new gods, that is, one's bosses and the exigencies of an impersonal market (1988, pp. 191–192).

This is not a pretty picture, but it captures the experience of many managers. Productive politics is a possible alternative, although hard to achieve. In the next chapter, we explore ways that a manager can become a constructive politician.

CONCLUSION

Traditional views see organizations as created and controlled by legitimate authorities who set goals, design structure, hire and manage employees, and ensure pursuit of the right objectives.

The political view frames a different world. Organizations are coalitions composed of individuals and groups with enduring differences who live in a world of scarce resources. That puts power and conflict at the center of organizational decision making.

Authorities have position power, but they must vie with many other contenders for other forms of leverage. Different contenders bring distinct beliefs, values, and interests. They seek access to various forms of power and compete for their share of scarce resources in a finite organizational pie.

From a political perspective, goals, structure, and policies emerge from an ongoing process of bargaining and negotiation among major interest groups. Sometimes legitimate authorities are the dominant members of the coalition, as is often true in small, owner-managed organizations. Large corporations are often controlled by senior management rather than by stockholders or the board of directors. Government agencies may be controlled more by the permanent civil servants than by the political leaders at the top. The dominant group in a school district may be the teachers' union instead of the school board or the superintendent. In such cases, rationalists recoil because they see the wrong people setting the agenda. But the political view suggests that exercising power is a natural part of ongoing contests. Those who get and use power to their advantage will be winners.

There is no guarantee that those who gain power will use it wisely or justly. But power and politics are not inevitably demeaning and destructive. Constructive politics is a possibility—indeed, a necessary option if we are to create institutions and societies that are both just and efficient.

The Manager as Politician

*Nobody made a greater mistake than he who did nothing
because he could do only a little.*

—Edmund Burke

Born to a wealthy but unorthodox family, Aruna Roy decided early in life
that her mission was to do something for India's poor. After getting a
master's degree from the University of Delhi, she became one of the few
women who passed the national test to join India's elite civil service. Thrilled
at first, she gradually became disillusioned with the rigid, top-down Indian
bureaucracy and concluded she could do more out of government.

She joined a nonprofit her husband had founded in a poor rural village. It was not an
easy transition. She had to walk miles to get there, the village lacked electricity and running
water, and the women she hoped to work with were initially suspicious. But Roy persisted,
adapted to village life, made friends, and worked on issues of incomes and children's
education. Through several years of travel and discussion, she came to a clearer sense of
what rural women needed and built a support network of individuals and agencies willing to
help on her goal of systemic change.

Roy then took another, even more radical step. She recruited a few allies who shared her
vision, and together they moved into a two-room hut in a remote village. They began by
building relationships, listening, learning, and looking for opportunities. One came when
they helped a nearby village reclaim 1,500 acres previously misappropriated by a well-
connected landowner. Over time, Roy and her group built a support base. In May, 1990,

they were able to bring a thousand people together to form a new organization, Mazdoor Kisan Shakti Sangathan (MKSS), or Worker and Peasant Empowerment Union.

As they continued to press for better village conditions, they realized that money intended for workers' pay or village improvements was often disappearing. On the rare occasions that they could get access to government records, they found that officials were generating reams of falsified documents to hide corruption. Roy and her allies began a campaign for more government transparency and drew support from the middle class as well as the poor—both suffered when money to repair roads or put a roof on the local school disappeared into someone's pocket. Roy and her allies began to hold public hearings, with little more than a tent and an open mike for people to voice grievances. The government tried to shut down the hearings, which only intensified support for the campaign. Trade unions got on board, national media covered the story, and approximately 400 organizations joined the cause. It took years of hard work, but in 2005 India enacted the National Right to Information Act (Krishnamurthy and Winston, 2010). Aruna Roy's ability to mobilize power, assemble coalitions, and champion a noble cause paid off.

It may not be obvious that political skill is as vital in business as in community organizing, but a case from Microsoft provides an example. Bill Gates and his tiny software business got their big break in the early 1980s when they obtained the contract to supply an operating system, DOS, for IBM's new line of personal computers. IBM PC's and clones soon dominated the PC business, and Microsoft began a meteoric rise.

Ten years later, everyone knew that DOS was obsolete and woefully deficient. The replacement was supposed to be OS/2, a new operating system developed jointly by Microsoft and IBM, but it was a tense partnership. IBMers saw "Microsofties" as undisciplined adolescents. Microsoft folks moaned that "Big Blue" was a hopelessly bureaucratic producer of "poor code, poor design, and poor process" (Manes and Andrews, 1994, p. 425). Increasingly pessimistic about the viability of OS/2, Gates decided to hedge his bets by developing his own new operating system to be called Windows NT. Gates recruited the brilliant but crotchety Dave Cutler from Digital Equipment to head the effort.

Gates recognized that Cutler was known "more for his code than his charm" (Zachary, 1993, p. A1). Things started well, but Cutler insisted on keeping his team small and wanted no responsibility beyond the "kernel" of the operating system. He figured someone else could worry about details like the user interface. Gates began to see a potential disaster looming, but issuing orders to the temperamental Cutler was as promising as telling Picasso how to paint. So Gates put the calm, understated Paul Maritz on the case. Born in South Africa, Maritz had studied mathematics and economics in Cape Town before deciding that software was his destiny. He joined Microsoft in 1986 and became the leader of its OS/2 effort. When he was assigned informal oversight of Windows NT, he got a frosty welcome:

> As he began meeting regularly with Cutler on NT matters, Maritz often found himself the victim of slights. Once Maritz innocently suggested to Cutler that "We should—" Cutler interrupted, "We! Who's we? You mean you and the mouse in your pocket?" Maritz brushed off such retorts, even finding humor in Cutler's apparently inexhaustible supply of epithets. He refused to allow Cutler to draw him into a brawl. Instead, he hoped Cutler would "volunteer" for greater responsibility as the shortcomings of the status quo became more apparent (Zachary, 1994, p. 76).

Maritz enticed Cutler with tempting challenges. In early 1990, he asked Cutler if he could put together a demonstration of NT for COMDEX, the industry's biggest trade show. Cutler took the bait. Maritz knew that the effort would expose NT's weaknesses (Zachary, 1994). When Gates subsequently seethed that NT was too late, too big, and too slow, Maritz scrambled to "filter that stuff from Dave" (p. 208). Maritz's patience eventually paid off when he was promoted to head all operating systems development:

> The promotion gave Maritz formal and actual authority over Cutler and the entire NT project. Still, he avoided confrontations, preferring to wait until Cutler came to see the benefits of Maritz's views. Increasingly Cutler and his inner circle viewed Maritz as a powerhouse, not an empty suit. "He's critical to the project," said [one of Cutler's most loyal lieutenants]. "He got into it a little bit at a time. Slowly he blended his way in until it was obvious who was running the show. Him" (Zachary, 1994, p. 204).

Chapter 9's account of the *Columbia* and *Challenger* cases drives home a chilling lesson about political pressures sidetracking momentous decisions. The implosion of firms such as Enron, WorldCom, and Portugal's oldest bank, Banco Espírito Santo, shows how the unfettered pursuit of self-interest by powerful executives can bring even a huge corporation to its knees. Many believe that the antidote is to get politics out of management. But this is unrealistic. Enduring differences lead to multiple interpretations of what's true and what's important. Scarce resources trigger contests about who gets what. Interdependence means that people cannot ignore one another; they need each other's assistance, support, and resources. Under such conditions, efforts to eliminate politics are futile and counterproductive. Aruna Roy's passion and persistence and Paul Maritz's deft combination of patience and diplomacy offer hope—positive examples of the manager as constructive politician.

Kotter (1985) contends that too many managers are either naive or cynical about organizational politics. Pollyannas view the world through rose-colored glasses, assuming that most people are good, kind, and trustworthy. Cynics believe the opposite: Everyone is selfish, things are always cutthroat, and "get them before they get you" is the best survival tactic. Brown and Hesketh (2004) documented parallel stances among college job seekers. The naive "purists" believed hiring was fair and they'd be rewarded on their merits if they presented themselves honestly. The more cynical "players" gamed the system and tried to present themselves as whatever they thought employers wanted. In Kotter's view, neither extreme is realistic or effective: "Organizational excellence . . . demands a sophisticated type of social skill: a leadership skill that can mobilize people and accomplish important objectives despite dozens of obstacles; a skill that can pull people together for meaningful purposes despite the thousands of forces that push us apart; a skill that can keep our corporations and public institutions from descending into a mediocrity characterized by bureaucratic infighting, parochial politics, and vicious power struggles" (p. 11).

In a world of chronic scarcity, diversity, and conflict, the nimble manager walks a tightrope: developing a direction, building a base of support, and cobbling together working relations with both allies and opponents. In this chapter, we discuss why this is vital and then lay out the basic skills of the manager as politician. Finally, we tackle ethical issues, the soft underbelly of organizational politics. Is it possible to play politics and still do the right thing? We discuss four instrumental values to guide ethical choice.

POLITICAL SKILLS

The manager as politician exercises four key skills: agenda-setting (Kanter, 1983; Kotter, 1988; Pfeffer, 1992; Smith, 1988), mapping the political terrain (DeLuca, 1999; Pfeffer, 1992; Pichault, 1993), networking and building coalitions (Brass and Krackhardt, 2012; Burt, 1992; DeLuca, 1999; Kanter, 1983; Kotter, 1982, 1985, 1988; Kurchner-Hawkins and Miller, 2006; Pfeffer, 1992; Smith, 1988), and bargaining and negotiating (Bellow and Moulton, 1978; Fisher and Ury, 1981; Lax and Sebenius, 1986).

Agenda Setting

Structurally, an agenda outlines a goal and a schedule of activities. Politically, an agenda is a statement of interests and a scenario for getting the goods. In reflecting on his experience as a university president, Warren Bennis arrived at a deceptively simple observation: "It struck me that I was most effective when I knew what I wanted" (1989, p. 20). Kanter's study of internal entrepreneurs in American corporations (1983), Kotter's analysis of effective corporate leaders (1988), and Smith's examination of effective U.S. presidents (1988) all reached a similar conclusion: Regardless of the role you're in, the first step in effective political leadership is setting an agenda.

The effective leader creates an "agenda for change" with two major elements: a vision balancing the long-term interests of key parties, and a strategy for achieving the vision while recognizing competing internal and external forces (Kotter, 1988). Aruna Roy always knew she wanted to do something for the poor, but she had to live and work with them over time to develop an agenda rooted in their needs and concerns. Her effectiveness increased dramatically when she seized on information transparency. The agenda must convey direction while addressing concerns of major stakeholders. Kanter (1983) and Pfeffer (1992) underscore the intimate tie between gathering information and developing a vision. Pfeffer's list of key political attributes includes "sensitivity"—knowing how others think and what they care about so that your agenda responds to their concerns: "Many people think of politicians as arm-twisters, and that is, in part, true. But in order to be a successful arm-twister, one needs to know which arm to twist, and how" (p. 172).

Kanter adds: "While gathering information, entrepreneurs can also be 'planting seeds'—leaving the kernel of an idea behind and letting it germinate and blossom so that it begins to float around the system from many sources other than the innovator" (1983, p. 218). Paul Maritz did just that. Ignoring Dave Cutler's barbs and insults, he focused on getting information, building relationships, and formulating an agenda. He quickly concluded that the NT project was in disarray and that Cutler had to take on more responsibility. Maritz's strategy was attuned to his quarry: "He protected Cutler from undue criticism and resisted the urge to reform him. [He] kept the peace by exacting from Cutler no ritual expressions of obedience" (Zachary, 1994, pp. 281–282).

A vision without a strategy remains an illusion. A strategy has to recognize major forces working for and against the agenda. Smith's point about U.S. presidents captures the importance of focus for managers at every level:

> The paramount task and power of the president is to articulate the national purpose: to fix the nation's agenda. Of all the big games at the summit of American politics, the agenda game must be won first. The effectiveness of the presidency and the capacity of any president to lead depend on focusing the nation's political attention and its energies on two or three top priorities. From

the standpoint of history, the flow of events seems to have immutable logic, but political reality is inherently chaotic: it contains no automatic agenda. Order must be imposed (1988, p. 333).

Agendas never come neatly packaged. The bigger the job, the harder it is to wade through the clutter and find order amid chaos. Contrary to Woody Allen's dictum, success requires more than just showing up. High office, even if the incumbent enjoys great personal popularity, is no guarantee. In his first year as president, Ronald Reagan was remarkably successful following a classic strategy for winning the agenda game: "First impressions are critical. In the agenda game, a swift beginning is crucial for a new president to establish himself as leader—to show the nation that he will make a difference in people's lives. The first 100 days are the vital test; in those weeks, the political community and the public measure a new president—to see whether he is active, dominant, sure, purposeful" (Smith, 1988, p. 334).

Reagan began with a vision but without a strategy. He was not a gifted manager or strategist, despite extraordinary ability to portray complex issues in broad, symbolic brushstrokes. Reagan's staff painstakingly studied the first 100 days of four predecessors. They concluded that it was essential to move with speed and focus. Pushing competing issues aside, they focused on two: cutting taxes and reducing the federal budget. They also discovered a secret weapon in David Stockman, the one person in the Reagan White House who understood the federal budget process. "Stockman got a jump on everyone else for two reasons: he had an agenda and a legislative blueprint already prepared, and he understood the real levers of power. Two terms as a Michigan congressman plus a network of key Republican and Democratic connections had taught Stockman how to play the power game" (Smith, 1988, p. 351). Reagan and his advisers had the vision; Stockman provided strategic direction.

Mapping the Political Terrain

It is foolhardy to plunge into a minefield without knowing where explosives are buried, yet managers unwittingly do it all the time. They launch a new initiative with little or no effort to scout and master the political turf. Pichault (1993) suggests four steps for developing a political map:

1. Determine channels of informal communication.
2. Identify principal agents of political influence.
3. Analyze possibilities for mobilizing internal and external players.
4. Anticipate counterstrategies that others are likely to employ.

Pichault offers an example of planned change in a large government agency in Belgium. The agency wanted to replace antiquated manual records with a fully automated paperless computer network. Proponents of the new system had little understanding of how work got done. Nor did they anticipate the interests and power of key middle managers and frontline bureaucrats. It seemed obvious to the techies that better data meant higher efficiency. In reality, frontline bureaucrats made little use of the data. They applied standard procedures in 90 percent of cases and asked their bosses what to do about the rest. They checked with supervisors partly to get the "right" answer but even more to get political cover. Because they saw no need for the new technology, street-level bureaucrats had incentives to ignore or work around it. After a consultant clarified the political map, a new battle erupted between unrepentant techies, who insisted their solution was correct, and senior managers who argued for a less ambitious approach. The two sides ultimately compromised.

A simple way to develop a political map for any situation is to create a two-dimensional diagram mapping players (who is in the game), power (how much clout each player is likely to exercise), and interests (what each player wants). Exhibits 10.1 and 10.2 present two hypothetical versions of the Belgian bureaucracy's political map. Exhibit 10.1 shows the map as the techies saw it. They expected little opposition and assumed they held the high cards; their map implied a quick and easy win. Exhibit 10.2, a more objective map, paints a very

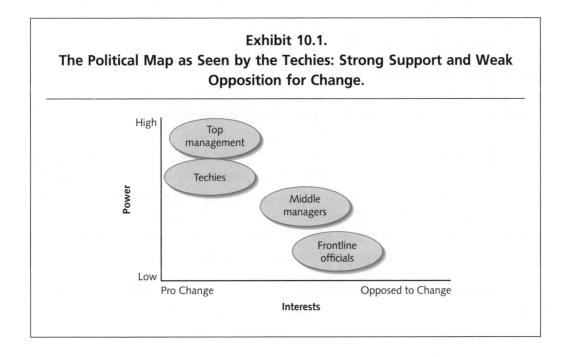

Exhibit 10.1.
The Political Map as Seen by the Techies: Strong Support and Weak Opposition for Change.

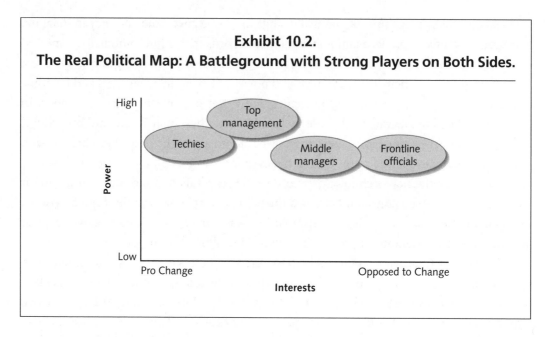

Exhibit 10.2.
The Real Political Map: A Battleground with Strong Players on Both Sides.

different picture. Resistance is more intense and opponents more powerful. This view forecasts a stormy process with protracted conflict. Though less comforting, the second map has an important message: Success requires substantial effort to realign the political force field. The third and fourth key skills of the manager as politician, discussed in the next two sections, respond to that challenge.

Networking and Building Coalitions

Managers often fail to get things done because they rely too much on reason and too little on relationships. In both the *Challenger* and *Columbia* space shuttle catastrophes (discussed in Chapter 9), engineers pitched careful, data-based arguments to their superiors about potentially lethal safety risks—and failed to dent their bosses' resistance (Glanz and Schwartz, 2003; Vaughan, 1995). Six months before the *Challenger* accident, for example, an engineer at Morton Thiokol wrote to management: "The result [of an O-ring failure] would be a catastrophe of the highest order—loss of human life" (Bell and Esch, 1987, p. 45). A memo, if it is clear and powerful, may work, but is often a sign of political innocence. Kotter (1985) suggests four basic steps for exercising political influence:

1. Identify relevant relationships. (Figure out which players you need to influence.)

2. Assess who might resist, why, and how strongly. (Determine where the leadership challenges will be.)

3. Develop, wherever possible, links with potential opponents to facilitate communication, education, or negotiation. (Hold your enemies close.)

4. If step three fails, carefully select and implement either more subtle or more forceful methods. (Save your more potent weapons until you really need them, but have a Plan B in case Plan A falls short.)

These steps underscore the importance of developing a power base. Moving up the managerial ladder confers authority but also creates more dependence, because success requires the cooperation of many others (Kotter, 1985, 1988; Butcher and Clarke, 2001). People rarely give their best efforts and fullest cooperation simply because they have been ordered to do so. They accept direction better when they perceive the people in authority as credible, competent, and sensible.

The first task in building networks and coalitions is to figure out whose help you need. The second is to develop relationships so people will be there when you need them. Successful middle-management change agents typically begin by getting their boss on board (Kanter, 1983). They then move to "preselling," or "making cheerleaders": "Peers, managers of related functions, stakeholders in the issue, potential collaborators, and sometimes even customers would be approached individually, in one-on-one meetings that gave people a chance to influence the project and [gave] the innovator the maximum opportunity to sell it. Seeing them alone and on their territory was important: the rule was to act as if each person were the most important one for the project's success" (p. 223).

Once you cultivate cheerleaders, you can move to "horse trading": promising rewards in exchange for resources and support. This builds a resource base that helps in "securing blessings"—getting the necessary approvals and mandates from higher management (Kanter, 1983). Kanter found that the usual route to success in securing blessings is to identify critical senior managers and to develop a polished, formal presentation to nail down their support. The best presentations respond to both substantive and political concerns. Senior managers typically care about two questions: Is it a good idea? How will my constituents react? Once innovators get a nod from higher management, they can formalize the coalition with their boss and make specific plans for pursuing the project.

The basic point is simple: As a manager, you need friends and allies to get things done. To sew up their support, you need to build coalitions. Rationalists and romantics often rebel against this scenario. Why should you have to play political games to get something accepted if it's the right thing to do? One of the great classics of French drama, Molière's *The Misanthrope*, tells the story of a protagonist whose rigid rejection of all things political is destructive for him and everyone close by. The point that Molière made four centuries ago still holds: It is hard to dislike politics without also disliking people. Like it or not, political dynamics are inevitable under three conditions most managers face every day: ambiguity, diversity, and scarcity.

Informal networks perform a number of functions that formal structure may do poorly or not at all—moving projects forward, imparting culture, mentoring, and creating "communities of practice." Some organizations use measures of social networking to identify and manage who's connected to whom. When Procter & Gamble studied linkages among its 25 research and development units around the world, it discovered that its unit in China was relatively isolated from all the rest—a clear signal that linkages needed strengthening to corner a big and growing market (Reingold and Yang, 2007).

Ignoring or misreading people's roles in networks is costly. Consider the mistake that undermined John LeBoutillier's political career. Shortly after he was elected to Congress from a wealthy district in Long Island, LeBoutillier fired up his audience at the New York Republican convention with the colorful quip that Speaker of the House Thomas P. O'Neill was "fat, bloated, and out of control, just like the Federal budget." Asked to comment, Tip O'Neill was atypically terse: "I wouldn't know the man from a cord of wood" (Matthews, 1999, p. 113). Two years later, LeBoutillier unexpectedly lost his bid for reelection to an unknown opponent who didn't have the money to mount a real campaign—until a mysterious flood of contributions poured in from all over America. When LeBoutillier later ran into O'Neill, he admitted sheepishly, "I guess you were more popular than I thought you were" (Matthews, 1999, p. 114). LeBoutillier learned the hard way that it is dangerous to underestimate or provoke people when you don't know how much power they have or who their friends are.

Bargaining and Negotiation

We often associate bargaining with commercial, legal, and labor transactions. From a political perspective, though, bargaining is central to decision making. The horse trading that Kanter describes as part of coalition building is just one of many examples. Negotiation occurs whenever two or more parties with some interests in common and others in conflict need to reach agreement. Labor and management may agree that a firm should make money and offer good jobs to employees but part ways on how to balance pay and profitability. Engineers and managers in the NASA space program had a common interest in the success of the shuttle flights, but at key moments differed sharply on how to balance technical and political tradeoffs.

A fundamental dilemma in negotiations is choosing between "creating value" and "claiming value" (Lax and Sebenius, 1986). Value creators believe that successful negotiators must be inventive and cooperative in searching for a win-win solution. Value claimers see "win-win" as naively optimistic. For them, bargaining is a hard, tough process in which you have to do what it takes to win as much as you can.

One of the best-known win-win approaches to negotiation was developed by Fisher and Ury (1981) in their classic *Getting to Yes*. They argue that parties too often engage in "positional bargaining": They stake out positions and then reluctantly make concessions to reach agreement. Fisher and Ury contend that positional bargaining is inefficient and misses opportunities to create something that's better for everyone. They propose an alternative: "principled bargaining," built around four strategies.

The first strategy is to separate people from the problem. The stress and tension of negotiations can easily escalate into anger and personal attack. The result is that a negotiator sometimes wants to defeat or hurt the other party at almost any cost. Because every bargaining situation involves both substance and relationship, the wise negotiator will "deal with the people as human beings and with the problem on its merits." Paul Maritz demonstrated this principle in dealing with the prickly Dave Cutler. Even though Cutler continually baited and insulted him, Maritz refused to be distracted and persistently focused on the task at hand.

The second strategy is to focus on interests, not positions. If you get locked into a particular position, you might overlook better ways to achieve your goal. A classic example is the 1978 Camp David treaty between Israel and Egypt. The sides were at an impasse over where to draw the boundary between the two countries. Israel wanted to keep part of the Sinai; Egypt wanted all of it back. Resolution became possible only when they looked at underlying interests. Israel was concerned about security: no Egyptian tanks on the border. Egypt was concerned about sovereignty: The Sinai had been part of Egypt from the time of the Pharaohs. The parties agreed on a plan that gave all of the Sinai back to Egypt while demilitarizing large parts of it (Fisher and Ury, 1981). That solution led to a durable peace agreement.

Fisher and Ury's third strategy is to invent options for mutual gain instead of locking in on the first alternative that comes to mind. More options increase the chance of a better outcome. Maritz recognized this in his dealings with Cutler. Instead of bullying, he asked innocently, "Could you do a demo at COMDEX?" It was a new option that created gains for both parties.

Fisher and Ury's fourth strategy is to insist on objective criteria—standards of fairness for both substance and procedure. Agreeing on criteria at the beginning of negotiations can produce optimism and momentum, while reducing the use of devious or provocative tactics that get in the way of a mutually beneficial solution. When a school board and a teachers' union are at loggerheads over the size of a pay increase, they can look for independent standards, such as the rate of inflation or the terms of settlement in other districts. A classic example of fair procedure finds two sisters deadlocked over how to divide the last wedge of pie between them. They agree that one will cut the pie into two pieces and the other will choose the piece that she wants.

Fisher and Ury devote most of their attention to creating value—finding better solutions for both parties. They downplay the question of claiming value. Yet there are many examples in which shrewd value claimers have come out ahead. In 1980, Bill Gates offered to license an operating system to IBM about 48 hours before he had one to sell. Then he neglected to mention to Tim Paterson of Seattle Computer that Microsoft was buying his operating system to resell it to IBM. Gates gave IBM a great price: only $30,000 more than the $50,000 he'd paid for it. But he retained the rights to license it to anyone else. At the time, Microsoft was a flea atop IBM's elephant. Almost no one except Gates saw the possibility that consumers would want an IBM computer made by anyone but IBM. IBM negotiators might well have thought they were stealing candy from babies in buying DOS royalty-free for a measly $80,000. Meanwhile, Gates was already dreaming about millions of computers running his code. As it turned out, the new PC was an instant hit, and IBM couldn't make enough of them. Within a year, Microsoft had licensed MS-DOS to 50 companies, and the number kept growing (Mendelson and Korin, n.d.). Twenty years later, onlookers who wondered why Microsoft was so aggressive and unyielding in battling government antitrust suits might not have known that Gates had long been a dogged value claimer.

A classic treatment of value claiming is Schelling's 1960 essay *The Strategy of Conflict*, which focuses on how to make credible threats. Suppose, for example, that I want to buy your house and am willing to pay $250,000. How can I convince you that I'm willing to pay only $200,000? Contrary to a common assumption, I'm not always better off if I'm stronger and have more resources. If you believe that I'm very wealthy, you might take my threat less seriously than you would if I can get you to believe that $200,000 is the highest I can go. Common sense also suggests that I should be better off if I have considerable freedom of action. Yet I may get a better price if I can convince you my hands are tied. Perhaps I'm representing a very stubborn buyer who won't go above $200,000, even if the house is worth more. Such examples suggest that the ideal situation for a bargainer is to have substantial resources and freedom while convincing the other side of the opposite. Value claiming provides its own slant on the bargaining process:

- *Bargaining is a mixed-motive game.* Both parties want an agreement but have differing interests and preferences, so that what seems valuable to one may be negligible to the other.

- *Bargaining is a process of interdependent decisions.* What each party does affects the other. Each player wants to be able to predict what the other will do while limiting the other's ability to reciprocate.

- *The more player A can control player B's level of uncertainty, the more powerful A is.* The more A can keep private—as Bill Gates did with Seattle Computer and IBM—the better.

- *Bargaining involves judicious use of threats rather than sanctions.* Players may threaten to use force, go on strike, or break off negotiations. In most cases, they prefer not to bear the costs of carrying out the threat.

- *Making a threat credible is crucial.* A threat works only if your opponent believes it. Noncredible threats weaken your bargaining position and confuse the process.

- *Calculation of the appropriate level of threat is also critical.* If I underthreaten, you may think I'm weak. If I overthreaten, you may not believe me, may break off the negotiations, or may escalate your own threats.

Creating value and claiming value are both intrinsic to the bargaining process. How do you decide how to balance the two? At least two questions are important: How much opportunity is there for a win-win solution? And will you have to work with these people again? If an agreement can make everyone better off, it makes sense to emphasize creating value. If you expect to work with the same people in the future, it is risky to use scorched-earth tactics that leave anger and mistrust in their wake. Managers who get a reputation for being manipulative, self-interested, or untrustworthy have a hard time building the networks and coalitions they need for long-term success.

Axelrod (1980) found that a strategy of conditional openness works best when negotiators need to work together over time. This strategy starts with open and collaborative behavior and maintains the approach if the other responds in kind. If the other party becomes adversarial, however, the negotiator responds accordingly and remains adversarial until the opponent makes a collaborative move. It is, in effect, a friendly and forgiving version of tit for tat: do unto others as they do unto you. Axelrod's research found that this conditional openness approach worked better than even the most fiendishly diabolical adversarial strategy.

A final consideration in balancing collaborative and adversarial tactics is ethics. Bargainers often misrepresent their positions—even though society almost universally condemns lying as unethical (Bok, 1978). This leads to a tricky question for the manager as politician: What actions are ethical and just?

MORALITY AND POLITICS

Burns (1978), Lax and Sebenius (1986), Messick and Ohme (1998), and Svara (2007) explore ethical issues in bargaining and organizational politics. Burns's conception of positive politics (1978) draws on examples as diverse and complex as Franklin Roosevelt and Adolf Hitler, Gandhi and Mao, Woodrow Wilson and Joan of Arc. He sees conflict and power as central to leadership. Searching for firm moral footing in a world of cultural and ethical diversity, Burns turned to Maslow's (1954) theory of motivation and Kohlberg's (1973) treatment of ethics.

From Maslow, he borrowed the hierarchy of motives (see Chapter 6). Moral leaders, he argued, appeal to higher-order human needs. Kohlberg supplied the idea of stages of moral reasoning. At the lowest, "preconventional" level, moral judgment rests primarily on perceived consequences: An action is right if you are rewarded and wrong if you are punished. In the intermediate or "conventional" level, the emphasis is on conforming to authority and following the rules. At the highest, "postconventional" level, ethical judgment rests on general principles: the greatest good for the greatest number, or universal moral principles.

Maslow and Kohlberg, intertwined, gave Burns a foundation for constructing a positive view of politics: "If leaders are to be effective in helping to mobilize and elevate their constituencies, leaders must be whole persons, persons with full functioning capacities for thinking and feeling. The problem for them as educators, as leaders, is not to promote narrow, egocentric self-actualization, but to extend awareness of human needs and the means of gratifying them, to improve the larger social situation for which educators or leaders have responsibility and over which they have power" (1978, pp. 448–449).

Burns's view provides two expansive criteria: Does your leadership rest on general moral principles? And does it appeal to the "better angels" in your constituents' psyches? Lax and Sebenius (1986) see ethical issues as inescapable quandaries but provide a concrete set of questions for assessing leaders' actions:

- *Are you following rules that are mutually understood and accepted?* In poker, for example, players understand that bluffing is part of the game but pulling cards from your sleeve is not.

- *Are you comfortable discussing and defending your choices?* Would you want your colleagues and friends to know what you're doing? Your spouse, children, or parents? Would you be comfortable if your deeds appeared on the Web or in your local newspaper?

- *Would you want to be on the receiving end of your own actions?* Would you want this done to a member of your family?

- *Would the world be better or worse if everyone acted as you did?* If you were designing an organization, would you want people to follow your example? Would you teach your children the ethics you have embraced?

- *Are there alternatives you could consider that rest on firmer ethical ground?* Could you test your strategy with a trusted advisor and ask about other possibilities?

These questions embody four principles of moral judgment:

Mutuality. Are all parties to a relationship operating under the same understanding about the rules of the game? Enron's Ken Lay was talking up the company's stock to analysts and employees even as he and others were selling their shares. In the period when WorldCom improved its profits by cooking the books, it made its competitors look bad. Top executives at competing firms such as AT&T and Sprint felt the heat from analysts and shareholders and wondered, "Why can't we get the results they're getting?" Only later did they learn the answer: "They're cheating, and we're not."

Generality. Does a specific action follow a principle of moral conduct applicable to comparable situations? When Enron and WorldCom violated accounting principles to inflate their results, they were secretly breaking the rules, not adhering to a broadly applicable rule of conduct.

Openness. Are we willing to make our thinking and decisions public and confrontable? As Justice Oliver Wendell Holmes observed many years ago, "Sunlight is the best disinfectant." That was why Aruna Roy was so passionate about making government more transparent. Keeping others in the dark has been a consistent theme in corporate ethics scandals. Enron's books were almost impenetrable, and the company attacked analysts who questioned the numbers.

Caring. Does this action show concern for the legitimate interests and concerns of others? Enron's effort to protect its share price by locking in employees so they couldn't sell the stock in their retirement accounts, even as the value of the shares plunged, put the interests of senior executives ahead of everyone else's.

Business scandals come in waves; they are a predictable feature of the trough following every business boom. After the market boom of the Roaring Twenties and the crash that began the Great Depression, the president of the New York Stock Exchange went to jail in his three-piece suit (Labaton, 2002). There was another wave of corporate scandals in the 1970s. The 1980s gave us Ivan Boesky and the savings and loan crisis. And in the early years of the twenty-first century, we have seen scandals at Enron, Siemens, Volkswagen, Wells Fargo Bank, and WorldCom, among many others. There will always be temptation whenever big egos and large sums of money are at stake. Too many managers rarely think or talk about the moral dimension of management and leadership. Porter notes the dearth of such conversation:

> In a seminar with seventeen executives from nine corporations, we learned how the privatization of moral discourse in our society has created a deep sense of moral loneliness and moral illiteracy; how the absence of a common language prevents people from talking about and reading the moral issues they face. We learned how the isolation of individuals—the taboo against talking about spiritual matters in the public sphere—robs people of courage, of the strength of heart to do what deep down they believe to be right (1989, p. 2).

If we banish moral discourse and leave managers to face ethical issues alone, we invite dreary and brutish political dynamics. An organization can and should take a moral stance. It can make its values clear, hold employees accountable, and validate the need for dialogue about ethical choices. Positive politics without an ethical framework and moral dialogue is as unlikely as bountiful harvests without sunlight or water.

CONCLUSION

The question is not whether organizations are political, but what kind of politics they will encompass. Political dynamics can be sordid and destructive. But politics can also be a vehicle for achieving noble purposes. Organizational change and effectiveness depend on managers' political skills. Constructive politicians know how to fashion an agenda, map the political terrain, create a network of support, and negotiate with both allies and adversaries. In the process, they will encounter a predictable and inescapable ethical dilemma: when to adopt an open, collaborative strategy or when to choose a tougher, more adversarial approach. In making such choices, they have to consider the potential for collaboration, the importance of long-term relationships, and, most important, their own and their organization's values and ethical principles.

Organizations as Political Arenas and Political Agents

Peace extends only to private life. In business it is war all the time.

—George Eastman, Founder of Eastman Kodak

Sam Walton started his merchant career in 1945 as proprietor of the second-best variety store in a small rural Arkansas town. From that humble beginning, he built the world's largest retail chain. With more than 2 million "associates," Walmart became the world's largest employer and, for both better and worse, one of the most powerful companies on the globe. More than 90 percent of American households shop at Walmart stores every year, expecting the company to keep its promise of "always low prices" (Fishman, 2006).

Walmart's subtle and pervasive impact is illustrated in a little-known story about deodorant packaging. Deodorant containers used to come packed in cardboard boxes until Walmart decided in the early 1990s that the boxes were wasteful and costly—about a nickel apiece for something consumers would just toss. When Walmart told suppliers to kill the cardboard, the boxes disappeared across the industry. Good for Walmart had to be good enough for everyone. The story is but one of countless examples of the "Walmart effect"—an umbrella term for multiple ways Walmart influences consumers, vendors, employees, communities, and the environment (Fishman, 2006).

Yet, for all its power and success, Walmart has struggled in recent years to cope with an assortment of critics and image problems. The company has been accused of abusing workers, discriminating against women, busting unions, destroying small businesses, damaging the environment, and bribing government officials in Mexico and elsewhere. Circled by enemies, it has mounted major public relations campaigns in defense of its image.

Like all organizations, Walmart is both an arena for internal conflict and a political agent or player operating on a field crammed with other organizations pursuing their own interests. As arenas, organizations house an ongoing interplay of players and agendas. As agents, organizations are powerful tools for achieving the purposes of whoever calls the shots. Walmart's enormous size and power have made its political maneuvers widely visible; almost everyone has feelings about Walmart, one way or another. The company's historic penchant for secrecy and its secluded location in Bentonville, Arkansas, have sometimes shielded its internal politics from the spotlight, but tales of political skullduggery still emerge, including a titillating story about a superstar marketing executive who was fired amid rumors of an office romance and conflict with her conservative bosses. The same year also spawned the strange tale of a Walmart techie who claimed he'd been secretly recording the deliberations of the board of directors. Walmart has historically resisted any efforts to unionize its workers, but in the fall of 2012, the company had its first experience with strikes by workers in multiple cities. Ambivalent shoppers told reporters that they sympathized with the workers but still shopped at Walmart because they could not afford to pass up the low prices.

This chapter explores organizations as both arenas and political agents. Viewing organizations as political arenas is a way to reframe many organizational processes. Organization design, for example, can be viewed not as a rational expression of an organization's goals but as a political embodiment of contending claims. In our discussion of organizations as arenas, we examine the political dimensions of organizational change, contrasting directives from the top with pressures from below. As political agents, organizations operate in complex ecosystems—interdependent networks of organizations engaged in related activities and occupying particular niches. We illustrate several forms that ecosystems can take—business, public policy, business-government, and society. Finally, we look at the dark side of the power wielded by big organizations. We explore the concern that corporate giants represent a growing risk to the world because they are too powerful for anyone to control.

ORGANIZATIONS AS ARENAS

From a political view, "happily ever after" exists only in fairy tales. Today's winners may quickly become tomorrow's losers or vice versa. Change and stability are paradoxical: Organizations constantly change and yet never change. As in competitive sports, players come and go, but the game goes on. In the annals of organizational politics, few have illustrated these precepts as well as Ross Johnson, who once made the cover of *Time* magazine as an emblem of corporate greed and insensitivity. In *Barbarians at the Gate*, Bryan Burrough and John Helyar (1990) explain how.

Barbarians at the Gate

Ross Johnson began his career in the 1960s. His charm, humor, and charisma moved him ahead, and by the mid-1970s he was second in command to Henry Weigl at the consumer products firm Standard Brands. Johnson's lavish spending (on limousines and sumptuous entertainment, for example) soon put him on a collision course with his tightfisted boss, who tried to get him fired. But Johnson had wooed members of Standard's board of directors so successfully that he had more friends on the board than Weigl. Johnson argued that Weigl's conservative style was strangling the company, and the board bought his pitch. Weigl was kicked upstairs, and Johnson took over. He fired many of Weigl's people and enjoyed a spectacular period of lavish spending on executive perks. After four years of mediocre business results, the company got an unexpected call from the chairman of the food giant Nabisco, who proposed a merger of the two companies. Within two weeks, the transaction was done: a $1.9 billion stock swap—a big deal in 1981.

Everyone knew Nabisco would be in charge after the deal; it was by far the stronger player. But they underestimated Ross Johnson. He was so successful at ingratiating himself with Nabisco's chairman, while quietly shedding the old Nabisco executives, that he was able to take over the company after a few years. Once in charge, Johnson showed more interest in hobnobbing with celebrities than in running the business. And then, in 1985, he received another call: Tylee Wilson, chief executive of R.J. Reynolds, the huge tobacco company, wanted to talk merger. Wilson needed a corporate partner to help Reynolds reduce its heavy dependence on the tainted cigarette business. Johnson held out for more than Wilson wanted to pay, but the deal was soon done: Reynolds coughed up $4.9 billion for Nabisco.

Although more than one of his friends warned him about Johnson, Wilson figured it was his deal, and he would be in charge. But Wilson, who lacked Johnson's awesome skills at ingratiation, had alienated some members of his board. After cultivating alliances with board members, Johnson used the same gambit that had worked at Standard Brands. He told friends on the board that he would be leaving because there was room for only one CEO. A few weeks later, Wilson was startled when his board pushed him out.

Political Dimensions of Organizational Processes

As arenas, organizations house contests and set the stakes, the rules of the game, and the parameters for players. In this light, every organizational process has a political dimension. Consider the task of shaping and structuring an organization. Theories built on the rational premises of the structural frame assume that the best design is the one that contributes most to efficient strategy and successful attainment of goals. Pfeffer offers an explicitly political conception as an alternative: "Since organizations are coalitions, and the different participants have varying interests and preferences, the critical question becomes not how organizations should be designed to maximize effectiveness, but rather, whose preferences and interests are to be served by the organization. . . . What is effective for students may be ineffective for administrators. . . . Effectiveness as defined by consumers may be ineffectiveness as defined by stockholders. The assessment of organizations is dependent upon one's preferences and one's perspective" (1978, p. 223).

Even though groups have conflicting preferences, they have a shared interest in avoiding incessant conflict. So they agree on ways to distribute power and resources, producing settlements reflected in organizational design. Structures are "the resolution, at a given time, of the contending claims for control, subject to the constraint that the structures permit the organization to survive" (Pfeffer, 1978, p. 224).

An example is a controversial decision made by Ross Johnson when he headed RJR Nabisco. Johnson moved RJR's headquarters from Winston-Salem, where it had been for a century, to Atlanta. Reynolds was the commercial heart of Winston-Salem. It engendered fierce pride and loyalty among the citizenry, many of whom were substantial stockholders. Structural logic suggests placing your headquarters in a location that best serves the business, but Johnson and his key lieutenants saw the small city in the heart of tobacco country as boring and provincial. The move to Atlanta had scant business justification, was unpopular with the RJR board, and made Johnson the most hated man in Winston-Salem. But he headed the dominant coalition. He got what he wanted.

Sources of Political Initiative

Gamson's distinction (1968) between authorities and partisans (see Chapter 9) implies two major sources of political initiative: bottom-up, relying on mobilization of groups to assert their interests; and top-down, relying on authorities' capacity to influence subordinates. We discuss examples of both to illustrate some of the basic premises of political action.

Bottom-Up Political Action

The rise of trade unions, the emergence of the American civil rights movement, the antiwar movement of the 1970s, environmental activism in recent decades, and the "Arab Spring" and Occupy Wall Street initiatives that began in 2011 all exemplify the process of bottom-up change. In every case, the impetus for change was a significant disruption in old patterns. Trade unions developed in the context of the industrial revolution, rapid urbanization, and the decline of family farms. The civil rights movement arose after massive occupational and geographic shifts for black citizens. The antiwar movement emerged from the juxtaposition of an unpopular war with a draft lottery that affected every 18-year-old male in the United States. "Green" activism developed as the costs of growing prosperity—including pollution, destruction of habitats and species, and global warming—became increasingly visible and hard to discount. In each case, changing conditions intensified dissatisfaction for disenfranchised groups. Each reflected a classic script for revolutions: a period of rising expectations followed by widespread disappointment.

The initial impetus for change came from grassroots mobilizing and organizing—the formation of trade unions, civil rights groups, student movements, or environmental groups. Elites contested the legitimacy of grassroots action and launched coercive blocking tactics. Employers often resisted unions, using everything from lawsuits to violence. The civil rights movement, particularly in its early stages, experienced violent repression by whites. Efforts to suppress the antiwar movement reached their apogee at Kent State University, when members of the Ohio National Guard fired on student demonstrators. Greens have been engaged in a long battle against business and political leaders who dispute the significance of environmental threats and resist what they see as the excessive costs of proposed remedies. In every Arab Spring country, authorities tried to clamp down, producing thousands of deaths in Libya and Syria.

In every case, despite intense opposition, grassroots groups fought to have their rights embodied in law, policy, or political change. Some achieved success, but many ultimately failed to achieve their most important goals.

Barriers to Control from the Top

The difficulties of grassroots political action lead many people to believe that you have to begin at the top to get anything done. Yet studies of top-down initiatives catalogue many failures. Deal and Nutt (1980), for example, conducted a revealing analysis of local school districts that received generous, long-term federal funding to develop experimental programs for comprehensive changes in rural education. These projects followed a recurring scenario:

1. The central administration learned of the opportunity to obtain a sizable chunk of government funding.

2. A small group of administrators met to develop a proposal for improving some aspect of the educational program. (Tight deadlines meant that the process was usually rushed, with only a few people involved.)

3. When funding was approved, the administration announced with pride and enthusiasm that the district had won a national award that would bring substantial funds to support an exciting new project to improve instruction.

4. Teachers were dismayed to learn that the administration had committed to new teaching approaches without faculty input. Administrators were startled and perplexed when teachers greeted the news with resistance, criticism, and anger.

5. Caught in the middle between teachers and the funding agency, administrators interpreted teacher resistance as a sign of defensiveness and unwillingness to change.

6. The new program became a political football. Teachers joined with parents, community members, and the school board in opposing the project's primary goals. The ensuing battles produced more disharmony, mistrust, and conflict than tangible improvement in education.

The programs studied by Deal and Nutt represented examples of top-down change efforts under favorable circumstances. The districts were not in crisis. The change efforts were well funded and blessed by the federal government. Yet across the board, the new initiatives set off heated political battles. In many cases, administrators found themselves outgunned. Only one superintendent survived over the program's five-year funding cycle.

In most instances, administrators never anticipated a major political battle. They were confident their proposed programs were progressive, effective, and good for everyone. They overlooked the risks in proposing change that someone else was expected to carry out. As a result, they were showered with antagonism instead of the expected huzzahs.

A similar pattern appears repeatedly in other attempts at change from above. Countless efforts mounted by chief executives, frustrated managers, hopeful study teams, and high-status management consultants end in failure. The usual mistake is assuming that the right idea (as perceived by the idea's champions) and legitimate authority ensure success. This assumption neglects the agendas and power of the "lowerarchy"—partisans and groups in midlevel and lower-level positions, who devise creative and maddening ways to resist, divert, undermine, ignore, or overthrow innovative plans.

ORGANIZATIONS AS POLITICAL AGENTS

Organizations are lively arenas for internal politics. They are also active political agents in larger arenas, or "ecosystems" (Moore, 1993). Because organizations depend on their environment for resources they need to survive, they are inevitably enmeshed with external constituents whose expectations or demands must be heeded. These constituents often speak with loud but conflicting voices, adding to the challenge of managerial work (Hoskisson et al., 2002). As political actors, organizations need to master many of the basic skills of individual managers as politicians: develop an agenda, map the environment, manage relationships with both allies and enemies, and negotiate compacts, accords, and alliances.

An example is the "framing contests" (Gurses and Ozcan, 2015) that can arise between competing sides in a business battle. Uber, founded in 2009 by two young entrepreneurs in San Francisco, grew rapidly into an international powerhouse, with some estimates putting its value at more than $50 billion by 2015. Offering a new transportation option in cities around the globe, Uber found itself in pitched battles with regulators and incumbent taxi operators in almost every market it entered. Uber framed the issue as one of choice, innovation, customer service, and freedom from the grip of an antiquated industry. Opponents framed the contest very differently: a rogue operator was routinely breaking the law, ignoring public safety, and competing unfairly. Uber's pattern—enter first and worry about legalities later—illustrates Funk and Hirschman's (2017) argument that firms use market as well nonmarket tactics to influence their policy and regulatory environment.

Uber's most important allies were its customers, who saw the service as a big improvement over traditional cab companies. While writing this book, one of the authors phoned a local taxi company 2 hours in advance to arrange a ride to the airport. When the cab failed to arrive at the promised time, he called to learn that the company had lost track of the pickup but might be able to get him a cab in another 45 minutes. He switched to Uber. A genial driver in a late-model car arrived quickly and got him to the airport on time. Uber has leveraged similar customer experiences to build a powerful coalition that helps it win more battles than it loses and keep growing (Griswold, 2015).

Many of an organization's key constituents are other enterprises. Just as frogs, flies, and water lilies coevolve in a swamp, organizations develop in tandem in a shared environment. Moore (1993) illustrates this with two ecosystems in the personal computer business, one pioneered by Apple Computer and the other by IBM. Apple's ecosystem dominated the PC industry before IBM's entry. But IBM's ecosystem rapidly surpassed Apple's. IBM had a very powerful brand, and the open architecture of its PC induced new players to flock to it. Some of these players competed head on (for example, Compaq and Dell in hardware, Microsoft and Lotus in software). Others were related much like bees and flowers, each performing an indispensable service to the other. One symbiotic pairing was particularly fateful. As Microsoft gained control of the operating system and Intel of the microprocessor in the IBM ecosystem, the two increasingly became mutually indispensable. More sophisticated software needed faster microprocessors and vice versa, so the two had every reason to cheer each other on. "Intel giveth, and Microsoft taketh away," as some cynics put it. Two companies that began as servants to IBM eventually took over what became the "Wintel" ecosystem. IBM eventually dropped out of the business, and industry terminology changed to reflect the shift in power—what were once called "IBM clones" and proudly advertised as "100 percent IBM compatible!" became simply "Windows PCs."

Meanwhile, the Apple ecosystem, which nearly died in the 1990s, came back to life in stunning fashion early in the twenty-first century with the introduction of a series of highly successful mobile devices, including the iPod, iPhone, and iPad. Wintel continued to dominate the world of microcomputers, but most of the growth and excitement were in mobile. Microsoft was in the smartphone business before Apple or Google and invested billions of dollars in the business but fell to less than 1 percent market share by 2016.

POLITICAL DYNAMICS OF ECOSYSTEMS

The same factors that spawn politics inside organizations also create political dynamics within and between ecosystems. Organizations have parochial interests and compete for scarce resources. Ross Johnson again provides an example. After he became CEO of RJR Nabisco, Johnson made a fateful decision to engage in a management craze of the time—a leveraged buyout (LBO). The basic idea of an LBO is to find an undervalued company, buy up shares with someone else's money, fix it up or break it up, and sell it at a profit. It's a high-risk venture.

Johnson's plan was to use a leveraged buyout to take RJR Nabisco private. But once he had announced the LBO, the company was in play; it was open season for anyone to enter the bidding. *Anyone* in this case meant Henry Kravis and his secretive firm, KKR, with some $45 billion in buying power. Johnson gave Kravis a cold shoulder, expecting Kravis to stay out because the deal was too big. He underestimated a dangerous adversary. What followed was one of business history's biggest six-week poker games. Huge coalitions formed around both players. Millions of dollars in fees gushed into the laps of bankers, lawyers, and brokers. When the dust cleared, Henry Kravis and KKR had won by a nose. RJR Nabisco was theirs for a cool $25 billion.

The bidding war created a fluid, temporary ecosystem illustrating many of the complexities of such arrangements. Dozens of individuals, groups, and organizations were involved, but the big prize in the contest, RJR Nabisco, was largely a bystander; its board was on the sidelines for most of the game. Johnson and his allies pursued their private interests more than the corporation's. Financial stakes were enormous, yet the game was often driven by issues of power, reputation, and personal animosity. Everyone wanted the prize, but you could win by losing and lose by winning. In the competitive frenzy, both sides bid too much, and the winner was stuck with an overpriced albatross.

The RJR Nabisco LBO ecosystem lasted only until the brutal bidding war was over. But many ecosystems, like Wintel's and Walmart's, are durable, lasting for decades. In such cases, an organization's role in an ecosystem affects how it can balance pursuit of its own interests with the overall well being of the ecosystem. This may not be a major issue for small players with only marginal influence, but is vital for "keystone" firms like Walmart that sit at the hub of an ecosystem:

> Walmart is successful because it figured out how to create, manage, and evolve an incredibly powerful business ecosystem. Over the years Walmart took advantage of its ability to gather consumer information to coordinate the distributed assets of its vast network of suppliers. Walmart made a point of tracking demand information in real time. The key was that it decided to share this information with its supplier network. It introduced Retail Link, the system that still delivers the most accurate, real-time sales information in the industry to Walmart partners. Walmart was unique in the retail space in offering this kind of service, turning Retail Link into a critical supply chain hub (Iansiti and Levien, 2004, pp. 1–2).

Fishman agrees about Walmart's dominant role in its ecosystem, but sees less rosy results:

> The ecosystem isn't a metaphor; it is a real place in the global economy where the very metabolism of business is set by Walmart. The fear of Walmart isn't just the fear of losing a big account. It's the fear that the more business you do with Walmart, the deeper you end up inside the Walmart ecosystem, and the less you are actually running your own business. Walmart's leadership virtually

never acknowledges this control, but the company clearly understands it, and even takes a sly pride in it (2006, p. 16).

But Walmart's ecosystem is not a gated community. Much as it might like to, Walmart has limited ability to exclude other players—including the firm's many competitors and critics—who choose to spend time in its neighborhood, even if uninvited. Walmart initiatives to build new stores are routinely countered by opponents who decry the economic and environmental costs that they claim the new outlet would create. Walmart's low wages and benefits create a tempting target for union organizers, though the company's antiunion stance has mostly been successful so far in keeping unions out.

Organizational ecosystems come in many forms and sizes. Some, like Walmart's, are huge and global. Others are small and local (like the ecosystem of laundries in Oslo or policing in Omaha). Next, we examine how ecosystem dynamics vary across sectors.

Public Policy Ecosystems

In the public sector, policy arenas form around virtually every government activity. One example is the commercial aviation ecosystem, in which air carriers, airplane manufacturers, travelers, legislators, and regulators are all active participants. In the United States, the Federal Aviation Administration has been a troubled key player for decades. Charged with divergent goals of defending safety, promoting the economic health of the industry, and keeping its own costs down, the FAA has perennially come under heavy fire from virtually every direction. Feeble oversight sometimes permitted marginal carriers to shortcut safety but continue flying. An air traffic modernization plan rang up billions of dollars in bills but 20 years later had yielded few results:

> When Marion C. Blakey took over at the Federal Aviation Administration in 2002, she was determined to fix an air travel system battered by terrorism, antiquated technology, and the ever-turbulent finances of the airline industry. Five years later, as she prepares to step down on Sept. 13, 2007, it's clear she failed. Almost everything about flying is worse than when she arrived. Greater are the risks, the passenger headaches, and the costs in lost productivity. Almost everyone has a horror story about missed connections, lost baggage, and wasted hours on the tarmac (Palmeri and Epstein, 2007, p. 1).

Fast forward to 2016, and the story was little changed: "The Federal Aviation Administration has little to show for a decade of work on modernizing air traffic control, and faces barriers and billions more in spending to realize its full benefits, says a report released Tuesday by a government watchdog" (Lowy, 2016).

Some of the FAA's troubles were internal. An earlier report from what was then called the General Accounting Office had faulted the agency's lack of a "performance-oriented culture essential to establishing a culture of accountability and coordination" (Dillingham, 2001). But almost every move it made to solve one constituency's problem created trouble for others. Much of the fault lay in its ecosystem: "Nobody is in charge. The various players in the system, including big airlines, small aircraft owners, labor unions, politicians, airplane manufacturers, and executives with their corporate jets, are locked in permanent warfare as they fight to protect their own interests. And the FAA, a weak agency that needs Congressional approval for how it raises and spends money, seems incapable of breaking the gridlock" (Palmeri and Epstein, 2007).

In recent years, drones presented a new test of the FAA's ability to balance conflicting interests and pressures. In August 2016, the FAA issued long-awaited drone regulations that sought to balance considerations of safety and commerce. At the time, there were about 20,000 commercial drones in operation in the United States, but the FAA was expecting that number to increase to approximately 600,000 in another year.

Education is another illustration of a complex policy ecosystem. Everyone thinks good schools are important. Families want their children to acquire the ingredients for success. Businesses need well-trained, literate graduates. Economists and policy analysts stress the importance of human capital. Teachers want better pay and working conditions. Taxpayers want to cut frills and keep costs down. Almost no one believes that American schools are as good as they should be, but there is little agreement about how to make them better.

One popular remedy, enshrined in the federal "No Child Left Behind" Act, emphasizes tests and incentives: measure how well schools are doing, reward the winners, and penalize the losers. But high-stakes testing may have generated more political heat than educational light. Some research suggests that the testing emphasis has improved learning outcomes (Wang, Beckett, and Brown, 2006), while others see "distortion, corruption, and collateral damage" (Nichols and Berliner, 2007) as the primary impact. The strenuous opposition to No Child Left Behind led the federal Department of Education into state-by-state negotiations to modify the requirements, making it even harder to assess how well the program is working (Sunderman, 2006).

Another popular cure for educational ills is giving parents more choice about which schools their children attend. One version of school choice is vouchers, grants that families can use to send their children to private schools. Another is charter schools—publicly funded, quasi-independent educational enterprises. Proponents of choice argue that parents would seek the best school for their children and that the ensuing competition would have an invigorating effect on public schools. But school administrators maintain that vouchers and charter schools drain away resources and exacerbate the challenges for the neediest students. Coalitions have formed on both sides of the choice issue and have lobbied vigorously at the state and national levels. Available research suggests that, on the whole, some charter schools are very good and others are not, but, on average, student learning outcomes are neither better nor worse than conventional public schools.

Business-Government Ecosystems

Government and business inevitably intersect in a multitude of ecosystems. Perrow (1986) discusses one example: pharmaceutical companies, physicians, and government. A major threat to drug companies' profit margins is generic drugs, which sell at a much lower price than brand-name equivalents. In the United States, the industry trade association, an interorganization coalition, successfully lobbied many state legislatures to prohibit the sale of generic drugs, ostensibly to protect consumers. The industry also persuaded the American Medical Association (AMA) to permit drugs to be advertised by brand name in its journals. Consumers normally buy whatever the doctor prescribes, and drug companies wanted doctors to think brands rather than chemical names. As a result of the policy shift, the AMA's advertising income tripled in seven years, and the manufacturers strengthened the position of their respective brands (Perrow, 1986).

The ecosystem shifted with the rapid rise of a newly powerful group of players: insurers and managed-care providers. The growing market dominance of a few large insurers dramatically reduced the bargaining power of physicians and drug companies. Insurers used their growing political leverage to push physicians to prescribe less expensive generic drugs. In an effort to save consumers' money, state legislatures began to require pharmacists to offer the generic equivalent when a brand name is prescribed. Pharmaceutical companies fought back with televised ads encouraging patients to ask their doctors for brand name drugs.

Drug companies are not alone in their attention to politics. Government policy can be a powerful source of competitive advantage because it "determines the rules of commerce; the structure of markets (through barriers to entry and changes in cost structures due to regulations, subsidies, and taxation); the offerings of goods and services that are permissible; and the sizes of markets based on government subsidies and purchases. Consequently, gaining and maintaining access to those who make public policy may well be a firm's most important political goal" (Schuler, Rehbein, and Cramer, 2002, p. 659).

Politically active firms use a range of strategies for influencing government agencies (Schuler, Rehbein, and Cramer, 2002). FedEx illustrates the possibilities. In Chapter 7, we noted the company's sophisticated approach to managing people. FedEx has been equally agile in managing its political environment. The *New York Times* described it as "one of the most formidable and successful corporate lobbies in the capital" (Lewis, 1996, p. A17). FedEx CEO Fred Smith "spends considerable time in Washington, where he is regarded as Federal Express's chief advocate. It was Mr. Smith who hit a lobbying home run in 1977 when he persuaded Congress to allow the fledgling company to use full-sized jetliners to carry its cargo, rather than the small planes to which it had been restricted. That was the watershed event that allowed the company to grow to its present dominating position with almost $10.3 billion in business" (p. A30).

FedEx's political action committee ranked among the nation's top ten, making generous donations to hundreds of congressional candidates. Its board was adorned with former political leaders from both major political parties. Its corporate jets regularly ferried officeholders to events around the country. All this generosity paid off. In October 1996, when FedEx wanted two words inserted into a 1923 law regulating railway express companies, the Senate stayed in session a few extra days to get it done, even with elections only a month away. A first-term senator commented, "I was stunned by the breadth and depth of their clout up here" (Lewis, 1996, p. A17).

A similar coevolution of business and politics occurs around the world:

No one would dispute that business and politics are closely intertwined in Japan. As one leading financial journalist puts it, "If you don't use politicians, you can't expand business these days in Japan—that's basic." Businessmen provide politicians with funds, politicians provide businessmen with information. If you wish to develop a department store, a hotel, or a ski resort, you need licenses and permissions and the cooperation of leading local political figures. And it is always useful to hear that a certain area is slated for development, preferably several years before development starts, when land prices are still low (Downer, 1994, p. 299).

The same intertwining of business and politics is even more dominant in China. It is almost impossible to start or build a business without the support of party and government officials. *Guanxi* (relationships) generally matters more than laws and regulations. Negotiating the ethical terrain is treacherous in a country where bribes are technically illegal but the exchange of cash-filled "red envelopes" is deeply rooted in a culture that sees gift-giving as basic to building relationships.

Society as Ecosystem

On a still grander scale, we find society: the massive, swirling ecosystem in which business, government, and the public are embedded. A critical question in this arena is the power relationship between organizations and everyone else. All organizations have power. Large organizations have a lot: "Of the 100 largest economies in the world, 51 are corporations, and only 49 are countries. Walmart is bigger than Israel, Poland, or Greece. Mitsubishi is bigger than Indonesia. General Motors is bigger than Denmark. If governments can't set the rules, who will? The corporations? But they're the players. Who's the referee?" (Longworth, 1996, p. 4).

This question is becoming more urgent as big companies get bigger. In 1954, it took more than 60 companies to equal 20 percent of the American economy; in 2005, it took only 20 companies. "We don't often talk about the concentration of corporate power, but it is almost unfathomable that the men and women who run just 20 companies make decisions every day that steer one-fifth of the U.S. economy" (Fishman, 2006, p. 22). A number of writers (including Bakan, 2004; Korten, 1995; Perrow, 1986; and Stern and Barley, 1996) emphasize that whoever controls a multibillion-dollar tool wields enormous power. Bakan (2004, p. 2) sees the corporation as "a pathological institution, a dangerous possessor of the great power it wields over individuals and societies." Korten's view is similarly dark:

> An active propaganda machinery controlled by the world's largest corporations constantly reassures us that consumerism is the path to happiness, government restraint of market excess is the cause of our distress, and economic globalization is both a historical inevitability and a boon to the human species. In fact, these are all myths propagated to justify profligate greed and mask the extent to which the global transformation of human institutions is a consequence of the sophisticated, well-funded, and intentional interventions of a small elite whose money enables them to live in a world of illusion apart from the rest of humanity. These forces have transformed once beneficial corporations and financial institutions into instruments of a market tyranny that is extending its reach across the planet like a cancer, colonizing ever more of the planet's living spaces, destroying livelihoods, displacing people, rendering democratic institutions impotent, and feeding on life in an insatiable quest for money (Korten, 1995, p. 12).

Greatest Hits from Organization Studies

Hit Number 2: Jeffrey Pfeffer and Gerald Salancik, *The External Control of Organizations* (New York: HarperCollins, 1978)

Pfeffer and Salancik's book fell out of print for several years and is little known outside academic circles, but scholars love it; it occupies the second rung in our ranking of most-cited works. As its title suggests, the book's principal theme is that organizations are much more creatures than creators of their environment. In the authors' words: "The perspective [in this book] denies the validity of the conceptualization of organizations as self-directed, autonomous actors pursuing their own ends and instead argues that organizations are other-directed, involved in a constant struggle for autonomy and discretion, confronted with constraint and external control" (p. 257). The authors follow Cyert and March (1963) in viewing organizations as coalitions that are both "markets in which influence and control are transacted" (p. 259) and players that need to negotiate their relationships with a range of external constituents.

Pfeffer and Salancik emphasize that organizations depend on their environment for inputs that they need to survive. Much of the job of management is to understand and respond to demands of key external constituents whose support is vital to survival. This job is made more difficult by two challenges:

- Organizations' understanding of their environment is often distorted or imperfect (because organizations act on only the information they're geared to collect and know how to interpret).
- Organizations confront multiple constituents whose demands are often inconsistent.

Organizations comply where they have to, but they also look for ways to increase their autonomy by making their environment more predictable and favorable. They may merge to gain greater market supremacy, form coalitions (alliances, joint ventures) to gain greater influence, or enlist government help (by seeking subsidies, tax breaks, or protective tariffs, for example). But there is a dilemma: every entanglement, even as it garners greater influence over a part of the environment, also produces erosion of the organization's autonomy. There's no free lunch.

Pfeffer and Salancik describe three roles for managers, two political and one symbolic: (1) a responsive role in which managers adjust the organization's activities to comply with pressures from the environment; (2) a discretionary role in which they seek to alter the organization's relationship with its environment; and (3) a symbolic role arising from the widely accepted myth that managers make a difference. If a team is losing but you can't change the players, you fire the coach, creating the appearance of change without actually changing anything (an important idea that we address in the next chapter).

Do sophisticated consumer marketing firms create and control consumer tastes, or do they simply react to needs created by larger social forces? Critics like Korten (1995) are convinced that the advantage lies with the corporations, but Pfeffer and Salancik (1978) see it the other way around, as do many proponents of "the marketing concept":

> The marketing concept of management is based on the premise that over the longer term all businesses are born and survive or die because people (the market) either want them or don't want them. In short, the market creates, shapes, and defines the demand for all classes of products and services. Almost needless to say, many managers tend to think that they can design goods and services and then create demand. The marketing concept denies this proposition. Instead, the marketing concept emphasizes that the creative aspect of marketing is discovering, defining, and fulfilling what people want or need or what solves their life-style problems (Marshall, 1984, p. 1).

Proponents of this view note that even the most successful marketers have had their share of Edsels—products released with great fanfare and huge marketing budgets that fluttered briefly and then sank like stones. Consumers, in this view, are in charge because they can buy what they want and walk away from what they don't want.

Slee (2006) provides a contrary view. He uses game theory and the concept of market failures to argue that, even though consumers generally make rational choices in terms of the options they have, their collective behavior can lead to a world that is worse for everyone. If, for example, Walmart opens a store on the outskirts of a medium-sized community, consumers may flock to it for the low prices and wide variety of merchandise. At first everyone is happy. But then, downtown merchants who can't match Walmart go out of business, throwing employees out of work and making the town center bleak and empty. Not all the newly unemployed can get jobs at Walmart, and those who do get paid less. Some of the wealth that used to circulate in the community now flies away to Walmart headquarters in Arkansas. The community as a whole may be worse off, even though everyone still likes Walmart's low prices.

Are large multinational corporations so powerful that they have become a law unto themselves, or are they heavily constrained by the need to respond to customers, cultures, and governments? An ecological view suggests that the answer is some of both. Ecosystems and competitors within them rise and fall. Power relations are never static, and even the most powerful have no guarantee of immortality. Of the top twenty-five U.S. companies at the beginning of the twentieth century, all but one had dropped off the list or vanished altogether when the century came to a close. The lone survivor? General Electric.

Fishman frames both sides of this issue in the case of Walmart:

> The easiest response to the Walmart critics comes from people who shrug and say, the United States economy is capitalistic and market-based. Walmart is large and ubiquitous—and powerful—because it does what it does so well. Walmart is winning for no other reason than personal choice: Customers vote for Walmart with their wallets; suppliers vote for Walmart with their products. Any consumer, any businessperson who doesn't care for the way Walmart does business is free to buy and sell products somewhere else.
>
> The problem is that this free choice has become an illusion. In many categories of products it sells, Walmart is now 30 percent or more of the entire market. It sells 31 percent of the pet food used in the United States, 37 percent of the fresh meat, 45 percent of the office and school supplies bought by consumers, and 24 percent of the bottled water. That kind of dominance at both ends of the spectrum—dominance across a huge range of merchandise and dominance of geographic consumer markets—means that market capitalism is being strangled with the kind of slow inexorability of a boa constrictor. It's not free-market capitalism; Walmart is running the market. The newly merged Procter & Gamble and Gillette has sales in excess of $64 billion a year—not only bigger by far than any other consumer products company, but bigger than all but 20 public companies of any kind in the United States. But remember: Walmart isn't just P&G's number-one customer; it's P&G's business. Walmart is bigger than P&G's next nine customers combined. That's why businesspeople are scared of Walmart. They should be. And if a corporation with the scale, vigor, and independence of P&G must bend to Walmart's will, it's easy to imagine the kind of influence Walmart wields over the operators of small factories in developing nations, factories that just want work and have almost no leverage with Walmart or Walmart's vendors (Fishman, 2006, p. 20. Copyright © 2006. Academy of Management).

Walmart's clout remains formidable, but its future is less clear. After years of embattled, slow growth, in 2016 Walmart's sales and profits declined for the first time in decades. Will it grow and prosper in the future? Or will it follow companies like Sears into a long downhill slide from the pinnacle it now commands? Whatever happens to Walmart, the battle over corporate power will continue on a global scale.

In recent years, across industries and around the globe, wealth and power have been increasingly concentrated in a shrinking number of very large "superstar" firms. This is not always good news for workers because as industries become more concentrated, the share of the economic pie that goes to labor shrinks (Autor et al., 2017). The power of large multinational companies has continued to grow, but they must still cope with the demands of other powerful players: governments, labor unions, investors, and consumers. In a cacophonous global village, this is the biggest political contest of all.

CONCLUSION

Organizations are both arenas for internal politics and political agents with their own agendas, resources, and strategies. As arenas, they house competition and offer a setting for the ongoing interplay of divergent interests and agendas. An arena's rules and parameters shape the game to be played, the players on the field, and the interests to be pursued. From this perspective, every significant organizational process is inherently political.

As agents, organizations are tools, often very powerful tools, for achieving the purposes of whoever controls them. But they are also inevitably dependent on their environment for needed support and resources. They exist, compete, and coevolve in business or political ecosystems with clusters of organizations, each pursuing its own interests and seeking a viable niche. As in nature, relationships within and between ecosystems are sometimes fiercely competitive, sometimes collaborative and symbiotic.

A particularly urgent and controversial question is the relative power of organizations and society. Giant multinational corporations have achieved scale and resources unprecedented in human history. Critics worry that they are dominating and distorting politics, society, and the environment. Optimists argue that organizations retain their clout only by adapting to larger social forces and responding to the needs and demands of customers and constituents.

PART FIVE

The Symbolic Frame

When the Catholic Church changed the liturgy from Latin to English many parishioners rebelled even though the change made sacred tenets more accessible. For many it was the first time that they could grasp and grapple with the sacred values of their faith. In *Hunger of Memory*, one parishioner describes vividly his reaction to the change:

> But now that I no longer live as a Catholic in a Catholic world, I cannot expect the liturgy—which reflects and cultivates my faith—to remain what it was. I will continue to go to the English mass. I will go because it is my liturgy. I will, however, often recall with nostalgia the faith I have lost . . . The church is no longer mine (Rodriguez, 1997, p. 107).

In 1995 The Coca-Cola Company changed its 99-year-old recipe for its flagship soft drink. Pepsi, the company's chief competitor, was making inroads into Coke's market share; and in a series of blind taste tests, the new recipe was consistently preferred over Pepsi. This gave the company executives confidence that a new product would corner the market. The New Coke was launched with an elaborate advertising campaign.

Public reaction was swift and unanticipated. Some consumers filled their basements with the original Coke. Protest groups popped up across the country. Songs were written to honor the old taste. Protestors at an event in Atlanta carried placards: "We want the real thing," "Our children will never know refreshment." Other reactions carried the same sentiment.

Both the Latin liturgy and Coca-Cola are laden with symbolism. Symbols carry powerful intellectual and emotional messages; they speak to the heart and the soul. They are embedded in myths which are truer than true. "It is through myths that men are lifted above their capacity in the ordinary, attain powerful visions of the future, and realize such visions" (Berger, 1974, p. 26).

The symbolic frame focuses on how myth and symbols help humans make sense of the chaotic, ambiguous world in which they live. Meaning, belief, and faith are its central concerns. Meaning is not given to us; we create it. There are, for example, many who revere the American flag and many others who burn it. The flag is symbolically powerful for both groups but for different reasons. It represents patriotism for one group, oppression or imperialism for the other. Symbols are the basic materials of the meaning systems, or cultures, we inhabit. Leaders are *bricoleurs*, people who survey and use the materials at hand to help construct meaning systems. We experience our way of life in the same way that fish live in water. Many contemporary leaders highlight the critical role culture plays in organizations:

- Lou Gerstner (IBM): "I came to see, in my time at IBM, that culture is not just one aspect of the game—it is the game."

- Peter Drucker: "Culture eats strategy for breakfast."

- Jim Sinegal (Costco): "What else have we got besides stories? It's what brings meaning to the work we do."

- Howard Schultz (Starbucks): "A company can grow big without losing the passion and personality that built it, but only if it's driven not by profits but by values and people."

- John Mackey (Whole Foods): "Culture is no less than 'how we do things around here.' Less tangible than other physical assets on a company balance sheet, it is nonetheless the most valuable asset a company has—for it stitches people together in common beliefs, values and purpose and represents the basis for authenticity of experience for both team members and customers."

Chapter 12 explores the many forms cultural symbols take in social life, including myth, vision, story, heroes and heroines, ritual, and ceremony. It then uses a variety of examples to demonstrate what culture is and why it is so important.

In Chapter 13, we apply symbolic concepts to team dynamics. We use a detailed case of a legendary and highly successful computer development team to show that the essence of its success was cultural and spiritual. The team relied on initiation rituals, humor, play, specialized language, ceremony, and other symbolic forms to weld a diverse and fractious group of individuals into a spirited, successful team.

Chapter 14 highlights dramaturgical and institutional perspectives, viewing organizations as akin to theater companies seeking recognition and support by staging dramas that both please and influence their audiences. We show that many activities and processes in organizations—such as evaluation and strategic planning—rarely achieve their supposed goals. Yet they persist, because they convey vital symbolic messages that internal and external audiences yearn for.

Organizational Symbols and Culture

A people without the knowledge of their past history, origin and culture is like a tree without roots.

—Marcus Garvey

For 800 years, neighborhoods in Siena, Italy, have competed twice each summer in a horse race known as the *palio*. Each side has its club, hymn, costumes, museum, and elected head. A crowd of more than 100,000 gathers to witness a 75-second event that people live for throughout the year. Riding under banners of the goose, seashell, or turtle, jockeys attack one another with whips and hang on desperately around 90-degree turns. The first horse to finish, with or without rider, wins. "The winners are worshipped. The losers embarrass their clan" (Saubaber, 2007, p. 42).

In July 2007, 22-year-old Giovanni Atzeni won the race in a photo finish. His followers were ecstatic. A young woman shouted, "We've waited 10 years," as she showered him with kisses. An old man almost fainted with joy at the chance to see a victory before he died. The legendary Aceto, a 14-time winner, once said, "*Palio* is a drug that makes you a God . . . and then crucifies you." The rest of Italy considers the event barbaric, but locals are proudly unfazed. Unless you were born in Siena, they insist, you will never understand the *palio*.

Rooted in a time when Siena was a proud and powerful republic, the occasion embodies the town's unique identity.

Building distinctive identity or community around a brand name in business updates ancient traditions based on tribe and homeland, like those surrounding the *palio*. Consider the characteristics of a unique modern business: Carnival-like zaniness. Free food and vending machines. Corporate values placing a premium on delivering "wow" and "creating fun and weirdness" (Heathfield, 2012). New recruits offered shots of vodka during hiring interviews and offered $2,000 to quit after their first round of training (Chafkin, 2009).

The 95 percent who turn down the $2,000 graduate in full ceremony to "Pomp and Circumstance" in front of families and members of their new, nontraditional departments: "Each department has its own décor, ranging from the rain forest–themed to Elvis-themed, and employees are encouraged to decorate their work spaces . . ." (Rogers-Kante, 2011.)

Employees carrying cowbells and noisemakers lead spontaneous office parades in costume (Frei, Ely, and Winig, 2010). Departments sponsor cookouts and other fun events throughout the year. Managers are required to spend 10 to 20 percent of their hours "goofing off" with employees. Managers and employees are encouraged to fraternize outside normal office hours. Three big company events—a summer picnic, a January party at the Boss's home, and a vendor party—fill out the year's cycle of fun and happiness.

Welcome to Zappos, CEO Tony Hsieh's "Culture of Happiness" (introduced in Chapter 3). All the merriment and spirit captures the hearts of the company's employees. But it also pays off in employee satisfaction and business results. Hsieh credits the company's phenomenal success to its distinctive culture with carnival-like zaniness that bears some resemblance to Siena's *palio*.

Zappos and the *palio* are two examples of how symbols permeate every fiber of society and organizations. "A symbol is something that stands for or suggests something else; it conveys socially constructed meanings beyond its intrinsic or obvious functional use" (Zott and Huy, 2007, p. 72). Distilled to the essence, people seek meaning in life. Because life is mysterious, symbols arise to sustain hope, belief, and faith. They express themselves in analogies. Symbols are metaphoric expression of psychic energy. Their content is far from obvious; it is expressed in unique and individual ways while embodying universal and collective imagery (Ghareman, 2016). These intangibles then shape our thoughts, emotions, and actions. Symbols cut deeply into the human psyche and tap the collective unconscious (Jung, [1912] 1965).

Symbols are basic elements of culture that pop up to fit unique circumstances. Symbols and symbolic actions are part of everyday life and are particularly perceptible at weekly, monthly, or seasonal high points. Symbols stimulate energy in moments of triumph and offer solace in times of tribulation. After 9/11, Americans relied on symbols to cope with the aftermath of a devastating terrorist attack. Flags flew. Makeshift monuments honored victims and the heroic acts of police and firefighters who gave their lives. Members of Congress sang "God Bless America" on the Capitol steps. Across the country, people gathered in both formal and informal healing ceremonies.

A comparably intense expression of shock, grief, and compassion came in the wake of the senseless 2012 shootings of 20 young schoolchildren and their adult caretakers at the Sandy Hook School in Newtown, Connecticut. Mourners from all over the nation sent flowers and toys, which were piled up in huge mounds in front of the school. Memorials of white angels appeared across the country. President Obama shed a tear in his nationally televised speech. It was another example of the spiritual magic that symbols represent.

The symbolic frame interprets and illuminates the basic issues of meaning and belief that make symbols so potent. It depicts a world distinct from popular canons of rationality, certainty, and linearity. This chapter journeys into the symbolic inner sanctum. We discuss symbolic assumptions and highlight various forms that symbols take in human organizations. We then move on to discuss organizations as cultures or tribes. Finally, we describe how two distinctive companies—BMW and Nordstrom department stores—have successfully applied symbolic ideas.

SYMBOLIC ASSUMPTIONS

The symbolic frame forms an umbrella for ideas from several disciplines, including organization theory and sociology (Selznick, 1957; Blumer, 1969; Schutz, 1967; Clark, 1975; Corwin, 1976; Hatch and Cunliffe, 2013; March and Olsen, 1976; Maitlis and Christianson, 2014; Meyer and Rowan, 1978; Weick, 1976; Davis et al., 1976; Hofstede, 1984), political science (Dittmer 1977; Edelman, 1971), magic (O'Keefe, 1983), and neurolinguistic programming (Bandler and Grinder, 1975).

Jung relied heavily on symbolic concepts to probe the human psyche and unconscious archetypes. Anthropologists have traditionally focused on symbols and their place in the lives of humans (Mead, 1928, 1935; Benedict, 1934; Goffman, 1974; Ortner, 1973; Bateson, 1972). In the early 1980s, business books began to apply cultural ideas to corporations, health care, and nonprofit enterprises (Deal and Kennedy, 1982; Peters and Waterman, 1982; Schein, 1992).

The symbolic frame distills ideas from diverse sources into five suppositions:

- What is most important is not what happens but what it means.
- Activity and meaning are loosely coupled; events and actions have multiple interpretations as people experience situations differently.

- In the face of uncertainty and ambiguity, symbols arise to help people resolve confusion, find direction, and anchor hope and faith.

- Events and processes are often more important for what they express or signal than for their intent or outcomes. Their emblematic form weaves a tapestry of secular myths, heroes and heroines, rituals, ceremonies, and stories to help people find purpose and passion.

- Culture forms the superglue that bonds an organization, unites people, and helps an enterprise to accomplish desired ends.

The symbolic frame sees life as allegorical, mystical, and more serendipitous than linear. Organizations are like constantly changing organic pinball machines. Issues, actors, decisions, and policies carom through an elastic labyrinth of cushions, barriers, and traps. Managers turning to Peter Drucker's *The Effective Executive* (1967) might do better to seek advice from Lewis Carroll's *Through the Looking Glass*. But apparent chaos has an underlying pattern and an emblematic order increasingly appreciated in corporate life (Kotter and Heskett, 1992).

ORGANIZATIONAL SYMBOLS

An organization's culture is revealed and communicated through its symbols: GEICO's gecko, Target's bullseye, Airbnb's Bélo or Aflac's duck. McDonald's franchises are unified as much by golden arches, core values, and the legend of Ray Kroc as by sophisticated control systems. Harvard professors are bound less by structural constraints than by rituals of teaching, values of scholarship, and the myths and mystique of Harvard. Symbols take many forms in organizations. Myth, vision, and values imbue an organization with deep purpose and resolve. The words and deeds of heroes and heroines serve as icons or logos for others to admire or emulate. Fairy tales and stories tender explanations, reconcile contradictions, and resolve dilemmas (Cohen, 1969). Rituals and ceremonies offer direction, faith, and hope (Ortner, 1973). Metaphor, humor, and play loosen things up and form communal bonds (Lewin, 1998; Romero and Cruthirds, 2006; Statler and Roos, 2007). We look at each of these symbolic forms in the following sections.

Myths, Vision, and Values

A myth is a collective dream (Jung, 1965). Myths, operating at a mystical level, are the story behind the story (Campbell, 1988). They explain, express, legitimize, and maintain solidarity and cohesion. They communicate unconscious wishes and conflicts, mediate contradictions, and offer a narrative anchoring the present in the past (Cohen, 1969). All organizations rely on myths or sagas of varying strength and intensity (Clark, 1975). Myths can transform a place of work into a beloved, revered, hallowed institution and an all-encompassing way of life.

Myths often originate in the launching of an enterprise. The original plan for Southwest Airlines, for example, was sketched on a cocktail napkin in a San Antonio bar. It envisioned connecting three Texas cities: Dallas, Houston, and San Antonio. As legend has it, Rollin King, one of the founders, said to his counterpart Herb Kelleher, "Herb, let's start an airline." Kelleher, who later became Southwest's CEO, replied, "Rollin, you're crazy. Let's do it!" (Freiberg and Freiberg, 1998, p. 15).

As the new airline moved ahead, it met fierce resistance from established carriers. Four years of legal wrangling kept the upstart grounded. In 1971, the Texas Supreme Court ruled in Southwest's favor, and its planes were ready to fly. A local sheriff's threat to halt flights under a court injunction prompted a terse directive from Kelleher: "You roll right over the son of a bitch and leave our tire tracks on his uniform if you have to" (Freiberg and Freiberg, 1998, p. 21). (That directive, of course, signaled resolve, not homicidal intent.) The persistence and zaniness of Southwest's mythologized beginnings shape its unique culture: "The spirit and steadfastness that enabled the airline to survive in its early years is what makes Southwest such a remarkable company today" (p. 14).

Myths undergird an organization's values. Values characterize what an organization stands for, qualities worthy of esteem or commitment. Unlike goals, values are intangible and define a unique character that helps people find meaning and feel special about what they do.

The values that count are those an organization lives, regardless of what it articulates in mission statements or formal documents. Southwest Airlines has never codified its values formally. But its Symbol of Freedom billboards and banners once expressed the company's defining purpose: extending freedom to fly to everyone, not just the elite, and doing it with an abiding sense of fun. Other organizations make values more explicit. The Edina (Minnesota) School District, following the suicide of a superintendent, involved staff, parents, and students in formally articulating values in a document: "We care. We share. We dare." The values of the U.S. Marine Corps are condensed into a simple phrase: "Semper Fi" (short for *semper fidelis*—always faithful). More than a motto, it stands for the traditions, sentiments, and solidarity instilled into recruits and perpetuated by veteran Marines: "The values and assumptions that shape its members . . . are all the Marines have. They are the smallest of the U.S. military services, and in many ways the most interesting. Theirs is the richest culture: formalistic, insular, elitist, with a deep anchor in their own history and mythology" (Ricks, 1998, p. 19).

Vision turns an organization's core ideology, or sense of purpose, into an image of the future. It is a shared fantasy, illuminating new possibilities within the realm of myths and values. Martin Luther King's "I have a dream" speech, for example, articulated poetically a new future for race relations rooted in the ideals of America's founding fathers.

Vision is deemed vital in contemporary organizations. In *Built to Last*, Collins and Porras profile a number of extraordinary companies and conclude, "The essence of a visionary company comes in the translation of its core ideology and its own unique drive for progress into the very fabric of the organization" (1994, p. 201). Johnson & Johnson's commitment to the elimination of "pain and disease" and to "the doctors, nurses, hospitals, mothers, and all others who use our products" motivated the company to make the costly decision to pull Tylenol from store shelves when several tainted bottles were discovered. 3M's principle of "thou shalt not kill a new product idea" came to life when someone refused to stop working on an idea that became Scotch Tape. The same principle paved the way for Post-it® notes, a product resurrected from the failed development of an adhesive. A vision offers mental pictures linking historical legend and core precepts to future events. Shared, it imbues an organization with spirit, resolve, and élan.

Myths, values, and visions often overlap. Take eBay, which emerged as a highly visible success amid a sea of 1990s dot-com disasters. Its interplay of myth, values, and vision contributes to its success even in a tough economic environment. Pierre Omidyar, eBay's founder, envisioned a marketplace where buyers would have equal access to products and prices, and sellers would have an open outlet for goods. Laws of supply and demand would govern prices.

But Omidyar's vision incorporated another element: community. Historically, people have used market stalls and cafés to swap gossip, trade advice, and pass the time of day. Omidyar wanted to combine virtual business site and caring community. That vision led to eBay's core values of commerce and community. Embedded in these are corollary principles: "Treat other people online as you would like to be treated, and when disputes arise, give other people the benefit of the doubt."

eBay is awash in myths and legends. Omidyar's vision is said to have taken root over dinner with his fiancée. She complained that their move from Boston to Silicon Valley severed her ties with fellow collectors of Pez dispensers. He came to her rescue by writing code and laying the foundation for a new company. Did it happen this way? Not quite. Mary Lou Song, an eBay publicist, hatched this story in an effort to get media exposure. Her rationale: "Nobody wants to hear about a 30-year-old genius who wanted to create a perfect market. They want to hear that he did it for his fiancée" (CNN Money, 2011). Her version persists because myths are truer than truth.

Airbnb, like Uber, is a young brand in the upcoming "sharing economy." Success has come so quickly that the 2008 start-up is now valued at $30 billion and has become a verb in everyday communication: "Let's 'Airbnb' in Los Angeles this weekend."

The company's rise had not been without its challenges, but one of its key successes is its search for a mission. The cofounders have succeeded in identifying the company's soul and how it interplays with employees, hosts, guests, and the outside world (Gallagher, 2016).

The quest for a unifying identity began in 2013 and was guided by key questions: Why does Airbnb exist? What's its purpose? What's its role in the world? The questions were put to founders, employees, hosts, and guests around the world. The answers would become the "rudder that guides the whole ship."

Early on, consensus began to emerge around "belonging." This formed the cornerstone for Airbnb's new mission: to make people around the world feel like they could "Belong Anywhere." Airbnb would become the place where anyone could engage with people and cultures as insiders, to meet the "universal human yearning to belong." The Company fashioned a new logo, the "Bélo," a cute squiggly shape resembling a heart, a location pin and the "A" in Airbnb. It stands for four things: people, places, love, and Airbnb (Gallagher, 2017).

Heroes and Heroines

Organizations often rely on CEOs or other prominent leaders as exemplars. They may not be media celebrities, like Jeff Bezos or Elon Musk, or symbols of corporate greed, like Ken Lay, Bernie Ebbers, and Dennis Kozlowski. They are solid leaders who build time-tested companies and deliver results.

One is Mary Barra, the first woman to serve as CEO of General Motors. She took the helm at a challenging time for the venerable automaker, which had barely survived bankruptcy and was under heavy fire for concealing a defective ignition switch that produced 13 deaths in GM Cobalts. Barra handled that with a directness and transparency that were new to General Motors and used it as an opportunity to begin to change GM's sclerotic culture. Since becoming GM's chief in 2014, she has tripled profits and engineered a dramatic revival (Colvin, 2014; Varchaver, 2016).

Another, Costco's James Sinegal, took pride in his disdain for corporate perks. He answered his own phone and personally escorted guests to his spartan office—no executive bathroom, no walls, 20-year-old furniture. He commented: "We're low-cost operators, and it would be a little phony if we tried to pretend that we're not and had all the trappings" (Byrnes et al., 2002, p. 82).

Executives like Barra and Sinegal embrace their role as cultural heroes. They act as living logos, human icons, whose words and deeds exemplify and reinforce core values. Bernie

Marcus, cofounder of Home Depot, underscores the impact of well-placed cultural heroes and heroines: "People watch the titular heads of companies, how they live their lives, and they know [if] they are being sold a bill of goods. If you are a selfish son-of-a-bitch, well that usually comes across fairly well. And it comes across no matter how many memos you send out [stating otherwise]" (Roush, 1999, p. 139).

Not all icons are at the top of organizations. Ordinary people often perform exemplary deeds. The late Joe Vallejo, custodian at a California junior high school, kept the place immaculate. He was also a liaison between the school and its community. His influence knew few limits. When emotions ran high, he attended parent conferences and often negotiated a compromise acceptable to all parties. He knew the students and checked report cards. He was not bashful about telling seasoned teachers how to tailor lessons to student interests and needs. When he retired, a patio was named in his honor. It remains today, commemorating a hero who made a difference well beyond his formal assignment.

Some heroic exploits go unrecognized because they happen out of view. Southwest Airlines annually recognizes its behind-the-scenes employees in a "Heroes of the Heart" award ceremony. The honor goes to the backstage individual or group that contributes most to Southwest's unique culture and successful performance. The year following the award, a Southwest aircraft flies with the winner's name on its fuselage. A song written for the occasion expresses the value Southwest places on its heroes and heroines whose important work is often hidden:

> Heroes come in every shape and size;
> Adding something very special to others in their lives
> No one gives you medals and the world won't know your name
> But in Southwest's eyes you're heroes just the same.

The Twin Towers tragedy reminded Americans of the vital role heroism plays in the human spirit. New York City police officers and firefighters touched people's hearts by risking their lives to save others. Many perished as a result. Their sacrifices reaffirmed Americans' spirit and resolve in enduring one of the nation's most costly tragedies. Every day, less dramatic acts of courage come to light as people go out of their way to help customers or serve communities. NBC's *Nightly News* airs a recurring segment recognizing people who "have made a difference." In 2007, Colin Powell proposed an "Above the Call" citizen award, recognition on par with the Congressional Medal of Honor.

Exploits of heroes and heroines are lodged in our psyches. We call on their examples in times of uncertainty and stress. American POWs in North Vietnamese prisons drew upon stories of the courage of Captain Lance Sijan, Admiral James Stockdale, and Colonel Bud Day, who refused to capitulate to Viet Cong captors. "[Their examples] when passed along the clandestine prison communications network . . . helped support the resolve that eventually defeated the enemy's efforts" (McConnell, 2004, p. 249). During the Bosnian conflict, the ordeal of Scott O'Grady, a U.S. Air Force fighter pilot, made headlines. To survive after being shot down, O'Grady drew on the example of Sijan: "His strong will to survive and be free was an inspiration to every pilot I knew" (O'Grady, 1998, p. 83). Although drawn from nightmares of warfare, these examples demonstrate how human models influence our decisions and actions. We carry lessons of teachers, parents, and others with us. Their exploits, animated through stories, serve as guides to choices we make in our personal lives and at work.

Stories and Fairy Tales

It is said that God made people because he loves stories. "Human life is so bound up in stories that we are desensitized to their weird and witchy power" (Gottschall, 2012, p. 1). Stories, like folk or fairy tales, offer more than entertainment or moral instruction for small children. They grant comfort, reassurance, direction, and hope to people of all ages. They externalize inner conflicts and tensions (Bettelheim, 1977). We tend to dismiss stories as the last resort of people without substance. As an older retiree remarked, "Why, I have a perfect memory. I even remember things that never happened." We denigrate professors and elders for telling "war stories." Yet stories convey information, morals, and myths vividly and convincingly (Mitroff and Kilmann, 1975; Denning, 2005; Gottschall, 2012). They perpetuate values and keep heroic feats alive. This helps account for the recent proliferation of business books linking stories and leadership (Clark, 2004; Denning, 2004, 2005; Simmons, 2006, 2007; Seely et al., 2004). Barry Lopez captures poetically why stories are significant:

Remember only this one thing,
The stories people tell have a way of taking care of them.
If stories come to you, care for them.
And learn to give them away where they are needed.
Sometimes a person needs a story more than food to stay alive.
That is why we put these stories in each other's memories.
This is how people care for themselves (Lopez, 1998).

Stories are deeply rooted in the human experience. It is through story that we can see into each other's souls, and apprehend the soul of the organization. The stories that both individuals and organizations tell about themselves anchor identity and hope. Vough and Caza (2017) note that when individuals experience career setbacks, they do better going forward if they tell a positive story. For example, one manager said about a career setback: "I actually don't regret . . . [not being promoted], because it helped me better understand how to navigate the political landscape, to really trust myself, and not allow others' opinions to influence my own sense of self-worth" (p. 203).

Stories are told and retold around campfires and during family reunions (Clark, 2004). David Armstrong, CEO of Armstrong International, notes that storytelling has played a commanding role in history through the teachings of Jesus, the Buddha, and Mohammed, among many others. It can play an equally potent role in contemporary organizations: "Rules, either in policy manuals or on signs, can be intimidating. But the morals in stories are invariably inviting, fun, and inspiring. Through storytelling our people can know very clearly what the company believes in and what needs to be done" (Armstrong, 1992, p. 6). To Armstrong, storytelling is a simple, timeless, and memorable way to have fun, train newcomers, recognize accomplishments, and spread the word. Denning (2005) puts the functions of stories into eight categories:

- Sparking action
- Communicating who you are
- Communicating who the company is—branding
- Transmitting values
- Fostering collaboration
- Taming the grapevine
- Sharing knowledge
- Leading people into the future

Effective organizations are full of good stories. They often focus on the legendary exploits of corporate heroes. Marriott Hotels founder J. W. Marriott Sr. died many years ago, but his presence lives on. Stories of his unwavering commitment to customer service linger. His aphorism "Take good care of your employees and they'll take good care of your customers" is still part of Marriott's philosophy. According to fable, Marriott visited new general managers and took them for a walk around the property. He pointed out broken branches, sidewalk pebbles, and obscure cobwebs. By tour's end, the new manager had a long to-do list—and, more important, an indelible lesson in what mattered at Marriott.

Not all stories center on the founder or chief executive. Ritz-Carlton is famous for the upscale treatment it offers guests. It begins with the Ritz-Carlton credo and service values, reviewed at the daily "lineup" in every property and carried by every employee in a wallet-sized card. (Another hotel chain planned to implement a similar approach but then canceled the initiative to save the cost of the cards.) "My pleasure" is employees' traditional response to requests, no matter how demanding or trivial. One hurried guest jumped into a taxi to the airport but left his briefcase on the sidewalk. The doorman retrieved the briefcase, abandoned his post, sped to the airport, and delivered it to the panicked guest. Instead of being fired, the doorman became part of the legends and lore—a living example of the company's commitment to service (Deal and Jenkins, 1994).

Stories are a key medium for communicating corporate myths. They establish and perpetuate tradition. Recalled and embellished in formal meetings and informal coffee breaks, they convey and buttress an organization's values and identity to insiders, building loyalty and support. At a company's annual celebration banquet, a nervous executive serving as the night's emcee introduced all the VIPs seated at the head dais. As he was completing his obviously compulsory assignment, a younger man stepped up behind him and whispered, "You forgot to mention the chairman."

A red-faced, flustered emcee turned to the crowd and apologized, "Oh yes, and of course our esteemed chairman of the board, Dr. Frye. Excuse me, Dr. Frye, my secretary left your name off the list." Frye turned to his COO: "John, I want that guy fired tomorrow. That's not the way we do things around here. Honesty and owning your mistakes are a big part of who we are." The story spread quickly through the cultural network. Point made.

Or take Costco, widely recognized for its low prices and high value. Jim Sinegal, founder and former CEO of Costco, is known as a masterful storyteller constantly spinning yarns that reinforce the value of putting the interests of customers and employees ahead of stockholders:

> In 1996 we were selling between $150,000 and $200,000 worth of salmon fillet every week at $5.99 a pound. Then our buyers were able to get an improved product with belly fat, back fins, and collarbones removed, at a better price. As a result we reduced our retail price to $5.29. So they improved the product and lowered the price. The buyers weren't finished with the improvements, though. Next our buyers negotiated for a product with the pin bone out and all of the skin removed, and it was at an even better price, which enabled us to lower our price to $4.99 a pound. Then, because we had continued to grow and had increased our sales volume, we

were able to buy direct from Canadian and Chilean farms, which resulted in an even lower price of $4.79 (Denning, 2005, p. 137).

The "salmon story" is a widely shared symbolic reminder that low prices and high value are central to Costco's core purpose. The story's meaning is reinforced by a "salmon award" given to an employee or supplier who shows great diligence in contributing to Costco's mission. Each award celebrates new stories and creates new lore.

"What else have we got besides stories?" Sinegal asks, "It's what brings meaning to the work we do" (Fisher, Harris, and Jarvis, 2008).

Costco does not advertise, because fans and the media tell their story for them. Costco couldn't say it better than "GearheadGrrrl" in a *Daily Kos* post:

> Been looking for a small tool set to carry in the cars and sidecars, and Costco had the best deal with an American made Craftsman set for $100, now marked down to $80 . . . I was still looking for a better floor jack and Costco had one for $100 that goes down as low as 4" to get under my cars and up to 18" to get the car up where it's easier on my back to work on. Shopped local, but anything equivalent was at least $150 . . . My back is much happier now! So folks, that's the "Costco effect." How Costco saves consumers dollars on mass market merchandise in major markets, while leaving opportunities for small local businesses to cater to our needs for specialty merchandise. Add in the living wages that Costco pays that allow Costco employees to funnel more dollars back into the economy, and we have a "Costco effect" that benefits workers, consumers, and businesses of all sizes instead of funneling wealth to the few like Walmart does! (GearheadGrrrl, 2013).

CNBC ran a TV story that focused on low prices, customer loyalty, and the "treasure hunt," crediting Costco with reinventing shopping; the clip has more than 500,000 periodic views on YouTube (CNBC, 2013). The webmaster for addictedtocostco.com maintained her devotion to the store even after moving from Texas to the United Kingdom, despite a longer and initially scarier drive. Similar fanaticism was exemplified by two customers who held their engagement party at a local Costco. The story garnered national media attention.

Ritual

As a symbolic act, ritual is routine that "usually has a stateable purpose, but one that invariably alludes to more than it says, and has many meanings at once" (Moore and Meyerhoff, 1977, p. 5). Enacting a ritual connects an individual or group to something mystical, more than words or rational thinking can capture. At home and at work, ritual gives structure and meaning to each day: "We find these magical moments every day—drinking our morning coffee, reading the daily paper, eating lunch with a friend, drinking a glass of wine while admiring the sunset, or saying, 'Good night, sleep tight . . .' at bedtime. The holy in the daily; the sacred in the single act of living . . . A time to do the dishes. And a time to walk the dog" (Fulghum, 1995, pp. 3, 254).

Humans create both personal and communal rituals. The ones that carry meaning become the dance of life. "Rituals anchor us to a center," Fulghum writes, "while freeing us to move on and confront the everlasting unpredictability of life. The paradox of ritual patterns and sacred habits is that they simultaneously serve as a solid footing and springboard, providing a stable dynamic in our lives" (1995, p. 261).

The power of ritual becomes palpable if one experiences the emptiness of losing it. Campbell (1988) underscores this loss: "When you lose rituals, you lose a sense of civilization; and that's why society is so out of kilter." As mentioned earlier, many Catholics lost their faith in the 1960s when the Roman Catholic Church changed its liturgy from Latin to vernacular. Later the Church reversed its earlier position and gave local priests permission to conduct the mass in Latin. Conversely, when the Catholic Church was hit later with a series of scandals involving sexual abuse of children and adolescents by priests, shaken laypersons turned to rituals of the mass for comfort and reassurance.

Rituals of initiation induct newcomers into communal membership. "Greenhorns" often encounter powerful cultural pressures as they join a group or organization. A new member must gain entry to the inner sanctum. Transitioning from stranger to full-fledged member grants access to cherished organizational secrets. The key episode is the rite of passage affirming acceptance. In tribes, simply attaining puberty is insufficient for young males: "There must be an accompanying trial and appropriate ritual to mark the event. The so-called primitives had the good sense to make these trials meaningful and direct. Upon attaining puberty you killed a lion and were circumcised. After a little dancing and whatnot, you were admitted as a junior member and learned some secrets. The [men's] hut is a symbol of, and a medium for maintaining, the status quo and the good of the order" (Ritti and Funkhouser, 1982, p. 3).

We are not beyond the primitive drives, sexism, and superstition that gave rise to age-old institutions such as the men's hut. Consider the experience of a newly elected member of the U.S. Congress:

One of the early female novices was a representative who was a serious feminist. Soon after arriving in Congress, she broke propriety by audaciously proposing an amendment to a military bill of Edward Hebert, Chief of the Defense Clan. When the amendment received only a single vote, she supposedly snapped at the aged committee chairman: "I know the only reason my amendment failed is that I've got a vagina." To which Hebert retorted, "If you'd been using your vagina instead of your mouth, maybe you'd have gotten a few more votes" (Weatherford, 1985, p. 35).

That exchange seems particularly harsh and offensive, but its multiple interpretations take us to the heart of symbolic customs. A kinder and gentler anecdote would blunt the power in a multilayered transaction with multiple meanings. Let's look at some possible versions.

One version highlights the age-old battle between the sexes. The female representative raises the specter of sexual discrimination; Hebert uses a sexist jibe to put her in her place. Another view sees the exchange as a classic give-and-take. Newcomers bring new ideas as agents of evolution and reform. Old-timers are supposed to pass along time-tested values and traditions. As an initiation ritual, the exchange is a predictable clash between a new arrival and an established veteran. The old-timer is reminding the rookie who's in charge. Newcomers don't get free admission. The price is higher for those who, because of race, gender, or ethnicity, question or threaten existing values, norms, or patterns. If newcomers succumb, an organization risks stultification and decay; if old-timers fail to induct new arrivals properly, chaos and disarray lie ahead. Only a weak culture accepts newcomers without some form of testing, rite of passage, or "hazing." The rite of passage reinforces the existing culture while testing the newcomer's ability to become a member.

Initiation rituals in other organizations also reveal cultural values and ways to the newcomer. At Ritz Carlton, the process is called "Onboarding." The two-day experience is as intense as the Congressional example but not as coarse. Newcomers learn the Credo and Gold Standards from current employees and high-ranking executives. They are imbued with their role as "ladies and gentlemen serving ladies and gentlemen." They learn about the "Wow Effect" and their role in assuring that each guest has a superlative experience (each Ritz employee has a $4,000 discretionary fund to make sure this happens).

One new employee describes how the "Wow Effect" took place at the end of the event's second day:

> We took a break. But before being dismissed our leaders asked each of us to write down our favorite food. Mine was Belgian chocolate. We handed in our

slips of paper and left. Upon the return, there was a plate of our favorite food at each place. Belgian chocolate for me. I never forgot that and now look for any chance I have to make a guest exclaim "WOW."

Initiation is one important role of ritual. Rituals also bond a group together and imbue the enterprise with traditions and values. They prepare combat pilots to slip into a fighter cockpit knowing they may not return:

For me, there can be no fighter pilots without fighter pilot rituals. The end result of these rituals is a culture that allows individuals to risk their lives and revel in it (Broughton, 1988, p. 131).

Some rituals become ceremonial occasions to recognize momentous accomplishments. When Captain Lance Sijan received his posthumous Medal of Honor, the president of the United States attended:

In the large room, men in impressive uniforms and costly vested suits and women [in uniforms] and cheerful spring pastels stood motionless and silent in their contemplation of the words. The stark text of the citation contained a wealth of evocative imagery, some of it savage, some tender to the point of heartbreak. President Ford left the rostrum: a group of senior officers drew up beside him to hand forward the glass-covered walnut case containing the medal. There was a certain liturgical quality to this passing of a sanctified object among a circle of anointed leaders (McConnell, 2004, p. 217).

At the other end of the scale are many light-hearted rituals, but even these have a more serious side:

On a Friday night at a base officers' club, four Marine A-6 Intruder pilots joined a packed crowd of Air Force officers. One of the Marine aviators put his cap on the bar while fishing for some money to pay for his drink. The bartender rang a foot-tall bell and yelled "Hat on the bar!" This infraction automatically means the guilty party buys a round of drinks. Surveying the size of the crowd, the Marine . . . refused to pay. An Air Force colonel approached him and asked him if he really intended to flout the tradition. When the Marine responded in the affirmative, the colonel called the base security and ordered the A-6 [aircraft] on the ramp impounded. The Marine left and called his superior to report the colonel's action. Shortly thereafter, he returned and asked sheepishly, "What's everyone having?" (R. Mola, cited in Reed, 2001, p. 6).

Rituals also delineate key relationships. One of the most important relationships in a fighter squadron is that between a pilot and crew chief.

A preflight ritual transfers ownership between someone who cares for an aircraft on the ground and the one who will take it aloft. The ground ritual has several phases. A first salute reinforces rank and signifies respect between mechanic and pilot. A handshake takes the formal greeting to a new level, cementing the personal bond between the two. A second salute after the pilot has checked the aircraft indicates the aircraft's airworthiness. It is now officially under the pilot's command. Finally, a thumbs-up is a personal gesture wishing the pilot a good flight. Interwoven, the many rituals of combat flying bond the participants and bind them to the service's traditions and values (R. Mola, cited in Reed, 2001, p. 5).

Ceremony

Historically, cultures have relied on ritual and ceremony to create order, clarity, and predictability—particularly around mysterious and random issues or dilemmas. The distinction between ritual and ceremony is elusive. As a rule of thumb, rituals are more frequent, everyday routines imbued with special meaning. Ceremonies are more episodic, grander, and more elaborate. Ceremonies often weave several rituals in concert and are convened at times of transition or on special occasions. Rain dances, harvest celebrations, the darkest days of winter, the new beginnings and hope of spring bring people together to remember the past and to renew faith, hope, and spirit. Annual business meetings invoke supernatural assistance in explaining dips in the stock price or in building new market share. Annual conventions renew old ties and revive deep, collective commitments. "Convention centers are the basilicas of secular religion" (Fulghum, 1995, p. 96).

Both ritual and ceremony are illustrated in an account from Japan:

It has been the same every night since the death in 1964 of Yasujiro Tsutsumi, the legendary patriarch of the huge Seibu real-estate and transportation group. Two employees stand an overnight vigil at his tomb . . . On New Year's, the weather is often bitter, but at dawn the vigil expands to include five or six hundred top executives—directors, vice presidents, presidents—arrayed by company and rank, the most senior in front. A limousine delivers Yasujiro's third son, Yoshiaki Tsutsumi, the head of the family business and Japan's richest man. A great brass bell booms out six times as Yoshiaki approaches his father's tomb. He claps his hands twice, bows deeply, and says, "Happy New Year, Father, Happy New Year." Then he turns to deliver a brief-but-stern sermon to the assembled congregation. The basic themes change little from year to year: last year was tough, this year will be even tougher, and you'll be washing dishes in one of the hotels if your performance is bad. Finally, he toasts his father with warm sake and departs (Downer, 1994).

Ceremonies serve four major roles: they socialize, stabilize, reassure, and convey messages to external constituencies. Consider the example of Mary Kay Cosmetics. Several thousand people gather at the company's annual seminars to hear (now posthumous) personal messages from Mary Kay, to applaud the achievements of star salespeople, to hear success stories, and to celebrate. The ceremony brings new members into the fold and helps maintain faith, hope, and optimism in the Mary Kay family. It is a distinctive pageant and makes the Mary Kay culture accessible to outsiders, particularly consumers. Failure recedes and obstacles disappear in the "you can do it" spirit of the company symbol, the bumblebee—a creature that, according to mythical aerodynamics experts, should not be able to fly. Unaware of its limitations, it flies anyway.

Some events, like retirement dinners and welcoming events for new employees, are clearly ceremonial. Other ceremonies happen at moments of triumph or transition. When Phil Condit took over the reins of Boeing in 1996, he invited senior managers to his home for dinner. Afterward, the group gathered around a giant fire pit to tell stories about Boeing. Condit asked them to toss negative stories into the flames. It was an emblematic way to banish the dark side of the company's past (Deal and Key, 1998).

Condit resigned his chairman position at Boeing, under pressure, in 2003 but returned as part of the crowd to witness the ceremonial rollout of an aircraft his team had begun work on a decade earlier—the 787 Dreamliner. As the *Seattle Post-Intelligencer* reported, "With some 15,000 people gathered Sunday inside the world's largest building—Boeing's Everett factory—and tens of thousands more watching the event live around the world—Boeing opened the hangar doors to reveal the 787 Dreamliner, the first commercial passenger plane that will have a mostly composite airframe rather than aluminum . . . Those 15,000 employees, past and current executives, airline customers and others crowded around the new jet for an up-close look" ("Thousands Welcome the Long-Awaited 787 Dreamliner," 2007).

Condit mingled with employees to give and receive congratulations. Tom Brokaw served as master of ceremonies. Rock music roused the crowd. The event gave VIPs and politicians an opportunity to bask in the glory of a momentous accomplishment. As those who had launched every plane from the 707 through the 747 rubbed elbows and swapped tales, the roots of the past fused with the joy of the present and the promise of tomorrow's next leap forward.

Ceremonies do not have to be as lavish as Boeing's launch of the Dreamliner. Every organization has its moments of achievement and atonement. Expressive events provide order and meaning and bind an organization or a society together.

Ceremony is equally evident in other arenas. In the United States, political conventions select candidates, even though in recent decades the winner is usually determined well in advance. After the conventions come several months in which competing candidates trade clichés. The same pageantry unfolds each election year. Rhetoric and spontaneous demonstrations are staged in advance. Campaigning is repetitious and superficial, reporters play up the skirmish of the day, and voting often seems disconnected from the main drama. The denouement is often just what everyone expected, but occasionally the drama takes an unexpected turn, as in 2016 when Donald Trump won even though he was expected to lose.

Even so, the process of electing a president is still a momentous ceremony. It entails a sense of social involvement. It is an outlet for expression of discontent and enthusiasm. It stages live drama for citizens to witness and debate and gives millions of people a sense of participating in an exciting adventure. It lets candidates reassure the public that there are answers to important questions and solutions to vexing problems. It draws attention to common social ties and to the importance of America's peaceful transfer of power (Edelman, 1977).

When properly conducted and attuned to valued myths, both ritual and ceremony fire the imagination and deepen faith; otherwise, they become cold, empty forms that people resent and avoid. They can release creativity and transform meanings, but they can also cement the status quo and block adaptation and learning. In some organizations, whining and complaining evolve as rituals of choice. Negative symbols perpetuate evil, just as positive symbols reinforce goodness. Symbols cut both ways.

Metaphor, Humor, and Play

Metaphor, humor, and play illustrate the important "as if," "suppose that" quality of symbols. Metaphors make the strange familiar and the familiar strange. They capture subtle themes that normal language can obscure. Consider these metaphors from managers asked to depict their agency as it is and as they hope it might become:

As the Agency Is	As It Might Become
A maze	A well-oiled wheel
Wet noodle	Oak tree
Aggregation of competing tribes	Symphony orchestra
Three-ring circus	Championship team
An unsolvable puzzle	A smooth-running machine
Twilight zone	Utopia
Herd of rampaging cattle	Fleet of ships

Metaphors compress complicated issues into understandable images, influencing our attitudes and actions. A university head who views the institution as a factory leads differently than one who conceives of it as a craft guild, shopping center, or beloved alma mater.

Humor plays a number of important roles: It integrates, expresses skepticism, contributes to flexibility and adaptiveness, and lessens status differences. Hansot (1979) argues that instead of asking why people use humor in organizations, we should ask why people are so serious. Humor is a classic device for distancing, but it also draws people together. It establishes solidarity and facilitates face saving. Above all, it is a way to illuminate and break frames, indicating that any single definition of a situation is arbitrary.

Play and humor are often distinguished from work. Play is what people do away from the office. Images of play among managers typically connote aggression, competition, and struggle ("We've got to beat them at their own game"; "We dropped the ball on that one"; "We knocked that one out of the park") rather than relaxation and fun. But if play is viewed as a state of mind (Bateson, 1972; Goffman, 1974), any activity can become playful. Play relaxes rules to explore alternatives, encouraging experimentation, flexibility, and creativity. Playfulness has created many remarkable innovations. March (1976) suggests some guidelines for encouraging play in organizations: treat goals as hypotheses, intuition as real, hypocrisy as transition, memory as an enemy, and experience as a theory.

ORGANIZATIONS AS CULTURES

What is culture? What is its role in an organization? Both questions are contested. Some argue that organizations *have* cultures; others insist that organizations *are* cultures. Schein (1992, p. 12) offers a formal definition: "a pattern of shared basic assumptions that a group learned as it solved its problems of external adaptation and integration, that has worked well enough to be considered valid and therefore to be taught to new members as the correct way to perceive, think, and feel in relation to those problems." Deal and Kennedy (1982, p. 4) portray culture more succinctly as "the way we do things around here." Culture is both a product and a process. As a product, it embodies wisdom accumulated from experience. As a process, it is renewed and recreated as newcomers learn the old ways and eventually become teachers themselves.

There is a long-standing controversy about the relationship between culture and leadership. Do leaders shape culture, or are they shaped by it? Is symbolic leadership empowering or manipulative? Another debate swirls around the link between culture and results. Do organizations with robust cultures outperform those relying on structure and strategy? Does success breed a cohesive culture, or is it the other way around? Books like Kotter and Heskett's *Corporate Culture and Performance* (1992), Collins and Porras's *Built to Last* (1994), and Collins's *Good to Great* (2001) offer impressive longitudinal evidence linking culture to the financial bottom line.

Over time, an organization develops distinctive beliefs, values, and customs. Managers who understand the significance of symbols and know how to evoke spirit and soul can shape more cohesive and effective organizations—so long as the cultural patterns align with the challenges of the marketplace. To be sure, culture can become a negative force, as it did at Volkswagen and Wells Fargo Bank. But two cases demonstrate how positive, cohesive business cultures can be fashioned and perpetuated.

BMW's Dream Factory

In 1959, BMW was in a financial hole as deep as the one General Motors and Ford experienced more recently (Edmondson, 2006. Copyright © 2006. McGraw-Hill Companies, Inc.). During the 1950s, BMW executives misjudged the consumer market, and customers shunned two new models—one too big and pricey even for the luxury market, the other a two-seater too small and impractical for the sporty crowd. BMW almost went bankrupt and almost had to sell out to Mercedes. A wealthy shareholder stepped in and, with concessions from the unions, bailed the company out. The memory of this close call is part of BMW's lore: "Near death experiences are healthy for companies. BMW has been running scared for years" (p. 4, Copyright © 2006. McGraw-Hill Companies, Inc.). The near-death story is retold often and is one of the first things newcomers learn.

Old ways become especially vulnerable in times of crisis. BMW shucked off its top-down mentality in 1959 and cultivated a new cultural mind-set to guard against making the same mistake again.

A visit to BMW's Leipzig plant shows how far the company has come. The plant's modern, artsy, open-air feeling reflects the company's cultural values and demonstrates its commitment to breaking down barriers among workers, designers, engineers, and managers. Openness encourages chance encounters and a freewheeling exchange of ideas. People "meet simply because their paths cross naturally. And they say 'Ah, glad I ran into you, I have an idea'" (Edmondson, 2006, p. 1. Copyright © 2006. McGraw-Hill Companies, Inc.).

At BMW, the bedrock value is innovation:

> Just about everyone working for the Bavarian automaker—from the factory floor to the design studios to the marketing department—is encouraged to speak out. Ideas bubble up freely, and there is never a penalty for proposing a new way of doing things, no matter how outlandish. Much of BMW's success stems from an entrepreneurial culture that's rare in corporate Germany, where management is usually top-down and the gulf between workers and management is vast. BMW's 100,000 employees have become a nimble network of true believers with few barriers to hinder innovation (Edmondson, 2006, pp. 1–2. Copyright © 2006. McGraw-Hill Companies, Inc.).

Commitment to its workers is another core value of BMW. It is not easy to get a job at a company that fields 200,000 applications annually. Those who pass initial screening have to survive intense interviews and a day of working in teams. The goal: to screen out those who don't fit. The lucky few who are hired move into the mix right away. They are forced to rely on veteran workers to learn the ropes. But once part of the BMW workforce, workers have unparalleled job security. Layoffs, once common at Ford and GM, don't happen at BMW. The company is loyal to its employees, and they respond in kind.

From the start, workers receive indoctrination into the BMW Way. They are steeped "with a sense of place, history, and mission. Individuals from all strata of the corporation work elbow-to-elbow, creating informal networks where they can hatch even the most unorthodox ideas for making better Bimmers or boosting profits. The average BMW buyer may not know it, but he is driving a machine born of thousands of important brainstorming sessions. BMW, in fact, may be the chattiest company ever" (Edmondson, 2006, p. 2. Copyright © 2006. McGraw-Hill Companies, Inc.).

Rituals are a way of tribal life at BMW—building bonds among diverse groups, connecting employees' hearts with the company's soul, and pooling far-flung ideas for better products. After BMW acquired Rolls-Royce, an assemblage of designers, engineers, marketers, and line workers was thrown together to redesign the signature Rolls Phantom.

The result was a superluxurious best seller. When management decided to drop the Z3, a designer persuaded some other designers and engineers to join him in an "off the books, skunk-works" effort. The outcome of their collective endeavor: the successful Z4 sports car.

The flexibility of BMW's manufacturing process allows buyers to select engine types, interior configuration, and trim, customizing almost every key feature. They can change their minds up to 5 hours before the vehicle is assembled—and they do. The assembly line logs 170,000 alterations a month. This level of personal attention lets assemblers visualize who the driver might be. Making identical cars only every nine months creates a sense of personal touch and creativity. That's a prime reason work at BMW has meaning beyond a paycheck. Everyone's efforts are aimed at building a distinctive automobile that an owner will be proud to drive.

The vitality and cohesiveness of the idea-driven BMW culture is reflected in the company's bottom line. From its nadir in the 1950s, BMW grew past Mercedes to become the world's largest premium carmaker (Vella, 2006). But that growth may also be its biggest vulnerability. "Losing its culture to sheer size is a major risk" (Edmondson, 2006, p. 3. Copyright © 2006. McGraw-Hill Companies, Inc.). So far, BMW seems to be meeting the challenge of nurturing recollections of 1959 as a defense against complacency. In 2012, *Forbes* named BMW the most reputable company in the world.

Greatest Hits from Organization Studies

Hit Number 28: Geert Hofstede, *Culture's Consequences: International Differences in Work-Related Values* (Newbury Park, CA: Sage, 1984)

Geert Hofstede pioneered research on the impact of national culture on the workplace. Although other studies, such as GLOBE (House et al., 2004), are more current, his work remains the most frequently cited.

Defining culture as "the collective programming of the mind that distinguishes the members of one human group from another" (p. 21), Hofstede focused particularly on work-related values. The heart of his book is a survey of a large U.S. multinational company's employees. Approximately 117,000 surveys were collected from workers and managers in 40 countries and 20 languages. Data were collected in two waves, one in 1968 and another in 1972. Hofstede then identified variables that reliably differentiated managers of various nations. He ultimately settled on four dimensions of national culture:

1. *Power distance:* A measure of power inequality between bosses and subordinates. High power-distance countries (such as the Philippines, Mexico, and Venezuela) display more autocratic relationships between bosses and subordinates. Low power-distance countries (including Denmark, Israel, and Austria) show more democratic and decentralized patterns.

2. *Uncertainty avoidance:* The level of comfort with uncertainty and ambiguity. Countries high on uncertainty avoidance (Greece, Portugal, Belgium, and Japan) tend to make heavy use of structure, rules, and specialists to maintain control. Those low on the index (Hong Kong, Denmark, Sweden, and Singapore) put less emphasis on structure and are more tolerant of risk taking.

3. *Individualism:* The importance of the individual versus the collective (group, organization, or society). Countries highest on individualism (the United States, Australia, Great Britain, and Canada) put emphasis on autonomous, self-reliant individuals who care for themselves. Countries lowest on individuality (Peru, Pakistan, Colombia, and Venezuela) emphasized mutual loyalty.

4. *Masculinity-femininity:* The degree to which a culture emphasizes ambition and achievement versus caring and nurture. In countries highest in masculinity (Japan, Austria, Venezuela, Italy), men tend to feel strong pressures for success, relatively few women hold high-level positions, and job stress is high. The opposite is true in countries low in masculinity (such as Denmark, Norway, the Netherlands, and Sweden).

Hofstede argues that management practices and theories are inevitably culture bound. Most management theory has been developed in the United States, which is culturally similar to nations where people speak English and other northern-European languages but distinct from most countries in Asia (as well as those speaking Romance languages). To Hofstede, managers and scholars have too often assumed that what works in their culture will work anywhere, an assumption that can have disastrous results.

Hofstede also explores the relationship between national and organizational culture, noting that a common culture is a powerful form of organizational glue. This is most likely to occur in multinationals in which a home country culture reigns companywide, which in turn requires that managers from outside the home country become bicultural. Many American managers who work abroad, in Hofstede's view, tend to live in American enclaves and remain both monolingual and monocultural.

Hofstede's research was limited in many ways. His sample came from only one American company (IBM), and many nations were absent (China, Russia, most of Africa and Eastern Europe). His data are now about four decades old. But no other work has been as influential in demonstrating the pervasive impact of national culture on organizations.

Nordstrom's Rooted Culture

Nordstrom department stores are renowned for customer service and employee satisfaction. Customers rave about its no-hassle, no-questions-asked commitment to high-quality service: "not service the way it used to be, but service that never was" (Spector and McCarthy, 1995, p. 1). Year after year, Nordstrom has been ranked at or near the top in retail service ratings, and in 2016 it continued to hold the top spot for department stores. The company is consistently listed on *Fortune's* list of the 100 Best Companies to Work for.

Founder John Nordstrom was a Swedish immigrant who settled in Seattle after an odyssey across America and a brief stint hunting gold in Alaska. He and Carl Wallin, a shoemaker, opened a shoe store. Nordstrom's sons Elmer, Everett, and Lloyd joined the business. Collectively, they anchored the firm in an enduring philosophical principle: the customer is always right. The following generations of Nordstroms expanded the business while maintaining a close connection with historical roots.

The company relies on acculturated "Nordies" to induct new employees into customer service the Nordstrom way. Newcomers begin in sales, learning traditions from the ground up: "When we are at our best, our frontline people are lieutenants because they control the business. Our competition has foot soldiers on the front line and lieutenants in the back" (Spector and McCarthy, 1995, p. 106).

Nordstrom's unique commitment to customer service is heralded in its "heroics"—tales of heroes and heroines going out of their way:

- A customer fell in love with a particular pair of pleated burgundy slacks on sale at Nordstrom's downtown Seattle store. Unfortunately, the store was out of her size. The sales associate got cash from the department manager, marched across the street, bought the slacks at full price from a competitor, brought them back, and sold them to the customer at Nordstrom's reduced price (Spector and McCarthy, 1995, p. 26).

- According to legend, a Nordie once refunded a customer's payment for a set of automobile tires, even though the company had never stocked tires. In 1975, Nordstrom had acquired three stores from Northern Commercial in Alaska. The customer had purchased the tires from Northern Commercial, so Nordstrom took them back—as the story goes (Spector and McCarthy, 1995, p. 27).

Nordstrom's commitment to customer service is reinforced in storewide rituals. Newcomers encounter the company's values in the initial employee orientation. For many years, they were given a 5″ × 8″ card labeled the "Nordstrom Employee Handbook," which listed only one rule: *Use your sound judgment in all situations.* Newcomers still get the card, but Nordstrom has added a handbook that lists a few rules and legal considerations. The emphasis on pleasing the customer is still dominant. At staff meetings, sales associates compare and discuss sales techniques and role-play customer encounters.

Periodic ceremonies reinforce the company's cherished values. From the company's early years, the Nordstrom family sponsored summer picnics and Christmas dance parties, and the company continues to create occasions to celebrate customer service: "We do crazy stuff. Monthly store powwows serve as a kind of revival meeting, where customer letters of appreciation are read and positive achievements are recognized, while coworkers whoop and cheer for one another. Letters of complaint about Nordstrom customer service are also read over the intercom (omitting the names of offending salespeople)" (Spector and McCarthy, 1995, pp. 120, 129).

At one spirited sales meeting, a regional manager asked all present to call out their sales targets for the year, which he posted on a large chart. Then the regional manager uncovered his own target for each person. Anyone whose target was below the regional manager's was roundly booed. Those whose individual goals were higher were acclaimed with enthusiastic cheers (Spector and McCarthy, 1995).

The delicate balance of competition, cooperation, and customer service has served Nordstrom well. Its stellar identity has created a sterling image. In a sermon titled "The Gospel According to Nordstrom," one California minister "praised the retailer for carrying out the call of the gospel in ways more consistent and caring than we sometimes do in the church" (Spector and McCarthy, 1995, p. 21).

Nordstrom, like every business, has stumbled occasionally. But its steadfast loyalty to proven values and ways keeps the company on a successful course.

CONCLUSION

In contrast to traditional views emphasizing rationality, the symbolic frame highlights the tribal aspect of contemporary organizations. It centers on complexity and ambiguity and emphasizes the idea that symbols mediate the meaning of work.

Myths, values, and vision bring cohesiveness, clarity, and direction in the presence of confusion and mystery. Heroes carry values and serve as powerful icons. Rituals and ceremonies provide scripts for celebrating success and facing calamity. Metaphors, humor, and play offer escape from the tyranny of facts and logic; they stimulate creative alternatives to timeworn choices. Symbolic forms and activities are the basic elements of culture, accumulated over time to shape an organization's unique identity and character. In *The Feast of Fools*, Cox (1969, p. 13) summarizes: "Our links to yesterday and tomorrow depend also on the aesthetic, emotional, and symbolic aspects of human life—on saga, play, and celebration. Without festival and fantasy, man would not really be a historical being at all."

Culture in Action

*Not a having and a resting, but a growing and becoming is
the character of perfection as culture conceives it.*

—Matthew Arnold

The public has been fascinated with the U.S. Navy's secret SEAL strike teams ever since one of them, SEAL Team Six Red Squadron, tracked down Osama bin Laden in 2012. The public eye typically focuses on the modern weaponry, awesome firepower, and sheer bravado of the SEAL operators. At least three books and a hit movie, *Zero Dark Thirty*—each with its own interpretation of that operation—came out in 2013. But lurking beneath the surface of Red Squadron's successful foray is another story about the culture of SEAL Team Six, which has not been fully told.

The books written by SEALs generally underscore the important contributions of the team's tightly knit culture. The members of Team Six "are bound together not only by sworn oaths, but also by the obligations of their brotherhood" (Pfarrer, 2011, p. 28). As one SEAL described it, "My relationship with Team Six has been more important than my marriage" (Wasdin and Templin, 2011, p. 254). Posttraumatic stress disorder among returning soldiers has been attributed to the loss of brotherhood. Published sources sometimes mention pranks, humor, ritual, and specialized language, but they don't describe in depth the essential cultural components that create these intense emotional and spiritual bonds.

Descriptions, prescriptions, and theories about improving teamwork often miss the deeper secrets and mysteries of how groups and teams reach the elusive state of grace and peak performance. Former Visa CEO Dee Hock captured the heart of the issue: "In the field of group endeavor, you will see incredible events in which the group performs far beyond the sum of its individual talents. It happens in the symphony, in the ballet, in the theater, in sports, and equally in business. It is easy to recognize and impossible to define. It is a mystique. It cannot be achieved without immense effort, training, and cooperation, but effort, training, and cooperation alone rarely create it" (quoted in Schlesinger, Eccles, and Gabarro, 1983, p. 173).

With a population of only slightly more than 2 million people in the 1770s, how was the United States able to produce an extraordinary leadership team that included John Adams, Benjamin Franklin, Alexander Hamilton, Thomas Jefferson, and George Washington? In World War II, did anyone believe that Britain's Royal Air Force could defend the island nation against the overwhelming power of Hitler's Luftwaffe? As Winston Churchill later commented, "Never have so many owed so much to so few."

Did anyone expect the Iraqi soccer team to take home the Asian Cup in 2007? With all the turmoil and strife at the time in Iraq, it is hard to picture the country even fielding a team. And how could two graduate students who came from opposite ends of the earth (Michigan and Moscow), and who initially didn't like each other, create a company whose name—Google—became a global household word?

Are such peak performances simply a great mystery—beautiful when they happen but no more predictable or controllable than California's next earthquake? Too often we try to attribute success to extraordinary individuals, enlightened structural design, or political harmony. In this chapter, we scrutinize a classic case of a team that achieved a state of transcendence. Tracy Kidder spent a year embedded in a group of engineers, intimately observing it in operation. The unusually in-depth and close-grained story takes us directly to the symbolic roots of flow, spirit, and magic. Very few studies of teams can match Kidder's rigor and attention to detail.

THE EAGLE GROUP'S SOURCES OF SUCCESS

Kidder's *Soul of a New Machine* (1981) is the dazzling and detailed account of the extensive period of time he spent at the minicomputer firm Data General in the 1970s with a group of engineers who created a new computer in record time. Despite scant resources and limited support, the Eagle Group outperformed all other Data General divisions to produce a new state-of-the-art machine. The technology they developed is now antiquated, but lessons drawn from how they pulled it off are as current and instructive ever.[1]

Why did the Eagle Group succeed? So many groups of engineers—or educators, physicians, executives, or graduate students—start out with high hopes but falter and fail.

Were the project members extraordinarily talented? Not really. Each was highly skilled, but there were equally talented engineers working on other Data General projects.

Were team members treated with dignity and respect? Quite the contrary. As one engineer noted, "No one ever pats anyone on the back" (p. 179). Instead, the group experienced what they called mushroom management: "Put 'em in the dark, feed 'em shit, and watch 'em grow" (p. 109). For over a year, group members jeopardized their health, their families, and their careers: "I'm flat out by definition. I'm a mess. It's terrible. It's a lot of fun" (p. 119).

Were financial rewards a motivating factor? Group members said explicitly that they did not work for money. Nor were they motivated by fame. Heroic efforts were rewarded neither by formal appreciation nor by official applause. The group quietly dissolved shortly after completing the new computer, and most members moved unrecognized to other parts of Data General or to other companies. Their experience fits later successes at Cisco Systems, about which Paulson concludes, "All personnel are driven by the desire to be a part of a winning organization" (2001, p. 187).

Perhaps the group's structure accounted for its success. Were its members pursuing well-defined and laudable goals? The group leader, Tom West, offered the precept that "not everything worth doing is worth doing well." Pushed to translate his maxim, he elaborated, "If you can do a quick-and-dirty job and it works, do it" (p. 119). Did the group have clear and well-coordinated roles and relationships? According to Kidder, it kept no meaningful charts, graphs, or organization tables. One of the group's engineers put it bluntly: "The whole management structure—anyone in Harvard Business School would have barfed" (p. 116).

Can the political frame unravel the secret of the group's phenomenal performance? Possibly group members were motivated more by power than by money: "There's a big high in here somewhere for me that I don't fully understand. Some of it's a raw power trip. The reason I work is because I win" (p. 179). They were encouraged to circumvent formal channels to advance group interests: "If you can't get what you need from some manager at your level in another department, go to his boss—that's the way to get things done" (p. 191).

Group members were also unusually direct and confrontational: "Feeling sorely provoked, [David] Peck one day said to this engineer, 'You're an asshole.' Ordered by his boss to apologize, Peck went to the man he had insulted, looking sheepish, and said, 'I'm sorry you're an asshole'" (p. 224).

The group was highly competitive with others in the company: "There's a thing you learn at Data General, if you work here for any period of time . . . that nothing ever happens unless you push it" (p. 111). They also competed with one another. Their "tube wars" are a typical example. Carl Alsing, head of a subgroup known as the Microkids, returned from lunch one day to find that all his files had become empty shells: the names were there, but the contents had vanished. It took him an hour to find where the real files were. Alsing counterattacked by creating an encrypted file and tantalizing the team, "There's erotic writing in there and if you can find it, you can read it" (p. 107).

Here we begin to encounter the secrets of the group's success. The tube wars—and other exchanges among group members—were more than power struggles. They were a form of play that released tensions, created bonds, and contributed to an unusual group spirit. A shared and cohesive culture rather than a clear, well-defined structure was the invisible force that gave the team its drive.

From the Eagle Group's experience, we can distill several important tenets of the symbolic frame that are broadly applicable to groups and teams:

- How someone becomes a group member is important.
- Diversity supports a team's competitive advantage.
- Example, not command, holds a team together.
- A specialized language fosters cohesion and commitment.
- Stories carry history and values and reinforce group identity.
- Humor and play reduce tension and encourage creativity.
- Ritual and ceremony lift spirits and reinforce values.
- Informal cultural players contribute disproportionately to their formal roles.
- Soul is the secret of success.

Becoming a Member

Joining a team involves more than a rational decision. It is a mutual choice marked by some form of ritual. In the Eagle Group, the process of becoming a member was called "signing up." When interviewing recruits, Alsing conveyed the message that they were volunteering to climb Mount Everest without a rope despite lacking the "right stuff" to keep up with other climbers. When the new recruits protested they wanted to climb Mount Everest anyway, Alsing told them they would first have to find out whether they were good enough. After the selections were made, Alsing summed it up this way: "It was kind of like recruiting for a suicide mission. You're gonna die, but you're gonna die in glory" (p. 66).

Through the signing-up ritual, an engineer became part of a special effort and agreed to forsake family, friends, and health to accomplish the impossible. It was a sacred declaration: "I want to do this job and I'll give it my heart and soul" (p. 63).

Diversity Is a Competitive Advantage

Though nearly all the group's members were engineers, each had unique skills and style. Tom West, the group's leader, was by reputation a highly talented technical debugger. He was also aloof and unapproachable, the "Prince of Darkness." Steve Wallach, the group's computer architect, was a highly creative maverick. According to Kidder (p. 75), before accepting West's invitation to join the group, he went to Edson de Castro, the president of Data General, to find out precisely what he'd be working on:

"Okay," Wallach said, "what the fuck do you want?"

"I want a 32-bit Eclipse," de Castro told him.

"If we can do this, you won't cancel it on us?" Wallach asked. "You'll leave us alone?"

"That's what I want, a 32," de Castro assured him, "a 32-bit Eclipse and no mode bit."

Wallach signed up. His love of literature, stories, and verse provided a literary substructure for the technical architecture of the new machine. Alsing, the group's microcode expert, was as warm and approachable as West was cold and remote. Alsing headed the Microkids, the group of young engineers who programmed the new machine. Ed Rasala, Alsing's counterpart, headed the Hardy Boys, the group's hardware design team. Rasala was a solid, hyperactive, risk-taking, detail-oriented mechanic: "I may not be the smartest designer in the world, a CPU giant, but I'm dumb enough to stick with it to the end" (p. 142).

Diversity among the group's other top engineers was evident in specialty as well as personality. One engineer, for example, was viewed as a creative genius who liked inventing an esoteric idea and then trying to make it work. Another was a craftsman who enjoyed fixing things, working tirelessly until the last bug had been tracked down and eliminated.

West buffered the team from upper management interference and served as a group "devil." Wallach created the original design. Alsing and the Microkids created "a synaptic language that would fuse the physical machine with the programs that would tell it what to do" (p. 60). Rasala and the Hardy Boys built the physical circuitry. Understandably, there was tension among these diverse, highly specialized individuals and groups. Harnessing the resulting energy galvanized the parts into a working team.

Example, Not Command

Wallach's design generated modest coordination for Eagle's autonomous individuals and groups. The group had some rules but paid little attention to them. Members viewed de Castro, the CEO, as a distant god. He was never there physically, but his presence was. West, the group's official leader, rarely interfered with the actual work, nor was he around in the laboratory. One Sunday morning in January, however, when the team was supposed to be resting, a Hardy Boy happened to come by the lab and found West sitting in front of one of the prototypes. The next Sunday, West wasn't in the lab, and after that they rarely saw him. For a long time he did not hint that he might again put his hands inside the machine.

West contributed primarily by causing problems for the engineers to solve and making mundane events and issues appear special. He created an almost endless series of "brush-fires" so he could inspire his staff to douse them. He had a genius for finding drama and romance in everyday routine. Other members of the group's formal leadership followed de Castro and West in creating ambiguity, encouraging inventiveness, and leading by example. Heroes of the moment gave inspiration and direction. Subtle and implicit signals rather than concrete and explicit guidelines or decisions held the group together and directed it toward a common goal.

Specialized Language

Every group develops words, phrases, and metaphors unique to its circumstances. A specialized language both reflects and shapes a group's culture. Shared language allows team members to communicate easily, with minimal misunderstanding. To the members of the Eagle Group, for example, a *kludge* was a poor, inelegant solution—such as a machine with loose wires held together with duct tape. A *canard* was anything false. *Fundamentals* were the source of enlightened thinking. The word *realistically* typically prefaced flights of fantasy. "Give me a *core dump*" meant tell me your thoughts. A *stack overflow* meant that an engineer's memory compartments were too full, and a *one-stack-deep mind* indicated shallow thinking. "Eagle" was a label for the project, and "Hardy Boys" and "Microkids" gave identity to the subgroups. Two prototype computers received the designations "Woodstock" and "Trixie."

Shared lingo binds a group together and is a visible sign of membership. It also sets a group apart and reinforces unique values and beliefs. Asked about the Eagle Group's headquarters, West observed, "It's basically a cattle yard. What goes on here is not part of the real world." Asked for an explanation, West remarked, "Mm-hmm. The language is different" (p. 50).

Stories Carry History, Values, and Group Identity

In high-performing organizations and groups, stories keep traditions alive and provide examples to channel everyday behavior. Group lore extended and reinforced the subtle yet powerful influence of Eagle's leaders—some of them distant and remote. West's reputation as a "troublemaker" and an "excitement junkie" spread through stories about computer wars of the mid-1970s. Alsing said of West that he was always prepared and never raised his voice. But he coolly conveyed intensity and the conviction that he knew the way out of whatever storm was currently battering the group.

West also possessed the skills of a good politician. He knew how to develop agendas, build alliances, and negotiate with potential supporters or opponents. When he had a particular objective in mind, he would first sign up senior executives.

Then he went to people one at a time, telling them the bosses liked the idea and asking them to come on board: "They say, 'Ah, it sounds like you're just gonna put a bag on the side of the Eclipse,' and Tom'll give 'em his little grin and say, 'It's more than that, we're really gonna build this fucker and it's gonna be fast as greased lightning.' He tells them, 'We're gonna do it by April'" (p. 44).

Stories of persistence, irreverence, and creativity encouraged others to go beyond themselves, adding new exploits and tales to Eagle's lore. For example, as the group neared completion, a debugging problem threatened the entire project. Jim Veres, one of the engineers, worked day and night to find the error. Ken Holberger, one of the Hardy Boys, drove to work early one morning, pondering the state of the project and wondering if it would ever get done.

He was startled out of his reverie by an unexpected scene as he entered the lab. "A great heap of paper lies on the floor, a continuous sheet of computer paper streaming out of the carriage at [the] system console. Stretched out, the sheet would run across the room and back again several times. You could fit a fairly detailed description of American history . . . on it. Veres sits in the midst of this chaos, the picture of the scholar. He's examined it all. He turns to Holberger. 'I found it,' he says" (p. 207).

Humor and Play

Groups often focus single-mindedly on the task, shunning anything not directly work related. Seriousness replaces playfulness as a cardinal virtue. Effective teams balance seriousness with play and humor. Surgical teams, cockpit crews, and many other groups have learned that joking and playful banter are essential sources of invention and team spirit. Humor releases tension and helps resolve issues arising from day-to-day routines as well as from sudden emergencies.

Play among the members of the Eagle project was an innate part of the group's process. When Alsing wanted the Microkids to learn how to manipulate the computer known as Trixie, he made up a game. As the Microkids came on board, he told each of them to figure how to write a program in Trixie's assembly language. The program had to fetch and print contents of a file stored inside the computer. The Microkids went to work, learned their way around the machine, and felt great satisfaction—until Alsing's perverse sense of humor tripped them up. When they finally found the elusive file, a message greeted them: "Access Denied."

Through such play, the Microkids learned to use the computer, coalesced into a team, and practiced negotiating their new technical environment. They also learned that their playful leader valued creativity.

Humor was a continuous thread as the team struggled with its formidable task. Humor often stretched the boundaries of good taste, but that too was part of the group's identity:

> [Alsing] drew his chair up to his terminal and typed a few letters—a short code that put him in touch with Trixie, the machine reserved for the use of his micro coding team. "We've anthropomorphized Trixie to a ridiculous extent," he said.
>
> He typed, WHO.
>
> On the dark-blue screen of the cathode-ray tube, with alacrity, an answer appeared: CARL.
>
> WHERE, typed Alsing.
>
> IN THE ROAD, WHERE ELSE! Trixie replied.
>
> HOW.
>
> ERROR, read the message on the screen.
>
> "Oh, yeah, I forgot," said Alsing, and he typed, PLEASE HOW.
>
> THAT'S FOR US TO KNOW AND YOU TO FIND OUT.
>
> Alsing seemed satisfied with that, and he typed, WHEN.

RIGHT FUCKING NOW, wrote the machine.

WHY, wrote Alsing.

BECAUSE WE LIKE TO CARL (pp. 90–91).

Throughout the year and a half it took to build their new machine, engineers of the Eagle project relied on play and humor as a source of relaxation, stimulation, enlightenment, and spiritual renewal.

Ritual and Ceremony

Rituals and ceremonies are expressive occasions. As parentheses in an ordinary workday, they enclose and define special forms of symbolic behavior. What occurs on the surface is not nearly as important as the deeper meaning communicated below ground. With little time for anything not related to the task of building the machine, the Eagle Group intuitively understood the importance of symbolic activity. From the beginning, leadership encouraged ritual and ceremony.

As one example, Rasala, head of the Hardy Boys, established a rule requiring that changes in public boards of the prototype be updated each morning. This activity allowed efforts to be coordinated formally. More important, the daily update was an occasion for informal communication, bantering, and gaining a sense of the whole. The engineers disliked the daily procedure, so Rasala changed it to once a week—on Saturday. He made it a point always to be there himself.

Eagle's leaders met regularly, but their meetings focused more on symbolic issues than on substance. "We could be in a lot of trouble here,' West might say, referring to some current problem. And Wallach or Rasala or Alsing would reply, 'You mean you could be in a lot of trouble, right, Tom?' It was Friday, they were going home soon, and relaxing, they could half forget that they would be coming back to work tomorrow" (p. 132). Friday afternoon is a customary time at the end of the workweek to wind down and relax. Honoring such a tradition was all the more important for a group whose members often worked all week and then all weekend. West made himself available to anyone who wanted to chat. Near the end of the day, before hurrying home, he would lean back in his chair with his office door open and entertain any visitor.

In addition to recurring rituals, the Eagle Group members convened intermittent ceremonies to raise their spirits and reinforce their dedication to a shared, intensely zealous mission. Toward the end of the project, Alsing instigated a ceremony to trigger a burst of renewed energy for the final push. The festivities called attention to the values of creativity, hard work, and teamwork. A favorite pretext for parties was presentation of the Honorary

Microcoder Awards that Alsing and the Microcoder Team instituted. Not to be outdone, the Hardy Boys cooked up the PAL Awards (named for the programmable array logic chips used in the machines). The first presentation came after work at a local establishment called the Cain Ridge Saloon. The citation read as follows (p. 250):

Honorary PAL Award

In recognition of unsolicited contributions to the advancement of Eclipse hardware above and beyond the normal call of duty, we hereby convey unto you our thanks and congratulations on achieving this "high" honor.

The same values and spirit were reinforced again and again in a continued cycle of celebratory events:

> Chuck Holland [Alsing's main submanager] handed out his own special awards to each member of the Microteam, the Under Extraordinary Pressure Awards. They looked like diplomas. There was one for Neal Firth, "who gave us a computer before the hardware guys did," and one to Betty Shanahan, "for putting up with a bunch of creepy guys." After dispensing the Honorary Microcoder Awards to almost every possible candidate, the Microteam instituted the All-Nighter Award. The first of these went to Jim Guyer, the citation ingeniously inserted under the clear plastic coating of an insulated coffee cup (p. 250).

The Contribution of Informal Cultural Players

Alsing was the main organizer and instigator of parties. He was also the Eagle Group's conscience and nearly everyone's confidant. For a time when he was still in college, Alsing had wanted to become a psychologist. He acted like one now. He kept track of his team's technical progress but was more visible as the social director of the Microteam and often of the entire Eclipse Group. Fairly early in the project, Chuck Holland had complained, "Alsing's hard to be a manager for, because he goes around you a lot and tells your people to do something else." But Holland also conceded, "The good thing about him is that you can go and talk to him. He's more of a regular guy than most managers" (p. 105).

Every group or organization has a "priest" or "priestess" who ministers to spiritual needs. Informally, these people hear confessions, give blessings, maintain traditions, encourage ceremonies, and intercede in matters of gravest importance. Alsing did all these things and, like the tribal priest, acted as a counterpart to and interpreter of the intentions of the chief:

> West warned him several times, "If you get too close to the people who work for you, Alsing, you're gonna get burned." But West didn't interfere, and he soon stopped issuing warnings.
>
> One evening, while alone with West in West's office, Alsing said: "Tom, the kids think you're an ogre. You don't even say hello to them."
>
> West smiled and replied. "You're doing fine, Alsing" (pp. 109–110).

The duties of Rosemarie Seale, the group's secretary, also went well beyond formal boundaries. If Alsing was the priest, she was the mother superior. She performed the usual secretarial chores—answering the phones, preparing documents, and constructing budgets. But she found particular joy in serving as a kind of den mother who solved minor crises that arose almost daily. When new members came on, it was Rosemarie Seale who worried about finding them a desk and some pencils. When paychecks went astray, she would track them down and deliver them to their intended recipients. She liked the job, she said, because she felt that she was doing something important.

In any group, a network of informal players deals with human issues outside formal channels. On the Eagle project, their efforts were encouraged, appreciated, and rewarded outside the formal chain of command; they helped keep the project on track.

Soul Is the Secret of Success

The symbolic tenor of the Eagle Group was the actual secret of its success. Its soul, or culture, created a new machine: "Ninety-eight percent of the thrill comes from knowing that the thing you designed works, and works almost the way you expected it would. If that happens, part of you is in that machine" (p. 273).

All the members of the Eagle Group put something of themselves into the new computer. Individual efforts went well beyond the job, supported by a unique way of life that encouraged each person to commit to doing something of significance. Their deep commitment and unwavering spirit jelled in the ritual of signing up. Both were then intensified and expanded by diversity, exceptional leaders, common language, stories, rituals, ceremonies, play, and humor. In the best sense of the word, the Eagle Group was a team, and the efforts of the individual members were interwoven by symbolic fibers. Cultural elements were the heart and soul of the group's success.

The experience of the Eagle Group is not an outlier. After extensive research on high-performing groups, Vaill (1982) concluded that spirit was at the core of every such group he studied. Members of such groups consistently "felt the spirit," a feeling essential to the meaning and value of their work. Bennis (1997) could have been writing about the Eagle Group when he concluded, "All Great Groups believe that they are on a mission from God, that they could change the world, make a dent in the universe. They are obsessed with their work. It becomes not a job but a fervent quest. That belief is what brings the necessary cohesion and energy to their work" (p. 1).

More and more teams and organizations, like the Eagle project or SEAL Team Six, realize that culture, soul, and spirit are the wellspring of high performance. The U.S. Air Force, in the aftermath of the Vietnam War, embarked on a vigorous effort to reaffirm traditions and rebuild its culture. The air warfare arm of the U.S. military added "Cohesion is a principle of war" to its list of core values. Project Warrior brought heroes—living and dead—forward as visible examples of the right stuff. The Air Force also instituted a "reblueing" ceremony to encourage recommitment to its traditions and values.

Other organizations have taken similar steps. In 2006 Starbucks's performance had begun to slide, then dip. By 2007, the company's stock price had fallen by 42 percent. In February, Starbucks Chairman Howard Schultz sent a confidential memo to top executives linking the downturn to slippage in the firm's culture: "Over the past 10 years, in order to achieve the growth, development and scale necessary to go from less than 1,000 stores to 13,000 stores and beyond, we have had to make a series of decisions that, in retrospect, have led to the watering down of the Starbucks Experience, and what some might call the commoditization of our brand" (Schultz and Gordon, 2011, p. 23).

The "confidential" memo became public, and bedlam reigned at Starbucks. Schultz resumed his former role as CEO and took immediate steps to breathe new spirit into the company's once vibrant way of life:

- A brainstorming meeting of company leaders to ponder the question: What is the soul of Starbucks?

- A ritual closing of 7,100 Starbucks outlets nationwide for an evening to refresh baristas in the texture and magic of a perfect espresso

- A meeting of top executives and managers to review, refine, revive, and recommit themselves to the company's values

- A large meeting of shareholders featuring, with dramatic panache, new products, a frequent customer reward program, and a new espresso machine

- A meeting in New Orleans of almost 10,000 Starbucks managers—a gigantic celebration with themes of "Onward" and "Believe"; a recommitment to the company's cultural history, values, and ways; and, to seal the deal, a rousing speech from Bono

The Air Force and Starbucks confirm that too much emphasis on sorties flown or quarterly numbers can divert attention from sustaining and revitalizing culture. That, in turn, can jeopardize the outcomes an organization or team is trying to maximize. Team Six, Starbucks, Zappos, and other successful companies and teams understand and live this lesson. When asked, "How much of your time do you spend dealing with cultural issues?" a wise executive said, "Not enough—maybe half my time."

CONCLUSION

Symbolic perspectives question the traditional view that building a team mainly entails putting the right people in the right structure. The essence of high performance is spirit. If we were to banish play, ritual, ceremony, and myth from the workplace, we would destroy teamwork, not enhance it. There are many signs that contemporary organizations are at a critical juncture because of a crisis of meaning and faith. Managers wonder how to build team spirit when turnover is high, resources are tight, and people worry about losing their jobs. Such questions are important, but by themselves, they limit imagination and divert attention from deeper issues of faith and purpose. Managers are inescapably accountable for budget and bottom line; they have to respond to individual needs, legal requirements, and economic pressures. Leaders serve a deeper and more durable function if they recognize that team building at its heart is a spiritual undertaking. It is both a search for the spirit within and creation of a community of believers united by shared faith and shared culture. Burton Clark calls this an organization's saga, a story "between the coolness of rational purpose and the warmth of sentiment found in religion or magic . . . it includes affect that turns a formal place into a beloved institution" (Baldridge and Deal, 1975, p. 98). Peak performance emerges as a team discovers its soul.

NOTE

1. Unless otherwise attributed, page number citations in this chapter are to Kidder's book. From *The Soul of a New Machine* by Tracy Kidder. Copyright © 1981 by John Tracy Kidder. Reprinted by permission of Little, Brown and Company, Inc. All rights reserved.

chapter
14

Organization as Theater

All the world's a stage, and all the men and women
merely players.

—William Shakespeare, *As You Like It*

More than 400 years ago, Shakespeare captured an enduring truth we sometimes neglect in our love affair with facts and logic. Much of human behavior aims at getting things accomplished. The assumption of linear causality works sometimes when outcomes are tangible and a link between means and ends is clear. A factory, we surmise, rises or falls on what it produces. But the logic falters when outcomes are less tangible and the connection between actions and outcomes is more elusive.

Think about a church or temple. Shall we rely on income statements and congregation size to gauge success? How do we capture the value of souls saved and lives enriched? Such elusive variables are hard to quantify, but focusing on what we can measure rather than what we care about is a formula for disappointment and failure. In theater, what appears on stage is draped in perception. The same is true of organizations. We judge them by how they appear and how well they follow the script we expect. Shared faith and liturgy tie believers together and bestow legitimacy. As in theater, performance, faith, and devotion matter more than data and logic.

This is illustrated in a story and its accompanying drama that are central to the faith of Ethiopian Christians. The existence and location of the Ark of the Covenant is one of

279

history's greatest mysteries . . . but not to Ethiopians. They know that the Ark is now enshrined in a modest Chapel surrounded by a small courtyard in Azum. The Ark is overseen by a High Priest who, it is alleged, chooses his successor on his deathbed. Very few Ethiopians have seen the Ark's caretaker. No one, including religious leaders and the president of Ethiopia, has ever laid eyes on the Ark, though they have seen models because every Orthodox church in Ethiopia has one (Raffaele, 2007).

A reporter once approached the chapel and was able to talk briefly to the guardian. He said, "I have heard of the Ethiopian tradition that the Ark of the Covenant is kept here . . . in this Chapel. I have also heard that you are the Guardian of the Ark. Are these things true?"

"They are true."

"But in other countries, nobody believes these stories."

"People can say what they wish. People can believe what they wish. Nevertheless, we do possess the Ark of the Covenant and I am its Guardian. It is not a lesson. It is history."

"But no one has seen the Ark. Don't people need some proof that it's really here?"

"I've seen the Ark as did my predecessor and will my successor. The story of the Ark has passed through generations. What other proof do we need? In the very distant past, the Ark was brought out for religious rituals at Tikrit. But we don't do that anymore because of the turmoil and civil war around us. It is much too dangerous to have the Ark exposed."

"Do people have memories of seeing it before, in more peaceful times?"

"The Ark was always draped. Its brilliance would have blinded onlookers."

The ongoing drama surrounding the Ark creates its own kind of proof. Belief suffices; facts are irrelevant. Any attempt to challenge the truth of the historical interpretation is thwarted by a dramatic explanation that reinforces the prevailing account.

Even in technical environments, a dramaturgical view of situations offers enlightenment. The story of the U.S. Navy's Polaris missile system is a classic example of the role show business can play. One of its outstanding attributes was reliance on modern management techniques such as PERT (Program Evaluation Review Techniques) and PPBS (Program Planning and Budgeting Systems)—both better known by their acronyms than by their names. Specialist roles, technical divisions, management meetings, and the Special Projects Office embodied the methods.

In the wake of the project's success—on time and under budget—analysts credited the project's innovative management approach. The admiral in charge received recognition for his leadership in bringing modern management techniques to the U.S. Navy. A team of British experts visiting the project were impressed and, upon returning home, highly recommended PERT and PPBS to their Admiralty.

A later study by Sapolsky (1972) revealed a very different explanation for the project's accomplishments. Management innovations were highly visible but only marginally connected to the actual work. Specialists' activities linked loosely to other elements of the project. Plans and charts produced by the technical division received scant attention. Management meetings served as public arenas to chide poor performers and to stoke the project's religious fervor. The Special Projects Office served as an official briefing area. Visiting dignitaries were regaled with impressive diagrams and charts almost entirely unrelated to the project's progress. The team from the British Navy apparently surmised all this and still recommended a similar approach back home (Sapolsky, 1972).

Instead of serving intended rational purposes, modern management techniques contributed to a saga that built external legitimacy and support and kept critics and legislators at bay. The myth afforded breathing space for work to go forward and elevated participants' spirits and self-confidence. The Polaris story demonstrates the virtues of drama in engaging the attention and appreciation of both internal and external audiences: "An alchemist's combination of whirling computers, bright-colored charts, and fast-talking public relations officers gave the Special Projects Office a truly effective management system. It mattered not whether the parts of the system functioned, or even existed. It mattered only that certain people, for a certain period of time, believed that they did" (Sapolsky, 1972, p. 129).

Of course, not all theater has a happy conclusion. The drama in theater or on television features tragedy as well as triumph. U2's music video "The Saints Are Coming" demonstrates the power of drama in driving home the meaning of an experience. The video, which focuses on the effects of Hurricane Katrina, opens with scenes of the storm's traumatic aftermath: New Orleans under water, survivors trapped on roofs pleading for help, the horror of conditions at the Superdome, widespread devastation. The song lyrics plaintively call for the next act: When will aid arrive?

CNN news flashes appeared periodically on the screen below images of the ravaged city: "U.S. Iraq Troops Redeployed to New Orleans," "U.S. Troops Come Home to Help Katrina Victims," "Air Force Launches Aid Drops." With the melancholic lyrics as musical background, the video shows swarms of Black Hawk helicopters arriving to pluck victims from roofs, and larger helicopters and Harrier fighters dropping food and medical supplies. The video fades and a large sign appears: "Not as seen on TV."

The U2 video packs a wallop for several reasons: Bono himself is a heroic symbol on the world stage. The opening acts reveal the pathos all Americans observed initially. The "troops to the rescue" imagery conveys what everyone wanted to believe; the final scene transports us back to the reality viewers actually saw firsthand on their television sets.

During previous hurricanes, drama played quite differently. The Federal Emergency Management Agency (FEMA) came onstage as a heroic rescuer. The script was clear. A hurricane hits, bringing devastation and suffering. FEMA arrives with symbolic fanfare to dispense aid and hope to victims. A world audience applauds the performance. FEMA takes a bow. In New Orleans, the drama went off track. The hero missed most of the show. The audience waited for an actor who arrived too late and then muffed his lines. The world saw a once-heroic agency become a bumbling performer in a bad play.

The juxtaposed theatrical masks of comedy and tragedy capture the different dramas played out by Polaris and FEMA. Polaris staged a drama that wowed its audience and became a smash hit. FEMA blew its act. Hurricane Sandy in 2012 gave FEMA an opportunity for a comeback with a new director, a new cast, and a revised script from a skilled playwright. This time the performance received an ovation from the audience, including the governor of New Jersey and the mayor of New York City.

Theater arouses emotions and kindles our spirit or reveals our fears. It reduces bewilderment and soothes open wounds. It provides a shared basis for understanding the present and imagining a more promising tomorrow. Dramaturgical and institutional theorists have explored the role of theater in organizations, and we begin this chapter by discussing their views. We then look at structure and other organizational processes as theater.

DRAMATURGICAL AND INSTITUTIONAL THEORY

Institutional theory, a fairly recent addition to the management literature, draws on ideas from earlier dramaturgical theories. We can identify two traditions (Boje, Luhman, and Cunliffe, 2003): one represented by the work of Erving Goffman (1959, 1974), who pioneered in the use of theater as a metaphor for understanding organizations, and the other by the work of Kenneth Burke (1937, 1945, 1972), who drew his inspiration from philosophy and literary criticism. Goffman approached organizations as if they were theatrical; Burke saw them as theater. Despite their differences, both theorists opened a window for seeing organizations in a new way: "Most of our organizational life is carefully scripted; we play out our scenes in organizationally approved dress codes and play the game by acceptable roles of conduct" (Boje, Luhman, and Cunliffe, 2003, p. 4).

Whereas dramaturgical theorists focus on social interaction among individuals and on internal situations, institutional scholars extend theatrical examples like Polaris and FEMA to the interface between organizations and their various publics. Scott (2014) sees the institutional view encompassing three schools of thought, each embedded in different literatures.

The first views institutions as providing the rules of the game in which organizations are the players (North, 1989). A second view holds that "individual organizations devise distinctive characteristics over time, developing commitments that channel and constrain future behavior in the service of their basic values (Williamson 1985; Selznick, 1957).

The third view argues that structure in institutional organizations reflects prevailing social myths and ideas in good currency about what constitutes a good organization. Contemporary organizations gain legitimacy through isomorphism—reflecting current thinking about modern management technology. Accordingly, technical organizations plan in order to change, whereas institutionalized organizations plan instead of changing. "Plans are regarded as ends in themselves—as evidence that we are a humane and scientific people who have brought yet another problem under rational control" (Meyer and Rowan, 1983, p. 126).

DiMaggio and Powell agree that in some contexts organizations worry more about how innovations appear than what they add to effectiveness: "New practices become infused with value beyond the technical requirements of the task at hand . . . As an innovation spreads, a threshold is reached beyond which adoption provides legitimacy rather than improves performance" (1983, p. 142). Staw and Epstein (2000) present evidence that adoption of modern management techniques accentuates a company's legitimacy and increases CEO compensation—even if the methods are not fully put into action. Performance may not improve, but perceptions of innovativeness and confidence in management still rise.

Institutional theory has been criticized for focusing more on why organizations don't change than how they do and for attending to why organizations are irrational instead of how they might become more effective (see Peters, 2000; Scott and Davis, 2007). But the ideas provide a counterweight to traditional views of organizations as closed, rational systems (Meyer, 2008). In such views, functional demands shape social architecture. The environment serves as a source of raw materials and a market for finished products. Efficiency, internal control of the means of production, and economic performance are key concerns. Exterior fluctuations and production uncertainties are buffered by rational devices such as forecasting, stockpiling, leveling peaks and valleys of supply and demand, and growth (so as to get more leverage over the environment).

Institutional theorists present a dramaturgical retake on rational imagery. Organizations, particularly those with vague goals and weak technologies, cannot seal themselves off from external events and pressures. They are constantly buffeted by larger social, political, and economic trends. The challenge is sustaining isomorphism—that is, schools need to look like schools "ought to" and churches need to look like churches "should" in order to project legitimacy and engender belief, support, faith, and hope among a variety of constituents. Structure and processes must reflect widely held myths and expectations. When production and results are hard to measure, correct appearance and dramatic presentation become the principal gauge of an organization's effectiveness.

Greatest Hits from Organization Studies

Hit Number 1: Paul J. DiMaggio and Walter Powell, "The Iron Cage Revisited: Institutional Isomorphism and Collective Rationality in Organizational Fields," *American Sociological Review*, April 1983, *48*, 147–160

At the top of our list of greatest hits is an article by Paul J. DiMaggio and Walter Powell that parallels our view of organization as theater. Isomorphism, as DiMaggio and Powell use the word, refers to processes that cause organizations to become more like other organizations, particularly members of the same "organizational field." The authors define an organizational field as a set of organizations that "constitute a recognized area of institutional life: key suppliers, resource and product consumers, regulatory agencies, and other organizations that produce similar services or products" (p. 148). This is similar to the concept of an organizational ecosystem, discussed in Chapter 11. As an example, think about public schools. They are like each other but unlike most other kinds of organization. They have similar buildings, classrooms, curricula, staffing patterns, gyms, and parent-teacher organizations. The structural frame explains these similarities as resulting from the need to align structure with goals, task, and technology. DiMaggio and Powell counter that isomorphism occurs for reasons unrelated to efficiency or effectiveness.

They describe three kinds of isomorphism: coercive, mimetic, and normative. Coercive isomorphism occurs when organizations become more similar in response to outside pressures or requirements. For example, MBA programs tend to have similar admission requirements, curricula, and faculty credentials because so many of them are accredited by the same body using the same standards. Mimetic isomorphism occurs when one organization simply copies another, as when a university of modest reputation adopts a set of freshman requirements borrowed from those at Harvard or Yale. To DiMaggio and Powell, imitation is particularly likely in the presence of fuzzy goals and uncertain technology. When uncertainty makes it hard to prove one approach better than another, imitation saves time and may buy legitimacy.

Normative isomorphism, the third type, occurs because professionals (such as lawyers, doctors, engineers, and teachers) bring shared ideas, values, and norms from their training to the workplace. DiMaggio and Powell argue that professionally trained individuals are becoming more numerous and predominant. Managers with MBAs from accredited business schools carry shared values, beliefs, and practices wherever they go. New ideas from business schools may or may not produce better results, but they spread rapidly because the newly minted professionals believe in them.

The primary benefit of isomorphism is to improve an organization's image rather than its products and services: "Each of the institutional isomorphic processes can be expected to proceed in the absence of evidence that they increase internal organizational efficiency. To the

---

> extent that organizational effectiveness is enhanced, the reason will often be that organizations are rewarded for being similar to other organizations in their fields. This similarity can make it easier for organizations to transact with other organizations, to attract career-minded staff, to be acknowledged as legitimate and reputable, and to fit into administrative categories that define eligibility for public and private grants and contracts" (p. 153).

The idea that appearance can be more important than tangible outcomes may seem heretical. Such heresy can easily lead to cynicism, undercutting confidence in organizations and undermining faith and morale for those struggling to make a difference. Skepticism is also spawned by rationalists who champion a tidy cause-and-effect world where concrete outcomes matter most.

The symbolic frame offers a more hopeful interpretation. Institutionalized structures, activities, and events become expressive components of organizational theater. They create ongoing drama that entertains, creates meaning, and portrays the organization to itself and outsiders. They undergird life's meaning. Geertz observed this phenomenon in Balinese pageants, where "the carefully crafted and scripted, assiduously enacted ritualism of court culture was . . . 'not merely the drapery of political order but its substance'" (Mangham and Overington, 1987, p. 39).

ORGANIZATIONAL STRUCTURE AS THEATER

Recall that the structural frame depicts a workplace as a formalized network of inter-dependent roles and units coordinated through a variety of horizontal and vertical linkages. Structural patterns align with purpose and are determined by goals, technologies, and environment (Lawrence and Lorsch, 1967; Perrow, 1979; Woodward, 1970). In contrast, a symbolic view approaches structure as stage design: an arrangement of space, lighting, props, and costumes that make the drama vivid and credible to its audience.

One dramaturgical role of structure is reflecting and conveying prevailing social values and myths. Settings and costumes should be appropriate: a church should have a suitable building, religious artifacts, and a properly attired member of the clergy. A clinic should have examination rooms, uniformed nurses, and licensed physicians, with diplomas prominently featured on the wall. Meyer and Rowan (1978) depict the structure of public schools as largely symbolic. A school has difficulty sustaining public support unless it offers fashionable answers to three questions: Does it offer appropriate topics (for example, third-grade mathematics or world history)? Are topics taught to age-graded students by certified teachers? Does it look like a school (with classrooms, a gymnasium, a library, and a flag near the front door)?

An institution of higher education is judged by the age, size, and beauty of the campus, the amount of its endowment, its faculty-student ratio, and the number of professors who received doctorates from prestigious institutions. Kamens (1977) suggests that the major function of a college or university is to redefine novice students as graduates who possess special qualities or skills. The value of the status transformation is negotiated with important constituencies through constant references to the quality and rigor of educational programs. The significance of the conversion from novice to graduate is validated by structural characteristics, reputation of faculty, success of former students, or appearance of the institution.

A valid structural configuration, in Kamens's view, depends on whether an institution is elite or not and whether it allocates graduates to a specific social or corporate group. Each type of institution espouses its own myth and dramatizes its own aspects of structure. Ivy League schools such as Harvard, Yale, and Princeton are known for producing graduates who occupy elite roles in society. Elite schools dramatize selectivity, maintain an attractive residential campus, advertise a favorable ratio of faculty to students, and develop a core curriculum that restrains specialization in favor of a unified core of knowledge.

If an institution or its environment changes, theatrical refurbishing is needed. Audiences call for revisions in actors, scripts, or settings. Because legitimacy and worth are anchored in the match between structural characteristics and prevailing myths, organizations alter appearances to mirror changes in social expectations. For example, if total quality management, reengineering, or Six Sigma becomes the fashionable addition to the screenplay for progressive companies, corresponding programs and consultants spread like fire in a parched forest.

New structures reflect legal and social expectations and represent a bid for legitimacy and support from the attending audience. An organization without an affirmative action program, for example, is suspiciously out of step with prevailing concerns for diversity and equity. Nonconformity invites questions, criticism, and inspection. It is easier to appoint a diversity officer than to change hiring practices deeply embedded in both individual and institutional beliefs and practices. Because the presence of a diversity officer is more visible than revisions in hiring priorities, the addition of a new role may signal to external constituencies that there has been a new development in the drama even if the appointment is "window dressing" and no real change has occurred.

In this light, government agencies serve mostly political and symbolic functions: "Congress passes on to these agencies a type of symbolic control; they represent our belief in the virtues of planning and the value of an integrated program of action. But the agencies are given no formal authority over the organizations whose services they are to control and few funds to use as incentives to stimulate the cooperation of these existing organizations" (Scott, 1983, p. 126).

In practice, agencies reduce tension and uncertainty and increase the public's sense of confidence and security. Only in a crisis—as when people or pets die from eating contaminated food—do people ask why regulators failed to do their job. Theatrically, agencies enact their roles to create a drama showing that violators will be identified and punished and flaws will be remedied so that the problems never recur.

ORGANIZATIONAL PROCESS AS THEATER

Rationally, procedures produce results. Administrative protocols coordinate work. Technology improves efficiency. Lectures impart information, knowledge, and wisdom. Medical care cures illness. Social workers manage cases and write reports to, occasionally, identify and remedy social ills.

People in organizations spend much of their time engaged in such endeavors. To justify their toil, they want to believe that their efforts produce the intended outcomes. Even if the best intentions or the most sophisticated technologies do not yield expected results, the activities play a vital theatrical role. They serve as scripts and stage markings for self-expressive opportunities, improvisation for airing grievances, and amphitheaters for negotiating new understandings. We illustrate how these figurative forms alter the context of meetings, planning, performance appraisals, collective bargaining, the exercise of power, and symbolic management.

Meetings

March and Olsen (1976) were ahead of their time in depicting meetings as improvisational "garbage cans." In this imagery, meetings are magnets attracting individuals looking for something to do, problems seeking answers, and people bringing solutions in search of problems. The results of a meeting depend on a serendipitous interplay among items that show up: Who came to the meeting? What problems, concerns, or needs were on their minds? What solutions or suggestions did they bring?

Garbage-can scripts are likely to play out in meetings dealing with emotionally charged, symbolically significant, or technically fuzzy issues. The topic of mission, for example, attracts a more sizable collection of people, problems, and solutions than the topic of cost accounting. Meetings may not always produce rational discourse, sound plans, or meaningful improvements. But they serve as expressive occasions to clear the air and promote collective bonding. Some players get opportunities to practice and polish their lines in the drama. Others revel in the chance to add excitement to work. Audiences feel reassured that issues are getting attention and better times may lie ahead. But problems and solutions characteristically linger on, detached from one another.

Planning

An organization without a plan is in peril of being seen as reactive, shortsighted, and rudderless. Planning, then, is an essential ceremony that organizations stage periodically to maintain legitimacy. A plan is a decoration displayed conspicuously and with pride. A strategic plan carries even higher status. A new leader in a school, college, or public agency almost invariably initiates a strategic planning process shortly after arrival. Mintzberg's insightful book *The Rise and Fall of Strategic Planning* (1994) presents an array of survey and anecdotal evidence questioning the link between strategic planning and its stated objectives. He shows that the presumed linear progression from analysis to objectives to action to results is more fanciful than factual. Many executives recognize the shortcomings of strategic planning yet continue to champion the process: "Recently I asked three corporate executives what decisions they had made in the last year that they would not have made were it not for their corporate plans. All had difficulty identifying one such decision. Since each of their plans [was] marked 'secret' or 'confidential,' I asked them how their competitors might benefit from the possession of their plans. Each answered with embarrassment that their competitors would not benefit. Yet these executives were strong advocates of corporate planning" (Russell Ackoff, quoted in Mintzberg, 1994, p. 98).

Planning persists because it plays an eminent role in an organization's enduring drama. Quinn notes: "A good deal of the corporate planning I have observed is like a ritual rain dance; it has no effect on the weather that follows, but those who engage in it think it does. Moreover, it seems to me that much of the advice and instruction related to corporate planning is directed at improving the dancing, not the weather" (quoted in Mintzberg, 1994, p. 139).

Discussing universities, Cohen and March (1974) list four symbolic roles that plans play:

- *Plans are symbols.* Academic organizations have few real pieces of objective evidence to evaluate performance. They have nothing comparable to profit or sales figures. How are we doing? No one really knows. Planning is a signal that all is well or improvement is just around the corner. A school or university undergoing an accreditation review engages in a "self-study" and lays out an ambitious strategic plan, which can then gather a decade of dust until it is time to repeat the process.

- *Plans become games.* Especially where goals and technology are unclear, planning becomes a test of will. A department that wants a new program badly must justify the expenditure by substantial planning efforts. An administrator who wishes to avoid saying yes but has no real basis for saying no can test commitment by asking for a plan. Benefits lie more in the process than the result.

- *Plans become excuses for interaction.* Developing a plan forces discussion and may increase interest in and commitment to new priorities. Occasionally, interaction yields positive results. But rarely does it yield an accurate forecast. Conclusions about what will happen next year are notoriously susceptible to alteration as people, politics, policies, or preferences change, but discussions of the future seldom modify views of what should be done differently today.

- *Plans become advertisements.* What is frequently labeled as a plan is more like an investment brochure. It is an attempt to persuade private and public donors of an institution's attractiveness. Plans are typically adorned with glossy photographs of beautiful people in pristine settings, official pronouncements of excellence, and a noticeable dearth of specifics.

Cohen and March (1974) asked college presidents their views of the linkage between plans and decisions. Responses fell into four main categories:

> "Yes, we have a plan. It is used in capital project and physical location decisions."
> "Yes, we have a plan. Here it is. It was made during the administration of our last president. We are working on a new one."
> "No, we do not have a plan. We should. We're working on one."
> "I think there's a plan around here someplace. Miss Jones, do we have a copy of our comprehensive, ten-year plan?" (p. 113).

Evaluation

Assessing the performance of individuals, departments, or programs is a major undertaking. Organizations devote considerable time, energy, and resources to appraising individuals, even though many doubt that the procedures connect closely with improvements, and Culbert (2010) insists that they do more harm than good. Organization-wide reviews yield lengthy reports presented with fitting pomp and ceremony. Universities convene visiting committees or accrediting teams to evaluate schools or departments. Government requires routine assessment of program efficacy. Social service agencies commission studies or audits whenever an important problem or issue arises.

Occasionally, actions follow insights or recommendations. Sometimes suggestions yield tangible improvements. At other times they trigger changes that are primarily symbolic. Most higher education accreditors, for example, insist on currently fashionable "assurance of learning" processes, which in practice typically assure additional paperwork more than enhanced learning. Often, results disappear into the recesses of people's minds or the far reaches of administrators' files. But evaluation still plays a decisive role in helping organizations foster faith, belief, and confidence among constituents.

Evaluation as drama assures spectators that an organization is responsible, serious, and well managed. It shows that an organization takes goals seriously and cares about performance and improvement. The evaluation process gives participants an opportunity to share opinions and have them recognized publicly. It helps people relabel old practices, escape normal routine, and build new beliefs (Rallis, 1980). Although the impact on decisions or behavior may be marginal, methodical evaluation and its magic numbers serves as a potent weapon in political battles or as a compelling justification for a decision already made (Weiss, 1980).

In public organizations, Floden and Weiner argue, "Evaluation is a ritual whose function is to calm the anxieties of the citizenry and to perpetuate an image of government rationality, efficiency, and accountability. The very act of requiring and commissioning evaluations may create the impression that government is seriously committed to the pursuit of publicly espoused goals, such as increasing student achievement or reducing malnutrition. Evaluations lend credence to this image even when programs are created to appease interest groups" (1978, p. 17).

Collective Bargaining

In collective bargaining, labor and management negotiate to forge divisive standoffs into workable agreements. The process typically pits two sets of interests against each other: Unions want better wages, benefits, and working conditions for members; management aims to keep costs down and maximize profits for shareholders. Negotiating teams follow a familiar script: "Negotiators have to act like opponents, representatives and experts, showing that they are aligned with teammates and constituents, willing to push hard to achieve constituent goals, and constantly in control. On the public stage, anger and opposition dominate; rituals of opposition, representation, and control produce a drama of conflict. At the same time, there are mechanisms for private understanding between opposing lead bargainers, such as signaling and sidebar discussions" (Friedman, 1994, pp. 86–87).

On the surface, the negotiation process appears as a strife-ridden political brawl where persistence and power determine the distribution of scarce resources. On a deeper level, negotiation is a carefully crafted pugilistic performance that delivers the show various audiences demand. Going off script carries high risk: "A young executive took the helm of a firm with the intention of eliminating bickering and conflict between management and labor. He commissioned a study of the company's wage structure and went to the bargaining table to present his offer. He informed the union representatives what he had done and offered them more than they had expected to get. The astonished union leaders berated the executive for undermining the process of collective bargaining and asked for another five cents an hour beyond his offer" (Blum, 1961, pp. 63–64).

Similar problems have been documented by Friedman in his studies of mutual-gains bargaining (which emphasizes cooperation and a win-win outcome rather than conflict). A disillusioned participant in an abortive mutual gains process lamented: "It hurt us. We got real chummy. Everyone talked. Then in the final hours, it was the same old shit. Maybe we should have been pounding on the table" (Friedman, 1994, p. 216).

In theater, actors who deviate from the script disrupt everyone else's ability to deliver their lines. The bargaining drama is designed to convince each side that the outcomes were the result of a heroic battle—often underscored by desperate, all-night, after-the-deadline rituals of combat that produce a deal just when hope seems lost. If well performed, the drama conveys the message that two determined opponents fought hard and persistently for what they believed was right (Blum, 1961; Friedman, 1994). It obscures the reality that actors typically know in advance how the play will end.

A perennial example in U.S. politics is periodic budget stand-offs between the White House and Congress. One came in late 2012, as the United States confronted a "fiscal cliff." Without congressional action by December 31, the country faced a set of spending cuts and tax increases that spelled economic turmoil. President Obama, who had just been re-elected in November, and a Republican Congress were at loggerheads. A final compromise failed to pass before Congress adjourned for the holidays. Technically, the U.S. went over the cliff at 12:01 AM on January 1. But then at 2 AM the Senate passed the compromise bill, and the House followed suit later in the day. It was a stopgap measure that postponed all the key decisions.

The real drama was a play within a play, a struggle for power between two divided parties. It ended as many expected. No agreement reached. No catastrophe. Both sides fought hard. Republicans in the House demonstrated that they were a powerful force.

Obama reminded everyone that he was still the president. But to the American public the Washington drama portrayed government as a Keystone Cops comedy.

Power

Power is typically viewed as a commodity that individuals or systems possess—something that can be seized, exercised, contested, or redistributed. But power is inherently ambiguous and slippery. It is rarely easy to determine what power is, who has it, or how to get it. Sometimes it is even harder to know when someone actually wields power. You are powerful if others think you are.

Certain performances are widely believed to portray power. People often attribute power to those who talk a lot, belong to committees, and seem close to the action. Yet there may be little relationship between such actions and their impact. The relationship between actions and real clout may even be negative; the frustrated may talk a lot, and the disgruntled may resort to futile political intrigue or posturing (Enderud, 1976).

People also attribute power to individuals or groups in an effort to account for observed outcomes. If the unemployment or crime rates drop, political incumbents take credit. If a firm's profits jump, we credit the influence and power of the chief executive. If a program launches just as things are getting better, its advocates inherit success. Myths of leadership attribute causality to individuals in high places. Whether things are going well or badly, we like to hold someone responsible. Cohen and March have this to say about college presidents:

> Presidents negotiate with their audiences on the interpretations of their power. As a result, during . . . years of campus troubles, many college presidents sought to emphasize the limitations of presidential control. During the more glorious days of conspicuous success, they solicited a recognition of their responsibility for events. This is likely to lead to popular impressions of strong presidents during good times and weak presidents during bad times. Persons who are primarily exposed to the symbolic presidency (for example, outsiders) will tend to exaggerate the power of the presidency. Those people who have tried to accomplish something in the institution with presidential support (for example, educational reforms) will tend to underestimate presidential power or presidential will (1974, pp. 198–199).

As Edelman puts it: "Leaders lead, followers follow, and organizations prosper. While this logic is pervasive, it can be misleading. Serendipitously marching one step ahead of a crowd moving in a specific direction may suggest a spurious connection between leadership and followership. Successful leadership is having followers who believe in the power of the leader. By believing, people are encouraged to link positive events with leadership behaviors" (1977, p. 73).

Though reassuring, the assumption that powerful leaders make a difference is often misleading. Cohen and March compare the command and control of college presidents to that of the driver of a skidding automobile: "The marginal judgments he makes, his skill, and his luck will probably make some difference to the life prospects of his riders. As a result, his responsibilities are heavy. But whether he is convicted of manslaughter or receives a medal for heroism is largely outside his control" (1974, p. 203).

As with other processes, a leader's power is less a matter of action than of appearance. When a leader does make a difference, it is mostly by enriching and updating the drama—constructing new myths that alter beliefs and generate faith.

Managing Impressions

Peter Vaill (1989) characterized management as a performing art. This rings especially true for those trying to launch a business. One of the chief challenges confronting entrepreneurs is acquiring the resources needed to get embryonic ideas to the marketplace. This requires convincing investors of the future worth of an idea or product. Entrepreneurs typically concentrate on developing a persuasive business plan that projects a rosy financial future, coupled with an impressive PowerPoint presentation full of information about the new idea's potential.

Zott and Huy's two-year field study suggests that symbols may be more powerful than numbers in determining who gets funded (2007). They compared entrepreneurs who garnered a lion's share of resources with others who did not fare as well. Their results depict "the entrepreneur as an active shaper of perceptions and a potentially skilled user of cultural tool kits . . . By enacting symbols effectively entrepreneurs can shape a compelling symbolic universe that complements the initially weak and uncertain quality of their ventures" (pp. 100–101).

Resources flowed to entrepreneurs who presented themselves, their companies, and their products with dramatic flair rather than relying solely on technical promise and financial analyses. The winners knew their audience, capitalized on credentials and business associations, wore appropriate costumes to blend with clients and investors, spotlighted the symbolic value of their products, stressed the cultural vigor of their enterprises, called attention to unique processes, highlighted personal commitment, pointed to short-term achievements, and told good stories.

Fundraisers often say that giving is a matter of heart more than head. By invoking meaningful symbols, successful entrepreneurs were able to loosen the purse strings of investors. They skillfully managed impressions through carefully crafted theatrical performances.

CONCLUSION

From an institutional perspective, organizations are judged as much on appearance as on outcomes. The right drama gives audiences the performance they expect. The production reassures, fosters belief in the organization's purposes, and cultivates hope and faith. Structures that do little to coordinate activity and protocols that rarely achieve their intended outcomes still play a significant symbolic role. They provide internal glue. They help participants cope, believe, find meaning, and play their roles without reading the wrong lines, upstaging the lead actors, or confusing tragedy with comedy. To outside audiences, they provide a basis for confidence and support.

Dramaturgical concepts sharply redefine organizational dynamics. Historically, theories of management and organization have focused on instrumental issues. We see problems, try to solve them, and then ask, "What did we accomplish?" Often, the answer is "nothing" or "not much." We find ourselves repeating the old saw that the more things change, the more they remain the same. Such a message can be disheartening and disillusioning. It often produces a sense of helplessness and a belief that things will never get much better.

In *Hope Dies Last*, Studs Terkel says it well: "In all epochs, there were first doubts and the fear of stepping forth and speaking out, but the attribute that spurred the warriors on was hope. And the *act*. Seldom was there a despair or a sense of hopelessness. Some of those on the sidelines, the spectators, feeling hopeless and impotent, had by the very nature of the passionate act of others become imbued with hope themselves" (2004, p. xviii). Theatrical imagery offers a hopeful note. For a variety of reasons, we may be restless, frustrated, lost, or searching to renew our faith and beliefs. We commission a new play called *Change*. At the end of the pageant, we can ask: What was expressed? What was recast? And what was legitimized? A good play assures us that each day is potentially more exciting and full of meaning than the last. If things go badly, buff up the symbols, revise the drama, develop new myths—or dance to another tune.

PART SIX

Improving Leadership Practice

A messy, turbulent world rarely presents bounded, well-defined problems, and decoding complex situations is not a single-frame activity. In this part of the book, we focus on combining lenses to achieve multiframe approaches to managing and leading.

In Chapter 15, we contrast a stereotype of crisp, orderly rationality with the more frantic, reactive reality of managerial life. We show how routine activities and processes such as strategic planning, decision making, and conflict take on different meanings depending on how they are viewed. We provide an example to illustrate the cacophony that arises when parties are seeing different realities. Finally, we look at studies of effective organizations and senior managers to examine how research aligns with our framework.

In Chapter 16, we examine a case of a middle manager who encounters an unexpected crisis on the first day in a new job. We show how each lens spawns both helpful and unproductive scenarios in a situation where the stakes and risks are high.

We turn to a discussion of leadership in Chapter 17. We begin by examining the 2016 U.S. presidential election to examine the interaction between leader and circumstances. We explore the concept of leadership and tour 100 years of leadership research. We review issues of culture and gender in leadership. Then we illustrate each frame's image of leaders and leadership.

Chapter 18 takes us to a perennial challenge: creating change. We examine predictable barriers identified in each frame and point out different remedies. We then integrate the frames with a stage model of change. The two in combination provide a powerful map.

Ethics and spirit take center stage in Chapter 19. We begin with a look at cases of dubious ethics at Siemens and Walmart. We discuss four criteria for ethical behavior: authorship, love, justice, and significance.

Chapter 20 presents an integrative case in which we zoom in on a new principal in his perilous early weeks at a troubled urban high school. We illustrate how the frames in tandem generate a more comprehensive diagnosis of the issues and offer more promising options for moving ahead.

Finally, in the Epilogue, we summarize the basic messages of the book and lay out implications for the development of future leaders.

Integrating Frames for Effective Practice

The world is but canvas to our imaginations.

—Henry David Thoreau

Can a natural disaster determine a presidential election?

Crises are an acid test of leadership. In the heat of the moment, leaders sometimes hesitate until events pass them by. Other times they jump too quickly, making bad decisions. Either way, they look weak, foolish, or out of touch. A deft response to crisis bolsters a leader's credibility. When Superstorm Sandy roared out of the Atlantic Ocean a week before the U.S. presidential election in 2012, it posed a major test for elected officials up and down the East Coast but even more for the two men locked in a close contest for the presidency, Mitt Romney and Barack Obama. Romney struggled to find his footing, hampered by the ambiguity of the challenger's role and by comments he had made months earlier suggesting he favored defunding the Federal Emergency Management Agency (FEMA), the arm of the U.S. government responsible for coming to the rescue in major natural disasters.

Obama could have stumbled, as his predecessor, President George W. Bush, had during Hurricane Katrina in 2005. Just before Sandy hit, Obama was campaigning in Florida. He almost got stuck there, which would have painted a picture of a misguided president who cared more about getting elected than helping storm victims. Instead, he got back to Washington to do what presidents are supposed to do in such an emergency—convey an image of being concerned and in charge. Leveraging the advantages of incumbency, he ordered relief to the affected areas, coordinated with governors and mayors and travelled to scenes of destruction to offer comfort and reassurance. He garnered rave reviews from two prominent Republicans, New York City's Mayor Michael Bloomberg and New Jersey's Governor Chris Christie. Christie's praise was particularly potent—he had given a fiery speech in support of Romney at the Republican convention and had recently described Obama as a flailing president who couldn't find the light switch.

Obama could always give a good speech—otherwise he would never have attained the presidency in 2008. But many critics and supporters alike saw him as bloodless, remote, and passive, deficient in the strength and passion needed to cope with the leadership challenges of the presidency. But in the face of Superstorm Sandy, his sure-footed response captured elements of every frame. He cut through red tape and bureaucracy to speed help to victims. He worked the phones to develop personal relationships with key leaders like Bloomberg and Christie. He visited affected areas, hugged victims, and promised swift and effective help. He recognized both the political and symbolic benefits of getting off the campaign trail for several days to focus on the biggest natural disaster to hit the United States since Hurricane Katrina hit New Orleans in 2005. Just before Sandy hit, the election polls showed the race as a virtual tie. A few days later, Obama began to pull away and he easily won reelection.

Harmonizing the frames and crafting inventive responses to new circumstances are essential to both management and leadership. This chapter considers questions about using the frames in combination. How do you decide how to frame an event? How do you integrate multiple lenses in responding to the same situation? We begin by revisiting the turbulent world of managers. We then explore what happens when people diverge in viewing the same challenge. We offer questions and guidelines to stimulate thinking about aligning perspectives with specific situations. Finally, we examine literature on effective managers and organizations to see which modes of thought dominate current theory.

LIFE AS MANAGERS KNOW IT

Traditional mythology depicts managers as rational people who plan, organize, coordinate, and control the activities of subordinates. Periodicals, books, and business schools sometimes paint a pristine image of modern managers: unruffled and well organized, with clean desks, power suits, and sophisticated information systems. Such "super managers" develop and implement farsighted strategies, producing predictable and robust results. It is a reassuring picture of clarity and order. Unfortunately, it's wrong.

An entirely different picture appears if you watch managers at work (Carlson, 1951; Florén and Tell, 2013; Kahneman, 2011; Klein, 1999; Kotter, 1982; Luthans, 1988; Mintzberg, 1973; Tengblad, 2013). It's a hectic life, shifting rapidly from one situation to another. Much of it involves dealing with people and emotions. Decisions emerge from a fluid, swirling vortex of conversations, meetings, and memos. Information systems ensure an overload of detail about what happened yesterday or last month. Yet they fail to answer a far more important question: What next?

McCloskey (1998) maintains that only two important European novels have depicted managers in a positive light. One is Thomas Mann's *Buddenbrooks*, published in 1902. The other is David Lodge's *Nice Work* (1988), whose central figure is Victor Wilcox, the manager of a struggling British factory. The novel opens with Wilcox struggling through a sleepless night that provides an all-too-realistic glimpse of managerial life:

> Worries streak towards him like an enemy spaceship in [a video game]. He flinches, dodges, zaps them with instant solutions, but the assault is endless: the Avco account, the Rawlinson account, the price of pig-iron, the value of the pound, the competition from Foundrax, the incompetence of his Marketing Director, the persistent breakdowns of the core blowers, the vandalizing of the toilets in the fettling shop, the pressure from his divisional boss, the last month's account, the quarterly forecast, the annual review (Lodge, 1988, p. 3).

The work of managers, Tengblad (2013) concludes, is more akin to juggling hot potatoes than engaging in analytic contemplation. In deciding what to do next, managers operate largely on the basis of intuition, drawing on firsthand observations, hunches, and judgment derived from experience. Too swamped to spend much time thinking, analyzing, or reading, they get most of their information in meetings, on the Internet, on the fly, or over the phone. They are hassled priests, modern muddlers, and corporate wheeler-dealers.

How does one reconcile the actual work of managers with the heroic imagery? "Whenever I report this frenetic pattern to groups of executives," says Harold Leavitt, "regardless of hierarchical level or nationality, they always respond with a mix of discomfiture and recognition. Reluctantly, and somewhat sheepishly, they will admit that the description fits, but they don't like to be told about it. If they were really good managers, they seem to feel, they would be in control, their desks would be clean, and their shops would run as smoothly as a Mercedes engine" (1996, p. 294). Led to believe that they should be rational and on top of things, managers may instead become bewildered and demoralized. They are supposed to plan and organize, yet they find themselves muddling and playing catch-up. They want to solve problems and make decisions. But when problems are ill defined and options murky, control is mostly an illusion and rationality an elusive dream.

ACROSS FRAMES: ORGANIZATIONS AS MULTIPLE REALITIES

Life in organizations is packed with activities and happenings that can be interpreted in a number of ways. Exhibit 15.1 examines familiar processes through four lenses. As the chart shows, any event can be framed in different ways and serve multiple purposes. Planning, for example, produces specific objectives. But it also creates arenas for airing conflict and becomes a sacred occasion to renegotiate symbolic meanings.

Exhibit 15.1.
Four Interpretations of Organizational Processes.

Process	Structural Frame	Human Resource Frame	Political Frame	Symbolic Frame
Strategic planning	Process to set objectives and coordinate resources	Activities to promote participation, build support	Arenas to air conflicts and realign power	Ritual to signal responsibility, produce symbols, negotiate meanings
Decision making	Rational sequence to produce correct decision	Open process to produce commitment	Opportunity to gain or exercise power	Ritual to confirm values and provide opportunities for bonding
Reorganizing	Realign roles and responsibilities to fit tasks and environment	Improve balance between human needs and formal roles	Redistribute power and form new coalitions	Maintain an image of accountability and responsiveness; negotiate a new social order
Evaluating	Way to distribute rewards or penalties and control performance	Feedback for helping individuals grow and improve	Opportunity to exercise power	Occasion to play roles in shared ritual

---

Exhibit 15.1. (*continued*)

Process	Structural Frame	Human Resource Frame	Political Frame	Symbolic Frame
Approaching conflict	Authorities maintain organizational goals by resolving conflict	Individuals confront conflict to develop relationships	Use power to defeat opponents and achieve goals	Use conflict to negotiate meaning and develop shared values
Goal setting	Keep organization headed in the right direction	Open communications and keep people committed to goals	Provide opportunity for individuals and groups to express interests	Develop symbols and shared values
Communication	Transmit facts and information	Exchange information, needs, and feelings	Influence or manipulate others	Tell stories
Meetings	Formal occasions for making decisions	Informal occasions for involvement, sharing feelings	Competitive occasions to win points	Sacred occasions to celebrate and transform the culture
Motivation	Economic incentives	Growth and self-actualization	Coercion, manipulation, and seduction	Symbols and celebrations

Multiple realities produce confusion and conflict as individuals see the same event through different lenses. A hospital administrator once called a meeting to make an important decision. The chief technician viewed it as a chance to express feelings and build relationships. The director of nursing hoped to gain power vis-à-vis physicians. The medical director saw it as an occasion for reaffirming the hospital's distinctive approach to medical care. The meeting became a cacophonous jumble, like a group of musicians each playing from a different score.

The confusion that can result when people view the world through different lenses is illustrated in this classic case:

Doctor Fights Order to Quit Maine Island

Dr. Gregory O'Keefe found himself the focus of a fierce battle between 1,200 year-round residents of Vinalhaven, Maine (an island fishing community), and the National Health Service Corps (NHSC), which paid his salary and insisted he take a promotion to an administrator's desk in Rockville, Maryland. He didn't want to go, and his patients felt the same way. The islanders were so distressed they lobbied Senator William Cohen (R-Maine) to keep him there:

> It's certainly not the prestige or glamour of the job that is holding O'Keefe, who drives the town's only ambulance and, as often as twice a week, takes critically ill patients to mainland hospitals via an emergency ferry run or a Coast Guard cutter, private plane, or even a lobster boat.
>
> Apparently unyielding in their insistence that O'Keefe accept the promotion or resign, NHSC officials seemed startled last week by the spate of protests from angry islanders, which prompted nationwide media attention and inquiries from the Maine congressional delegation. NHSC says it probably would not replace O'Keefe on the island, which, in the agency's view, is now able to support a private medical practice.
>
> Cohen described himself as "frustrated by the lack of responsiveness of lower-level bureaucrats." But to the NHSC, O'Keefe is a foot soldier in a military organization of more than 1,600 physicians assigned to isolated, medically needy communities. And he's had the audacity to question the orders of a superior officer.
>
> "It's like a soldier who wanted to stay at Ft. Myers and jumped on TV and called the defense secretary a rat for wanting him to move," Shirley Barth, press officer for the federal Public Health Service, said in a telephone interview Thursday (Goodman, 1983, p. 1).

The NHSC officials had trouble seeing beyond the structural frame; they had a job to do and a structure for getting it done. O'Keefe's resistance was illegitimate. O'Keefe saw the situation in human resource terms. He felt the work he was doing was meaningful and satisfying, and the islanders needed him. For Senator Cohen, it was a political issue; could minor bureaucrats be allowed to harm his constituents through mindless abuse of power? For the hardy residents of Vinalhaven, O'Keefe was a heroic figure of mythic proportions: "If he gets one night's sleep out of 20, he's lucky, but he's always up there smiling and working." The islanders were full of stories about O'Keefe's humility, skill, humaneness, dedication, wit, confidence, and caring.

With so many people peering through different filters, confusion, and conflict were predictable. The inability of NHSC officials to understand and acknowledge the existence of other perspectives illustrates the risks of clinging to a single view of a situation. Whenever someone's actions seem to make no sense, it is worth asking whether you and they are seeing contrasting realities. You know better what you're up against when you understand their perspective, even if you're sure they're wrong. Their mind-set—not yours—determines how they act.

MATCHING FRAMES TO SITUATIONS

In a given situation, one lens may be more helpful than others. At a strategic crossroads, a rational process focused on gathering and analyzing information may be exactly what is needed. At other times, developing commitment or building a power base may be more critical. In times of great stress, decision processes may become a form of ritual that brings comfort and support. Choosing a frame to size things up or understanding others' perspectives involves a combination of analysis, intuition, and artistry. Exhibit 15.2 poses questions to facilitate analysis and stimulate intuition. It also suggests conditions under which each way of thinking is most likely to be effective.

• *Are commitment and motivation essential to success?* The human resource and symbolic approaches need to be considered whenever issues of individual dedication, energy, and skill are vital to success. A new curriculum launched by a school district will fail without teacher support. Support might be strengthened by human resource approaches, such as participation and self-managing teams or through symbolic approaches linking the innovation to values and symbols teachers cherish.

Exhibit 15.2.
Choosing a Frame.

Question	If Yes:	If No:
Are individual commitment and motivation essential to success?	Human resource Symbolic	Structural Political
Is the technical quality of the decision important?	Structural	Human resource Political Symbolic
Are there high levels of ambiguity and uncertainty?	Political Symbolic	Structural Human resource
Are conflict and scarce resources significant?	Political Symbolic	Structural Human resource
Are you working from the bottom up?	Political Symbolic	Structural Human resource

- *Is the technical quality important?* When a good decision needs to be technically sound, the structural frame's emphasis on data and logic is essential. But if a decision must be acceptable to major constituents, then human resource, political, or symbolic issues loom larger. Could the technical quality of a decision ever be unimportant? A college found itself embroiled in a three-month battle over the choice of a commencement speaker. The faculty pushed for a great scholar, the students for a movie star. The president was more than willing to invite anyone acceptable to both groups; she saw no technical criterion for judging that one choice was better than the other.

- *Are ambiguity and uncertainty high?* If goals are clear, technology well understood, and behavior reasonably predictable, the structural and human resource approaches are likely to apply. As ambiguity increases, the political and symbolic perspectives become more relevant. The political frame expects that the pursuit of self-interest will often produce confused and chaotic contests that require political intervention. The symbolic lens sees symbols as a way of finding order, meaning, and "truth" in situations too complex, uncertain, or mysterious for rational or political analysis.

- *Are conflict and scarce resources significant?* Human resource logic fits best in situations favoring collaboration—as in profitable, growing firms or highly unified schools. But when conflict is high and resources are scarce, dynamics of conflict, power, and self-interest regularly come to the fore. In situations like a bidding war or an election campaign, sophisticated political strategies are vital to success. In other cases, skilled leaders may find that an overarching symbol helps potential adversaries transcend their differences and work together.

In 1994, after decades of increasing turmoil, the Republic of South Africa finally ended its system of white rule and held a national election in which the black majority could vote for the first time. The African National Congress and its leader, Nelson Mandela, came to power with more than 60 percent of the vote, but it was a sudden and wrenching adjustment for many South Africans. Historic tensions plagued the new government, and there was a serious threat of violence and guerilla warfare from armed and dangerous white bitter-enders.

Looking for a way to build unity, Mandela alighted on an unlikely vehicle: rugby. White South Africans loved the sport and the national team, the Springboks. Black South Africans hated rugby and routinely cheered for the Springboks' opponents. Mandela lobbied to bring the rugby world cup tournament to South Africa, and he charmed the Springbok captain in order to enlist him as a champion of a united nation. Mandela then undertook the even harder task of persuading black South Africans to support a team they hated. He was initially booed by distressed supporters, but his credibility, persuasive skills, and a mantra of "one team, one nation" eventually persuaded most of his followers to get on board. Then something magical happened. No one expected the Springboks to go very far in the tournament, but they kept winning until they reached the finals.

> Mandela's coup de grâce, the final submission of white South Africa to his charms, came minutes before the final itself when the old terrorist-in-chief went onto the pitch to shake hands with the players dressed in the colors of the ancient enemy, the green Springbok shirt.
>
> For a moment, Ellis Park Stadium, 95 per cent white on the day, stood in dumb, disbelieving silence. Then someone took up a cry that others followed, ending in a thundering roar: "Nel-son! Nel-son! Nel-son!"
>
> . . . With Mandela playing as an invisible 16th man, Joel Stransky, the one Jewish player in the Springbok team, kicked the winning drop goal in extra time.
>
> Mandela emerged again, still in his green jersey, and, to even louder cries of "Nel-son! Nel-son!," walked onto the pitch to shake the hand of [Springbok captain] François Pienaar.
>
> As he prepared to hand over the cup to his captain, he said: "François, thank you for what you have done for our country." Pienaar, with extraordinary presence of mind, replied: "No, Mr President. Thank you for what you have done" (Carlin, 2007. Reprinted with permission).

There wasn't a dry eye in the house. There wasn't a dry eye in the country. Everybody celebrated: one country at last.

- *Are you working from the bottom up?* Restructuring is an option primarily for those in a position of authority. Human resource approaches to improvement—such as training, job enrichment, and participation—usually need support from the top to be successful. The political frame, in contrast, is more likely to work for changes initiated from below. Change agents lower in the pecking order rarely can rely on formal clout, so they have to find other bases of power, such as symbolic acts, to draw attention to their cause and embarrass opponents. The 9/11 terrorists could have picked from an almost unlimited array of targets, but the World Trade Towers and the Pentagon were deliberately selected for their symbolic value.

The questions in Exhibit 15.2 cannot be followed mechanically. They won't substitute for judgment and intuition in deciding how to size up or respond to a situation. But they can guide and augment the process of choosing a promising course of action. Finding a workable strategy is a matter of playing probabilities. In some cases, your line of thinking might lead you to a familiar frame. But if the tried-and-true approach seems likely to fall short, reframe again. You may discover an exciting and creative new lens for deciphering the situation. Then you can take on the challenge of communicating your breakthrough to others who still champion the old reality.

EFFECTIVE MANAGERS AND ORGANIZATIONS

Does the ability to use multiple frames actually help managers decipher events and determine alternative ways to respond? If so, how are the frames embedded and integrated in everyday situations? We examine several strands of research to answer these questions. First, we look at four influential guides to organizational excellence: *In Search of Excellence* (Peters and Waterman, 1982), *Built to Last* (Collins and Porras, 1994), *Good to Great* (Collins, 2001), and *Great by Choice* (Collins and Hansen, 2011). We then review three studies of managerial work: *The General Managers* (Kotter, 1982), *Managing Public Policy* (Lynn, 1987), and *Real Managers* (Luthans, Yodgetts, and Rosenkrantz, 1988). Finally, we look at studies of managers' frame orientations to see whether current thinking is equal to present-day challenges.

Organizational Excellence

Peters and Waterman's best-seller *In Search of Excellence* (1982) explored the question, "What do high-performing corporations have in common?" Peters and Waterman studied more than 60 large companies in six major industries: high technology (Digital Equipment and IBM, for example), consumer products (Kodak, Procter & Gamble), manufacturing (3M, Caterpillar), service (McDonald's, Delta Airlines), project management (Boeing, Bechtel), and natural resources (Exxon, DuPont). The companies were chosen on the basis of both objective performance indicators (such as long-term growth and profitability) and the judgment of knowledgeable observers.

Collins and Porras (1994) attempted a similar study of what they termed "visionary" companies but tried to address two methodological limitations in the Peters and Waterman study. Collins and Porras included a comparison group (missing in Peters and Waterman) by matching each of their top performers with another firm in the same industry with a comparable history. Their pairings included Citibank with Chase Manhattan, General

Electric with Westinghouse, Sony with Kenwood, Hewlett-Packard with Texas Instruments, and Merck with Pfizer. Collins and Porras emphasized long-term results by restricting their study to companies at least 50 years old with evidence of consistent success over many decades.

Built to Last was the first in a series of works that Jim Collins, alone and with colleagues, has produced that attempt to draw lessons from successful companies. *Good to Great* (2001) used a comparative approach similar to that of Collins and Porras but focused on a different criterion for success: instead of organizations that had excelled for many years, he identified a group of companies that had made a dramatic breakthrough from middling to superlative and compared them with similar companies that had remained ordinary. In *Great by Choice*, Collins and Hansen focused on seven companies (Amgen, Biomet, Intel, Microsoft, Progressive Insurance, Southwest Airlines, and Stryker) that had dramatically outperformed the stock market and their respective industries over a period of two to three decades.

All of these studies identified roughly seven or eight critical characteristics of excellent companies, similar in some respects and distinct in others, as Exhibit 15.3 shows. All suggest that excellent companies manage to embrace paradox. They are loose yet tight, highly disciplined yet entrepreneurial. Peters and Waterman's "bias for action" and Collins and Porras's "try a lot, keep what works" both point to risk taking and experimenting as ways to learn and avoid bogging down in analysis paralysis. All four studies emphasize a clear core identity that helps firms stay on track and be clear about what they will not do.

All of the Collins studies emphasized a nonfinding that ran afoul of conventional wisdom: They did not find that success was associated with larger-than-life charismatic leaders. All three books highlighted leaders who were typically homegrown and focused on building their organization rather than their own reputation. Collins's "level 5" leaders were driven but self-effacing, extremely disciplined, and hardworking but consistent in attributing success to their colleagues rather than themselves.

As Exhibit 15.3 shows, all four studies produced three-frame models of excellence. Notice that none of the characteristics of excellence are political. Does an effective organization eliminate politics? Or did the authors miss something? By definition, their samples focused on companies with a strong record of growth and profitability. Infighting and backbiting tend to be less visible on a winning team than on a losing one. When resources are relatively abundant, political dynamics are less prominent because it's easier to use slack assets to keep everyone happy. Recall, too, that a strong culture breeds people who share both values and habits of mind. A unifying culture reduces conflict and political strife—or at least makes them easier to manage.

Exhibit 15.3.
Characteristics of Excellent or Visionary Companies.

Frame	Peters and Waterman, 1982	Collins and Porras, 1994	Collins, 2001	Collins and Hansen, 2011
Structural	Autonomy and entrepreneurship; bias for action; simple form, lean staff	Clock building, not time telling; try a lot, keep what works	Confront the brutal facts; "hedgehog concept" (best in the world, economic engine); technology accelerators; "flywheel," not "doom loop"	"20-mile march," "Specific, methodological and consistent," "Fire bullets, then cannon-balls"
Human resource	Close to the customer; productivity through people	Home-grown management	"Level 5 leadership;" first who, then what	"Level 5 leadership"
Political				
Symbolic	Hands-on, value-driven; simultaneously loose and tight; stick to the knitting	Big hairy audacious goals; cult-like cultures; good enough never is; preserve the core, stimulate progress; more than profits	Never lose belief or faith; hedgehog concept (deeply passionate); culture of discipline	Fanatic discipline, productive paranoia

Even in successful companies, it is likely that power and conflict are more important than these studies suggest. Ask a few managers, "What makes your organization successful?" They rarely talk about coalitions, conflict, or jockeying for position. Even if it is a prominent issue, politics is typically kept in the closet—known to insiders but not on public display. But if we change our focus from effective organizations to effective managers, we find a different picture.

The Effective Senior Manager

Kotter (1982) conducted an intensive study of 15 corporate general managers (GMs). His sample included "individuals who hold positions with some multifunctional responsibility for a business" (p. 2); each managed an organization with at least several hundred employees. Lynn (1987) analyzed five subcabinet-level executives in the U.S. government—political appointees with responsibility for a major federal agency. Luthans, Yodgetts, and Rosenkrantz (1988) studied a larger but less elite sample of managers. They examined the day-to-day activities of 450 managers at a variety of levels and described how those activities related to success and effectiveness. Exhibit 15.4 shows the characteristics that these studies emphasize as being the keys to effectiveness.

Kotter and Lynn described jobs of enormous complexity and uncertainty, coupled with substantial dependence on networks of people whose support and energy were essential for the executives to do their job. They described leaders who focused on three basic challenges: setting an agenda, building a network, and using the network to get things done. Lynn's work is consistent with Kotter's observation: "As a result of these demands, the typical GM faced significant obstacles in both figuring out what to do and in getting things done" (Kotter, 1982, p. 122).

Kotter and Lynn both emphasized the political dimension in senior managers' jobs. Lynn described the need for a significant dose of political skill and sophistication: "building legislative support, negotiating, and identifying changing positions and interests" (1987, p. 248). Kotter's model includes elements of all four frames; Lynn's includes all but the symbolic.

A somewhat different picture emerges from the study by Luthans, Yodgetts, and Rosenkrantz. In their sample, middle- and lower-level managers spent about three-fifths of their time on structural activities (routine communications and traditional management functions like planning and controlling), about one-fifth on "human resource management" (people-related activities like motivating, disciplining, training, staffing), and about one-fifth on "networking" (political activities like socializing, politicking, and relating to external constituents). The results suggest that, compared with the senior executives Kotter and Lynn studied, middle managers spend less time grappling with complexity and more time on routine.

Luthans, Yodgetts, and Rosenkrantz distinguished between "effectiveness" and "success." The criteria for effectiveness were the quantity and quality of the unit's performance and the level of subordinates' satisfaction with their boss. Success was defined in terms of promotions per year—how fast people got ahead. Effective managers and successful managers used time differently. The most "effective" managers spent much of their

Exhibit 15.4.
Challenges in Managers' Jobs.

Frame	Kotter (1982)	Lynn (1987)	Luthans, Yodgetts, and Rosenkrantz (1988)
Structural	Keep on top of large, complex set of activities Set goals and policies under conditions of uncertainty	Attain intellectual grasp of policy issues	Communication* (paperwork, exchange routine information) Traditional management (planning, goal setting, controlling)
Human resource	Motivate, coordinate, and control large, diverse group of subordinates	Use own personality to best advantage	Human resource management* (motivating, managing conflict, staffing, and so on)
Political	Achieve "delicate balance" in allocating scarce resources Get support from bosses Get support from corporate staff and other constituents	Exploit all opportunities to achieve strategic gains	Networking† (politics, interacting with outsiders)
Symbolic	Develop credible strategic premises Identify and focus on core activities that give meaning to employees		

*Most relevant to managers who were judged "effective" by their subordinates.
†Most relevant to managers who were considered "successful" (achieved rapid promotions to higher positions faster than peers).

time on communications and human resource management and relatively little time on networking. But networking was the only activity that was strongly related to getting ahead. "Successful" managers spent almost half their time on networking and only about 10 percent on human resource management.

At first glance, this might seem to confirm the cynical suspicion that getting ahead in a career is more about politics than performance. More likely, though, the results confirm that performance is in the eye of the beholder. Subordinates rate their boss primarily on criteria internal to the unit—effective communications and treating people well. Bosses, on the other hand, focus on how well a manager handles relations to external constituents, including, of course, the bosses themselves. The researchers found that the 10 percent or so of their sample who were high on both success and effectiveness had a balanced approach emphasizing both internal and external issues. A multiframe approach made them both effective and successful.

Comparing all these studies—those focusing on organizations and those focusing on managers—reveals both similarities and differences. All give roughly equal emphasis to structural and human resource considerations. But political issues are invisible in the organizational excellence studies, whereas they are prominent in all the studies of individual managers. Politics was as important for Kotter's corporate executives as for Lynn's political appointees and was the key to getting ahead for middle managers. Conversely, symbols and culture were more prominent in the studies of organizational excellence. For various reasons, each study tended to neglect one frame or another. In assessing any prescription for improving organizations, ask whether any frame is omitted. The overlooked perspective could be the one that derails the effort.

MANAGERS' FRAME PREFERENCES

Yet another line of research has yielded additional data on how frame preference influences leadership effectiveness. Bolman and Deal (1991, 1992a, 1992b) and Bolman and Granell (1999) studied populations of managers and administrators in both business and education. They found that the ability to use multiple frames was a consistent correlate of effectiveness. Effectiveness as a manager was particularly associated with the structural frame, whereas the symbolic and political frames tended to be the primary determinants of effectiveness as a leader.

Bensimon (1989, 1990) studied college presidents and found that multiframe presidents were viewed as more effective than presidents wedded to a single frame. In her sample, more than a third of the presidents relied only one frame, and only a quarter depended on more than two. Single-frame presidents tended to be less experienced, relying mainly on structural or human resource perspectives. Presidents who relied solely on the structural frame were particularly likely to be seen as ineffective leaders. Heimovics, Herman, and Jurkiewicz Coughlin (1993) found the same thing for chief executives in the nonprofit sector, and Wimpelberg (1987) found comparable results in a study of school principals. He found that principals of ineffective schools relied almost entirely on the structural frame, whereas principals in effective schools used multiple frames. When asked about hiring teachers, principals in less effective schools talked about standard procedures (how vacancies are posted, how the central office sends a candidate for an interview), whereas more effective principals emphasized "playing the system" to get the teachers they needed.

Bensimon found that presidents thought they used more frames than their colleagues observed. They were particularly likely to overrate themselves on the human resource and symbolic frames, a finding also reported by Bolman and Deal (1991). Only half of the presidents who saw themselves as symbolic leaders were perceived that way by others.

Despite the low image of organizational politics in the minds of many managers, political savvy appears to be a primary determinant of success in managerial work. Heimovics, Herman, and Jurkiewicz Coughlin (1993, 1995) found this for chief executives of nonprofit organizations, and Doktor (1993) found the same thing for directors of family service organizations in Kentucky.

CONCLUSION

The image of firm control and crisp precision often attributed to managers has little relevance to the messy world of complexity, conflict, and uncertainty they actually inhabit. They need multiple frames to survive. They need to understand that any event or process can serve several purposes and that participants are often operating from different views of reality. Managers need a diagnostic map that helps them assess which lenses are likely to be salient and helpful in a given situation. Among the key variables are motivation, technical constraints, uncertainty, scarcity, conflict, and whether an individual is operating from the top down or from the bottom up.

Several lines of research have found that effective leaders and effective organizations rely on multiple frames. Studies of effective corporations, of individuals in senior management roles, and of public and nonprofit administrators all point to the need for multiple perspectives in developing a holistic picture of complex systems.

Reframing in Action
Opportunities and Perils

When you are face to face with a difficulty,
you are up against a discovery.

—William Thomson (Lord Kelvin)

Life in organizations is often governed by routine, with undercurrents of suppressed conflicts, jealousies, or unhealed egos from past skirmishes. Periodically, however, past or present issues come to the surface, and tensions are laid bare. One likely scenario is a transition from one boss to another. How participants frame their circumstances is fateful for the outcomes.

Reach and Grasp

Put yourself in the shoes of Cindy Marshall. You're headed to the office for your first day in a new job. Your company has transferred you to Kansas City to manage a customer service unit. It's a big promotion, with a substantial increase in pay and responsibility, but you know you face a major challenge. You are inheriting a department with a reputation for slow, substandard service. Senior management places much of the blame on your predecessor, Bill Howard, seen as too authoritarian and rigid. Howard is moving to another job, but the company asked him to stay on for a week to help you get oriented. One potential sticking point: He hired most of your new staff. Many may still feel loyal to him.

(continued)

(continued)

When you arrive, you get a frosty hello from Susan Bond, the department secretary. As you walk into your new office, you see Howard behind the desk in a conversation with three other staff members. You say hello, and he responds by saying, "Didn't the secretary tell you that we're in a meeting right now? If you'll wait outside, I'll be able to see you in about an hour."

As Cindy Marshall, what would you do? You're in the glare of the spotlight, and the audience eagerly awaits your response. If you feel threatened or attacked—as most of us would—those feelings will push you toward either fight or flight. Escalating the conflict is risky and could damage everyone. Backing away or fleeing could suggest that you are too emotional or not tough enough.

This is a classic example of a manager's nightmare: an unexpected situation that threatens to explode in your face. Howard's greeting tries to throw you off stride and put you in a bind. It carries echoes of historic patterns of male arrogance and condescension in relating to women (similar to those that surfaced in the Anne Barreta case in Chapter 8). Whether or not he intended it that way, Howard's response appears well designed for disconcerting a younger female colleague. He makes it likely that, as Cindy, you will feel trapped and powerless, or you will do something rash and regrettable. Either way, he wins and you lose.

The frames suggest another set of possibilities. They offer the advantage of multiple angles to size up the situation. What's really going on here? What options do you have? What script does the situation demand? How might you reinterpret the scene to create a more effective scenario? Reframing is a powerful tool in a tough situation for generating possibilities other than fight or flight.

An immediate question facing you, as Cindy Marshall, is whether to respond to Howard on the spot or to buy time. If you're at a loss for what to say or if you fear you will make things worse instead of better, take time to "go to the balcony"—try to get above the confusion of the moment long enough to get a sharper perspective. Better yet, find an effective response on the spot.

Each of the frames generates its own possibilities, creatively translated into alternative scenarios. They can also be misapplied or misused. Success depends on the skill and artistry of the person following a given script. In this chapter, we describe setups Marshall might compose, showing that each of the four lenses can produce both effective and ineffective reactions. We conclude with a summary of the power and risks of reframing and highlight its importance for outsiders and newcomers taking on new responsibilities.

Structural Frame

A Structural Scenario

A structural scenario casts managers and leaders in fundamental roles of clarifying goals, attending to the relationship between structure and environment, and developing a clearly defined array of roles and relationships appropriate to what needs to be done. Without a workable structure, people become unsure about what they are supposed to be doing. The result is confusion, frustration, and conflict. In an effective organization, individuals understand their responsibilities and their contribution. Policies, linkages, and lines of authority are straightforward and accepted. With the right structure, the organization can achieve its goals, and individuals can see their role in the big picture.

The main job of a leader is to focus on task, facts, and logic, rather than personality and emotions. Most people problems stem from structural flaws, not personal limitations or liability. The structural leader is not rigidly authoritarian and does not attempt to solve every problem by issuing orders (although that is sometimes appropriate). Instead, the leader tries to design and implement a process or architecture appropriate to the circumstances.

You may wonder what structure has to do with a direct, personal confrontation, but the structural scenario in the box can be scripted to generate a variety of responses.

Here's one example:

Howard: Didn't the secretary tell you that we're in a meeting right now? If you'll wait outside, I'll be able to see you in about an hour.

Marshall: My appointment as manager of this office began at nine this morning. This is now my office, and you're sitting behind my desk. Either you relinquish the desk immediately, or I will call headquarters and report you for insubordination.

Howard: I was asked to stay on the job for one more week to try to help you learn the ropes. Frankly, I doubt that you're ready for this job, but you don't seem to want any help.

Marshall: I repeat, I am now in charge of this office. Let me also remind you that headquarters assigned you to stay this week to assist me. I expect you to carry out that order. If you don't, I will submit a letter for your file detailing your lack of cooperation. Now, [firmly] I want my desk.

Howard: Well, we were working on important office business, but since the princess here is more interested in giving orders than in getting work done, let's move our meeting down to your office, Joe. Enjoy your desk!

In this exchange, Marshall places heavy emphasis on her formal authority and the chain of command. By invoking her superiors and her legitimate authority, she takes charge and gets Howard to back down, but at a price. She unwittingly colludes with Howard in making the encounter a personal confrontation. She risks long-term tension with her new subordinates, who surely feel awkward during this combative encounter. They may conclude that the new boss is like the old one—autocratic and rigid.

There are other options. Here's another example of how Marshall might exercise her authority:

Howard: Didn't the secretary tell you that we're in a meeting right now? If you'll wait outside, I'll be able to see you in about an hour.

Marshall: She didn't mention it, and I don't want to interrupt important work, but we also need to set some priorities and work out an agenda for the day anyway. Bill, have you developed a plan for how you and I can get to work on the transition?

Howard: We can meet later on, after I get through some pressing business.

Marshall: The pressing business is just the kind of thing I need to learn about as the new manager here. What issues are you discussing?

Howard: How to keep the office functioning when the new manager is not ready for the job.

Marshall: Well, I have a lot to learn, but I feel up to it. With your help, I think we can have a smooth and productive transition. How about if you continue your meeting and I just sit in as an observer? Then, Bill, you and I could meet to work out a plan for how we'll handle the transition. After that, I'd like to schedule a meeting with each manager to get an individual progress report. I'd like to hear from each of you about your major customer service objectives and how you would assess your progress. Now, what were you talking about before I got here?

This time, Marshall is still clear and firm in establishing her authority, but she does it without appearing harsh or dictatorial. She underscores the importance of setting priorities. Note the deft use of a question when she asks whether Howard has a plan for making the transition productive. That lets her engage Howard while declining his invitation for combat. She emphasizes shared goals and defines a temporary role for herself as an observer. She focuses steadfastly on the task and not on Howard's provocations. In keeping the exchange on a rational level and outlining a transition plan, she avoids escalating or submerging the conflict. She also communicates to her new staff that she has done her homework, is organized, and knows what she wants. When she says she would like to hear their personal objectives and progress, she communicates an expectation that they should follow her example.

Human Resource Frame

A Human Resource Scenario

The human resource leader believes that people are the center of any organization. If people feel the organization is responsive to their needs and supportive of their personal goals, they will deliver commitment and loyalty. Administrators who are authoritarian or insensitive, who don't communicate effectively, or who don't care can never be effective leaders. The human resource leader works on behalf of both the organization and its people, seeking to serve the best interests of both.

The job of the leader is support and empowerment. Support takes a variety of forms: showing concern, listening to people's aspirations and goals, and communicating personal warmth and openness. The leader empowers through participation and inclusion, ensuring that people have the autonomy and support needed to do their job.

The human resource frame favors listening and responsiveness, but some people go a little too far in trying to be responsive:

Howard: Didn't the secretary tell you that we're in a meeting right now? If you'll wait outside, I'll be able to see you in about an hour.

Marshall: Oh, gosh, no, she didn't. I just feel terrible about interrupting your meeting. I hope I didn't offend anyone because to me, it's really important to establish good working relationships right from the outset. While I'm waiting, is there anything I can do to help? Would anyone like a cup of coffee?

Howard: No. We'll let you know when we're finished.

Marshall: Oh . . . Um, well, have a good meeting, and I'll see you in an hour.

In the effort to be friendly and accommodating, Marshall is acting more like a waitress than a manager. She defuses the conflict, but her staff are likely to see their new boss as weak. She could instead capitalize on an interest in people:

Howard: Didn't the secretary tell you that we're in a meeting right now? If you'll wait outside, I'll be able to see you in about an hour.

Marshall: I'm sorry if I'm interrupting, but I'm eager to get started, and I'll need all your help. [She walks around, introduces herself, and shakes hands with each member of her new staff. Howard scowls silently.] Bill, could we take a few minutes to talk about how we can work together on the transition, now that I'm coming in to manage the department?

(continued)

(continued)

Howard: You're not the manager yet. I was asked to stay on for a week to get you started—though, frankly, I doubt that you're ready for this job.

Marshall: I understand your concern, Bill. I know how committed you are to the success of the department. If I were you, I might be worried about whether I was turning my baby over to someone who wouldn't be able to take care of it. But I wouldn't be here if I didn't feel ready. I want to benefit as much as I can from your experience. Is it urgent to get on with what you were talking about, or could we take some time first to talk about how we can start working together?

Howard: We have some things we need to finish.

Marshall: Well, as a manager, I always prefer to trust the judgment of the people who are closest to the action. I'll just sit in while you finish up, and then we can talk about how we move forward from there.

Here, Marshall is unfazed and relentlessly cheerful; she avoids a battle and acknowledges Howard's perspective. When he says she is not ready for the job, she resists the temptation to debate or return his salvo. Instead, she recognizes his concern but calmly communicates her confidence and focus on moving ahead. She demonstrates an important skill of a human resource leader: the ability to combine advocacy with inquiry. She listens carefully to Howard but gently stands her ground. She asks for his help while expressing confidence that she can do the job. When he says they have things to finish, she responds with the agility of a martial artist, using Howard's energy to her own advantage. She expresses part of her philosophy—she prefers to trust her staff's judgment—and positions herself as an observer, thus gaining an opportunity to learn more about her staff and the issues they are addressing. By reframing the situation, she has gotten off to a better start with Howard and is able to signal to others the kind of people-oriented leader she intends to be.

Political Frame

A Political Scenario

The political leader believes that managers have to recognize political reality and know how to deal with conflict. Inside and outside any organization, a range of people and interest groups, each with their own agenda, compete for scarce resources. There are never enough to give all parties what they want, so there will always be struggles.

The job of the leader is to recognize major constituencies, develop ties to their leadership, and manage conflict as productively as possible. Above all, leaders need to build a power base and use power carefully. They can't give every group everything it wants, but they can create arenas where groups can negotiate differences and come up with a reasonable compromise. They also need to work at articulating interests everyone has in common. It is wasteful for people to expend energy fighting each other when there are plenty of enemies outside to battle. Any group that doesn't get its act together internally tends to get trounced by outsiders.

Some managers translate the political approach described in this box to mean management by intimidation and manipulation. It sometimes works, but the risks are high. Here's an example:

Howard: Didn't the secretary tell you that we're in a meeting right now? If you'll wait outside, I'll be able to see you in about an hour.

Marshall: In your next job, maybe you should train your secretary better. Anyway, I can't waste time sitting around in hallways. Everyone in this room knows why I'm here. You've got a choice, Bill. You can cooperate with me, or you can lose any credibility you still have in this company.

Howard: If I didn't have any more experience than you do, I wouldn't be so quick to throw my weight around. But if you think you know it all already, I guess you won't need any help from me.

Marshall: What I know is that this department has gone downhill under your leadership, and it's my job to turn it around. You can go home right now, if you want—you know where the door is. But if you're smart, you'll stay and help. The vice president wants my report on the transition. You'll be a lot better off if I can tell him you've been cooperative.

Moviegoers cheer when bullies get their comeuppance. It can be satisfying to give the verbal equivalent of a kick in the groin to someone who deserves it. In this exchange, Marshall establishes that she is tough, even dangerous. But such coercive tactics can be expensive in the long run. She is likely to win this battle because her hand is stronger. But she may lose the war. She increases Howard's antagonism, and her attack may offend him and frighten her new staff. Even if they dislike Howard, they may see Marshall as arrogant and callous. She lays the ground for a counterattack, and she may have done political damage that will be difficult to reverse.

Sophisticated political leaders prefer to avoid naked demonstrations of power, looking instead for ways to appeal to the self-interests of potential adversaries:

> *Howard:* Didn't the secretary tell you that we're in a meeting right now? If you'll wait outside, I'll be able to see you in about an hour.
>
> *Marshall:* [pleasantly] Bill, if it's okay with you, I'd prefer to skip the games and go to work. I expect this department to be a winner, and I hope that's what we all want. I also would like to manage the transition in a way that's good for your career, Bill, and for the careers of others in the room.
>
> *Howard:* If I need advice from you on my career, I'll ask.
>
> *Marshall:* Okay, but the vice president has asked me to let him know about the cooperation I get here. I'd like to be able to say that everyone has been helping me as much as possible. Is that what you'd like, too?
>
> *Howard:* I've known the vice president a lot longer than you have. I can talk to him myself.
>
> *Marshall:* I know, Bill; he's told me that. In fact, I just came from his office. If you'd like, we could both go see him right now.
>
> *Howard:* Uh, no, not right now.
>
> *Marshall:* Well, then, let's get on with it. Do you want to finish what you were discussing, or is this a good time for us to develop some agreement on how we're going to work together?

In this politically based response, Marshall is both direct and diplomatic. She uses a light touch in dismissing Howard's opening salvo. ("I'd prefer to skip the games.") She speaks directly to both Howard's interest in his career and her subordinates' interest in theirs. She deftly deflates his posturing by asking whether he wants to go with her to talk to the vice president. Clearly, she is confident of her political support and knows that his bluster has little to back it up.

Note that in both political scenarios, Marshall draws on her power resources. In the first, she uses those resources to humiliate Howard, but in the second, her approach is subtler. She conserves her political capital and takes charge while leaving Howard with as much pride as possible, achieving something closer to a win-win than a win-lose outcome.

Symbolic Frame

A Symbolic Scenario

The symbolic leader believes that the most important part of a leader's job is inspiration—giving people something they can believe in. People become excited about and committed to a place with a unique identity, a special place where they feel that what they do is really important. Effective symbolic leaders are passionate about making the organization unique in its niche and

---

communicating that passion to others. They use dramatic symbols to get people excited and to give them a deep sense of the organization's mission. They are visible and energetic. They create slogans, tell stories, hold rallies, give awards, appear where they are least expected, and manage by wandering around.

Symbolic leaders are sensitive to an organization's history and culture. They seek to use the best in an organization's traditions and values as a base for building a culture with cohesiveness and meaning. They articulate a vision that communicates the organization's unique capabilities and mission.

At first glance, Cindy Marshall's encounter with Bill Howard might seem a poor candidate for the symbolic approach just outlined. An ineffective effort could produce embarrassing results, making the would-be symbolic leader look foolish:

Howard: Didn't the secretary tell you that we're in a meeting right now? If you'll wait outside, I'll be able to see you in about an hour.

Marshall: It's great to see that you're all hard at work. It's proof that we all share a commitment to excellence in customer service. In fact, I've already made up buttons for all the staff. Here—I have one for each of you. They read, "The customer is always first." They look great, and they communicate the spirit that we all want in the department. Go on with your meeting. I can use the hour to talk to some of the staff about their visions for the department. [She walks out of the office.]

Howard: [to remaining staff] Did you believe that? I told you they hired a real space cadet to replace me. Maybe you didn't believe me, but you just saw it with your own eyes.

Marshall's symbolic direction might be on the right track, but symbols work only when attuned to the context—both people and place. As a newcomer to the department culture, she needs to pay close attention to her audience. Meaningless symbols antagonize, and empty symbolic events backfire.

Conversely, a skillful symbolic leader understands that a situation of challenge and stress can serve as a powerful opportunity to articulate values and build a sense of mission. Marshall demonstrates how, in a well-formed symbolic approach to Howard's gruffness:

Howard: Didn't the secretary tell you that we're in a meeting right now? If you'll wait outside, I'll be able to see you in about an hour.

(continued)

(continued)

Marshall: [smiling] Maybe this is just the traditional initiation ritual in this department, Bill, but let me ask a question. If one of our customers came through the door right now, would you ask her to wait outside for an hour?

Howard: If she just came barging in like you did, sure.

Marshall: Are you working on something that's more important than responding to our customers?

Howard: They're not your customers. You've only been here 5 minutes.

Marshall: True, but I've been with this company long enough to know the importance of putting customers first.

Howard: Look, you don't know the first thing about how this department functions. Before you go off on some customer crusade, you ought to learn a little about how we do things.

Marshall: There's a lot I can learn from all of you, and I'm eager to get started. For example, I'm very interested in your ideas on how we can make this a department where as soon as people walk in, they get the sense that this is a place where people care, are responsive, and genuinely want to be helpful. I'd like that to be true for anyone who comes in—a staff member, a customer, or just someone who got lost and came into the wrong office. That's not the message I got from my initiation just now, but I'm sure we can think of lots of ways to change that. How does that fit with your image of what the department should be like?

Notice how Marshall recasts the conversation. She recognizes newcomers usually experience an initial test or "hazing." Instead of engaging in a personal confrontation with Howard, she focuses on the department's core values. She brings her "customer first" commitment with her, but she avoids positioning that value as something imposed from outside. Instead, she grounds it in an experience everyone in the room has just shared: the way she was greeted when she entered. Like many successful symbolic leaders, she is attuned to the cues about values and culture that are expressed in everyday life. She communicates her philosophy, but she also asks questions to draw out Howard and her new staff members. If she can use the organization's history to an advantage in rekindling a commitment to customer service, she passes her first test and is off to a good start.

BENEFITS AND RISKS OF REFRAMING

The multiple replays of the Howard–Marshall incident illustrate both the power and the risks of reframing. The frames are powerful because of their ability to spur imagination and generate new insights and options. But each frame has limits as well as strengths, and each can be applied well or poorly.

Frames generate scripts, or scenarios, to guide action in high-stakes circumstances. By changing your script, you can change how you appear, what you do, and how your audience sees you. You can create the possibility of a makeover in everyday life. Few of us have the dramatic skill and versatility of a professional actor, but you can alter what you do by choosing an alternative script or scenario. You have been learning how to do this since birth. Both men and women, for example, typically employ different scenarios for same-sex and opposite-sex encounters. Students who are guarded and formal when talking to a professor become energized and intimate when talking to friends. Managers who are polite and deferential with the boss may be gruff and autocratic with subordinates and then come home at night to romp playfully with their kids. The tenderhearted neighbor becomes a ruthless competitor when his company's market share is threatened. The tough-minded drill instructor bows to authority when facing a colonel. Consciously or not, we all read situations to figure out the scene we're in and the role we should fill so that we can respond in character. But it's important to ask ourselves whether the drama is the one we want and to recognize that we can choose which character to play and how to interpret or alter the script.

The essence of reframing is examining the same situation from multiple vantage points. The effective leader changes lenses when things don't make sense or aren't working. Reframing offers the promise of powerful new options, but it cannot guarantee that every new strategy will be successful. Each lens offers distinctive advantages, but each has its blind spots and shortcomings.

The structural frame risks ignoring everything outside the rational scope of tasks, procedures, policies, and organization charts. Structural thinking can overestimate the power of authority and underestimate the authority of power. Paradoxically, overreliance on structural assumptions and a narrow emphasis on rationality can lead to an irrational neglect of human, political, and cultural variables crucial to effective action.

Adherents of the human resource frame sometimes cling to a romanticized view of human nature in which everyone hungers for growth and collaboration. When they are too optimistic about integrating individual and organizational needs, they may neglect both structure and the stubborn realities of conflict and scarcity.

The political frame captures dynamics that other frames miss, but it has its own limits. A fixation on politics easily becomes a cynical self-fulfilling prophecy, reinforcing conflict and mistrust while sacrificing opportunities for rational discourse, collaboration, and hope. Political action too often is interpreted as amoral, scheming, and oblivious to the common good.

The symbolic frame offers powerful insight into fundamental issues of meaning and belief, as well as possibilities for bonding people into a cohesive group with a shared mission. But its concepts are subtle and elusive; effectiveness depends on the artistry of the user. Symbols are sometimes mere fluff or camouflage, the tools of a scoundrel who seeks to manipulate the unsuspecting, or awkward gimmicks that embarrass more than energize people at work. But in the aura of an authentic leader, symbols can bring magic to the workplace.

REFRAMING FOR NEWCOMERS AND OUTSIDERS

Marshall's initial encounter with Howard exemplifies many of the challenges and tests that managers confront as they move forward in their careers. The different scenarios offer a glimmer of what they might run into, depending on how they size up a situation. Managers feel powerless and trapped when they rely on only one or two frames. This is particularly true for newcomers, as well as for women and outsiders who experience "the dogged frustration of people living daily in a system not made for them and with no plans soon to adjust for them or their differences" (Gallos and Ramsey, 1997, p. 216). These outsiders are less likely to get a second or third chance when they fail.

Though progressive organizations have made heroic strides in building fairer, more just opportunity structures (Bell, 2011; Esposito et al., 2002; Daniels et al., 2004; Levering and Moskowitz, 1993; Morrison, 1992), the path to success is still fraught with obstacles blocking particularly women and minorities. Judicious reframing can enable them to transform an imprisoning managerial trap into a promising leadership opportunity. And the more often individuals break through the glass ceiling or out of the corporate ghetto, the more quickly those barriers will fade. Career barriers can feel as foreboding and impenetrable as the Berlin Wall did—until it suddenly fell.

CONCLUSION

Managers can use frames as scenarios, or scripts, to generate alternative approaches to challenging circumstances. In planning for a high-stakes meeting or a tense encounter, they can imagine and try out novel ways to play their roles. Until reframing becomes instinctive, it takes more than the few seconds that Cindy Marshall had to generate an effective response in every frame. In practicing any new skill—playing tennis, flying an airplane, or handling a tough leadership challenge—the process is often slow and painstaking at first. But as skill improves, it gets easier, faster, more fluid, and comes almost as second nature.

Reframing Leadership

A leader is a dealer in hope.

—Napoléon Bonaparte

The pitched battle between Hillary Clinton and Donald Trump for the U.S. presidency in 2016 sent shockwaves around the world and was unprecedented in many ways. Clinton was the first woman nominated to run for president by a major party, while Trump was the first major candidate who had no previous political or military experience. Few, if any, could remember an election where both candidates were so widely disliked, nor one where one of the candidates, Trump, spent so much time battling leaders of his own party. Historians will no doubt spend years trying to sort this out, but a look through the four frames reveals important lessons for leadership. Structure, people, politics, and symbols all contributed to the outcome.

Structure

Two key structural issues were the process for nominating candidates and the Electoral College system for choosing the winner. In U.S. presidential elections, a party's nominee emerges over several months from a state-by-state process of caucuses and primary elections that select delegates to each party's national convention. The two major parties had different rules. On the Republican side, it was winner-take-all in many states, and a candidate could garner all of a state's delegates with less than half the votes. Running in a multicandidate field, Trump racked up a majority of all Republican delegates with less than 40 percent of the total votes. The race ended early but produced an unconventional candidate opposed by many grassroots Republicans and much of the party's leadership. Meanwhile, the Democratic race dragged on longer because the party awarded delegates on a proportional basis. Over the primary season, Clinton got a majority of the votes but had trouble pulling away from her major opponent, Bernie Sanders. Even when she won a state, she often got only a slightly larger share of the delegates.

The Electoral College, a quaint eighteenth century compromise enshrined in the U.S. Constitution,[1] gives each state a number of electors equivalent to its representation in Congress. Beginning in the 1990s, America became sharply divided between red (Republican) and blue (Democratic) states. In the 2016 election, most of the 50 states and the District of Columbia were sure to vote either red or blue, leaving only a few states that were real battlegrounds and three that were critical. Trump was almost sure to win if, but only if, he carried Florida, Ohio, and Pennsylvania.

Human Needs

Turning to the human resource frame, we can ask about the concerns and attitudes that were motivating American voters. It was a year of surprises as both sides of the political spectrum saw major shifts in the electorate toward greater anger and dissatisfaction with the status quo. Many voters wanted wholesale change because they believed Washington was broken. On the Democratic side, almost everyone expected that Clinton, who had narrowly lost the nomination to Barack Obama eight years earlier, had an easy path to the nomination. But Bernie Sanders, a relatively obscure senator from Vermont, mounted a ferocious challenge from the left on a platform of economic justice, universal health care, and free college tuition. Liberals and young voters flocked to him. Caught off guard, Clinton struggled to adjust her positions to catch up with a leftward drift among Democratic primary voters. She ultimately prevailed but emerged weaker than expected amid concerns that many Sanders voters might never support her.

Meanwhile, the surprises were even greater on the Republican side. When Donald Trump first announced that he was running for the nomination, almost everyone saw it as a publicity stunt that would quickly flame out. How could a brash real estate developer and television personality with no government experience and a crazy idea about building a wall along the U.S./Mexican border get anything more than a fringe vote? But Trump tapped into a huge reservoir of disenchantment among voters who felt that they were being left behind and that the America they knew was being undermined by globalization, immigrants, bureaucrats, and condescending coastal elites. Trump gave voice to their feelings. His promise to deport immigrants, bring jobs back, and make America great again resonated powerfully, and he overwhelmed the large field of more traditional Republicans running against him.

The human resource frame also underscores the importance of the personal characteristics of the two candidates. Clinton and Trump had a few things in common. Long before the election, both were household names and both had very high unfavorable ratings. The two were also the oldest pair of candidates in U.S. history; Trump would be 70 on Election Day, and Clinton would be 69. But they had very different personas. Trump was hot where Clinton was cool, flamboyant where she was restrained, shoot-from-the-hip where she was disciplined, and outrageous where she was cautious. To almost every issue, Trump offered dramatic but vague promises, while Clinton delineated specific policies and plans. Voters who liked one rarely liked the other. Many disliked both and lamented that they were forced to choose the lesser of two evils.

The candidates also had contrasting leadership styles. Trump was an entertainer, a business magnate, and perhaps the least-disciplined presidential candidate in American history. He was notorious for over-the-top 3 AM Twitter storms attacking his various enemies. He was a relentless warrior who mostly embodied the political and symbolic frames, both central to effective leadership. Clinton was a cool-headed policy wonk—strong on details but weaker on assembling them into a compelling vision. She was more attuned to the structural and human resource frames. Her picture of the future was clearer on the details but fuzzier in terms of the big picture. Voters knew that Trump promised to "Make America great again," but were less clear about Clinton's core message.

Changing Coalitions

The political frame points to the importance of coalitions and scarce resources, and the 2016 election occurred in the context of a deeply polarized nation and a changing electorate. Beginning in the 1960s, the Republicans had evolved from the party of the industrial north to a coalition of economic conservatives (including much of the business elite) and white social conservatives (particularly in the south and the Plains states). The party appealed to the first group with support for low taxes, free markets, and free trade and kept the second group happy by opposing abortion, gay marriage, and government programs many whites saw as mostly benefitting persons of color.

The Democratic coalition, meanwhile, underwent its own evolution in the late twentieth and early twenty-first centuries. Members of the white working class, particularly religious and social conservatives, drifted toward the Republicans, but a new Democratic coalition emerged that brought together groups heavily concentrated in and around major cities—the poor, minorities, and upscale progressives.

The differences between Clinton and Trump backers in the 2016 campaign reflected the evolution in both parties. Democrats increased their share of college-educated voters, and Clinton won among women and people of color. But Trump won among whites, particularly white men without college degrees. Tellingly, 81 percent of Trump supporters, but only 19 percent of Clinton's said that life for people like them was worse now than 50 years earlier (Smith, 2016).

Culture and Narrative

The symbolic frame underscores the importance of culture and narrative in understanding the election. A critical cultural shift in the U.S. electorate was the gradual decline of non-Hispanic whites as a percentage of the population. People of color had become a majority in four states (California, Hawaii, New Mexico, and Texas) and were gaining in many others. This worked both for and against Trump: demographics were shifting toward the Democrats, but that shift triggered powerful levels of distress and anger among many whites. The specter of terrorism, beginning with 9/11 and continuing with the rise of ISIS, exacerbated voters' suspicions toward immigrants in general and Muslims in particular. Trump supporters were not poorer than Clinton voters, but they had the lowest opinions of Muslims and were most likely to favor mass deportation of undocumented immigrants (Matthews, 2016).

What followed was one of the bitterest, most divisive presidential campaigns in U.S. history. Many Trump supporters saw Clinton as a corrupt, lying criminal who would confiscate their guns, open the door to terrorists, and destroy everything good in America if she became president. They cheered when Trump said that she would be in jail if he became president and nodded assent when he told them that "this election is our last chance to save our country." Many Clinton supporters found the prospect of a Trump presidency genuinely terrifying. They saw him as a homegrown version of Adolf Hitler—an authoritarian, narcissistic, racist misogynist.

In the end, Clinton got some 2.8 million more votes, but Trump won the presidency. He took the battleground states he had to get (Florida, Ohio, and Pennsylvania) and picked up narrow victories in two blue states in the upper Midwest, Michigan, and Wisconsin.

Leadership Lessons from the 2016 Election

In the tale of the 2016 election we can find many of the lessons for leadership that form the backbone of this chapter. Structure matters but is not always sufficient for leadership success. Clinton won on campaign infrastructure, but that was not enough to win the presidency. During the primaries, both candidates had to appeal to the partisan zealots who form the party's base, but Trump defied the conventional wisdom that a candidate needs to move to the center in a general election to pick up independents and undecideds. He thrived on huge rallies where his passionate supporters devoured his message and showered him with approval. That passion turned out to be critical.

Symbolically, elections are always about shaping the narrative in order to control how voters perceive you and your opponent. Trump framed himself as the only leader strong enough to save America from terminal decline. In his story, the United States had become a weak, borderless nation that was failing on almost every front, and he knew how to "Make America great again." That catchphrase crystallized his message and rallied his supporters. Clinton, better on policy specifics than grand narrative, struggled to communicate an equally focused and compelling message. Her catchphrases included "I'm with her," "Stronger together," "America is already great," and "Love trumps hate." They added up to a fuzzy rationale for her candidacy. In a change election, Trump offered a clearer message of making things better.

Both campaigns' efforts to develop a positive image for their candidate were sometimes overshadowed by efforts to persuade the public that their opponents were terrible leaders and vile human beings. Trump consistently referred to Clinton as "crooked Hillary" and labeled her the worst candidate for president in American history. That narrative drew support from an FBI investigation into Clinton's use of a personal e-mail server while she was Secretary of State and from an ongoing drip-drip of e-mails hacked from her campaign by Russian operatives and distributed through Wikileaks. Clinton supporters believed that her momentum was seriously damaged when FBI director James Comey announced days before the election that new e-mails had been discovered that "might be pertinent" to the investigation. A week later, Comey said that it had been a false alarm, but Democrats believed the new announcement served only to keep the e-mails in the news.

Although the Democrats got no help from the FBI or Wikileaks, they benefited from a continuing flow of new material from investigative reporters and from Trump himself to support their framing of him as a liar, misogynist, racist, and tax cheat who lacked the judgment and self-control to be trusted in the White House.

Gender was a central issue for the first time in a U.S. presidential election. It both helped and hindered Clinton. She was a powerful symbol to millions who hoped to see the first woman president. But leadership has historically been associated with maleness, and research (that we examine later in this chapter) shows that women who seek high office often face discrimination and higher expectations than men. Both men and women are often uncomfortable with women who are powerful or who seem to want power.

In the end, much of the public believed the worst about both candidates—polls suggested that Clinton was viewed unfavorably by 57 percent of the public and Trump by 62 percent. Even many Trump supporters feared that he lacked the maturity and steadiness required in a president. But they saw him as the candidate who could bring change to Washington. That was enough to make him president.

We begin this chapter with a historical tour of theory and research on leadership, examining quantitative and qualitative strands that have run in parallel to one another. This will lead us into an exploration of the idea of leadership—what it is, what it is not, and what it can and cannot accomplish. We look at the differences between leadership and power and between leadership and management. We examine the intersection of leadership with gender and culture. Finally, we explore how each of the four frames generates its own image of leadership.

LEADERSHIP IN ORGANIZATIONS: A BRIEF HISTORY

In nearly every culture, the earliest literature includes sagas of heroic figures who led their people to physical or spiritual victory over internal or external enemies. In Egypt and China, we find narratives about pharaohs and emperors and the rise and fall of dynasties that date back thousands of years. Ancient Chinese chronicles tell a cyclical story that begins when a dynamic leader leverages disorder and discontent and amasses sufficient force to found a new dynasty. For a time the new dynasty produces vigorous and far-sighted leaders who create a stable and prosperous state. But eventually corruption spreads, leadership falters, and the dynasty collapses in the face of a new challenger. Then the cycle begins anew. This saga still has a powerful resonance in modern China because the Communist party leaders understand that their dynasty, like all that have come before, may someday lose the "mandate of heaven."

From ancient times to the late nineteenth century, the leadership literature consisted mostly of narratives about monarchs, generals, and political leaders. Then the rise of big business triggered an interest in the qualities of the giants who founded great enterprises, like Cornelius Vanderbilt, Andrew Carnegie, J. P. Morgan, and John D. Rockefeller. In the same era, social science began to separate from philosophy and emerge as a distinct academic field. Scholars like Harvard psychologist William James and the sociologists Herbert Spencer in England and Emile Durkheim in France began to lay the intellectual foundations for a science of society and human behavior based on systematic research.

Out of this ferment emerged two distinct approaches to understanding leadership in organizations that have coexisted for more than a century, traveling more or less side by side, with only occasional nods to one another. One track, which we label *quantitative-analytic*, emphasizes testing hypotheses with quantitative data to develop leadership theory. The work is typically published as articles in scholarly journals (an overview of eras in the evolution of this strand appears in Exhibit 17.1). A second track, *qualitative-holistic*, relies

Exhibit 17.1.

A Short History of Quantitative-Analytic Leadership Research.

Leadership Theory	Examples	Central Idea	Current Status
Trait theory: how are leaders different?	Galton, 1869; Terman, 1904; Kirkpatrick and Locke, 1991; Zaccaro, 2007	Leaders possess distinctive personal characteristics (intelligence, self-confidence, integrity, extraversion, and so on).	Fell out of favor in the 1950s when reviewers found weak empirical support, but has returned to favor in recent decades.
Leadership style theory: how do leaders act?	Lewin, Lippitt, and White, 1939; Likert, 1961; Fleishman and Harris, 1962	Leadership depends on style (democratic vs. autocratic, task-oriented vs. people-oriented, etc.).	Mixed evidence stimulated move toward contingency theories, which often include leader style variables.
Contingency theory: how do circumstances affect leadership?	Fiedler, 1967; Lawrence and Lorsch, 1967; Evans, 1970; House, 1971, 1996	Effective leadership depends on the characteristics of followers and context: what works in one situation may not work in another.	No single contingency view has found consistent empirical support or wide acceptance, but most modern leadership research incorporates the idea that leadership depends on circumstances.
Leader-member exchange (LMX) theory: what happens in the leader-follower relationship?	Dansereau, Graen, and Haga, 1975; Graen and Uhl-Bien, 2008	Leadership is rooted in the quality of the relationships between leaders and individual followers.	Advocates of LMX theory have been actively conducting research since the 1970s; many LMX propositions have empirical support, but the approach is criticized for complexity and viewing leadership too narrowly.
Transformational leadership theory: how do leaders transform followers?	Burns, 1978; Bass, 1985; Conger and Kanungo, 1998	Transformational (or charismatic) leaders use inspiration, idealized influence, and the like to generate followers' trust and willingness to go above and beyond.	Evidence suggests transformational leadership makes a difference, but more research is needed on when and how it works best.

on case studies and interviews with practitioners to develop ideas and theory about how leadership works in practice. Such work is often published in books aimed at an audience that includes both practitioners and scholars. We will survey quantitative and then qualitative work before trying to capture the current state of the field.

Quantitative-Analytic Research

Since the early twentieth century, quantitative research has moved through several eras, gradually evolving from simpler to more complex views of leadership. The initial research, flowing from the "great man" theory of leadership (Carlyle, 1841), focused on finding the distinctive traits that made leaders different from everyone else. Around 1950, multiple reviews (Stogdill, 1948; Gibb, 1947; Jenkins, 1947) concluded that there was little consistency in leadership traits across people and circumstances. That gave rise to two lines of research in the 1950s and subsequent decades: one on leadership style and another on situational contingencies. Style research focused particularly on the difference between task-oriented and people-oriented leaders. The results suggested that leaders who focused on people generated higher morale although not necessarily higher productivity, and that the most effective leaders were good at dealing with both tasks and people (Fleishman and Harris, 1962).

Contingency theorists examined characteristics of situations that interacted with leader behavior. One influential line, for example, found that task-oriented leaders did best in situations that were either highly favorable or highly unfavorable for the leader, while people-oriented leaders did best in situations in the middle (Fiedler, 1964, 1967).

Another contingency theory, Hersey and Blanchard's situational leadership model (1969, 1977), had less research support (Hambleton and Gumpert, 1982; Graeff, 1983; Blank, Weitzel, and Green, 1990) but became more popular with practitioners because it is more intuitive and offers clearer practical guidance to practitioners. The model incorporates its own version of the distinction between task and people, using a two-by-two table to develop four different leadership styles (see Exhibit 17.2). Hersey and Blanchard argued that each style was appropriate for a different level of subordinate "readiness," which they defined in terms of how able and willing subordinates were to do the work. If subordinates are neither willing nor able, then the leader should tell them how to do the job. If they want to do the job but lack skill, then the leader should sell or coach to build capacity. When subordinates are able but unwilling or insecure, then the leader should use a participative style to build motivation. If they are both able and willing, the leader should delegate and get out of the way.

Exhibit 17.2.

Situational Leadership Model.

High Relationship, Low Task:	**High Relationship, High Task:**
Participate	*Sell (or Coach)*
Use when followers are "able" but "unwilling" or "insecure."	Use when followers are "unable" but "willing" or "motivated."
Low Relationship, Low Task:	**Low Relationship, High Task:**
Delegate	*Tell*
Use when followers are "able" and "willing" or "motivated."	Use when followers are "unable" and "unwilling" or "insecure."

Hersey and Blanchard's model continues to be popular for leadership training but has been criticized for lack of research support and for generating self-fulfilling prophesies. If, for example, managers give unwilling and unable subordinates high direction and low support, what would cause their motivation to improve? The manager of a computer design team told us ruefully, "I treated my group with a 'telling' management style and found that in fact they became both less able and less willing."

The 1970s spawned a new line of research: leader-member exchange theory (LMX). LMX research began with the insight that leaders create different relationships with different followers, and, in particular, they create in-groups and out-groups by interacting with some subordinates in a more personal way while focusing strictly on task with others (Dansereau, Graen, and Haga, 1975; Graen and Uhl-Bien, 2008). One practical implication from this research is that leaders can get better results by creating strong relationships with all, not just some, of their subordinates (Graen and Uhl-Bien, 2008, p. 225).

A major new strand that emerged in the 1980s emphasized a distinction between transactional and transforming leadership (Burns, 1978). Transactional leadership involves practical, give-and-take exchanges, such as pay for performance. Transforming leaders, on the other hand, "champion and inspire followers . . . to rise above narrow interests and work together for transcending goals" (Burns, 2003, p. 26). Over the next two decades, research on transformational, or charismatic, leadership became a dominant research strand, producing a number of studies confirming that transformational leaders had a more powerful impact than those who relied only on transactional approaches (Shamir, House, and Arthur, 1993; Conger and Kanungo, 1998).

Qualitative-Holistic Leadership Studies

The quantitative research tradition has both strengths and limits. Over more than a century, scholars have tested hypotheses, discarded ideas that don't work, and gradually built theory that fits the data. But the work has often simplified the complexities of leadership by treating only a few variables at a time and by treating leadership as equivalent to what happens between managers and their subordinates. Qualitative research on real-world practice has viewed leadership in more nuanced and holistic ways, often developing ideas decades before they make their way into quantitative studies. Mary Parker Follett (1896, 1918, 1941), for example, was well ahead of her time in exploring distributed leadership, charisma, and the importance of the human element. Many of the major themes in Follett's work were extended by two of the most influential management thinkers of the early twentieth century: Elton Mayo and Chester Barnard. Mayo, often viewed as the founder of the "human relations" school of management, conducted the famous studies that gave rise to the "Hawthorn effect" and promoted the idea, viewed as radical at the time, that human and social factors mattered as much as technical and economic ones (Mayo, 1933).

Chester Barnard, a telephone executive, was a practitioner rather than an academic, but he wrote one of the most influential management books of the midtwentieth century, *The Functions of the Executive* (Barnard, 1938). Barnard argued that the task of leadership is to balance technical and human factors to achieve cooperation among the many groups and individuals within an organization. Organizations rarely survive indefinitely, he noted, because it is so challenging to solve two central issues: achieving goals while satisfying the needs of those who do the work.

The idea that leadership is about balancing or integrating concerns for task and people remained a central theme in qualitative work on leadership for the next several decades (examples include Argyris, 1962; Bennis, 1961; Likert, 1961; McGregor, 1960), but in later years researchers began to give greater attention to political and symbolic issues in the workplace (Dalton, 1959; Mintzberg, 1973; Kotter, 1985; Heifetz and Linsky, 2002).

Interest in the symbolic dimension of leadership exploded in the 1980s when students of organization discovered something long known to anthropologists—organizations had cultures, and those cultures mattered (Deal and Kennedy, 1982; Peters and Waterman, 1982; Schein, 1992). Symbolic elements such as charisma, vision, and transformational leadership became dominant themes in discussions of leadership, although Collins and Porras (1994) and Collins (2001) led a kind of counterrevolution, arguing that charisma was overrated (Collins and Porras, 1994). Instead, they argued, leaders of successful companies were disciplined and determined but humble (attributing success to the team, not to themselves) and even self-effacing. Heifetz and Linsky (2002), focusing particularly on leadership in the public sector, took a similar position, arguing that the essence of leadership is not vision but mobilizing followers to work on solving hard problems.

EVOLUTION OF THE IDEA OF LEADERSHIP

Prior to the twentieth century, leadership was usually equated to high position, and the dominant theme in leadership studies was that leaders were born with special gifts that made them different from ordinary mortals. That view is dying, brought down by leadership research and by the complex challenges of leading in contemporary organizations. Our tour of more than 100 years of leadership history shows a gradual shift from a simpler view centered on the individual to a more complex view that takes account of individual, relationship, and context. Five propositions capture this evolution:

Leadership Is an Activity, Not a Position

Leadership is distinct from authority and position, although authorities may be leaders. Weber (1947) and Barnard (1938) both linked authority to legitimacy. People consent and choose to obey authority only as long as they believe it is legitimate. Authority and leadership are both built on voluntary compliance. Leaders cannot lead without legitimacy, but many examples of authority fall outside the domain of leadership. As Gardner put it, "The meter maid has authority, but not necessarily leadership" (1989, p. 7).

Heifetz (1994) argues that authority often impedes leadership because in times of distress we expect those in authority to know and do more than they can and to solve our problems for us. This tempts leaders to overpromise and underdeliver, a recurring setup for failure and disappointment. After the 2016 election, many observers wondered how Donald Trump would be able to deliver on the many promises that he made during his election campaign.

The management literature has often equated leadership to whatever managers do with their subordinates, but this defines leadership too narrowly. Leaders need skill in managing relationships with all significant stakeholders, including superiors, peers, and external constituents (Burns, 1978; Gardner, 1986; Kotter and Cohen, 2002; Heifetz and Linsky, 2002).

Leadership Is Different from Management

You can be a leader without being a manager, and many managers could not "lead a squad of seven-year-olds to the ice-cream counter" (Gardner, 1989, p. 2). Bennis and

Nanus (1985) suggest that "managers do things right, and leaders do the right thing" (p. 21); that is, managers focus on execution, leaders on purpose and values. Barnard (1938) argued that a moral dimension is central to leadership because it rests on "creating faith: faith in common understanding, in the probability of success, in the ultimate satisfaction of personal motives, in the integrity of objective authority, and in the superiority of common purpose" (Barnard, 1938, p. 239). A managerially oriented navy officer gave a ringing endorsement of his more leaderlike successor: "I go by the book; he writes the book."

Kotter (1988) sees management as being primarily about structural nuts and bolts: planning, organizing, and controlling. He views leadership as a change-oriented process of visioning, networking, and building relationships. But Gardner argues against contrasting leadership and management too sharply, because leaders may "end up looking like a cross between Napoleon and the Pied Piper, and managers like unimaginative clods" (1989, p. 3). He suggests several dimensions for distinguishing leadership from management. Leaders think in the long term, look outside as well as inside, and influence constituents beyond their immediate formal jurisdiction. They emphasize vision and renewal and have the political skills to cope with the demands of multiple constituencies.

Leadership Is Multilateral, Not Unilateral

Heroic images of leadership convey the notion of a one-way transaction: leaders show the way and followers tag along. But leaders are not independent actors; they both shape and are shaped by their constituents (Gardner, 1989; Simmel, 1950; Heifetz and Linsky, 2002). Leaders often promote a new initiative only after a large number of constituents favor it (Cleveland, 1985). Leaders' actions generate responses that in turn affect the leaders' capacity for taking further initiatives (Murphy, 1985). As Briand puts it, "A 'leader' who makes a decision and then attempts to 'sell' it is not wise and will likely not prove effective. The point is not that leaders should do less but that others can and should do more. Everyone must accept responsibility for the people's well being, and everyone has a role to play in sustaining it" (1993, p. 39).

Leadership Is Distributed Rather Than Concentrated at the Top

In times of crisis we expect leadership from people in high places, and we are grievously disappointed if they fail to provide it. But it is misleading to imagine that leadership comes only from people in prominent positions. Such a view leads us to ask too much of too few. It relegates the rest of us to a passive role and reinforces a tendency for those at the top to take on more responsibility than they can discharge (Oshry, 1995). The turbulent world of the twenty-first century pushes organizations to be fast, flexible, and decentralized, which requires leadership from many quarters (Barnes and Kriger, 1986; Kanter, 1983).

Leadership does not come automatically with high position, as Follett (1896) documented long ago in a study of the U.S. Congress. Speakers of the House were always elected by their colleagues, but Follett found that some were able to leverage and expand the potential in the job, while others failed to lead. Conversely, it is possible and often necessary to lead without a position of formal authority. In 1991, the year that she was awarded the Nobel Peace Prize, Aung San Suu Kyi was the most credible and respected leader in Myanmar, even though she held no office and was under house arrest. Finally set free in 2010, she was elected to parliament in 2012, and her party won control of the Myanmar government in 2015.

Leadership Is Contextual and Situated Not in the Leader but in the Exchange between Leader and Constituents

In story and myth, leaders are often lonely heroes and itinerant warriors, wed only to honor and a noble cause. Think of Batman, Ellen Ripley, Han Solo, James Bond, Joan of Arc, Rambo, or every character ever played by Clint Eastwood. But images of solitary, heroic leaders mislead by suggesting that leaders go it alone and by focusing the spotlight too much on individuals and too little on the stage where they play their parts. Leaders make things happen, but things also make leaders happen. The transformation in Rudy Giuliani's image after 9/11 from has-been to hero in 24 hours is a perfect illustration. An unpopular, lame-duck New York mayor found himself center stage in an unplanned theater of horror and delivered the performance of his life. But Giuliani's heroic image was fleeting. *Time* magazine named him person of the year for 2001, but he left the mayor's office at the end of the year and struggled to find another opportunity to demonstrate such visible and heroic leadership. He ran for the Republican presidential nomination in 2008, but his early lead in the polls evaporated after a series of gaffes. He disappeared from the public eye until he bobbed up again in 2016 as a loyal surrogate promoting Donald Trump for president.

No single formula is possible for the great range of situations leaders encounter. Three of the most dominant and destructive figures of the twentieth century were Adolf Hitler, Joseph Stalin, and Mao Zedong. All were able to come to power because they came of age when their respective countries were in disarray, and people were looking for someone strong enough to lead them out of chaos. Had they been born in different times or places, no one would remember them.

Leadership is thus a subtle process of mutual influence fusing thought, feeling, and action. It produces cooperative effort in the service of purposes embraced and enhanced by both leader and led. Single-frame managers are unlikely to understand and attend to the intricacies of this lively process.

WHAT DO WE KNOW ABOUT GOOD LEADERSHIP?

Threading through the literature on leadership have been two divergent propositions. One asserts that good leaders need the right stuff—qualities like vision, strength, and commitment. The other holds that good leadership is situational; what works in one setting will not work in another. A proposition from the "effective schools" literature illustrates the right-stuff perspective: A good school is headed by a strong and visionary instructional leader. An example of the situational view is the belief that it takes a different kind of person to lead when you're growing and adding staff than when you're cutting budgets and laying people off.

Despite the tension between these one-best-way and contingency views, both capture part of the truth. Studies have found shared characteristics among effective leaders across sectors and situations. Another body of research has identified situational variables that determine the kind of leadership that works best.

Recent decades have produced a steady stream of studies of effective leadership. Modern trait research (reviewed in Zaccaro, Kemp, and Bader, 2004) tells us that leaders, compared to nonleaders, tend to be smarter, more creative, more extroverted and agreeable, and better at thinking outside the box. They have more social skills and stronger needs for power and achievement. But this research tells us more about what leaders are like than what they do. A list of leadership traits may help in selecting leaders but provides limited guidance for how to lead (Zaccaro, 2007).

We get a different picture if we look at the many qualitative studies of leadership in recent decades. No characteristic is universally associated with good leadership in these studies, but vision and focus show up most often. Effective leaders help articulate a vision, set standards for performance, and create focus and direction. A related characteristic, explicit in some reports (Clifford and Cavanagh, 1985; Kouzes and Posner, 2007; Peters and Austin, 1985) and implicit in others, is the ability to communicate a vision effectively, often through the use of symbols. Another quality often mentioned is passion, determination, or will (Clifford and Cavanagh, 1985; Collins, 2001; Collins and Hansen, 2011; George, 2004; Peters and Austin, 1985; Vaill, 1982). Good leaders care deeply about their work and the people who do it and are doggedly persistent in pushing the cause forward. Yet another characteristic is the ability to inspire trust and build relationships (Bennis and Nanus, 2007; Kotter, 1988; Kouzes and Posner, 1987, 2007; Maccoby, 1981). But beyond vision, focus, passion, and trust, there is less consensus. The many reviews of the literature (Bass, 1990; Gardner, 1987; Hollander, 1978; Yukl, 2012) generate a long list of attributes associated with effective leadership, but they do not add up to a coherent picture.

Research has made progress in one area of growing importance: the intersection of culture and leadership. We'll discuss results from the GLOBE program, a large international research project, in the next section.

CULTURE AND LEADERSHIP

Organizational culture (as we discussed in Chapter 12) is a pattern of basic assumptions and values shared among members of a group. This definition applies to groups of any size, from a small work group or family to a nation like China or the United States. Much of the research on leadership in organizations has been conducted in a Western context, particularly in the United States, but globalization drives a need to better understand what happens when citizens of one culture try to lead those of another. What do they need to understand? What adjustments do they have to make?

The GLOBE researchers surveyed more than 17,000 middle managers in 950 organizations across 62 countries (see Exhibit 17.3). They found that some leadership characteristics seemed to be universal, but others were not. Managers around the world wanted leaders who were trustworthy, planful, positive, motivating, decisive, and intelligent, and not unfriendly, irritable, or self-centered. But other characteristics—such as autonomous, ambitious, cunning, intuitive, logical, and risk-taking—were valued much more highly in some cultures than others.

The GLOBE researchers identified six different leadership styles in their data:

1. *Charismatic/values based:* leader sets high standards, seeks to inspire people around a vision, emphasizes core values

2. *Team-oriented:* leader evokes pride, loyalty, and cooperation, values team cohesiveness and shared goals

3. *Participative:* leader encourages input in decisions, emphasizes delegation and equality

4. *Humane:* leader is patient, supportive, concerned for others' welfare

5. *Autonomous:* leader is independent and individualistic and puts self at the center

6. *Protective:* leader emphasizes procedure, status, face-saving, and safety and security of individual and group

Exhibit 17.3.
GLOBE Country Clusters.

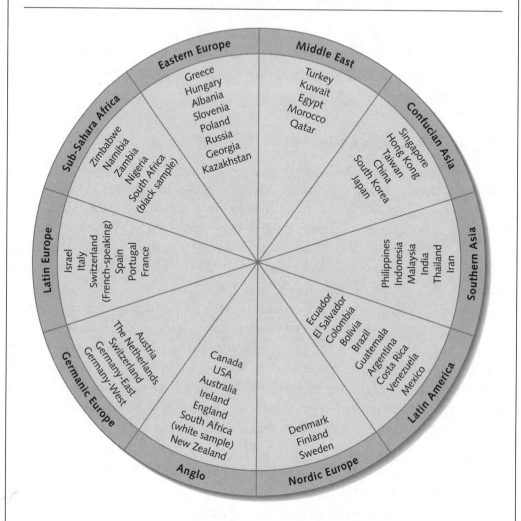

Source: Adapted from House, Hanges, Javidan, Dorfman, and Gupta (eds.), *Culture, Leadership, and Organizations: The GLOBE Study of 62 Societies.* Copyright © 2004 by Sage Publications, Inc. Reprinted with permission.

Which of those styles is most like you? Which do you think works best? Your answer is likely to be different depending on the culture you grew up in. The GLOBE researchers categorized their 62 countries into 10 regional clusters, shown in Exhibit 17.3. Countries that are near one another on the wheel are more similar in terms of culture and views of leadership. Those that are opposite one another are least alike. Thus the English-speaking Anglo cluster is least like the Middle-Eastern cluster of Islamic nations. The Anglo managers preferred the charismatic/values-based, participative, and humane styles. They liked the protective style least. Middle-Eastern managers liked the protective style best and the charismatic/values-based style least. It is easy to imagine how an American or Australian trying to lead in the Middle East could flame out while implementing a leadership approach—charismatic or participative, for example—that was perfect back home but wrong for a new and unfamiliar context. Instead of recognizing the cultural dynamics, the failed manager might blame the locals for having bad attitudes or a poor work ethic. Globalization increases the chance that at some point in your career you will be working in another culture that has different values and ideas about leadership. Your cultural intelligence and willingness to learn will be vital to your success.

GENDER AND LEADERSHIP

When Carlyle (1841) laid out his influential "great man theory" of leadership, his story included women only as wives and mothers. He omitted Vietnam's national heroines, the Trung sisters, who raised a mostly female army almost 2,000 years ago and succeeded for a time in pushing out Chinese overlords. Nor did he mention Joan of Arc, revered in France for leading her dispirited prince to the victories over the English that he needed in order to be coronated as King of France. The implicit, taken-for-granted assumption was that leadership is a male activity. Recent decades, however, have seen a dramatic shift in women's roles and accomplishments. At the end of 2016, some of the world's most prominent leaders were women, including Germany's long-serving chancellor, Angela Merkel, and Theresa May, the new prime minister in the United Kingdom. In breaking through old barriers and bringing their own strengths and styles to traditionally male roles, an increasing number of women have blazed new paths.

One example is Karren Brady, who became managing director of the Birmingham (England) City Football Club in 1993. At 23, she was the youngest and the only female head of an English professional soccer team. As you might expect, she ran into some challenges. There was the strapping forward who told her on the team bus that he liked her blouse because he could see her breasts through it. She looked him in the eye and replied, "Where

I'm going to send you, you won't be able to see them from there." A week later, he was downgraded to a club a hundred miles away. There was the time the directors of another team told her how fortunate she was that they were willing to let her into their owners' box. She fired back, "The day I have to feel grateful for half a lager and a pork pie in a dump of a little box with a psychedelic carpet is the day I give up" (Hoge, 2002, p. A14. Copyright © 2002 by The New York Times Co. Reprinted by permission.).

Brady got plenty of media attention, but it often focused on her looks and wardrobe. One newspaper ran a full-page photo of her in a short skirt under the headline "Sex Shooter." Another described her entry into a meeting: "Every inch the modern woman, she totters into the room on high-heeled strappy sandals and a short and sexy black suit." Brady was continually perplexed: "I came here to run a business, to put right a dilapidated, rundown operation with a series of business solutions. But the media, with the combination of my age, the way I look, and obviously the fact that I was a female—the first in a male-dominated world—went into a frenzy. It was unbelievable. I'd be in press conferences, and journalists would actually ask me my vital statistics" (Hoge, 2002, p. A14. Copyright © 2002 by The New York Times Co. Reprinted by permission). Brady did not have the benefit of later research showing that "self-sexualizing" women suffered a backlash related to discomfort with women being powerful (Infanger, Rudman, and Sczesny, 2014)

Still, Brady understood that publicity, even tinged with notoriety, was good for business. She took a team that had never shown a profit from the edge of bankruptcy to become one of the England's strongest teams, both on the field and at the cash register. The club was sold in 2009 for almost $130 million. She even overcame the complications that might have arisen after she married one of her players. She bought and sold her husband twice, making over a million pounds in the process. She won businesswoman-of-the-year awards, and even her fellow football executives recognized her talent, naming her to represent them in negotiations for the national television contract that provided much of their revenue.

Women like Karren Brady have proven that they can lead in a man's world. But do men and women lead differently? Are they seen differently in leadership roles? Why do men still have such a disproportionate hold on positions of institutional and organizational power? Research on gender and leadership has asked these and other questions, and we turn next to some of the answers that have emerged.

Do Men and Women Lead Differently?

Book (2000), Helgesen (1990), Rosener (1990), and others have argued that women bring a "female advantage" to leadership. They believe that modern organizations need the leadership style that women are more likely to offer, including concern for people, nurturance, and willingness to share information. But the evidence is equivocal. We might expect, for example, that women would be higher on people attributes (warmth, support, participation) and lower on political characteristics (power, shrewdness, aggression), more "communal" and less "agentic." But examples like Karren Brady and "the Iron Lady," British prime minister Margaret Thatcher, tell us that things are not so simple. In fact, research gives such stereotypes limited support (Van Engen, Van der Leeden, and Willemsen, 2001; Dobbins and Platz, 1986; Eagly and Johnson, 1990; Bolman and Deal, 1991, 1992a).

For the most part, the available evidence suggests that men and women in similar positions are more alike than different, at least in the eyes of their subordinates (Bolman and Deal 1991, 1992a; Carless, 1998; Komives, 1991; Morrison, White, and Van Velsor, 1987; Paustian-Underdahl, Walker, and Woehr, 2014; Thompson, 2000). When differences are detected, they often show women scoring somewhat higher than men on a variety of measures of leadership and managerial behavior (Bass, Avolio, and Atwater, 1996; Eagly and Carli, 2003; Edwards, 1991; Hallinger, Bickman, and Davis, 1990; Weddle, 1991; Wilson and Wilson, 1991). But the differences are not large, and it is not clear that they have practical significance, except among physicians—female doctors get better outcomes in terms of mortality and hospital readmission rates (Tsugawa et al., 2016).

Why the Glass Ceiling? And the Glass Cliff?

If women lead at least as well as men, why does the so-called glass ceiling cap their rise to top positions? Growing numbers are now in the pipeline leading to the executive suite. In the United States, they are a substantial majority of college students and an expanding presence in professional schools—more than half of education and law students and close to half in business and medical schools. This is a dramatic shift (except in education, where they have long been a majority).

Nevertheless, in 2014, women made up less than 10 percent of CEOs in Fortune 500 companies (Glass and Cook, 2016). More than half the companies did not have a single female officer. The story is similar in education. In American schools, women constitute the great majority of teachers and a growing percentage of middle managers, yet in 2010 they accounted for slightly less than a quarter of school superintendents (Kowalski et al., 2010). That was only slightly more than in 1930, though it was up from a low of 1.2 percent in 1981 (Keller, 1999).

There is no consensus about what sustains the glass ceiling, but evidence points to several contributing factors:

- *Stereotypes associate leadership with maleness.* Both men and women tend to link leadership characteristics to men more than women (Schein, 1975, 1990). Job applicants with more masculine voices get rated as more competent (Ko, Judd, and Stapel, 2009), Even with identical backgrounds, female CEOs are seen as less capable, and therefore less worthy of investment, than men (Bigelow, Parks, and Wuebker, 2012).

- *Women walk a tightrope of conflicting expectations.* Simply put, high-level jobs are "powerful, but women, in the minds of many people, should not be" (Keller, 1999). Women have the difficult challenge of being powerful and "feminine" at the same time. Expressing anger and wanting power are viewed as positive or neutral traits for men, but negative ones for women (Brescoll and Uhlmann, 2008; Okimoto and Brescoll, 2010). Women are attracted to intelligent men, but men are not enthusiastic about women who are smarter than they are (Fisman et al., 2006). As a woman running for president in 2016, Hillary Clinton had to negotiate this tightrope. How could she prove that she was tough enough to be commander-in-chief without seeming too angry or too smart? How could she show feminine warmth and caring without seeming weak?

- *Women encounter discrimination.* In ancient fairy tales as well as modern films, powerful women often turn out to be witches (or worse). Shakespeare's *The Taming of the Shrew* is typical of many stories with the message that a strong woman is dangerous unless tamed by a stronger man. The historical association of powerful men with leadership and of powerful women with evil produces unspoken and often unconscious bias. Subtle gender biases associate competence with maleness and inhibit women's ability to accumulate the "career capital" that leads to success (Valian, 1999; Fitzsimmons and Callan, 2016).

- *Parenting has a positive career impact for men but a negative one for women.* Women are rated lower on almost everything if they are parents, but the opposite is true for men (Correll and Benard, 2007). Bosses, regardless of gender, see women as having greater family-work conflict than men, even when their family situations are the same (Hoobler, Wayne, and Lemmon, 2009). Those perceptions in turn led them to see women as less promotable.

- *Women pay a higher price.* Shakeshaft (cited in Keller, 1999) argues that the rewards of senior positions are lower for women because, compared with men, they have higher needs for success in their family and personal lives but lower needs for esteem and status. Almost 70 percent of women in one study named personal and family responsibilities as by far the biggest barrier to their career success (Morris, 2002). Executive jobs impose a crushing workload on incumbents. The burden is even more overwhelming for women, who still do the majority of the housework and child rearing in most dual-career families. That helps to explain why fast-track women are less likely to marry and, if they do marry, are more likely to divorce (Heffernan, 2002; Keller, 1999). It also clarifies why many women who do make it to the top are blessed with "trophy husbands"—those hard-to-find stay-at-home dads (Morris, 2002).

- *Women in high positions are pushed toward the "glass cliff" where they are more likely to fail.* Glass and Cook (2016) studied male and female Fortune 500 CEOS—including all 52 of the women who had held one of those jobs by 2014. They report, "Women are more likely than men to be promoted to high-risk leadership positions and often lack the support or authority to accomplish their strategic goals As a result, women leaders often experience shorter tenures compared to male peers." Women in powerful positions have a harder time than men eliciting respect and admiration from subordinates. As a result, female power-holders are seen as less legitimate than male counterparts (Viall, Napier, and Brescoll, 2016, p. 400).

Despite the challenges, women have made progress. Attitudes are changing, support mechanisms (such as day care) have increased, and cultural views have shifted. A study of gender and leadership in higher education underscores the importance of culture and the policy context that it spawns:

> In secular Sweden there are strong policies that are implemented at all political levels supported by the public discourse, while in Ireland such measures are few and the equality infrastructures and discourse have been weakened by the state. In Sweden women have come to dominate the Rector/President/Vice Chancellor positions, and each gender has between 40 and 50 percent of the other leading positions. In Ireland, there are no women in the top position and their percentage of other leading positions is between 13 to 25 percent (O'Connor and Goransson, 2015, p. 323).

Perhaps the strongest force for continued advancement is the talent pool that women represent—they make up more than half the population and have a growing educational edge over their male counterparts. Glass and Cook (2016, p. 55) note that, despite the many barriers, an increasing number of women are getting to the top of large corporations. "Prior to the year 2000, only seven women had been CEO of a Fortune 500 company. Twenty-four women became CEO between 2001 and 2010, and from 2011 to 2014, 22 women became CEO." In 2009, Ursula Burns at Xerox became the first African American woman to head a major U.S. corporation and the first woman to succeed another woman.

Between 1986 and 2006, the proportion of female presidents of American universities more than doubled—to almost one in four—and Harvard put a woman in the job for the first time in 2007. Princeton accepted no women until 1969, and 30 years later, some of its mostly male alumni worried that their beloved alma mater might be on the skids when the first woman president appointed the first female provost. But grumbling at alumni gatherings could not change the fact that women were making gains even in America's most elite academic institutions.

REFRAMING LEADERSHIP

Each of the frames offers a distinctive image of leadership. Depending on leader and circumstance, each turn of the kaleidoscope can reveal compelling and constructive leadership opportunities, even though no one image is right for all times and seasons. In this section, we discuss four images of leadership summarized in Exhibit 17.4. For each, we examine skills and processes and propose rules of thumb for successful leadership practice.

Architect or Tyrant? Structural Leadership

Structural leadership may evoke images of petty tyrants and rigid bureaucrats who never met a command or rule they didn't like. Compared with other frames, literature on structural leadership is sparse, and some structural theorists have contended that leadership is neither important nor basic (Hall, 1987). But the effects of structural leadership can be

Exhibit 17.4.
Reframing Leadership.

	Leadership is effective when		Leadership is ineffective when	
Frame	Leader is:	Leadership process is:	Leader is:	Leadership process is:
Structural	Analyst, architect	Analysis, design	Petty bureaucrat or tyrant	Management by detail and fiat
Human resource	Catalyst, servant	Support, empowerment	Weakling, pushover	Abdication
Political	Advocate, negotiator	Advocacy, coalition building	Con artist, thug	Manipulation, fraud
Symbolic	Prophet, poet	Inspiration, meaning-making	Fanatic, charlatan	Mirage, smoke and mirrors

powerful and enduring, even if the style is subtler and more analytic than other forms. Collins and Hansen (2011) argue that great companies develop and adhere to a set of durable operating principles that are specific, methodical, and consistent.

One of the great architects in business history is Jeff Bezos, who has built Amazon into one of America's most dominant firms with a relentless focus on building structure and technology to support a relentless focus on customers. Bezos follows in a long line of structural leaders that can be traced back at least to Alfred P. Sloan Jr., who became president of General Motors in 1923 and remained a dominant force until his retirement in 1956. The structure and strategy he established made GM the world's largest corporation. Lee (1988) described Sloan as "the George Washington of the GM culture" (p. 42), even though his "genius was not in inspirational leadership, but in organizational structures" (p. 43).

GM founder, Billy Durant, had built GM by buying everything he could, forming a loose combination of previously independent firms. "GM did not have adequate knowledge or control of the individual operating divisions. It was management by crony, with the divisions operating on a horse-trading basis. The main thing to note here is that no one had the needed information or the needed control over the divisions" (Sloan, 1965, pp. 27–28).

Uncontrolled costs and a business slump in 1920 created a financial crisis, and GM almost sank (Sloan, 1965). In 1923, Sloan's first year at the helm, GM's market share dropped from 20 percent to 17 percent, while Ford's increased to 55 percent. But change was afoot. Henry Ford had a disdain for organization and clung to his vision of a single low-priced, mass-market car. His cheap, reliable Model T—the "Tin Lizzie"—was a marketing miracle at a time when customers would buy anything with four wheels and a motor if the price was right. But Ford stayed with the same design for almost 20 years and dismissed the need for creature comforts. Sloan surmised that consumers would pay more for amenities like windows to keep out rain and snow. His strategy worked, and Chevrolet soon began to gnaw off large chunks of Ford's market share. By 1928, Model T sales had dropped so precipitously that Henry Ford was forced to close his massive River Rouge plant for a year to retool. General Motors took the lead in the great auto race for the first time in 20 years. For the rest of the twentieth century, no one sold more cars than General Motors.

The dominant structural model of the time was a centralized, functional organization, but Sloan felt that GM needed something better. He developed the world's first division-alized organization The basic principle was simple: Centralize planning and resource allocation; decentralize operating decisions. Under Sloan's model, divisions focused on making and selling cars, while top management worked on long-range strategy and major funding decisions, relying on headquarters staff for the information and control systems they needed.

The structure worked. By the late 1920s, GM had a more versatile organization with a broader product line than Ford's. With the founder still dominating his highly centralized company, Ford was poorly positioned to compete with GM's multiple divisions, each producing its own cars and chasing distinct market niches at different price points. GM's pioneering structural form eventually set the standard for others: "Only two basic organizational structures have been used for the management of large industrial enterprises. One is the centralized, functional departmentalized type perfected by General Electric and Du Pont before World War I. The other is the multidivisional, decentralized structure initially developed at General Motors and also at Du Pont in the 1920s" (Chandler, 1977, p. 463).

In the 1980s, GM found itself with another structural leader, Roger Smith, at the helm. The results were less satisfying. Like Sloan, Smith ascended to the top at a difficult time. In 1980, his first year as GM's chief executive, every American carmaker lost money. It was GM's first loss since 1921. Recognizing that the company had serious competitive problems, Smith banked on structure and technology to make it "the world's first twenty-first century corporation" (Lee, 1988, p. 16). He restructured vehicle operations and spent billions of dollars in a quest for paperless offices and robotic assembly plants. The changes were dramatic, but the results were dismal: "[Smith's] tenure has been a tragic era in General Motors history. No GM chairman has disrupted as many lives without commensurate rewards, has spent as much money without returns, or has alienated so many along the way" (Lee, 1988, pp. 286–287).

Why did Smith stumble where Sloan had succeeded? The answer comes down to how well each implemented the right structural form. Effective structural leaders share several characteristics:

- *Structural leaders do their homework.* Sloan was a brilliant engineer who had grown up in the auto industry. Before coming to GM, he ran an auto accessories company where he implemented a divisional structure. He pioneered the development of better information systems and market research. He was an early convert to group decision making and created a committee structure to make major decisions. Roger Smith had spent his career with General Motors, but most of his jobs were in finance. His numbers told him machines were cheaper than people, so much of his vision for General Motors involved changes in production technology, an area where he had little experience or expertise.

- *Structural leaders rethink the relationship of structure, strategy, and environment.* Sloan's new structure was intimately tied to a strategy for reaching the automotive market. He foresaw growing demand, better cars, and more discriminating consumers. In the face of

Henry Ford's stubborn attachment to the Model T, Sloan initiated the "price pyramid" (cars for every pocketbook) and the annual introduction of new models, which soon became the industry norm.

For a variety of reasons, GM in the 1960s began to move away from Sloan's concepts. Fearing a government effort to break up the corporation, GM reduced the independence of the car divisions and centralized design and engineering. Increasingly, the divisions became marketing groups tasked to build and sell the cars that corporate gave them. "Look-alike cars" confused consumers who found it hard to tell a Chevrolet from a Cadillac.

Instead of addressing this marketing challenge, Smith focused more on reducing costs than on making better cars. As he saw it, GM's primary competitive problem was high costs driven by high wages. He showed little interest in efforts already under way at GM to improve working conditions on the shop floor. Ironically, one of his best investments—a joint venture with Toyota—succeeded because Toyota brought innovative approaches to managing people: "With only a fraction of the money invested in GM's heavily robotized plants, [the NUMMI plant at] Fremont is more efficient and produces better-quality cars than any plant in the GM system" (Hampton and Norman, 1987, p. 102).

- *Structural leaders focus on implementation.* Structural leaders often miscalculate the difficulties of putting their designs in place. They underestimate resistance, skimp on training, fail to build a political base, and misread cultural cues. Sloan was no human resource specialist, but he intuitively saw the need to cultivate understanding and acceptance of major decisions. He did that by continually asking for advice and by establishing committees and task forces to address major issues.

- *Effective structural leaders experiment.* Sloan tinkered constantly with GM's structure and strategy and encouraged others to do likewise. The Great Depression produced a drop of 72 percent in sales at GM between 1929 and 1932, but the company adapted adroitly to hard times. Sales fell, but GM increased its market share and made money every year. In the 1980s, Smith spent billions on his campaign to modernize the company and cut costs, yet GM lost market share every year and remained the industry's highest-cost producer.

Catalyst or Wimp? Human Resource Leadership

The tiny trickle of writing about structural leadership is swamped by a torrent of human resource literature (including Argyris, 1962; Bennis and Nanus, 1985, 2007; Blanchard and Johnson, 1982; Bradford and Cohen, 1984; Boyatzis and McKee, 2005; Fiedler and Chemers,

1974; Goleman, Boyatzis, and McKee, 2004; Hersey, 1984; Hollander, 1978; House, 1971; Levinson, 1968; Likert, 1967; Vroom and Yetton, 1973; and Waterman, 1994). Human resource theorists typically advocate openness, caring, mutuality, listening, coaching, participation, and empowerment. They view the leader as a facilitator and catalyst who uses emotional intelligence and social skill to motivate and empower subordinates. The leader's power comes from talent, caring, sensitivity, and service rather than position or force.

Greenleaf contends that followers "will freely respond only to individuals who are chosen as leaders because they are proven and trusted as servants" (1973, p. 4). He adds, "The servant-leader makes sure that other people's highest priority needs are being served. The best test [of leadership] is: do those served grow as persons; do they, while being served, become healthier, wiser, freer, more autonomous, more likely themselves to become servants?" (p. 7). Research confirms that servant leadership improves employee attitudes, job performance, and loyalty (Liden et al., 2014; Ling, Liu, and Wu, 2016)

Martín Varsavsky is one example of a human resource leader whose skill and artistry have produced extraordinary results. Varsavsky, a native of Argentina, wound up in New York as a teenager after violence forced his family to flee the military dictatorship in his homeland. Over two decades, Varsavsky founded seven companies and picked up entrepreneur-of-the-year awards on both sides of the Atlantic. He made his first millions in New York City real estate before moving to Europe. There he founded two high-tech companies that he later sold for more than a billion dollars each. In 2005, he partnered with venture capitalists and Google to found FON, which soon became the world's largest Wi-Fi network. His approach to managing people was pivotal to his success: "Martín developed management practices that would be keys throughout his career: create horizontal organizations without any hierarchy, communicate clearly what you intend before doing it, delegate as much as possible, trust your colleagues, and leave operating decisions in the hands of others" (Ganitsky and Sancho, 2002, p. 101).

Gifted human resource leaders such as Varsavsky typically apply a consistent set of people-friendly leadership principles:

- *Human resource leaders communicate a strong belief in people.* They are passionate about "productivity through people" (Peters and Waterman, 1982). They express this faith in both words and actions, often formalized in a core philosophy or credo. Fred Smith, founder and CEO of Federal Express, sees "putting people first" as the cornerstone of his company's success: "We discovered a long time ago that customer satisfaction really begins with employee satisfaction. That belief is incorporated in our corporate philosophy statement: "People—Service—Profit . . . In that order" (Waterman, 1994, p. 89).

- *Human resource leaders are visible and accessible.* Peters and Waterman (1982) popularized "management by wandering around"—the idea that managers need to get out of their offices and spend time with workers and customers. Patricia Carrigan, the first female plant manager at General Motors, modeled this technique in the course of turning around two manufacturing plants, each with a long history of union–management conflict (Kouzes and Posner, 1987). In both situations, she began by going to the plant floor to introduce herself to workers and to ask how they thought the operation could be improved. One worker commented that before Carrigan, "I didn't know who the plant manager was. I wouldn't have recognized him if I saw him."

- *Effective human resource leaders empower others.* People-oriented leaders often refer to their employees as "partners," "owners," or "associates." They make it clear that workers have a stake in the organization's success and a right to be involved in making decisions. In the 1980s, Jan Carlzon, CEO of Scandinavian Air Systems (SAS), turned around a sluggish business with the intent of making it "the best airline in the world for business travelers" (Carlzon, 1987, p. 46). To find out what the business traveler wanted, he turned to SAS's frontline service employees. Focus groups generated hundreds of ideas and emphasized the importance of frontline autonomy to decide on the spot what passengers needed. Carlzon concluded that SAS's image was built on countless "moments of truth:" 15-second encounters between employees and customers:

> "We have to place responsibility for ideas, decisions, and actions with the people who are SAS during those 15 seconds. If they have to go up the organizational chain of command for a decision on an individual problem, then those 15 golden seconds will elapse without a response and we will have lost an opportunity to earn a loyal customer" (Carlzon, 1987, p. 66).

Advocate or Hustler? Political Leadership

Even in the results-driven private sector, leaders find that they have to plunge into the political arena to move their company where it needs to go. Lee Iacocca, who became chief executive of Chrysler in the late 1970s when the company was near death, provided one of the most impressive examples of political leadership in American business history.

Iacocca's career had taken him to the presidency of Ford Motor Company. But then in 1978 his boss, Henry Ford II, fired him, reportedly with the simple explanation, "Let's just say I don't like you" (O'Toole, 1984, p. 231). Iacocca's unemployment was brief. Chrysler Corporation, desperate for new leadership, saw Iacocca as the best answer to the company's business woes.

Iacocca had done his homework before accepting Chrysler's offer but still found things were worse than he expected. Chrysler was losing money so fast that bankruptcy seemed almost inevitable. He concluded that the only way out was to persuade the U.S. government to guarantee massive loans. It was a tough sell; much of Congress, the media, and the American public was against the idea. Iacocca had to convince them all that government intervention was in their best interest as well as Chrysler's.

Ultimately, Iacocca got his guarantees. He won by artfully employing rules for political leaders:

- *Political leaders clarify what they want and what they can get.* Political leaders are realists. They don't let hope cloud judgment. Iacocca translated Chrysler's survival into the realistic goal of getting enough help to eke out a couple of difficult years. He was always careful to ask not for money but for loan guarantees. He insisted that it would cost taxpayers nothing because Chrysler would pay back its loans.

- *Political leaders assess the distribution of power and interests.* Political leaders map the political terrain by thinking carefully about the key players, their interests, and their power, asking: Whose support do I need? How do I go about getting it? Who are my opponents? How much power do they have? What can I do to reduce or overcome their opposition? Is this battle winnable? Iacocca needed the support of Chrysler's employees and unions, but they had little choice. The key players were Congress and the public. Congress would vote for the guarantees only if Iacocca's proposal had sufficient popular support.

- *Political leaders build linkages to key stakeholders.* Political leaders focus their attention on building relationships and networks. They recognize the value of personal contact and face-to-face conversations.

- *Iacocca worked hard to build linkages.* He spent hours meeting with members of Congress and testifying before congressional committees. After he met with 31 Italian American members of Congress, all but one voted for the loan guarantees. Said Iacocca, "Some were Republicans, some were Democrats, but in this case they voted the straight Italian ticket. We were desperate, and we had to play every angle" (Iacocca and Novak, 1984, p. 221).

- *Political leaders persuade first, negotiate second, and coerce only if necessary.* Wise political leaders recognize that power is essential to their effectiveness; they also know to use it judiciously. William P. Kelly, a veteran public administrator, put it well:

> "Power is like the old Esso [gasoline] ad—a tiger in your tank. But you can't let the tiger out, you just let people hear him roar. You use power terribly sparingly

because it has a short half-life. You let people know you have it and hope that you don't have to use it" (Ridout and Fenn, 1974, p. 10).

Sophisticated political leaders know that influence begins with understanding others' concerns and interests. Iacocca knew that he had to address a widespread fear that federal guarantees would throw taxpayer dollars down a rat hole. He used a big ad campaign to respond to public concerns. Does Chrysler have a future? Yes, he said, we've been here 54 years, and we'll be here another 54 years. Would the loan guarantees be a dangerous precedent? No, the government already carried $400 billion in other loan guarantees, and in any event, Chrysler was going to pay its loans back. Iacocca also spoke directly to Congressional concerns with data painting a grim picture of jobs lost in every district if Chrysler went under.

Iacocca got what he wanted—enough breathing room for Chrysler to pull out of its tailspin. The company repaid its loans, ignited the minivan craze, and had many profitable years before the return of bad times in the 1990s (which led to a sale to German automaker Daimler Benz in 1998 and then to a private equity firm in 2007).

Prophet or Zealot? Symbolic Leadership

The symbolic frame represents a fourth turn of the leadership kaleidoscope, portraying organization as both theater and temple. As theater, an organization creates a stage on which actors play their roles and hope to communicate the right impression to their audience. As temple, an organization is a community of faith, bonded by shared beliefs, traditions, myths, rituals, and ceremonies.

Symbolically, leaders lead through both actions and words as they interpret and reinterpret experience. What are the real lessons of history? What is really happening in the world? What will the future bring? What mission is worthy of our loyalty and investment? Data and analysis offer few compelling answers to such questions. Symbolic leaders interpret experience so as to impart meaning and purpose through phrases of beauty and passion. Franklin D. Roosevelt reassured a nation in the midst of its deepest economic depression that "the only thing we have to fear is fear itself." At almost the same time, Adolf Hitler assured Germans that their severe economic and social problems were the result of betrayal by Jews and communists. Germans, he said, were a superior people who could still fulfill their nation's destiny of world mastery. Though many saw the destructive paranoia in Hitler's message, millions of fearful citizens were swept up in Hitler's bold vision of German preeminence.

Symbolic leaders follow a consistent set of practices and scripts:

- *Symbolic leaders lead by example.* They demonstrate their commitment and courage by plunging into the fray. In taking risks and holding nothing back, they reassure and inspire others. When Ann Mulcahy took the top job at Xerox in 2001, the building was burning and few thought she had much chance of putting the fire out. Her financial advisors told her bankruptcy was the only choice. Determined to save the company she loved, Mulcahy became a tireless, visible cheerleader working to get the support she needed to make Xerox a success: "Constantly on the move, Mulcahy met with bankers, reassured customers, galvanized employees. She sometimes visited three cities a day" (Morris, 2003, p. 1).

- *They use symbols to capture attention.* When Diana Lam became principal of the Mackey Middle School in Boston, she faced a substantial challenge. Mackey had the typical problems of an urban school: decaying physical plant, poor discipline, racial tension, disgruntled teachers, and limited resources (Kaufer and Leader, 1987a). In such a situation, a symbolic leader looks for something visible and dramatic to signal that change is on the way. During the summer before assuming her duties, Lam wrote personal letters to every teacher requesting individual meetings. She met teachers wherever they wanted (in one case driving for 2 hours). She asked them how they felt about the school and what changes they wanted. Then she recruited her family to repaint the school's front door and some of its ugliest classrooms. "When school opened, students and staff members immediately saw that things were going to be different, if only symbolically. Perhaps even more important, staff members received a subtle challenge to make a contribution themselves" (Kaufer and Leader, 1987b, p. 3).

  When Iacocca became president of Chrysler, one of his first steps was to announce that he was reducing his salary to $1 a year. "I did it for good, cold pragmatic reasons. I wanted our employees and our suppliers to be thinking: 'I can follow a guy who sets that kind of example'" (Iacocca and Novak, 1984, pp. 229–230).

- *Symbolic leaders frame experience.* In a world of uncertainty and ambiguity, a key function of symbolic leadership is to offer plausible and hopeful interpretations of experience. President John F. Kennedy channeled youthful exuberance into the Peace Corps and other initiatives with his stirring inaugural challenge: "Ask not what your country can do for you; ask what you can do for your country." When Martin Luther King Jr. spoke at the March on Washington in 1963 and gave his extraordinary "I Have a Dream" speech, his opening line was, "I am happy to join with you today in what will go down in history as the greatest demonstration for freedom in the history of our nation."

He could have interpreted the event in a number of other ways: "We are here because nothing else has worked"; "We are here because it's summer and it's a good day to be outside." Each version is about as accurate as the next, but accuracy is not the issue. King's assertion was bold and inspiring; it told members of the audience that they were making history by their presence at a momentous event.

- *Symbolic leaders communicate a vision.* One powerful way in which a leader can interpret experience is by distilling and disseminating a vision—a persuasive and hopeful image of the future. A vision needs to address both the challenges of the present and the hopes and values of followers. Vision is particularly important in times of crisis and uncertainty. When people are in pain, when they are confused and uncertain, or when they feel despair and hopelessness, they desperately seek meaning and hope. In the 2016 U.S. presidential election, Donald Trump's vow to "Make America Great Again" was accompanied by very few policy specifics, but that did not trouble millions of voters who longed to see their country get back on the right track.

  Where does such vision come from? One view is that leaders create a vision and then persuade others to accept it (Bass, 1985; Bennis and Nanus, 1985). A different take is that leaders discover and articulate a vision that is already there, even if unexpressed (Cleveland, 1985). Kouzes and Posner put it well: "Corporate leaders know very well that what seeds the vision are those imperfectly formed images in the marketing department about what the customers really wanted and those inarticulate mumblings from the manufacturing folks about the poor product quality, not crystal ball gazing in upper levels of the corporate stratosphere. The best leaders are the best followers. They pay attention to those weak signals and quickly respond to changes in the corporate course" (1987, p. 114).

  Leadership is a two-way street. No amount of charisma or rhetorical skill can sell a vision that reflects only the leader's values and needs. Effective symbolic leadership is possible only for those who understand the deepest values and most pressing concerns of their constituents. But leaders still play a critical role in articulating a vision by bringing a unique, personal blend of history, poetry, passion, and courage in distilling and shaping direction. Most important, they can choose which stories to tell to express a shared quest.

- *Symbolic leaders tell stories.* Symbolic leaders often embed their vision in a mythical story—a story about "us" and about "our" past, present, and future. "Us" could be a school's faculty, a plant's employees, the people of Thailand, or any other audience a leader hopes to reach. The past is usually golden, a time of noble purposes, of great deeds, of legendary heroes and heroines. The present is troubled, a critical moment when we have to make fateful choices. The future is a dreamlike vision of hope and greatness, often tied to past glories.

A version of this story line helped Ronald Reagan, a master storyteller, become America's thirty-ninth president. Reagan's golden past was rooted in the frontier, a place of rugged, sturdy, self-reliant men and women who built a great nation. They took care of themselves and their neighbors without interference from a monstrous national government. America had fallen into crisis, said Reagan, because "the liberals" had created a federal government that levied oppressive taxes and eroded freedom through bureaucratic regulation and meddling. Reagan promised a return to American greatness by "getting government off the backs of the American people" and restoring traditional values of freedom and self-reliance. Reagan's story line worked for him and for a Reagan acolyte, George W. Bush, in 2000. It worked still a third time in 2016 for Donald Trump. Trump did not spell out the golden past that was implicit in his campaign mantra "Make America great again." But he was clear that America was in crisis because of a toxic combination of terrorism, uncontrolled immigration, increasing crime and violence, the loss of jobs to foreign competitors, and bad leadership in Washington. His vision for the future offered resolution of all those problems: "Together, we will lead our party back to the White House, and we will lead our country back to safety, prosperity, and peace. We will be a country of generosity and warmth. But we will also be a country of law and order" (Politico Staff, 2016).

Leaders' stories succeed when they offer something that people want to believe, regardless of historical validity or empirical support. Even a flawed story will work if it taps persuasively into the experience, values, and hopes of listeners.

CONCLUSION

Although leadership is universally accepted as a cure for social and organizational ills, it is also widely misunderstood. Many views of leadership fail to recognize its relational and contextual nature and its distinction from power and position. Shallow ideas about leadership mislead managers. A multiframe view provides a more comprehensive map of a complex and varied terrain.

Each frame highlights significant possibilities for leadership, but each by itself is incomplete. A century ago, models of managerial leadership were narrowly rational. In the 1960s and 1970s, human resource leadership became fashionable. In recent years, symbolic and political leadership have become more prominent, and the literature abounds with advice on how to become a powerful or visionary leader. Ideally, managers combine multiple frames into a comprehensive approach to leadership. Wise leaders understand their own strengths, work to expand them, and build diverse teams that can offer an organization leadership in all four modes: structural, political, human resource, and symbolic.

Note

1. In the constitutional convention, delegates were divided over whether the president should be selected by Congress or elected directly by the voters. The Electoral College was the compromise solution. Usually, the winner of the national popular vote wins the presidency, but there have been exceptions, including two in this century. In 2000, Al Gore won the popular vote, and would have been president if he had carried Florida, which he lost by 537 votes out of almost 4 million total. In 2016, as we discuss, Hillary Clinton won the popular vote by more than 2.8 million votes but lost in the electoral college when Donald Trump carried key swing states.

Reframing Change
in Organizations

> *There is no more delicate matter to take in hand,
> nor more dangerous to conduct, nor more doubtful
> in its success, than to set up as a leader in the introduction
> of changes. For he who innovates will have for his enemies
> all those who are well off under the existing order of things,
> and only the lukewarm support in those who might be
> better off under the new.*
>
> —Machiavelli, 1514, p.27

Running for president in 2008, Barack Obama ran on a platform promising "change." Running for reelection in 2012, President Obama defended his record against Governor Mitt Romney's campaign promise of "change." And so it goes in one presidential race after another. In the 2016 campaign, Hillary Clinton promised both change and continuity with the policies of the popular incumbent, Obama. Donald Trump ran as an unabashed change candidate, promising a return to greatness. After the election, Trump supporters rejoiced and Clinton voters were horrified. Yet the status quo is often remarkably durable, hanging on until the next election and a renewed promise of change and hope.

A similar pattern is observable in American businesses. When profits dip, when employees become restless or when some other calamity looms, executives think about "pursuing a different path." They scan prevailing ideas in "good currency" for the latest magical remedies to make things better. They do not always realize that many panaceas for solving problems have already been tried and found wanting. Henry Mintzberg, for example, was a proponent of strategic planning in the 1970s and 1980s as a more systematic way. In his 1994 book, *The Rise and Fall of Strategic Planning*, he concluded: ". . . strategic planning did not work . . . the form ('the rationality of planning') did not conform to the function ('the needs of strategy making')" (p. 415). Countless other modern management theories and techniques have suffered a similar fate.

Successful change efforts often reach back to the past. In 1993, Lou Gerstner Jr., the new CEO of IBM, pulled the company out of a downward spiral by harking back to the time when Tom Watson Sr. was CEO and IBM was the most admired company in the world. He reinvigorated old values and refurbished dormant cultural practices. Howard Schultz followed a similar path when Starbucks took a dive in 2007 (see Chapter 13). He made public his concern that the company had wandered from the cultural values and ways that enabled it to become a household name. He put Starbucks back on a path to growth and profitability and restored the spirit that had once made the company unique.

Yet clinging to the status quo can also stifle progress. The United States is one of only three nations that have not yet officially converted to the metric system. This seems odd, given that the United States has little in common with the other two holdouts—Liberia and Myanmar. It seems even stranger because the system was first officially authorized in the United States in 1866, and as far back as 1958, the *Federal Register* contained provisions that "all calibrations in the U.S. customary system of weights and measurements carried out by the National Bureau of Standards will continue to be based on metric measurement and standards."

And it seems even more puzzling because in 1996 all federal agencies were ordered to adopt the metric system. Adhering to a thousand-year-old English system that even the English have been abandoning imposes many disadvantages. It handicaps international commerce, for example, and it led to measurement confusion in the design of the Hubble space telescope, costing taxpayers millions of dollars. Yet the United States has made little progress in going metric, despite cosmetic changes such as putting kilometers alongside miles on vehicle speedometers.

America's inertia in implementing the metric system illustrates pervasive and predictable challenges of change that repeatedly scuttle promising innovations. Organizations spend millions of dollars on change strategies that produce little improvement or make things worse. Mergers sour. Technology falls short of its potential. Vital strategies never wend their way into practice. In elections, challengers promise change, but winners struggle to deliver on even a fraction of their pledges.

To shrink the gap between change advocates' intentions and outcomes, a voluminous body of literature has flourished. The sheer volume of change models, case studies, and prescriptive remedies is overwhelming. Some contain productive insights. Beer and Nohria (2001), for example, compare two distinct change models—a hard, top-down approach that emphasizes shareholder value (Theory E) and a softer, more participative strategy (Theory O) that targets organizational culture. Kanter, Stein, and Jick's "Big Three" model (1992) helps managers sort through the interplay of change strategies, implementers, and recipients.

But despite growing knowledge, the same mistakes keep repeating themselves. It's like reading a stream of books on dieting but never losing weight. The target is never easy to reach, and it often seems that everyone *wants* things to be different, so long as they don't have to do anything differently. The key question is: What keeps the innovations that organizations need from taking hold? This chapter opens by examining the innovation process at two different companies. It then moves to a multiframe analysis to show how participation, training, structural realignment, political bargaining, and symbolic rituals of letting go can help achieve more positive outcomes. It concludes with a discussion integrating the frames with Kotter's influential analysis of the stages of change.

THE INNOVATION PROCESS

What makes organizational change so difficult? When Bain and Company surveyed 250 American companies to determine their experience with making needed changes, they discovered a disturbing trend:

- Only 12 percent achieved what they set out to accomplish

- 38 percent failed by a wide margin, capturing less than half of their original target

- 50 percent settled for a significant shortfall (Bain Insights, 2016)

Comparing two typically flawed change efforts with an atypical success story offers insights.

Six Sigma at 3M

Beginning at Motorola in 1986 and later enhanced at General Electric, Six Sigma evolved from a statistical concept to a range of metrics, methods, and management approaches intended to reduce defects and increase quality in products and services (Pande, Neuman, and Cavanagh, 2000). It became the new corporate shibboleth in the 1990s after its successful, widespread use at GE. Essentially the approach has two components, one emphasizing metrics and control and the other emphasizing systems design. It has spawned acronyms like DMAIC (define, measure, analyze, improve, and control) and DFSS (design for Six Sigma—by building quality in from the start). GE executives groomed in the Six Sigma way brought the techniques with them when they moved to other corporations. One example was James McNerney, who missed the chance to succeed Jack Welch as GE's CEO but was snapped up by 3M in 2001 to bring some discipline to a legendary enterprise that seemed to be losing its edge. Profit and sales growth had been erratic, and the stock price had languished.

McNerney got people's attention by slashing eight thousand jobs (11 percent of the workforce), putting teeth in the performance review process, and tightening the free-flowing spending spigot. Thousands of 3M workers trained to earn the Six Sigma title of "Black Belt." These converts pioneered companywide Six Sigma initiatives such as boosting production by reducing variation and eliminating pointless steps in manufacturing. The Black Belts trained rank-and-file employees as "Green Belts," in charge of local Six Sigma initiatives. The Black Belt elite maintained metrics that tracked both overall and "neighborhood" efforts to systematize and streamline all aspects of work—including research and development.

In the short run, McNerney's strategy paid off. Indicators of productivity improved, costs were trimmed, and the stock price soared. But Six Sigma's standardization began to intrude on 3M's historical emphasis on innovation. Prior to McNerney's arrival, new ideas were accorded almost unlimited time and funding to get started. Fifteen percent of employees' on-the-clock time was devoted to developing groundbreaking products—with little accountability. This approach had given birth to legendary products like Scotch Tape and Post-it notes.

Six Sigma systematized the research and development process. Sketchy, blue-sky projects gave way to scheduled, incremental development. Funds carried an expiration date, and progress through a planned pipeline was measured and charted. Development of new products began to wane. "The more you hardwire a company on total quality management, [the more] it is going to hurt breakthrough innovation," says Vijay Govindarajan, a management professor at Dartmouth. "The mindset that is needed, the capabilities that are needed, the metrics that are needed, the whole culture that is needed for discontinuous innovation, are fundamentally different." Art Fry, the inventor of the Post-it, agreed: "We all came to the conclusion that there was no way in the world that anything like a Post-it note would ever emerge from this new system" (Hindo, 2007, p. 9).

With the lethargy ended but the damage done, McNerney left 3M in 2005 to become the new CEO at Boeing. Fry observed, "What's remarkable is how fast a culture can be torn apart. [McNerney] didn't kill it, because he wasn't here long enough. But if he had been here much longer, I think he would have." George Buckley, McNerney's successor, observed in retrospect, "Perhaps one of the mistakes that we made as a company—it's one of the dangers of Six Sigma—is that when you value sameness more than you value creativity, I think you potentially undermine the heart and soul of a company like 3M" (Hindo, 2007, p. 9).

Benner and Tushman (2015) rely on the 3M case to argue that organizations need the capacity to manage paradox in order to foster both incremental and discontinuous innovation. Process improvements like Six Sigma, along with many other management "panaceas," may make incremental innovation more efficient and reliable but also tend to block break-the-mold innovations. So organizations may become very good at improving existing products or services but fall to more nimble and creative competitors at times of dramatic changes in markets and technology.

Take another example, JC Penney, an American institution where generations of Americans had shopped for almost everything for more than a century. More than a few remember it as "the place your mom dragged you to buy clothes you hated in 1984" (Morran, 2013). By 2011, the firm was treading water, and CEO Myron Ullman retired after seven years at the helm. Ullman's initial years had gone well, but the recession of 2008 hit Penney's middle-income shoppers hard, and the company had been going downhill since.

The board looked for a savior and found him in Ron Johnson, a wunderkind merchant who had worked his magic at two of the most successful retailers in America. He'd made Target hip and led Apple Stores as they became the most profitable retail outlets on the planet. Johnson moved quickly to create a new, trendier JC Penney. His vision went well beyond changing the system of metrics and measurement or making the company more profitable. He wanted to graft an entirely new vision of retail merchandising onto ailing old root stock: ". . . to analysts and employees, Johnson was Willy Wonka asking [them] to go with him on a trip through his retail imagination" (Macke, 2013).

Wanting to move fast, Johnson skipped market tests and staged rollouts. "No need," said Johnson, "we didn't test at Apple" (Heisler, 2013). Creative new floor plans divided stores into boutique shops featuring brands like Martha Stewart, Izod, Joe Fresh, and Dockers. Centralized locations provided places for customers to lounge, share a cup of coffee, have their hair done, or grab a quick lunch. Games and other entertainment kept children occupied while customers visited boutique offerings or just "hung out."

Johnson quickly did away with Penney's traditional coupons, clearance racks and sales events, part of a model that relied on inflating prices, then marking them down to create the illusion of bargains. Johnson replaced all that with everyday "Fair and Square" prices. To Johnson's rational way of thinking, this move made perfect sense. But shopping is more of a ritual than rational undertaking:

> JCP's Ron Johnson was . . . clueless about what makes shopping meaningful for women. It's the thrill of the hunt, not the buying . . . women love to shop and deals are what make the game worth playing. Bargain hunting is now like playing a game—and finding deeply discounted goods on sale is part of the game (Phillips, quoted in Denning, 2013).

Johnson replaced much of Penney's leadership with executives from other top retailers. Many, like Johnson, lived in California, far from company headquarters in Plano, Texas. They often looked down on the customers and the JC Penney culture they had inherited. One of Johnson's recruits, COO Michael Kramer, another Apple alum, told the *Wall Street Journal*, "I hated the JC Penney culture. It was pathetic" (Tuttle, 2013). Inside and outside the company, perceptions grew that Johnson and his crew blamed customers rather than themselves as results went from bad to worse. Traditionally, great merchants, like Costco's Jim Sinegal or Walmart's Sam Walton, have loved spending time in their stores, chatting up staff and customers, asking questions, and studying everything to stay in touch with their business. Johnson, on the contrary, gave the impression that he wouldn't shop in one of his own stores and didn't particularly understand the people who did (Tuttle, 2013).

Johnson substituted broadcasts for store visits. He sent out company-wide video updates every 25 days. Staff gathered in training rooms to hear what the CEO had to say and struggled to make sense of the gap between Johnson's rosy reports and the chaos they were experiencing firsthand in the stores. It didn't help that Johnson liked to broadcast from his home in Palo Alto or from the Ritz-Carlton in Dallas, where he stayed during visits to headquarters. Instead of marking milestones in Johnson's turnaround effort, the broadcasts deepened a perception that he was out of touch and self-absorbed.

Johnson's reign at JC Penney lasted 17 months. Customers left, sales plummeted, and losses piled up. A board with few good options sacked Johnson and reappointed Ullman, the man who had left under a cloud less than two years earlier.

The change initiatives at 3M and Penney's reveal a familiar scenario: New CEO introduces new techniques and scores a short-term victory; political pressures and cultural resistance start to mount; CEO leaves to try again; organization licks its wounds and moves both backward and onward. In short, an optimistic beginning, tumultuous middle, and controversial conclusion.

Ford Motor Company: An Atypical Case

In 2006, the Ford Motor Company was chalking up a $13 billion loss and expected to lose even more the following year. Chairman William Ford III reluctantly concluded that his best efforts were no match for the executive infighting and entrenched mind-sets that were dragging the company down. His search for a tougher successor yielded Alan Mulally, the number two executive at Boeing. Mullaly had been passed over for the top job in favor of James McNerney, who had left 3M with mixed reviews. Ford convinced Mulally that Ford could give him what Boeing wouldn't. Mullaly accepted what he knew would be a formidable challenge.

To begin with, deteriorating political dynamics needed attention. First up was the media, who would give the public its first impression of the new Ford chief. Step one was leaked memos from Bill Ford bemoaning the lack of honesty at the top of the company and calling for immediate and dramatic change. Mullaly and his media staff cultivated key news sources and carefully staged the public announcement of his selection to assure that the new show opened to mostly rave reviews.

A second challenge was to make sure employees came aboard for a new direction. On his second day of work Mullaly and Bill Ford led a joint town hall meeting in Detroit that was broadcast to workers around the world. After Ford introduced him, Mullaly said he was honored to be asked to join such a storied organization. Then he opened the floor to questions and gave upbeat but honest answers. Would he bring in a new executive team? No, he said, his team was right there. When the head of a strategic planning group asked if her unit would have a bigger role, he told her no, strategy is a job for "our team," not a staff group.

Two weeks later, Mullaly sent a frank e-mail message to everyone at Ford that described his "first impressions." He was upfront about some bad news: Ford's "gut-wrenching" circumstances meant that "some very good and loyal people are going to leave this company" in the months to come. But, he added, he was excited about the many people who were "bursting with ideas" and wanted to share them in e-mails, hallways, or the cafeteria. He ended on an upbeat note: "Everyone loves a comeback story. Let's work together to write the best one ever."

Two more key constituencies were the board of directors and the Ford family. Mulally tested the same message with both groups: Ford needed to simplify its product line, produce cars that customers wanted, and develop a clear view of the future. Both groups responded enthusiastically, and many of Henry Ford's descendants happily signed their names on a diagram of the family tree that Mulally had brought with him to their first meeting.

Mulally also understood that Ford needed help from the United Automobile Workers (UAW). Both company and union were in a tough spot. Ford's survival depended on negotiating a lower cost structure in its UAW contracts. The autoworkers' leadership knew that Ford was in deep trouble and feared a disaster for its members if the company failed. Top leadership from both company and union held many meetings, at which Mulally promoted his mantra of "profitable growth for all." His case centered on the fact that Ford was losing money on every car it made in North America. He argued that Ford had only three options: keep losing money and go out of business, move production offshore, or get a union contract that would let them build cars in the United States. The union reluctantly bought the argument, and after many rounds of bargaining and some last-minute high drama, company and union agreed on a deal that enabled Ford to build more cars in America.

Still another critical political challenge was getting the support of Ford's senior executives, including some who had hoped to become CEO. The proud, intensely competitive group of longtime Ford veterans was initially unimpressed with the new chief. To some, Mulally seemed like a smiling, overgrown Boy Scout who lacked the smarts, toughness, and gravitas to run Ford. He apparently didn't even know how to dress, showing up in a dark-suit culture wearing a sport coat and olive pants. Many in the room felt that the auto industry was too tough for Mulally to understand, and Ford's technical officer put it to him directly: "We appreciate you coming here from a company like Boeing, but you've got to realize that this is a very, very capital-intensive business with long product development lead times. The average car is made up of thousands of different parts, and they all have to work together flawlessly."

"That's really interesting," Mulally replied, with his usual genial smile and unflappable aura. "The typical passenger jet has four million parts, and if just one of them fails the whole thing can fall out of the sky. So I feel pretty comfortable with this." This quieted naysayers for the moment, but Mulally knew that much of his team still wondered if he could do the job. Instead of trying to convince them directly, he turned to structural changes to bring clarity and focus to the top team as well as Ford's global operations.

Mulally quickly concluded that Ford needed a major overhaul of a "convoluted management structure riddled with overlapping responsibilities and tangled chains of command." He implemented what had worked for him at Boeing, a matrix structure that crisscrossed the strong regional organizations with upgraded global functional units (as described in Chapter 4).

Mulally knew that the structure would work only if the top executives came together as a team. He pulled out another structural device he had developed at Boeing: the Business Plan Review (BPR). He replaced dozens of high-level gatherings with one key meeting—same time, same place, every week. Attendance was required, in person or via video hookup, for everyone who reported to him. He put in new rules. In the old days, no one wanted to admit that anything was going wrong, so executives ritualistically came to meetings with thick binders and a bevy of assistants to help them hide problems under a blizzard of details. Executives now had to make their own 5-minute reports, using a standard format, on progress against plan. Mulally asked lots of questions but told them it was okay if someone didn't know an answer. "Because we'll all be here again next week, and I *know* you'll know by then." Every item in each report had to be color coded: green for on track, yellow for needs attention, and red for anything that was off plan or behind schedule. "This is the only way I know to operate," he told them. "We need to have everybody involved. We need to have a plan. And we need to know where we are on the plans."

The head of Ford's international operations, Mark Schultz, had hoped to be CEO himself and didn't like the new rules. He dug in his heels. At the first BPR meeting, he said he wanted his chief financial officer to report for him. When Mulally told Schultz to do it himself, he tried, but was obviously unprepared. After a few minutes, Mulally had heard enough and tried to cut him off, but it took four tries before Schultz got the hint. After the meeting an angry Schultz told Mulally that he would not be able to attend all the BPR meetings because he had important work to do in Asia. With his usual smile, Mulally told him he didn't have to come to meetings—but couldn't stay on the team if he didn't. Schultz figured he could play by his own rules because his longtime fishing buddy, Bill Ford, would protect him. That was a misjudgment. When Mulally eliminated his job and offered him a smaller one, Schultz retired rather than accept the demotion.

Other executives got the message: Mulally was in charge, and Bill Ford was solidly behind him. As executives began to fall in line, Mulally was able to turn his attention to two pressing human resource issues: talent at the top and morale throughout the company. He respected Ford's executive talent and felt that the company needed continuity rather than massive turnover in the senior leadership. He asked his HR chief to develop retention plans for all key executives. If Mulally heard that one of them was thinking about leaving, he would drop by his or her office to ask directly, "Are you going to stay?" Usually the executive did.

Mulally's major HR challenge was rebuilding the commitment and morale of Ford's workforce in a time of downsizing and dismal business results. At headquarters, he was a master of leading by wandering around. He often skipped the executive dining room to eat in the company cafeteria, standing in line with his tray and chatting up accountants or sales analysts. He popped into meeting where he wasn't expected, asking, "What are you guys talking about?" Lifers who had waited forever for a CEO who would listen started sending e-mails to Mulally. He answered them all and sometimes followed up with a telephone call.

One engineer showed up at Mulally's office with a pile of schematics, including drawings for more than a dozen different hood structures. He wanted to show the new chief just how muddled Ford's design and engineering were. The drawings confirmed what Mulally already suspected. He asked if there was a way to reduce the complexity. When the engineer said yes, Mulally put him in charge of the effort.

To reach the thousands of employees beyond Detroit, Mulally traveled to locations around the world, asking questions and reinforcing the message that Ford was coming back. He issued every employee a wallet card that carried the essence of the plan going forward: "One Ford. One Team. One Plan. One Goal."

Symbolically, Mulally's biggest challenge was to change the perception that Ford was on a path to oblivion because it had become too bloated, bureaucratic, and self-absorbed to understand or adapt to the realities of the twenty-first century. As he sought a more hopeful story about the future, he followed the lead of wise symbolic leaders such as Lou Gerstner at IBM. He looked to the past. Mulally combed Ford's corporate archives, believing that a key to Ford's future was a return to the principles that had make it great in the first place. He hit pay dirt with an ad that Henry Ford had run in 1925 in the *Saturday Evening Post* (America's most widely read publication at the time). Under a picture of an American family standing atop a grassy knoll next to their Model T, the caption read, "Opening the highways to all mankind." In the text, Henry Ford outlined his vison: "A wholehearted belief that riding on the people's highways should be within easy reach of all the people." That ad gave Mulally the touchstone he was looking for. He wrote stream-of-consciousness notes about what needed to happen: pull stakeholders together, form tight relationships with the board and the Ford family, respect the heritage, implement reliable discipline and a business plan, and include everyone. Then he took another sheet of paper and sketched his "Alan Legacy." Bottom line: "One Ford," anchored on a glorious past, moving toward a future that replaced chaos and infighting with simplicity, teamwork, and unity—worldwide.

How Frames Can Improve the Odds

Comparing the stories of change at 3M, JC Penney, and Ford illustrates an iron law: Limited, top-down thinking almost always fails. Changes that are more employee driven and comprehensive have a better chance. Organizations today face a persistent dilemma. Changes in leadership or the environment pressure them to adapt, yet the more they try to change, the more often their reach exceeds their grasp (Nickerson and Silverman, 2003; Barnett and Freeman, 2001). Ormerod (2007) argues that "things usually fail" because decision makers don't understand their circumstances well enough to anticipate the consequences of their actions. They march blindly down their chosen path ignoring warning signs that they are headed in the wrong direction. In studying scores of innovations, we continue to see managers whose strategies are limited because their thinking is employs only one or two cognitive lenses.

Think about the challenges of rebuilding Iraq. The architects of the U.S. invasion foresaw a relatively quick and painless transition to democratic stability. Instead, eliminating the Saddam Hussein regime opened a Pandora's box of political and symbolic issues seething beneath the surface (as happened subsequently in Libya, Egypt, and many other nations that have undergone cataclysmic regime change). It is much better to spot quicksand before rather than after you're mired in it. The frames can help change agents see pitfalls and roadblocks ahead, thereby increasing their odds of success.

Changing an organization is a complex, systemic undertaking. It rarely works to retrain people without revising roles or to revamp roles without retraining. Planning without broad-based participation that gives voice to the opposition almost guarantees stiff resistance later on. Change alters power relationships and undermines existing agreements and pacts. Even more profoundly, it intrudes on deeply rooted symbolic forms, traditional ways, icons, and rituals. Below the surface, an organization's cultural tapestry begins to unravel, threatening time-honored traditions, prevailing cultural values and ways, and shared meaning.

Too many change efforts fail, but there are bright spots that offer hope. Arnold (2015) cites five cases of dramatically successful change. One was Santander, the giant Spanish bank, which entered the U.K. market by buying two old-line British banks. The two were very different from one another and neither had much in common with Santander in terms of culture, systems, and practices. Santander needed to establish a common brand and to get both banks to align with its cultural values of "Simple, Personal, and Fair." Santander's change process emphasized both people and systems, including extensive opportunities for involvement and training. Reading between the lines of such case descriptions, one can detect the importance of the four frames in approaching change. In the remainder of the chapter, we look more closely at the human resource, structural, political, and symbolic aspects of organizational change and integrate them with Kotter's model of the change process. Exhibit 18.1 summarizes the views of major issues in change that each frame offers. The human resource view focuses on needs, skills, and participation; the structural approach, on alignment and clarity; the political lens, on conflict and arenas; and the symbolic frame, on loss of meaning and the importance of creating new symbols and ways. Each mode of thought highlights a distinctive set of barriers and offers some possibilities for making change stick.

Exhibit 18.1.
Reframing Organizational Change.

Frame	Barriers to Change	Essential Strategies
Human resource	Anxiety, uncertainty; people feel incompetent and needy	Training to develop new skills; participation and involvement; psychological support
Structural	Loss of direction, clarity, and stability; confusion, chaos	Communicating, realigning, and renegotiating formal patterns and policies
Political	Disempowerment; conflict between winners and losers	Developing arenas where issues can be renegotiated and new coalitions formed
Symbolic	Loss of meaning and purpose; clinging to the past	Creating transition rituals; mourning the past, celebrating the future

CHANGE, TRAINING, AND PARTICIPATION

It might seem obvious that investment in change calls for collateral investments in training and in development of active channels for employee input. Yet countless innovations falter because managers neglect to spend time and money to develop needed knowledge and skills and to involve people throughout the process. The human resource department is too often an afterthought no one takes seriously.

At one large firm, for example, top management decided to purchase state-of-the-art technology. They expected a 50-percent cut in cycle time from customer order to delivery, leading to a decisive competitive advantage. Hours of careful analysis went into crafting the strategy. They launched the new technology with great fanfare. The CEO assured a delighted sales force it would now have a high-tech competitive edge. After the initial euphoria faded, though, the sales force realized that its old methods and skills were obsolete; years of experience were useless. Veterans felt like neophytes.

When the CEO heard that the sales force was shaky about the new technology, he said, "Then get someone in human resources to throw something together. You know, what's-her-name, the new vice president of human resources. That's why we hired her. That's her job: to put together training packages." A year later, the new technology had failed to deliver. The training never materialized. Input from the front lines never reached the right ears. The company's investment ultimately yielded a costly, inefficient process and a demoralized sales force. The window of opportunity was lost to the competition.

Management Best Sellers

Spencer Johnson, *Who Moved My Cheese? An A-Mazing Way to Deal with Change in Your Work and Your Life* (New York: Putnam, 1998)

Spencer Johnson's brief (94-page) parable about mice, men, and change topped *Businessweek*'s best-seller list for three consecutive years (1999, 2000, and 2001), making it one of the most successful management books ever.

The essence of the book is a story about a maze and its four inhabitants: two mice named Sniff and Scurry and two "little people" named Hem and Haw. Life is good because they have found a place in the maze where they reliably discover a plentiful supply of high-quality cheese. But then the quality and quantity of cheese decline, and eventually the cheese disappears altogether.

The mice, being relatively simple creatures, figure "No cheese here? Let's go look somewhere else." Sniff is very good at sniffing out new supplies, and Scurry excels in scurrying after them once they're found. Before long, they're both back in cheese heaven.

But Hem and Haw, being human, are reluctant to abandon old ways. They figure someone has made a mistake because they're entitled to get cheese where they always have. They're confident that, if they wait, the cheese will return. It doesn't. As they get hungrier, Hem and Haw gripe and complain about the unfairness of it all. Eventually, Haw decides it's time to explore and look for something better. Hem, however, insists on staying where he is until the cheese comes back.

As he searches, Haw develops a new outlook. He posts signs on the walls to express his new thinking, with messages such as "Old beliefs do not lead you to new cheese." Haw's explorations eventually reunite him with Sniff, Scurry, and the new cache of cheese. Hem continues to starve.

Cheese, as the book points out, is a metaphor for whatever you might want in life. The maze represents the context in which you work and live; it could be your family, your workplace, or your life. The basic message is simple and clear: clinging to old beliefs and habits when the world around you has changed is self-defeating. Flexibility, experimentation, and the willingness to try on new beliefs are critical to success in a fast-changing world.

The book certainly has critics, including many who believe that the story downplays the possibility that some change is wrongheaded and deserves to be resisted. But *Cheese* has far more fans, for whom its simplicity is a virtue. The parable often enables its ardent readers to see aspects of themselves and their own experience—times when, like Hem, they have hurt themselves by refusing to adapt to new circumstances.

A more favorable experience unfolded in a large hospital that invested millions of dollars in a new integrated information system. The goal was to improve patient care by making updates in clinical care and technology quickly available to everyone involved in treatment plans. Widespread involvement ensured that relevant ideas and concerns made their way into the innovative system. Terminals linked patients' bedsides to nursing stations, attending physicians, pharmacy, and other services.

To ensure that the new system would work, hospital administrators created a simulation lab. Individual representatives from all affected groups came into a room and sat at terminals. Hypothetical scenarios gave them a chance to practice and work out the kinks. Many staff members, particularly physicians, needed to improve their computer skills. Coaches were there to help. Each group became its own self-help support system. Skills and confidence improved in the training session. Relationships that formed because of extensive involvement and participation were invaluable as the new technology went into operation.

From a human resource perspective, people often have good reason to resist change. Very often, resistance is sensible because the new methods embody a management infatuation that might take the organization in the wrong direction. Even if changes are for the good, people don't like feeling anxious, voiceless, or incompetent. Changes in routine practice and protocol typically undermine existing knowledge and skills and undercut people's ability to perform with confidence and success. When asked to do something they don't understand, haven't had a voice in developing, don't know how to do, or don't believe in, people feel puzzled, anxious, and insecure. Lacking skills and confidence to implement the new ways, they resist or even engage in sabotage, awaiting the return of the status quo. Alternatively, they may comply outwardly while covertly dragging their feet. Even if they try to carry out the new ways, the results are predictably elusive. Training, psychological support, and participation increase the likelihood that people will understand and feel comfortable with the new methods.

Often overlooked in the training loop are the change agents responsible for promoting and guiding the change. Kotter and Cohen (2002) present a vivid example of how training can prepare people to communicate the rationale for a new order of things. A company moving to a team-based structure developed at the top was concerned about how workers and trade unions would react. To make sure people would understand and accept the changes, the managers went through an intensive training regimen: "Our twenty 'communicators' practiced and practiced. They learned the responses, tried them out, and did more role-plays until they felt comfortable with nearly anything that might come at them. Handling 200 issues well may sound like too much, but we did it . . . I can't believe that what we did is not applicable nearly everywhere. I think too many people wing it" (Kotter and Cohen, 2002, p. 86). Taking the time to hear people's ideas and concerns and to make sure that those involved have the talent, confidence, and expertise to carry out their new responsibilities is a requisite of successful innovation.

CHANGE AND STRUCTURAL REALIGNMENT

Involvement and training will not ensure success unless existing roles and relationships are realigned to fit the new initiative. As an example, a school system created a policy requiring principals to assume a more active role in supervising classroom instruction. Principals were trained in how to observe and counsel teachers. When they set out to apply their new skills, morale problems and complaints soon began to surface. Failure to anticipate how changes in principals' duties might affect teachers and impinge on existing agreements about authority produced pushback. Not all teachers welcomed principals' spending time in classrooms observing and suggesting ways to improve teaching. Most important, no one had asked who would handle administrative duties for which principals no longer had time. As a result, supplies were delayed and relationships between principals and parents deteriorated. By midyear, most principals returned to their administrative duties and teachers were again left with little formal feedback.

Change undermines existing structural arrangements, creating ambiguity, confusion, and distrust. People no longer know what is expected of them or what they can expect from others. Everyone may think someone else is in charge when in fact no one is. A hospital, facing rapid changes in health care, struggled with employee turnover and absenteeism, a shortage of nurses, poor communication, low staff morale, and rumors of an impending effort to organize a union. A consultant's report identified several structural problems: The members of the executive committee were confused about their roles and authority. They suspected the new hospital administrator was making key decisions behind closed doors prior to meetings. Individuals believed the administrator was making "side deals" in return for support at committee meetings. Members of the executive committee felt manipulated, baffled, and dissatisfied.

The consultant noted similar structural troubles at the nursing level. The director of nursing seemed to be taking her management cues from the new hospital administrator—with unhappy results. Nursing supervisors and head nurses bemoaned their lack of authority. Staff nurses complained about a lack of direction and openness on the part of their superiors. "Nurses were unaware of what their jobs were, whom they should report to, and how decisions were made" (McLennan, 1989, p. 211). Labor disputes, loss of accreditation, and other problems loomed until the consultant's report brought to light the structural deficiencies and helped the participants work them out.

As the school and hospital examples illustrate, when things start to shift, people become unsure of what their new duties are, how to relate to others, and who has authority to decide what. Clarity, predictability, and rationality give way to confusion, loss of control, pervasive, and a sense that politics trumps policy. To minimize such difficulties, innovators need to anticipate structural issues and work to redesign the existing architecture of roles and relationships. In some situations, reworking the structure can be done informally. In others, structural arrangements require renegotiations in a more formal setting.

In Exhibit 18.1, Reframing Organizational Change, think of the line separating Human Resource/Structural from Political/Symbolic as a "waterline." Innovation in organizations often deals only with what is above the surface. Below the waterline lurk the issues we shy away from because we consider them "distasteful" or overlook because they are too opaque to comprehend: politics and symbols. In the next sections, we delve into the depths of change that tend to torpedo even the noblest efforts to improve organizations.

Greatest Hits from Organization Studies

Hit Number 9: Richard R. Nelson and Sidney G. Winter, *An Evolutionary Theory of Economic Change* (Cambridge, MA: Harvard University Press, 1982)

How do economists think about change in organizations? Nelson and Winter argue against the neoclassical view that has dominated among economists. At its core, the neoclassical view sees both humans and organizations as rational decision makers who maximize their own interests (utility) in the face of available options and incentives. In this view, the problem of change is simple: rational maximizers will alter their behavior if their preferences change or if the environment changes the options and incentives they face. This view assumes that decision makers have complete information about themselves and their world and that they can turn on a dime.

An example of the neoclassical approach is Jensen and Meckling's paper on agency theory, discussed in Chapter 4 as Greatest Hit Number 7. Nelson and Winter are dissenters. (So are the authors of two other works on our hit list: Number 3, Cyert and March, discussed in Chapter 9, and Number 8, March and Simon, discussed in Chapter 2.) Nelson and Winter criticize maximization on the grounds that decision makers find it hard to know their options and hard to evaluate the alternatives they see. Borrowing from Darwinian concepts of evolution, Nelson and Winter develop a theory that is intended to conform more closely to how change works in practice. Three concepts are central:

- *Routine:* A regular and predictable pattern of behavior; a way of doing something that a firm uses repeatedly. This is akin to what March and Simon (1958) refer to as "programmed activity."
- *Search:* The process of assessing current options, acquiring new information, and altering routines. "Routines play the role of genes in our evolutionary theory. Search routines stochastically generate mutations" (p. 400).
- *Selection environment:* The set of considerations determining whether an organization adopts an innovation and how an organization learns about an innovation from others.

In other words, Nelson and Winter see organizations as combining ongoing routines, which produce stability and continuity, with activities for scouting new options. When an organization finds promising new alternatives, it tries them out. As with natural selection, mutations that work are kept; others are discarded. Nelson and Winter's view is distinct from the "population ecology" perspective in organization theory, even though both borrow from Darwin. Nelson and Winter see selection affecting the routines that live or die within organizations; population ecologists see selection determining which organizations survive or fail.

CHANGE AND CONFLICT

Change invariably generates conflict, a supercharged tug-of-war between innovators and traditionalists to determine winners and losers. Changes usually benefit some while neglecting or harming others. This ensures that some individuals and groups support the innovations while others oppose, sit on the fence, or become isolated. Clashes often go underground and smolder beneath the surface. Occasionally they erupt into unregulated warfare. What began with enthusiasm and an expectation of wide support is lost. A classic case in point comes from a U.S. government initiative to improve America's rural schools. Public cries for innovation consistently grab their share of media exposure. The following was one U.S. government response.

> The Experimental Schools Project provided funds for comprehensive educational changes in ten participating rural school districts. It also placed anthropologists on each site to carefully document the experiences of the districts over a five-year period.
>
> The first year's planning was free of conflict. But as plans became realities, hidden issues boiled to the surface. A Northwest school district illustrates a common pattern:
>
> > In the high school, a teacher evaluator explained the evaluation process while emphasizing the elaborate precautions to insure the raters would be unable to connect specific evaluations with specific teachers . . . Because of the tension the subject aroused, he joked that teachers could use the list to "grade" their own [forms]. He got a few laughs; he got more laughs when he encouraged teachers to read the evaluation plan by suggesting, "If you have fifteen minutes to spare and are really bored, you should read this section." [This was] followed by nervous and derisive questions and more laughter (Firestone, 1977, pp. 174–175).
>
> The superintendent got up to speak shortly afterward:
>
> > . . . he was furious. He cautioned teachers for making light of the teacher evaluators . . . Several times, he repeated that because teachers did not support the [project] they did not care for students. "Your attitude," he concluded, "is damn the children and full speed ahead!" He then rushed out of the room . . . As word of the event spread through the system, it caused reverberations in other buildings as well (ibid.).
>
> After the heated exchange, the gloves came off. Conflict between the administration and teachers intensified. The issue was broader than evaluation. Teachers were angry about the entire project. Parents became concerned. Soon the school board got involved and reduced the superintendent's authority. Rumors that he might be fired further undermined his authority.

Such scenarios are common to change initiatives. As changes emerge, different camps form around supporters, opponents, and those who prefer to wait and see. Players avoid or smooth over differences until conflict explodes in divisive battles. Coercive power, rather than legitimate authority, may determine the victor. Often, the status quo prevails and change agents lose.

From a political perspective, conflict is natural. People manage quarrels best through processes of negotiation and bargaining, in which they hammer out settlements and agreements. If ignored, disputes explode into street fights—no rules, anything goes. People get hurt, and scars linger for years.

Arenas with rules, referees, and spectators are alternatives to street fights. Arenas create opportunities to forge divisive issues into shared agreements. Through bargaining, supporters of the status quo and those bringing innovative ideas arrive at compromises. Grafting new ideas onto existing practices is essential to successful change. An astute hospital administrator said, "The board and I had to learn how to wrestle in a public forum."

Mitroff (1983) describes a drug company facing competitive pressure on its branded prescription drug from generic substitutes. Management split into three factions: One group wanted to raise the price of the drug, another wanted to lower it, and still another wanted to keep it the same but cut costs. Each group collected information, constructed models, and developed reports showing that its solution was correct. The process degenerated into a frustrating downward spiral. Mitroff intervened to get each group to identify major stakeholders and articulate assumptions about them. All agreed that the most critical stakeholders were physicians prescribing the drug. Each group had its own suppositions about how physicians would respond to a price change. But no one really knew. The three groups finally agreed to test their assumptions by implementing a price increase in selected markets. The intervention worked by convening an arena with a more productive set of rules.

Successful change requires an ability to frame issues politically, confronting conflict, building coalitions, and establishing arenas for negotiating differences into workable pacts. One insightful executive remarked: "We need to confront, not duck, and face up to disagreements and differences of opinions and conflicting objectives . . . All of us must make sure—day in and day out—that conflicts are aired and resolved before they lead to internecine war."

CHANGE AND LOSS

Symbols tap a deep reservoir of meaning, belief, and faith: national flags, the cross or crescent, fraternity or sorority pins, team mascots, wedding bands—even the symbols of companies and their products.

In a classic 1980s case, the venerable Coca-Cola company introduced New Coke. It seemed to make good business sense. America's cola wars—a battle between Coke and Pepsi—had intensified. A head-to-head taste test, the "Pepsi Challenge," was making inroads because many avowed Coke drinkers preferred Pepsi in blind tasting. Pepsi won narrowly in a Coke counterchallenge held at its corporate headquarters in Atlanta. Coca-Cola executives became even more nervous when Pepsi stunned the industry by signing Michael Jackson to a $5 million celebrity advertising campaign.

Coke struck back with one of the most startling announcements in the company's 99-year history—Old Coke was gone:

> Shortly before 11:00 AM [on Tuesday, April 23, 1985], the doors of the Vivian Beaumont Theater at Lincoln Center opened . . . The stage was aglow with red. Three huge screens, each solid red and inscribed with the company logo, rose behind the podium and a table draped in red. The lights were low; the music began: "We are. We will always be. Coca-Cola. All-American history."
>
> Robert Goizueta [CEO of Coca-Cola] came to the podium . . . [he] claimed that in the process of concocting Diet Coke, the company flavor chemists had "discovered" a new formula. And research had shown that consumers preferred this new one to old Coke (Oliver, 1986, p. 132).

The rest is history. Coke drinkers overwhelmingly rejected the new product. They felt betrayed; many were outraged:

> Duane Larson took down his collection of Coke bottles and outside of his restaurant hung a sign, "They don't make Coke anymore." . . . Dennis Overstreet of Beverly Hills hoarded 500 cases of old Coke and advertised them for $30 a case. He almost sold out . . . *San Francisco Examiner* columnist Bill Mandel called it "Coke for wimps." . . . Finally, Guy Mullins exclaimed, "When they took old Coke off the market, they violated my freedom of choice—baseball, hamburgers, Coke—they're all the fabric of America" (Morganthau, 1985, pp. 32–33).

Bottlers and Coca-Cola employees were aghast: "By June the anger and resentment of the public was disrupting the personal lives of Coke employees, from the top executives to the company secretaries. Friends and acquaintances were quick to attack, and once-proud employees now shrank from displaying to the world any association with the Coca-Cola company" (Oliver, 1986, pp. 166–167).

Coca-Cola rebounded quickly with Classic Coke. Misreading your customers is not usually a recommended route to better results, but the company's massive miscalculation led to one of the strangest serendipitous triumphs in marketing history. A brilliant stratagem, *if* anyone had planned it.

What led Coke's executives into such a quagmire? In their zeal to compete with Pepsi, Coke's executives overlooked a central tenet of the symbolic frame: The meaning of an object or event can be far more powerful than the reality. What people believe trumps the facts of taste tests. Strangely, Coke's leadership had lost touch with their product's significance to consumers. To many people, old Coke was a piece of Americana linked to cherished memories. Coke represented something far deeper than just a soft drink.

In introducing New Coke, company executives unintentionally announced the passing of a beloved American symbol, but they were not the first or last executives to misread their own symbols. In 2010, the clothing retailer Gap unveiled a new logo that was intended to signal a change in Gap's image from "classic, American design to modern, sexy, cool." Instead, the logo encountered "a chorus of caustic criticism" (Weiner, 2010) and died in a week. Two years later, the University of California crashed into a similar wall of criticism and quickly retreated after a new logo designed to be a simple, bold expression of California identity was savaged as corporate, shallow, and ugly. Symbols create meaning and generate emotional attachment (Jung, 1964). When one is destroyed or replaced, people experience feelings akin to those at the passing of a spouse, child, old friend, or pet. When a relative or close friend dies, we feel a deep sense of loss (Kübler-Ross, 1997; Marris, 2016). We harbor similar feelings when a computer operating system replaces old procedures, a logo changes after a merger, or a new leader replaces an old one. When these transitions take place in the workplace rather than in a family, feelings of loss are often denied or attributed to other causes.

Rituals of Loss

Significant change often triggers two conflicting responses. The first is to keep things as they were, to replay the past. The second is to ignore the loss and plunge into the future. Individuals or groups get stuck in denial or bog down vacillating between the two responses.

For much of the twentieth century, AT&T had a near monopoly of telephones in the United States. Then, in 1982, a federal judge forced AT&T to divest its local phone operations. Four years later, an executive commented: "Some mornings I feel like I can set the world on fire. Other mornings I can hardly get out of bed to face another day." Nurses in a hospital's intensive care unit, caught in a loss cycle for 10 years following their move from an old facility, finally determined the cause of their hard-to-pinpoint anguish. Loss is an unavoidable byproduct of improvement, particularly for those who are the target of someone else's change initiative. As change accelerates, executives and employees become mired in endless cycles of unresolved grief.

In our personal lives, tradition prescribes the pathway from loss to healing. Every culture sets forth a sequence for transition rituals following significant loss: always a collective experience allowing pain to be expressed, felt, and often juxtaposed with humor and hope. Think of Irish actor Malachy McCourt, who, as his mother lay dying, said to her distressed physician, "Don't worry, Doctor, we come from a long line of dead people" (McCourt, 2012).

In many societies, the sequence of ritual steps involves a wake, a funeral, a period of mourning, and some form of commemoration. From a symbolic perspective, ritual is an essential companion to significant change. A naval change-of-command ceremony, for example, is scripted by tradition: After a wake for the outgoing commander, the mantle of command passes to the new one in a full-dress ceremony attended by friends, relatives, officers, and sailors. The climactic moment of transition occurs as the incoming and outgoing skippers face each other at attention. The new commander salutes and says, "I relieve you, sir." The retiring commander salutes and responds, "I stand relieved." During the ceremony, sailors post the new commander's name at the unit's entrance. After a time, the old commander's face or name appears in a picture or plaque on a wall honoring previous commanders (personal communication with author, 2006).

Transition rituals initiate a sequence of steps that help people let go of the past, deal with a painful present, and move into a meaningful future. The form of these rites varies widely, but they are essential to the ability to face and transcend loss. Otherwise, people vacillate between clinging to the old and rushing to the future. An effective ritual helps them let go of old ways and embrace a new beginning.

Releasing a Negative Past

Many find it hard to understand how villains, negative stories, and tragedies can hold a culture together, but downbeat symbols hold sway when people have nothing more positive to bond them together. In such cultural voids, griping can become the predominant ritual. Evil heroes emerge as popular icons.

In one example, new owners acquired a newspaper mired in a negative past. Letting go of old tyrants and wounds was essential to a new, more positive beginning. The new owners sensed they needed to create something dramatic to help people let go of their historic attachment to pessimism. They invited all employees to an unusual event. Employees arrived to find a room filled with black balloons. Pictures of reviled managers were affixed to the lid of an open coffin positioned prominently in the front. The startled employees silently took their places. The new CEO opened the ceremony: "We are assembled today to say farewell to the former owners of this newspaper. But it only seems fitting that we should say a few words about them before they leave us forever."

On cue, without prompting or rehearsal, individuals rose from their seats, came forward, and, one by one, grabbed a picture. Each then briefly described life under the sway of "the bastards," tore up the person's photograph, and threw it into the coffin. When all the likenesses were gone, a group of New Orleans style jazz musicians filed in playing a mournful dirge. Coffin bearers marched the coffin outside. Employees followed and released the black balloons into the sky. A buffet lunch followed, festooned by balloons with the colors of the new company logo.

The CEO admitted later, "What a risk. I was scared to death. It came off without a hitch and the atmosphere is now completely different. People are talking and laughing together. Circulation has improved. So has morale. Who would have 'thunk' it?"

CHANGE STRATEGY

The frames offer a checklist of issues for change agents to recognize and respond to. How can they be combined in an integrated model? How does the change process move through time? John Kotter, an influential student of leadership and change, has studied both successful and unsuccessful change efforts in organizations around the world. In his book *The Heart of Change* (2002, written with Dan S. Cohen), he summarizes what he has learned. His basic message is very much like ours. Too many change initiatives fail because they rely too much on "data gathering, analysis, report writing, and presentations" (p. 8) instead of a more creative approach aimed at grabbing the "feelings that motivate useful action" (p. 8). In other words, change agents fail when they rely mostly on reason and structure while neglecting human, political, and symbolic elements.

Kotter describes eight stages that he repeatedly found in successful change initiatives:

1. Creating a sense of urgency
2. Pulling together a guiding team with the needed skills, credibility, connections, and authority to move things along

3. Creating an uplifting vision and strategy
4. Communicating the vision and strategy through a combination of words, deeds, and symbols
5. Removing obstacles, or empowering people to move ahead
6. Producing visible symbols of progress through short-term victories
7. Sticking with the process and refusing to quit when things get tough
8. Nurturing and shaping a new culture to support the emerging innovative ways

Kotter's stages depict a dynamic process moving through time, though not necessarily in linear sequence. In practice, stages overlap, and change agents sometimes need to cycle back to earlier phases.

Combining Kotter's stages with the four frames generates the model presented in Exhibit 18.2. The table lists each of Kotter's stages and illustrates actions that change agents might take. Not every frame is essential to each stage, but all are critical to overall success.

Consider, for example, Kotter's first stage: developing a sense of urgency. Strategies from the human resource, political, and symbolic strategies all contribute. Symbolically, leaders can construct a persuasive story by painting a picture of the current challenge or crisis and emphasizing why failure to act would be catastrophic. Human resource techniques of skill building, participation, and open meetings can help to get the story out and gauge audience reaction. Behind the scenes, leaders can meet with key players, assess their interests, and negotiate or use power as necessary to get people on board.

As another example, Kotter's fifth step calls for removing obstacles and empowering people to move forward. Structurally, that means identifying rules, roles, procedures, and patterns that block progress and then working to realign the system. Meanwhile, the human resource frame counsels training, support, and resources to enable people to master new behaviors. Symbolically, a few "public hangings" (for example, firing, demoting, or exiling prominent opponents) could reinforce the message. Public celebrations could honor successes and herald a new beginning.

Exhibit 18.2 is an illustration, not an exhaustive plan. Every situation and change effort is unique. Creative change agents can use the ideas to stimulate thinking and spur imagination as they develop an approach that fits local circumstances.

Exhibit 18.2.
Reframing Kotter's Change Stages.

Kotter's Stage of Change	Structural frame	Human resource frame	Political frame	Symbolic frame
1. Sense of urgency		Involve people throughout organization; solicit input	Network with key players; use power base	Tell a compelling story
2. Guiding team	Develop coordination strategy	Do team-building for guiding team	Stack team with credible, influential members	Put chief executive and organizational heroes on team
3. Uplifting vision and strategy	Build implementation plan		Map political terrain; manage conflict; develop agenda	Craft hopeful vision of future rooted in organization's history
4. Communicate vision and strategy through words, deeds, and symbols	Create structures to support change process	Hold meetings to communicate direction, get feedback	Create arenas; build alliances; defuse opposition	Visible leadership involvement; kickoff ceremonies
5. Remove obstacles and empower people to move forward	Remove or alter structures and procedures that support the old ways	Provide training, resources, support		Public demotion or discharge of opponents
6. Early wins	Plan for short-term victories		Invest resources and power to ensure early wins	Communicate and celebrate early signs of progress
7. Keep going when going gets tough	Keep people on plan			Hold revival meetings
8. New culture to support new ways	Align structure to new culture	Create a "culture" team; broad involvement in developing culture		Mourn the past; celebrate heroes of the revolution; share stories of the journey

CONCLUSION

Innovation inevitably generates four issues. First, it affects individuals' ability to feel effective, valued, and in control. Without support, training, and a chance to participate in the process, people become anchored to the past, blocking forward motion. Second, change disrupts existing patterns of roles and relationships, producing confusion and uncertainty. Structural patterns need revamping and realignment to support the new direction. Third, change creates conflict between winners and losers—those who benefit from the new direction and those who do not. Conflict requires creation of arenas where players negotiate the issues and redraw the political map. Finally, change creates loss of meaning for recipients of the change. Transition rituals, mourning the past, and celebrating the future help people let go of old attachments and embrace new ways of doing things. Kotter's model of successful change includes eight stages. Integrated with the frames, it offers an orchestrated, integrated design for responding to needs for learning, realignment, negotiation, and grieving.

Reframing Ethics and Spirit

*For what shall it profit a man, if he shall gain
the whole world, and lose his own soul?*

—Mark 8:36 (King James Version)

Starbucks chairman Howard Schultz asked that question in a memo to his
company's leadership team in 2007, wondering if the stores had lost the
soul of the past. But for many business leaders around the globe, soul has no
place in business, and ethics comes down to the slippery concept of "the
morals of the marketplace"—meaning "Anything for a buck," or "If other
people do it, it must be okay."

That was how German electronics giant Siemens approached the question, "Should we
pay someone a bribe if that will help us bring in business?" Under the Foreign Corrupt
Practices Act, it has been illegal since 1977 for U.S. businesses to pay bribes to government
officials, but in Germany bribes were a legal and deductible business expense until 1999.
Like many other German firms, Siemens routinely paid bribes in foreign countries whenever
that seemed to be the local custom. When German law changed in 1999, Siemens changed
too—not by stopping bribes, but by finding creative ways to hide them.

It wasn't easy to hide more than $1 billion in slush money spread around the globe: $5
million to the prime minister's son in Bangladesh, $12.7 million to officials in Nigeria
(government contracts), $14 million in China (medical equipment), $16 million in Venezuela
(urban rail lines), $20 million in Israel (power plants), and $40 million in Argentina (a $1
billion contract to produce national identity cards). The $1.7 million to Saddam Hussein and

his cronies was modest by comparison. But Siemens leadership was resourceful in hiding the money trail. They stashed funds in hard-to-trace offshore bank accounts and hired local "consultants" with ties to government officials whose job was to put cash into the right hands. To heap camouflage atop the camouflage, Siemens established a toothless monitoring process—which was supposed to ensure that no bribes were being paid—and even ordered Siemens managers who oversaw the bribery to sign pledges attesting that they had *not done* what they and their bosses knew they *had done* (Schubert and Miller, 2008).

Reinhard Siekaczek, a former midlevel Siemens executive, was not surprised when German police woke him up early one November morning in 2006. He and his colleagues at Siemens had occasionally joked that they might someday share a jail cell and a deck of cards. Siekaczek had been assigned to move millions of dollars into front companies and offshore bank accounts to support the bribery program. He got the job because of his integrity and loyalty to Siemens—he was honest, the kind of man who could be trusted not to take a cut for himself. He knew he was breaking the law, and he suspected that the police would show up sooner or later. He even kept personal copies of financial records to ensure that when he went down, he wouldn't be alone. Siemens ultimately wound up paying $1.6 billion in fines and at least another $1 billion to clean up the mess. Several executives went to jail (Schubert and Miller, 2008). But the biggest cost for Siemens was the undermining of its image as a company that customers could trust to obey the law and act with integrity.

Siemens' story is far from unique. The sordid history of Walmart's Mexican subsidiary, as recounted in the *New York Times*, makes Siemens look almost respectable by comparison: "Wal-Mart de Mexico was not the reluctant victim of a corrupt culture that insisted on bribes as the cost of doing business. Nor did it pay bribes merely to speed up routine approvals. Rather, Wal-Mart de Mexico was an aggressive and creative corrupter, offering large payoffs to get what the law otherwise prohibited. It used bribes to subvert democratic governance—public votes, open debates, transparent procedures. It used bribes to circumvent regulatory safeguards that protect Mexican citizens from unsafe construction. It used bribes to outflank rivals" (Barstow and Xanic von Bertrag, 2012, p. 1).

As at Siemens, the bribes went well beyond pocket change—eight bribes totaling $341,000 to get permits for a Sam's Club in Mexico City and nine bribes totaling $765,000 to build a distribution center in an environmentally sensitive flood basin north of the city. Was it a case of rogue executives ignoring the parent company's ethical stance? Would the executives back at headquarters in Bentonville, Arkansas, have tolerated such blatantly unethical and illegal action? Maybe not, but after a lawyer in the Mexican subsidiary briefed top executives on the bribes, Walmart first investigated—and then squelched the investigation: "They did so even though their investigators had found a wealth of evidence supporting the lawyer's allegations.

The decision meant authorities were not notified. It also meant basic questions about the nature, extent and impact of Wal-Mart de Mexico's conduct were never asked, much less answered" (Barstow and Xanic von Bertrag, 2012, p. 1).

As we write in 2017 amid ongoing investigations and shareholder lawsuits, the ultimate consequences of this case are still unknown, but Walmart has altered its compliance practices and spent hundreds of millions of dollars in trying to clean up the mess. Over the years, similar corporate ethics imbroglios (including the Volkswagen and Wells Fargo scandals discussed in Chapter 1) have recurred around the world. What can managers and organizations do about this abysmal state of moral lapse? We argue in this chapter that ethics must reside in *soul*, a sense of bedrock character that anchors core beliefs and values. We discuss why soul is important and how it sustains spiritual conviction and ethical behavior. We then present a four-frame approach to leadership ethics.

SOUL AND SPIRIT IN ORGANIZATIONS

Medtronic states its core purpose as serving patients rather than shareholders. Its CEO from 1989 to 2001, Bill George, was an outspoken advocate of authentic leadership and a vocal critic of short-term thinking. His position on Medtronic's mission was clear: "Medtronic is not in business to maximize shareholder value. We are in business to maximize value to the patients we serve." This principle was rooted in Medtronic's original mission statement, developed by founder Earl Bakken in the 1960s. To reinforce the message, Bakken created the "Mission and Medallion Ceremony." He met personally with every new employee, reviewed the mission, shared stories of how it played out in practice, and gave the employee a bronze medallion with an image of a patient rising from the operating table and walking into a full life. The tradition continued even as Medtronic grew much larger. During his term as CEO Bill George conducted medallion ceremonies for thousands of employees around the world—sometimes at 2 AM for night shift workers.

Do such noble sentiments make a difference in practice? George thought so. Shortly after he promoted a talented executive to head Medtronic's European operations, George learned that the individual was maintaining a secret account in a Swiss bank, apparently for making payments to doctors. At Siemens, this might have been just a line item, and the executive argued that American values shouldn't be imposed in Europe. Not American values, George responded, but Medtronic values, and these were the same everywhere. Though it was painful, he asked the executive to resign immediately, released details to regulators in both the United States and Europe, and publicized the incident so that people inside and outside of the company clearly understood Medtronic's unyielding ethical position.

How did this squeaky-clean approach work out for shareholders? During George's tenure, Medtronic's share price increased at a rate of 36 percent per year, and its market capitalization rose from $1 billion to $60 billion. Other fast-growth companies in the same period, such as Enron and WorldCom, also shot up very fast—only to crash into bankruptcy. Medtronic, in contrast, had an orderly CEO transition and kept growing.

Some people have such strong ethical convictions that it matters little where they work, but most of us are at greater risk—like Reinhard Siekaczek, the honest Siemens executive. His integrity and company loyalty led to a conviction for corruption in one of the biggest ethics scandals in German business history. We are social beings, attuned to cues and expectations from our workplace and our colleagues about what to do and not to do. In recent years one organization after another has lost its soul in the race for innovation, growth, and a rising share price. A company that loses track of any redeeming moral purpose doesn't provide credible ethical guardrails for its employees. The result is often a spiritual and financial disaster.

Many would scoff at the notion that organizations possess soul, but there is growing evidence that a bedrock sense of values and identity is a critical element in long-term success. A dictionary definition of *soul* uses terms such as "animating force," "immaterial essence," and "spiritual nature." For an organization, group, or family, soul can also be viewed as a resolute sense of character, a deep confidence about who we are, what we care about, and what we deeply believe in. Siemens lost it and had to struggle to regain it. Walmart is still struggling. Medtronics deploys a chief ethics and compliance officer and mandatory training in corporate integrity to buttress continuing commitment to its core values of customer focus, candor, trust, respect, courage, and accountability.

Why should an organization—a company, a school, or a public agency—be concerned about soul? Many organizations and management writers discount or scoff at the idea. As an example, two best sellers on strategy, Treacy and Wiersema's *The Discipline of Market Leaders* (1995) and Hamel and Prahalad's *Competing for the Future* (1994), linked the enormous success of Southwest Airlines to its strategic prowess. But founder Herb Kelleher offered a very different explanation for what made Southwest work, one that featured people, humor, love, and soul. "Simply put, Kelleher 'cherishes and respects' his employees, and his 'love' is returned in what he calls 'a spontaneous, voluntary overflowing of emotion'" (Farkas and De Backer, 1996, p. 87).

At Southwest, soul and the "Southwest spirit" are shared throughout the company. Kelleher claimed that the most important group in the company was the "Culture Committee," a 70-person cross-section of employees established to perpetuate the company's values and spirit. His charge to the committee was to "carry the spiritual message of Southwest Airlines" (Farkas and De Backer, 1996, p. 93). There were plenty of skeptics, and a competing airline executive grumbled, "Southwest runs on Herb's bullshit" (Petzinger, 1995, p. 284). But, as we write in 2017, Southwest is the only airline in the industry that has turned a profit for 44 consecutive years.

A growing number of successful leaders embrace a philosophy much like Kelleher's. Ben Cohen, cofounder of the ice cream company Ben & Jerry's Homemade, observes: "When you give love, you receive love. I maintain that there is a spiritual dimension to business just as there is to the lives of individuals" (Levering and Moskowitz, 1993, p. 47). Howard Schultz of Starbucks echoes those sentiments in his emphasis on culture and heart.

Evidence suggests that tapping a deeper level of human energy pays off. Collins and Porras (1994) and De Geus (1995) both found that a central characteristic of organizations that succeeded over the long haul was a core ideology emphasizing "more than profits" and offering "guidance and inspiration to people inside the company" (Collins and Porras, 1994, pp. 48, 88). When they are authentic and part of everyday life, such core ideologies—love at Southwest, maximizing value to patients at Medtronics—give a company soul.

Soul and ethics are inextricably intertwined. Recent decades have regularly produced highly public scandals of major corporations engaging in unethical, if not illegal, behavior. It happened in the 1980s, a decade of remarkable greed and corruption in business. It happened again with the spate of scandals in 2001 and 2002 (Enron, WorldCom, Tyco, and the like), and in the subprime mortgage mess of 2007–2008. In recent years, the rogues' gallery included Toyota (cooking the books), FIFA (bribery and fraud in connection with marketing rights to soccer games), Volkswagen (cheating on emissions tests), Wells Fargo (fake sales of "solutions") and two health care giants that put profits ahead of patients: Johnson & Johnson (dubious marketing and defective products) and Hospital Corporation of America (HCA) (inducing patients to undergo unnecessary and dangerous cardiac procedures).

Efforts to do something about the ethical void in management have ebbed and flowed as dishonor comes and goes. One proposed remedy is a greater emphasis on ethics in business schools and training programs. A second proposed remedy is corporate ethics statements. A third is stronger legal and regulatory muscle, such as the United Nations Convention Against Corruption (signed by more than 140 nations), and "SOX"—the controversial Sarbanes-Oxley Act of 2002[1]—which mandated a variety of measures to combat fraud and increase corporate transparency.

These are important and useful initiatives, but they only skim the surface. Solomon calls for a deeper "Aristotelian ethic:"

> There is too little sense of business as itself enjoyable (the main virtue of the "game" metaphor), that business is not a matter of vulgar self-interest but of

vital community interest, that the virtues on which one prides oneself in personal life are essentially the same as those essential to good business—honesty, dependability, courage, loyalty, integrity. Aristotle's central ethical concept, accordingly, is a unified, all-embracing notion of "happiness" (or, more accurately, eudaimonia, perhaps better translated as "flourishing" or "doing well"). The point is to view one's life as a whole and not separate the personal and the public or professional, or duty and pleasure (1993, p. 105).

Solomon settled on the term *Aristotelian* because it makes no pretense of imparting the latest cutting-edge theory or technique of management. Rather, he reminds us of a perspective and debate reaching back to ancient times. The central motive is not to commission a new wave of experts and seminars or to kick off one more downsizing bloodbath; rather, "It is to emphasize the importance of continuity and stability, clearness of vision and constancy of purpose, corporate loyalty and individual integrity" (1993, p. 104). Solomon reminds us that ethics and soul are essential for living a good life as well as managing a fulfilling organization. Since the beginning, humanity's philosophical and spiritual traditions have proffered wisdom to guide our search for better ways to accomplish both.

We have emphasized the four frames as cognitive lenses for understanding and tools for influencing collective endeavors. Our focus has been the heads and hands of leaders. Both are vitally important. But so are hearts and souls. The frames also carry implications for creating ethical communities and for reviving the moral virtues of leadership. Exhibit 19.1 summarizes our view.

Exhibit 19.1.
Reframing Ethics.

Frame	Metaphor	Organizational Ethic	Leadership Contribution
Structural	Factory	Excellence	Authorship
Human resource	Extended family	Caring	Love
Political	Jungle	Justice	Power
Symbolic	Temple	Faith, Belief	Significance

The Factory: Excellence and Authorship

One of our oldest images of organizations is that of factories engaged in a production process. Raw materials (steel, peanuts, or five-year-olds) come in the door and leave as finished products (refrigerators, peanut butter, or educated graduates). The ethical imperative of the factory is excellence: ensuring that work is done as effectively and efficiently as possible to produce high-quality yields. Since the 1982 publication of Peters and Waterman's famous book, almost everyone has been searching for excellence, although flawed products and mediocre services keep reminding us that the hunt does not always bring home the quarry.

One source of disappointment is that excellence requires more than pious sermons from top management; it demands commitment and autonomy at all levels of an enterprise. How do leaders foster such dedication? As we've said before, "Leading is giving. Leadership is an ethic, a gift of oneself" (Bolman and Deal, 2011, p. 122). Critical for creating and maintaining excellence is the gift of authorship:

> Authorship turns the classic organizational pyramid on its side and provides space within boundaries. Leaders increase their influence and build more productive organizations. Workers experience the satisfactions of creativity, craftsmanship, and a job well done. Authorship transcends the traditional adversarial relationship in which superiors try to increase control while subordinates resist them at every turn. Trusting people to solve problems generates higher levels of motivation and better solutions. The leader's responsibility is to create conditions that promote authorship. Individuals need to see their work as meaningful and worthwhile, to feel personally accountable for the consequences of their efforts, and to get feedback that lets them know the results (Bolman and Deal, 2011, pp. 128–129).

Google provides a contemporary example of the power of authorship. Among the many ways that Google supports both the expression and development of talent is its 70/20/10 time allocation model—10 percent of an engineer's time is allocated for "innovation, creativity, and freedom to think," and 20 percent is for "personal development that will ultimately benefit the company." In terms of revenue per employee, Google's staff are among the most productive on the planet. Internet retailer Zappos has a different approach. Zappos' core value #3 is "create fun and a little weirdness," followed by #4, "be adventurous, creative, and open-minded." Does Zappos take those values seriously? Maybe, but they definitely take them playfully. Where else do employees in the finance department do a weekly parade around the office performing random acts of kindness? How many companies encourage their people to create video musicals and skits that can be posted on the website? Zappos believes that a culture of fun and family underpins core value #1, "deliver WOW through service." The business results support their faith.

The Family: Caring and Love

Caring—one person's compassion and concern for another—is both the primary purpose and the ethical glue that holds a family together. Parents care for children and, eventually, children care for their parents. A compassionate family or community requires servant-leaders concerned with the needs and wishes of members and stakeholders. This creates a challenging obligation for leaders to understand and to provide stewardship of the collective well being. The gift of the servant-leader is love.

Love is largely absent from most modern corporations. Most managers would never use the word in any context more profound than their feelings about food, family, films, or games. They shy away from love's deeper meanings, fearing both its power and its risks. Caring begins with knowing; it requires listening, understanding, and accepting. It progresses through a deepening sense of appreciation, respect, and ultimately love. Love is a willingness to reach out and open one's heart. An open heart is vulnerable. Confronting vulnerability allows us to drop our mask, meet heart to heart, and be present for one another. We experience a sense of unity and delight in those voluntary, human exchanges that mold "the soul of community" (Whitmyer, 1993, p. 81).

At Southwest Airlines, they talk openly about love. Former president Colleen Barrett reminisced, "Love is a word that isn't used often in corporate America, but we used it at Southwest from the beginning." The word *love* is woven into the culture. They fly out of Love Field in Dallas; their symbol on the New York Stock Exchange is LUV; the employee newsletter is called *Luv Lines*; and their twentieth anniversary slogan was "Twenty Years of Loving You" (Levering and Moskowitz, 1993). They hold an annual "Heroes of the Heart" ceremony to honor members of the Southwest family who have gone above and beyond even Southwest's high call of duty. There are, of course, ups and downs in any family, and the airline industry certainly experiences both. Through life's peaks and valleys, love holds people—both employees and passengers—together in a caring community.

The Jungle: Justice and Power

Woody Allen captured the political frame's competitive, predator-prey imagery succinctly: "The lion and the calf shall lie down together, but the calf won't get much sleep" (Allen, 1986, p. 28). As the metaphor suggests, the jungle is a politically charged environment of conflict and pursuit of self-interest. Politics and politicians are routinely viewed as objects of scorn—often for good reason. Their behavior tends to prompt the question: Is there any ethical consideration associated with political action? We believe there is: the commitment to justice. In a world of competing interests and scarce resources, people are continually compelled to make trade-offs. No one can give everyone everything they want, but it is possible to adhere to a value of fairness in making decisions about who gets what. Solomon (1993, p. 231) sees justice as the ultimate virtue in corporations, because the perception that employees, customers, and investors are all getting their due is the glue that holds everyone together.

Justice is never easy to define, and disagreement about its application is inevitable. The key gift that leaders can offer in pursuit of justice is sharing power. People with a voice in key decisions are far more likely to feel a sense of fairness than those with none. Leaders who hoard power produce powerless organizations. People stripped of power look for ways to fight back: sabotage, passive resistance, withdrawal, or angry militancy. Giving power liberates energy for more productive use. If people have a sense of efficacy and an ability to influence their world, they are more likely to direct their energy and intelligence toward making a contribution rather than making trouble. The gift of power enrolls people in working toward a common cause. It also creates difficult choice points. If leaders clutch power too tightly, they activate old patterns of antagonism. But if they cave in and say yes to anything, they put an organization's mission at risk.

During the Reagan administration, House Speaker "Tip" O'Neill was a constant thorn in the side of the president, but they carved out a mutually just agreement: They would fight ferociously for their independent interests but stay civil and find fairness wherever possible. Their rule: "After six o'clock, we're friends, whatever divisiveness the political battle has produced during working hours." Both men gave each other the gift of power. During one acrimonious public debate between the two, Reagan reportedly whispered, "Tip, can we pretend it's six o'clock?" (Neuman, 2004, p. 1).

Power and authorship are related; autonomy, space, and freedom are important in both. Still, there is an important distinction between the two. Artists, authors, and craftspeople can experience authorship even working alone. Power, in contrast, is meaningful only in relation to others. It is the capacity to wield influence and get things to happen on a broader scale. Authorship without power is isolating and splintering; power without authorship can be dysfunctional and oppressive.

The gift of power is important at multiple levels. As individuals, people want power to control their immediate work environment and the factors that impinge on them directly. Many traditional workplaces still suffocate their employees with time clocks, rigid rules, and authoritarian bosses. A global challenge at the group level is responding to ethnic, racial, and gender diversity. Gallos, Ramsey, and their colleagues get to the heart of the complexity of this issue:

> Institutional, structural, and systemic issues are very difficult for members of dominant groups to understand. Systems are most often designed by dominant group members to meet their own needs. It is then difficult to see the ways in which our institutions and structures systematically exclude others who are not "like us." It is hard to see and question what we have always taken for granted and painful to confront personal complicity in maintaining the status quo. Privilege enables us to remain unaware of institutional and social forces and their impact (1997, p. 215).

Justice requires that leaders systematically enhance the power of excluded or vulnerable groups—ensuring access to decision making, creating internal advocacy groups, building diversity into information and incentive systems, and strengthening career opportunities (Cox, 1994; Gallos and Ramsey, 1997; Morrison, 1992). All this happens only with a rock-solid commitment from top management, the one condition that Morrison (1992) found to be universal in organizations that led in responding to diversity.

Justice also has important implications for the increasingly urgent question of "sustainability:" How long can a production or business process last before it collapses as a result of the resource depletion or environmental damage it produces? Decisions about sustainability inevitably involve trade-offs among the interests of constituencies that differ in role, place, and time. How do we balance our company's profitability against damage to the environment, or current concerns against those of future generations? Organizations with a commitment to justice will take these questions seriously and look for ways to engage and empower diverse stakeholders in making choices.

The Temple: Faith and Significance

An organization, like a temple, can be seen as a hallowed place, an expression of human aspirations and beliefs, a monument to faith in human possibility. A temple is a gathering place for a community of people with shared traditions, values, and beliefs. Members of a community may be diverse in many ways (age, background, economic status, personal interests), but they are tied together by shared faith and bonded by a sanctified spiritual covenant. In work organizations, faith is strengthened if individuals feel the organization is characterized by excellence, caring, and justice. Above all, people must believe that the organization is doing something worth doing—a calling that adds something of value to the world, making a difference. Significance is partly about the work itself but even more about how the work is embraced. This point is made by an old story about three stonemasons giving an account of their work. The first said he was "cutting stone." The second said that he was "building a cathedral." The third said simply that he was "serving God."

Temples need spiritual leaders. This does not mean promoting religion or a particular theology; rather, it means bringing a genuine concern for the human spirit. The dictionary defines spirit as "the intelligent or immaterial part of man," "the animating or vital principle in living things," and "the moral nature of humanity." Spiritual leaders help people find meaning and faith in work and help them answer fundamental questions that have confronted humans of every time and place: Who am I as an individual? Who are we as a people? What is the purpose of my life, of our collective existence? What ethical principles should we follow? What legacy will we leave?

Spiritual leaders offer the gift of significance, rooted in confidence that the work is precious, that devotion and loyalty to a beloved institution can offer hard-to-emulate intangible rewards. Work is exhilarating and joyful at its best, arduous, frustrating, and exhausting in less happy moments. Many adults embark on their careers with enthusiasm, confidence, and a desire to make a contribution. Some never lose that spark, but many do. They become frustrated with sterile or toxic working conditions and discouraged by how hard it is to make a difference, or even to know if they have made one. Tracy Kidder puts it well in writing about teachers: "Good teachers put snags in the river of children passing by, and over time, they redirect hundreds of lives. There is an innocence that conspires to hold humanity together, and it is made up of people who can never fully know the good they have done" (Kidder, 1989, p. 313). The gift of significance helps people sustain their faith rather than burn out or retire from a meaningless job and end up wondering if their work made any difference at all.

Significance is built through the use of many expressive and symbolic forms: rituals, ceremonies, stories, and music. An organization without a rich symbolic life grows empty and barren. The magic of special occasions is vital in building significance into collective life. Moments of ecstasy are parentheses that mark life's major passages. Without ritual and ceremony, transition remains incomplete, a clutter of comings and goings; "life becomes an endless set of Wednesdays" (Campbell, 1983, p. 5).

When ritual and ceremony are authentic and attuned, they fire the imagination, evoke insight, and touch the heart. Ceremony weaves past, present, and future into life's ongoing tapestry. Ritual helps us face and comprehend life's everyday shocks, triumphs, and mysteries. Both help us experience the unseen web of significance that ties a community together. When inauthentic, such occasions become meaningless, repetitious, and alienating—wasting our time, disconnecting us from work, and splintering us from one another. "Community must become more than just gathering the troops, telling the stories, and remembering things past. Community must also be rooted in values that do not fail, values that go beyond the self-aggrandizement of human leaders" (Griffin, 1993, p. 178).

Stories give flesh to shared values and sacred beliefs. Everyday life in organizations brings many heartwarming moments, dramatic encounters, and rib-splitting, humorous screwups. Transformed into stories, these events fill an organization's treasure chest with lore and legend. Told and retold, they draw people together and connect them with the significance of their work.

Music captures and expresses life's deeper meaning. When people sing or dance together, they bond to one another and experience emotional connections otherwise hard to express. The late Harry Quadracci, chief executive officer of the printing company Quadgraphics, convened employees once a year for an annual gathering. A management chorus sang the year's themes. Quadracci himself voiced the company philosophy in a solo serenade.

Max DePree, famed both as both a business leader and an author of elegant books on leadership, is clear about the role of faith in business: "Being faithful is more important than being successful. Corporations can and should have a redemptive purpose. We need to weigh the pragmatic in the clarifying light of the moral. We must understand that reaching our potential is more important than reaching our goals" (1989, p. 69). Spiritual leaders have the responsibility of sustaining and encouraging their own faith and recalling others to the faith when they have wandered away.

CONCLUSION

Ethics ultimately must be rooted in soul: an organization's commitment to deeply rooted identity, beliefs, and values. Each frame offers a perspective on the ethical responsibilities of organizations and the moral authority of leaders. Every organization needs to evolve for itself a profound sense of its own ethical and spiritual core. The frames offer spiritual guidelines for the quest.

Signs are everywhere that institutions around the globe suffer from crises of meaning and moral authority. Rapid change, high mobility, globalization, and racial, ideological, and ethnic conflict tear at the fabric of community. The most important responsibility of leaders is not to answer every question or get every decision right. They cannot escape their responsibility to track budgets, motivate people, respond to political pressures, and attend to culture, but they serve a deeper and more enduring role if they are models and catalysts for values like excellence, caring, justice, and faith.

Note

1. The Sarbanes-Oxley Act is officially the Public Company Accounting Reform and Investor Protection Act of 2002.

Bringing It All Together
Change and Leadership in Action

*We can't always control the music life plays for us
but we can choose how we dance to it.*

—Anonymous

Life's daily challenges rarely arrive clearly labeled or neatly packaged. Instead, they come upon us in a murky, turbulent, and unrelenting flood. The art of reframing uses knowledge and intuition to read the flow and to find sensible and effective ways to channel the incoming tide.

In this chapter, we illustrate the process by following a new principal through his first week in a deeply troubled urban high school. Had this been a corporation in crisis, a struggling hospital, or an embattled public agency, the basic leadership issues would have been much the same. Our protagonist is familiar with the frames and reframing. How might he use what he knows to figure out what's going on? What strategies can he mull over? What will he do?

Read the case thoughtfully.* Ask yourself what you think is going on and what options you would consider. Then compare your reflections with his.

---

* From Harvard Business School case study, copyright © 1974 by the President and Fellows of Harvard College. Harvard Business Case #9-474-183. This case was prepared by J. Gabarro as the basis for class discussion rather than to illustrate either effective or ineffective handling of an administrative situation. Reprinted by permission of Harvard Business School.

ROBERT F. KENNEDY HIGH SCHOOL

On July 15, David King became principal of Robert F. Kennedy High School, the newest of six high schools in Great Ridge, Illinois. The school had opened two years earlier amid national acclaim as one of the first schools in the country designed and built on the "house system" concept. Kennedy High was organized into four "houses," each with 300 students, 18 faculty, and a housemaster. Each house was in a separate building connected to the "core facilities"—cafeteria, nurse's room, guidance offices, boys' and girls' gyms, offices, shops, and auditorium—and other houses by an enclosed outside passageway. Each had its own entrance, classrooms, toilets, conference rooms, and housemaster's office. The building was widely admired for its beauty and functionality and had won several national architectural awards.

Hailed as a major innovation in urban education, Kennedy High was featured during its first year in a documentary on a Chicago television station. The school opened with a carefully selected staff of teachers, many chosen from other Great Ridge schools. At least a dozen were specially recruited from out of state. King knew that his faculty included graduates from several elite East Coast and West Coast schools, such as Yale, Princeton, and Stanford, as well as several of the very best Midwestern schools. He knew, too, that the racial mix of students had been carefully balanced so that blacks, whites, and Latinos each made up a third of the student body. And King also knew—perhaps better than its planners—that Kennedy's students were drawn from the toughest and poorest areas of the city.

Despite careful and elaborate preparations, Kennedy High School was in serious trouble by the time King arrived. It had been racked by violence the preceding year—closed twice by student disturbances and once by a teacher walkout. It was also widely reported (although King did not know whether this was true) that achievement scores of its ninth- and tenth-grade students had declined during the preceding two years, and no significant improvement could be seen in the scores of the eleventh and twelfth graders' tests. So far, Kennedy High School had fallen far short of its planners' hopes and expectations.

David King

David King was born and raised in Great Ridge, Illinois. His father was one of the city's first black principals. King knew the city and its school system well. After two years of military service, King followed in his father's footsteps by going to Great Ridge State Teachers College, where he received B.Ed and M.Ed degrees. King taught English and coached in a predominantly black middle school for several years, until he was asked to become the school's assistant principal. He had been in that post for five years when he was asked to take over a large middle school of 900 pupils—believed at the time to be the most "difficult" middle school in the city. While there, King gained a citywide reputation as a gifted and popular administrator. He was credited with changing the worst middle school in the system into one of the best. He had been very effective in building community support, recruiting new faculty, and raising academic standards. He was also credited with turning out basketball and baseball teams that had won state and county championships.

The Great Ridge superintendent made it clear that King had been selected for the Kennedy job over several more senior candidates because of his ability to handle tough situations. The superintendent also told him that he would need every bit of skill and luck he could muster. King knew of the formidable credentials of Jack Weis, his predecessor at Kennedy High. Weis, a white man, had been the superintendent of a small local township school system before becoming Kennedy's first principal. He had written one book on the house system concept and another on inner-city education. Weis held a PhD from the University of Chicago and a divinity degree from Harvard. Yet despite his impressive background and ability, Weis had resigned in disillusionment. He was described by many as a "broken man." King remembered seeing the physical change in Weis over that two-year period. Weis's appearance had become progressively more fatigued and strained until he developed what appeared to be permanent dark rings under his eyes and a perpetual stoop. King remembered how he had pitied the man and wondered how Weis could find the job worth the obvious personal toll it was taking on him.

History of the School

The First Year

The school's troubles began to manifest themselves in its first year. Rumors of conflicts between the housemasters and the six subject-area department heads spread throughout the system by the middle of the year. The conflicts stemmed from differences in interpretations of curriculum policy on required learning and course content. In response, Weis had instituted a "free market" policy: subject-area department heads were supposed to convince housemasters which course to offer, and housemasters were supposed to convince department heads which teachers should be assigned to their houses. Many felt that this policy exacerbated the conflicts.

To add to the tension, a teacher was assaulted in her classroom in February of that first school year. The beating frightened many of the staff, particularly older teachers. A week later, eight teachers asked Weis to hire security guards. This request precipitated a debate in the faculty about the desirability of guards in the school. One group felt that the guards would instill a sense of safety and promote a better learning climate. The other faction felt that the presence of guards in the school would be repressive and would destroy the sense of community and trust that was developing. Weis refused the request for security guards because he believed they would symbolize everything the school was trying to change. In April, a second teacher was robbed and beaten in her classroom after school hours, and the debate was rekindled. This time, a group of Latino parents threatened to boycott the school unless better security measures were implemented. Again, Weis refused the request for security guards.

The Second Year

The school's second year was even more troubled than the first. Financial cutbacks ordered during the summer prevented Weis from replacing eight teachers who had resigned. As it was no longer possible for each house to staff all of its courses with its own faculty, Weis instituted a "flexible staffing" policy. Some teachers were asked to teach a course outside their assigned house, and students in the eleventh and twelfth grades were able to take elective and required courses in other houses. One of the housemasters, Chauncey Carver, publicly attacked the new policy as a step toward destroying the house system. In a letter to the *Great Ridge Times*, he accused the board of education of trying to subvert the house concept by cutting back funds.

The debate over the flexible staffing policy was heightened when two of the other housemasters joined a group of faculty and department heads in opposing Carver's criticisms. This group argued that interhouse cross-registration should be encouraged, because the 15 to 18 teachers in each house could never offer the variety of courses that the schoolwide faculty of 65 to 70 could.

Further expansion of the flexible staffing policy was halted, however, because of difficulties in scheduling fall classes. Errors cropped up in the master schedule developed during the preceding summer. Scheduling problems persisted until November, when the vice principal responsible for developing the schedule resigned. Burtram Perkins, a Kennedy housemaster who had formerly planned the schedule at Central High, assumed the function on top of his duties as housemaster. Scheduling took most of Perkins's time until February.

Security again became an issue when three sophomores were assaulted because they refused to give up their lunch money during a shakedown. The assailants were believed to be outsiders. Several teachers approached Weis and asked him to request the board of education to provide security guards. Again Weis declined, but he asked Bill Smith, a vice principal at the school, to secure all doors except for the entrances to each of the four houses, the main entrance to the school, and the cafeteria. This move seemed to reduce the number of outsiders roaming through the school.

In May of the second year, a fight in the cafeteria spread and resulted in considerable damage, including broken classroom windows and desks. The disturbance was severe enough for Weis to close the school. A number of teachers and students reported that outsiders were involved in the fight and in damaging the classrooms. Several students were taken to the hospital for minor injuries, but all were released. A similar disturbance occurred two weeks later, and again the school was closed. Against Weis's advice, the board of education ordered a temporary detail of municipal police to the school. In protest to the assignment of police, 30 of Kennedy's 68 teachers staged a walkout, joined by over half the student body. The police detail was removed, and an agreement was worked out by an ad hoc subcommittee composed of board members and informal representatives of teachers who were for and against a police detail. The compromise called for the temporary stationing of a police cruiser near the school.

King's First Week at Kennedy High

King arrived at Kennedy High on Monday, July 15, and spent most of his first week individually interviewing key administrators (see box). On Friday, he held a meeting with all administrators and department heads. King's purpose in these meetings was to familiarize himself with the school, its problems, and its key people.

ADMINISTRATIVE ORGANIZATION OF ROBERT F. KENNEDY HIGH SCHOOL

Principal: David King, 42 (black) B.Ed., M.Ed., Great Ridge State Teachers College

Vice principal: William Smith, 44 (black) B.Ed., Breakwater State College; M.Ed., Great Ridge State Teachers College

Vice principal: Vacant

Housemaster, A House: Burtram Perkins, 47 (black) B.S., M.Ed., University of Illinois

Housemaster, B House: Frank Czepak, 36 (white) B.S., University of Illinois; M.Ed., Great Ridge State Teachers College

Housemaster, C House: Chauncey Carver, 32 (black) A.B., Wesleyan University; B.F.A., Pratt Institute; M.A.T., Yale University

Housemaster, D House: John Bonavota, 26 (white) B.Ed., Great Ridge State Teachers College; M.Ed., Ohio State University

Assistant to the principal: Vacant

Assistant to the principal for community affairs: Vacant

King's first interview was with Bill Smith, a vice principal. Smith was black and had worked as a counselor and then vice principal of a middle school before coming to Kennedy. King knew Smith's reputation as a tough disciplinarian who was very much disliked by many of the younger faculty and students. King had also heard from several teachers whose judgment he respected that Smith had been instrumental in keeping the school from "blowing apart" the preceding year. It became clear early in the interview that Smith felt that more stringent steps were needed to keep outsiders from wandering into the buildings. Smith urged King to consider locking all the school's 30 doors except for the front entrance so that everyone would enter and leave through one set of doors. Smith also told him that many of the teachers and pupils were scared and that "no learning will ever begin to take place until we make it so people don't have to be afraid anymore." At the end of the interview, Smith said he had been approached by a nearby school system to become its director of counseling but that he had not yet made up his mind. He said he was committed enough to Kennedy High that he did not want to leave, but his decision depended on how hopeful he felt about the school's future.

As King talked with others, he discovered that the "door question" was highly controversial within the faculty and that feelings ran high on both sides of the issue. Two housemasters in particular—Chauncey Carver, who was black, and Frank Czepak, who was white—were strongly against closing the house entrances. The two men felt such an action would symbolically reduce house "autonomy" and the feeling of distinctness that was a central aspect of the house concept.

Carver, master of C House, was particularly vehement on this issue and on his opposition to allowing students in one house to take classes in another house. Carver contended that the flexible staffing program had nearly destroyed the house concept. He threatened to resign if King intended to expand cross-house enrollment. Carver also complained about what he described as "interference" from department heads that undermined his teachers' autonomy.

Carver appeared to be an outstanding housemaster, from everything King had heard about him—even from his many enemies. Carver had an abrasive personality but seemed to have the best-operating house in the school and was well liked by most of his teachers and pupils. His program appeared to be the most innovative, but it was also the one most frequently attacked by department heads for lacking substance and ignoring requirements in the system's curriculum guide. Even with these criticisms, King imagined how much easier running the school would be if he had four housemasters like Chauncey Carver.

During his interviews with the other three housemasters, King discovered that they all felt infringed upon by the department heads, but only Carver and Czepak were strongly against locking the doors. The other two housemasters actively favored cross-house course enrollments. King's fourth interview was with Burtram Perkins, also a housemaster. Perkins, mentioned earlier, was a black man in his late forties who had served as assistant to the principal of Central High before coming to Kennedy. Perkins spent most of the interview discussing how schedule pressures could be relieved. Perkins was currently developing the schedule for the coming school year until a vice principal could be appointed to perform that job (Kennedy High had allocations for two vice principals and two assistants in addition to the housemasters).

Two bits of information concerning Perkins came to King during his first week at the school. The first was that several teachers were circulating a letter requesting Perkins's removal as a housemaster. They felt that he could not control the house or direct the faculty. This surprised King because he had heard that Perkins was widely respected within the faculty and had earned a reputation for supporting high academic standards and for working tirelessly with new teachers. As King inquired further, he discovered that Perkins was genuinely liked but was also widely acknowledged as a poor housemaster. The second piece of information concerned how Perkins's house compared with the others. Although students had been randomly assigned to each house, students in Perkins's house had the highest absence rate and the greatest number of disciplinary problems. Smith had told him that Perkins's dropout rate the preceding year was three times that of the next highest house.

While King was in the process of interviewing his staff, he was called on by David Crimmins, chairman of the history department. Crimmins was a native of Great Ridge, white, and in his late forties. Though scheduled for an appointment the following week, he had asked King whether he could see him immediately. Crimmins had heard about the letter asking for Perkins's removal and wanted to present the other side. He became very emotional, saying that Perkins was viewed by many of the teachers and department chairmen as the only housemaster trying to maintain high academic standards; his transfer would be seen as a blow to those concerned with quality education. Crimmins also described in detail Perkins's devotion and commitment to the school. He emphasized that Perkins was the only administrator with the ability to straighten out the schedule, which he had done in addition to all his other duties. As Crimmins departed, he threatened that if Perkins were transferred, he would write a letter to the regional accreditation council decrying the level to which standards had sunk at Kennedy. King assured Crimmins that such a drastic measure was unnecessary and offered assurance that a cooperative resolution would be found. King knew that Kennedy High faced an accreditation review the following April and did not wish to complicate the process unnecessarily.

Within 20 minutes of Crimmins's departure, King was visited by Tim Shea, a young white teacher. He said he had heard that Crimmins had come in to see King. Shea identified himself as one of the teachers who had organized the movement to get rid of Perkins. He said that he liked and admired Perkins because of the man's devotion to the school but that Perkins's house was so disorganized and that discipline there was so bad that it was nearly impossible to do any good teaching. Shea added, "It's a shame to lock the school up when stronger leadership is all that's needed."

King's impressions of his administrators generally matched what he had heard before arriving at the school. Carver seemed to be a very bright, innovative, and charismatic leader whose mere presence generated excitement. Czepak came across as a highly competent though not very imaginative administrator who had earned the respect of his faculty and students. Housemaster John Bonavota, age 26, seemed smart and earnest but unseasoned and unsure of himself. King felt that with a little guidance and training, Bonavota might have the greatest promise of all; at the moment, however, the young housemaster seemed confused and somewhat overwhelmed. Perkins impressed King as a sincere and devoted person with a good mind for administrative details but an incapacity for leadership.

King knew that he had the opportunity to make several administrative appointments because of the three vacancies that existed. Indeed, should Smith resign as vice principal, King could fill both vice principal positions. He also knew that his recommendations for these positions would carry a great deal of weight with the central office. The only constraint King felt was the need to achieve some kind of racial balance among the Kennedy administrative group. With his own appointment as principal, black administrators out-numbered white administrators two to one, and Kennedy did not have a single Latino administrator, even though a third of its pupils were Hispanic.

The Friday Afternoon Meeting

In contrast to the individual interviews, King was surprised to find how quiet and conflict-free these same people seemed in the staff meeting he called on Friday. He was amazed at how slow, polite, and friendly the conversation was among people who had so vehemently expressed negative opinions of each other in private. After about 45 minutes of discussion about the upcoming accreditation review, King broached the subject of housemaster–department head relations. There was silence until Czepak made a joke about the uselessness of discussing the topic. King probed further by asking if everyone was happy with the current practices. Crimmins suggested that the topic might be better discussed in a smaller group. Everyone seemed to agree—except for Betsy Dula, a white woman in her late twenties who chaired the English department. She said that one of the problems with the school was that no one was willing to tackle tough issues until they exploded. She added that relations between housemasters and department heads were terrible, and that made her job very difficult. She then attacked Chauncey Carver for impeding her evaluation of a nontenured teacher in Carver's house. The two argued for several minutes about the teacher and the quality of an experimental sophomore English course the teacher was offering. Finally, Carver, by now quite angry, coldly warned Dula that he would "break her neck" if she stepped into his house again. King intervened in an attempt to cool both their tempers, and the meeting ended shortly thereafter.

The following morning, Dula called King at home and told him that unless Carver publicly apologized for his threat, she would file a grievance with the teachers' union and take it to court if necessary. King assured Dula that he would talk with Carver on Monday. King then called Eleanor Debbs, a Kennedy High math teacher he had known well for many years, whose judgment he respected. Debbs was a close friend of both Carver and Dula and was also vice president of the city's teachers' union. Debbs said that the two were longtime adversaries but both were excellent professionals.

She also reported that Dula would be a formidable opponent and could muster considerable support among the faculty. Debbs, who was black, feared that a confrontation between Dula and Carver might stoke racial tensions in the school, even though both Dula and Carver were generally popular with students of all races. Debbs strongly urged King not to let the matter drop. She also told him that she had overheard Bill Smith, the vice principal, say at a party the night before that he felt King didn't have the stomach or the forcefulness to survive at Kennedy. Smith said that the only reason he was staying was that he did not expect King to last the year, in which case Smith would be in a good position to be appointed principal.

· · ·

David King inherited a job that had broken his predecessor and could destroy him as well. His new staff greeted him with a jumble of problems, demands, maneuvers, and threats. His first staff meeting began with an undercurrent of tension and ended in outright hostility.

Sooner or later, you may encounter a chaotic situation like this that leaves you feeling confused and overwhelmed. Nothing makes any sense, and good options are hard to find. Can King avoid disaster?

There is one potential bright spot. As the case ends, King is talking to Eleanor Debbs on a Saturday morning. She is a supportive colleague. He also has some slack—the rest of the weekend—to regroup. Where should he begin? We suggest that he start by actively reflecting and reframing. A straightforward way to do that is to examine the situation one frame at a time, asking two simple questions: From this perspective, what's going on?

And what options does this view suggest? This reflective process deserves ample time and careful thought. It requires "going to the balcony" (see Heifetz, 1994) to get a panoramic view of the scene below. Ideally, King would include one or more other people—a valued mentor, principals in other schools, close friends, his spouse—for alternative perceptions in pinpointing the problem and developing a course of action. We present a streamlined version of the kind of thinking that David King might entertain.

STRUCTURAL ISSUES AND OPTIONS

King sits down at his kitchen table with a cup of coffee, a pen, a fresh yellow pad, and his laptop computer. He starts to review structural issues at Kennedy High. He recalls the "people-blaming" approach (Chapter 2), in which individuals are blamed for everything that goes wrong. He smiles and nods his head. That's it! Everyone at Kennedy High School is blaming everyone else. He recalls the lesson of the structural frame: We blame individuals when the real problems are systemic.

So what structural problems does Kennedy High have? King thinks about the two cornerstones of structure: differentiation and integration. He sees immediately that Kennedy High School has an ample division of labor but weak overall coordination. He scribbles on his pad, trying to sketch the school's organization chart. He realizes that the school has a matrix structure—teachers have an ill-defined dual reporting relationship to both department chairs and housemasters. He remembers the downside of the matrix structure: It's built for conflict (teachers wonder which authority they're supposed to answer to, and administrators bicker about who's in charge). The school has no integrating devices to link the approaches of housemasters like Chauncey Carver (who wants a coherent, effective program for his house) with those of department chairs like Betsy Dula (who is concerned about the schoolwide English curriculum and adherence to district guidelines). It's not just personalities; the structure is pushing Carver and Dula toward each other's throats. Goals, roles, and responsibilities are all vaguely defined. Nor is there a structural protocol (say, a task force or a standing committee) in place to diagnose and resolve such problems. If King had been in the job longer, he might have been able to rely more heavily on the authority of the principal's office. It helps that he's been authorized by the superintendent to fix the school. But so far, he's seen little evidence that the Kennedy High staff is endorsing his say-so with much enthusiasm.

King's musings are making sense, but it isn't clear what to do about the structural gaps. Is there any way to get the school back under control when it is teetering on the edge of irrational chaos? It doesn't help that his authority is shaky. He is having trouble controlling the staff, and they are having the same problem with the students. The school is an underbounded system screaming for structure and boundaries.

King notes, ruefully, that he made things worse in the Friday meeting. "I knew how these people felt about one another," he thinks. "Why did I push them to talk about something they were trying to avoid? We hadn't done any homework. I didn't give them a clear purpose for the conversation. I didn't set any ground rules for how to talk about the issue. When it started to heat up, I just watched. Why didn't I step in before it exploded?" He stops and shakes his head. "Live and learn, I guess. But I learned these lessons a long time ago—they served me well in my last school. In the confusion, I forgot that even good people can't function very well without some structure. What did I do the last time around?"

King begins to brainstorm options. One possibility is responsibility charting: Bring people together to define tasks and responsibilities. It has worked before. Would it work here? He reviews the language of responsibility charting, a technique for clarifying roles and relationships. The acronym CAIRO (Consulted, Approves, Informed, Responsible, and Omitted) helps him remember. *Who's responsible? Who has to approve? Who needs to be consulted? Who should be informed? Who doesn't need to be in the loop, and so can be omitted?*

As he applies these questions to Kennedy High, the overlap between the housemasters and the department chairs is an obvious problem. Without a clear definition of roles and relationships, conflict and confusion are inevitable. He wonders about a total overhaul of the structure: "Is the house system viable in its current form? If not, is it fixable? Maybe we need a process to look at the structure: What if I chaired a small task force to examine it and develop recommendations? I could put Dula and Carver on it—let them see firsthand what's causing their conflict. Get them involved in working out a new design. Give each authority over specific areas. Develop some policies and procedures."

It is clear from even a few minutes of reflection that Kennedy High School has major structural problems that have to be addressed. But what to do about the immediate crisis between Dula and Carver? The structure helped create the problem in the first place, and fixing it might prevent dustups like this in the future. But Dula's demand for an immediate apology didn't sound like something a rational approach would easily fix. King is ready to try another angle. He turns to the human resource frame for counsel.

HUMAN RESOURCE ISSUES AND OPTIONS

"Ironic," King muses. "The original idea behind the school was to respond better to students. Break down the big, bureaucratic high school. Make the house a community, a family even, where people know and care about each other. But it's drifted off course. Everyone's marooned on the bottom of Maslow's needs hierarchy: No one even feels safe. Until they do, they'll never focus on caring. The problem isn't personalities. Everyone's frustrated because no one is getting personal or professional needs met. Not me, not Carver, not Dula. We're all so frustrated, we don't realize everyone else is in the same boat."

With the Dula–Carver mess staring him in the face, King shifts his thoughts from individual needs to interpersonal relationships. Tense relationships everywhere. People talking only to people who agree with them. Why? How to get a handle on it? He remembers reading, "Lurking in Model I is the core assumption that an organization is a dangerous place where you have to look out for yourself or someone else will do you in."

"That's us!" he says. "Too bad they don't give a prize for the most Model I school in America. We'd win hands down. Everything here is win–lose. Nothing is discussed openly, and if it is, people just attack each other. If anything goes wrong, we blame other people and try to straighten *them* out. They get defensive, which proves we were right. But we never test our assumptions. We don't ask questions. We just harbor suspicions and wait for people to prove us right. Then we hit them over the head. We've got to find better ways to deal with one another.

"How do you get better people management?" King wonders. "Successful organizations start with a clear human resource philosophy. We don't have one, but it might help. Invest in people? We've got good people. They're paid pretty well. They've got job security. We're probably okay there. Job enrichment? Jobs here are plenty challenging. Empowerment? That's a big problem. Everyone claims to be powerless, yet they expect me to fix everything—the way they want it fixed. Is there something we could do to get people to own more of the problem? Convince them we've got to work together to make things better? The trouble is, if we go that way, people may not have the emotional intelligence or the group skills they'd need. Staff development? With all the conflict, mediation skills might be a place to start." Conflict. Politics. Politics is normal in an organization. He knows it's true. "But we don't seem to have a midpoint between getting along and getting even."

POLITICAL ISSUES AND OPTIONS

King reluctantly shifts to a political lens. He knows it's relevant, but he's always hated political games. Still, he's never seen a school with more intense political strife. His old school is beginning to seem tame by comparison; he tackled some things head-on there. Kennedy is a lot more volatile, with a history of explosions. Threats and coercion seem to be the power tactics of choice. But that's not an option he's comfortable with.

Things might get even more vicious if he tackles the conflict openly. He mulls over the basic elements of the political frame: enduring differences, scarce resources, conflict, and power. "Bingo! We've got 'em all. We've got factions for and against the house concept. Housemasters want to run their houses and guard their turf. Department chairs want to run the faculty and expand their territory. One group wants to close the doors and bring in guards. Another wants open doors and no guards. We've got race issues simmering under the surface. No Latino administrators. This Carver–Dula thing could blow up the school. Black male says he'll break white female's neck. A recipe for disaster. We need some damage control.

"Then we've got all those outside folks looking over our shoulder. Parents worry about safety. The school board doesn't trust us. They want higher test scores. The media are looking for a story. Accreditation is coming in the spring. Could we get people thinking about the enemies outside instead of inside? A common devil might pull people together—for a while anyway.

"Scarce resources? They're getting scarcer. We lost 10 percent of our teachers—that got us into the flexible staffing mess. Housemasters and department chairs are fighting over turf. Bill Smith wants my job. It's a war zone. We need some kind of peace settlement. But who can lead the diplomatic effort? Almost no one is neutral. Eleanor Debbs would respond to the call. People respect her. But she's not an administrator."

King's attention turns to the issue of power. "Power can be used to do people in. That's what we're doing right now. But you can also use power to get things done. That's the constructive side of politics. Too bad no one here seems to have a clue about it. If I'm going to be a constructive politician, what can I do? First, I need an agenda. Without that, I'm dead in the water. Basically, I want everyone working in tandem to make the school better for kids. Most people could rally behind that. I also need a strategy. Networking—I need good relationships with key folks like Smith, Carver, and Dula. The interviews were a good place to start. I learned a lot about who wants what. The Friday meeting was a mistake, a collision of special interests with no common ground. It's going to take some horse trading. We need a deal the housemasters and the department chairs can both buy into. And I need some allies—badly."

He smiles as he remembers all the times he's railed against analysis paralysis. But he feels he's getting somewhere. He turns to a clean sheet on his pad. "Let's lay this thing out," he says to the quiet, empty kitchen. Across the top he labels three columns: allies, fence-sitters, and opponents. At the top left, he writes "High power." At the bottom left, "Low power." Over the next half-hour, he creates a political map of Kennedy High School, arranging individuals and groups in terms of their interests and their power. When he finishes, he winces. Too many powerful opponents. Too few supportive allies. A bunch of fence-sitters waiting to choose sides. He begins to think about how to build a coalition and reshape the school's political map.

"No doubt about it," King says, "I have to get on top of the political mess. Otherwise they'll carry me out the same way they did Weis. But it's a little depressing. Where's the ray of hope?" He smiles. He's ready to think about symbols and culture. "Where's Dr. King when I need him?" He recalls the famous words from 1963: "For even though we face the difficulties of today and tomorrow, I still have a dream." What happened to Kennedy High's dream?

He decides to take a break, get some fresh air. He takes stock of his surroundings. Moonlit night. Crowded sidewalks. Young and old, poor and affluent, black, white, and Latino. Merchandise pours out of stores into sidewalk bins: clothes, toys, electronic gear, fruit, vegetables—you name it. It makes him feel better. King runs into some students from his old school. They're at Kennedy now. "We're tellin' our friends we got a *good* principal now," they say. He thanks them, hoping they're right.

SYMBOLIC ISSUES AND OPTIONS

Back to the kitchen and the yellow pad. Buoyed by the walk and another cup of coffee, he reviews the school's history. "Interesting," he observes. "That's one of the problems: The school's too new to have many roots or traditions. What we have is mostly bad. We've got a hodgepodge of individual histories people brought from someplace else. Deep down, everyone is telling a different story. Maybe that's why Carver is so attached to his house and Dula to her English department. There's nothing schoolwide for people to bond to. Just little pockets of meaning."

He starts to think about symbols that might create common ground. Robert Kennedy, the school's namesake. He has only a vague recollection of Bobby Kennedy's speeches. Anything there? He remembers the man. What was he like? What did he stand for? What were the founders thinking when they chose his name for the school? What signals were they trying to send? Any unifying theme? A search engine takes him to Ted Kennedy's eulogy for his brother, where he quoted one of Bobby's favorite sayings: "Some people see things as they are, and say why? I dream things that never were, and say why not?"

"That's the kind of thinking we need here," King realizes. "We need to get above all the factions and divisions. We need a banner or icon that we all can rally around. Celebrate Kennedy's legacy now? Can we have a ceremony in the midst of warring chaos? It could backfire, make things worse. But it seems the school never had any special occasions—even at the start. No rituals, no traditions. The only stories are downbeat ones. The high road might work. We've got to get back to the values that launched the school in the first place. Rekindle the spark. What if I pull some people together? Start from scratch—this time paying more attention to symbols and ceremony? We need some glue to weld this thing together."

Meaning. Faith. He rolls the words around in his mind. Haunting images. Ideas start to tumble out. "We're supposed to be pioneers, but somehow we got lost. A lighthouse where the bulb burned out. Not a beacon anymore. We're on the rocks ourselves. A dream became a nightmare. People's faith is pretty shaky. There's a schism—folks splitting into two different faiths. Like a holy war between the church of the one true house system and the temple of academic excellence. We need something to pull both sides together. Why did people join up in the first place? How can we get them to sign up again—renew their vows?" He smiles at the religious overtones in his thoughts. His mother and father would be proud.

He catches himself. "We're not a church; we're a school. But maybe the symbolic concept bridges the gap. Organization as temple. A lot of it is about meaning. What's Kennedy High School really about? Who are we? What happened to our spirit? What's our soul, our values? That's what folks are fighting over! Deep down, we're split over two versions of what we stand for. Department chairs promoting excellence. Housemasters pushing for caring. We need both. That was the original dream. Bring excellence and caring together. We'll never get either if we're always at war with one another."

He thinks about why he got into public education in the first place. It was his calling. Why? Growing up in a racist society was tough, but his father had it a lot tougher—he was a principal when it was something black men didn't do. King had always admired his dad's courage and discipline. More than anything, he remembered his father's passion about education. The man was a real champion for kids—high standards, deep compassion. Growing up with this man as a role model, there was never much question in King's mind. As far back as he could remember, he'd wanted to be a principal too. It was a way to give to the community and to help young people who really needed it. To give everyone a chance.

In the midst of a firefight, it was easy to forget his mission. It felt good to remember.

A FOUR-FRAME APPROACH

Before going further, King senses that it is a good time for a review. Over yet another cup of coffee, he goes back over his notes. They strike him as stream of consciousness, with some good stuff and a little whining and self-pity. He smiles as he remembers himself in graduate school, fighting against all that theory. "Don't think; do! Be a leader!" "Avoid analysis paralysis." Now, here he is, thinking, reflecting, struggling to pull things together. In a strange way, it feels natural.

Exhibit 20.1.
Reframing Robert F. Kennedy High School.

Frame	What's Going On?	What Options Are Available?
Structural	Weak integration—goals, roles, responsibilities, linkages unclear	Responsibility charting
	Ill-defined matrix structure	Task force on structure
	Underbounded	Establish his authority as principal
Human resource	Basic needs not met (safety and so on)	Improve safety, security
	Poor conflict management	Training in communication, conflict management
	People feel disempowered	Participation
		Teaming
Political	House-department conflict	Create arenas for negotiation
	Doors and guards issue	Damage control
	Carver–Dula and racial tension	Unite against outside threats
	Outside constituents—parents, board, media, and so on	Build coalitions, negotiate
Symbolic	No shared symbols (history, ceremony, ritual)	Hoist a banner (common symbol: RFK?)
	Loss of faith, religious schism	Develop symbols (meld excellence and caring?)
	Lack of identity (What is RFK's soul?)	Ceremony, stories
		Leadership gifts

He organizes his ideas into a chart (see Exhibit 20.1). He's starting to feel better now. The picture is coming into focus. He feels he has a better sense of what he's up against. It's reassuring to see he has options. There are plenty of pitfalls, but some real possibilities. He knows he can't do everything at once; he needs to set priorities. He needs a plan of action, an agenda anchored in basic values. Where to begin? Soul? Values? He has to find a rallying point somewhere.

He has already embraced two values: excellence and caring. He turns his attention to leadership as gift giving. "I've mostly been listening and learning. Now what? What are my gifts? If I want excellence, the gift I have to offer is authorship. That's what people want. They don't want to be told what to do. They want to put their signature on this place. Make a contribution. They're fighting so hard because they care so much. That's what brought them to Kennedy in the first place. They wanted to be a part of something better. Create something special. They all want to do a good job. How can I help them do it without tripping over or maiming each other?

"What about caring? The leadership gift is love. No one's getting much of that around here." (He smiles as a song fragment comes to mind: "Looking for love in all the wrong places.") "I've been waiting for someone else to show caring and compassion," he realizes. "I've been holding back."

The thought leads him to pick up the phone. He calls Betsy Dula. She is out, but he leaves a message on the machine: "Betsy, Dave King. I've been thinking a lot about our conversation. One thing I want you to know is that I'm glad you're part of the Kennedy High team. You bring a lot, and I sure hope I can count on your help. We can't do it without you. We need to finish what we started out to do. I care. I know you do, too. I'll see you Monday."

He senses he's on a roll. But it's one thing to leave a message on someone's machine and another to deliver it in person—particularly if you don't know how receptive the other person will be. *She may think I'm just shining on, faking it.*

On his next call, to Chauncey Carver, King takes a deep breath. He gets through immediately. "Chauncey? Dave King. Sorry to bother you at home, but Betsy Dula called me this morning. She's upset about what you said yesterday. Particularly the part about breaking her neck."

King listens patiently as Carver makes it clear that he was only defending himself against an unprovoked public attack. "Chauncey, I hear you . . . Yeah, I know you're mad. So is she." King listens patiently through another one-sided tirade. "Yes, Chauncey, I understand. But look, you're a key to making this school work. I know how much you care about your house and the school. The word on the street is clear—you're a terrific housemaster. You know it, too. I need your help, man. If this thing with Betsy blows up and goes public, what's it going to do to the school? . . . You're right, we don't need it. Think about it. Betsy's pushing hard for an apology."

He feared that the word *apology* might set Carver off again, and it does. This is getting tough. He reminds himself why he made the call. He shifts back into listening mode. After several minutes of venting, Chauncey pauses. Softly, King tries to make his point.

"Chauncey, I'm not telling you what to do. I'm just asking you to think about what's best for the school. Let me know what you come up with. Can we meet first thing Monday? . . . Thanks for your time. Have a good rest of the weekend."

King puts down the phone. Things are still tense, but he hopes he's made a start. Carver is a loose cannon with a short fuse. But he's also smart, and he cares about the school. Get him thinking, King figures, and he'll see the risks in his comment to Dula. Push him too hard, and he'll fight like a cornered badger. With some space, he might just figure out something on his own. The gift of authorship. Would Chauncey bite? Or would the problem wind up back on the principal's doorstep—with prejudice?

After the conversation with Chauncey, King needs another breather. He goes back to his yellow pad, which has become something of a security blanket. More than that, it's helping him find his way to the balcony. It has given him a better view of the situation. He's made notes about excellence and caring. Is he making progress or just musing? It doesn't matter. He feels better; the situation seems to be getting clearer and his options more promising.

King's thoughts move on to justice. "Do people feel the school is fair?" he asks. "I'm not hearing a lot of complaints about injustice. But it wouldn't take much to set off another war. The Chauncey–Betsy thing is scary. A man physically threatening a woman could send a terrible message. There's too much male violence in the community already. Make it a black man and a white woman, and it gets worse. The fact that Chauncey and I are black men is good and bad: It makes for a better chance of getting Chauncey's help—brothers united and all that. But it could be devastating if people think I'm siding with Chauncey against Betsy— sisters in defiance. It's like being on a tightrope: One false step and I'm history. And the school, too. All the more reason to encourage Chauncey and Betsy to work this out. If I could get the two together, what a symbol of unity that would be! Maybe just what we need. A positive step at least."

Finally, King thinks about the ethic of faith and the gift of significance. Symbols again, revisited in a deeper way. "How did Kennedy High go from high hopes to no hope in two years? How do we rekindle the original faith? How do we recapture the dream that launched the school? Well," he sighs, "I've been around this track before. My last school was a snake pit when I got there. Not as bad as Kennedy, but still pretty awful. We turned that one around, and I learned some things in the process—including be patient, but hang tough. It's gonna be hard. But maybe fun, too. And it *will* happen. That's why I took this job in the first place. So what am I moaning about? I knew what I was getting into. It's just that knowing it in my head is one thing. Feeling it in my gut is another."

By Sunday night, King has pages of notes. They help—but not as much as his conversation with himself in an empty kitchen. Going to the gallery, getting a fresh look, reflecting instead of just fretting. The inner dialogue has led to new conversations with others, on a deeper level. He's made a lot of phone calls, talked to almost every administrator in the building. A lot of them have been surprised—a principal who calls on the weekend isn't business as usual.

He is making headway. He needs to hear from Betsy but has some volunteers for a task force on structural issues. He's done some relationship building. A second call to Chauncey to commend him for devotion to the mission. A deeper connection. Crediting Frank Czepak for excellent counsel, even if the principal isn't smart enough to pay attention—a frank admission.

Some has been pure politics. Negotiating a deal with Bill Smith: "I *could* help you, Bill, next time the district needs a principal, but right now I need your help. You scratch my back, I'll scratch yours." Gently persuading Burt Perkins that he was needed much more for scheduling than running a house, and that moving to assistant principal would be a step up. A call to Dave Crimmins to tell him Perkins has decided to make a change. An encouraging conversation with Luz Hernandez, a stalwart in his previous school. She might be willing to come to Kennedy High as a housemaster. Planting seeds with everyone about ways to resolve the door problem.

Above all, King has worked on creating symbolic glue, renewing the hopes and dreams people felt at the time the school was founded. A cohesive group pulling together for a common purpose: a school everyone can feel proud of. His to-do list is ambitious. But at least he has one. A month and a half until the first day of school and a lot to accomplish. He isn't sure what the future will bring, but he feels a little more hope in the air. The knot in his stomach is mostly gone. So are the images of being carried off like his predecessor, a broken man with a shattered career.

The phone rings. It's Betsy Dula. She's been away for the weekend but wants to thank King for his message. It was important to know he cared, she told him. "By the way," she says, "Chauncey Carver called me. Said he felt bad about Friday. Told me he'd lost his temper and said some things he didn't really mean. He invited me to breakfast tomorrow."

"Are you going?" King asks, as nonchalantly as possible. He holds his breath, thinking, *If she declines, we could be back to square one.*

"Yes," she says. "Even a phone call is a big step for Chauncey. He's a proud and stubborn man. But we're both professionals. It's worth a try."

A sigh of relief. "I agree. One more question," King says. "When you came to the school, you knew it wouldn't be easy. Why did you sign up for this in the first place?"

She is silent for a long time. He can almost hear her thinking. "I love English and I love kids," she says. "And I want kids to love English."

"And now?" he asks.

"Can't we get past all the bickering and fighting? That's not why we launched this noble experiment. Let's get back to why we're here. Work together to make this a good school for our kids. They really need us."

"Maybe even a great school we can all be proud of?" he asks.

"Sounds even better," she says. Maybe she doesn't grasp what he means. But they are closer to being on the same page. It will take time, but they can work it out.

At the end of a very busy weekend, David King is still a long way from solving all the problems of Kennedy High. "But," he tells himself, "I made it through the valley of confusion, and I'm feeling more like my old self. The picture of what I'm up against is a lot clearer. I'm seeing a lot more possibilities than I was seeing on Friday. In fact, I've got some exciting things to try. Some may work; some may not. But deep down, I think I know what's going on. And I know which way is west. We're now moving roughly in that direction."

He can't wait for Monday morning.

CONCLUSION: THE REFRAMING PROCESS

A different David King would probably raise other questions and see other options. Reframing, like management and leadership, is more art than science. Every artist brings a distinctive vision and produces unique works. King's reframing process necessarily builds on a lifetime of skill, knowledge, intuition, and wisdom. Reframing guides him in accessing what he already knows. It helps him feel less confused and overwhelmed by the doubt and disorder around him. A cluttered jumble of impressions and experiences gradually evolves into a manageable image. His reflections help him see that he is far from helpless—he has a rich array of actions to choose from. He has also rediscovered a very old truth: Reflection is a spiritual discipline, much like meditation or prayer. A path to faith and heart. He knows the road ahead is still long and difficult. There is no guarantee of success. But he feels more confident and more energized than when he started. He is starting to dream things that never were and to say, "Why not?"

EPILOGUE
ARTISTRY, CHOICE, AND LEADERSHIP

The wheel is come full circle.

—William Shakespeare, *King Lear*

In 1983 we published *Modern Approaches to Understanding and Managing Organizations.* We laid out for the first time the four frames as a way to better understand organizations and leadership. Much has happened in the years since. Prominent corporations have disappeared; new ones have arisen to take their place. We wrote the first book using pen on paper and a primitive early personal computer—in a time before cell phones, the Internet, or female CEOs in Fortune 500 companies.

Since then, we have gained more confidence in our framework. Thousands of readers and students throughout the world have told us how much our ideas helped them master the leadership challenges they faced. A large body of research has confirmed the validity and power of the frames. We've worked with organizations in the United States and around the world—corporations, professional and military organizations, schools, colleges, churches, hospitals, unions, and many others. The combination of research evidence and our own experience has confirmed our initial hope that the frames help leaders expand their capacity to see more of what's going on. Then, and only then, can they figure out what to do amid the complexities of organizational life, particularly the subtle, often-mystifying political and symbolic realms.

We hope *Reframing Organizations* continues to inspire inventive management and wise leadership. Both managers and leaders require high levels of personal artistry if they are to respond to today's challenges, ambiguities, and paradoxes. They need a sense of choice and

419

personal freedom to find new patterns and possibilities in everyday life at work. They need versatile thinking that fosters flexibility in action. They need capacity to act inconsistently when uniformity fails, diplomatically when emotions are raw, intuitively when reason flags, politically in the face of vocal parochial self-interests, and playfully when fixating on task and purpose backfires.

Leaders face a paradox: how to maintain integrity and mission without making organizations rigid and intractable. They walk a fine line between rigidity and spinelessness. Rigidity saps energy, stifles initiative, misdirects resources, and leads ultimately to catastrophe. This pattern can be seen graphically in the decline of great corporations (such as Circuit City, Digital Equipment, Lehman Brothers, Arthur Andersen, Pan American Airlines, Polaroid, and TWA) and the disappearance of many others into corporate mergers. We see it in the escalation of chronic ethnic violence and terrorism. In a world of "permanent white water" (Vaill, 1989), nothing is fixed and everything is in flux. It is tempting to track familiar paths in a shifting terrain and to summon timeworn solutions, even when problems have changed. Doing what's familiar is comforting. It reassures us that our world is orderly and that we are in command. But when old ways fail, managers often flip-flop: They cave in and try to appease everyone. The result is aimlessness and anarchy, which kill or maim concerted, purposeful action. Collins and Porras (1994) made it clear. "Visionary" companies have the paradoxical capacity to stimulate change and pursue high-risk new ventures while simultaneously maintaining their commitment to core ideology and values.

Good managers and leaders sustain a tension-filled poise between extremes. They combine core values with elastic strategies. They get things done without being done in. They know what they stand for and what they want and communicate their vision with clarity and power. But they also understand and respond to the vortex of forces that propel organizations in conflicting trajectories. They think creatively about how to make things happen. They develop strategies with enough elasticity to respond to the twists and turns of the path to a better future.

There is a misguided notion that a leader ventures into uncharted terrain with omniscient foresight and unlimited courage. Keller comes closer to the reality: "The greatest leaders are often, in reality, skillful followers. They do not control the flow of history, but by having the good sense not to stand in its way, they seem to (1990, p. 1).

Leaders need confidence to confront gnarly problems and deep divisions. They must expect conflict, knowing their actions may unleash forces beyond their control. They need courage to follow uncharted routes, expecting surprise and pushing ahead when the ultimate destination is only dimly foreseeable. Most important, they need to be in touch with their hearts and souls as well as their heads. It has been said that the heart has a mind of its own. Good leaders listen.

COMMITMENT TO CORE BELIEFS

Poetry and philosophy are neglected in managerial training, and business schools seldom ask if spiritual development is central to their mission. It is no wonder that managers are often viewed as chameleons who can adapt to anything, guided only by expediency. Analysis and agility are necessary but not enough. Organizations need leaders who can provide a durable sense of purpose and direction, rooted deeply in values and the human spirit. "We have a revolution to make, and this revolution is not political, but spiritual" (Guéhenno, 1993, p. 167). There is cause for hope.

Leaders need to be deeply reflective and dramatically explicit about core values and beliefs. Many of the world's legendary corporate heroes articulated their philosophies and values so strikingly that they are still visible in today's behavior and operations. In government, Franklin Delano Roosevelt, Charles de Gaulle, Margaret Thatcher, and Lee Kuan Yew were controversial, but each espoused enduring values and beliefs. These served as a guiding beacon for their respective nations.

MULTIFRAME THINKING

Commitment to both resilient values and elastic strategies involves a paradox. Franklin Roosevelt's image as lion and fox, Mao's reputation as tiger and monkey, and Mary Kay Ash's depiction as fairy godmother and pink panther were not so much inconsistencies as signs that they could embrace contradiction. They intuitively recognized the multiple dimensions of society and moved flexibly to implement their visions. The use of multiple frames permits leaders to see and understand more—*if* they are able to employ the different logics that accompany diverse ways of thinking.

Leaders fail when they take too narrow a view. Unless they can think flexibly and see organizations from multiple angles, they will be unable to deal with the full range of issues they inevitably encounter. Jimmy Carter's preoccupation with details and rationality made it hard for him to marshal support for his programs or to capture the hearts of most Americans. Even FDR's multifaceted approach to the presidency—he was a superb observer of human needs, a charming persuader, a solid administrator, a political manipulator, and a master of ritual and ceremony—miscarried when he underestimated the public reaction to his plan to enlarge the Supreme Court.

Multiframe thinking is challenging and often counterintuitive. To see the same organization as machine, family, jungle, and theater requires the capacity to think in different ways at the same time about the same thing. Like surfers, leaders must ride the waves of change. Too far ahead, they will be crushed. If they fall behind, they will become irrelevant. Success requires artistry, skill, and the ability to see organizations as organic forms in which needs, roles, power, and symbols must be integrated to provide direction and shape behavior. The power to reframe is vital for modern leaders. The ability to see new possibilities and to create new opportunities enables leaders to discover alternatives when options seem severely constrained. It helps them find hope and faith amid fear and despair. Choice is at the heart of freedom, and freedom is essential to achieving the twin goals of commitment and flexibility.

Organizations everywhere are struggling to cope with a shrinking planet and a global economy. The accelerating pace of change continues to produce grave political, economic, and social discontinuities. A world ever more dependent on organizations now finds them evolving too slowly to meet pressing social demands. Without wise leaders and artistic managers to help close the gap, we will continue to see misdirected resources, massive ineffectiveness, and unnecessary human pain and suffering. All these afflictions are already present and there is no guarantee that they will not worsen—unless we can enlarge our palette of options.

We see prodigious challenges ahead for organizations and those who guide them, yet we remain optimistic. We want this revised volume to lay the groundwork for a new generation of managers and leaders who recognize the importance of poetry and philosophy as well as analysis and technique. We need pioneers who embrace the fundamental values of human life and the human spirit. Such leaders and managers will be playful theorists who can see organizations through a complex prism. They will be negotiators able to design resilient strategies that simultaneously shape events and adapt to changing circumstances. They will understand the importance of knowing and caring for themselves and the people with whom they work. They will be architects, catalysts, advocates, and prophets who lead with soul.

APPENDIX
THE BEST OF ORGANIZATIONAL STUDIES

One goal for our book is to cover the most important and influential works in the field and cite or summarize them where appropriate. There is no perfect way to determine the best or most important books and articles, but we can assess which ones scholars pay the most attention to.

SCHOLARS' HITS

Our list of scholars' "greatest hits" relies on citation analysis—how often a work is cited in the scholarly literature. This method is often used to measure scholarly impact. We began by conducting a citation analysis of the two journals that Trieschmann, Dennis, and Northcraft (2000) cited as the most visible and influential in the field of management: *Academy of Management Journal* (AMJ, for the years 1996 to 2009) and the *Administrative Science Quarterly* (ASQ, for the years 1993 to 2009). We combined the analyses from those two journals to get a list of the "top 20" articles and books based on citation frequency. (In identifying our top 20, we excluded purely methodological works that dealt with statistical analysis or research methods.)

We then conducted an additional analysis using Google Scholar (GS) as of November 2016. GS provides a broadly inclusive analysis of citation data for scholarly work. This gave us three separate rankings: AMJ, ASQ, and GS. The first two are specific to the field of organization studies. The GS data provide a broader indication of influence both within and beyond the management field. For the items in our top 20, the correlations among AMJ, ASQ, and GS are positive but low (ranging between .09 for AMJ/ASQ to .27 for ASQ/GS). We believe this reflects reality. Scholars who publish in different journals or come from

Exhibit A.1.
Top 20 "Scholars' Hits" from Citation Analysis.

AMJ Rank	ASQ Rank	GS Rank	Overall Rank	Author	Year	Title
1	1	4	1	DiMaggio, P. J., and Powell, W. W.	1983	"The Iron Cage Revisited: Institutional Isomorphism and Collective Rationality in Organizational Fields"
2	2	9	2	Pfeffer, J., and Salancik, G.	1978	*The External Control of Organizations: A Resource Dependence Perspective*
3	2	8	3	Cyert, R. M., and March, J. G.	1963	*A Behavioral Theory of the Firm*
9	3	10	4	Meyer, J., and Rowan, B.	1977	"Institutionalized Organizations: Formal Structure as Myth and Ceremony"
7	4	12	5	Thompson, J. D.	1967	*Organizations in Action: Social Science Bases of Administrative Theory*
11	6	7	6	Granovetter, M. S.	1985	*Economic Action and Social Structure: The Problem of Social Embeddedness*
4	20	1	7	Jensen, M. C., and Meckling, W. H.	1976	"Theory of the Firm: Managerial Behavior, Agency Costs, and Ownership Structure"
10	10	12	8	March, J. G., and Simon, H. A.	1958	*Organizations*
9	17	8	9	Nelson, R. R., and Winter, S. G.	1982	*An Evolutionary Theory of Economic Change*
11	8	18	10	Burt, R. S.	1992	*Structural Holes: The Social Structure of Competition*
16	15	20	12	Williamson, O. E.	1975	*Markets and Hierarchies*

AMJ Rank	ASQ Rank	GS Rank	Overall Rank	Author	Year	Title
13	10	19	13	Hannan, M. T., and Freeman, J.	1984	"Structural Inertia and Organizational Change"
16	5	33	15	Hannan, M. T., and Freeman, J.	1989	*Organizational Ecology*
17	11	24	14	Levitt, B., and March, J. G.	1988	"Organizational Learning"
21	24	4	11	Williamson, O. E.	1985	*The Economic Institutions of Capitalism*
21	16	25	17	Uzzi, B.	1992	"Social Structure and Competition in Interfirm Networks: The Paradox of Embeddedness"
21	12	35	18	Levinthal, D. A., and March, J.G.	1993	"The Myopia of Learning"
6	30	23	16	Scott, W. R.	1985	*Institutions and Organizations*
21	21	27	19	Stinchcombe, A. L.	1965	"Social Structure and Organizations"
4	40	28	20	Hambrick, D. C., and Mason, P. A.	1984	"Upper Echelons: The Organization as a Reflection of Its Top Managers"

different disciplines have different tastes and prefer different sources. It also suggests that our results are somewhat arbitrary, because a different set of journals might have produced different results. The results for the top 20 are shown in Exhibit A.1.

The results are not definitive, but they identify some of the works that have had the greatest influence on scholars. To reduce our list to a single rank order, we averaged the rankings across the three separate databases. For example, our highest ranking went to an article by DiMaggio and Powell (1983) that ranked first in AMJ and ASQ and fourth in GS.

Though the citation analysis is based on articles published in the 1990s and 2000s, many of the works that appear at the high end of the list were published much earlier, in the 1960s, 1970s, and 1980s. The oldest item in the top 20 was published in 1958, the newest in 1993. The results suggest that there is typically a lag of a decade or more before a new work can become a widely cited "classic."

BIBLIOGRAPHY

Ackman, D. 2002. "Pay Madness at Enron." *Forbes*, March 22. www.forbes.com/2002/03/22/0322enronpay.html.

Adams, S. 1996. *The Dilbert Principle*. New York: Harper Business.

Adams, S. 2015. "The World's Most Reputable Companies in 2015." *Forbes*, April 21. https://www.forbes.com/sites/susanadams/2015/04/21/the-worlds-most-reputable-companies-in-2015/#5ec295dc425c.

Adler, P. S., and B. Borys. 1996. "Two Types of Bureaucracy: Enabling and Coercive." *Administrative Science Quarterly 41*: 61–89.

Agrawal A., J. F. Jaffe, and G. N. Mandelker. 1992. "The Post-merger Performance of Acquiring Firms: A Reexamination of an Anomaly." *Journal of Finance 47*: 1605–1621.

Ajila, C. O. 1997. "Maslow's Hierarchy of Needs Theory: Applicability to the Nigerian Industrial Setting." *IFE Psychologia 5*: 162–74.

Alderfer, C. P. 1972. *Existence, Relatedness, and Growth*. New York: Free Press.

Alderfer, C. P. 1979. "Consulting to Underbounded Systems." In Vol. 2 of *Advances in Experiential Social Processes*, edited by C. P. Alderfer and C. Cooper. New York: Wiley.

Allen, W. 1986. *Without Feathers*. Cambridge, MA: Ballantine.

Allison, G. 1971. *Essence of Decision: Explaining the Cuban Missile Crisis*. New York: Little, Brown.

Alterman, E. 1989. "Wrong on the Wall, and Most Else." *New York Times*, November 12.

Amar, V. 2004. *Pouvoir et leadership: Enquête sur les archétypes culturels du management [Power and Leadership: An Inquiry into the Cultural Archetypes of Management]*. Paris: Village Mondial.

Amazon.com Inc. 2015. "2015 Annual Report." Amazon.com. http://www.annualreports.com/Click/4710.

American Customer Satisfaction Index. 2016. "Benchmarks By Industry." *American Customer Satisfaction Index*. http://www.theacsi.org/index.php?option=com_content&view=article&id=147&catid=&Itemid=212&i=Specialty+Retail+Stores.

Anderlini, J. 2013. "Chinese Parliament Holds 83 Billionaires." *Financial Times*, March 7. https://www.ft.com/content/4568598e-8731-11e2-9dd7-00144feabdc0.

Anders, G. 2012. "Jeff Bezos Gets It." *Forbes*, April 23. http://www.forbes.com/sites/georgeanders/2012/04/04/inside-amazon.

Appelbaum, E., T. Bailey, P. Berg, and A. L. Kalleberg. 2000. *Manufacturing Advantage: Why High-Performance Work Systems Pay Off*. New York: Cornell University Press.

Arnold, P. 2015. "The Five Greatest Examples of Change in Business History." Chartered Management Institute, July. http://www.managers.org.uk/insights/news/2015/july/the-5-greatest-examples-of-change-management-in-business-history.

Argyris, C. 1957. *Personality and Organization*. New York: HarperCollins.

Argyris, C. 1962. *Interpersonal Competence and Organizational Effectiveness*. Homewood, IL: Irwin.

Argyris, C. 1964. *Integrating the Individual and the Organization*. New York: Wiley.

Argyris, C. 1998. "Empowerment: The Emperor's New Clothes." *Harvard Business Review 76*, no. 3: 98.

Argyris, C., and D. A. Schön. 1974. *Theory in Practice: Increasing Professional Effectiveness*. San Francisco: Jossey-Bass.

Argyris, C., and D. A. Schön. 1978. *Organizational Learning: A Theory of Action Perspective*. Reading, MA: Addison-Wesley.

Argyris, C., and D. A. Schön. 1996. *Organizational Learning II: Theory, Method, and Practice*. Reading, MA: Addison-Wesley.

Armstrong, D. 1992. *Managing by Storying Around: A New Method of Leadership*. New York: Currency/Doubleday.

Arndt, M. 2007. "Knock Knock, It's Your Big Mac: From São Paulo to Shanghai, McDonald's Is Boosting Growth with Speedy Delivery." *Bloomberg*, July 12. https://www.bloomberg.com/news/articles/2007-07-12/knock-knock-its-your-big-macbusinessweek-business-news-stock-market-and-financial-advice.

Arteta, F. 2006. "Historia de Ascardio." [History of Ascardio.] http://www.ascardio.org/ascardioweb/saciverinformacion.php?id=0000000002.

Autin, F., and J.-C., Croizet. 2012. "Improving Working Memory Efficiency by Reframing Metacognitive Interpretation of Task Difficulty." *Journal of Experimental Psychology: General 141*, no. 4: 610–618.

Autor, D., D. Dorn, L. G. Katz, C. Patterson and J. van Reenan, 2017. "Concentrating on the Fall of the Labor Share." IZA Institute of Labor Economics Discussion Paper Series, Jan. http://ftp.iza.org/dp10539.pdf.

Axelrod, R. 1980. "More Effective Choice in the Prisoner's Dilemma." *Journal of Conflict Resolution 24*: 379–403.

Baily, M. N., and B. Katz. 2012. "U.S. Manufacturing Makes a Comeback." *Washington Post*, May 18. http://www.washingtonpost.com/opinions/us-manufacturing-makes-a-comeback/2012/05/18/gIQA6dyVZU_story.html.

Bakan, J. 2004. *The Corporation: The Pathological Pursuit of Profit and Power*. New York: Free Press.

Baker, C. 2004. *Behavioral Genetics: An Introduction to How Genes and Environments Interact Through Development to Shape Differences in Mood, Personality, and Intelligence*. Washington, D.C.: American Association for the Advancement of Science.

Baldridge, J. V. 1971. *Power and Conflict in the University*. New York: Wiley.

Baldridge, J. V., and T. E. Deal, eds., 1975. *Managing Change in Educational Organizations*. Berkeley, CA: McCutchan.

Bales, F. 1970. *Personality and Interpersonal Behavior*. Austin, TX: Holt, Rinehart and Winston.

Balkundi, P., and D. A. Harrison. 2006. "Ties, Leaders, and Time in Teams: Strong Inference About the Effects of Network Structure on Team Viability and Performance." *Academy of Management Journal 49*: 49–68.

Bandler, R., and J. Grinder. 1975. Vol. 1 of *The Structure of Magic: A Book about Magic and Therapy*. Palo Alto, CA: Science and Behavior Books.

Barboza, D. 2007. "My Time as a Hostage, and I'm a Business Reporter." *New York Times*, June 24. http://www.nytimes.com/2007/06/24/weekinreview/24barboza.html.

Bardach, E. 1977. *The Implementation Game: What Happens After a Bill Becomes Law*. Cambridge, MA: MIT Press.

Barley, S. R. 1990. "The Alignment of Technology and Structure Through Roles and Networks." *Administrative Science Quarterly 35*: 61–103.

Barnard, C. I. 1938. *The Functions of the Executive*. Cambridge, MA: Harvard University Press.

Barnes, L. B., and M. P. Kriger. 1986. "The Hidden Side of Organizational Leadership." *Sloan Management Review*, Fall: 15–25.

Barnett, W. P., and J. Freeman. 2001. "Too Much of a Good Thing? Product Proliferation and Organizational Failure." *Organization Science 12*: 539–558.

Barrick, M. S., G. R. Thurgood, T. A. Smith, and S. H. Courtright. 2015. "Collective Organizational Engagement: Linking Motivational Antecedents, Strategic Implementation, and Firm Performance." *Academy of Management Journal 58*, no. 1: 111–135.

Barstad, A., D. Ellingsen, and O. Hellevik. 2005. "Wealthier, But So What?" Oslo: Statistics Norway. https://www.ssb.no/en/sosiale-forhold-og-kriminalitet/artikler-og-publikasjoner/wealthier-but-so-what.

Barstow, D., and L. Bergman. 2003a. "At a Texas Foundry, an Indifference to Life." *New York Times*, January 8.

Barstow, D., and L. Bergman. 2003b. "Family's Profit, Wrung from Blood and Sweat." *New York Times*, January 9.

Barstow, D., and L. Bergman. 2003c. "Deaths on the Job, Slaps on the Wrist." *New York Times*, January 10.

Barstow, D., and A. Xanic von Bertrag. 2012. "The Bribery Aisle: How Wal-Mart Used Payoffs to Get Its Way in Mexico." *New York Times*, December 17. http://www.nytimes.com/2012/12/18/business/walmart-bribes-teotihuacan.html?src=un&feedurl=http%3A%2F%2Fjson8.nytimes.com%2Fpages%2Fbusiness%2Findex.jsonp.

Bass, B. M. 1985. *Leadership and Performance Beyond Expectations*. New York: Free Press.

Bass, B. M. 1990. *Bass & Stogdill's Handbook of Leadership: Theory, Research, and Managerial Application*. 3rd ed. New York: Free Press.

Bass, B. M., B. Avolio, and L. Atwater. 1996. "The Transformational and Transactional Leadership of Men and Women." *Applied Psychology: An International Review 45*: 5–34.

Bateson, G. 1972. *Steps to an Ecology of Mind*. New York: Ballantine.

Batstone, D. 2003. *Saving the Corporate Soul—And (Who Knows?) Maybe Your Own*. San Francisco: Jossey-Bass.

Becker, B. E., and M. A. Huselid. 1998. "High Performance Work Systems and Firm Performance: A Synthesis of Research and Managerial Implications." *Research in Personnel and Human Resource Management 16*: 53–101.

Beer, M., and N. Nohria. 2001. "Resolving the Tension Between Theories E and O of Change." In *Breaking the Code of Change*, edited by M. Beer and N. Nohria, 1–34. Boston: Harvard Business School Press.

Bell, M. P. 2011. *Diversity in Organizations*. Mason, OH: South-Western.

Bell, T. E., and K. Esch. 1987. "The Fatal Flaw in Flight 51-L." *IEEE Spectrum*, February: 36–51.

Bellow, G., and B. Moulton. 1978. *The Lawyering Process: Cases and Materials*. Mineola, NY: Foundation Press.

Belluck, P., and J. Steinberg. 2002. "Defector Indignant at President of Harvard." *New York Times*, April 16. http://www.nytimes.com/2002/04/16/us/defector-indignant-at-president-of-harvard.html.

Benedict, R. 1934. *Patterns of Culture*. New York: Houghton Mifflin.

Benner, M. J. and M. L. Tushman. 2015. "Reflections on the 2013 Decade Award—'Exploration, Exploitation, and Process Management: The Productivity Dilemma Revisited' Ten Years Later." *Academy of Management Review 40:*, no. 4: 497–514.

Bennis, W. G. 1961. "Revisionist Theory of Leadership." *Harvard Business Review 39*, no. 1, January–February.

Bennis, W. G. 1989. *Why Leaders Can't Lead: The Unconscious Conspiracy Continues*. San Francisco: Jossey-Bass.

Bennis, W. G. 1997. "The Secrets of Great Groups." *Leader to Leader*, no. 3, Winter. https://www.leader-values.com/FCKfiles/File/Bennis_Secret_of_great_groups.pdf.

Bennis, W. G., and B. Nanus. 2007. *Leaders: Strategies for Taking Charge*. New York: HarperCollins.

Bensimon, E. M. 1989. "The Meaning of 'Good Presidential Leadership': A Frame Analysis." *Review of Higher Education 12*: 107–123.

Bensimon, E. M. 1990. "Viewing the Presidency: Perceptual Congruence Between Presidents and Leaders on Their Campuses." *Leadership Quarterly 1*: 71–90.

Benson, B. 2016. "Cognitive Bias Cheat Sheet: Because Thinking Is Hard." *Better Humans*, September 1. https://betterhumans.coach.me/cognitive-bias-cheat-sheet-55a472476b18#.xtdf23qsh.

Berenson, A. 2004. "Survey Finds Profit Pressure Is Leading to Poor Decisions." *New York Times*, February 7.

Berger, P. 1974. *Pyramids of Sacrifice*. New York: Basic Books.

Bergquist, W. H. 1992. *The Four Cultures of the Academy: Insights and Strategies for Improving Leadership in Collegiate Organizations*. San Francisco: Jossey-Bass.

Bernstein, A. 1996. "Why ESOP Deals Have Slowed to a Crawl." *Businessweek*, March 18.

Bernstein, E., J. Bunch, N. Canner, and M. Lee. 2016. "Beyond the Holocracy Hype." *Harvard Business Review*, July-August.

Berger, Warren (2014). *A More Beautiful Question*. New York: Bloomsbury.

Besharov M. L., and W. K. Smith. 2014. "Multiple Institutional Logics in Organizations: Explaining Their Varied Nature and Implications." *Academy of Management Review 39*: 364–381.

Bethune, G., and S. Huler. 1999. *From Worst to First: Behind the Scenes of Continental's Remarkable Comeback*. New York: Wiley.

Bettelheim, B. 1977. *The Uses of Enchantment*. New York: Vintage Books.

Bigelow, L., J. M. Parks, and R. Wuebker. 2012. "Skirting the Issues: Experimental Evidence of Gender Bias in IPO Prospectus Evaluations." *Journal of Management 40*, no. 6: 1732–1759.

Bion, W. R. 1961. *Experiences in Groups*. London: Tavistock.

Bird, Alan, Torsten Lichtenau, and David Michels. 2016. "Three Questions to Spur Corporate Change Efforts." *Forbes*, April 15. https://www.forbes.com/sites/baininsights/2016/04/15/three-questions-to-spur-corporate-change-efforts/#62c088ba512f.

Birnbaum, R. 1988. *How Colleges Work: The Cybernetics of Academic Organization and Leadership*. San Francisco: Jossey-Bass.

Birnbaum, R. 1992. *How Academic Leadership Works: Understanding Success and Failure in the College Presidency*. San Francisco: Jossey-Bass.

Blair, M. M., D. L. Kruse, and J. R. Blasi. 2000. "Employee Ownership: An Unstable Form or a Stabilizing Force?" In *The New Relationship: Human Capital in the American Corporation*, edited by M. M. Blair and T. Kochan. Washington, D.C.: Brookings Institution Press. http://ssrn.com/abstract=142146.

Blake, R., and J. S. Mouton. 1969. *Building a Dynamic Corporation Through Grid Organizational Development*. Reading, MA: Addison-Wesley.

Blakeman, C. 2014. "Companies Without Managers Do Better by Every Metric." Inc.com, July 22. http://www.inc.com/chuck-blakeman/companies-without-managers-do-better-by-every-metric.html

Blanchard, K., and S. Johnson. 1982. *The One-Minute Manager*. New York: Morrow.

Blank, W., J. R. Weitzel, and S. G. Green. 1990. "A Test of the Situational Leadership Theory." *Personnel Psychology 43*: 579–597.

Blasi, J. R., D. Kruse, and A. Bernstein. 2003. *In the Company of Owners: The Truth about Stock Options (And Why Every Employee Should Have Them)* New York: Basic.

Blau, P. M., and Scott, W. R. 1962. *Formal Organizations: A Comparative Approach*. Novato, CA: Chandler & Sharp.

Block, P. 1987. *The Empowered Manager: Positive Political Skills at Work*. San Francisco: Jossey-Bass.

Blum, A. 1961. "Collective Bargaining: Ritual or Reality." *Harvard Business Review*, November–December.

Blumberg, P. 1968. *Industrial Democracy: The Sociology of Participation*. New York: Schocken Books.

Blumer, H. 1969. *Symbolic Interaction: Perspective and Method*. Upper Saddle River, NJ: Prentice Hall.

Boivie, S., S. D. Graffin, and R. J. Gentry. 2016. "Understanding the Direction, Magnitude, and Joint Effects of Reputation When Multiple Actors' Reputations Collide." *Academy of Management Journal 59*, no. 1: 188–206.

Boje, D. M., J. T. Luhman, and A. L. Cunliffe. 2003. "A Dialectic Perspective on the Organization Theatre Metaphor." *American Communication Journal 6*.

Bok, S. 1978. *Lying: Moral Choice in Public and Private Life*. New York: Vintage Books.

Bolman, L. G., and E. Granell. 1999. "Versatile Leadership: A Comparative Analysis of Reframing in Venezuelan Managers." Paper presented at the World Conference of the Ibero-American Academy of Management, Madrid, December.

Bolman, L. G., and T. E. Deal. 1984. *Modern Approaches to Understanding and Managing Organizations*. San Francisco: Jossey-Bass.

Bolman, L. G., and T. E. Deal. 1991. "Leadership and Management Effectiveness: A Multi-Frame, Multi-Sector Analysis." *Human Resource Management 30*: 509–534.

Bolman, L. G., and T. E. Deal. 1992a. "Leading and Managing: Effects of Context, Culture, and Gender." *Education Administration Quarterly 28*: 314–329.

Bolman, L. G., and T. E. Deal. 1992b. "Reframing Leadership: The Effects of Leaders' Images of Leadership." In *Impact of Leadership*, edited by K. E. Clark, M. B. Clark, and D. Campbell. Greensboro, NC: Center for Creative Leadership.

Bolman, L. G., and T. E. Deal. 2011. *Leading with Soul: An Uncommon Journey of Spirit*. 3rd ed. San Francisco: Jossey-Bass.

Book, E. W. 2000. *Why the Best Man for the Job Is a Woman*. New York: HarperCollins.

Bower, J. L. 1970. *Managing the Resource Allocation Process*. Boston: Division of Research, Harvard Business School.

Boyatzis, R., and McKee, A. 2005. *Resonant Leadership: Renewing Yourself and Connecting with Others Through Mindfulness, Hope, and Compassion*. Boston: Harvard Business School Press.

Brachmann, S. 2014. "The Rise and Fall of the Company that Invented Digital Cameras." *IPWatchdog*. November 1. http://www.ipwatchdog.com/2014/11/01/the-rise-and-fall-of-the-company-that-invented-digital-cameras/id=51953/.

Bradford, D. L., and A. R. Cohen. 1984. *Managing for Excellence*. New York: Wiley.

Brass, D. J., and D. M. Krackhardt. 2012. "Power, Politics and Social Networks in Organizations." In *Politics in Organizations: Theory and Research Considerations*, edited by G. R. Ferris and D. C. Treadway. New York: Routledge.

Brescoll, V. L., and E. L. Uhlmann. 2008. "Can an Angry Woman Get Ahead? Status Conferral, Gender, and Expression of Emotion in the Workplace." *Psychological Science 19*, no. 3: 268–275.

Briand, M. 1993. "People, Lead Thyself." *Kettering Review*. Summer: 38–46.

Brief, A. P., and H. K. Downey. 1983. "Cognitive and Organizational Structure: A Conceptual Analysis of Implicit Organizing Theories." *Human Relations 36*, no. 12: 1065–1090.

Broder, J. M., and E. Schmitt. 2003. "U.S. Attacks on Holdouts Dealt Iraqis Final Blow." *New York Times*, April 13.

Broughton, I. 1988. *Hangar Talk: Interview with Fliers 1920s to 1990s*. Spokane: Eastern Washington University Press.

Brown, D. J. 2014. *The Boys in the Boat: Nine Americans and Their Epic Quest for Gold at the 1936 Berlin Olympics*. New York: Penguin.

Brown, L. D. 1983. *Managing Conflict at Organizational Interfaces*. Reading, MA: Addison-Wesley.

Brown, L. D. 1986. "Power Outside Organizational Paradigms: Lessons from Community Partnerships." In *The Functioning of Executive Power: How Executives Influence People and Organizations*, edited by S. Srivastva and Associates. San Francisco: Jossey-Bass.

Brown, P., and A. Hesketh. 2004. *The Mismanagement of Talent: Employability and Jobs in the Knowledge Economy*. New York: Oxford University Press.

Bryan, L. L., and C. I. Joyce. 2007. "Better Strategy Through Organizational Design." *McKinsey Quarterly Number 2*. May. http://www.vvka.net/downloads/Mckinsey_Better%20Strategy_2007.pdf.

Bunker, B. B., and B. T. Alban. 1996. *Large Group Interventions: Engaging the Whole System for Rapid Change*. San Francisco: Jossey-Bass.

Bunker, B. B., and B. T. Alban. 2006. "Large Group Interventions and Dynamics." In *Organization Development: A Jossey-Bass Reader*, edited by J. V. Gallos. San Francisco: Jossey-Bass.

Bureau of Labor Statistics. 2012. "Mass Layoff Events and Initial Claimants for Unemployment Insurance, Nov. 2008 to Oct. 2012, Seasonally Adjusted." *Bureau of Labor Statistics*. https://www.bls.gov/news.release/archives/mmls_11202012.pdf.

Bureau of Labor Statistics. 2016. "Databases, Tables, and Calculators by Subject." *Bureau of Labor Statistics*. http://data.bls.gov/timeseries/CES3000000001/htm.

Burke, K. 1937. *Attitudes Toward History*. Boston: Beacon Press.

Burke, K. 1945. *A Grammar of Motives*. Berkeley: University of California Press.

Burke, K. 1972. *Dramatism and Development*. Barre, MA: Clark University Press.

Burke, W. 2006. "Where Did OD Come From?" In *Organization Development: A Jossey-Bass Reader*, edited by J. V. Gallos. San Francisco: Jossey-Bass.

Burkus, D. 2016. "Why Whole Foods Builds Its Entire Business on Teams." *Forbes*, June. http://www.forbes.com/sites/davidburkus/2016/06/08/why-whole-foods-build-their-entire-business-on-teams/#58715d20483d

Burnes, B. 2006. "Kurt Lewin and the Planned Approach to Change: A Reappraisal." In *Organization Development: A Jossey-Bass Reader*, edited by J. V. Gallos. San Francisco: Jossey-Bass.

Burns, J. M. 1978. *Leadership*. New York: HarperCollins.

Burns, J. M. 2003. *Transforming Leadership: The Pursuit of Happiness*. New York: Atlantic Monthly Press.

Burns, N., and D. Kiley. 2007. "Executive Churn: Hello, You Must Be Going." *Businessweek*, February 12.

Burrough, B., and J. Helyar. 1990. *Barbarians at the Gate: The Fall of RJR Nabisco*. New York: HarperCollins.

Burt, R. 1992. *Structural Holes: The Social Structure of Competition*. Cambridge, MA: Harvard University Press.

Business Week. 2005. "The Best & Worst Managers of 2004, Best Manager: Robert Nardelli, Home Depot." *Businessweek*, January 10.

Butcher, D., and M. Clarke. 2001. *Smart Management: Using Politics in Organizations*. London: Palgrave MacMillan.

Byrne, J. A. 1996. "The Shredder: Did CEO Dunlap Save Scott Paper—or Just Pretty It Up?" *Businessweek*, January 15.

Byrne, J. A. 2002a. "Inside McKinsey." *Businessweek*, July 8.

Byrnes, N., and M. Arndt. 2006. "The Art of Motivation." *Businessweek*, May 1.

Byrnes, N., J. A. Byrne, C. Edwards, and L. Lee. 2002. "The Good CEO." *Businessweek*, September 23.

Cable, J. P., and D. S. DeRue. 2002. "The Convergent and Discriminant Validity of Subjective Fit Perceptions." *Journal of Applied Psychology 87*: 875–884.

Caldicott, S. M. 2014 "Why Ford's Alan Mulally Is An Innovation CEO for The Record Books." *Forbes*, June 25. http://www.forbes.com/sites/sarahcaldicott/2014/06/25/why-fords-alan-mulally-is-an-innovation-ceo-for-the-record-books/#42347cbd779b

Campbell, D. 1983. "If I'm in Charge, Why Is Everyone Laughing?" Paper presented at the Center for Creative Leadership, Greensboro, N.C.

Campbell, J. 1988. *The Power of Myth*. New York: Doubleday.

Campbell, J. P., and M. D. Dunnette. 1968. "Effectiveness of T-Group Experiences in Managerial Training and Development." *Psychological Bulletin 70*: 73–104.

Carless, S. A. 1998. "Gender Differences in Transformational Leadership: An Examination of Superior, Leader, and Subordinate Perspectives." *Sex Roles: A Journal of Research*, December: 1–10.

Carlin, J. 2007. "How Nelson Mandela Won the Rugby World Cup." *The Telegraph*, October 19, London: UK. http://www.telegraph.co.uk/news/features/3634426/How-Nelson-Mandela-won-the-rugby-World-Cup.html.

Carlson, S. 1951. *Executive Behavior*. Stockholm: Strombergs.

Carlyle, T. 1841. *On Heroes, Hero-Worship, and the Heroic in History*. https://www.gutenberg.org/files/1091/1091-h/1091-h.htm. London: James Fraser.

Carlzon, J. 1987. *Moments of Truth*. New York: Ballinger.

Cascio, W. 2006. "The High Cost of Low Wages." *Harvard Business Review*, December. http://hbr.org/2006/12/the-high-cost-of-low-wages/ar/1

Cascio, W., and J. Boudreau. 2008. *Investing in People: Financial Impact of Human Resource Initiatives*. Philadelphia: Wharton School Publishing.

Cascio, W., C. E. Young, and J. R. Morris. 1997. "Financial Consequences of Employment-Change Decisions in Major U.S. Corporations." *Academy of Management Journal 40*: 1175–1189.

Case, J. 1995. *Open Book Management: The Coming Business Revolution*. New York: Harper Business.

Chafkin, M. 2009. "The Zappos Way of Managing." *Inc.* May. http://www.inc.com/magazine/20090501/the-zappos-way-of-managing.html.

Chamberlain, A. 2015. "CEO to Worker Pay Ratios: Average CEO Earns 204 Times Median Worker Pay." https://www.glassdoor.com/research/ceo-pay-ratio/.

Champy, J. M. 1995. *Reengineering Management: The Mandate for New Leadership*. New York: HarperCollins.

Chandler, A. D., Jr. 1962. *Strategy and Market Structure*. Cambridge, MA: MIT Press.

Chandler, A. D., Jr. 1977. *The Visible Hand: The Managerial Revolution in American Business*. Cambridge, MA: Harvard University Press.

Cherniss, C. 2000. "Emotional Intelligence: What It Is and Why It Matters." Paper presented at Annual Meeting of the Society for Industrial and Organizational Psychology, New Orleans, October.

Chicago Project on Security and Terrorism (CPOST). 2016. Suicide Attack Database. October 12. http://cpostdata.uchicago.edu/

"China Says 'No' to Pirated Software." 2002. *People's Daily*, April 5.

Christensen, C. M. 1997. *The Innovator's Dilemma: When New Technologies Cause Great Firms to Fail*. Boston: Harvard Business School Press.

Christensen C. M., R. Alton, C. Rising, and A. Waldeck. 2011. "The Big Idea: The New M&A Playbook." *Harvard Business Review 89*, no. 3. http://hbr.org/2011/03/the-big-idea-the-new-ma-playbook/ar/1"\t"_blank.

Chunka, M. 2012. "How Kodak Failed." *Forbes*, January 18. http://www.forbes.com/sites/chunkamui/2012/01/18/how-kodak-failed/#2964a31ebd6a.

Cialdini, R. B. 2008. *Influence: Science and Practice*. 5th ed. New York: Pearson.

Cialdini, R. B. 2016. *Pre-Suasion: A Revolutionary Way to Influence and Persuade*. New York: Simon & Schuster.

Ciulla, J. B. 1998. "Leadership and the Problem of Bogus Empowerment." In *Ethics: The Heart of Leadership*, edited by J. B. Ciulla. Westport, CT: Praeger.

Clark, B. R. 1975. "The Organizational Saga in Higher Education." In *Managing Change in Educational Organizations*, edited by J. V. Baldridge and T. E. Deal. Berkeley, CA: McCutchan.

Clark, E. 2004. *Around the Corporate Campfire: How Great Leaders Use Stories to Inspire Success*. Sevierville, TN: Insight Publishing.

Cleveland, H. 1985. *The Knowledge Executive: Leadership in an Information Society*. New York: Dutton.

Clifford, D. K., and R. E. Cavanagh. 1985. *The Winning Performance*. New York: Bantam Books.

CNBC. 2013. "Costco Craze: Inside the Warehouse Giant." http://www.cnbc.com/the-costco-craze-inside-the-warehouse-giant/.

CNN Money. 2011. "Startup Lies Companies Tell You." CNN.com. http://money.cnn.com/galleries/2011/smallbusiness/1103/gallery.business_creation_myths/index.html.

Cochran, S. 2000. *Encountering Chinese Networks: Western, Japanese and Chinese Corporations in China, 1880–1937*. Berkeley: University of California Press.

Cohen, M., and J. G. March. 1974. *Leadership and Ambiguity*. New York: McGraw-Hill.

Cohen, P. S. 1969. "Theories of Myth." *Man 4*: 337–353.

Cohen, S. G., and D. E. Bailey. 1997. "What Makes Teams Work: Group Effectiveness Research from the Shop Floor to the Executive Suite." *Journal of Management 23*, no. 3: 239–290.

Cohen, S. G., and G. E. Ledford, Jr. 1994. "The Effectiveness of Self-Managing Teams: A Quasi-Experiment." *Human Relations 47*: 13–43.

Collins, B. E., and H. Guetzkow. 1964. *A Social Psychology of Group Processes for Decision Making*. New York: Wiley.

Collins, J. C. 2001. *Good to Great: Why Some Companies Make the Leap and Others Don't*. New York: HarperCollins.

Collins, J. C., and J. I. Porras. 1994. *Built to Last: Successful Habits of Visionary Companies*. New York: Harper Business.

Collins, J. C., and M. T. Hansen. 2011. *Great by Choice: Uncertainty, Chaos, and Luck—Why Some Thrive Despite Them All.* New York: Harper Business.

Collinson, D. L. and M. Collinson (1989). "Sexuality in the Workplace: The Domination of Men's Sexuality." In J. Hearn, D. L. Sheppard, P. Tancred-Sheriff, and G. Burrell (eds.), *The Sexuality of Organization.* London: Sage

Columbia Accident Investigation Board. 2003. *Final Report.* Washington, D.C.: National Aeronautics and Space Administration. https://history.nasa.gov/columbia/CAIB_reportindex.html.

Colvin, G. 1999. "The 50 Best Companies for Asians, Blacks, and Hispanics." *Fortune,* July 19.

Colvin, G. 2014. "Mary Barra's (Unexpected) Opportunity." *Fortune,* September 18. http://fortune.com/2014/09/18/mary-barra-general-motors/.

Conger, J. A., and Kanungo, R. N. 1998. *Charismatic Leadership in Organizations.* Thousand Oaks, CA: Sage.

Conley, C. 2007. *Peak: How Great Companies Get Their Mojo from Maslow.* San Francisco: Jossey-Bass.

Cooper, C., and R. Block. 2006. *Disaster: Hurricane Katrina and the Failure of Homeland Security.* New York: Holt.

Corkery, M. and S. Cowley. 2016. "Wells Fargo Warned Workers Against Sham Accounts, but 'They Needed a Paycheck.'" *New York Times,* September 17. http://www.nytimes.com/2016/09/17/business/dealbook/wells-fargo-warned-workers-against-fake-accounts-but-they-needed-a-paycheck.html?emc=edit_th_20160917&nl=todaysheadlines&nlid=17437576&_r=0

Cornelissen, J. P., and M. D. Werner. 2014 "Putting Framing in Perspective: A Review of Framing and Frame Analysis across the Management and Organizational Literature." *Academy of Management Annals 8,* no. 1: 181–235.

Correll, S. J., and S. Benard. 2007. Getting a Job: Is There a Motherhood Penalty? *American Journal of Sociology 112,* no. 5: 1297–1339. http://gender.stanford.edu/sites/default/files/motherhoodpenalty.pdf

Corwin, R. 1976. "Organizations as Loosely Coupled Systems: Evolution of a Perspective." Paper presented at the Conference on Schools as Loosely Coupled Organizations, Stanford University, November.

Cowley, S. 2016. "At Wells Fargo, Complaints About Fraudulent Accounts Since 2005." *New York Times,* October 11. http://www.nytimes.com/2016/10/12/business/dealbook/at-wells-fargo-complaints-about-fraudulent-accounts-since-2005.html?ref=business

Cox, H. 1969. *The Feast of Fools.* Cambridge, MA: Harvard University Press.

Cox, T., Jr. 1994. *Cultural Diversity in Organizations: Theory, Research, and Practice.* San Francisco: Berrett-Koehler.

Coy, P., M. Conlin, and M. Herbst. 2010. "The Disposable Worker." *Businessweek,* Jan. 7. http://www.businessweek.com/magazine/content/10_03/b4163032935448.htm.

Cronshaw, S. F. 1987. "Effects of Categorization, Attribution, and Encoding Processes on Leadership Perspectives." *Journal of Applied Psychology 72,* no. 1: 91–106.

Crozier, M., and E. Friedberg. 1977. *L'acteur et le système* [The Actor and the System]. Paris: Points/Politique Seuil.

Culbert, S. 2010. *Get Rid of the Performance Review!: How Companies Can Stop Intimidating, Start Managing—and Focus on What Really Matters.* New York: Business Plus.

Cyert, R. M., and J. G. March. 1963. *A Behavioral Theory of the Firm*. Upper Saddle River, NJ: Prentice Hall.

Dalton, M. 1959. *Men Who Manage*. New York: Wiley.

Dane, E., and M. G. Pratt. 2007. "Exploring Intuition and Its Role in Managerial Decision Making." *Academy of Management Review 32*, no. 1: 33–54.

Daniels, C., J. Hickman, C. Y. Chen, A. Harrington, A. Lustgarten, J. Mero, and C. Tkaczyk. 2004. "50 Best Companies for Minorities." *Fortune*, June 28. http://money.cnn.com/magazines/fortune/fortune_archive/2004/06/28/374393/index.htm.

Dansereau, F., G. Graen, and W. J. Haga. 1975. "A Vertical Dyad Linkage Approach to Leadership Within Formal Organizations." *Organizational Behavior and Human Performance 13*: 46–78.

David, G. 2003. "Can McDonald's Cook Again?" *Fortune*, April 14.

Davis, M., and others. 1976. "The Structure of Educational Systems." Paper presented at the Conference on Schools as Loosely Coupled Organizations, Stanford University, November.

Davis, S. M., and P. R. Lawrence 1978. "Problems of Matrix Organizations." *Harvard Business Review, 56*, no. 3: 131–142.

De Geus, A. 1995. "Companies: What Are They?" *RSA Journal*, June: 26–35.

Deal, T. E., and A. A. Kennedy. 1982. *Corporate Cultures*. Reading, MA: Addison-Wesley.

Deal, T. E., and M. K. Key. 1998. *Corporate Celebration: Play, Purpose, and Profit at Work*. San Francisco: Berrett-Koehler.

Deal, T. E., and S. C. Nutt. 1980. *Promoting, Guiding, and Surviving Change in School Districts*. Cambridge, MA: Abt Associates.

Deal, T. E., and W. A. Jenkins. 1994. *Managing the Hidden Organization: Strategies for Empowering Your Behind-the-Scenes Employees*. New York: Warner Books.

DeBecker, G. 1997. *The Gift of Fear*. New York: Dell.

DeLuca, J. 1999. *Political Savvy: Systematic Approaches to Leadership Behind the Scenes*. Berwyn, PA: EBG Publications.

Demick, B. 2012. "China's New Party Leader Eschews Predecessors' Rhetoric." *Los Angeles Times*, November 15.

Denning, S. 2004. *Squirrel, Inc.: A Fable of Leadership Through Storytelling*. San Francisco: Jossey-Bass.

Denning, S. 2005. *The Leader's Guide to Storytelling: Mastering the Art and Discipline of Business Narrative*. San Francisco: Jossey-Bass.

Denning, S. 2013. "J.C. Penney: Was Ron Johnson's Strategy Wrong?" *Forbes*, April 9. http://www.forbes.com/sites/stevedenning/2013/04/09/j-c-penney-was-ron-johnsons-strategy-wrong.

DePree, M. 1989. *Leadership Is an Art*. New York: Dell.

Dillingham, D. L. 2001. "Air Traffic Control: Role of the FAA's Modernization Program in Reducing Delays and Congestion." *Testimony to Congress*, May 10. Washington, D.C.: General Accounting Office.

DiMaggio, P. J., and W. W. Powell. 1983. "The Iron Cage Revisited: Institutional Isomorphism and Collective Rationality in Organizational Fields." *American Sociological Review 48*, April: 147–160.

Dittmer, L. 1977. "Political Culture and Political Symbolism: Toward a Theoretical Synthesis." *World Politics 29*: 552–583.

Dobbins, G. H., and S. J. Platz. 1986. "Sex Differences in Leadership: How Real Are They?" *The Academy of Management Review 11*, no. 1: 118–127. doi: 10.2307/258335.

Doktor, J. 1993. "The Early Implementation of the Family Resource and Youth Services Centers of Kentucky: Multi-Frame Perspective." Unpublished doctoral dissertation, Vanderbilt University.

Donadio, R., and J. Yardley. 2013. "Vatican's Bureaucracy Tests Even the Infallible." *New York Times*, March 18. http://www.nytimes.com/2013/03/19/world/europe/pope-francis-faces-an-entrenched-curia.html?_r=0&pagewanted=print.

Dornbusch, S., and W. R. Scott. 1975. *Evaluation and the Exercise of Authority*. San Francisco: Jossey-Bass.

Downer, L. 1994. *The Brothers: The Hidden World of Japan's Richest Family*. New York: Random House.

Drucker, P. F. 1989. "Peter Drucker's 1990s: The Futures That Have Already Happened." *Economist*, October 21.

Drucker, P. F. 1993. *Managing the Future: The 1990s and Beyond*. New York: Plume.

Druskat, V. U., and J. V. Wheeler. 2003. "Managing from the Boundary: The Effective Leadership of Self-Managing Work Teams." *Academy of Management Journal 46*: 435–457.

Druskat, V. U., F. Sala, and G. Mount, 2005. *Linking Emotional Intelligence and Performance at Work: Current Research Evidence With Individuals and Groups*. New York: Psychology Press.

Duesenberry, J. 1960. "Comment on Gary S. Becker's 'An Economic Analysis of Fertility'." In National Bureau of Economic Research, *Demographic and Economic Change in Developed Countries*, p. 233. http://www.nber.org/chapters/c2387.pdf.

Duhigg, C., 2016. "What Google Learned From Its Quest to Build the Perfect Team." *New York Times*, Feb. 26. https://www.nytimes.com/2016/02/28/magazine/what-google-learned-from-its-quest-to-build-the-perfect-team.html?_r=0.

Duhigg, C., and D. Barboza. 2012. "In China, Human Costs Are Built Into an iPad." *New York Times,* January 25. http://www.nytimes.com/2012/01/26/business/ieconomy-apples-ipad-and-the-human-costs-for-workers-in-china.html?_r=1&nl=todaysheadlines&emc=tha2.

Dumaine, B. 1994. "The Trouble with Teams." *Fortune,* September 5.

Dunford, R. W., and I. C. Palmer. 1995. "Claims About Frames: Practitioners' Assessment of the Utility of Reframing." *Journal of Management Education 19*: 96–105.

Dwyer, J., K. Flynn, and F. Fessenden. 2002. "9/11 Exposed Deadly Flaws in Rescue Plan." *New York Times,* July 7.

Eagleman, D. 2011. *Incognito: The Secret Lives of the Brain*. New York: Pantheon.

Eagly, A. H., and L. L. Carli. 2003. "The Female Leadership Advantage: An Evaluation of the Evidence." *Leadership Quarterly 14*: 807–834.

Eagly, A. H., and B. T. Johnson. 1990. "Gender and Leadership Style: A Meta-Analysis." *Psychological Bulletin 111*: 233–256.

Edelman, M. J. 1971. *Politics as Symbolic Interaction: Mass Arousal and Quiescence*. Orlando, FL: Academic Press.

Edelman, M. J. 1977. *The Symbolic Uses of Politics*. Madison: University of Wisconsin Press.

Edmondson, A. 1999. "Psychological Safety and Learning Behavior in Work Teams." *Administrative Science Quarterly 44*, no. 2: 350–383.

Edmondson, G. 2006. "BMW's Dream Factory." *Businessweek,* October 16, pp.70–80. Copyright © 2006 McGraw-Hill Companies, Inc.

Edwards, M. R. 1991. "In-Situ Team Evaluation: A New Paradigm for Measuring and Developing Leadership at Work." Paper presented at conference on The Impact of Leadership at the Center for Creative Leadership, Colorado Springs, CO, May.

Eichenwald, K. 2002. "Flinging Billions of Dollars to Buy Assets No One Else Would Touch." *New York Times,* October 3.

Elden, M. 1983. "Client as Consultant: Work Reform Through Participative Research." *National Productivity Review,* Spring: 136–147.

Elden, M. 1986. "Sociotechnical Systems Ideas as Public Policy in Norway: Empowering Participation Through Worker-Managed Change." *Journal of Applied Behavioral Science 22*: 239–255.

Elmore, R. F. 1978. "Organizational Models of Social Program Implementation." *Public Policy 26*: 185–228.

Elson, C. M., and C. K. Ferrere. 2012. "Executive Superstars, Peer Groups, and Overcompensation: Cause, Effect, and Solution." SSRN. http://ssrn.com/abstract=2125979.

Emery, C. R., and L. D. Fredendall. 2002. "The Effect of Teams on Firm Profitability and Customer Satisfaction." *Journal of Service Research 4*: 217–229.

Enderud, H. G. 1976. "The Perception of Power." In *Ambiguity and Choice in Organizations,* edited by J. G. March and J. Olsen. Bergen, Norway: Universitetsforlaget.

Esposito, F., S. Garman, J. Hickman, N. Watson, and A. Wheat. 2002. "America's 50 Best Companies for Minorities." *Fortune,* July 9.

Evans, M. G. 1970. "The Effects of Supervisory Behavior on the Path-goal Relationship." *Organizational Behavior and Human Performance 5*: 277–298.

Ewing, J. 2015. "Volkswagen Says Whistle-Blower Pushed It to Admit Broader Cheating." *New York Times,* November 9. http://www.nytimes.com/2015/11/09/business/international/volkswagen-says-whistle-blowers-pushed-it-to-admit-gas-car-cheating.html.

Ewing, J. 2017. "German Police Raid Audi Offices, Escalating Volkswagen Diesel Inquiry." *New York Times,* March 15. https://www.nytimes.com/2017/03/15/business/audi-vw-diesel-emissions.html.

Farkas, C. M., and P. De Backer. 1996. *Maximum Leadership: The World's Leading CEOs Share Their Five Strategies for Success.* New York: Henry Holt.

Fast, N. J., E. R. Burris, and C. A. Bartel. 2014. "Managing to Stay in the Dark: Managerial Self-Efficacy, Ego Defensiveness, and the Aversion to Employee Voice." *Academy of Management Journal 57,* no. 4: 1013–1034.

Fayol, H. 1949. *General and Industrial Management,* translated by C. Stours. London: Pitman. [Originally published 1919.].

Feinberg, M., and J. J. Tarrant. 1995. *Why Smart People Do Dumb Things.* New York: Simon & Schuster.

Fiedler, F. E. 1964. "A Contingency Model of Leadership Effectiveness." In *Advances in Experimental Social Psychology,* edited by L. Berkowitz. New York: Academic Press.

Fiedler, F. E. 1967. *A Theory of Leadership Effectiveness.* New York: McGraw-Hill.

Fiedler, F. E., and M. Chemers. 1974. *Leadership and Effective Management*. Glenview, IL: Scott Foresman.

Fiedler, K. 1982. "Casual Schemata: Review and Criticism of Research on a Popular Construct." *Journal of Personality and Social Psychology 42*: 1001–1013.

Firestone, D. 2002. "Senate Votes, 90-9, to Set Up Homeland Security Department Geared to Fight Terrorism." *New York Times,* November 20.

Firestone, W. A. 1977. "Butte-Angels Camp: Conflict and Transformation." In *The Dynamics of Planned Educational Change*, edited by R. Herriot and N. Gross. Berkeley, CA: McCutchan.

Fisher, R., and W. Ury. 1981. *Getting to Yes*. Boston: Houghton Mifflin.

Fisher, R., A. Harris, and C. Jarvis 2008. *Education in Popular Culture*. New York: Routledge.

Fishman, C. 1996a. "The Whole Foods Recipe for Teamwork." *Fast Company,* April. https://www.fastcompany.com/26641/whole-foods-recipe-teamwork.

Fishman, C. 1996b. "Whole Foods Is All Teams." *Fast Company,* April. https://www.fastcompany.com/26671/whole-foods-all-teams.

Fishman, C. 2006. "The Wal-Mart Effect and a Decent Society: Who Knew Shopping Was So Important." *Academy of Management Perspectives,* August.

Fiske, S. T., and L. M. Dyer. 1985. "Structure and Development of Social Schemata: Evidence from Positive and Negative Transfer Effects." *Journal of Personality and Social Psychology 48*, no. 4: 839–852.

Fisman, R., S. S. Iyengar, E. Kamenica, and I. Simonson. 2006. "Gender Differences in Mate Selection: Evidence from a Speed Dating Experiment." *Quarterly Journal of Economics 121*, no. 2: 673–697.

Fitzsimmons, T. W., and V. J. Callan. 2016. "Applying a Capital Perspective to Explain Continued Gender Inequality in the C-suite." *The Leadership Quarterly 27*: 354–370.

Fleishman, E. A., and E. F. Harris. 1962. "Patterns of Leadership Behavior Related to Employee Grievances and Turnover." *Personnel Psychology 15*: 43–56.

Floden, R. E., and S. S. Weiner. 1978. "Rationality to Ritual." *Policy Sciences 9*: 9–18.

Florén, H., and J. Tell. 2013. "Managerial Behaviour in Small Firms: Does it Matter What Managers Do?" In *The Work of Managers: Toward a Practice Theory of Management*, edited by S. Tengblad. Oxford: Oxford University Press.

Follett, M. P. 1896. *The Speaker of the House of Representatives*. New York: Longmans, Green.

Follett, M. P. 1918. *The New State: Group Organization and the Solution of Popular Government*. London: Longmans.

Follett, M. P. 1941. *Dynamic Administration: The Collected Papers of Mary Parker Follett*. New York: Harper.

Fortune Magazine. 2006. "Six Teams That Changed the World." *Fortune,* May 31. http://archive.fortune.com/2006/05/31/magazines/fortune/sixteams_greatteams_fortune_061206/index.htm.

Fortune Magazine. 2017. "100 Best Companies to Work for 2017." http://beta.fortune.com/best-companies.

Fortune: SAS Institute. 2017. http://fortune.com/best-companies/sas-institute-8.

Foss, N. J., and L. Webber. 2016. "Moving Opportunism to the Back Seat: Bounded Rationality, Costly Conflict, and Hierarchical Forms." *Academy of Management Review 41*: 61–79.

Foucault, M. 1975. *Surveiller et punir [Supervise and Punish]*. Paris: NRF-Gallimard.

Frei, F. X., R. J. Ely, and L. Winig. 2010. *Zappos.com 2009: Clothing, Customer Service, and Company Culture*. Boston: Harvard Business School Publishing.

Freiberg, K., and J. Freiberg. 1998. *Nuts: Southwest Airlines' Crazy Recipe for Business and Personal Success*. New York: Broadway.

French, J. R. P., and B. H. Raven. 1959. "The Bases of Social Power." In *Studies in Social Power*, edited by D. Cartwright. Ann Arbor, MI: Institute for Social Research.

Frensch, P. A., and R. J. Sternberg. 1991. "Skill-Related Differences in Chess Playing." In *Complex Problem Solving*, edited by R. J. Sternberg and P. A. Frensch. Hillsdale, NJ: Erlbaum.

Freudenberg, W. R., and R. Gramling. 1994. "Bureaucratic Slippage and Failures of Agency Vigilance." *Social Problems 4*, no. 1: 214–239.

Friedman, R. A. 1994. *Front Stage, Backstage: The Dramatic Structure of Labor Negotiations*. Cambridge, MA: MIT Press.

Frost, P. J. 1986. "Power, Politics, and Influence." In *The Handbook of Organizational Communication*, edited by L. W. Porter and others. Thousand Oaks, CA: Sage.

Fulghum, R. 1995. *From Beginning to End: The Rituals of Our Lives*. New York: Villard Books.

Funk, R. J., and D. Hirschman. 2017. "Beyond Nonmarket Strategy: Market Actions as Corporate Political Activity." *Academy of Management Review 42*, no. 1: 32–52.

Gaar, B. 2010. "At Whole Foods, Team Management Goes All the Way to the Top." *Austin Statesman*, http://www.statesman.com/news/business/employment/at-whole-foods-team-management-goes-all-the-way-to/nRyBq/.

Galbraith, J. R. 2001. *Designing Organizations: An Executive Briefing on Strategy, Structure, and Process*. Revised ed. San Francisco: Jossey-Bass.

Gallagher, L. 2017. *The Airbnb Story*. Boston: Houghlin Mifflin and Harcourt.

Gallagher, L. 2016. "How Airbnb Found a Mission—and a Brand." *Fortune*, December 22. http://fortune.com/airbnb-travel-mission-brand/

Gallos, J. V., and V. J. Ramsey. 1997. *Teaching Diversity: Listening to the Soul, Speaking from the Heart*. San Francisco: Jossey-Bass.

Gallos, J. V., ed. 2006. *Organization Development: A Jossey-Bass Reader*. San Francisco: Jossey-Bass.

Gallup. 2015. "State of the American Manager: Analytics and Advice for Leaders." Washington, D. C.: Gallup.

Galton, F. 1869. *Hereditary Genius: An Inquiry into Its Laws and Consequences*. London: Macmillan.

Gamson, W. A. 1968. *Power and Discontent*. Florence, KY: Dorsey Press.

Ganitsky, J., and A. Sancho. 2002. "Martín Varsavsky (A)." *Revista de Empresa 1*, no. 1, July–September: 97–126.

Gardner, H. 1993. *Frames of Mind: The Theory of Multiple Intelligences*. 10th anniversary ed. New York: Basic Books.

Gardner, J. W. 1986. *Handbook of Strategic Planning*. New York: Wiley.

Gardner, J. W. 1987. *The Moral Aspects of Leadership*. Washington, D.C.: Independent Sector.

Gardner, J. W. 1989. *On Leadership*. New York: Free Press.

Garfield, L. 2015. "The 10 Best Countries to Live in Around the World." http://www.businessinsider.com/the-top-countries-to-live-in-2015–12.

Garland, H. 1990. "Throwing Good Money After Bad: The Effect of Sunk Costs on the Decision to Escalate." *Journal of Applied Psychology 75*: 728–731.

GearheadGrrrl. 2013. "The Costco Effect . . ." Daily Kos, November 30. http://www.dailykos.com/story/2013/11/30/1259290/-The-Costco-Effect.

Gegerenzer, G., U. Hoffrage, and H. Kleinbölting. 1991. "Probabilistic Mental Models: A Brunswikian Theory of Confidence." *Psychological Review 98*: 506–528.

George, B. 2004. *Authentic Leadership: Rediscovering the Secrets to Creating Lasting Value*. San Francisco: Jossey-Bass: *2004*.

Gertz, D., and J. P. A. Baptista. 1995. *Grow to Be Great: Breaking the Downsizing Cycle*. New York: Free Press.

Ghareman, A. 2003. *Soul of World, Soul of Word*. San Luis Obispo, CA: Self-published.

Ghoshal, S., and C. A. Bartlett. 1990. "The Multinational Corporation as an Interorganizational Network." *Academy of Management Review 15*: 603–625.

Gibb, C. A. 1947. "The Principles and Traits of Leadership." *Journal of Abnormal and Social Psychology 42*, no. 3: 267–284.

Gibb, J. R. 1975. "A Research Perspective on the Laboratory Method." In *The Laboratory Method of Changing and Learning*, edited by K. D. Benne, L. P. Bradford, J. R. Gibb, and R. O. Lippitt. Palo Alto, CA: Science and Behavior Books.

Ginsburg, S. "The Spurs Were Simply Better: James." Reuters, June 16, 2014. http://www.reuters.com/article/us-nba-finals-heat-idUSKBN0ER0BF20140616.

Giroux, H. 1998. "The Business of Public Education." *Z Magazine*, August.

Gladwell, M. 2005. *Blink: The Power of Thinking Without Thinking*. New York: Little, Brown.

Glanz, J., and J. Schwartz. 2003. "Dogged Engineer's Effort to Assess Shuttle Damage." *New York Times*, September 26.

Glass, C., and A. Cook. 2016. "Leading at the Top: Understanding Women's Challenges above the Glass Ceiling." *The Leadership Quarterly 27*: 51–63. http://ac.els-cdn.com/S1048984315001034/1-s2.0-S1048984315001034-main.pdf?_tid=b8fac7f4-80ef-11e6-88d4-00000aab0f27&acdnat=1474567957_5c1afee6299113ceca8fcb91aa102416.

Goffman, E. 1959. *The Presentation of Self in Everyday Life*. New York: Anchor.

Goffman, E. 1974. *Frame Analysis*. Cambridge, MA: Harvard University Press.

Goldberg, L. R. 1992. "The Development of Markers for the Big Five Factor Structure." *Psychological Assessment 4*: 26–42.

Goleman, D. 1995. *Emotional Intelligence*. New York: Bantam.

Goleman, D., R. E. Boyatzis, and A. McKee. 2004. *Primal Leadership: Learning to Lead with Emotional Intelligence*. Boston: Harvard Business School Press.

Goodman, D. 1983. "Doctor Fights Order to Quit Maine Island." *Boston Globe*, October 15.

Gottfried, M. A., and G. Q. Conchas. 2016. "Facing the Facts: Why School Policies Backfire." *School Administrator*, October.

Gottschall, J. 2012. *The Storytelling Animal: How Stories Make Us Human*. New York: Houghton Mifflin Harcourt.

Graeff, C. L. 1983. "The Situational Leadership Theory: A Critical View." *Academy of Management Review*, April.

Graen, G. B. and M. Uhl-Bien (2008, Aug.) "Relationship-Based Approaches to Leadership: Development of Leader Member Exchange Theory (LMX) Over 25 Years." *Leadership Quarterly*, 6(2), 219–247.

Graffin, S. D., J. Haleblian, and J. T. Kiley. 2016. "Ready, AIM, Acquire: Impression Offsetting and Acquisitions." *Academy of Management Journal 59*, no. 1: 232–252.

Granovetter, M. S. 1985. "Economic Action and Social Structure: The Problem of Social Embeddedness." *American Journal of Sociology 91*, no. 3: 481–510.

Gray, B., J. M. Purdy, and S. Ansari. 2015. "From Interactions to Institutions: Microprocesses of Framing and Mechanisms for the Structuring of Institutional Fields." *Academy of Management Review 40*, no. 1: 115–143.

Greenleaf, R. K. 1973. *The Servant as Leader*. Newton Center, MA: Robert K. Greenleaf Center.

Gregory, K. L. 1983. "Native View Paradigms: Multiple Cultures and Cultural Conflict in Organizations." *Administrative Science Quarterly 28*: 359–376.

Greiner, L. E. 1972. "Evolution and Revolution as Organizations Grow." *Harvard Business Review*, July–August.

Griffin, E. 1993. *The Reflective Executive: A Spirituality of Business and Enterprise*. New York: Crossroad.

Griswold, A. 2015. "Uber Won New York." *Slate*, November 18. http://www.slate.com/articles/business/moneybox/2015/11/uber_won_new_york_city_it_only_took_five_years.html.

Groopman, J. 2007. *How Doctors Think*. Boston: Houghton Mifflin.

Guéhenno, J. M. 1993. *La fin de la démocratie [The end of democracy]*. Paris: Flammarion.

Gulati, R., and M. Gargiulo, 1999. "Where Do Interorganizational Networks Come From?" *American Journal of Sociology, 104*, no. 5, 1439–1493.

Gulick, L., and L. Urwick, eds., 1937. *Papers on the Science of Administration*. New York: Columbia University Press.

Gunther, M. 2006. "Queer Inc.: How Corporate America Fell in Love with Gays and Lesbians. It's a Movement." *Fortune*, December 11, pp. 94–110.

Gurses, K., and P. Ozcan., 2015. "Entrepreneurship in Regulated Markets: Framing Contests and Collective Action to Introduce Pay TV in the U.S." *Academy of Management Journal 58*, no. 6: 1709–1739.

Hackman, J. R. 2002. *Leading Teams: Setting the Stage for Great Performances*. Boston: Harvard Business School Press.

Hackman, J. R. ed., 1989. *Groups That Work (and Those That Don't): Creating Conditions for Effective Teamwork*. San Francisco: Jossey-Bass.

Hackman, J. R., G. R. Oldham, R. Janson, and K. Purdy. 1987. "A New Strategy for Job Enrichment." In *The Great Writings in Management and Organizational Behavior*, edited by L. E. Boone and D. D. Bowen. New York: Random House.

Hærem, T., B. T. Pentland, and K. D. Miller. 2015. "Task Complexity: Extending a Core Concept." *Academy of Management Review 40*, no. 3: 446–460.

Hagey, K. 2007. "Would-Be Robber Stays for Wine and Hugs." Associated Press, July 13. http://www.cbsnews.com/news/would-be-robber-stays-for-wine-and-hugs.

Hahn, T., L. Preuss, J. Pinkse, and F. Figge. 2014. "Cognitive Frames in Corporate Sustainability: Managerial Sensemaking with Paradoxical and Business Case Frames." *Academy of Management Review 39*, no. 4: 463–487.

Hall, R. H. 1963. "The Concept of Bureaucracy: An Empirical Assessment." *American Journal of Sociology 49*: 32–40.

Hall, R. H. 1987. *Organizations: Structures, Processes, and Outcomes*. 4th ed. Englewood Cliffs, NJ: Prentice Hall.

Hallinger, P., L. Bickman, and K. Davis. 1990. "What Makes a Difference? School Context, Principal Leadership, and Student Achievement." Occasional Paper # 3. National Center for Educational Leadership.

Hambleton, R. K., and R. Gumpert. 1982. "The Validity of Hersey and Blanchard's Theory of Leader Effectiveness." *Group and Organization Studies*, June: 225–242.

Hambrick, D. C., and P. A. Mason. 1984. "Upper Echelons: The Organization as a Reflection of Its Top Managers." *Academy of Management Review 9*: 193–206.

Hamel, G. 2006. "The Why, What, and How of Management Innovation." *Harvard Business Review*, February. https://hbr.org/2006/02/the-why-what-and-how-of-management-innovation.

Hamel, G. 2010. "Innovation Democracy: W. L. Gore's Original Management Model." *ManagementExchange.com*, September 23. http://www.managementexchange.com/story/innovation-democracy-wl-gores-original-management-model.

Hamel, G., and C. K. Prahalad. 1994. *Competing for the Future: Breakthrough Strategies for Seizing Control of Your Industry and Creating the Markets of Tomorrow*. Boston: Harvard Business School Press.

Hamm, S. 2005. "Linux Inc." *Businessweek*, January 31.

Hammer, M., and J. Champy. 1993. *Reengineering the Corporation*. New York: HarperCollins.

Hampden-Turner, C. 1992. *Creating Corporate Culture: From Discord to Harmony*. Reading, MA: Addison-Wesley.

Hamper, B. 1992. *Rivethead: Tales from the Assembly Line*. New York: Grand Central Publishing.

Hampton, W. J., and J. R. Norman. 1987. "General Motors: What Went Wrong—Eight Years and Billions of Dollars Haven't Made Its Strategy Succeed." *Businessweek*, March 16.

Handy, C. 1993. *Understanding Organizations*. New York: Oxford University Press.

Hannan, M. T., and J. Freeman. 1984. "Structural Inertia and Organizational Change." *American Sociological Review 49*: 149–164.

Hannan, M. T., and J. Freeman. 1989. *Organizational Ecology*. Cambridge, MA: Harvard University Press.

Hannaway, J., and L. S. Sproull. 1979. "Who's Running the Show? Coordination and Control in Educational Organizations." *Administrator's Notebook 27*, no. 9: 1–4.

Hansot, E. 1979. "Some Functions of Humor in Organizations." Unpublished paper, Kenyon College, Gambier, Ohio.

Harnish, V. and the Editors of *Fortune*. 2012. *The Greatest Business Decisions of All Time*. New York: Fortune Books.

Harrison, J., and R. E. Freeman. 2004. "Special Topic: Democracy in and Around Organizations." *Academy of Management Executive 18*: 49–53.

Hatch, M. J., and A. L. Cunliffe. 2013. *Organization Theory: Modern, Symbolic and Postmodern Perspectives*. Oxford: Oxford University Press.

Healey, M. P., T. Vuori, and G. P. Hodgkinson, 2015. "When Teams Agree While Disagreeing: Reflexion and Reflection in Shared Cognition." *Academy of Management Review 40*, no. 3: 399–422.

Heathfield, S. M. 2012. "20 Ways Zappos Reinforces Its Company Culture." *About.com Human Resources*, April 12. http://humanresources.about.com/b/2012/04/02/20-ways-zappos-reinforces-culture.htm.

Hedberg, B. L. T., P. C. Nystrom, and W. H. Starbuck. 1976. "Camping on Seesaws: Prescriptions for a Self-Designing Organization." *Administrative Science Quarterly 21*: 41–65.

Heffernan, M. 2002. "The Female CEO." *Fast Company,* August.

Heffron, F. 1989. *Organization Theory and Public Organizations: The Political Connection*. Upper Saddle River, NJ: Prentice Hall.

Heifetz, R. A. 1994. *Leadership Without Easy Answers*. Cambridge, MA: Belknap Press.

Heifetz, R. A., and M. Linsky. 2002. *Leadership on the Line: Staying Alive Through the Dangers of Leading*. Boston: Harvard Business School Press.

Heimovics, R. D., R. D. Herman, and C. L. Jurkiewicz Coughlin. 1993. "Executive Leadership and Resource Dependence in Nonprofit Organizations: A Frame Analysis." *Public Administration Review 53*: 419–427.

Heimovics, R. D., R. D. Herman, and C. L. Jurkiewicz Coughlin. 1995. "The Political Dimension of Effective Nonprofit Executive Leadership." *Nonprofit Management and Leadership 5*: 233–248.

Heisler, Y. 2013. "Former Apple Retail Guru Ron Johnson Shown the Door at JC Penney." http://www.networkworld.com/community/blog/former-apple-retail-guru-ron-johnson-shown-door-jc-penney.

Helgesen, S. 1990. *The Female Advantage: Women's Ways of Leadership*. New York: Doubleday.

Helgesen, S. 1995. *The Web of Inclusion: A New Architecture for Building Great Organizations*. New York: Currency/Doubleday.

Heller, F. 2003. "Participation and Power: A Critical Assessment." *Applied Psychology 52*, no. 1: 144–163.

Henderson, R. M., and K. B. Clark, 1990. "Architectural Innovation: The Reconfiguration of Existing Product Technologies and the Failure of Established Firms." *Administrative Science Quarterly 35*: 9–30.

Hernández, J. C. 2016. "Across China, Walmart Faces Labor Unrest as Authorities Stand Aside." *New York Times*, November 16. http://www.nytimes.com/2016/11/17/world/asia/across-china-walmart-faces-labor-unrest-as-authorities-stand-aside.html.

Hersey, P. 1984. *The Situational Leader*. New York: Warner Books.

Hersey, P., and K. H. Blanchard. 1969. "Life Cycle Theory of Leadership." *Training and Development Journal*: 26–34.

Hersey, P., and K. H. Blanchard. 1977. *The Management of Organizational Behavior*. 3rd ed. Upper Saddle River, NJ: Prentice Hall.

Herzberg, F., B. Mausner, and B. B. Snyderman. 1959. *The Motivation to Work*. New York: Wiley.

Herzberg, F. 1966. *Work and the Nature of Man*. Cleveland, Ohio: World.

Hill, L. A., and M. T. Farkas. 2000. *Meg Whitman at eBay, Inc.* Boston: Harvard Business School Publishing.

Hindo, B. 2007. "At 3M, A Struggle Between Efficiency and Creativity." *Businessweek*, June 11.

Hoffman, B. G. 2012. *American Icon: Alan Mulally and the Fight to Save Ford Motor Company*. New York: Crown Business.

Hofstede, G. 1984. *Culture's Consequences: International Differences in Work-Related Values*. Thousand Oaks, CA: Sage.

Hogan, R., G. J. Curphy, and J. Hogan. 1994. "What We Know About Leadership." *American Psychologist 49*: 493–504.

Hoge, W. 2002. "Crashing, and Saving, the Old Lads' Front Office." *New York Times*, September 14, p. A14, New York: The New York Times Co.

Hollander, E. P. 1978. *Leadership Dynamics*. New York: Free Press.

Holloway, P. "Tamir Rice's Death: A Lawful Tragedy." *CNN.com,* December 28, 2015. http://www.cnn.com/2015/12/28/opinions/holloway-tamir-rice-case/.

Hoobler, J. M., S. J. Wayne, and G. Lemmon. 2009. "Bosses' Perceptions of Family-Work Conflict and Women's Promotability: Glass Ceiling Effects." *Academy of Management Journal 52*, no. 5: 939–957.

Hoskisson, R. E., M. A. Hitt, R. A. Johnson, and W. Grossman. 2002. "Conflicting Voices: The Effects of Institutional Ownership Heterogeneity and Internal Governance on Corporate Innovation Strategies." *Academy of Management Journal 45*, no. 4: 697–716.

House, R. J. 1971. "The Path-Goal Theory of Effectiveness." *Administrative Science Quarterly 16*: 321–338.

House, R. J. 1996. "Path-Goal Theory of Leadership: Lessons, Legacy, and a Reformulated Theory." *Leadership Quarterly 7*, no. 3: 323–352.

House, R. J., P. J. Hanges, M. Javidan, P. W. Dorfman, and V. Gupta, eds., 2004. *Culture, Leadership, and Organizations: The GLOBE Study of 62 Societies*. Thousand Oaks, CA: Sage.

Hróbjartsson, A., and P. C. Gøtzsche. 2010. "Placebo Interventions for All Clinical Conditions." *Cochrane Database of Systematic Reviews 1*, January. CD003974. doi: 10.1002/14651858. CD003974.pub3. PMID 20091554.

Iacocca, L., and W. Novak. 1984. *Iacocca*. New York: Bantam Books.

Iansiti, M., and R. Levien. 2004. *The Keystone Advantage: What the New Dynamics of Business Ecosystems Mean for Strategy, Innovation, and Sustainability*. Boston: Harvard Business School Press.

Infanger, M., L. A. Rudman, and S. Sczesny. 2014. "Sex as a Source of Power? Backlash Against Self-sexualizing Women." *Group Processes and Intergroup Relations 10*, no. 1: 110–124.

Jackall, R. 1988. *Moral Mazes: The World of Corporate Managers*. New York: Oxford University Press.

Jacobs, A. 2013 "Elite in China Face Austerity Under Xi's Rule." *New York Times,* March 27. http://www.nytimes.com/2013/03/28/world/asia/xi-jinping-imposes-austerity-measures-on-chinas-elite.html?pagewanted=all.

Jamieson, J. P., W. B. Mendes, E. Blackstock, and T. Schmader. 2010. "Turning the Knots in Your Stomach into Bows: Reappraising Arousal Improves Performance on the GRE." *Journal of Experimental Social Psychology 46*: 208–212.

Jehn, K. A. 1995. "A Multimethod Examination of the Benefits and Detriments of Intragroup Conflict." *Administrative Science Quarterly 40*: 256–282.

Jenkins, William O. 1947. "A Review of Leadership Studies with Particular Reference to Military Problems." *Psychological Bulletin 44*, no. 1: 54–79.

Jensen, C. 1995. *No Downlink: A Dramatic Narrative About the Challenger Accident and Our Time.* New York: Farrar, Straus & Giroux.

Jensen, M. C., and W. H. Meckling. 1976. "Theory of the Firm: Managerial Behavior, Agency Costs, and Ownership Structure," *Journal of Financial Economics 3*: 305–360.

Jensen, M. C., and W. H. Meckling. 1994. "The Nature of Man." *Journal of Applied Corporate Finance 7*, no. 2: 4–19.

John, O. P. 1990. "The 'Big Five' Factor Taxonomy: Dimensions of Personality in the Natural Language and in Questionnaires." In *Handbook of Personality: Theory and Research*, edited by L. A. Pervin. 66–100. New York: Guilford.

Johnson, S. 1998. *Who Moved My Cheese? An A-Mazing Way to Deal with Change in Your Work and Your Life.* New York: Putnam.

Judge, T. A., J. E. Bono, R. Ilies, and M. W. Gerhardt. 2002. "Personality and Leadership: A Qualitative and Quantitative Review." *Journal of Applied Psychology 87*, no. 4: 765–780.

Jung, C. 1965. *Memories, Dreams, and Reflections.* New York: Random House [Originally published 1912.].

Jung, C. G. 1964. *Man and His Symbols.* London: Aldus.

Kacmar, K. M., M. C. Andrews, D. L. Van Rooy, R. C. Steilberg, and S. Cerrone. 2006. "Sure Everyone Can Be Replaced. But at What Cost? Turnover as a Predictor of Unit-Level Performance." *Academy of Management Journal 49*, no. 1, February: 133–144.

Kahn, J. 2001. "Diversity Trumps the Downturn." *Fortune,* July 9.

Kahneman, D. 2011. *Thinking, Fast and Slow.* New York: Farrar, Straus & Giroux.

Kahneman, D., and A. Tversky. 1979. "Prospect Theory: An Analysis of Decisions Under Risk." *Econometrica 47*: 263–291.

Kalleberg, A. A., T. Nesheim, and K. M. Olsen. 2009. "Is Participation Good or Bad for Workers? Effects of Autonomy, Consultation and Teamwork on Stress Among Workers in Norway." *Acta Sociologica 52*, no. 2: 99–116.

Kamens, D. H. 1977. "Legitimating Myths and Education Organizations: Relationship Between Organizational Ideology and Formal Structure." *American Sociological Review 42*: 208–219.

Kanter, R. M. 1977. *Men and Women of the Corporation.* New York: Basic Books.

Kanter, R. M. 1983. *The Change Masters: Innovations for Productivity in the American Corporation.* New York: Simon & Schuster.

Kanter, R. M. 1989a. *When Giants Learn to Dance.* New York: Simon & Schuster.

Kanter, R. M. 1989b. "The New Managerial Work." *Harvard Business Review,* December.

Kanter, R. M., B. A. Stein, and T. D. Jick. 1992. *The Challenge of Organizational Change: How Companies Experience It and Leaders Guide It.* New York: Free Press.

Kantor, J., and D. Streitfeld. 2015. "Inside Amazon: Wrestling Big Ideas in a Bruising Workplace." *New York Times,* August 16. http://www.nytimes.com/2015/08/16/technology/inside-amazon-wrestling-big-ideas-in-a-bruising-workplace.html?ref=business&_r=0.

Katzell, R. A., and D. Yankelovich. 1975. *Work, Productivity, and Job Satisfaction.* New York: Psychological Corporation.

Katzenbach, J. R., and D. K. Smith. 1993. *The Wisdom of Teams: Creating the High-Performance Organization.* Boston: Harvard Business School Press.

Kaufer, N., and G. C. Leader. 1987a. "Diana Lam (A)." Case. Boston University.

Kaufer, N., and G. C. Leader. 1987b. "Diana Lam (B)." Case. Boston University.

Kauffman, E. M. 1996. "Creating the Uncommon Company." In *Leadership and Entrepreneurship: Personal and Organizational Development in Entrepreneurial Values,* edited by R. W. Smilor and D. L. Sexton. Westport, CT: Quorum/Greenwood.

Kegan, R. 1998. *In Over Our Heads: The Mental Demands of Modern Life.* Cambridge: Harvard University Press.

Keidel, R. W. 1984. "Baseball, Football, and Basketball: Models for Business." *Organizational Dynamics,* Winter: 5–18.

Keller, B. 1990. "While Gorbachev Gives In, the World Marvels at His Power." *New York Times,* February 11.

Keller, B. 1999. "Women Superintendents: Few and Far Between." *Education Week,* November 10.

Kenny, C. 2014. "Why Manufacturing Jobs Are Shrinking Everywhere." *Bloomberg,* April 28. https://www.bloomberg.com/news/articles/2014-04-28/why-factory-jobs-are-shrinking-everywhere.

Kidder, T. 1981. *The Soul of a New Machine.* New York: Little, Brown.

Kidder, T. 1989. *Among School Children.* Boston: Houghton Mifflin.

Killian, K., F. Perez, and C. Siehl. 1998. "Ricardo Semler and Semco S. A." Glendale, AZ: Thunderbird, The American Graduate School of International Management.

King D. R., D. R. Dalton, C. M. Daily, and J. G. Covin. 2004. "Meta-analyses of Post-acquisition Performance: Indications of Unidentified Moderators." *Strategic Management Journal 25,* no. 2: 187–200.

Kirkman, B. L., and D. L. Shapiro. 1997. "The Impact of Cultural Values on Employee Resistance to Teams: Towards a Model of Globalized Self-Managing Work Team Effectiveness." *Academy of Management Review 22:* 730–757.

Kirkpatrick, S. A., and E. A. Locke. 1991. "Leadership: Do Traits Matter?" *Academy of Management Executive 5:* 48–60.

Klein, G. 1999. *Sources of Power: How People Make Decisions.* Cambridge: MIT Press.

Ko, S. J., C. M. Judd, and D. A. Stapel. 2009. "Stereotyping Based on Voice in the Presence of Individuating Information: Vocal Femininity Affects Perceived Competence but Not Warmth." *Personality & Social Psychology Bulletin 35,* no. 2, February: 198–211.

Kohlberg, L. 1973. "The Claim to Moral Adequacy of a Highest Stage of Moral Judgment." *Journal of Philosophy 70:* 630–646.

Komives, S. R. 1991. "Gender Differences in the Relationship and Hall Directors' Transformational and Transactional Leadership and Achieving Styles." *Journal of College Student Development 32*: 155–164.

Kopelman, R. E. 1985. "Job Redesign and Productivity: A Review of the Evidence." *National Productivity Review 4*: 237–255.

Korten, D. C. 1995. *When Corporations Rule the World*. San Francisco: Berrett-Koehler.

Kotter, J. P. 1982. *The General Managers*. New York: Free Press.

Kotter, J. P. 1985. *Power and Influence: Beyond Formal Authority*. New York: Free Press.

Kotter, J. P. 1988. *The Leadership Factor*. New York: Free Press.

Kotter, J. P., and D. S. Cohen. 2002. *The Heart of Change: Real Life Stories of How People Change Their Organizations*. Boston: Harvard Business School Press.

Kotter, J. P., and J. L. Heskett. 1992. *Corporate Culture and Performance*. New York: Free Press.

Kouzes, J. M., and B. Z. Posner. 1987. *The Leadership Challenge*. 2nd ed. San Francisco: Jossey-Bass.

Kouzes, J. M., and B. Z. Posner. 2007. *The Leadership Challenge*. 4th ed. San Francisco: Jossey-Bass.

Kowalski, T. J., R. S. McCord, G. J. Peterson, P. I. Young, and N. M. Ellerson. 2010. *The American School Superintendent: 2010 Decennial Study*. Lanham, MD: R & L Education.

KPMG. 2000. "Unlocking Shareholder Value: The Keys to Success." http://people.stern.nyu.edu/adamodar/pdfiles/eqnotes/KPMGM&A.pdf.

Krishnamurthy, P., and K. Winston. 2010. "Aruna Roy and the Birth of a People's Movement in India." Cambridge, MA: Kennedy School of Government, Harvard University, Case HKS128.

Kruger, J., and D. Dunning. 1999. "Unskilled and Unaware of It: How Difficulties in Recognizing One's Own Incompetence Lead to Inflated Self-Assessments." *Journal of Personality and Social Psychology 77*: 1121–1134.

Kruse, D. L. 1993. "Does Profit Sharing Affect Productivity?" NBER Working Paper No. W4542. Washington, D.C.: National Bureau of Economic Research. http://papers.ssrn.com/sol3/papers.cfm?abstract_id=375304.

Kruse, D. L., J. R. Blasi, and R. Park. 2010. "Shared Capitalism in the U.S. Economy: Prevalence, Characteristics, and Employee Views of Financial Participation in Enterprises." In *Shared Capitalism at Work: Employee Ownership, Profit and Gain Sharing, and Broad-based Stock Options*, edited by D. L. Kruse, R. B. Freeman, and J. R. Blasi. Washington, D.C.: National Bureau of Economic Research.

Kübler-Ross, E. 1997. *On Death and Dying*. New York: Scribner.

Kühberger, A. 1995. "The Framing of Decisions: A New Look at Old Problems." *Organizational Behavior and Human Decision Processes 62*: 230–240.

Kuhn, T. S. 1970. *The Structure of Scientific Revolutions*. 2nd ed. Chicago: University of Chicago Press.

Kurchner-Hawkins, R., and R. Miller. 2006. "Organizational Politics: Building Positive Political Strategies in Turbulent Times." In *Handbook of Organizational Politics*, edited by E. Vigoda-Gadot and A. Drory. Northampton, MA: Edward Elgar.

Labaton, S. 2002. "Downturn and Shift in the Population Feed Boom in White Collar Crime." *New York Times*, June 2. www.nytimes.com/2002/06/02/business/02CRIM.html?.

Labich, K. 1994. "Is Herb Kelleher America's Best CEO?" *Fortune,* May 2.

Lagarde, D. 2008. "Benazir Bhutto: My Country Is in Danger." *L'Express,* January 3.

Lakoff, G. 2004. *Don't Think of an Elephant: Know Your Values and Frame the Debate—The Essential Guide for Progressives.* White River Junction, VT: Chelsea Green.

Lam, C. K., Xu Huang, and S. C. H. Chan. 2015. "The Threshold Effect of Participative Leadership and the Role of Leader Information Sharing." *Academy of Management Journal 58,* 3: 836–855.

Langer, E. 1989. *Mindfulness.* Reading, MA: Addison-Wesley.

Langer, E. 2009. *Counterclockwise: Mindful Health and the Power of Possibility.* New York: Ballantine.

Latham, G. P., and C. C. Pinder. 2005. "Work Motivation Theory and Research at the Dawn of the Twenty-First Century." *Annual Review of Psychology 56*: 485–516.

Lawler, E. E., III. 1986. *High-Involvement Management: Participative Strategies for Improving Organizational Performance.* San Francisco: Jossey-Bass.

Lawler, E. E., III. 1996. *From the Ground Up: Six Principles for Building the New Logic Corporation.* San Francisco: Jossey-Bass.

Lawler, E. E., III, and C. Worley. 2006. *Built to Change: How to Achieve Sustained Organizational Effectiveness.* San Francisco: Jossey-Bass.

Lawler, E. E., III, and J. L. Shuttle. 1973. "A Causal Correlation Test of the Need Hierarchy Concept." *Organizational Behavior and Human Performance 7*: 265–287.

Lawrence, P. R., and J. Lorsch. 1967. *Organization and Environment.* Boston: Division of Research, Harvard Business School.

Lawrence, P. R., and N. Nohria. 2001. *Driven: How Human Nature Shapes Our Choices.* San Francisco: Jossey-Bass, 2002.

Lax, D. A., and J. K. Sebenius. 1986. *The Manager as Negotiator.* New York: Free Press.

Leavitt, H. J. 1978. *Managerial Psychology.* 4th ed. Chicago: University of Chicago Press.

Leavitt, H. J. 1996. "The Old Days, Hot Groups, and Managers' Lib." *Administrative Science Quarterly 41*: 288–300.

Ledford, G. E. 1993. "Employee Involvement: Lessons and Predictions." In *Organizing for the Future: The New Logic of Managing Complex Organizations,* edited by J. R. Galbraith, E. E. Lawler, III, and Associates. San Francisco: Jossey-Bass.

Lee, A. 1988. *Call Me Roger.* Chicago: Contemporary Books.

Lesgold, A., and S. Lajoie. 1991. "Complex Problem Solving in Electronics." In *Complex Problem Solving,* edited by R. J. Sternberg and P. A. Frensch. Hillsdale, NJ: Erlbaum.

Levering, R., and M. Moskowitz. 1993. *The 100 Best Companies to Work for in America.* New York: Plume.

Levine, D. I., and L. D. Tyson. 1990. "Participation, Productivity, and the Firm's Environment." In *Paying for Productivity: A Look at the Evidence,* edited by A. S. Blinder. Washington, D.C.: Brookings Institution.

Levinson, H. 1968. *The Exceptional Executive.* Cambridge, MA: Harvard University Press.

Levinthal, D. A., and J. G. March. 1993. "The Myopia of Learning." *Strategic Management Journal 14*: 95–112.

Levitt, B. and J. G. March. 1988. "Organizational Learning." *Annual Review of Sociology 14*: 319–340.

Lewin, A. Y. 1998. "Introduction—Jazz Improvisation as a Metaphor for Organization Theory." *Organization Science 9*, no. 5.

Lewin, K., R. Lippitt, and R. White. 1939. "Patterns of Aggressive Behavior in Experimentally Created Social Climates." *Journal of Social Psychology 10*: 271–299.

Lewis, N. A. 1996. "This Mr. Smith Gets His Way in Washington." *New York Times*, October 12.

Likert, R. 1961. *New Patterns of Management*. New York: McGraw-Hill.

Ling, Q., F. Liu, and X. Wu. 2016. "Servant Versus Authentic Leadership: Assessing Effectiveness in China's Hospitality Industry." *Cornell Hospital Quarterly*, April.

Lingle, C. 2002. "China's Economy Faces Severe Pain." *Taipei Times*, February 3.

Lipsky, M. 1980. *Street-Level Bureaucracy*. New York: Russell Sage Foundation.

Litmanovitz, M. 2011. "Beyond the Classroom: Women in Education Leadership." *Harvard Kennedy School Review*.

Locke, E. A., and G. P. Latham, 2002. "Building a Practically Useful Theory of Goal Setting and Task Motivation." *American Psychologist 9*: 705–717.

Locke, E. A., and G. P. Latham. 2004. "What Should We Do About Motivation Theory? Six Recommendations for the Twenty-First Century." *Academy of Management Review 29*: 388–403.

Lodge, D. 1988 *Nice Work*. Hammondsworth, Middlesex: Viking.

Longworth, R. C. 1996. "Old Rules of Economics Don't Work the Way Textbooks Say They Should." *Kansas City Star*, October 27.

Lopez, B. 1998. *Crow and Weasel*. New York: North Point.

Lord, R. G., and R. J. Foti. 1986. "Schema Theories, Information Processing, and Organizational Behavior." In *The Thinking Organization*, edited by H. P. Sims Jr., D. A. Gioia, and Associates. San Francisco: Jossey-Bass.

Love, E. G., and M. Kraatz. 2005. "How Do Firms' Actions Influence Corporate Reputation? The Case of Downsizing at Large U.S. Firms." *Academy of Management Proceedings*.

Love, J. F. 1986. *McDonald's: Behind the Arches*. New York: Bantam Books.

Lowy, J. 2016. "No Price Tag, End Date for FAA's Air Traffic Control Plan." *USNews*, November 15.

Lubans, J. 2001. "A Reason for Rain: Hoop Lessons for Library Leaders." *LA&M On Managing*, Winter. www.lubans.org.

Lukes, S. 1974. *Power: A Radical View*. New York: Macmillan.

Luthans, F. 1988. "Successful vs. Effective Real Managers." *Academy of Management Executive 2*, no. 2: 127–132.

Luthans, F., Yodgetts, R. M., and Rosenkrantz, S. A. (1988). *Real Managers*. Cambridge, MA: Ballinger.

Lutz, B. 2015. "One Man Established the Culture That Led to VW's Emissions Scandal: A Diesel Dictatorship." *Roadandtrack.com* November 4. http://www.roadandtrack.com/car-culture/a27197/bob-lutz-vw-diesel-fiasco/.

Lynch, P. 1996. "In Defense of the Invisible Hand." *Worth*, June.

Lynn, L. E., Jr. 1987. *Managing Public Policy*. New York: Little, Brown.

Maccoby, M. 1981 *The Leader*. New York: Ballantine.

Maccoby, M. 2003 *The Productive Narcissist: The Promise and Peril of Visionary Leadership*. New York: Broadway.

Machan, D. 1987. "DEC's Democracy." *Forbes,* March 23.

Machiavelli, N. 1961 *The Prince*. New York: Penguin Books. [Originally published 1514.].

Macke, J. 2013. "Ron Johnson's JCPenney: Anatomy of a Retail Failure." http://finance.yahoo.com/blogs/breakout/ron-johnson-jcpenney-anatomy-retail-failure-114635276.html

Maier, N. 1967. "Assets and Liabilities in Group Problem Solving." *Psychological Review 74*: 239–249.

Maitlis, S., and M. Christianson. 2014. "Sensemaking in Organizations: Taking Stock and Moving Forward." *Academy of Management Annals 8*, no. 1: 57–125.

Malavé, J. 1995. *Gerencia en salud: Un modelo innovador [Health Management: An Innovative Model]*. Caracas, Venezuela: Ediciones IESA.

Manes, S., and P. Andrews., 1994 *Gates*. New York: Touchstone.

Mangham, I. L., and M. A. Overington. 1987. *Organizations as Theater: A Social Psychology of Dramatic Appearances*. New York: Wiley.

Mann, M. 1986. *The History of Power from the Beginning to AD 1760*. Vol. 1 of *The Sources of Social Power*. Cambridge: Cambridge University Press.

Mann, M. 2013. *Globalizations, 1945–2011*. Vol. 4 of *The Sources of Social Power*. Cambridge: Cambridge University Press.

Manz, C. C., and H. P. Sims, Jr. 1995 *Business Without Bosses: How Self-Managing Teams Are Building High Performance Companies*. New York: Wiley.

March, J. G. 1976. "The Technology of Foolishness." In *Ambiguity and Choice in Organizations*, edited by J. G. March and J. Olsen. Bergen, Norway: Universitetsforlaget.

March, J. G., and H. A. Simon. 1958. *Organizations*. New York: Wiley.

March, J. G., and J. Olsen, eds. 1976. *Ambiguity and Choice in Organizations*. Bergen, Norway: Universitetsforlaget.

Maremont, M. 2016. "EpiPen Maker Dispenses Outsize Pay." *Wall Street Journal*, September 13. http://www.wsj.com/articles/epipen-maker-dispenses-outsize-pay-1473786288?mod=djemalertNEWS.

Markels, A., and M. Murray. 1996. "Call It Dumbsizing: Why Some Companies Regret Cost-Cutting." *Wall Street Journal*, May 14.

Marris, P. 2016. *Loss and change*. 2nd ed. New York: Routledge.

Marshall, M. V. 1984. *"An Introduction to the Marketing Concept of Managing an Institution's Future."* Cambridge, MA: Institute for Educational Management.

Maruping, L. M., V. Venkatesh, S. M. B Thatcher, and P. C. Patel. 2015 "Folding Under Pressure or Rising to the Occasion? Perceived Time Pressure and the Moderating Role of Team Temporal Leadership." *Academy of Management Journal 58*, no. 5: 1313–1333.

Marx, R., C. Stubbart, V. Traub, and M. Cavanaugh. 1987. "The NASA Space Shuttle Disaster: A Case Study." *Journal of Management Case Studies 3*: 300–318.

Maslow, A. H. 1943. "A Theory of Human Motivation." *Psychological Review 50*, no. 4: 370–96.

Maslow, A. H. 1954. *Motivation and Personality*. New York: HarperCollins.

Matthews, C. 1999. *Hardball*. New York: Free Press.

Matthews, C. 2012. "Can Robots Bring Manufacturing Jobs Back to the U.S.?" *Time*, September 27. http://business.time.com/2012/09/27/can-robots-bring-back-manufacturing-jobs-to-the-u-s/.

Matthews, D. 2016. "Taking Trump Voters' Concerns Seriously Means Listening to What They're Actually Saying." *Vox*, October 15. http://www.vox.com/policy-and-politics/2016/10/15/13286498/donald-trump-voters-race-economic-anxiety.

Mayo, E. 1933. *The Human Problems of an Industrial Civilization*. New York: MacMillan.

Mayo, E. 1945. *The Social Problems of an Industrial Civilization*. Boston: Division of Research, Graduate School of Business Administration, Harvard University.

McCall, M. W., M. M. Lombardo, and A. M. Morrison. 1988. *Lessons of Experience: How Successful Executives Develop on the Job*. New York: Free Press.

McCaskey, M. B. 1982. *The Executive Challenge: Managing Change and Ambiguity*. Marshfield, MA: Pitman.

McClelland, D. C. 1985. *Human Motivation*. Glenview, IL: Scott Foresman.

McCloskey, D. N. 1998. Bourgeois Virtue and the History of P and S. *The Journal of Economic History 58*, no. 2.

McConnell, M. 1987. *Challenger: A Major Malfunction*. New York: Doubleday.

McConnell, M. 2004. *Into the Mouth of the Cat: The Story of Lance Sijan, Hero of Vietnam*. New York: Norton.

McCourt, M. 2012. "Another Expiration Date." In Zackheim, V. *Exit Laughing: How Humor Takes the Sting Out of Death*. New York: North Atlantic Books.

McGrath, J. E. 1984. *Groups: Interaction and Performance*. Upper Saddle River, NJ: Prentice Hall.

McGregor, D. 1960. *The Human Side of Enterprise*. New York: McGraw-Hill.

McLennan, R. 1989. *Managing Organizational Change*. Upper Saddle River, NJ: Prentice Hall.

McNamee, M., and A. Borrus. 2002. "Out of Control at Enron." *Businessweek*, April 8.

Mead, M. 1928. *Coming of Age in Samoa*. New York: William Morrow.

Mead, M. 1935. *Sex and Temperament in Three Primitive Societies*. New York: William Morrow.

Mellahi, K., and A. Wilkinson. 2006. "The Impact of Downsizing on Innovation Output." *Academy of Management Proceedings*.

Mendelson, H., and A. Korin. (n.d.) *The Computer Industry: A Brief History*. Palo Alto, CA: Stanford Business School.

Meredith, R. 1996. "New Blood for the Big Three's Plants: This Hiring Spree Is Rewarding Brains, Not Brawn." *New York Times*, April 21.

Messick, D. M., and D. K. Ohme. 1998. "Some Ethical Aspects of the Social Psychology of Social Influence." In *Power and Influence in Organizations*, edited by R. M. Kramer and M. A. Neale. Thousand Oaks, CA: Sage.

Meyer, J. W. 2008. "Reflections on Institutional Theories of Organizations." In *The Sage Handbook of Organizational Institutionalism*, edited by R. Greenwood, C. Oliver, R. Suddaby, and K. Sahlin-Andersson. Thousand Oaks, CA: Sage.

Meyer, J. W., and B. Rowan. 1977. "Institutionalized Organizations: Formal Structure as Myth and Ceremony." *American Journal of Sociology 83*: 340–63.

Meyer, J. W., and B. Rowan. 1978. "The Structure of Educational Organizations." In *Environments and Organizations: Theoretical and Empirical Perspectives*, by M. W. Meyer and Associates. San Francisco: Jossey-Bass.

Meyer, J. W., and B. Rowan. 1983. "Institutionalized Organizations: Formal Structure as Myth and Ceremony." In *Organizational Environments: Ritual and Rationality*, edited by J. W. Meyer and W. R. Scott. Thousand Oaks, CA: Sage.

Mihalopoulos, D., and J. Kimberly. 2006. "Inside Daley's Machine." *Chicago Tribune*, June 21.

Miller, D., and P. H. Friesen. 1984. *Organizations: A Quantum View*. Upper Saddle River, NJ: Prentice Hall.

Mintzberg, H. 1973. *The Nature of Managerial Work*. New York: HarperCollins.

Mintzberg, H. 1979. *The Structuring of Organizations*. Upper Saddle River, NJ: Prentice Hall.

Mintzberg, H. 1987. "The Strategy Concept I: Five Ps For Strategy." *California Management Review 30*, no. 1: 11–24.

Mintzberg, H. 1994. *The Rise and Fall of Strategic Planning: Reconceiving Roles for Planning, Plans, Planners*. New York: Free Press.

Mirvis, P. H. 1988. "Organization Development, Part I: An Evolutionary Perspective." *Research in Organizational Change and Development 2*: 1–57.

Mirvis, P. H. 2006. "Revolutions in OD: The New and the New, New Things." In *Organization Development: A Jossey-Bass Reader*, edited by J. V. Gallos. San Francisco: Jossey-Bass.

Mirvis, P. H. 2014. "JABS at 50: Applied Behavioral Science and Something More?" *Journal of Applied Behavioral Science 50*, no. 4: 1–31.

Mitroff, I. I. 1983. *Stakeholders of the Organizational Mind: Toward a New View of Organizational Policy Making*. San Francisco: Jossey-Bass.

Mitroff, I. I., and R. H. Kilmann. 1975. "Stories Managers Tell: A New Tool for Organizational Problem Solving." *Management Review*, July: 18–28.

Moeller, J. 1968. "Bureaucracy and Teachers' Sense of Power." In *Sociology of Education*, edited by N. R. Bell and H. R. Stub. Florence, KY: Dorsey Press.

Mohr, R. D., and C. Zoghi. 2006. "Is Job Enrichment Really Enriching?" Washington, D.C.: Bureau of Labor Statistics. www.bls.gov/ore/abstract/ec/ec060010.htm.

Moore, J. F. 1993. "Predators and Prey: A New Ecology of Competition." *Harvard Business Review*, May–June: 75–86.

Moore, S., and B. Meyerhoff. 1977. *Secular Ritual*. Assen, Netherlands: Van Gorcum.

Morgan, A. 1995. *Prescription for Success: The Life and Values of Ewing Marion Kauffman*. Kansas City, MO: Andrews & McMeel.

Morgan, G. 1986. *Images of Organization*. Thousand Oaks, CA: Sage.

Morganthau, T. 1985. "Saying 'No' to New Coke." *Newsweek*, June 23.

Morgeson, F. P., M. D. Johnson, M. A. Campion, G. J. Medsker, and T. V. Mumford. 2006. "Understanding Reactions to Job Redesign: A Quasi-Experimental Examination of the Moderating Effects of Organizational Context on Perceptions of Performance Behavior." *Personnel Psychology 59*: 333–363.

Morran, C. 2013. "JCPenney Ends Ron Johnson Experiment, Sends CEO Packing." *Consumerist,* April 8. http://consumerist.com/2013/04/08/jcpenney-ends-ron-johnson-experiment-sends-ceo-packing.

Morris, B. 2002. "Trophy Husbands." *Fortune,* October 14.

Morris, B. 2003. "The Accidental CEO." *Fortune,* June 9.

Morrison, A. M. 1992. *The New Leaders: Guidelines on Leadership Diversity in America.* San Francisco: Jossey-Bass.

Morrison, A. M., R. P. White, and E. Van Velsor. 1987. *Breaking the Glass Ceiling.* Reading, MA: Addison-Wesley.

Moyers, B. 2007. "Payday for CEOs." *Bill Moyers Journal.* http://www.pbs.org/moyers/journal/06082007/profile.html.

Murphy, J. T. 1985. *Managing Matters: Reflections from Practice.* Monograph. Cambridge, MA: Graduate School of Education, Harvard University.

Myers, I. 1980. *Introduction to Type.* Palo Alto, CA: Consulting Psychologists Press.

Nadler, D. A., M. S. Gerstein, and R. B. Shaw. 1992. *Organizational Architecture: Designs for Changing Organizations.* San Francisco: Jossey-Bass.

Nelson, R. R., and S. G. Winter. 1982. *An Evolutionary Theory of Economic Change.* Cambridge, MA: Harvard University Press.

Neuman, J. 2004. "Former President Reagan Dies at 93." *Los Angeles Times, 1.* http://www.latimes.com/news/specials/obituaries/la-reagan,1,5246827,full.story.

Nichols, S. L., and D. C. Berliner. 2007. "High-stakes Testing and the Corruption of American Schools." *Harvard Educational Letter 23,* no. 2: 1–2.

Nickerson, J. A., and B. S. Silverman. 2003. "Why Firms Want to Organize Efficiently and What Keeps Them from Doing So: Inappropriate Governance, Performance, and Adaptation in a Deregulated Industry." *Administrative Science Quarterly 48:* 433–465.

Niemann, G. 2007. *Big Brown: The Untold Story of UPS.* San Francisco: Jossey-Bass.

North, D. C. 1989. "Institutional Change and Economic History," *Journal of Institutional and Theoretical Economics 145,* no. 1, March: 238–245.

O'Connor, P., and A. Goransson. 2015. "Constructing or Rejecting the Notion of the Other in University Management." *Educational Management, Administration, & Leadership, 43,* no. 2: 323–340.

O'Grady, S. 1998. *Basher Five-Two.* New York: Yearling.

Ohmae, K. 1990. *The Borderless World: Power and Strategy in the Interlinked Economy.* New York: Harper Business.

O'Keefe, D. L. 1983. *Stolen Lightning: The Social Theory of Magic.* New York: Vintage Books.

Okimoto, T. G., and V. L. Brescoll. 2010 "The Price of Power: Power Seeking and Backlash Against Female Politicians." *Personality and Social Psychology Bulletin,* vol. *36,* no. 7, 923–936.

Oliver, T. 1986. *The Real Coke, the Real Story.* New York: Random House.

Organ, D. W., and K. A. Ryan. 1995. "A Metaanalytic Review of Attitudinal and Dispositional Predictors of Organizational Citizenship Behavior." *Personnel Psychology 48:* 775–802.

Orgogozo, I. 1991. *Les paradoxes du management [The Paradoxes of Management].* Paris: Les Éditions d'Organisation.

Ormerod, P. 2007. *Why Most Things Fail: Evolution, Extinction and Economics*. New York: Wiley.

Ortner, S. 1973. "On Key Symbols." *American Anthropologist 75*: 1338–1346.

Oshry, B. 1995. *Seeing Systems: Unlocking the Mysteries of Organizational Life*. San Francisco: Berrett-Koehler.

O'Toole, J. 1995. *Leading Change: Overcoming the Ideology of Comfort and the Tyranny of Custom*. San Francisco: Jossey-Bass.

O'Toole, P. 1984. *Corporate Messiah: The Hiring and Firing of Million-Dollar Managers*. New York: Morrow.

Owen, H. 1993. *Open Space Technology*. Potomac, MD: Abbott.

Owen, H. 1995. *Tales from Open Space*. Potomac, MD: Abbott.

Owen, M., and K. Maurer. 2012, *No Easy Day: The Firsthand Account of the Mission That Killed Osama Bin Laden*. New York: Dutton.

Palmeri, C., and K. Epstein. 2007. "Fear and Loathing at the Airport." *Businessweek*, September 10.

Palumbo, G. 1991. *Gerencia participativa: Un caso exito en el sector salud [Participative Management: A Successful Case in the Health Sector]*. Caracas, Venezuela: Fundación Antonio Cisneros Bermudez.

Pande, P. S., R. P. Neuman, and R. R. Cavanagh. 2000. *The Six Sigma Way: How GE, Motorola, and Other Top Companies Are Honing Their Performance*. New York: McGraw-Hill.

Pape, R. 2006. *Dying to Win: The Strategic Logic of Suicide Terrorism*. New York: Random House.

Parker, G. 2008. *Team Players and Teamwork: New Strategies for Developing Successful Collaboration*. San Francisco: Jossey-Bass.

Parker, S., and T. D. Wall. 1998. *Job and Work Design: Organizing Work to Promote Well-Being and Effectiveness*. Thousand Oaks, CA: Sage.

Pasquier, S., and A. Chevelkina. 2007. "Gasprom: L'Arme de Pression." [Gazprom: The Pressure Weapon.] *L'Express,* January 25.

Paulson, E. 2001. *Inside Cisco: The Real Story of Sustained M&A Growth*. New York: Wiley.

Paustian-Underdahl, S. C., L. S. Walker, and D. J. Woehr. 2014. "Gender and Perceptions of Leadership Effectiveness: A Meta-analysis of Contextual Moderators." *Journal of Applied Psychology 99*, no. 6: 1129–1145.

Peck, S. 1998. *The Different Drum: Community Making and Peace*. New York: Touchstone.

Perrow, C. 1979. *Complex Organizations: A Critical Essay*. 2nd ed. Glenview, IL: Scott, Foresman.

Perrow, C. 1986. *Complex Organizations: A Critical Essay*. 3rd ed. New York: Random House.

Peters, B. G. 1999. *American Public Policy: Promise and Performance*. New York: Chatham House.

Peters, B. G. 2000. "Institutional Theory: Problems and Prospects." *Political Science Series*. Institute for Advanced Studies, Vienna.

Peters, T. J. 1979. "Beyond the Matrix Organization." *Business Horizons, 22*, No. 6, 15–27.

Peters, T. J., and N. Austin. 1985. *A Passion for Excellence*. New York: Random House.

Peters, T. J., and R. H. Waterman. 1982. *In Search of Excellence*. New York: HarperCollins.

Petzinger, T. 1995. *Hard Landing: The Epic Contest for Power and Profits That Plunged the Airlines into Chaos*. New York: Times Business.

Pfarrer, C. 2011. *SEAL Target Geronimo: The Inside Story of the Mission to Kill Osama bin Laden*. New York: Macmillan.

Pfeffer, J. 1978. *Organizational Design*. Arlington Heights, IL: AHM Publishing.

Pfeffer, J. 1981. *Power in Organizations*. Boston: Pitman.

Pfeffer, J. 1992. *Managing with Power: Politics and Influence in Organizations*. Boston: Harvard Business School Press.

Pfeffer, J. 1994. *Competitive Advantage Through People: Unleashing the Power of the Work Force*. Boston: Harvard Business School Press.

Pfeffer, J. 1998. *The Human Equation: Building Profits by Putting People First*. Boston: Harvard Business School Press.

Pfeffer, J. 2007. *What Were They Thinking? Unconventional Wisdom About Management*. Boston: Harvard Business School Press.

Pfeffer, J., and G. Salancik. 1978. *The External Control of Organizations*. New York: HarperCollins.

Pichault, F. 1993. *Ressources humaines et changement stratégique: Vers un management politique [Human Resources and Strategic Change: Toward a Political Approach to Management]*. Brussels, Belgium: DeBoeck.

Pink, D. H. 2009. *Drive: The Surprising Truth About What Motivates Us*. New York: Riverhead.

Pitt, R. N., and S. A. Tepper. 2012. "Double Majors: Influences, Identities and Impacts." Nashville: Curb Center, Vanderbilt University.

Politico Staff. 2016. "Full Text: Donald Trump 2016 RNC Draft Speech Transcript." *Politico*, July 17. http://www.politico.com/story/2016/07/full-transcript-donald-trump-nomination-acceptance-speech-at-rnc-225974.

Powell, B. 2007. "Trade: No Faking It." *Time*, April 12.

Powell, W. W., K. W. Koput, and L. Smith-Doerr. 1996. "Interorganizational Collaboration and the Locus of Innovation: Networks of Learning in Biotechnology." *Administrative Science Quarterly 41*: 116–145.

Pressman, J. L., and A. B. Wildavsky. 1973. *Implementation*. Berkeley: University of California Press.

Pyzdek, T. 2003. *The Six Sigma Handbook: The Complete Guide for GreenBelts, BlackBelts, and Managers at All Levels*. New York: McGraw-Hill.

Quenllas, A. 2013. "Whole Foods Case Study: A Benchmark Model of Management for Hospitality." *HospitalityNet.org*, February. http://www.hospitalitynet.org/news/4059396.html

Quinn, R. E. 1988. *Beyond Rational Management: Mastering the Paradoxes and Competing Demands of High Performance*. San Francisco: Jossey-Bass.

Quinn, R. E., and K. Cameron. 1983. "Organizational Life Cycles and Shifting Criteria of Effectiveness." *Management Science 29*: 33–51.

Quinn, R. E., S. R. Faerman, M. P. Thompson, and M. R. McGrath. 1996. *Becoming a Master Manager: A Competency Framework*. New York: Wiley.

Raffaele, P. 2007. "Keepers of the Lost Ark?" *Smithsonian* Magazine, December. http://www.smithsonianmag.com/people-places/keepers-of-the-lost-ark-179998820/?no-ist=&=&preview=&pa=&page=1

Rallis, S. 1980. "Different Views of Knowledge Use by Practitioners." Unpublished paper, Graduate School of Education, Harvard University.

Randall, D. 2010. "How Wells Fargo Cheated its Customers." *Forbes,* August 11. http://www.forbes
.com/sites/davidrandall/2010/08/11/how-wells-fargo-cheated-its-customers/#6147747f56c8.

Rao, P., and A. Kulkarni. 1998. "Perceived Importance of Needs in Relation to Job Level and Personality Make-Up." *Journal of the Indian Academy of Applied Psychology 24*: 37–42.

Rappaport, C. 1992. "A Tough Swede Invades the U.S." *Fortune,* January 29.

Reed, K. 2001. "Rituals of Combat: Air War." Unpublished manuscript, University of Southern California.

Reed, S., and A. Sains. 2002. "Outraged in Europe Over ABB." *Businessweek,* March 4.

Reichheld, F. F. 1993. "Loyalty-Based Management." *Harvard Business Review*, March–April.

Reichheld, F. F. 1996. *The Loyalty Effect: The Hidden Force Behind Growth, Profits, and Lasting Value.* Boston: Harvard Business School Press.

Reingold, J., and J. L. Yang. 2007. "The Hidden Workplace." *Fortune,* July 18. http://archive.fortune
.com/magazines/fortune/fortune_archive/2007/07/23/100135706/index.htm

RetailSails. 2012. *2012 Chain Store Productivity Guide – Overall Rankings.* http://www.retailsails
.com.php53-12.dfw1-1.websitetestlink.com/site-content/live/3/rs200_rankings.pdf.

Rice, A. K. 1953. *The Enterprise and Its Environment.* London: Tavistock.

Ricks, T. 1998. *Making the Corps.* New York: Touchstone.

Ridout, C. F., and D. H. Fenn. 1974. *Job Corps.* Boston: Harvard Business School Case Services.

Riebling, M. 2002. *Wedge: From Pearl Harbor to 9/11—How the Secret War between the FBI and CIA Has Endangered National Security.* New York: Touchstone.

Ritti, R. R., and G. R. Funkhouser. 1982. *The Ropes to Skip and the Ropes to Know.* 2nd ed. Columbus, Ohio: Grid.

Roberts, J. 2004. *The Modern Firm: Organizational Design for Performance and Growth.* Oxford: Oxford University Press.

Roberts, M. 2007. "Southwest CEO's 2006 Pay Less Than $1M." *Forbes.com,* March 30.

Rodriguez, R. 1997. "Credo." In Wolfe, G. *The New Religious Humanists: A Reader.* New York: Free Press.

Roethlisberger, F. J. 1945. "The Foreman: Master and Victim of Doubletalk." *Harvard Business Review 23*, no. 3.

Rogers-Kante, J. 2011. "A Trip to Zappos Headquarters." https://senegencebyjoni.com/page/15/.

Romero, E. J., and K. W. Cruthirds. 2006. "The Use of Humor in the Workplace." *Academy of Management Perspectives 20*, no. 2: 58–69.

Rosen, C., J. Case, and M. Staubus. 2005. *Equity: Why Employee Ownership Is Good for Business.* Boston: Harvard Business School Press.

Rosener, J. B. 1990. "Ways Women Lead." *Harvard Business Review 68*: 119–125.

Rosenthal, R., and L. Jacobson. 1968. *Pygmalion in the Classroom: Teacher Expectations and Pupils' Intellectual Development.* Austin, TX: Holt, Rinehart and Winston.

Rosovsky, H. 1990. *The University: An Owner's Manual.* New York: Norton.

Rossiter, C. 1966. *1787: The Grand Convention.* New York: New American Library.

Roush, C. 1999. *Inside Home Depot.* New York: McGraw-Hill.

Rundall, T., D. Starkweather, and B. Norrish. 1998. "If It Ain't Broke, Fix It: Beth Israel Hospital." Seattle: Cascade Center for Public Service, University of Washington.

Russ, J. 1994. *Les théories du pouvoir [Theories of Power].* Paris: Librairie Générale Française.

Salamone, A. 2016. "Foundry Operator McWane Ductile Tries to Repair Corporate Damage." *The Morning Call,* July 20. http://www.mcall.com/business/mc-mcwane-pipe-factory-tour-2016 0423-story.html.

Salancik, G. R., and J. Pfeffer. 1977. "An Examination of Need-Satisfaction Models of Job Attitudes." *Administrative Science Quarterly 22*: 427–456.

Salovey, P., and J. Mayer. 1990. "Emotional Intelligence." *Imagination, Cognition, and Personality 9,* no. 3: 185–211.

Salovey, P., B. Bedell, J. B. Detweiler, and J. D. Mayer. 1999. "Coping Intelligently: Emotional Intelligence and the Coping Process." In *Coping: The Psychology of What Works,* edited by C. R. Snyder. New York: Oxford University Press.

Sapolsky, H. 1972. *The Polaris System Development.* Cambridge, MA: Harvard University Press.

Saubaber, D. 2007. "Sienne: La cavalcade infernale." [Siena: The Horse Race from Hell.] *L'Express,* September 8.

Schein, E. H. 1969. *Process Consultation.* Reading, MA: Addison-Wesley.

Schein, E. H. 1992. *Organizational Culture and Leadership.* 2nd ed. San Francisco: Jossey-Bass.

Schein, V. E. 1975. "Relationships Between Sex Role Stereotypes and Requisite Management Characteristics Among Female Managers." *Journal of Applied Psychology 75*: 340–344.

Schein, V. E. 1990. "The Relationship Between Sex Role Stereotypes and Requisite Management Characteristics: A Cross-Cultural Look." Paper presented at the Twenty-Second International Congress of Applied Psychology, Kyoto, Japan, July.

Schelling, T. (1960). *The Strategy of Conflict.* Cambridge, MA: Harvard University Press.

Schlender, B. 2004. "The Man Who Built Pixar's Incredible Innovation Machine." *Fortune,* Nov. 15.

Schlesinger, L., R. Eccles, and J. Gabarro. 1983. *Managerial Behavior in Organizations.* New York: McGraw-Hill.

Schmidt, E., and H. Varian. 2005. "Google: Ten Golden Rules." *Newsweek,* December 2.

Schneider, B., and C. Alderfer. 1973. "Three Studies of Measures of Need Satisfaction in Organizations." *Administrative Science Quarterly 18*: 498–505.

Schubert, S., and T. C. Miller. 2008. "At Siemens, Bribery Was Just a Line Item." *New York Times,* December 20. http://www.nytimes.com/2008/12/21/business/worldbusiness/21siemens.html.

Schuler, D. A., K. Rehbein, and R. D. Cramer. 2002. "Pursuing Strategic Advantage Through Political Means: A Multivariate Approach." *Academy of Management Journal 45,* no. 4: 659–672.

Schutz, A. 1967. *The Phenomenology of the Social World.* Evanston, IL: Northwestern University Press.

Schultz, H., and J. Gordon. 2011. *Onward: How Starbucks Fought for Its Life without Losing Its Soul.* New York: Rodale.

Schwartz, H. S. 1986. "The Clockwork or the Snakepit: An Essay on the Meaning of Teaching Organizational Behavior." *Organizational Behavior Teaching Review 11*: 19–26.

Schwartz, N. D. 2009. "Job Losses Pose a Threat to Stability Worldwide." *New York Times,* February 14. http://www.nytimes.com/2009/02/15/business/15global.html?pagewanted=all&_r=0.

Schwartz, T., and C. Porath. 2014. "Why You Hate Work." *New York Times,* June 1. http://www.nytimes.com/2014/06/01/opinion/sunday/why-you-hate-work.html?action=click&content Collection=Asia%20Pacific&module=MostEmailed&version=Full&region=Marginalia&src= me&pgtype=article.

Scott, W. R. 1981. *Organizations: Rational, Natural, and Open Systems.* Upper Saddle River, NJ: Prentice Hall.

Scott, W. R. 1983. "The Organization of Environments: Network, Cultural, and Historical Elements." In *Organizational Environments: Ritual and Rationality,* edited by J. W. Meyer and W. R. Scott. Thousand Oaks, CA: Sage.

Scott, W. R. 1985. *Institutions and Organizations.* Thousand Oaks, CA: Sage.

Scott, W. R. 2014. *Institutions and Organizations.* 4th Ed. Thousand Oaks, CA: Sage.

Scott, W. R., and G. F. Davis. 2007. *Organizations and Organizing: Rational, Natural, and Open Systems Perspectives.* Englewood Cliffs, NJ: Prentice-Hall.

Seeger, J. A., J. W. Lorsch, and C. F. Gibson. 1975. *First National City Bank Operating Group (A) and (B)* Boston: Harvard Business School Case Services.

Seely Brown, J., S. Denning, K. Groh, and L. Prusak. 2004. *Storytelling in Organizations: Why Storytelling Is Transforming 21st Century Organizations and Management.* Burlington, MA: Butterworth-Heinemann.

Seelig, T. 2015. *inGenius: A Crash Course on Creativity.* New York: HarperOne.

Selznick, P. 1957. *Leadership and Administration.* New York: HarperCollins.

Semler, R. 1993. *Maverick: The Success Story Behind the World's Most Unusual Workplace.* New York: Warner Book.

Senge, P. M. 1990. *The Fifth Discipline: The Art and Practice of the Learning Organization.* New York: Currency/Doubleday.

Seper, J. 2005. "CIA Didn't Tell FBI About 9/11 Hijackers." *Washington Times,* June 10.

Sérieyx, H. 1993. *Le big bang des organisations [The Organizational Big Bang].* Paris: Calmann-Lévy.

Shamir, B., R. J. House, and M. Arthur. 1993. "The Motivational Effects of Charismatic Leadership: A Self-Concept Based Theory." *Organization Science 4:* 577–593.

Shani, G., and J. D. Westphal. 2016. "Persona Non Grata? Determinants and Consequences of Social Distancing from Journalists Who Engage in Negative Coverage of Firm Leadership." *Academy of Management Journal 59,* no. 1: 302–329.

Shermer, M. 2012. *The Believing Brain: From Ghosts and Gods to Politics and Conspiracies—How We Construct Beliefs and Reinforce Them as Truths.* New York: St. Martin's Griffin.

Shu, L., and A. S. Adams. 1995. "Is There Something More Important Behind Framing?" *Organizational Behavior and Human Decision Processes 62:* 216–219.

Simmel, G. 1950. *The Sociology of Georg Simmel.* New York: Free Press.

Simmons, A. 2006. *The Story Factor.* 2nd ed. New York: Perseus Books.

Simmons, A. 2007. *Whoever Tells the Best Story Wins: How to Use Your Own Stories to Communicate with Power and Impact.* New York: AMACOM.

Simon, H. 1996. *Hidden Champions: Lessons from 500 of the World's Best Unknown Companies*. Boston: Harvard Business School Press.

Simon, H. A. 1947. *Administrative Behavior*. New York: Macmillan.

Simon, H. A., and W. G. Chase. 1973. "Skill in Chess." *American Scientist 61*: 394–403.

Sirianni, C. 1995. "Tavistock Institute Develops Practices of Contemporary Work Reform." Civic Practices Network, Brandeis University.

Slee, T. 2006. *No One Makes You Shop at Wal-Mart: The Surprising Deceptions of Individual Choice*. Toronto: Between the Lines.

Sloan, A. P., Jr. 1965. *My Years with General Motors*. New York: Macfadden.

Smith, C. S. 2002. "China Faces Problems Creating Jobs, Officials Say." *New York Times,* April 20.

Smith, G. and R. Parloff. 2016. "Hoaxwagen." *Fortune,* March 16. http://fortune.com/inside-volkswagen-emissions-scandal/.

Smith, H. 1988. *The Power Game*. New York: Random House.

Smith, S. 2016. "6 Charts that Show Where Clinton and Trump Supporters Differ." Pew Research Center. http://www.pewresearch.org/fact-tank/2016/10/20/6-charts-that-show-where-clinton-and-trump-supporters-differ/.

Solomon, R. C. 1993. *Ethics and Excellence: Cooperation and Integrity in Business*. Oxford, England: Oxford University Press.

Soper, S. 2011. "Inside Amazon's Warehouse." *Allentown (PA) Morning Call,* September 18.

Sorkin, A. R. 2016. "Pervasive Sham Deals at Wells Fargo, and No One Noticed?" *New York Times,* September 13.

Spector, R., and D. McCarthy. 1995. *The Nordstrom Way: The Inside Story of America's #1 Customer Service Company*. New York: Wiley.

Springarn, N. D. 1982. "Primary Nurses Bring Back One-to-One Care." *New York Times,* December 26.

Stack, J., and B. Burlingham. 1994. *The Great Game of Business*. New York: Currency/Doubleday.

Statler, M., and J. Roos. 2007. "The Importance of Play in Organizations." In *Everyday Strategic Preparedness*, by M. Statler and J. Roos. Houndmills, Basingstoke, Hampshire: Palgrave MacMillan.

Staw, B. M., and H. Hoang. 1995. "Sunk Costs in the NBA: Why Draft Order Affects Playing Time and Survival in Professional Basketball." *Administrative Science Quarterly 40*: 474–494.

Staw, B. M., and L. D. Epstein. 2000. "What Bandwagons Bring: Effects of Popular Management Techniques on Corporate Performance, Reputation, and CEO Pay." *Administrative Science Quarterly 45*, no. 3: 523–556.

Stein, N. 2000. "Winning the War to Keep Top Talent." *Fortune,* May 29.

Stern, R. N., and S. R. Barley. 1996. "Organizations and Social Systems: Organization Theory's Neglected Mandate." *Administrative Science Quarterly 41*: 146–162.

Sternberg, R. J. 1985. *Beyond IQ: A Triarchic Theory of Human Intelligence*. New York: Cambridge University Press.

Steward, T. A. 1994. "Managing in a Wired Company." *Fortune,* July 11.

Stinchcombe, A. L. 1965. "Social Structure and Organizations." In *Handbook of Organizations*, edited by J. G. March. 142–193. Chicago: Rand McNally.

Stires, D. 2002. "Fallen Arches." *Fortune,* April 29.

Stogdill, R. 1948. "Personal Factors Associated with Leadership: A Survey of the Literature." *Journal of Psychology 35*: 25–71.

Stogdill, R. 1974. *Handbook of Leadership.* New York: Free Press.

Stone, B. 2013 "Costco CEO Craig Jelinek Leads the Cheapest, Happiest Company in the World." *Businessweek,* June 6.

Stross, R. E. 1996. "Microsoft's Big Advantage—Hiring Only the Supersmart." *Fortune,* November 25.

Sunderman, G. L. 2006. "The Unraveling of No Child Left Behind: How Negotiated Changes Transform the Law." The Civil Rights Project at Harvard University. http://files.eric.ed.gov/fulltext/ED490859.pdf.

Svara, J. G. 2007. *The Ethics Primer for Public Administrators in Government and Nonprofit Organizations.* Sudbury, MA: Jones & Bartlett.

Tagliabue, J. 1999. "McDonald's Gets a Lesson in, Well, the French Fry." *New York Times,* December 11.

Taleb, N. 2007. *The Black Swan: The Impact of the Highly Improbable.* New York: Random House.

Taylor, F. W. 1911. *The Principles of Scientific Management.* New York: Harper.

Tengblad, S. 2013. *The Work of Managers: Toward a Practice Theory of Management.* Oxford: Oxford University Press.

Terkel, S. 2004. *Hope Dies Last.* New York: New Press.

Terman, L. M. 1904. "A Preliminary Study of the Psychology and Pedagogy of Leadership." *Journal of Genetic Psychology 11*: 413–451.

Thompson, J. D. 1967. *Organizations in Action.* New York: McGraw-Hill.

Thompson, M. D. 2000. "Gender, Leadership Orientation, and Effectiveness: Testing the Theoretical Models of Bolman & Deal and Quinn." *Sex Roles 42*: 969–992.

Thorndike, E. L. 1920. "Intelligence and Its Uses." *Harper's.*

"Thousands Welcome the Long-Awaited 787 Dreamliner." 2007. *Seattle Post-Intelligencer,* July 8.

Tomsho, R. 1994. "How Greyhound Lines Re-Engineered Itself Right into a Deep Hole." *Wall Street Journal,* October 20.

Topoff, H. R. 1972. "The Social Behavior of Army Ants." *Scientific American,* November.

Treacy, M., and F. Wiersema. 1995. *The Discipline of Market Leaders: Choose Your Customers, Narrow Your Focus, Dominate Your Market.* Reading, MA: Addison-Wesley.

Trieschmann, J. S., A. R. Dennis, and G. B. Northcraft. 2000. "Serving Multiple Constituencies in the Business School: MBA Program vs. Research Performance." *Academy of Management Journal 43*: 1130–1142.

Trist, E., and K. Bamforth. 1951. "Some Social and Psychological Consequences of the Longwall Method of Coal Getting." *Human Relations 4*: 3–38.

Trost, A. H. 1989. "Leadership Is Flesh and Blood." In *Military Leadership: Traditions and Future Trends,* edited by L. Atwater and R. Penn. Annapolis, MD: Naval Institute Press.

Tsugawa, Y., B. J. Anupam, J. F. Figueroa, J. Orva, D. M. Blumenthal, and A. K. Jha. 2016. "Comparison of Hospitality Mortality and Readmission Rates for Medicare Patients Treated by Male vs Female Physicians." *JAMA Internal Medicine,* doi: 10.1001/jamainternalmed.2016.7875. http://jamanetwork.com/journals/jamainternalmedicine/fullarticle/2593255.

Turse, N. 2013. *Kill Anything That Moves: The Real American War in Vietnam.* New York: Metropolitan.

Tuttle, B. 2013 "The 5 Big Mistakes That Led to Ron Johnson's Ouster at JC Penney." *Time,* April 9. http://business.time.com/2013/04/09/the-5-big-mistakes-that-led-to-ron-johnsons-ouster-at-jc-penney.

Uchitelle, L. 2007. "The End of the Line as They Know It: Detroit's Displaced Are Struggling to Build New Lives." *New York Times,* April 1.

Urwick, L. 1937. "Organization as a Technical Problem." In *Papers on the Science of Administration,* edited by L. H. Gulick and L. Urwick. New York: Columbia University Press.

Uzzi, B. 1997. "Social Structure and Competition in Interfirm Networks: The Paradox of Embeddedness." *Administrative Science Quarterly 42*: 35–67.

Vaill, P. B. 1982. "The Purposing of High-Performance Systems." *Organizational Dynamics,* Autumn: 23–39.

Vaill, P. B. 1989. *Managing as a Performing Art: New Ideas for a World of Chaotic Change.* San Francisco: Jossey-Bass.

Valian, V. 1999. *Why So Slow? The Advancement of Women.* Cambridge, MA: MIT Press.

Van Engen, M. L., R. Van der Leeden, and T. M. Willemsen. 2001. "Gender, Context and Leadership Styles: A Field Study." *Journal of Occupational and Organizational Psychology 74*, no. 5: 581–598. doi: 10.1348/096317901167532.G.

Van Kerckhove, G. 2013. "Another View on China." Address to UMKC EMBA Group, Beijing, April.

Vantrappen, H., and F. Wirtz, 2016. "Making Matrix Organizations Actually Work." *Harvard Business Review,* March 1. https://hbr.org/2016/03/making-matrix-organizations-actually-work.

Varchaver, N. 2016 "Mary Barra." *Fortune,* December 1.

Vaughan, D. 1990. "Autonomy, Interdependence, and Social Control: NASA and the Space Shuttle Challenger." *Administrative Science Quarterly 35*: 225–257.

Vaughan, D. 1995. *The Challenger Launch Decision: Risky Technology, Culture, and Deviance at NASA.* Chicago: University of Chicago.

Vella, M. 2006. "German Throwdown: BMW vs. Mercedes-Benz." *Businessweek,* May 5.

Viall, A. C., J. L. Napier, and V. L. Brescoll, 2016. "A Bed of Thorns: Female Leaders and the Self-Reinforcing Cycle of Illegitimacy." *Leadership Quarterly,* vol. 27, 400–414.

Vough, H. C., and B. B. Caza. 2017. "Where Do I Go from Here? Sensemaking and the Construction of Growth-Based Stories in the Wake of Denied Promotions." *Academy of Management Review 42*, no. 1: 103–128.

Voss, J. F., C. R. Wolfe, J. A. Lawrence, and R. A. Engle. 1991. "From Representation to Decision: An Analysis of Problem Solving in International Relations." In *Complex Problem Solving,* edited by R. J. Sternberg and P. A. Frensch. Hillsdale, NJ: Erlbaum.

Vroom, V. H., and P. W. Yetton. 1973. *Leadership and Decision Making.* Pittsburgh: University of Pittsburgh Press.

Wahba, M. A., and L. G. Bridwell. 1976. "Maslow Reconsidered: A Review of Research on Need Hierarchy Theory." *Organizational Behavior and Human Performance 15*: 212–240.

Wald, M. L., and J. Schwartz. 2003a. "NASA Management Failings Are Linked to Shuttle Demise." *New York Times,* July 12.

Wald, M. L., and J. Schwartz. 2003b. "Part by Part, Investigators Relive the Shuttle's Demise." *New York Times,* July 22.

Wang, L., G. Beckett, and L. Brown. 2006. "Controversies of Standardized Assessment in School Accountability Reform: A Critical Synthesis of Multidisciplinary Research Evidence." *Applied Measurement in Education 19*, no. 4: 305–328.

Wasdin, H. E., and S. Templin. 2014. *SEAL Team Six: Memoirs of an Elite Navy SEAL Sniper.* New York: St. Martin's Press.

Waterman, R. H., Jr. 1994. *What America Does Right: Learning from Companies That Put People First.* New York: Norton.

Watson, T. 2000. *In Search of Management: Culture, Chaos and Control in Managerial Work.* Revised ed. London: Thomson Learning.

Weatherford, J. M. 1985. *Tribes on the Hill: The United States Congress—Rituals and Realities.* Westport, CT: Bergin & Garvey.

Weber, M. 1947. *The Theory of Social and Economic Organization,* translated by T. Parsons. New York: Free Press.

Weddle, C. J. 1991. "A Study of Leadership Styles and Personality of Successful Women Administrators in Higher Education: Implications for Organizations and Training." Paper presented at conference on "The Impact of Leadership," Center for Creative Leadership, Colorado Springs, CO.

Wegmans. 2016. "What We Believe." https://www.wegmans.com/about-us/company-overview.html.

Weick, K. E. 1976. "Educational Organizations as Loosely Coupled Systems." *Administrative Science Quarterly 21*: 1–19.

Weick, K. E., and M. G. Bougon. 1986. "Organizations as Cognitive Maps." In *The Thinking Organization,* edited by H. P. Sims Jr., D. A. Gioia, and associates. San Francisco: Jossey-Bass.

Weiner, J. 2010. "New Gap Logo, Despised Symbol of Corporate Banality, Dead at One Week." *Vanity Fair,* October 12. http://www.vanityfair.com/online/daily/2010/10/new-gap-logo-despised-symbol-of-corporate-banality-dead-at-one-week.

Weingart, L. R., K. J. Behfar, C. Bendersky, G. Todorova, and K. A. Jehn. 2015. "The Directness and Oppositional Intensity of Conflict Expression." *Academy of Management Journal 40*, no. 2: 235–262.

Weisbord, M. R., and S. Janoff. 1995. *Future Search: An Action Guide to Finding Common Ground in Organizations and Communities.* San Francisco: Berrett-Koehler.

Weiss, C. H. 1980. *Social Science Research and Decision Making.* New York: Columbia University Press.

White, R. W. 1960. "Competence and the Psychosexual Stages of Development." In *Nebraska Symposium on Motivation,* edited by M. R. Jones. Lincoln: University of Nebraska Press.

Whitmyer, C. 1993. *In the Company of Others.* New York: Putnam.

Whyte, W. F. 1955. *Money and Motivation.* New York: HarperCollins.

Williamson, O. E. 1975. *Markets and Hierarchies.* New York: Free Press.

Williamson, O. E. 1985. *The Economic Institutions of Capitalism.* New York: Macmillan.

Wilson, C., and J. Wilson. 1991. "The Impact of Personality, Gender and International Location on Multi-Level Management Ratings." Paper presented at conference on "The Impact of Leadership," Center for Creative Leadership, Colorado Springs, CO, July.

Wimpelberg, R. K. 1987. "Managerial Images and School Effectiveness." *Administrators' Notebook 32*: 1–4.

Wingfield, N. 2016. "Redfin Shies Away from the Typical Start-Up's Gig Economy." *New York Times,* July 9. http://www.nytimes.com/2016/07/10/technology/a-start-up-shies-away-from-the-gig-economy.html

Worldhappiness, report. 2017. "World Happiness Report 2017." http://worldhappiness.report/ed/2017/.

Woodward, J. ed., 1970. *Industrial Organizations: Behavior and Control.* Oxford, England: Oxford University Press.

Wooley, A. W., C. F. Chabris, A. Pentland, N. Hashmi, and T. W. Malone. 2010. "Evidence for a Collective Intelligence Factor in the Performance of Human Groups." *Science 330*: 686–688.

WuDunn, S. 1996. "When Lifetime Jobs Die Prematurely." *New York Times,* June 12.

Yorks, L., and D. A. Whitsett. 1989. *Scenarios of Change: Advocacy and the Diffusion of Job Redesign in Organizations.* New York: Praeger.

Yukl, G. 2012. *Leadership in Organizations.* 8th ed. Upper Saddle River, NJ: Prentice Hall.

Zaccaro, S. 2007. "Trait-Based Perspectives of Leadership." *American Psychologist 62*: 6–16.

Zaccaro, S., C. Kemp, and P. Bader, 2004. "Leader Traits and Attributes." In *The Nature of Leadership,* by J. E. Antonakis, A. T. Cianciolo, and R. J. Sternberg. Thousand Oaks, CA: Sage.

Zachary, G. P. 1993. "Climbing the Peak: Agony and Ecstasy of 200 Code Writers Beget Windows NT." *Wall Street Journal,* May.

Zachary, G. P. 1994. *Showstopper! The Breakneck Race to Create Windows NT and the Next Generation at Microsoft.* New York: Free Press.

Zappos Blogs. 2011. "Amazon & Zappos, 1 Year Later."

Zott, C., and Q. N. Huy. 2007. "How Entrepreneurs Use Symbolic Management to Acquire Resources." *Administrative Science Quarterly 52*: 70–105.

THE AUTHORS

Lee G. Bolman holds the Marion Block Missouri Chair in Leadership at the Bloch School of Management, University of Missouri–Kansas City. He received a BA (1962) in history and a PhD (1968) in administrative sciences, both from Yale University. Bolman's interests lie at the intersection of leadership and organizations, and he has published numerous articles, chapters, and cases. With Joan Gallos he is coauthor of *Engagement: Transforming Difficult Relationships at Work* (2016) and *Reframing Academic Leadership* (2011). Bolman has been a consultant to corporations, public agencies, universities, and public schools in the United States, Asia, Europe, and Latin America. For 20 years he taught at the Harvard Graduate School of Education, where he also chaired the Institute for Educational Administration and the School Leadership Academy. He has been director and board chair of the Organizational Behavioral Teaching Society and Director of the National Training Laboratories.

Bolman lives in Brookline, Massachusetts with his wife, Joan Gallos, and a mischievous Theory Y cockapoo, Douglas McGregor.

•   •   •

Terrence E. Deal has served on the faculties of Stanford, Harvard, Vanderbilt, and the University of Southern California. He received his BA (1961) in history from the University of La Verne (ULV), his MA (1966) in social science from California State University at Los Angeles, and his PhD (1972) in sociology and administration from Stanford University. Deal has been a police officer, public school teacher, high school principal, district administrator, and university professor.

His primary research interests are in organizations, symbolism, and change. He is the author of 37 books, including the bestseller *Corporate Cultures* (with A. A. Kennedy, 1982) and *Shaping School Culture* (with K. Peterson, 3rd ed., 2016). He has published articles on organizations, change, and leadership. He is a consultant to business, health care, military, educational, and religious organizations domestically and in Europe, Scandinavia, the Middle East, Canada, South America, Japan, and Southeast Asia. He is currently the founder of ULV's Deal Leadership Institute.

Deal lives in San Luis Obispo's Edna Valley, California, with his wife, Sandy, and their cats, Toby and Murphy. He is semiretired from university life. Along with writing, his current avocation is winemaking as a founder of the Edna Ranch Vintner's Guild.

• • •

Bolman and Deal first met in 1976 when they were assigned to co-teach a course on organizations at Harvard University. Steeped in different disciplines on opposite coasts, they disagreed on almost everything. It was the beginning of a challenging but very productive partnership. They have written a number of other books together, including *Leading with Soul: An Uncommon Journey of Spirit* and *How Great Leaders Think: the Art of Reframing*. Their books have been translated into many languages for readers in Asia, Europe, Latin America, and the Middle East.

For five years, Bolman and Deal also codirected the National Center for Educational Leadership, a research consortium of Harvard, Vanderbilt, and the University of Chicago.

The authors appreciate hearing from readers and welcome comments, questions, suggestions, or accounts of experiences that bear on the ideas in the book. Stories of success, failure, or chronic puzzlement are all welcome. Readers can contact the authors at the following addresses:

Lee Bolman
37 Salisbury Road
Brookline, MA 02445
lee@bolman.com

• • •

Terry Deal
6625 Via Piedra
San Luis Obispo, CA 93401
sucha@surfnetusa.com

NAME INDEX

Note: Page references in *italics* refer to exhibits.

Bellow, G., 204
Belluck, P., 80
Benard, S., 344
Benedict, R., 241
Benner, M. J., 7, 363
Bennis, Warren, 190, 205, 276, 334–336, 339, 349, 355
Bensimon, E. M., 20, 311–312
Benson, B., 36–37, *37*
Berenson, A., 131
Berg, P., 137, 147
Berger, P., 236
Berger, W., 13
Bergman, L., 132–133
Berliner, D. C., 227
Bernstein, A., 143
Bernstein, E. J., 63–64
Besharov, M. L., 7
Bettelheim, B., 247
Bezos, Jeff, 46, 63, 245, 347
Bhutto, Benazir, 179
Bickman, L., 343
Bierce, Ambrose, 181
Bies, Leann, 125
Bigelow, L., 344
bin Laden, Osama, 44, 93, 94, 106, 265
Bion, W. R., 170
Birnbaum, R., 20
Blair, M. M., 143
Blake, R., 168
Blakeman, C., 151
Blakey, Marion C., 226
Blanchard, K., 332, 333, 349
Blank, W., 332
Blasi, J. R., 143
Blau, P. M., 49
Block, P., 190
Block, R., 55
Bloomberg, Michael, 298
Blum, A., 291
Blumberg, P., 147
Blumer, H., 241
Boesky, Ivan, 216
Boivie, S., 192
Boje, D. M., 282
Bok, S., 213
Bolman, L. G., 16, 20, 311, 312, 343, 391, 419
Bonaparte, Napoléon, 325
Bono, 277, 281
Book, E. W., 342
Borrus, A., 75
Borys, B., 52
Boudreau, J., 131
Bower, J. L., 82
Boyatzis, R. E., 167, 349, 350

Brachmann, S., 51
Bradford, D. L., 349
Brady, Karren, 341–343
Brass, D. J., 204
Brescoll, V. L., 344, 345
Briand, M., 336
Bridwell, L. G., 121
Broder, J. M., 67
Brokaw, Tom, 256
Broughton, I., 253
Brown, D. J., 46
Brown, L., 227
Brown, L. D., 193, 195, 196
Brown, P., 204
Bryan, L. L., 53
Buckley, George, 363
Buddha, 248
Bunker, B. B., 155
Burke, Edmund, 201
Burke, Kenneth, 282
Burke, W., 155–156
Burkus, D., 108
Burlingham, B., 145
Burnes, B., 154
Burns, J. M., 214, *331*, 333, 335
Burns, N., 9
Burns, Ursula, 345
Burris, E. R., 147
Burrough, Bryan, 219
Burt, R. S., 204, *424*
Bush, George W., 55, 193, 297, 356
Butcher, D., 209
Byrne, J. A., 10, 131
Byrnes, N., 116, 151
Byrnes, N. J., 245

C
Cable, J. P., 118
Caldicott, S. M., 15
Callan, V. J., 344
Cameron, K., 65
Campbell, D., 395
Campbell, J., 242, 251
Campbell, J. P., 154
Capra, Fritjof, 83
Carless, S. A., 343
Carli, L. L., 343
Carlin, J., 305
Carlson, S., 299
Carlyle, T., 332, 341
Carlzon, Jan, 351
Carnegie, Andrew, 330
Carrigan, Patricia, 351
Carstedt, Goran, 11

Gargiulo, M., 60
Garland, H., 39
Garvey, Marcus, 239
Gates, Bill, 51, 139, 202, 203, 212, 213
GearheadGrrrl, 250
Gegerenzer, G., 39
Gentry, R. J., 192
George, B., 338
George, Bill, 387–388
Gerstein, M. S., 53
Gerstner, Lou, Jr., 236, 360, 368
Gertz, D., 131
Gibb, C. A., 154, 332
Gibson, C. F., 88–89
Ginsburg, S., 103
Giroux, H., 128
Giuliani, Rudy, 337
Gladwell, M., 12
Glanz, J., 208
Glass, C., 343, 345
Goffman, Erving, 11, 241, 257, 282
Goizueta, Robert, 377
Goldberg, L. R., 169
Goleman, D., 350
Goleman, Daniel, 166, 167, 177
Goodman, D., 302
Goodnight, Jim, 141
Goransson, A., 345
Gorbachev, Mikhail, 189, 195
Gordon, J., 276
Gore, William L., 82–83, 107
Gottfried, M. A., 11
Gottschall, J., 21, 247
Gøtzsche, P. C., 40
Govindarajan, Vijay, 362
Graeff, C. L., 332
Graen, G., *331,* 333
Graffin, S. D., 9, 192
Granell, E., 311
Granovetter, M. S., 159–160, *424*
Gray, B. J., 12
Green, S. G., 332
Greenberg, Jack, 79
Greenleaf, R. K., 350
Greiner, L. E., 65
Griffin, E., 396
Grinder, J., 241
Griswold, A., 223
Groopman, J., 13
Guéhenno, J. M., 421
Guetzkow, H., 170
Gulati, R., 60
Gulick, L., 48
Gumpert, R., 332

Gunther, M., 153
Gupta, Rajat, 10
Gupta, V., *340*
Gurses, K., 223
Guyer, Jim, 274

H
Hackman, J. R., *121,* 149, 170, 176
Haerem, T., 96
Haga, W. J., *331,* 333
Hagey, K., 14
Hahn, T. L., 12
Haleblian, J., 9
Hall, R. H., 49, 346
Hallinger, P., 343
Hambleton, R. K., 332
Hambrick, D. C., *425*
Hamel, G., 72, 82, 83, 388
Hamm, S., 84
Hammer, M., 87–88
Hampden-Turner, C., 11
Hamper, Ben, 124–128
Hampton, W. J., 349
Handy, C., 169
Hanges, P. J., *340*
Hannan, M. T., *425*
Hannaway, J., 61
Hansen, M. T., 306, 307, *308,* 338, 347
Hansot, E., 257
Harnish, V., 136
Harris, A., 250
Harris, E. F., *331,* 332
Harrison, D. A., 173
Harrison, J., 151
Hatch, M. J., 241
Haynes, Jan, 104
Haynes, Ron, 104–105
Healey, M. P., 173
Heathfield, S. M., 240
Hebert, Edward, 252
Hedberg, B. L. T., 82
Heffernan, M., 344
Heffron, F., 196
Heifetz, R. A., 196, 334, 335, 336
Heimovics, R. D., 20, 311, 312
Heisler, Y., 363
Helgesen, Sally, 72, 75, 76, 83–84, 89, 92, 100, 342
Heller, F., 147, 150
Hellevik, O., 151
Helyar, John, 219
Henderson, R. M., 66, 86
Herbst, M., 131
Herman, R. D., 20, 311, 312
Hernández, J. C., 117

Hersey, P., 332, 333, 350
Herzberg, F., 120, *121,* 148–149
Hesketh, A., 204
Heskett, J. L., 242, 258
Hewlett, William, 78
Hildebrand, Jeffrey, 145–146
Hill, L. A., 84
Hindo, B., 56, 362, 363
Hirschman, D., 223
Hitler, Adolf, 8, 214, 328, 337, 353
Hoang, H., 39
Hock, Dee, 266
Hodgkinson, G. P., 173
Hoffman, B. G., 91
Hoffrage, U., 39
Hofstede, Geert, 241, 260–261
Hogan, J., 9
Hogan, R. G., 9
Hoge, W., 342
Holberger, Ken, 271
Holland, Chuck, 274
Hollander, E. P., 339, 350
Holloway, P., 39
Holmes, Oliver Wendell, 215
Hoobler, J. M., 344
Hoover, J. Edgar, 19
Hoskisson, R. E., 223
House, R. J., *331,* 333, *340,* 350
Hróbjartsson, A., 40
Hsieh, Tony, 63, 64, 240
Huang, Xu, 147
Huselid, M. A., 137, 139
Hussein, Saddam, 195, 369, 385
Huy, Q. N., 240, 293

I
Iacocca, Lee, 351–354
Iansiti, M., 225
Infanger, M., 342

J
Jackall, R., 197, 198
Jackson, Michael, 377
Jacobs, A., 187
Jacobson, L., 39–40
Jaffe, J. F., 9
James, LeBron, 103
James, William, 330
Jamieson, J. P., 15
Janoff, S., 154
Jarvis, C., 250
Javidan, M., *340*
Jehn, K. A., 196
Jenkins, W. A., 137, 249

Jenkins, W. O., 332
Jensen, C., 183
Jensen, Michael C., 76, 118, 374, *424*
Jesus, 248
Jick, T. D., 361
Joan of Arc, 214, 341
Jobs, Steve, 5–6, 51, 78, 95
John, O. P., 169
Johnson, B. T., 343
Johnson, Kelly, 95
Johnson, Ron, 363–364
Johnson, Ross, 219, 220, 224–225
Johnson, S., 349
Johnson, Spencer, 371
Joyce, C. I., 53
Judd, C. M., 344
Judge, T. A., 169
Jung, C., 240, 241, 242, 378
Jurkiewicz Coughlin, C. L., 20, 311, 312

K
Kacmar, K. M., 140
Kahn, J., 152
Kahneman, D., 15, 39, 299
Kalleberg, A. A., 151
Kalleberg, A. L., 137, 147
Kamens, D. H., 286
Kanter, R. M., 143, 158, 192, 204, 205, 209, 210, 337, 361
Kantor, J., 115–116
Kanungo, R. N., *331,* 333
Katz, B., 130
Katzell, R. A., 147
Katzenbach, J. R., 105–106, 177
Kaufer, N., 354
Kauffman, Ewing, 132
Kegan, R., 7
Keidel, R. W., 102, 103, 104
Kelleher, Herb, 243, 388–389
Keller, B., 343, 344, 420
Keller, Helen, 93
Kelly, Terri, 82–83
Kelly, William P., 352
Kelman, Glenn, 129
Kemp, C., 338
Kennedy, A. A., 68, 241, 258, 334
Kennedy, John F., 18, 193, 354
Kenney, C., 131
Kerr, Clark, 195
Key, M. K., 255
Kidder, Tracy, 266–277, 395
Kiley, D., 9
Kiley, J. T., 9
Killian, K., 151
Kilmann, R. H., 247

Mann, Thomas, 299

Manz, C. C., 150

Mao Zedong, 187, 214, 337, 421

March, James G., 27–28, 29, 34, 49, 188, 189–190, 231, 241, 257, 287, 288, 289, 292, 293, 374, *425*

Marcus, Bernie, 245–246

Maremont, M., 152

Maritz, Paul, 202–203, 204, 205, 211

Markels, A., 131

Marriott, J. W., Sr., 248

Marris, P., 378

Marshall, M. V., 232

Maruping, L. M., 176

Marx, Karl, 214

Marx, R., 183

Maslow, Abraham, 119, 120–123, *121, 122,* 214

Mason, P. A., *425*

Matsushita, Konosuke, 78

Matthews, Chris, 130, 184, 210

Matthews, D., 328

Maurer, K., 94

Mausner, B., *121*

May, Theresa, 341

Mayer, J., 166–167, 177

Mayo, Elton, 117, 334

McAuliffe, Christa, 182, 184–185

McCall, M. W., 13

McCarthy, D., 261, 262, 263

McCaskey, M. B., *33*

McClelland, D. C., 119

McCloskey, D. N., 299

McConnell, M., 182, 183, 247, 253

McCourt, Malachy, 379

McGrath, J. E., 170

McGreevy, Brian, 3

McGregor, Douglas, 123, 125, 128, 334

McKee, A., 167, 349, 350

McLean, Bethany, 145

McLennan, R., 373

McNamee, M., 75

McNerney, James, 362, 363, 365

Mead, M., 241

Meckling, William H., 76, 118, 374, *424*

Mellahi, K., 131

Mendelson, H., 212

Meredith, R., 130

Merkel, Angela, 341

Messick, D. M., 214

Messier, Jean-Marie, 194–195

Meyer, J. W., 241, 283, 285, *424*

Meyerhoff, B., 250

Mihalopoulos, D., 192

Mill, John Stuart, 71

Miller, D., 86, 87

Miller, K. D., 96

Miller, R., 204

Miller, T. C., 386

Milne, A. A., 45

Mintzberg, Henry, 44, 50, 54, 57, 66, 72, 75–84, *77, 81,* 89, 92, 158, 288, 299, 334, 360

Mirvis, P. H., 155–156

Mitroff, I. I., 247

Moeller, J., 52

Mohammed, 248

Mohr, R. D., 149

Mola, R., 254

Molière, 209–210

Moore, J. F., 223–224

Moore, S., 250

Morgan, G., 132

Morgan, J. P., 330

Morganthau, T., 377

Morgeson, F. P., 149

Morran, C., 363

Morris, B., 345, 354

Morris, J. R., 131

Morrison, A. M., 13, 324, 343, 394

Moskowitz, M., 137, 139, 324, 389, 392

Moss, Frank, 182

Moulton, B., 204

Mount, G., 167

Mouton, J. S., 168

Moyers, B., 152

Mulally, Alan, 91, 365–368

Mulcahy, Anne, 189, 354

Müller, Mattias, 3–4

Mullins, Guy, 377

Murphy, J. T., 336

Murray, M., 131

Musk, Elon, 245

Myers, I., 168

N

Nadler, D. A., 53

Nanus, B., 190, 336, 339, 349, 355

Napier, J. L., 345

Nardelli, Robert, 34

Nelson, Richard R., 374, *424*

Nesheim, T., 151

Neuman, R. P., 361–362

Nichols, S. L., 227

Nickerson, J. A., 368

Niemann, G., 52

Nixon, Richard, 8

Nohria, N., 119, *121,* 361

Nordstrom, Elmer, 261

Nordstrom, Everett, 261

Nordstrom, John, 261

Nordstrom, Lloyd,   261
Norman, W. J.,   349
Norrish, B.,   90
Northcraft, G. B.,   423
Novak, W.,   352
Nutt, S. C.,   221–222
Nystrom, P. C.,   82

O
Obama, Barack,   37, 94, 106, 241, 291–292, 297–298, 326, 359
O'Connor, P.,   345
O'Grady, Scott,   247
Ohmae, K.,   68
Ohme, D. K.,   214
O'Keefe, D. L.,   241
O'Keefe, Gregory,   302
Okimoto, T. G.,   344
Oldham, G. R.,   *121*
Oliver, T.,   378
Olsen, J.,   241, 287
Olsen, K. M.,   151
Omidyar, Pierre,   84, 244
O'Neill, Thomas P. ("Tip"),   210, 393
Organ, D. W.,   169
Orgogozo, I.,   128
Ormerod, P.,   368
Ortner, S.,   241, 242
Oshry, Barry,   33–35, 336
O'Toole, P.,   351
O'Toole, J.,   136
Overington, M. A.,   285
Overstreet, Dennis,   377
Owen, H.,   155
Owen, M.,   94
Owen, Robert,   136, 137
Ozcan, P.,   223

P
Packard, David,   78
Palmer, I. C.,   20
Palmeri, C.,   226, 227
Palumbo, G.,   147
Pande, P. S.,   361–362
Pape, R.,   192
Park, R.,   143
Parker, G.,   170, 171
Parker, S.,   149
Parks, M.,   344
Parloff, R.,   4
Pasquier, S.,   189
Paterson, Tim,   212
Paulson, E.,   267
Paustian-Underdahl, S. C.,   343

Peck, David,   267–268
Peck, S.,   197
Pentland, B. T.,   96
Perez, F.,   151
Perrow, C.,   49, 56, 228, 230, 285
Peters, B. G.,   11, 283
Peters, T. J.,   59, 241, 307, *308,* 334, 338, 350, 351, 391
Petzinger, T.,   389
Pfarrer, C.,   94, 265
Pfeffer, Jeffrey,   118, 131, 137, 139, 142, 144, 145, 149, 150, 151, 186, 192, 193, 204, 205, 220, 231–232, *424*
Pichault, F.,   204, 206–207
Pienaar, François,   305
Pinder, C. C.,   121
Pink, D. H.,   119, *121*
Pinkse, J.,   12
Pitt, Brad,   120
Pitt, R. N.,   20–21
Platz, S. J.,   343
Porath, C.,   115, 137
Porras, J. I.,   137, 142, 244, 258, 306–307, *308,* 334, 389, 420
Posner, B. Z.,   338, 339, 351, 355
Powell, B.,   187
Powell, Colin,   153, 246
Powell, Walter W.,   60, 283, 284–285, *424,* 425
Prahalad, C. K.,   388
Pratt, M. G.,   12
Pressman, J. L.,   11
Preuss, L.,   12
Putin, Vladimir,   189
Pyzdek, T.,   56

Q
Quadracci, Harry,   396
Quenllas, A.,   110
Quinn, R. E.,   65

R
Raffaele, P.,   280
Rallis, S.,   290
Ramsey, V. J.,   324, 394
Randall, D.,   4
Rao, P.,   121
Rasala, Ed,   269, 273
Raven, B. H.,   192, 193
Reagan, Ronald,   185, 193, 206, 356, 393
Reed, John,   88–89
Reed, K.,   254
Rehbein, K.,   228, 229
Reichheld, F. F.,   131
Reingold, J.,   210
Rice, A. K.,   148
Rice, Tamir,   39

Wallach, Steve, 269, 273
Wallin, Carl, 261
Walton, Sam, 217, 364
Wang, L., 227
Wasdin, H. E., 265
Waterman, R. H., Jr., 122, 131, 137, 144, 241, 306, 307, *308,* 334, 350, 351, 391
Watson, T., 158
Watson, Tom, Sr., 360
Wayne, S. J., 344
Weatherford, J. M., 252
Webber, L., 12, 36
Weber, Max, 48–49, 335
Weddle, C. J., 343
Weick, K. E., 241
Weigl, Henry, 219
Weiner, J., 378
Weiner, S. S., 290
Weingart, L. R., 175
Weisbord, M. R., 154
Weiss, C. H., 290
Weitzel, J. R., 332
Welch, Jack, 34, 155, 194, 362
Werner, M. D., 12
West, Cornel, 80
West, Tom, 267, 269, 270, 271, 273, 275
Westphal, J. D., 193
Wheeler, J. V., 176
White, R., 168, *331*
White, Robert, 88–89
White, R. P., 343
White, R. W., 119
Whitman, Meg, 84
Whitmyer, C., 392
Whitsett, D. A., 149
Whyte, W. F., 146
Wiersema, F., 388
Wildavsky, A. B., 11
Wilkinson, A., 131
Willemsen, T. M., 343

Williamson, Oliver E., 159–160, 283, *424, 425*
Wilson, C., 343
Wilson, J., 343
Wilson, Tylee, 219
Wilson, Woodrow, 214
Wimpelberg, R. K., 20, 311
Wingfield, N., 129
Winig, L., 240
Winston, K., 202
Winter, Sidney G., 374, *424*
Winterkorn, Martin, 3, 6, 31–32
Wirtz, F., 59
Woehr, D. J., 343
Woodward, J., 285
Wooley, A. W., 172
Worley, C., 131
Wozniak, Steve, 78
Wu, X., 350
WuDunn, S., 129
Wuebker, R., 344

X
Xanic von Bertrag, A., 386–387
Xi Jinping, 187

Y
Yang, J. L., 210
Yankelovich, D., 147
Yardley, J., 84
Yeltsin, Boris, 189
Yetton, P. W., 350
Yorks, L., 149
Young, C. E., 131
Yukl, G., 339

Z
Zaccaro, S., *331,* 338
Zachary, G. P., 202, 203, 205
Zoghi, C., 149
Zott, C., 240, 293

SUBJECT INDEX

Note: Page references in *italics* refer to exhibits.

customer service
full-time employees for, 129
structural frame and organizing for, 46–47, 64

D

Daily Kos, 250
Data General, 266–277
deceptive nature, of organizations, 32
decision making
authorities and partisans, 191–192
authority of, 190
A Behavioral Theory of the Firm (Cyert, March), 189–190
distribution of power and, 195–196
interpersonal and group dynamics, 176–177
Organizations (March, Simon) on, 27–28
sources of power and, 192–195
Denny's Restaurants, 152
Digital Equipment, 86, 306
Dilbert (Adams), 10, 128
direct expression, of conflict, 175
disasters
leadership and, 297–298, 337
as organizational problem, 26, 28, 31–32
structural frame of, 46–47, 55, 73
symbolic frame of, 240–241, 282, 305
Discipline of Market Leaders, The (Treacy, Wiersema), 388
discrimination, gender and, 344
distribution of leadership responsibility, 336–337
diverse professions, of team members, 269–270
diversity
egalitarianian employment and, 152–153
gender, race, and leadership issues, 345
political frame of, 210
divisionalized organizations, 80–82, *81*
division of labor, 53–55, *61*
DOS (Microsoft), 202–203, 212
downsizing, 131
dramaturgical theory, 282–285
Dreamliner (Boeing), 255–256
dual authority teams, *98*
Duke University, 103
DuPont, 59, 306

E

Eagle Group (Data General team), 266–277
contribution of informal players, 274–275
diverse backgrounds of team members, 269–270
group identity of teams, 271
humor and play for, 272–273
inspirational leadership and, 270
membership and, 268–269

overview, 266–268
ritual and ceremony for, 273–274
soul as secret of success in, 275–277
specialized language of teams, 270–271
Eastman Kodak, 50–51, 66, 306
eBay, 84, 244
"Economic Action and Social Structure" (Granovetter), 159–160
ecosystems
business-government, 228–230
defined, 223–224
overview, 218
political dynamics, overview, 224–226
public policy, 226–228
society as ecosystem, 230–234
Edina (Minnesota) School District, 243
Effective Executive, The (Drucker), 242
egalitarianism, 150–152
Egypt, Camp David Accords and, 211
Electoral College, 326
emotional intelligence, 166–167
Emotional Intelligence (Goleman), 166, 167
employee retention, 140–144
employee stock ownership plans (ESOPs), 143
employment contract
global trends and, 128–130
investing in people and, 131–133
"lean and mean" approach to, 130–131, 133
empowerment
autonomy and participation, 146–147
egalitarianism and, 150–152
fostering self-managing teams for, 149–150
by human resource leaders, 351
overview, 144
providing information and support to employees, 145–146
redesigning work for, 148–149
Enron, 10, 28–29, 74–75, 145, 152, 215
Enterprise, 139
environmental factors
of organizational decision making, 27–28
of restructuring, 86
structural frame and, 348–349
EpiPen (Mylan), 152
espoused theories, 161
ethics, 385–397
authorship as criteria of, 391–392
justice as criteria of, 392–393
love as criteria of, 392
overview, 296, 385–387
political frame of, 214–216, 229–230
significance as criteria of, 394–396
soul and spirit in organizations, 387–390, *390*
Ethiopian Christians, 279–280

evaluation, organizational process of, 289–290

Evolutionary Theory of Economic Change, An (Nelson, Winter), 374

expectations
gender and leadership, 344
"spurters" example, 39–40
See also goals

Experimental Schools Project, 375

experimentation
in groups, 175
by structural leaders, 349

expertise, information and, 192

expression of conflict, 175

External Control of Organizations, The (Pfeffer, Salancik), 231

extrinsic motivation, 120

F

factories view of four frames model
authorship as ethics criteria, 391–392
defined, 17

fairy tales, symbolism of, 247–250

families
families view of four frames model, 17, 392
gender issues of leadership and, 344
socializing effects of, 158

Feast of Fools, The (Cox), 263

featherbedding, 126

features, structural. See organizing

Federal Aviation Administration, 226–227

Federal Bureau of Investigation (FBI), 18–19, 29, 73

Federal Emergency Management Agency (FEMA), 55, 282

Federal Express, 122, 229, 350

financial issues
employment practices and, 130–131
ethics and business scandals, 215–216
financial perspective of organizations, 137
job security and, 141–142
reward programs, 120, 143–144
symbolism of political budget stand-offs, 291

five-sector "logo," 76–84, *77, 81*

FON, 350

football teams, 102–103

Ford Motor Company
change at, 365–368
human resource frame of, 136
leadership of, 347, 349, 351–353
structural frame of, 91, 95

Foreign Corrupt Practices Act, 385

Fortune, 145

four-frame model
development of, 419
expanding managerial thinking, 21–22, *22*

factories view, 17, 391–392
families view, 17, 392
FBI and CIA example, 18–19
flexibility in, 74, 368–369, *370*
groups and informal roles, 170–172
jungles view, 17–18, 392–394
multiframe thinking, 19–21, 421–422
organizational complexity and, 40
overview, 15–18, *20*
reframing ethics with, *390*
reframing leadership with, *346,* 346–356 (*See also* leadership)
temples view, 18, 394–396
See also ethics; four-frame model, integrating; human resource frame; leadership; political frame; structural frame; symbolic frame

four-frame model, integrating, 297–312
interpretations of organizational processes, *300–301,* 300–302
managers' image *versus* actual work, 298–300
matching frames to situations, *303,* 303–306
overview, 295, 297–298
research on effectiveness of managers, 306–311, *308, 310*
research on frame preference of managers, 311–312

framing
decision making nad, 28
frame, defined, 43
framing contests, 223
framing effect, 39
sources of power and, 193

Fujifilm, 51

Functions of the Executive, The (Barnard), 334

FzioMed, 104

G

gain-sharing plans, 143–144

Gallup, 9

games, planning and, 289

gap, overlap *versus,* 73

"garbage-can" scripts, 287–288

gay rights, 153

Gazprom, 189

GEICO, 242

gender
egalitarianian employment and, 152–153
leadership issues affected by, 329, 341–346
masculinity-feminism and organizational culture, 261

General Electric, 155, 194–195, 232, 306, 361–362

generality, moral judgment and, 215

General Managers, The (Kotter), 306, 309, *310,* 311

General Motors, 59, 107, 230, 245, 347–349

Getting to Yes (Fisher, Ury), 211–212

"gig economy," 129

quantitative-analytic analysis of, 330, *331,* 332–333

See also Robert F. Kennedy High School (case study)

"lean and mean" employment practices, 130–131, 133

learning, by organizations, 33–36, *35*

liking, 194

linkage. *See* networks

Linux, 83–84

Lockheed, 95

Los Angeles Times, 5

loss, from change, 376–380

love, 392

"lowerarchy," 222–223

M

machine bureaucracy, 78–79, 85

"making cheerleaders," 209

management

    cluelessness of, 5, 8

    expanding managerial thinking, 21–22, *22*

    expectations of, 7–11

    leadership *versus,* 335–336

    political and symbolic roles of managers, 231

    restructuring and generic issues affecting, 84–85

    senior executives' skills, 9

    styles, 168–169

    symbolism of negotiation by, 290–292

    See also manager as politician

manager as politician, 201–216

    agenda setting, 204–206

    bargaining and negotiation, 210–213

    ethical considerations, 214–216

    mapping political terrain, 206–208, *207, 208*

    networking and building coalitions, 208–210

    overview, 180, 201–204

Manager's Guide (Federal Express), 122

Managing Public Policy (Lynn), 306, 309, *310,* 311

mapping political terrain, 206–208, *207, 208*

March of Dimes, 75

Marion Laboratories, 132

Marriott Hotels, 248

Mary Kay Cosmetics, 255

masculinity-feminism, organizational culture and, 261

MasterCard, 95

matrix structures, 59, 61–62

Mazda, 142

Mazdoor Kisan Shakti Sangathan (Worker and Peasant Empowerment Union; India), 202

McCann Ericson, 95

McDonald's

    research about, 306

    structural frame of, 57, 62–66, 68, 75, 78

    symbolic frame of, 241–242

McKinsey & Co., 10

McWane, 132–133

measurement, of team performance, 110–111

Medtronic, 387–388

meetings

    organizational process of, as theater, 287–288

    structural frame of, 58

membership, in teams, 268–269

metaphor, symbolism of, 256–257

metric system, change and, 360

"Microkids" (team dynamics example), 268–272

Microsoft, 51, 139, 212, 224, 307

Mindfulness (Langer), 38

"mindlessness," 21

Mintzberg's Ps (plan, perspective, pattern, position, ploy), 50–51

Misanthrope, The (Molière), 209–210

Model II theory-in-use, 163–166, *164*

modeling, by leaders, 270, 354

Model I theory-in-use, *161,* 161–163, 174–175

Modern Approaches to Understanding and Managing Organizations (Bolman, Deal), 419

Modern Times (film), 124

monocratic bureaucracy, 48–49

moral development, stages of, 214

"moral mazes," 197–198

Morton Thiokol Corporation, 182–184, 208

motivation

    downsizing and, 131

    human resources frame and, 349–351

    Maslow's hierarchy of needs, 120–123, *122, 214*

    matching frames to situations, 303

    models of, *121*

    overview, 119–120

    personality and organization, 124–128

    Theory X and Theory Y, 123

Motorola, 361

multiframe thinking

    defined, 19–21

    importance of, 421–422

    See also four-frame model

multilateral nature of leadership, 336

mutual-gains bargaining, 291

mutuality, moral judgment and, 215

Myers-Briggs Type Indicator, 168–169

Mylan, 152

myths, 242–245

N

Nabisco, 219

NASA, 9, 181–185, 208

National Health Service Corps (NHSC), 302

National Right to Information Act (India), 202

national security, organizational problems of, 25–26, 28, 31–32

nature *versus* nurture concept, 119

needs
    concept of human needs, 118–119
    hierarchy of needs, 120–123, *122,* 214
    "high growth"/"low growth" needs, 149
    See also people and organizations
negativity, releasing, 379–380
negotiation. *See* bargaining and negotiation
networks
    networking and building coalitions, 208–210
    political frame of, 352
    as sources of power, 192–193
    structural frame of, 59–60
newcomers, reframing for, 324
New Lanark (Scotland) knitting mill, 136
New Patterns of Management (Likert), 155
New York Times, 386–387
Nice Work (Lodge), 299
No Child Left Behind, 227–228
Nordstrom, 261–263
norms, informal, 172–173
Norway, egalitarianism in, 150–151
Novo-Nordisk, 11
Nucor Corporation, 116–117, 151

O

Office, The (television series), 128
"Onboarding" (Ritz-Carlton), 252–253
one-boss teams, *97,* 97–98
open-book management, 145–146
openness, moral judgment and, 215
operating core, of Mintzberg's five-sector "logo," 77
Operation Neptune Spear, 93–94
"organizational big bang," 7
organizational complexity, 25–41
    common fallacies of, 26–29
    coping with ambiguity and complexity, 36–40, *37*
    defined, 31–32
    organizational learning and, 33–36, *35*
    overview, 25–26
    peculiarities of organizations and, 30–33, *33*
organizational democracy, 150–152
organizational development (OD), 154–156
organizational symbols and culture, 239–263
    assumptions about, 241–242
    ceremonies, 254–256
    heroes and heroines, 245–247
    metaphor, humor, and play, 256–257
    myths, vision, and values, 242–245
    organizations as cultures, 257–263
    overview, 236, 239–240, 242
    rituals, 250–254
    stories and fairy tales, 247–250
    See also team dynamics
organization as theater, 279–294

    dramaturgical and institutional theory, 282–285
    organizational process and, 287–294
    organizational structure and, 285–287
    overview, 237, 279–282
Organizations (March, Simon), 27–28
organizations as political arenas and agents, 217–234
    organizations as arenas, 219–223
    organizations as political agents, 223–224
    overview, 180, 217–218
    political dynamics of ecosystems, 224–234
Organizations in Action (Thompson), 49–50
organizing, 45–69
    challenges of global organization, 68
    choosing structural design options for, 60–64, *61*
    lateral coordination of, 58–60
    origins of structural perspective, 48–50
    overview, 43–44, 45–47
    strategy for, 50–51
    structural assumptions for, 47–48
    structural forms and functions, 51–53
    structural imperatives for, *64,* 64–68
    vertical coordination of, 55–58
    work differentiation and division of labor for, 53–55
outsiders, reframing for, 324
overlap, gap *versus,* 73
overload, underuse *versus,* 73–74

P

palio, 239–240
Panasonic, 68
parenting, gender issues of leadership and, 344
participation
    for change, 361, 370–372
    GLOBE project on, 339
    participation studies, 146–147
partisan opposition, to power, 191–192
passion, 338
peer review systems, 110–111
people and organizations, 115–134
    changing employment contract, 128–133
    core assumptions about, 117–118
    human needs and, 118–119
    overview, 113, 115–117
    workplace motivation, 119–128, *121, 122*
Pepsi, 235, 377
performance, by teams, 105–106
performance control, 57–58
personality
    "Big 5" model of personality, 169
    Myers-Briggs Type Indicator, 168–169
    trait research, 338
    workplace motivation and, 124–128
personal power, 193
persuasion, by political leaders, 352–353

PERT (Program Evaluation Review Techniques), 280–281
Philips, 68
philosophy, for human resources management, 138–139
piracy, of intellectual property, 187–188
Pixar, 58
planning
    interpretations of organizational processes, 300
    organizational process of, as theater, 288–289
    structural frame of, 57–58
play
    symbolism of, 256–257
    team dynamics and, 272–273
Polaris missile system (U.S. Navy), 280–282
Polaroid, 51
policy, structural frame of, 56–57
political frame
    change and, *370*, 373–374
    FBI/CIA example of four frames model, 18–19
    interpretations of organizational processes, *300–301*, 300–302
    matching frames to situations, *303*, 303–306
    overview, 179–180
    presidential election of 2016 example, 327–328
    reframing example, 318–320, 323
    reframing leadership with, *346*, 351–353
    Robert F. Kennedy High School case study, 410–412
    symbolic frame compared to, 286–287
    See also manager as politician; organizations as political arenas and agents
power, conflict, and coalition, 181-199
    conflict generated by change, 375–376
    conflict in organizations, 196–197
    decision making, 189–196
    distribution of power, 352
    interpersonal conflict in groups, 173–176
    matching frames to situations, 303
    "moral mazes" of, 197–198
    networking and building coalitions, 208–210
    organizations as coalitions, 184–185, 188–190
    overview, 179, 181–184
    political assumptions about, 184–188
    position power, 192 (*See also* authority)
    power and ethical behavior, 392–394
    power distance, 260
    power relations and political ecosystems, 232
    symbolism of power, 292–293
POWs (prisoners of war), symbolism of, 246–247
PPBS (Program Planning and Budgeting Systems), 280–281
preparation, by structural leaders, 348
"preselling," 209
presidential election (2008), 359
presidential election (2016), 325–330
Pret à Manger, 11

Primal Leadership (Goleman, Boyatzis, McKee), 167
primary nursing concept, restructuring and, 90
Princeton University, 345–346
process level, of groups, 170
professional bureaucracy, 79–80
profit-sharing plans, 143–144
promotion
    "glass ceiling"/"glass cliff," 343–346
    promoting from within, 142
protective leadership, GLOBE project on, 339
Ps (plan, perspective, pattern, position, ploy), 50–51
psychological safety, 172–173
public policy ecosystems, 226–228
Publix, 144

Q
qualitative-holistic analysis of leadership, 330–332, 334–335
quantitative-analytic analysis of leadership, 330, *331*, 332–333

R
RadioShack, 9
Rashomon (film), 21
"rational man," 27
Raytheon, 153
reality
    cognitive bias and, 38–39
    reality-bound *versus* frame-bound preferences, 15
Real Managers (Luthans, Yodgetts, Rosenkrantz), 306, 309, *310*
reciprocation, 193
Redfin, 129
Reengineering Management (Champy), 88
referent power, 193
reframing, 3–24
    defined, 13–15
    expectation of management, 7–11
    four frames model, 15–22, *20, 22*
    framing, defined, 11–13
    overview, 3–7
    See also reframing example
reframing example, 313–324
    benefits and risks of reframing, 322–324
    human resource scenario of, 317–318, 323
    overview, 313–314
    political scenario of, 318–320, 323
    reframing for newcomers and outsiders, 324
    structural scenario of, 315–316, 323
    symbolic scenario of, 320–322, 324
relationship management
    emotional intelligence and, 167
    guanxi, 229–230
    leadership ability and, 339

Southwest Airlines
  human resource frame of, 132–133, 139, 152
  leadership of, 307, 388–389, 392
  symbolic frame of, 243, 246
specialization, 54–55
sports
  leadership examples, 304–305, 341–342
  organizing example, 43–44
  teamwork analogy, 101–103
Springboks, 304–305
Springfield Remanufacturing (SRC Holdings), 145
"spurters," 39–40
stages of moral development, 214
stagnant bureaucracies, restructuring by, 87
Standard Brands, 219
standard operating procedures (SOPs), 56–57
Starbucks, 236, 276–277, 360, 385, 389
star networks, 100, *101*
stereotypes, about gender, 343–344
stories
  symbolism of, 247–250
  team dynamics and, 271
  told by symbolic leaders, 355–356
strategy
  agenda setting and, 205–206
  human resource management success strategies,
    overview, 137–138, *138*
  organizing, 50–51
  The Rise and Fall of Strategic Planning
    (Mintzberg), 360
  structural frame and organizing, *64,* 66–67
Strategy of Conflict, The (Schelling), 212–213
structural frame
  change and, *370,* 373–374
  frame, defined, 43
  human resources frame compared to, 47–48
  interpretations of organizational processes, *300–301,*
    300–302
  matching frames to situations, *303,* 303–306
  overview, 43–44
  presidential election of 2016 example, 325–326
  principles of successful structural change, 91–92
  reframing example, 315–316, 323
  reframing leadership with, *346,* 346–349
  Robert F. Kennedy High School case study,
    408–409
  symbolic frame compared to, 285–287
  See also groups and teams; organizing; restructuring
structural realignment, for change, 372–374
suboptimization, 55
surprising nature, of organizations, 32
Survey Research Center (University of Michigan),
    155
  symbolic frame

change and, *370,* 373–374
interpretations of organizational processes, *300–301,*
    300–302
leadership theory and, 334–335
matching frames to situations, *303,* 303–306
overview, 235–237
presidential election of 2016 example, 328
reframing example, 320–322, 324
reframing leadership with, *346,* 353–356
Robert F. Kennedy High School case study, 412–413
symbolic roles of plans, 288–289
symbols and loss, 376–378
symbols as attention-getting devices, 354
See also organizational symbols and culture; organization
    as theater
system maps, 34–36, *35*

T

Taming of the Shrew, The (Shakespeare), 344
Target, 242, 363
task forces, structural frame of, 58, 60–61. *See also* groups
    and teams
task level, of groups, 170
Taurus (Ford Motor Company), 95
team dynamics, 265–277
  contribution of informal players, 274–275
  diverse backgrounds of team members,
    269–270
  Eagle Group example, overview, 266–268
  group identity of teams, 271
  humor and play for, 272–273
  inspirational leadership and, 270
  membership and, 268–269
  overview, 237, 265–266
  ritual and ceremony for, 273–274
  soul as secret of success in, 275–277
  specialized language of teams, 270–271
  See also groups and teams
Team Six (U.S. Navy SEALS), 93–96, 265–266
technical quality, 304
technostructure, of Mintzberg's five-sector "logo,"
    78, 85
temples view of four frames model
  defined, 18
  significance as ethics criteria, 394–396
  See also soul
tension, structural. *See* restructuring
terrorism. *See* September 11, 2001 terrorist attacks
Texaco, 152
T-groups, 154–155
theater, organization as. *See* organization as theater
theories-in-use, 160–166, *161, 164,* 174–175
Theory E/Theory O, 361
"Theory of the Firm" (Jensen, Meckling), 75–76

Theory X
    lack of employee participation and,   146
    Theory X and Theory Y, overview,   123, 137
    work redesign and,   148–149
Thiokol (Morton Thiokol Corporation),   182–184, 208
thirsting for power,   28–29
3M,   361–364
Time,   198
time management,   176
top-down initiatives,   220, 221–223
Toyota,   72, 349, 389
training
    for change,   370–372
    for employees,   144
trait research,   338
trait theory,   *331*
transactional leadership theory,   333
transformational leadership theory,   *331, 333*
trust,   339
two-factor theory,   120
Tyco,   76

U
Uber,   129, 223
uncertainty avoidance,   261
underuse, overload *versus*,   73–74
United Airlines,   144, 152
United Automobile Workers (UAW),   363
United Nations Against Corruption,   389
United Parcel Service (UPS),   52, 57
University of California,   195, 378
University of Michigan,   155
U.S. Air Force,   276
U.S. Army,   153
U.S. Congress,   251–252, 337
U.S. Department of Education,   227–228
U.S. Department of Homeland Security,   55, 73
U.S. Marine Corps,   243
U.S. Navy
    Polaris missile system,   280–282
    SEALS,   93–96, 265–266
U.S. presidents, vision of,   205–206
U2,   281–282

V
value, creating *versus* claiming,   210–213
values
    commitment to core beliefs,   421
    GLOBE project on values-based leadership,
        339
    symbolism of,   242–245
    team dynamics and,   274
vertical conflict,   196–197

vertical coordination
    choosing lateral coordination *versus*,   60–64, *61*
    defined,   55–58
    structural imperatives of,   *64*, 64–68
    See also organizing
Visa,   266
vision
    agenda setting and,   204–206
    communicating,   355
    of leaders,   338
    symbolism of,   242–245
    "visionary" companies,   420
Vivendi,   194–195
Volkswagen,   3–7, 31, 35–36, 129, 389
Volvo,   11

W
Wall Street Journal,   136
Walmart
    as ecosystem,   225–226, 230, 232–233
    ethics and,   386–387
    human resource frame of,   117, 140–141
    political frame of,   217–218
web of inclusion,   83–84
Wegmans,   118, 139
Wells Fargo,   3–7, 31, 389
whistleblowers,   198
Whole Foods,   108–111, 145, 150, 152, 236
Who Moved My Cheese? (Johnson),   371
Wikipedia,   11
"window dressing,"   286–287
Windows NT (Microsoft),   202–203
"Wintel" ecosystem,   224
win-win approaches,   211–213, 291
Wisdom of Teams, The (Katzenbach, Smith),   105–106
withdrawal, workplace motivation and,   125, 126
work differentiation
    integration *versus*,   73
    structural tensions/options,   53–55, *61*
Worker and Peasant Empowerment Union (Mazdoor Kisan
        Shakti Sangathan),   201–202
"Work-Out" conferences,   155
workplace motivation. *See* motivation
WorldCom,   87, 215
World Trade Organization,   187
"Wow Effects" (Ritz-Carlton),   252–253

X
Xerox,   51, 345

Z
Zappos,   63–64, 140, 240, 391–392
zones of indifference,   195